# THE STORY OF FAITH MISSIONS

Dedicated to the Association of German
Speaking Evangelical Missiologists (AFEM)
and its members.
Also as a sign of gratitude for the award of the
George W. Peters Prize in Missiology 1993.

# THE STORY OF
# FAITH MISSIONS

**Klaus Fiedler**

Regnum Books International

Oxford

Akropong   Buenos Aires   Irvine, CA   New Delhi

Published by Regnum Books International
in association with Paternoster Press, P.O. Box 300, Carlisle, Cumbria
CA3 0QS U.K.

Regnum Books International

P.O. Box 70, Oxford, OX2 6HB, UK

17951 Cowan, Irvine, California 92714, USA

P.O. Box 76, Akropong-Akuapem, Ghana

Jose Marmol 1734, 1602 Florida, Buenos Aires, Argentina

Post Bag No. 21, Vasant Kunj, New Delhi 110057, India

01  00  99  98  97  96  95     7  6  5  4  3  2  1

A catalogue record for this book is available from the British Library

ISBN 1-870345-18-5

Printed and bound in Great Britain

# Contents

Preface                                                              9

1   A plurality of missions: faith missions in
    the context of the Protestant missionary
    movement                                                        11

2   A new missionary movement: the early
    history of faith missions                                       32

3   Not an easy endeavour: faith missions in Africa    70

4   Born in revival: faith missions and the
    1859/1873 revival                                              112

5   Reaching the unreached: faith mission
    geography                                                      125

6   Interdenominational missions and
    denominational churches: the concept
    of individual unity                                            169

7   Power for service: faith missions and the
    holiness movement                                              210

8   The rigorous Christian life: faith missions
    and African holiness                                           247

9   A propelling vision: faith missions and
    the prophetic movement                                         272

10  Using (no longer) neglected forces: women          292

11  Continuity and change: faith mission
    churches in Africa                                             319

12  A vision taken up: African missions               364

13  Sufficient challenges for faith missions          392

Bibliography                                                       406

97023

# Illustrations and charts

The origin of the different Protestant missionary movements 12

National mission associations 14

A historical typology of the Protestant missionary movement 17

Precursors of the faith missions 23

The principles of the China Inland Mission 33

Hudson Taylor and the China Inland Mission 35

Fanny and Grattan Guinness and the faith mission movement in Africa 36

Fanny and Grattan Guinness and the missions connected with them 39

A. B. Simpson and the Church and Missionary Alliance 42

A. J. Gordon and A. T. Pierson: theologians and publicists of the faith missions 44

Fredrick Franson 45

Africa Inland Mission 49

Sudan Interior Mission 50

Sudan United Mission 51

'Industrial missions' founded in Africa by faith missions 54

The advance of faith missions and the Brethren movement missions in the 'unreached' parts of Africa 72

The chain in the strategy of the early faith missions 77

African churches originating in the faith missions founded before 1918 81

New mission work 1918–1940 85

1931: The Worldwide Evangelization Crusade's plans for West Africa 87

From mission to independent church 90

Churches with faith mission origins 92

Summary: 'faith mission Christians' in Africa 102

The denominational development of the early faith mission leaders 178

Comity agreements in northern Nigeria 189

Comity borders prescribed by the colonial government 191

Comity in Burundi 193

The worldwide structure of WEC International 261

Critical analysis of the Kenyan missons mentioned by Keyes 366

# Abbreviations

| | |
|---|---|
| ABMS | American Baptist Missionary Society |
| AEF | Africa Evangelical Fellowship* (originally SAGM) |
| AEM | Angola Evangelical Mission* |
| AGC | Africa Gospel Church (from WGM)* |
| AIC | Africa Inland Church (from AIM) |
| AICMB | Africa Inland Church Missionary Board |
| AIM | Africa Inland Mission* |
| AMZ | Allgemeine Missionszeitschrift |
| BMM | Baptist Mid Missions (formerly Mid Africa Mission*) |
| BMMF | Bible and Medical Missionary Fellowship* |
| BMS | Baptist Missionary Society |
| BTSSM | Bishop Taylor's Self-Supporting Missions* |
| CAPRO | Calvary Productions/Calvary Ministries, Nigeria* |
| CBFMS | Conservative Baptist Foreign Mission Society |
| CBM | Congo Balolo Mission* (later RBMU) |
| CECA20 | Communaut vang lique au Centre de l'Afrique (from AIM) |
| CECCA16 | Communaut vang lique du Christ au Coeur de l'Afrique (from WEB) |
| CIM | China Inland Mission* |
| CMA | Christian and Missionary Alliance* |
| CMM | Central Morocco Mission* |
| CMS | Church Missionary Society |
| CNEC | Christian Nationals Evangelism Commission* (now Partners International) |
| COCIN | Churches of Christ in Nigeria (from SUM) |
| CoIM | Congo Inland Mission* |
| CPC | Congo Protestant Council |
| ECWA | Evangelical Churches of West Africa (Nigeria, from SIM) |
| ECZ | Église du Christ au Zaire |
| EFMA | Evangelical Foreign Missions Association |
| ELTI | East London Training Institute* |
| EM | Evangelikale Missiologie |
| EMCM | Encyclopedia of Modern Christian Missions |
| EMM | Evangelisches Missionsmagazin |
| EMS | Evangelical Missionary Society, Jos, Nigeria |
| GMU | Gospel Missionary Union* |
| HD | Hearing and Doing |

| | |
|---|---|
| IBMR | International Bulletin of Missionary Research |
| IFMA | Interdenominational Foreign Missions Association |
| LIM | Livingstone Inland Mission* |
| LMS | London Missionary Society |
| MP | Mission Philafricaine* |
| MRW | Missionary Review of the World |
| NAM | North Africa Mission* (Arab World Ministries) |
| NAPMO | Mission Handbook: North American Protestant Ministries Overseas |
| NCCK | National Christian Council of Kenya |
| NIM | Nyassa Industrial Mission* |
| NTM | New Tribes Mission* |
| PIM | Providence Industrial Mission |
| QIM | Qua Iboe Mission* |
| RBMU | Regions Beyond Missionary Union* |
| SAGM | South Africa General Mission* (now AEF) |
| SIM | Sudan Interior Mission* (now SIM International) |
| SMF | Svenska Missionsförbundet* |
| SMM | Southern Morocco Mission* |
| SPM | Sudan-Pionier-Mission* |
| SUM | Sudan United Mission* |
| SvAM | Svenska Alliansmissionen* |
| TEAM | The Evangelical Alliance Mission (The Scandianavian Alliance Mission of North America)* |
| UAM | Unevangelized Africa Mission* |
| UFM | Unevangelized Fields Mission* |
| UMI | University Microfilm International |
| WCE | World Christian Encyclopedia |
| WEC | Worldwide Evangelization Crusade* (now WEC International) |
| WGM | World Gospel Mission* |
| WWW | *The Word, the Work and the World* |
| ZfM | Zeitschrift für Mission |
| ZIM | Zambezi Industrial Mission* |

For the meaning of other abbreviations, see the surrounding text. The branches of a mission in a given country are designated as follows: SIM-UK, SIM-RSA, SIM-AUS/NZ and so on. Faith missions are marked thus:*. For terminology, see Chapter 1.

# Preface

More than two centuries ago, in 1792, William Carey published *An Enquiry into the Obligation of Christians to Use Means for the Conversion of the Heathen*, which led to the establishment of the 'Particular Baptist Society for the Propagation of the Gospel among the Heathen'. This mission, now simply called the 'Baptist Missionary Society', was not the first Protestant mission, but it was the first mission of a new era, which in this book is called the era of classical missions. The book, and the mission resulting from it, ushered in what Latourette called 'the Great Century' of World Missions, a century (1800–1914) which changed the religious map of the world. It is not surprising, therefore, that most missiological interest was and is directed toward the classical missions and the churches to which they gave birth.

Two generations after the *Enquiry* (1865), Hudson and Maria Taylor founded the China Inland Mission, which was, as much as the Baptist Missionary Society had been in its time, not just another mission, but the first mission of a new era, the era of interdenominational faith missions.

These 'new' missions have attracted considerably less missiological interest, and this book is a first—though far from exhaustive—attempt to present an overall picture of the whole movement. As a mission historian, I have set myself the double task of describing past events and of trying to define and outline present identity. How far I have achieved this in this book I must leave to the judgment of my readers. I would be happy if the book led to a kind of dialogue between readers and author.

Although only I am responsible for the contents of the book, I wrote it with the help of many people and organizations.

In financial terms, the book was made possible, firstly, through a two-year scholarship (including eight months travel for research in Africa, America and Europe) from the Deutsche Forschungsgemeinschaft, Bonn, and, after that, by my wife Irene.

I want to thank all the missions which opened their archives to me, with special thanks to the many individuals who shared information with me and helped me to understand what I had seen and collected, and who, very often, also provided generous hospitality.

I also want to thank Professor Theo Sundermeier, my super-

9

visor at Heidelberg University, and those who read certain chapters and sections and commented on them. Thanks to Georg Weger for drawing most of the original maps and graphs, and to Regnum Books and Lynx Communications for their care over the manuscript of the English version.

Very personal thanks go to my wife, who shared the many years of work with me, and to Hochdahl Baptist/Brethren Church (near Düsseldorf), of which I had the privilege of being a member and of feeling at home there during 1984–92.

This English edition is the third version of the results of my research. In 1991, the original thesis was accepted by Heidelberg University for the degree of Doctor of Theology. In 1992, a slightly revised version of the dissertation was published in German by Brunnen Verlag, Giessen and Basel. This English version is partly a translation of the German version, but much of it has been restructured or rewritten. The material has also been condensed by about one- third.

The entire process of research, of writing, of translation and of production of the English version has taken about ten years, and this means that 'today' may refer to any one of those ten years. Though some attempt to update developments after the completion of the German version has been made, this has not been possible in all cases. But I am convinced that the general ideas still remain valid, even where details have changed.

That I write this preface in Malawi, where I am now a lecturer at the University of Malawi, Chancellor College, is as good a proof as any that missionary work in Africa, classical and post-classical (in this country, since 1875 and 1892 respectively), has not been in vain.

*Klaus Fiedler*
Zomba, September 1994

Note: If you find any mistakes or inaccuracies in this book, I would be grateful if you would communicate them to me, so that appropriate changes can be made in a later edition. My address is: Dr Klaus Fiedler, PO Box 280, Zomba, Malawi.

# 1
# A plurality of missions: faith missions in the context of the Protestant missionary movement

The term 'faith missions' was not coined by the faith missions themselves. They did not claim that other missions worked without faith, nor did they claim to have more faith than the missions that had started their work decades earlier. It was others who took one of the faith missions' innovative concepts—the 'faith principle' of financial support[1]—and referred to them under that name. This was only partially correct, because 'faith support' is not the most important characteristic of these missions. The most important characteristic is indeed brought out by the name they often use for themselves: 'interdenominational' missions.[2] Because not every interdenominational mission is necessarily a faith mission, however, in this book they will always be called 'faith missions'. After all, the Methodists, the Baptists and the Quakers did not fare badly with a name that others had chosen for them.

## Possible definitions of 'faith missions'

There are various ways to define what a faith mission is. For this book, the term is defined by history. A faith mission is a mission which traces its origin or (more often) the origin of its principles[3] directly or indirectly back to the China Inland Mission (CIM), which was founded by Hudson Taylor and his wife Maria in 1865—not simply as one new mission among others, but as the first mission of what turned out to be a completely new missionary movement.[4]

In order to define clearly what faith missions are, it is better to look at the various missionary movements in the context of the revival movements that shaped Protestant church history.

Looking at church history in this way, it is less a linear development of denominations than a succession of revival cross currents affecting the denominations and the non-Chris-

11

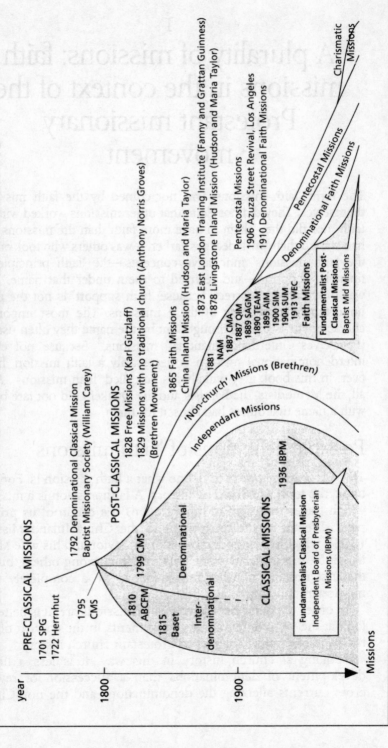

# THE ORIGIN OF THE DIFFERENT PROTESTANT MISSIONARY MOVEMENTS

year

**PRE-CLASSICAL MISSIONS**

1701 SPG
1722 Herrnhut

1795 CMS

1792 Denominational Classical Mission
Baptist Missionary Society (William Carey)

**POST-CLASSICAL MISSIONS**

1799 CMS

1810 ABCFM

1815 Basel

1828 Free Missions (Karl Gützlaff)
1829 Missions with no traditional church (Anthony Norris Groves)
(Brethren Movement)

1865 Faith Missions
China Inland Mission (Hudson and Maria Taylor)

1873 East London Training Institute (Fanny and Grattan Guinness)
1878 Livingstone Inland Mission (Hudson and Maria Taylor)

**Denominational**

**Inter-denominational**

1881 NAM
1887 CMA
1887 QIM
1889 SAGM
1890 TEAM
1895 AIM
1900 SIM
1904 SUM
1913 WEC

**Faith Missions**

'Non-church' Missions (Brethren)

Independant Missions

Pentecostal Missions
1906 Azusa Street Revival, Los Angeles
1910 Denominational Faith Missions

Denominational Faith Missions

Pentecostal Missions

Charismatic Missions

**CLASSICAL MISSIONS**

1936 IBPM

Fundamentalist Classical Mission
Independent Board of Presbyterian
Missions (IBPM)

Fundamentalist Post-
Classical Missions
Baptist Mid Missions

1800

1900

Missions

tian sectors of society in various ways. Because nearly all missions trace their origin back to a revival, the various movements of spiritual renewal from which they originated may well serve as a guide for classifying Protestant missions. This method of classification allows for the changes which inevitably occur over time—if it can be demonstrated that those changes usually take place within a given sector of the Protestant missionary movement and, therefore, do not blur the differences between them. This is indeed the case, for today's mission associations reflect to a large extent the revival movements that brought about the birth of their member missions.[5]

If one accepts historic origin as a valid base for the classification of missions, a 'historical typology' can be reached. The results of such an attempt are summarized in the table on page 16. On the following page the concept of historical typology is applied to the various national mission associations.

# Four successive missionary movements: the historical typology of Protestant missions

Kenneth Scott Latourette calls the period 1800–1914 the 'Great Century' of world missions, with William Carey at its very outset.[6] During this period, the mission society—independent of the churches but closely related to them—is the characteristic organizational form of missionary work.[7] The missions of the Great Century are known as the 'classical missions'; all missionary enterprises before 1793 look more like forerunners, and are therefore known as the 'pre-classical' missions. No one can minimize the crucial importance of the classical missions for the church worldwide[8]; however, many new mission agencies were formed alongside or after the classical missions. These were not just additional missions, but missions of a new type or types. These new (that is, new type) missions are known as the 'post-classical missions'; they comprise the major subdivisions of evangelical missions and pentecostal/charismatic missions, each of which can be further subdivided. This book deals exclusively with faith missions but, in order to perceive their characteristics clearly, faith missions must be seen in the overall context of the whole Protestant missionary movement.

## National Mission Associations

| | ECUMENICAL | EVANGELICAL | FUNDAMENTALIST | OTHERS |
|---|---|---|---|---|
| USA | DOM-NCCCUSA (Division of Overseas Ministries, National Council of the Churches of Christ in the USA) [Classical missions]<br><br>No Pentecostal missions<br><br>No double membership | IFMA (Interdenominational Foreign Missions Association) [Only faith missions]<br><br>EFMA (Evangelical Foreign Missions Association) [Denominational missions, including Pentecostal missions]<br><br>Double membership IFMA and EFMA possible for faith missions | TAM-ICCC (The Associated Missions, International Council of Christian Churches) [denominational—'fighting fundamentalism']<br><br>FOM (Fellowship) ['quiet' non-denominational fundamentalism]<br><br>Double membership of any kind impossible | A growing number of US missions are not members of any missions association, for example, Wycliffe Bible Translators, New Tribes Mission, Youth with a Mission |
| Canada | CCC-CWC (Canadian Council of Churches, Commission on World Concerns) [as USA] | As in the USA | Only TAM-ICCC has a Canadian member, World-wide Evangelical Mission | Similar to the USA |
| Switzerland (German Speaking) | Konferenz Evangelischer Missionen (KEM) [Classical missions and Kwango Mission] | Arbeitsgemeinschaft Evangelikaler Missionen (AEM) [Faith missions, no Pentecostal missions] | | Few, for example, Evangelischer Brüderverein |

National Mission Associations (continued)

| | ECUMENICAL | EVANGELICAL | FUNDAMENTALIST | OTHERS |
|---|---|---|---|---|
| **Great Britain** | Conference for World Mission [Classical missions: denominational, interdenominational, specialized. No Pentecostal missions] <br><br> Three Anglican missions (CMS, SAMS and BCMS) and three specialized missions hold double membership | Evangelical Missionary Alliance (EMA) [Post-classical, except Brethren and Fundamentalist missions. Also Pentecostal missions] | Only two fundamentalist missions (one 'fighting', one 'quiet') | Some small missions (classical and post-classical) |
| **Germany** | Evangelisches Missionswerk (EMW) [Classical missions, one Pentecostal mission (Vereinigte Missionsfreunde)] <br><br> Only the Baptists (Bund Evangelisch Freikirchlicher Gemeinden und EBM) hold double membership. Some AEM missions cooperate with the EMW in business matters. | Arbeitsgemeinschaft-Evangelikaler Missionen (AEM) [Faith missions, one classical mission (EBM), one non-church mission (Wiedenst)] | Bibletreue Mission Weltweit (small) | Some faith missions and a growing number of charismatic missions |
| **France** <br> **and French speaking** <br> **Switzerland** | Service Protestant de Mission et de Relations Internationales (Défap) | Fédération des Missions Evangéliques Francophones (FMEF) [Faith missions, one non-church mission, one charismatic mission, one classical specialized mission] | | |

National Mission Associations (continued)

| | ECUMENICAL | EVANGELICAL | FUNDAMENTALIST | OTHERS |
|---|---|---|---|---|
| **Netherlands** | Nederlandse Zendingsraad [Classical missions, mostly denominational, no Pentecostal missions] | Evangelische Zendings Alliantie (EZA) [Faith missions, Pentecostal missions, no non-church missions, no denominational evangelical missions] | | Few missions |
| **Sweden** | Svensk Missionsrådet [Classical and post-classical missions. New international missions partly as observers (1986)] | | | Few missions, especially new international faith missions |
| **Norway** | Norsk Missionsrådet | | | Moratorium for accepting new missions as members (1986) |
| **Denmark** | Dansk MissionsrÅd [Classical and post-classical missions] | | | One-fifth of all missions (of various types) |
| **Finland** | Finnish Missionary Council [Classical missions, Pentecostal missions, faith missions] | | | |
| **Nigeria** | | Nigeria Evangelical Missionary Alliance (NEMA) [Faith missions, denominational evangelical, independent and charismatic missions] | | |

# A historical typology of the Protestant missionary movement

| TYPE OF MISSION | OLDEST MISSION | IMPORTANT MISSION | NAME | FORM OF ORGANIZATION | POSITION | FINANCE | SPIRITUAL MOVEMENT |
|---|---|---|---|---|---|---|---|
| **Pre-Classical** | [SPCK 1699] [SPG 1701] | Dänisch-Hallesche 1706 Moravians 1732 | | Individual enterprises Colonial missions State directed | Employed | State support, contributions | Pietism Reformation |
| **Classical Denominational** | Baptist Missionary Society 1792 (Carey) | Church Missionary Society (CMS) 1799 Methodist Missionary Society 1813 [1786] | Name indicating origin, mostly denominational | Mission societies Rarely mission departments of churches | Employed | Gifts, membership fees | Revival of the late 18th and the early 19th century |
| **Classical Inter-denominational** | [London] Missionary Society 1795 | ABCFM 1810 Basel 1815 Paris 1819 Barmen 1828 | Name indicating geographical origin | Mission society | Employed | Gifts, membership fees | Revival of the late 18th and the early 19th century |
| **Classical Specialized** | Edinburgh Medical Missionary Society 1841 | BMMF 1852 WUMS 1860 Ludhiana F. 1894 | Job-oriented names | Mission society | Employed | Gifts | Revival of the late 18th and the early 19th century |

A historical typology of the Protestant missionary movement (continued)

| TYPE OF MISSION | OLDEST MISSION | IMPORTANT MISSION | NAME | FORM OF ORGANIZATION | POSITION | FINANCE | SPIRITUAL MOVEMENT |
|---|---|---|---|---|---|---|---|
| **Classical Fundamentalist** | Association of Baptists for World Evangelism 1927 | Independent Board of Presbyterian Missions 1933 | Denominational names, with fund indicator | Mission departments, mission societies | Employed | Gifts, contributions of churches | 'Fighting funda-mentalism', mainly in the United States |
| **Free Missions** | Karl Gützlaff 1828 | Hudson Taylor 1857 David Livingstone 1852 | Often geographical aim | Individual enterprises | Completely independent | Earnings, private property, gifts | Revivals of the 19th century |
| **Non-Church Missions** | Norris Anthony Groves' Mission in Baghdad 1829 | [Echoes of Service] (1872) CMML Wiedenest 1905 | Geographical aim, general Christian names | Individual enterprises. De facto organization by a magazin | Independent | 'Faith support' | Brethren movement (since about 1825) |
| **Faith Missions** | China Inland Mission 1865 | LIM 1878 [RBMU] NAM 1881 CMA 1887 SAGM 1889 SIM 1900 SUM 1904 WEC 1913 Neukirchen 1882 | Most geographical aim | Mission societies, often with characteristics of an order | Members of the mission | 'Faith support' gifts | Revival of the second half of the 19th century, Holiness movement, Brethren movement, Prophetic (pre-millennialist) movement (Fellowship movement) |

A historical typology of the Protestant missionary movement (continued)

| TYPE OF MISSION | OLDEST MISSION | IMPORTANT MISSION | NAME | FORM OF ORGANIZATION | POSITION | FINANCE | SPIRITUAL MOVEMENT |
|---|---|---|---|---|---|---|---|
| **Pentecostal Missions** | Apostolic Faith Mission 1907 | Assemblies of God Mission 1908 Zaire Evangelistic Mission 1915 | Often denominational name of origin, partly geographical aim | Mission societies partly similar to faith missions | Mostly members of the mission | Gifts, often 'faith support', partly denominational support | Pentecostal movement since 1900–06 |
| **Post-classical Denominational** | Evangelical Free Church (USA) 1887 | Evangelical Congregational Church 1922 | Denominational name of origin | Mission departments of churches | Varied | Gifts, contributions of churches | Evangelical denominations, often from revival of second half of 19th century |
| **Post-classical Fundamentalist** | Not clear | WEF ministries Sahara Desert M. | Geographical aim | Mission society, partly independent tendency | Members, independent | Gifts | 'Quiet' non-denominational fundamentalism |
| **Charismatic** | Not yet clear | Globe Missionary Evangelism 1973 WE GO 1974 | General names, often worldwide | Mission societies | Varied | Gifts | Charismatic movement since about 1960 |

## THE PRE-CLASSICAL MISSIONS

Because the pre-classical missions relate little to the topic of this book, they will not be further subdivided. The first pre-classical missions to gain literary prominence, though no measurable success, were those of the Austrian exile Justinian von Welz (1764)[9]. Two of these missions still exist: the Society for the Propagation of the Gospel (SPG, 1701)[10] and the Moravian Mission (Unitas Fratrum, 1732). In one case, a church resulting from such a mission is still in place (Danisch- Hallesche Mission, 1706).

The three missions mentioned above all have their origin in pietism/puritanism, the first great revival movement after the Reformation. The SPG, with its Royal Charter, and the Danisch-Hallesche Mission were closely bound to the state, whereas the Moravian Mission was part of what became a very peculiar Free Church, originating from one local congregation. They were all, in one way or another, clearly related to a denomination or to a group of related denominations. Today they belong to ecumenical mission councils and have largely conformed to the patterns of the classical missions.

## THE CLASSICAL MISSIONS

The first subdivision of the classical missions comprises the denominational missions, whose names normally indicate their denominational origin. These denominational missions were almost always organized independently of any church, but were nevertheless strongly related to one church or to a small group of churches of the same type, which ordained the missionaries. The concept of unity was corporate—the point of reference was the church as a corporate body, not the individual's faith.

The missions were organized as voluntary associations in which every member other than the missionaries—to whom the principle of voluntary association did not apply because they were employed by the mission—had a say.[11]

Today, most classical missions have an ecumenical tendency and belong to their respective mission associations. However, there are also some classical denominational missions (especially in the United States) which, like the church they are related to, are definitely evangelical in theology.[12]

During the past decades, nearly all classical denominational missions have been integrated and brought under the control of their respective churches. Such integration guaranteed considerable financial support from the churches' regular income. In most of the classical denominational missions, the number of missionaries has declined over the same period.

The second subdivision of the classical missions comprises the interdenominational classical missions, the first of which was the London Missionary Society (1795). All the early German, and most continental, missions were of this type. They can be recognized by their names, which contain an element indicating the geographical origin, for example, the American Board of Commissioners for Foreign Missions (1810), Evangelische Missionsgesellschaft in Basel (1815), Societé des Missions Evangéliques de Paris (1822)[13] and Ostfriesische Missionsgesellschaft (1834).[14]

All interdenominational classical missions worked vicariously for churches (mostly territorial folk-churches) practising infant baptism. Their missionaries, like those of the denominational missions, were ordained by one of the churches to which the respective mission was related. Missionaries from churches with believers' baptism were not welcome.

All classical denominational missions underwent a rapid process of denominationalization, so that it is no longer useful to differentiate between denominational and interdenominational classical missions. All interdenominational classical missions today belong to ecumenical mission associations.

A separate subdivision must be accorded to the specialized classical missions, the first of which was the Edinburgh Medical Missionary Society (1841), followed by the Zenana Bible and Medical Mission, also founded also in Edinburgh eléven years later.[15] In the United States, one of the very early specialized missions was the Woman's Union Missionary Society of America, founded in 1861 as a protest against male restrictions on the involvement of women in missions.[16] These specialized missions hold a special position. They were less concerned with doctrine, so they could be more widely interdenominational, and they also offered more scope for individualism. In both respects, they served to some extent as an example for faith missions. Nevertheless, the example could operate the other way as well, as can be seen with the two last-mentioned missions which, in the course of their history, accepted the principles of faith missions and joined the same mission associations as they. The Chinese Evangelization Society, the precursor of the CIM, can best be understood as a classical specialized mission, because its aim, unlike the classical, was not to start churches but ('only') to evangelize the whole of China by means of Chinese evangelists combined with the extensive use of Christian literature.

During the second generation of the classical missionary movement, two missions were founded which were, to some extent, precursors of the later faith missions. The Gossner Mission (1836) later became a regular classical mission,[17] but when it started, its missionaries—like those of the independent missions—felt their work to be subject to God alone. Nonetheless, Johannes Evangelista Gossner, the founder of the Gossner Mission, developed a style of authoritarian leadership strongly reminiscent of the role of the early faith mission founders and leaders.[18] The other mission which may have served, at least in one aspect, as an example for faith missions was the Pilgermission St Chrischona (1840) which, for its missionary work along the 'Apostles' Road' from Jerusalem to Ethiopia, consciously employed only 'craftsmen missionaries'. Craftsmen missionaries were not ordained but were missionaries in their own right, whereas in most classical missions, unordained missionaries were only assistants to those missionaries who were ordained. In faith missions, unordained missionaries were usually accorded equal rights to those who were ordained.

It was only in the 1930s that the classical missionary movement gave birth to another subdivision, the fundamentalist classical missions. These missions were born in enmity and strife about proper theology within the classical denominations but, as their organizational structures show, they are children of the denominational variety of the classical missionary movement.[19] In all cases, they separated from classical missions. They number barely a dozen. Today (1986), they usually belong to a fundamentalist mission association (The Associated Missions of the International Council of Christian Churches (TAM-ICCC)) and refuse to cooperate with any other group, whether 'ecumenical' or 'evangelical'. Their concept of unity is based on separation—the precondition for any cooperation is a far-reaching agreement on the interpretation of the Bible and a strict separation from all individuals who do not adhere to the same convictions and from all corporate entities (such as churches, missions and so on) that are in fellowship with individuals or groups of different convictions ('second degree separation').[20]

# Precursors of the faith missions

| | |
|---|---|
| 1836 | Gossner Mission |
| 1841 | Edinburgh Medical Missionary Society |
| 1840 | (1856) Pilgermission St Chrischona |
| 1852 | Zenana, Bible, and Medical Mission, or Indian Female Normal School and Instruction Society |
| 1856 | Ermeloosche Zendingsgemeente (until 1862, auxiliary of the Rhenish Mission, then independent) |
| 1860 | Women's United Missionary Society |
| 1862 | Scripture Gift Mission |

## THE POST-CLASSICAL MISSIONS

When the China Inland Mission was started in 1865, it was not the first post-classical mission, though it was to become the most influential. Two smaller post-classical missionary movements preceded it and provided innovative ideas: that is, the independent missions and the non-church missions.

The independent missions accepted no human authority beyond their own and were responsible to no church or mission.[21] They usually consisted of the founder, members of his family (if the founder was a man) and perhaps a limited number of co-workers. The continuity of an independent mission was limited, especially after the founder died or left the mission field. The independent missionaries' financial support came from what they earned, possibly from a secular job or as traders; sometimes they were people of independent means, and often they received support from friends at home.

The independent missions served as an example for faith missions insofar as, for them too, God's individual call was the starting point of their missiology. But this conviction was not opposed to effective and, if necessary, far-reaching organization, nor to the establishment of permanent structures.

Independent missions are prone to fluctuation and change. Quite a number of them, originally conceived as independent missions, soon turned themselves into faith missions and developed the necessary organizational structures. The first important faith mission missionary was Karl Gützlaff (1803–51), a German Lutheran[22] who, in 1828, left the Nederlandsch Zendelinggenootschap because his mission did not agree to his work among the Chinese in Indonesia. Gützlaff usually earned his support by working for a government. To help him to extend his work, the Chinesische Stiftung was founded in Kassel in 1846.[23] A similar society, the Chinese Evangelization Society (CES), was founded in 1849 in Tottenham, London.[24] In 1854, Hudson Taylor started his missionary career as a member of this specialized mission. In 1857, he left the mission to become an independent missionary, though remaining on good terms with the mission throughout its existence.[25]

When Hudson Taylor became an independent missionary, he took the decision to expect his support only 'as an answer to prayer in faith'.[26] By so deciding, he followed the innovative 'faith principle' of the non-church missions which, originating from the Brethren movement, came into existence at about the same time as the independent missions.[27] The first non-church missionary was Anthony Norris Groves (1795–1853), who went with his party to Baghdad in 1829.[28] Originally Groves, a self-employed dentist, wanted to work with the CMS; however, shortly before he was due to travel, he severed his connection to the CMS because he could not agree to being ordained by any denomination[29]. Soon after leaving the CMS, he became convinced that no ordination at all was necessary.[30] The Brethren did not see themselves as a church but as a movement, trying to achieve 'the unity of all believers' from all denominations and beyond all denominations. Movements of this kind can be called non-denominational, which means that they do not see themselves as a denomination, although to the outsider they seem to behave quite like one.[31]

The Brethren and, with it, the non-church missions are evangelical in piety,[32] but they are not included among faith missions because they are not interdenominational.[33] Because the Brethren do not ordain, ordination has no role in the non-church missions either. Non-church missions do not usually join mission associations,[34] but they do not refuse to cooperate with other evangelical missions.

Faith missions absorbed their basic ideas from the independent missions (the concept of direct and individual responsibility to God) and from the non-church missions (the concept of 'faith support'). Although they can rightly be seen as successors to these two movements, it is more appropriate to understand them not as continuing these movements but as a correction of their basic shortcoming: lack of organization and missionary effectiveness.

A somewhat later development among the post-classical missions are the post-classical denominational missions. These missions: are closely related to one Free Church which originated in an interdenominational faith mission; were strongly influenced by the concepts of faith missions; or belong to a church which, like the Evangelical Free Church of America[35] and faith missions, originated in the Great Revival of the second half of the nineteenth century. Missions of this type are mainly found in the United States.

A special group among the post-classical missions are the fundamentalist post-classical missions. Unlike faith missions, they are not interdenominational, but non-denominational. They do not accept the denominations and either ignore or

25

(very often) oppose them. In common with the classical fundamentalist missions, they demand second degree separation. They differ from the classical fundamentalist missions in that they did not originate in a quarrel for supremacy within a classical denomination. They are not 'fighting fundamentalists' but originated in a somewhat later movement of independent fundamentalist congregations. They did not fight for correct doctrine and supremacy in the denominations, but withdrew from them—not as a group, but individually. Therefore, they may be called 'quiet fundamentalists' and their tendency is known as 'non-denominational fundamentalism'.

## THE PENTECOSTAL/CHARISMATIC MISSIONS

Faith missions, new and revolutionary as they were, did not remain for ever 'new'. Just as the 1859/1873 revival had produced a new type of mission, so did the next great revival criss-crossing the Protestant denominations. The pentecostal movement originated in 1900 in Topeka, Kansas,[36] and gained worldwide influence after the Los Angeles Azusa Street Revival in 1906.[37] pentecostal missions have existed since at least 1907. They are basically evangelical in piety but have a distinct theology of their own, concentrating on spiritual gifts and the 'full Gospel'. Speaking in tongues is usually seen as the 'initial sign' of being filled with the Spirit. Their theological background is Arminian rather than Calvinist, whereas faith missions, strongly influenced by Arminianism as they were, drew their main support from Calvinist denominations. In the mission field, pentecostal missions often cooperate with faith missions, and in some countries they belong to the same mission association.[38] Most pentecostal missions are denominational, but there are interdenominational missions in which Christians from various pentecostal denominations cooperate. Youth With A Mission (YWAM, 1960), a specialized pentecostal mission,[39] outgrew the limits of pentecostalism and now includes even Lutheran branches (in Scandinavia). There is even one pentecostal faith mission[40] but, in general, the pentecostal missions are a quite distinct type of mission, though they have not formed their own mission associations.[41]

The most recent worldwide renewal movement, which has touched most Protestant churches (and strongly influenced the Roman Catholic Church and Orthodox churches), was the charismatic movement, starting in about 1960. Because during its first decades the charismatic movement largely ran its course within the classical denominations, many missionaries who were influenced by this movement joined existing missions, including faith missions. Nevertheless, as more and more charismatic denominations and independent congregations come into existence, a separate charismatic missionary movement is being born. The United States is ahead in this, but the process has also started in Great Britain, and is beginning in Germany and elsewhere.[42]

It is possible that the charismatic movement will develop a non-denominational bias, but denominational and interdenominational developments also seem possible. Though charismatic theology is basically pentecostal, the charismatic missions must be regarded as a separate missionary movement because they stem from a different revival movement and operate in a different historical context.

IDENTITY, UNITY AND SEPARATION

In this book a clear distinction will be maintained between classical, evangelical and fundamentalist missions. Classical churches and missions tend to claim that the whole of the missionary spectrum rightly belongs to them, and they often see no real reason for the existence of 'all these new missions'.[44] Yet they have to accept the fact, alongside them, there now exist missions with a different identity. Evangelical missions have their own identity, stressing the value of the scriptures and emphasizing the need for evangelization and individual conversion. That identity, however, allows some overlap and cooperation with the classical missions. In this respect, fundamentalists strongly differ from evangelicals: their identity is based on separation from all false doctrine and from all who do not separate themselves from people who hold false doctrines. Because of this, I differentiate between evangelicals and fundamentalists. Only those missions will be termed fundamentalist which use the term themselves or would not object to it being used of them. Fundamentalist missions do not cooperate with other missions, whether evangelical or ecumenical, and do not join the respective mission associations or Christian Councils.[44]

Each group has a different concept of unity: for classical missions, it is corporate (organizations or churches trying to reach corporate unity); for faith missions, it is individual (individuals praying and working together irrespective of the

27

corporate relationship of their churches); and for fundamentalist missions, it is separated (cooperation only with those who agree in doctrine and on separation).

## Notes

1   Hudson Taylor formulated it thus: 'God's work done in God's way will not lack God's supply.'

2   The association of North American faith missions bears the name Interdenominational Foreign Missions Association (IFMA). This term was chosen in order not to give the impression that denominational missions lacked faith (Edwin L. Frizen, *An Historical Study of the Interdenominational Foreign Mission Association in Relation to Evangelical Unity and Cooperation*, DMiss, Deerfield, 1981, p. 23). Nevertheless, IFMA published a booklet in which each member mission presented itself, under the title: 'Faith Mighty Faith' (J. Herbert Kane, Wheaton, 1956).

3   This includes the limited number of missions which did not start as faith missions, but at some point in their history consciously accepted the principles of faith missions. Some major examples are: Pilgermission St Chrischona (1840–56), Women's United Missionary Society (1860) and some industrial missions, such as the Zambezi Industrial Mission (1892), the Nyassa Industrial Mission (1893) and the Philafrican Liberators' League.

4   An exception is made to this historical definition in the rare case of a mission consciously repudiating faith mission principles. Possibly there is only one mission which did this: the Kieler Mission, which started as the German Branch of the CIM (Andreas Franz, 'Die Abkehr von den Prinzipien einer Glaubensmission, dargestellt am Beispiel der Kieler Mission' in Klaus Fiedler, *Missionswerke ohne Spendenkampagnen—Die Glaubensmissionen heute und in der Vergangenheit*, idea-dokumentation 9/11, pp. 55–59).

5   If this is true, the change of a mission from one 'type' to another would be a significant event in its history, requiring special interpretation.

6   'In 1793, five years before the death of Schwartz, there landed in Calcutta William Carey, who was to begin a new era in Protestant missions, not only in India, but also in the entire world' (Kenneth Scott Latourette, *A History of the Expansion of Christianity*, Grand Rapids, Zondervan Edition [5]1976 (1939/1967) III, p. 281).

7   William Carey, *An Enquiry into the Obligation of Christians to Use Means for the Conversion of the Heathen*, Leicester, 1792, especially pp. 81ff.

8   See Andrew F. Walls, 'Missionary Societies and the Fortunate Subversion of the Church', in *Evangelical Quarterly* 88:2 (1988), pp. 141–155.

9   Fritz Laubach, 'Justinian von Welz—Leben und Werk', pp. 14ff., in Fritz Laubach (ed.), *Justinian von Welz. Sämtliche Schriften*, Wuppertal/Zürich, 1989, pp. 7–32.

10 Today, United Society for the Propagation of the Gospel. In 1965, merged with Universities Mission to Central Africa (1857); in 1968, with Cambridge Mission to Delhi (1877).

11 Therefore, the organizational principle of the early classical missions has been termed 'voluntary absolutism' (Peter Hinchliff, 'Voluntary Absolutism: British Missionary Societies in the Nineteenth Century' in W. J. Sheils and Diana Wood, *Voluntary Religion*, London, 1986, pp. 363–379).

12 A prominent example in this respect are the American Southern Baptists.

13 The early leaders of the Paris Mission were Reformed, Lutheran and Congregationalist. (Burton L. Goddard (ed.), *The Encyclopedia of Modern Christian Missions. The Agencies*, Camden, NJ et al., 1967, p. 590f.).

14 This name pattern equally applied to Scandinavia, where the missions right from the beginning were *de facto* Lutheran: Danske Missionsselskab (1821); Svenska Missionssällskapet (1836); Norske Misjonsselskap (1842); and Suomen Lähetysseura/Finska Missionssällskapet (1859).

15 Since 1989, called Interserve. Before that, Bible and Medical Missionary Fellowship (BMMF). Since 1952, men can become members. BMMF has experienced considerable growth.

16 Until 1911, Woman's Union Missionary Society of America for Heathen Lands.

17 Walter Holsten, *Johannes Evangelista Gossner. Glaube und Gemeinde*, Göttingen, 1949, pp. 158ff.

18 In faith missions, the Gossner Mission is sometimes seen as a precedent. Bingham, for example, writes: 'Gossner and Harms were the fathers of the 'Faith Mission' movement which really emanated from Germany' (*The Missionary Witness*, October 1914, p. 293). But no trace of direct influence could be found, although remote literary influences do not seem impossible.

19 A typical case in point is the Independent Board for Presbyterian Missions which was founded in 1933 by Gresham Machen in protest against Presbyterian 'modernism' (details: *EMCM*, p. 323f.). This led to his, and Carl McIntire's, expulsion from the Presbyterian Church in 1936; they then established the Orthodox Presbyterian Church, which Carl McIntire left in 1937 to begin the even more fundamentalist Bible Presbyterian Church (Constant H. Jaquet (ed.), *Yearbook of American and Canadian Churches 1986*, Nashville, 1985, p. 79). Both churches have remained small.

20 Second-degree separation today is the main yardstick with which to separate fundamentalists and evangelicals. Evangelicals separate themselves individually from what they consider wrong teaching. Fundamentalists demand corporate separation from any corporate structure contaminated by wrong doctrine, compromise, pluralism and/or the World Council of Churches. This attitude possibly goes back to John Nelson Darby.

21 George Müller's attitude here is typical: 'I further had a conscientious objection against being led and directed by men in my missionary labours. As a servant of Christ it appeared to me, I ought to be guided by the Spirit, and not by men, as to time and place' (George Müller, *A Narrative of Some of the Lord's Dealings with George*

*Müller Written by Himself*, 9th edn, London, 1895, [1]1837, p. 50f.).

22  Early monographs were Herman Schlyter, *Karl Gützlaff als Missionar in China*, Lund 1946; *Der China-Missionar Karl Gützlaff und seine Heimatbasis. Studien über das Interesse des Abendlandes an der Mission des China-Pioniers Karl Gützlaff und über seinen Einsatz als Missionserwecker*, Lund, 1976.

23  For a detailed history of the Chinesische Stiftung see Günter Bezzenberger, *Mission in China. Die Geschichte der Chinesischen Stiftung*, Kassel, 1979. The Chinesische Stiftung was no classical mission, because Gützlaff stood in no official relationship to it.

24  For the British organizations supporting Gützlaff, and for an evaluation of their work from the viewpoint of CIM/OMF, see A. J. Broomhall, *Barbarians at the Gates*, London/Sevenoaks, 1981, pp. 323–349.

25  James Hudson Taylor, *Retrospect*, London, 18, 1974, p. 95f. ([1]1894); see: A. J. Broomhall, *If I had a Thousand Lives*, Sevenoaks, 1982, p. 31, p. 34f.

26  Taylor, *Retrospect*, p. 95f.

27  A good and scholarly book on the Brethren movement is Frederick Roy Coad, *A History of the Brethren Movement. Its Origins, its Worldwide Development and its Significance for the Present Day*, Exeter, 1968.

28  Anthony Norris Groves, *Memoir of Anthony Norris Groves, Compiled Chiefly From his Journals and Letters, to Which is Added a Supplement, Containing Recollections of Miss Paget, and Accounts of Missionary Works in India, etc.* By his widow, London, [3]1869. His biography is G. H. Lang, *Anthony Norris Groves*, London, 1949.

29  Groves, *Memoir*, p. 42.

30  'One day the thought was brought to my mind, that ordination of any kind to preach the gospel is no requirement of scripture. To me it was a removal of a mountain' (Groves, *Memoir*, p. 42).

31  An example is the Non-Church Movement in Japan. See Hannelore Kimura-Andres, *Mukyokai*, Erlangen, 1988.

32  The missionary work of the Brethren is described in W. I. Stunt, *Turning the World Upside Down*, Eastbourne, 1972. For Brethren influences on Hudson Taylor and the founders of the NAM, see p. 31.

33  Seen from the point of view of the more exclusive section of the Brethren movement, even CIM is not a 'pure' mission because it has organizational structures which a 'purely scriptural' mission is supposed not to have (Lang, *Groves*, p. 18f.).

34  An important exception is Missionshaus Bibelschule Wiedenest. Ernst Schrupp, its founder, was strongly influenced by interdenominational movements such as Youth for Christ and IFES, and he tried to combine the strong concept of the local church as the sending agency with effective organization, as he learned it from faith missions (Ernst Schrupp, 'Die gemeindliche Sendung' in *Evangelikale Missiologie* 1/1987, pp. 10–14.) Also important was his participation in the Youth for Christ 1948 Conference for World Evangelization at Beatenberg Bible School (Interview Ernst Schrupp, 12 October 1987).

35 Founded in 1884 as the Swedish Evangelical Free Mission, later renamed Swedish Evangelical Free Church and, after union with the Evangelical Free Church Association (originally Norwegian and Danish Free Church Association), Evangelical Free Church of America (Frank S. Mead and Samuel S. Hill, *Handbook of Denominations in the United States*, Nashville, [8]1985, p. 113).

36 Walter J. Hollenweger, *Enthusiastisches Christentum. Die Pfingstbewegung in Geschichte und Gegenwart*, Zürich/Wuppertal, 1969, pp. 21ff.

37 Frank Bartleman, *Azusa Street*, Logos International, 1980 (includes Frank Bartleman, *How 'Pentecost' came to Los Angeles—How It Was in the Beginning*, 1925).

38 For example, Nigeria, France and Britain, but not Germany, and usually not the United States.

39 Loren Cunningham with Janice Rogers, *Is That Really You, God?*, Lincoln, 1984.

40 The Örebro Missionsforening originated in the Holiness movement and did not leave it after accepting pentecostal doctrine.

41 A mine of information on pentecostal missions is provided in Stanley M. Burgess, Gary B. McGee and Patrick H. Alexander (eds), *Dictionary of Pentecostal and Charismatic Movements*, Regency Reference Library, Zondervan, Grand Rapids, [3]1989 (1988) (that is, *DPCM*).

42 Recently, attempts were made at charismatic mission cooperation, for example, the North American Congresses on the Holy Spirit and World Evangelization (New Orleans, 1986, 1987) and the Association of International Mission Services, originating in a 1985 meeting at Christ for the Nations Institute in Dallas (Gary B. McGee, 'Missions, Overseas (North American)' in Burgess, McGee and Alexander (eds), *DPCM*, Grand Rapids, 1988, p. 624).

43 This position was formulated frequently by Gustav Warneck, often called the 'father' of German Protestant Missiology.

44 Often the term 'fundamentalist' is defined more loosely, for example, by James Barr, *Fundamantalism*, London, 1977. Barr includes much of what I call 'evangelical' in his somewhat unspecific definition of 'fundamentalist'. He writes: 'There is a difficulty, in that American and British terms seem not to agree precisely. I am not sure where the American distinction between evangelicals and fundamentalists, as it is found in recent usage, lies in relation to my own following description. My impression is that both these terms are used in America to indicate a position more conservative or more extreme than is the common usage in Great Britain, so that fundamentalism as depicted here might fall into the more extreme segment of evangelicalism and the less extreme of fundamentalism, as the terms are used in the United States' (p. 6). Fundamentalism means, for Barr, 'a certain basic personal religious and existential attitude... which, when it appears, commonly appears within, and overlaps with, the ecclesiastical grouping known as 'conservative evangelical'(p. 5). Yet another definition of fundamentalism which differs from mine is used by Stephan Holthaus, *Protestantischer Fundamentalismus in Deutschland—Geschichte und Erscheinungsbild*, Bonn, 1993. Whereas I use second-degree separation as the primary mark to define fundamentalism, he uses the adherence to Biblical inerrancy as the primary mark.

# 2

# A new missionary movement: the early history of faith missions

## Origins and basic concepts of faith missions

It is the aim of this book to describe faith missions and their theology. Their theology will be deduced not from the comparatively few theological statements produced by faith missions, but from observing what faith missions do. To date, no overall history of faith missions has been written. This book does not fufil that role, either, but it aims to present an overview of the early development of faith missions insofar as they touched Africa. In order to facilitate a historical understanding, the China Inland Mission will be described in some detail, because all faith missions working in Africa trace their origin to the CIM. Because few early faith missions did not work in Africa, the picture presented here applies to faith missions in general. In order not to overburden the presentation, much factual information will be presented in tables and charts.

### HUDSON TAYLOR AND THE CHINA INLAND MISSION

The most important person to leave his imprint on faith missions was Hudson Taylor,[1] who founded the CIM[2] and thus defined the basic principles of a faith mission. During the history of the various faith missions, these principles underwent many changes,[3] but they still remain valid as a yardstick.

Hudson Taylor did not originally intend to found a new mission. He took this step only after all his attempts to entice the existing missions to increase considerably their efforts in the 'inland' of China, beyond the area of the treaty ports, had proved futile.[4] Still, the reason for founding the CIM is not to be seen only as a result of the reluctance of the classical missions but equally as a result of Hudson Taylor's theological conviction that all who do not believe in Christ are eternally lost.[5] Therefore,

32

# The principles of the China Inland Mission

1. The mission is interdenominational. Missionaries from all Protestant churches can become members if they agree to the statement of faith.

2. Church order is a secondary issue. Problems of church order may be solved in a pragmatic way.

3. Missionaries are not employees, but members of the mission.

4. Missionaries receive no salary, but expect that God will supply their every need through the hands of his children ('faith principle').

5. Missionaries with any type of training are equally welcome.

6. There is no difference between ordained and unordained missionaries.

7. Wives are full missionaries and all possibilities open to men are open to them as well.

8. Single women have the same possibilities as men. They may work on their own as pioneer evangelists.

9. Missionaries identify as far as possible with the culture of their host country. As a sign of this identification they wear Chinese dress.

10. Missionaries must be willing to accept sacrifice and suffering.

11. In missionary work, evangelism takes precedence over institutional work.

12. It is the first priority of all evangelistic work to give everyone at least one chance to hear the Gospel. Therefore, evangelistic itineration must receive special attention.

13. Converts are to be joined into local congregations and to be used to further evangelism.

14. The mission is international.

15. Leadership is centralistic. The mission is field-directed. Home Councils are only to represent the mission in a given country, not to direct the mission.

Christians must make every effort to present the gospel every-where so that everyone has a chance to hear or read it and to accept Christ as saviour.[6] Parallel to this was his conviction that Christ's second coming will only take place after the gospel has been preached to all peoples. These two theological convictions demanded a quicker expansion of missionary work, more effective methods and much larger numbers of missionaries. His independent ecclesiastical position made it possible for Hudson Taylor to win many missionaries, to expand the missionary work and to try out new methods.

Born as a Wesleyan Methodist, Taylor had joined the Brethren, who do not practise ordination, so it was possible for him to use 'laymen' as full missionaries—not, as in the classical missions, only as missionaries' assistants. His Methodist background, strengthened by influences from the holiness movement, even allowed him to give 'laywomen' the right of full evangelistic service. Since Taylor did not feel bound to any ecclesiastical tradition, he was able to win missionaries from almost all Protestant churches, even from churches with opposing doctrines on baptism, such as Baptists and Presbyterians. His guiding theological principle was not dogmatic correctness but effective evangelism.

THE 'GUINNESS MISSIONS'

The names of faith missions usually say much about where they were to work, and nothing about their origin or background—but much can be deduced from connections between their founders. Looking at their origins in this way, the centrality of Fanny and Grattan Guinness soon becomes obvious. The great majority of the early faith missions stood in some kind of relationship to them. These faith missions, therefore, together with the CIM, form the main body. Among the 'non-Guinness-related missions', those immediately obliged to the holiness movement form one group[7] and the other group comprises the industrial missions. They do not go back to Hudson Taylor, but to David Livingstone (1813–73) and to the Methodist holiness preacher (later Bishop) William Taylor (1821–1902); however, in the course of their history they conformed to faith mission principles.[8]

FANNY AND GRATTAN GUINNESS AND
THE EAST LONDON TRAINING INSTITUTE

The transfer of the faith mission concept from China to Africa and beyond was effected by the Irish couple Fanny and Grattan

# Hudson Taylor and the China Inland Mission

| | |
|---|---|
| 1832 | Hudson Taylor born to Methodist parents |
| 1834 | George Müller creates 'Scriptural Knowledge Institution for Home and Abroad' |
| 1837 | Maria Jane Dyer born |
| 1844–50 | Karl Gützlaff's 'Chinese Union', Hong Kong |
| 1849 | Hudson Taylor's conversion. Member of the Methodist church at Barnsley |
| 1849 | (2 December) Hudson Taylor's holiness experience |
| 1850 | H.T. and his parents decide for Free Methodists at split of Methodist Church Barnsley |
| 1851–52 | H.T. joins Brethren at Hull, is baptized |
| 1851 | Karl Gützlaff dies at Hong Kong |
| 1853 | H.T. as missionary of the Chinese Evangelisation Society in China |
| 1857 | H.T. leaves CES and becomes a free missionary, receives some support from George Müller (SKI) |
| 1858 | Hudson Taylor and Maria Jane Dyer marry |
| 1860 | CES dissolves itself |
| 1860 | Hudson Taylor returns to London |
| 1864 | (3 June) H.T. opens bank account under the name 'China Inland Mission' |
| 1865 | Founding of China Inland Mission |
| 1866 | Hudson Taylor meets Grattan Guinness |
| 1866 | First CIM party leaves on the Lammermuir |
| 1866 | H.T. baptizes two missionaries at Anjer (Java) |
| 1867 | First baptism (in Hangzhou) |
| 1870 | Maria Taylor dies |
| 1871 | Hudson Taylor marries Jane E. Faulding |
| 1872 | Leadership in Britain passes from William Berger to the London Council |
| 1874–75 | Hudson Taylor severely ill |
| 1875 | CIM: twenty-eight missionaries in ten areas |
| 1888 | H.T. attends Moody's Northfield Conference |
| 1888 | CIM-North America started in Canada |
| 1900 | Boxer Rebellion |
| 1905 | Hudson Taylor dies at Changsha |
| 1950 | CIM decides to withdraw from China |
| 1951 | CIM decides to work in other countries of East Asia. Headquarters in Singapore |
| 1951 | CIM dissolves relationship to all associated missions |
| 1964 | CIM (now Overseas Missionary Fellowship) constituted as an international missionary fellowship with missionaries from all races and nations |

# FANNY AND GRATTAN GUINNESS AND THE FAITH MISSION MOVEMENT IN AFRICA—AN OVERVIEW

Holiness Movement

Wesley

Karl Gützlaff

Chinese
Evangelisation
Society

George Müller

Anthony Norris Groves

Brethren Movement

Holiness Conferences
(Keswick and others)

Hudson Taylor 1865
China Inland Mission

1865, Hudson Taylor visits Fanny
and Grattan Guinness in Dublin

Bible Conferences

Prophetic Movement

Prophetic Conferences

Chicago Avenue Church

Fredrik Franson

The decisive influence in the
missionary work of:
Örebro Mission
Helgelseförbundet
Svenska Alliansmissionen
Svenska Missionsförbundet
Norsk Missionsförbundet
Allianzmission

TEAM (USA/CA)

Gratan Guinness meets
Emma Dryer

Moody Bible
Institute 1889

Lucy Guinness

Karl Kumm

C. T. Studd

WEC

Sudan
Pioneer
Mission
(EMO,
SENM)

Sudan
United
Mission

North
Africa
Mission

**Fanny and Grattan Guinness East
London Training Institute 1873**

1878 Livingstone
Inland Mission

Svenska Missions-
förbundet

Congo Balolo
Mission

Regions Beyond
Missionary
Union

G. S. Fisher

Qua Iboe
Mission

*Influenced*
*School Mission*

*Grattan Guinness plays a*
*decisive role in the life*
*of A. B. Simpson*

A. J. Gordon

Boston Missionary
Training Institute 1889

*Influences and wins R. V.*
*Bingham for mission*

A. T. Pierson

Gospel
Missionary
Union

R. V. Bingham

P. C. Scott

Africa
Inland
Mission

A. B. Simpson

New York Missionary
Training Institute 1882

Sudan
Interior
Mission

Christian and
Missionary
Alliance

Guinness.[9] Grattan Guinness was more the theologian, and he spread the idea of faith missions and of Missionary Training Institutes to the United States[10] Fanny Guinness (née Fitzgerald) was more the organizer and mission leader[11]. Not only did they belong to the famous Guinness family (brewery, banking), but they even began a new branch of it: the mission Guinnesses.[12] They had personal contacts with most early faith missions, often family ties. This is brought out by the following chart.

Like Hudson Taylor, Grattan Guinness underwent a denominational change, in this case from Congregationalist to Brethren. He broke off training for the ministry at New College, Edinburgh; preached as an evangelist in Ireland; and, after refusing an offer for full-time service with the independent Moorfield Tabernacle in London, was sent out by the same as an itinerant interdenominational evangelist in 1857.[13] During the 1858–59 revival, he worked successfully as an evangelist on both sides of the Atlantic. In 1865–66, Fanny and Grattan Guinness settled for a time in Dublin, where Grattan organized, for ten young men, a course on the basics of the Christian faith. Part of his intention was to find out if, in the future, he should concentrate on training evangelists and missionaries.[14] Grattan Guinness invited Hudson Taylor to give a guest lecture on this course. After the talk, four of the participants,[15] and Fanny and Grattan Guinness, applied to join the CIM. Hudson Taylor told the Guinness couple that, being over thirty years of age, they would have problems in mastering a new language, so he asked them to remain in Britain and to train missionaries instead.[16] Fanny and Grattan Guinness were not convinced and went to Paris to do evangelistic work but, in the long run, Hudson Taylor's advice led them to found the East London Training Institute (ELTI) in 1873.[17] This was the first interdenominational mission training institute.[18]

By 1887, more than five hundred young people had been trained at the ELTI, and about seventy had joined the CIM.[19] Four faith missions, closely related to the ELTI, came into existence. Two of them—the Livingstone Inland Mission (LIM, 1878–84)[20] and the Congo Balolo Mission (1889)[21]—were the direct responsibility of the ELTI. In 1887, at the suggestion of Grattan Guinness, one of his students, Samuel A. Bill, went to the Calabar Coast in Nigeria as an independent missionary, resulting in the establishment of the Qua Iboe Mission.[22] Due to a personal friendship, George Pearse and his wife contacted the Guinnesses. This led, in 1881, to the founding of the North Africa Mission

(NAM), which today bears the name Arab World Ministries.[23] Under the influence of Edward Glenny, the co-founder and long-term leader of the NAM, three smaller missions were founded: the Southern Morocco Mission, the Central Morocco (Medical) Mission and the Algiers Mission Band.[24]

All these missions were interdenominational, but each had a different group of supporters: the main support of the LIM came from Wales[25]; the NAM received its strongest support from the Brethren movement; and the QIM received its main support from the interdenominational mission halls and YMCA groups in Presbyterian Northern Ireland, which had come into existence after the 1873 revival. The CBM was, in some ways, successor to the LIM.

The Guinness family belonged to an independent congregation in East London.[26] In theological terms, they were still close to the Brethren, but had left them from a desire to give preference to missionary effectiveness over doctrinal correctness. Leadership of the ELTI was a family affair: Fanny managed the Institute, ran the LIM and was the mission writer. Grattan was the evangelist and teacher, and also one of the leading theologians and writers of the new prophetic movement. Their children shared in the work at the ELTI and in its outreach as soon as they could.[27] In addition, Lucy and Geraldine demonstrated that they had inherited their mother's literary gifts.[28]

The ELTI played a double role: it was founded in 1873 as an independent missionary training institute, independent not only of any church, but also of any mission. When Fanny Guinness became responsible for the LIM, every student remained free to join the mission of their choice, even though the school had its own mission. This was an additional burden to the Guinnesses, and could have led to divided loyalties among the supporters. This makes it understandable that Fanny Guinness, on learning that the American Baptist Missionary Union would like to take over the recently started NAM work, suggested to Adoniram Judson Gordon that they take over the work of the LIM instead.[29] By handing over the LIM to the ABMU,[30] ELTI regained its full independence—only to give it up again in 1889 when Harry Guinness started the Congo Balolo Mission in order to continue the advance into the interior which the ABMU had promised to press for but had not achieved. The ELTI became the pattern for many other institutes, and its importance for training missionaries cannot be underestimated, although its close relation to one mission was unusual.[31]

# Fanny and Grattan Guinness and the missions connected with them

| | |
|---|---|
| 1832 | Fanny Fitzgerald born in Southern Ireland |
| 1835 | Henry Grattan Guinness born in Cheltenham |
| 1853 | Grattan Guinness' conversion |
| 1857 | (29 June) Grattan Guinness ordained by the Moorfield Tabernacle (London) as a travelling interdenominational evangelist |
| 1857–60 | Evangelistic work, in the context of the 1859 revival in North America, Great Britain and Ireland |
| 1858 | A. B. Simpson (Chatham, Canada, later founder of CMA) experiences his conversion under the influence of Grattan Guinness |
| 1860 | Grattan Guinness marries Fanny Fitzgerald at Bath. Joins the Brethren movement |
| 1866 | The Guinnesses meet Hudson Taylor in Dublin |
| 1867–72 | Evangelistic work, especially in Paris |
| 1870 | Grattan Guinness turns from postmillennialism to a historical premillennial eschatology |
| 1873 | East London Training Institute |
| 1878 | Livingstone Inland Mission (Zaire) |
| 1881 | North Africa Mission |
| 1881 | Engvall becomes the first Swedish missionary (Svenska Missionsförbundet) of the Livingstone Inland Mission |
| 1884 | LIM handed over to the American Baptist Foreign Missionary Union |
| 1885 | The Swedish missionaries of the LIM start their own mission of the Svenska Missionsförbundet |
| 1887 | Qua Iboe Mission |
| 1888 | Lilias Trotter starts the Algiers Mission Band, influenced by Edward Glenny (North Africa Mission) |
| 1888 | John Anderson starts the Southern Morocco (Medical) Mission, influenced by Edward Glenny (NAM) |
| 1889 | Harry Guinness starts the Congo Balolo Mission |
| 1889 | Grattan Guinness causes A. J. Gordon to start the Boston Missionary Training Institute |
| 1889 | Grattan Guinness assists Emma Dryer to organize the future Moody Bible Institute |
| 1889 | Grattan Guinness causes the founding of the Gospel Missionary Union's Sudan Mission, later to become the Sierra Leone Mission of the Christian and Missionary Alliance |
| 1898 | Fanny Guinness dies |
| 1899 | Grattan Guinness receives honorary Doctorate of Divinity from Brown University, United States |

| | |
|---|---|
| 1900 | Missionary work in three continents connected to ELTI brought together in one organization under the name Regions Beyond Missionary Union |
| 1900 | Karl and Lucy Kumm start the Sudan-Pionier-Mission in Eisenach |
| 1900 | The number of ELTI students starts to decline |
| 1902 | The leaders of the Sudan-Pionier-Mission dismiss Karl Kumm |
| 1902 | Karl Kumm forms the Lightbearer's League to further missionary work in the Sudan |
| 1904 | Karl and Lucy Kumm and Grattan Guinness start the Sudan United Mission |
| 1906 | Lucy Guinness dies at Northfield, Moody's home |
| 1904–08 | Harry Guinness campaigns against the Congo atrocities |
| 1908 | Karl Kumm wins C. T. Studd for missionary work in the interior of Africa through a talk in Liverpool |
| 1910 | East London Training Institute closes for lack of students |
| 1910 | Grattan Guinness dies (the Edinburgh Conference of the International Missionary Council expressed its appreciation for his work) |
| 1910 | C. T. Studd's journey to South West Sudan, which led to the expansion of CMS missionary work into that area |
| 1912 | C. T. Studd goes to Zaire as Head of the 'Independent British Branch of the Africa Inland Mission' |
| 1913 | C. T. Studd begins the Heart of Africa Mission (Zaire) as nucleus of WEC (Worldwide Evangelization Crusade) |
| 1915 | Harry Guinness dies |
| 1915 | East London Training Institute finally closed |
| 1931 | WEC splits into Unevangelized Fields Mission and WEC |
| 1931 | C. T. Studd dies |

## A. B. SIMPSON AND THE CHRISTIAN AND MISSIONARY ALLIANCE

As a young man, A. B. Simpson,[32] who was to found the Christian and Missionary Alliance,[33] had experienced his conversion under the influence of Grattan Guinness, when he visited Canada.[34] A. B. Simpson started his career as a fully trained Presbyterian pastor but, through decisive contacts with the holiness movement and the healing movement, within sixteen years he had become the pastor of the independent New York Gospel Tabernacle[35] and the founder of an interdenominational fellowship movement, the Christian Alliance. By 1882, he had already started to train missionaries in his newly founded church and, in 1883, he opened the New York Missionary Training College after the pattern of the East London Training Institute.[36]

As a branch of his Tabernacle Church, A. B. Simpson started a mission with the far-flung name 'Missionary Union for the Evangelization of the World' which, in December 1884, sent its first (and only) missionaries to the mouth of the Congo.[37] This endeavour failed because of insufficient preparation and equipment. Only when the Christian Alliance, which he had founded as a fellowship movement to further Christian holiness and healing, at first hesitantly and then enthusiastically took up the missionary idea, could the Evangelical Missionary Alliance,[38] which he founded in 1887, become an effective worldwide mission.

By combining a fellowship movement (Christian Alliance) with his mission endeavour (Evangelical Missionary Alliance) in the Christian and Missionary Alliance, A. B. Simpson had created an effective base which drew support from all over the United States and Canada. But it was not just a matter of organization—both groups had discovered new spiritual truths, the 'fourfold gospel'.[39]

A. B. Simpson united three elements, which repeatedly played an important role in the faith mission context: Bible school, fellowship movement and mission. But he added one more element, which was not so common: an *independent* congregation. Although he did not expect others to follow his lead in this matter, he did provide a pattern for the change-over from fellowship movement to free church. For the CMA as a whole, this process took shape mainly during the first half of this century, and the CMA is now a worldwide denomination.[40]

# A. B. Simpson and the Christian and Missionary Alliance

| | |
|---|---|
| 1843 | Albert Benjamin Simpson born in Bayview near Chatham, Ontario, Canada |
| 1858 | Conversion under the influence of Grattan Guinness |
| 1865 | Pastor of Knox Presbyterian Church, Hamilton, Canada |
| 1873 | Pastor of Chestnut Street Presbyterian Church, Louisville, United States |
| 1874 | Contact with the holiness movement (evangelists Whittle and Bliss) |
| 1877 | A. B. Simpson wants to be a missionary to China |
| 1879 | Pastor of Thirteenth Street Presbyterian Church, New York |
| 1880–81 | Founder and editor of the illustrated missionary magazine *The Gospel in All Lands* |
| 1881 | New contact with the holiness movement (Dr Charles Cullis). Experiences dramatic healing |
| 1881 | Private (re-)baptism by the pastor of a small Italian Baptist Church in New York |
| 1881 | Gives up pastorate in the Presbyterian Church |
| 1882 | Founds the independent New York Gospel Tabernacle for evangelistic outreach |
| 1882 | Starts to train missionaries in the New York Gospel Tabernacle |
| 1883 | Founds New York Missionary Training College |
| 1883 | Founds Berachah ['blessing'] Healing Home, New York |
| 1884 | Founds the Missionary Union for the Evangelization of the World |
| 1884 | Grattan Guinness speaks at the first missionary conference at the New York Gospel Tabernacle |
| 1885 | Failure of missionary work in Zaire after the death of John Condit |
| 1885 | A. B. Simpson takes part in the International Conference for Holiness and Healing at Bethshan, London (Mrs Baxter) |
| 1887 | Founding of the Evangelical Missionary Alliance (for mission) and of the Christian Alliance (as fellowship movement) |
| 1888 | Missionary work in Zaire reopened |
| 1889 | Evangelical Missionary Alliance renamed International Missionary Alliance |
| 1890 | CMA begins missionary work in Sierra Leone ('Sudan Mission') in cooperation with World's Gospel Union, Kansas |
| 1890–92 | Peter Cameron Scott, later founder of the Africa Inland Mission, CMA missionary in Vungu, Zaire |
| 1897 | International Missionary Alliance and Christian Alliance united as Christian and Missionary Alliance |
| 1897 | New York Missionary Training College relocated at Nyack |
| 1907 | The birth of the pentecostal movement brings about great turmoil in the CMA, which leads to the loss of a third of the membership |
| 1919 | (29 October) A. B. Simpson dies |
| 1921 | Margaret Simpson dies, the last remaining woman in the CMA leadership |

## US INITIATIVES AND GRATTAN GUINNESS'
## JOURNEY TO THE UNITED STATES

When the doctors suggested to Grattan Guinness that he spend some time in a warmer climate, he took this advice as occasion for a comprehensive journey to the United States in the interest of (faith) missions. His journey brought about three important developments for faith missions. In Boston, he visited Adoniram Judson Gordon,[41] pastor of Clarendon Baptist Church and president of the American Baptist Missionary Union which, on Gordon's suggestion, had taken over the work of the Livingstone Inland Mission in 1884. It had not been able further to extend its missionary work upriver, because the mission could not find the personnel. Grattan Guinness suggested that Gordon train the missionaries himself. Therefore, he opened the Boston Missionary Training College.[42] Later, Emma Dryer invited him to Chicago to help her to organize the 'Bible Institute of the Chicago Evangelization Society' (later to become known as the Moody Bible Institute).[43]

In Kansas, Grattan Guinness managed to win over a fellowship similar to the CMA for worldwide mission work: the World's Gospel Union (1902, Gospel Missionary Union).[44] George S. Fisher, and those who cooperated with him, had originally worked within the YMCA, but felt increasingly less welcome because of their theology and piety.[45] There was influence from the holiness movement, but that of the prophetic movement was also strong: not only through Grattan Guinness, but also through James H. Brookes, who was very influential in the early phase of the World's Gospel Union.[46] The first missionaries worked under the auspices of the CMA and, later, joined it fully.[47]

## FREDRIK FRANSON (1852–1908) AND THE ALLIANCE MISSIONS[48]

Dwight Lyman Moody, the greatest evangelist of the revival of the second half of the nineteenth century,[49] showed little sympathy for the newly emerging faith missions.[50] Nevertheless, he strongly influenced them. One channel of influence was the (Moody) Bible Institute. More important were his evangelistic campaigns, during which he called for conversion, but for 'total surrender', too, which for many became the foundation of their missionary engagement.[51] Another indirect but, again, most important influence from Moody reached faith missions through the independent 'Chicago Illinois Street Church' (later, Chicago Avenue Church; today, Moody Memorial Church).[52]

# A. J. Gordon and A. T. Pierson: theologians and publicists of the faith missions

| | |
|---|---|
| 1836 | Adoniram Judson Gordon born at New Hampton |
| 1837 | Arthur Tappan Pierson born at New York |
| 1850 | A. T. Pierson's conversion. Joins Tarrytown Methodist Episcopal Church |
| 1852 | (14 March) A. T. Pierson member of Thirteenth Street Presbyterian Church New York, his home church |
| 1857 | A. T. Pierson finishes his studies at Hamilton College (Presbyterian) |
| 1857–60 | A. T. Pierson studies at Union Theological Seminary |
| 1860 | A. T. Pierson ordained at Thirteenth Street Presbyterian Church, (later pastored by A. B. Simpson). Pastor of several Presbyterian congregations until 1889 |
| 1863 | A. J. Gordon pastor in Jamaica Plain, Boston |
| 1869 | A. J. Gordon pastor of Clarendon Street Baptist Church, Boston (until his death 1895) |
| 1874 | A. T. Pierson's decisive contact with the Holiness movement (evangelists Whittle and Bliss). Sees evangelism as the major task of the church |
| 1875 | Gordon editor of *The Watchword* |
| 1878 | Start of a lifelong friendship between A. T. Pierson and George Müller |
| 1885 | A. T. Pierson, influenced by Webb-Peploe, joins the Holiness movement (Keswick type) |
| 1886 | A. T. Pierson plays an important role in the birth of the Student Volunteer Movement at Moody's Northfield Conference. Most probably it was Pierson who coined the watchword 'The Evangelization of the World in this Generation' |
| 1888 | A. J. Gordon Chairman of the American Baptist Missionary Board |
| 1888 | A. T. Pierson follows J.M. Sherwood as editor of the interdenominational missionary magazine *The Missionary Review of the World* |
| 1888 | A. T. Pierson participates in the London Missionary Conference |
| 1889 | A. T. Pierson pastor of Bethany Church in Philadelphia (originating from John Wanamaker's Bethany Mission) |
| 1891 | Gordon publishes *The Holy Spirit in Missions*. Report of the First International Convention of the Student Volunteer Movement for Foreign Missions, Cleveland 1891 |
| 1891–92 and 1893 | A. T. Pierson temporary pastor of Spurgeon's independent London Metropolitan Tabernacle (Spurgeon dies 31 January 1892) |
| 1891–95 | A. J. Gordon Associate Editor of *The Missionary Review of the World* |
| 1893 | A. J. Gordon publishes *The Holy Spirit in Missions* (New York) |
| 1895 | A. T. Pierson supports the founding of the Africa Inland Mission by Peter Cameron Scott |
| 1895 | A. J. Gordon dies at Boston |
| 1896 | A. T. Pierson in England baptized by Baptists, but does not become a Baptist. Expelled from his presbytery, but remains (independent) Presbyterian |
| 1897 | A. T. Pierson returns to the United States |
| 1897 | A. T. Pierson encourages Hurlbert to take responsibility for the work of the AIM after Scott's death and the crisis among the missionaries |
| 1897 | A. T. Pierson joins the Holiness movement |
| 1903–05 | A. T. Pierson in Wales, participates in the 1905 revival there |
| 1909 | A. T. Pierson participates for the last time in the Keswick Convention |
| 1911 | (3 June) A. T. Pierson dies |

# Fredrik Franson

| | |
|---|---|
| 1852 | Fredrik Franson born at Nora, Sweden into a Lutheran family |
| 1869 | Emigrates with his parents to the United States |
| 1872 | Conversion at Estina, Nebraska |
| 1874 | Fredrik Franson and his parents become members of Estina Baptist Church |
| 1875 | Fredrik Franson secretary of Scandinavian Baptist Conference of Nebraska, Western Iowa, and Dakota |
| 1875–76 | Most probably participates in Moody's interdenominational evangelistic campaigns in Brooklyn, Philadelphia and Manhattan |
| 1876–77 | Fredrik Franson cooperates in Moody's interdenominational evangelistic campaigns in Chicago |
| 1875–76 | Fredrik Franson changes his concept of the church from Baptist to interdenominational, and his eschatology from postmillennial to premillennial |
| 1877 | (February) Fredrik Franson's first (interdenominational) evangelistic campaign (in Swede Band, Iowa) |
| 1878 | (4 August) Member of the interdenominational Chicago Avenue Church, Chicago, founded by Moody |
| 1878 | (4 August) Chicago Avenue Church makes Fredrik Franson a travelling evangelist |
| 1879 | Fredrik Franson's first theological contribution to issues of church order |
| 1881 | (June) Start of his worldwide activities at Malmö, Sweden |
| 1882 | Visits London (May Meetings, Bethshan Home of Mrs Baxter). Begins his campaign for world missions. Contact with the Healing movement |
| 1882 | (11 May) Joins the British Branch of the Evangelical Alliance |
| 1884 | Fredrik Franson's first course for evangelists (in Oslo) |
| 1884 | Norske Misjonsförbundet founded in Oslo |
| 1884 | Participates in the World Conference of the Evangelical Alliance in Copenhagen. There he meets Professor Christlieb, who invites him to Germany |
| 1884 | Expelled from Denmark because of his public healing activities, which he does not carry on after that |
| 1884 | Evangelical Free Church of America founded at Minneapolis. The process which led to this was strongly influenced in its early phases by Fredrik Franson |
| 1885 | First visit to Germany |
| 1886 | First visit to Switzerland |
| 1887 | Helgelseförbundet founded at Kumla, central Sweden |
| 1887 | Svensk Kinamisionen founded |

| | |
|---|---|
| 1888 | Danske Missionsförbundet founded in Odense |
| 1888 | Fredrik Franson in Finland |
| 1888 | Founding of Mission Covenant in Finland |
| 1889 | Founding of Frieôstafrikanske Mission in Oslo (1899 taken over by Norsk Misjonsförbundet) |
| 1889 | Fredrik Franson inspires the founding of the Deutsche China-Allianz-Mission in Barmen by Carl Polnick of Wuppertal |
| 1890 | Fredrik Franson publishes in Emden, *Weissagende Töchter*, on the right of women to preach |
| 1890 | First contacts of the Deutsche China-Allianz-Mission to Switzerland, which later led to the founding of an independent Schweizer Allianz Mission (1894 Franson in Switzerland) |
| 1890 | Fredrik Franson returns to the United States |
| 1890 | (14 October) First course for evangelists in the United States (Pilgrim Church, Brooklyn), which led to the founding of the Scandinavian Alliance Mission of North America (later TEAM) |
| 1892–93 | Fredrik Franson seeks 200 missionaries for the Christian and Missionary Alliance in China. Problems about cooperation with CMA |
| 1894–95 | Journey to India (Himalaya) and China |
| 1895 | Finnish Alliance Mission (later Vapaakirkko) |
| 1897 | Swedish Mongol Mission |
| 1897 | Fredrik Franson writes *Himlauret* (*The heavenly clock*, 1898), historical and futurist premillennial eschatology |
| 1899 | Fredrik Franson inspires the founding of Deutscher Gemeinschaftsdiakonieverband in Borken, eastern Prussia (later Marburg) |
| 1900 | Svenska Alliansmissionen (at first, branch of the Scandinavian Alliance Mission of North America) |
| 1900 | Women's Missionary Association of Finland |
| 1901 | Norwegian Alliance Mission |
| 1903 | Starts a world tour. Participates in the Korean revival |
| 1905 | Fredrik Franson in South-east Asia |
| 1906 | Fredrik Franson in (Turkish) Armenia. Founding of the Armenian Spiritual Brotherhood |
| 1906–07 | Fredrik Franson in South Africa and South America |
| 1908 | (2 August) Fredrik Franson dies at Idaho Springs, Colorado |

The major medium of this influence was a Swedish American, Fredrik Franson. After his (re-)baptism in 1874, he became a member of the Swedish Baptist Church in Estina, Saunders County, and began evangelistic activities. When, in 1875–76, he cooperated in Moody's evangelistic campaigns, he changed his Baptist concept of the church into an interdenominational one.[53] On 4 August 1878, he joined the interdenominational Chicago Avenue Church. The same day, he received the congregation's credentials as a travelling evangelist.[54]

In 1881, Franson transferred his activities to Sweden. He called for conversion and to be ready for Christ's second coming. After a visit to London in 1882, where he attended the conference of the Evangelical Alliance,[55] took part in the famous 'May Meetings'[56] and was influenced by Mrs Baxter (preacher of holiness and healing, and founder of Beth Shan Healing Home),[57] he began to see his evangelistic activities as part of worldwide missions. Wherever he went, he found the most eager support in the young fellowship movements. He had them send out missionaries, so that the fellowship movements became missions, too. The common interest of the local fellowships in missionary work later helped to advance the process of their changing from fellowships to Free Church congregations.

At first, Franson directed his missionary interest towards China; the missionaries he arranged to send out were to work there in connection with the CIM or the CMA. Only after his return to the United States in 1890 did he found a mission that worked in Africa, the Scandinavian Missionary Alliance of North America (today, TEAM). This meant that, for the early fellowships in Scandinavia, Africa was not much in view. There were two exceptions: Franson's influence led to the founding of the short-lived Frie Østafrikanske Mission which worked in eastern South Africa[58] and even before Fredrik Franson came to Scandinavia, the Svenska Missionsförbundet (1878)[59] had sent its first missionary into the work of the Livingstone Inland Mission in 1881, in the person of Carl Johan Engvall.[60] Others followed him[61] and, after the handing over of the LIM to the ABMU by Fanny Guinness in 1884,[62] the Svenska Missionsförbundet decided, in 1885, to work independently of the ABMU.[63] In 1909, the SMF extended its work northwards into the (French) Congo.[64]

The Svenska Alliansmissionen[65], the other group of Scandinavian faith missions strongly influenced by Franson, works in South Africa: within the (US) Scandinavian Missionary Alliance, which began its work in South Africa in 1890, there were soon also some missionaries from Sweden,[66] whose work then became the starting point for the Svenska Alliansmissionen[67] and for the Helgelseförbundet[68].

## THE BIG 'SECOND GENERATION' FAITH MISSIONS

Until the end of the nineteenth century, faith missions working outside China had remained comparatively small. In Africa, they had achieved very little, compared to the classical missions. That began to change when the three largest missions (in terms of numbers and influence) were founded: the Africa Inland Mission[69] (Peter Cameron Scott,[70] Philadelphia, 1895); the Sudan Interior Mission[71] (Rowland Bingham,[72] Toronto, 1898); and the Sudan United Mission[73] (Karl[74] and Lucy[75] Kumm, Liverpool, 1904).

All three missions were 'second attempts': Scott had been a CMA missionary in the Lower Congo from 1891 to 1893. After he had returned to the United States for health reasons, he failed to win the CMA to his vision of reaching the interior of Africa from the East Coast.[76] Bingham had tried this in 1893, together with Walter Gowans and Tom Kent as independent missionaries. The attempt failed; Walter Gowans and Tom Kent died.[77] Karl Kumm founded the Sudan United Mission after he had been a NAM missionary and, in 1900, he began the Sudan-Pionier-Mission[78] at Eisenach (Thüringen) (which dismissed him only two years later).[79]

The Africa Inland Mission and the Sudan Interior Mission were strongly influenced by the prophetic movement and the holiness movement. The Baptist element did not dominate, but it was comparatively strong. The Sudan United Mission was, in its beginnings, closely linked to the ELTI but, over the years, it became the faith mission with the strongest participation of non-Free Church missionaries. This meant that the SUM was the only faith mission to develop both denominational and interdenominational branches. These three 'second generation' missions are still among the largest faith missions. The churches resulting from their work in Africa comprised between three and four million members in about 1975.[80]

Two other missions—the last of the faith missions founded before 1914—have their roots in one or other of these three missions (AIM, SIM, SUM). The two are the Congo Inland Mission and the Heart of Africa Mission.

Alma Doering,[81] an American of German descent, started the

# Africa Inland Mission

| | |
|---|---|
| 1860 | (11 June) Charles E. Hurlbert born |
| 1867 | (7 March) Peter Cameron Scott born (Presbyterian) |
| 1891 | P. C. Scott ordained by A. B. Simpson (Independent) |
| 1891–93 | P. C. Scott CMA missionary in Zaire |
| 1893 | P. C. Scott has to leave Africa on the point of death |
| 1893–94 | P. C. Scott travels in United States trying to gather support for a mission to reach the interior of Africa from the East Coast |
| 1894 | P. C. Scott fails ultimately to win CMA support for his plans |
| 1895 | P. C. Scott comes into contact with the newly founded Philadelphia Missionary Council (PMC) |
| 1895 | First missionaries leave for Kenya |
| 1895 | Africa Inland Mission (AIM) founded as a field-directed mission. PMC responsible for home representation only |
| 1895 | Nzawi founded in Kenya |
| 1896 | Sakai, Kilungu and Kangundu founded |
| 1896 | (4 December) P. C. Scott dies at Nzawi |
| 1897–98 | Severe crisis of the mission |
| 1897 | A. T. Pierson counsels Hurlbert not to dissolve AIM |
| 1897 | Hurlbert Director of AIM |
| 1900 | Hurlbert visits the remaining missionary work in Kenya |
| 1901 | C. E. Hurlbert becomes a missionary to Kenya |
| 1903 | Kijabe founded, becomes headquarters of AIM |
| 1909 | CMS transfers Nasa Mission (Tanzania) to AIM |
| 1910 | First attempt to reach North-east Zaire fails |
| 1912 | Kasengu first mission station in North-east Zaire |
| 1913 | Kikuyu Conference defines aim of a United Church in Kenya |
| 1918 | AIM starts work in Arua, West Nile (Uganda) in the context of Anglican Church in Uganda |
| 1924 | AIM starts work in the eastern part of Central Africa |
| 1926 | C. E. Hurlbert resigns as Director of AIM |
| 1928 | C. E. Hurlbert starts Unevangelized Africa Mission |
| 1949 | Opari mission station at the southern tip of the Sudan |
| 1950 | Start of the controversy with US 'fighting fundamentalism' (Carl McIntyre) |
| 1955–62 | R. T. Davies International Secretary/General Director of AIM |
| 1970 | International reorganization of AIM |
| 1976 | Start of work on the Comoro Islands |
| 1987 | Start of work in Chad |

# Sudan Interior Mission

| | |
|---|---|
| 1872 | Rowland V. Bingham born at East Grinstead, Sussex |
| 1885 | His father dies from a vaccination |
| 1886 | Bingham pupil-teacher |
| 1887 | Converted by the Salvation Army, which he then joins |
| 1888 | Emigration to Canada |
| 1890 | Bingham meets John Salmon, founder of the CMA in Canada |
| 1892 | Bingham leaves the Salvation Army, comes close to the Brethren |
| 1892–93 | Assistant pastor to John Salmon, pastor of an independent church related to the CMA |
| 1893 | A. J. Gordon's lectures 'The Holy Spirit and Missions' win Bingham to the cause of world mission |
| 1893 | Mrs Gowans wins Bingham for her son's idea of starting a mission to the interior of the Sudan |
| 1893 | Walter Gowans, Bingham and Tom Kent try to reach Lake Tchad as independent missionaries |
| 1894 | Toronto Bible College, soon closely related to SIM |
| 1895 | Bingham returns to America after the death of Gowans and Kent |
| 1895 | Bingham becomes Baptist |
| 1898 | Bingham founds the Africa Industrial Mission in Toronto |
| 1898 | Hudson Taylor in Toronto |
| 1899 | Missionaries to Malawi in cooperation with Zambezi Industrial Mission |
| 1900 | Another attempt at missionary work in Nigeria fails |
| 1902 | First mission station: Patigi |
| 1903 | Second mission station: Bida |
| 1903 | The idea of self-supporting Industrial Missions recognized as unsuitable for Nigeria |
| 1905 | Crisis of the mission |
| 1905 | Africa Industrial Mission renamed Africa Evangelistic Mission |
| 1906 | Joins Karl Kumm's Sudan United Mission |
| 1907 | Leaves Sudan United Mission |
| 1910 | First baptism in Nigeria |
| 1910 | Indigenous church principle formally accepted as mission policy |
| 1924 | Bingham starts Canadian Keswick |
| 1924 | Missionary work starts in Niger |
| 1927 | SIM takes over the Abyssinia Frontiers Mission (Alfred Buxton) |
| 1930 | SIM starts work in Burkina Faso |
| 1932 | Bingham reorganizes SIM-UK |
| 1936 | SIM starts missionary work in Sudan |
| 1942 | Death of Rowland Bingham |
| 1945 | SIM missionary work in Aden |
| 1946 | SIM missionary work in Benin |
| 1952 | SIM takes over Radio ELWA, Monrovia, Liberia |
| 1954 | SIM missionary work in Somalia |
| 1956 | SIM missionary work in Ghana |
| 1981 | Pan-African Fellowship of SIM-related churches |

# Sudan United Mission

| | |
|---|---|
| 1874 | (19 October) Karl Kumm born in Osterode, Germany |
| 1872 | Lucy Guinness born to Fanny and Grattan Guinness of ELTI, London |
| 1895 | Karl Kumm missionary of North Africa Mission |
| 1900 | (11 January) Lucy and Karl Kumm marry in Cairo |
| 1900 | Ali (Samweli) Hussein (formerly ELTI) missionary in Aswan |
| 1900 | Sudan-Pionier-Mission founded in Eisenach |
| 1902 | Sudan-Pionier-Mission dismisses Kumm |
| 1902 | Promotion by Freiburg University (PhD) |
| 1902 | Lightbearers' League founded in Britain |
| 1904 | Sudan Pioneer Mission/Sudan United Mission founded |
| 1904 | First mission station: Wase |
| 1905 | Dr Fallon starts SUM-RSA |
| 1906 | SUM-USA |
| 1906 | (11 August) Lucy Kumm dies in Northfield |
| 1907 | Karl Kumm visits South Africa |
| 1908 | Tom Aliyana baptized |
| 1908 | Kumm wins C. T. Studd for missionary work in Central Africa |
| 1910 | Cambridge University Mission Party (CUMP) starts Kabwir Mission |
| 1910 | Kumm's journey from Nigeria to the Sudan |
| 1910 | Inter Mission Conference, Lokoja |
| 1911 | Kumm in Australia and New Zealand |
| 1911 | First baptism (Istifanus Lar) |
| 1912 | SUM-AUS/NZ |
| 1912 | SUM-DK (Dr Brønnum) |
| 1913 | SUM-D (with Orientmission) |
| 1913 | SUM-AUS/NZ in Melut (Sudan) |
| 1914 | Kumm goes to the United States because of his former German citizenship |
| 1916 | Reformed leave SUM-RSA, receive the Tiv area |
| 1920 | Johanna Veenstra in Nigeria |
| 1922 | SUM-N (later, NMS) |
| 1926 | Union Church decided on for northern Nigeria |
| 1929 | Federation decided on instead of Union Church |
| 1930 | CUMP work taken over by SUM-UK, but infant baptism kept |
| 1930 | Karl Kumm dies at San Diego, California |
| 1933 | Johanna Veenstra's death |
| 1946 | First ordinations |
| 1948 | Swiss missionaries |
| 1952 | SUM-CH/F |
| 1954 | Churches of Christ in the Sudan (today, COCIN) |
| 1960 | SUM-F |

Congo Inland Mission,[82] and worked as an AIM missionary in Kenya from 1906 to 1909.[83] In 1912, C. T Studd (1860–1931),[84] founded the Heart of Africa Mission, which was to become the Worldwide Evangelization Crusade[85] (today, Worldwide Endeavour for Christ (WEC) International). He had been won for missionary work in the interior of Africa by a talk given by SUM founder Kumm in Liverpool in 1908.[86] Malaria prevented Studd joining Kumm on a trip across Africa in 1909 but, in 1911, he managed to travel to the extreme south-west of Sudan.[87] There he found too few people but heard of the densely populated areas of northwest Zaire[88] where, in 1913, together with Alfred Buxton,[89] he started to work.[90]

Both Alma Doering and C. T. Studd were strongly influenced by the holiness movement. Alma Doering, though technically a Lutheran, strongly cooperated with US Mennonites, who did not fully share her concept of an interdenominational mission.[91] In 1925, she left the Congo Inland Mission,[92] which then increasingly became a denominational mission.[93] In 1926, she founded the Unevangelized Tribes Mission.[94] C. T. Studd's imprint on WEC was very strong.[95] Under the leadership of Norman P. Grubb, C. T. Studd's son-in-law and successor, it developed into one of the most international and interdenominational faith missions.

## MISSIONS NOT RELATED TO THE GUINNESS FAMILY

During the second half of the nineteenth century, the holiness movement influenced almost all Protestant churches, but with certain groups its influence was stronger than elsewhere. Quite early among these groups, two faith missions were begun: the American Faith Mission (1885),[96] which centred around Oberlin College in Ohio;[97] and the Kurku and Central India Hill Mission (1890),[98] led by Mrs Elizabeth Baxter[99] in London with her Missionary Training Home.[100] Both missions gained little importance and neither touched Africa. Just as the 'hard core' holiness movement produced many small groups and later denominations, these groups developed only small missions. Some of them worked in Africa, for example, the Peniel Missionary Society (1897)[101] and the Hephzibah Faith Missionary Association (1895).[102]

The larger holiness missions worked in southern Africa, where they could follow a double calling: to evangelize among (non-European) non-Christians and to spread the holiness message among the (European) Christians there. The South Africa General Mission[103] (today, the Africa Evangelical Fellowship (AEF)),[104] whose constituent parts were founded between 1889 and 1891 by Spencer Walton[105] and by Mrs Osborne-Howe, handed over the work among whites—after a generation—to other organizations. However, the Africa Evangelistic Band,[106] founded in 1924 by the Garratt sisters Helena, May and Emma, concentrated its work increasingly on whites and 'coloureds'.

A mission closely related to the American holiness movement was the World Gospel Mission (1910).[107] Until 1929, it worked only in China, then it started missionary work also in Africa: Kenya (1929), Burundi (1938) and Egypt (1949).[108]

These holiness missions followed Hudson Taylor's principles but were not connected to the Guinness family.

## THE INDUSTRIAL MISSIONS

The industrial missions do not go back to Hudson Taylor, although those treated in this book later accepted faith mission principles.[109] In the beginning, these missions were all to be self-supporting industrial missions. In Britain, this idea can be traced back to David Livingstone (1813–73) (and, through him, to Karl Gützlaff);[110] and for the United States, to William Taylor (1821–1902).[111] David Livingstone pleaded for the establishment of industrial missions in the highland areas of Central Africa, to support themselves by agriculture and trade. William Taylor was a visionary leader from the Methodist holiness movement. He had started, often in some contact with European settlements, self-supporting missions, first in India[112] and then in Latin America.[113] In 1885, meanwhile, being 'Bishop of Africa',[114] he began to practise the same ideas in Angola and Zaire.[115]

William Taylor's work was an example and an incentive to the CMA.[116] Livingstone served as an example to Joseph Booth (1851–1932),[117] a Scotsman who had emigrated to Australia.[118] In Malawi, he started the Zambezi Industrial Mission (1892) and the Nyassa Industrial Mission (1893).[119] The Livingstone Inland Mission[120], the Qua Iboe Mission,[121] the SIM[122] and, partly, also the AIM[123] were originally planned as industrial missions. It quickly became clear that it was even more difficult to run a self-supporting mission at the mouth of the Congo[124] or on the coast of West Africa[125] than it was in the African highlands. Only the Zambezi Industrial Mission and the Nyassa Industrial Mission were successful—and then only for some decades.[126]

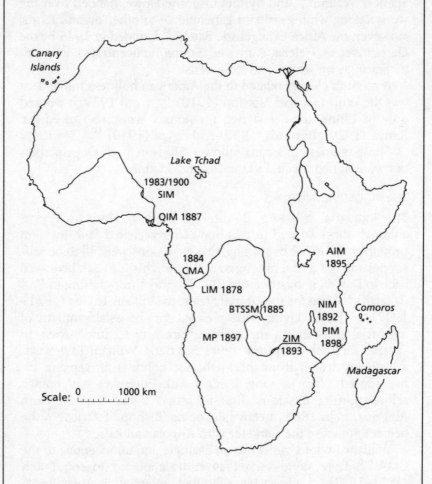

# 'INDUSTRIAL MISSIONS' FOUNDED IN AFRICA BY FAITH MISSIONS

Canary
Islands

Lake Tchad

1983/1900
SIM

QIM 1887

1884
CMA

LIM 1878

AIM
1895

BTSSM 1885

NIM
1892

Comoros

PIM
1898

MP 1897

ZIM
1893

Madagascar

Scale: 0   1000 km

**Abbreviations:**

| | |
|---|---|
| AIM: | Africa Inland Mission |
| BTSSM: | Bishop Taylor's Self-Supporting Missions |
| CMA: | Christian and Missionary Alliance (A. B. Simpson/USA) |
| LIM: | Livingstone Inland Mission |
| MP: | Mission Philafricaine |
| NIM: | Nyasa Industrial Mission |
| PIM: | Providence Industrial Mission |
| QIM: | Qua Iboe Mission |
| SIM: | Sudan Interior Mission |
| ZIM: | Zambezi Industrial Mission |

The most vehement advocate of the industrial mission concept was Héli Chatelin,[127] who was a member of Bishop Taylor's mission from 1885 to 1887.[128] In 1897, he designated Kalukembe in the Angolan Highlands as the first mission station of his Philafrican Liberators' League[129] (Mission Philafricaine).[130] Kalukembe (also called 'Lincoln' because it was to be a haven for freed slaves[131]), was meant to be the starting point for a whole chain of self-supporting industrial missions which were each to be financed by the profits of the preceding station.[132] Because slavery was coming to an end in those years, even in the Portuguese domains, Chatelin could only attract a limited number of slaves and he could not realize his economic ideas. He never managed to open even a second station and, after his death, the Mission Philafricaine gradually conformed to the usual patterns of faith missions in Africa. In 1952, it united with the Schweizer Allianz Mission, which goes back to Fredrik Franson.[133]

The idea of the industrial mission was at the same time useful and dangerous for faith missions: it encouraged the opening of new missions in unreached areas without having to secure a financial base first. On the other hand the industrial mission concept tempted the home constituencies to equip and supply their missionaries inadequately.

## GEORGE MÜLLER

Hudson Taylor took the 'faith principle' of financing a mission,[134] which assured its independence,[135] from George Müller (1805–98), who had founded several orphanages in Bristol.[136] Müller, in turn, had received the 'faith principle' from Anthony Norris Groves, the first Brethren missionary.[137] For independent missionaries (Brethren and non-Brethren), he created the 'Scriptural Knowledge Institution for Home and Abroad'.[138] Its support for a number of the missionaries of the early CIM, including Hudson Taylor, played an important role in the formative phase of the faith mission movement.[139]

George Müller worked more indirectly for foreign missionary work, but he nevertheless provided the impetus for the foundation of the first German faith mission. Ludwig Doll[140] (1846–83), (reformed) pastor at Neukirchen, heard George Müller when he visited the Rhineland in the spring of 1877. On the same faith principles as Müller, he started an orphanage in 1878, a mission magazine in 1879[141], and, in 1882, a missionary training institute.[142] The 'Waisen- und Missionsanstalt Neu-kirchen' (Neukirchener Mission)[143], the first German faith mission, was not greeted with enthusiasm by the German classical missions,[144] but in the end, even Gustav Warneck agreed that the mission had become an avenue to missionary service for many who would not have been acceptable for classical missions because of their different concepts of the church.[145]

During the first half century of their existence, faith missions managed to define their principles and to adapt them to the varied situations at home and overseas. They also managed to come to an arrangement with the classical missions. This was made easier by the fact that faith missions (with very few exceptions)[146] worked in unreached areas and that they often drew their support from quite different home constituencies than the classical missions. Perhaps the greatest achievement in missiological terms was that faith missions (in contrast to the independent missions and the non-church missions) managed to develop clear and effective organizational structures, and to defend them against widespread questioning.

This process was often cumbersome, especially in the early years. The faith missions worked with different personnel, with a different set of supporters, with different principles and, to a significant extent, with a different theology. This meant that faith missions could profit only slightly from the experience that classical missions had gained over a period of two generations. Still, they managed to push forward the frontiers of Christian missions in a remarkable way.

**Notes**

1  The basic Hudson Taylor biographies are: Geraldine and Howard Taylor, *Hudson Taylor in Early Years. The Growth of a Soul*, London, 1911; *Hudson Taylor and the China Inland Mission. The Growth of a Work of God*, London, 1918 (17 editions, translated into six European languages, shortened one-volume version in 1965; John Pollock, *Hudson Taylor and Maria*, London, 1965; A. J. Broomhall, *Hudson Taylor and China's Open Century*, 7 volumes: *Barbarians at the Gates*, 1981 (I); *Over the Treaty Wall*, 1982 (II); *If I had a Thousand Lives*, 1982 (III); *Survivors' Pact*, 1984 (IV); *Refiner's Fire*, 1985 (V); *Assault on the Nine*, 1988 (VI); *It is Not Death to Die*, 1989 (VII). The only autobiographical piece is: James Hudson Taylor, *Hudson Taylor's 'Retrospect'*, London, 1894, [2]1899, [3]1903, [18]1974. A piece of programmatic writing is: James Hudson Taylor, *China: Its Spiritual Need and Claims; With Brief Notices of Missionary Effort, Past and Present*, London, 1865, [2]1866, [3]1868, [5]1884 (revised and enlarged), [8]1890. For Hudson Taylor's

influence on Germany and Switzerland see: Andreas Franz, *Mission ohne Grenzen. Hudson Taylor and die Deutschen Glaubensmissionen*, Giessen/Basel, 1993.

2   For a CIM history, see: Geraldine Guinness, *Story of the China Inland Mission*, London, 1894; Marshall Broomhall, *The Jubilee Story of the China Inland Mission*, London, 1915.

3   Two dissertations can be helpful in assessing such changes: Moira J. McKay, *Faith and Facts in the History of the China Inland Mission 1832–1905*, MLitt, Aberdeen, 1981; and Daniel W. Bacon, *From Faith To Faith. The Influence of Hudson Taylor on Faith Missions Movement* (DMiss, Trinity, Deerfield, 1983), Singapore, 1984.

4   'Not a few abortive efforts had resulted in a deep conviction that a special agency was essential for the evangelization of Inland China. The grave difficulty of possibly interfering with existing missionary operations at home was foreseen; but it was concluded that, by simple trust in God, a suitable agency might be raised up and sustained without interfering injuriously with any existing work' (Taylor, *Retrospect*. London, [18]1974, p. 113).

5   This conviction is clearly expressed in: Hudson Taylor, *China: Its Spiritual Need and Claims*.

6   Klaus Fiedler, 'Die Bedeutung der Einzigartigkeit Jesu Christi für die Theologie der Glaubensmissionen' in *Jahrbuch für Evangelikale Theologie*, 1992.

7   For a comprehensive list, see: Charles Edwin Jones, *A Guide to the Study of the Holiness Movement*, Metuchen, NJ, 1974, pp. 388–416.

8   To be even more exact, these missions might be termed 'industrial faith missions', because industrial missions also developed among the classical missions which did not accept faith mission principles.

9   As long as no monograph exists about Fanny and Grattan Guinness, its place must be taken by the excellent: Michele Guinness, *The Guinness Legend*, London *et al.*, 1990. It deals with all the many Guinnesses, but pays special attention to the mission Guinnesses, for which Michele Guinness used excellent sources, including Lucy Guinness' diary. See also the booklet: Lucy Guinness, *Enter Thou. Pages from the Life Story of Fanny E. Guinness*, London, 1899.

10   Harry Guinness, *Not Unto Us. Record of Twenty One Years' Missionary Service*, London, n.d. (1908).

11   Michele Guinness—Fiedler, 2 February 1988.

12   Grattan Guinness was a grandson of Arthur Guinness, the founder of the brewery. Harry, Geraldine and Lucy met with their brewing cousins regularly for social occasions when they were young. The mission branch of the family developed naturally after Grattan's father, Captain John, became evangelical and teetotal, and gradually the two branches parted. Prominent members of the mission branch today are the missiologist Os Guinness and the writer Michele Guinness. For relationships between Grattan Guinness and the brewery Guinnesses, see Michele Guinness, *Guinness Legend*, pp. 48ff.

13   Fanny Guinness, *Enter Thou*, 15f.

14   Michele Guinness, *The Guinness Legend*, pp. 80ff.

15  McCarthy, Thomas Barnardo, Charles Fishe and probably Edward Fishe (A. J. Broomhall, *Survivors' Pact*, p. 119). Charles and Edward Fishe and McCarthy joined the CIM. Thomas Barnardo, whom Hudson Taylor had asked to study medicine first, became so absorbed in looking after the homeless boys of London and in missionary work in Eastern London that he never reached China.

16  Broomhall, *Survivors' Pact*, pp. 118–120. Elizabeth Pritchard, *For Such a Time as This. God's Faithfulness Through the Regions Beyond Missionary Union for a Hundred Years*, Lottbridge Drove, 1971, p. 14. Of the Guinness children, Geraldine and Whitfield joined the CIM.

17  The archives of the RBMU have now been deposited with the Centre for the Study of Christianity in the non-western World at New College, Edinburgh. They include the extant archival material for ELTI, LIM and CBM.

18  These institutes later became known as 'Bible Schools'. For this development, see: Klaus Fiedler, 'Aspects of the Early History of the Bible School Movement' in Festschrift Donald Moreland and Marthinus W. Pretorius (eds), *The Secret of Faith. In Your Heart—In Your Mouth*, Heverlee, 1992, pp. 62–77.

19  Until the Glasgow Bible Training Institute was founded in 1892, there were hardly any alternatives to ELTI for students wishing to receive an interdenominational training. The first Head of Glasgow BTI was John Anderson, the founder of the Southern Morocco Mission (Francis R. Steele, *Not in Vain. The Story of North Africa Mission*, Pasadena, 1981, p. 127).

20  Fanny Guinness, *The New World of Central Africa. With a History of the First Christian Mission on the Congo*, London, 1890; Holmes, *The Cloud Moves*, pp. 18ff; Pritchard, *For Such a Time as This*, pp. 28ff.

21  Holmes, *The Cloud Moves*, 23ff; Fanny Guinness, *The New World*, pp. 461–487; Pritchard, *For Such a Time as This*, 28ff. C. W. Mackintosh, *Dr Harry Guinness. The Life Story of Henry Grattan Guinness*, London, 1916, pp. 37–47; AMZ 25 (1898), p. 40f.

22  Robert L. M'Keown, *Twenty-Five Years in Qua Iboe. The Story of a Missionary Effort in Nigeria*, London/Belfast, 1912; Jean S. Corbett, *According to Plan. The Story of Samuel Alexander Bill, Founder of the Qua Iboe Mission, Nigeria*, Worthing, [2]1979 (1977).

23  Steele, *Not in Vain.*; Edward H. Glenny and J. Rutherford, *The Gospel in North Africa*, London, 1900. See also: John K. Cooley, *Baal, Christ and Mohammed. Religion and Revolution in North Africa*, New York/Chicago/San Francisco, 1965.

24  Southern Morocco Mission (founder: John Anderson (1888), 1892, principal of BTI Glasgow. For SMM history, see: Steele, *Not in Vain*, pp. 126–135); Algiers Mission Band (founder: Lilias Trotter (1888): Blanche A. F. Pigott, *I. Lilias Trotter. Founder of the Algiers Mission Band*, London/Edinburgh, n.d.); Central Morocco Mission (founder: Dr Kerr (1894)). Southern Morocco Mission (1961) and Algiers Mission Band (1964) joined NAM. Lilias Trotter influenced the founders of the Egypt General Mission (1897).

25  The first secretary of the LIM (1878–80) was the Baptist pastor Alfred Tilly of Cardiff. But the group around him was too small to support the LIM, which also needed a strong hand to guide it.

26  At first, Edinburgh Castle, Thomas Barnardo's Mission Hall in Stepney Green (Holmes, *The Cloud Moves*, p. 21), then Archibald Geikie Brown's East London Tabernacle, which was similar to Spurgeon's Metropolitan Tabernacle. Both congregations left the Baptist Union in the wake of the 'Down-Grade Controversy' in 1887. For the East London Tabernacle, see: George E. Page, *A.G.B., The Story of the Life and Work of Archibald Geikie Brown*, London, 1944. Even before 1887, Spurgeon and his Tabernacle behaved pretty independently. A. G. Brown only supported faith missions, not the Baptist Missionary Society.

27  Michele Guinness, *The Guinness Legend*, 128ff. Most important was Lucy, who was also influential in founding the Behar Mission (1898), the Sudan-Pionier-Mission (1900) and the Sudan United Mission (1902–04).

28  Geraldine Guinness joined the CIM and later became Hudson Taylor's biographer and daughter-in-law.

29  The NAM wanted to keep its identity. See: Fanny Guinness, *The New World of Central Africa*, p. 391. As to the facts, her account deserves precedence over that in the history of the ABMU (Robert G. Torbet, *Venture of Faith. The Story of the American Baptist Foreign Mission Society and the Woman's American Baptist Foreign Mission Society 1814–1954*, Philadelphia 1955, pp. 321–323).

30  Bror Walan, *Församlingstanken i Svenska Missionsförbundet*, Stockholm, 1964, pp. 512–521; 'Interdenominalismens kris i Kongo-Missionen'; Fanny Guinness, 'Transfer of the Congo Mission' in *WWW* 1884', pp. 148–150.

31  When ELTI was closed, only the missionary work remained. It was called the Regions Beyond Missionary Union and also had missionary work in Peru and India (Holmes, *The Cloud Moves*; Elizabeth Pritchard, *For Such a Time as This.*).

32  A. E. Thompson, *A. B. Simpson. His Life and Work* (originally *The Life of A. B. Simpson*, New York, 1920), Camp Hill, PA, 1960; A. W. Tozer, *Wingspread. A Study in Spiritual Altitude*, Harrisburg, 1943. For his theology, see: David F. Hartzfeld and Charles Nienkirchen (eds), *The Birth of a Vision. Essays on the Ministry and Thought of Albert B. Simpson*, Regina, 1986.

33  Robert L. Niklaus, John S. Sawin and Samuel J. Stoesz, *All for Jesus. God at Work in The Christian and Missionary Alliance Over One Hundred Years*, Camp Hill, PA, [2]1988 (1986); for Canada, see: Lindsay Reynolds, *Footprints. The Beginnings of the Christian and Missionary Alliance in Canada*, Toronto, 1981.

34  Thompson, *A. B. Simpson*, p. 26.

35  Simpson describes the beginnings in *WWW*, 1883, p. 45.

36  Because of Simpson's close connections with Dr Cullis, he may also have been influenced by his small Bible school which existed from 1875 to 1892 (Niklaus, Sawin and Stoesz, *All for Jesus*, p. 283). Although I found many references to ELTI in early CMA sources, I found none to Dr Cullis' school.

37  For a good overview, see: Cecilia Irvine, *The Church of Christ in Zaire. A Handbook of Protestant Churches, Missions and Communities, 1878–1978*, Indianapolis, 1978, p. 63.

38  In November 1889, the name was changed to 'International Missionary Alliance' to include Canada (Thompson, *A. B. Simpson*, p. 131).

39 Fourfold gospel: Christ the saviour, sanctifier, healer, coming king. For an analysis, see: J. Sawin, 'The Fourfold Gospel' in Hartzfeld and Nienkirchen, *The Birth of a Vision*, pp. 1–28.

40 It is often said that the CMA is a mission turned denomination. This is not correct: the mission did not turn itself into a denomination, but the fellowship movement of the same name did. This process ran parallel to a similar process in the Scandinavian fellowship movements.

41 His 'spiritual autobiography' is: A. J. Gordon, *How Christ Came to Church. The Pastor's Dream. A Spiritual Autobiography, With Life-Story By A. T. Pierson*, Philadelphia, 1895. His biography is: Ernest B. Gordon, *Adoniram Judson Gordon. A Biography*, New York, 1896. See also: George Gerald Houghton, *The Contribution of Adoniram Judson Gordon to American Christianity*, ThD, Dallas Theological Seminary, 1970.

42 BMTC later developed into Gordon Divinity School and is today part of Gordon-Conwell University. Up to 1967, more than 1,000 of its students had become missionaries. To honour its seventy-fifth jubilee in 1967, Gordon Divinity School produced *The Encyclopedia of Modern Christian Missions* (*EMCM*), the only extant dictionary of all Protestant missions. (Burton L. Goddard, *The Encyclopedia of Modern Christian Missions. The Agencies*, Camden, NJ, *et al.* 1967). The dictionary greatly facilitated the research for this book.

43 Gene A. Getz, *Moody Bible Institute*, Chicago, 1969. Most probably the MBI trained more faith mission missionaries than any other institute.

44 It had 'branches' and held 'conventions' as the CMA did, and it propagated a similar holiness theology.

45 'The movement was the outcome of the special work of grace in gospel and missionary lines carried on by the Y.M.C.A. in Kansas and the West from 1888 to 1891, and which was so strongly condemned and fought by the International Committee and other prominent leaders in the association work. The Bible teaching of Dr James H. Brookes, the missionary truths spoken by Dr Guinness, were used of God in laying the sure foundation of correct Bible doctrine, together with right living' (*World's Gospel Union*, 1893, p. 9).

46 *World's Gospel Union* 1892, p. 9.

47 Niklaus, Sawin and Stoesz, *All for Jesus*., pp. 87–89.

48 Until now, there has been no scholarly study of the Scandinavian Alliance Mission of America (today, TEAM), founded by Franson. The extant histories contain few details: J. F. Swanson (ed.), *Three Score Years . . . and Then. Sixty Years of Worldwide Missionary Advance*, Chicago, n.d. (1950)]; Paul H. Sheetz, *The Sovereign Hand*, Wheaton, 1971. See also: Vernon Mortenson, *This is TEAM*, Wheaton, [3]1985 ([2]1973, [1]1967).

49 The best (and almost only) book on his theology is Stanley N. Gundry, *Love Them In. The Life and Theology of D. L. Moody*, Grand Rapids, [2]1982 (1976). For further books, see pp. 228–243.

50 The CIM formed an exception in being fully accepted by Moody. It was not that he opposed faith missions, it was that he wanted no new missions, and in those days these were mostly faith missions. For this reason, he did not accept A.

T. Pierson's plans for a 'Northfield Missionary Board' (William R. Moody, *The Life of D. L. Moody*, New York, 1900, p. 381).

51  A. T. Pierson, 'Promoting Missions by Indirection. A Tribute to the Work of D. L. Moody' in *MRW*, 1910, pp. 276–280.

52  The best book for the early developments of this church is: W. H. Daniels, *D. L. Moody and his Work*, Hartford, 1876, pp. 103–120 (Full text 'Articles of Admission/Articles of Faith', pp. 108–110, 'Principles of Organization and Government', pp. 111–112). For its history, see: Robert G. Flood, *The Story of Moody Church. A Light in the City*, Chicago, 1985.

53  For the details of this change even Torjesen could find no primary sources, but his reconstruction of the process of change from October 1875 to February 1877 ('A Critical Data Gap' and 'A Suggested Reconstruction', pp. 47–50) is convincing.

54  Torjesen, *A Study of Fredrik Franson*, p. 80.

55  On 11 May 1882 he became a member of the British branch of the Evangelical Alliance (Torjesen, *A Study of Fredrik Franson*, p. 228).

56  Gene A. Getz, *Moody Bible Institute*, Chicago, 1969.

57  Nathaniel Wiseman, *Elizabeth Baxter (Wife of Michael Paget Baxter). Saint, Evangelist, Preacher, Teacher, and Expositor*, London, 1928.

58  This mission dramatically turned itself into an independent mission. After the failure of the mission which was originally to work on all the eastern coast of Africa, Ekutandaneni, its only mission station, was taken over by the Norske Misjonsforbund.

59  For the SMF's origins see: William Bredberg, *P. P. Waldenströms verksamhet till 1878. Till frågan om Svenska Missionsförbundets uppkomst*, Lund Akademisk avhandling, 1949, especially pp. 353–406. For its separation from Fosterlandsstiftelsen, see: William Bredberg and Oscar Lövgren, *Genom Guds Nåd. Svenska Missionsförbundet under 75 år*, Stockholm, 1953, 68ff. See also: Olof Wennås (ed.), *Liv och frihet. En bok om Svenska Missionsförbundet*, Stockholm, 1978, p. 303f. Older books are Theodor Anderson (ed.), *Svenska Missionsförbundet. Dess uppkomst och femtioårigs verksamhet*, Stockholm, 1928; J. E. Lundahl, *Vår yttre mission. Svenska Missionsförbundets mission i Kongo, Kina, Ost-Turkestan m.n.*, Stockholm, 1916.

60  *Förbundet* 1881, p. 116 contains Engvall's letter from Bonny, dated 24 August 1881. For health reasons, Engvall had to return to Sweden early in 1882 (Irvine, *The Church of Christ in Zaire* p. 105). See also *AMZ*, 13 (1886), p. 138.

61  Irvine, *The Church of Christ in Zaire*, p. 105.

62  In *WWW*, 1884, p. 148 Fanny Guinness describes the handover. She mentions that most missionaries hold a Baptist view of baptism, but does not explicitly mention the two SMF missionaries.

63  When Nils Westlind and Karl Johan Pettersson had to travel to Sweden in 1885, they suggested that the SMF start its own mission. The ABMU then transferred Mukimvungu to SMF, which was handed back to ABMU in 1939 (Irvine, *The Church of Christ in Zaire*, 105f.). A scholarly book dealing with this area is: Ragnar Widman, *Trosföreställningar i Nedre Zaire från 1880—talet*,

Stockholm, 1979 (with English summary).

64 Hilaire Nkounkou *et al.*, *75e Anniversaire de la fondation de Madzia et de l'Évangélisation du Congo par les Missionaires Protestants*, Brazzaville, 1984, p. 5. In 1906, the French colonial administration had refused entry to the Svenska Missionsförbundet (p. 5).

65 For the history of Svenska Alliansmissionen, especially in Sweden, see Fritz Hägg, *Svenska Alliansmissionen genom hundra år*, Jönköping, 1953. For a list of all missionaries (1900–53), see pp. 371–392.

66 William E. Dawson, *History of the Scandinavian Alliance Mission Work in Africa 1892–1920*, n.d. (1933) (unpublished); The biography of its most famous missionary is: Maria Nilsen and Paul H. Sheetz, *Malla Moe*, Chicago, [8]1980 (1956).

67 The first Svenska Alliansmissionen's missionary to work for the Scandinavian Alliance Mission (TEAM) was K. A. Hjelm (Dawson, *History* p. 79; Hägg, *Svenska Alliansmissionen genom hundra år*, p. 374). In 1909, the SvAM decided to work independently in South Africa. To this end, Hjelm was given the mission stations Ekukanyeni, Ekubonakaleni, Pataza and Piet Retief in Transvaal (Dawson, *History*, p. 156). For the history of the Svenska Alliansmissionen in South Africa, see: K. A. Hjelm, *Swedish Alliance Mission e South Africa 1901–51*, Piet Retief, 1951.

68 For the history of Helgelseförbundet, see: *Efter Tjugufem år. Minneskrift med anledning af Helgelseförbundets tjugufemårige verksamhet bland Kineser och Zuluer*, Torp (Kumla), 1915; *Minneskrift vid Helgelseförbundets fyrtioårsjubileum 1 Juni 1927*, Götabro, 1927; *Helgelseförbundet 1887–1937*, Torp, 1937; *Av Herren har det skett. Helgelseförbundet 60 år*, Götabro, 1947; Birger Davidsson, *Det började med ett bönemöte... Missionsslskapet Helgelsefrbundet. En presentation af Missionssälskapet Helgelseförbundets upkomst, utweckling och verksamhet*, Kumla, 1955.

69 Kenneth Richardson, *Garden of Miracles. The Story of the Africa Inland Mission*, London, 1976 (1968). This book is only brief and not so reliable. A thorough dissertation is: John A. Gration, 'The Relationship of the Africa Inland Mission and its National Church in Kenya Between 1895 and 1971', PhD, New York University, 1973, Ann Arbor (UMI) 1974. A good study of the African response is: David P. Sandgren: *Christianity and the Kikuyu. Religious Divisions and Social Conflict*, New York, 1989 (originally: 'The Kikuyu, Christianity and the Africa Inland Mission', PhD, University of Wisconsin-Madison, 1976 (UMI)). Books by AIM missionaries: Stuart M. Bryson, *Light in Darkness. The Story of the Nandi Bible*, London/Eastbourne, 1959; Gladys Stauffacher, *Faster Beats the Drum*, Pearl River, [2]1978 (1977) (based on diaries); K. N. Phillips, *Tom Collins of Kenya. Son of Valour*, London, n.d. (1965).

70 There is no current biography of Scott. The best is still Mrs E. M. Whittemore, *Promoted! A Brief Life Sketch of P. Cameron Scott*, New York (Door of Hope Publishing House), 1897, 125 pages. The voluminous AIM collection in Wheaton does not contain any primary sources on Scott except *Hearing and Doing*.

71 Rowland V. Bingham, *Seven Sevens of Years and a Jubilee. The Story of the Sudan Interior Mission*, Toronto, n.d. ([2]1958) 1943 (New York/Toronto); N. N., *Root from Dry Ground. The Story of the Sudan Interior Mission*, London, 1966. The SIM was founded as the Africa Industrial Mission. See: Rowland V. Bingham, 'A New Name for an Established Mission' in *The Missionary Witness*, 17 October 1905. For

SIM in Ethiopia, see: Raymond J. Davis, *Fire on the Mountains. The Story of a Miracle—the Church in Ethiopia*, Toronto *et al.*, [12]1981 (1980); Clarence W. Duff, *Cords of Love. A Testimony to God's Grace in Pre-Italian Ethiopia as Recorded in Memorabilia of One of the Sudan Interior Mission's 'C.O.D. Boys'*, Phillipsburg, NJ, 1980 (contains many original full text documents); Peter Cotterell, *Born at Midnight*, Chicago (Moody), 1973; Peter Cotterell, 'An Indigenous Church in Southern Ethiopia' in *Bulletin of the Society for African Church History* 1969–70, pp. 68–104; Peter Cotterell, 'Dr T. A. Lambie. Some Biographical Notes' in *Journal of Ethiopian Studies* 1972, pp. 43–53. For SIM in Liberia, see: Jane Reed and Jim Grant, *Voice under Every Palm. The Story of Radio Station ELWA*, Grand Rapids, [2]1970 (1968). For a traveller's overview, see: Harold Fuller, *Run While the Sun is Hot*, Toronto *et al.*, 1967. For a biography, see: Sophie de la Haye, *Tread upon the Lion. The Story of Tommie Titcombe*, Toronto *et al.*, [3]1980 (1974). Embedded within a far-flung theological and historical treatise is the (harmonizing) analysis of SIM-ECWA relations: Harold Fuller, *Mission-Church Dynamics. How to Change Bicultural Tensions into Dynamic Missionary Outreach*, Pasadena, 1980, pp. 193ff.

72 J. Hunter, *A Flame of Fire. The Life and Work of Dr Rowland V. Bingham*, Toronto *et al.*, 1961.

73 Lawry Maxwell, *Half a Century of Grace*, London, 1954; Mollie E. Tett, *The Road to Freedom. The Sudan United Mission 1904–1968*, Sidcup, 1968; Jan Harm Boer, *Missions: Heralds of Capitalism or Christ?*, Ibadan, 1984. For SUM in Sudan, see: Peter J. Spartalis, *To the Nile and Beyond. The Work of the Sudan United Mission*, Homebush, NSW, 1981 (carefully researched and documented); Roy E. Conwell, *Samwiil of Sudan*, Ashgrove, Queensland, 1985.

74 A biography written by a friend of his second wife Gertrude is: Irene V. Cleverdon, *Pools on the Glowing Sand.. The Story of Karl Kumm*, Melbourne, 1936. The current biography is: Peter Spartalis with Roy Conwell and Christof Sauer, *Karl Kumm: The Last of the Livingstones. Pioneer Missionary and Statesman*, Bonn, 1993. For a dissertation, see: John H. Boer, 'The Last of the Livingstones: a Study of H. Karl W. Kumm's Missiological Conceptions of Civilization', Free Reformed University of Amsterdam, 1973. Kumm's most important books are: *The Sudan. A Short Compendium of Facts and Figures about the Land of Darkness*, London, 1907; *From Hausaland to Egypt Through the Sudan*, London, 1910; *Khont Hon Nofer. The Lands of Ethiopia*, London, 1910.

75 Grattan Guinness, *Lucy Guinness Kumm. Her Life Story. With Extracts From Her Writings*, London, 1908.

76 *Sixth Annual Report International Missionary Alliance* (11 October 1893), p. 43 shows the CMA still in full accord with his plans.

77 Bingham, *Seven Sevens of Years*, pp. 18–23.

78 Grattan Guinness, 'Evangelizing Nubia' (unpublished), 5 pages; Eberhard von Dessien, Ulrich Ehrbeck and Eberhard Troeger, *Wasser auf dürres Land. 85 Jahre Sudan-Pionier-Mission/Evangelische Mission in Oberägypten*, Wiesbaden, 1985; Samuel Ali Hussein, *Aus meinem Leben*, Wiesbaden, 1920; Johannes Held, *Anfänge einer deutschen Muhammedanermission. Rückblick auf die ersten 25 Jahre der Sudan- Pionier-Mission 1900–1925*, Wiesbaden, 1925; Margarete Unruh, *Fünfzig Jahre evangelische Missionsarbeit unter Muhammedanern*, Wiesbaden, 1950; *Auftrag und Weg einer Muhammedanermission*, Wiesbaden, 1955.

79  Minutes Sudan-Pionier-Mission, 29 May 1902; 26 July 1902; 2 October 1902.

80  See statistics at the end of Chapter 3.

81  There is no biography of this extraordinary woman. The existing brief sketches of her life are more like legends. For when she joined the AIM and for the time before, see *Haigh Diary*, April–June 1906, 9f. Partly autobiographical is: *Leopard Spots or God's Masterpiece. Which? An Attempt to Answer After Eighteen Years of Missionary Service Among Races of Three Colors, White, Black and Copper*, Cleveland, Ohio, n.d. (1914, before the start of the war); Written by herself, but not dealing with missions: Alma E. Doering, *To Find His Way Out—Under Pressure, Not Rebellious*, St Petersburg, FL, n.d. (1957); Written by her closest associate: Stella C. Dunkelberger, *Crossing Africa. Being the Experiences of a Home Secretary in Primitive Parts of the Black Continent*, Germantown, 1935.

82  William B. Weaver and Harry E. Bertsche, *Twenty-five Years of Mission Work in Belgian Congo*, Chicago, 1938; *Thirty-five Years in the Congo. A History of Demonstrations of Divine Power in the Congo*, Chicago, 1945; Melvin J. Loewen, *Three Score. The Story of an Emerging Mennonite Church in Central Africa*, Elkhart, 1972.

83  An important source to account for her leaving the AIM is: Haigh Diary, 1908ff., in the possession of the Africa Inter Mennonite Mission. See especially the following entries: 11 November 1908; 14 November 1908; 17 December 1908; 6 December 1908; 31 December 1908; 28 December 1910. In 1896–1900, Alma Doering was a CMA missionary on the Lower Congo; in 1900–04, she worked with the Svenska Missionsförbundet there, which cooperated with the CMA.

84  Norman P. Grubb, *C. T. Studd. Cricketer and Pioneer*, London, 1933, Ft Washington *et al.*, 1965.

85  There is no WEC history yet, but see: Alfred Buxton, *The First Ten Years of the Heart of Africa Mission 1913–1922*, London, [5]1927; For the origin of the various Continental WEC branches, see the thorough: Bernd Schirrmacher, *Baumeister ist der Herr. Erfahrungen göttlicher Kleinarbeit in einem Missionswerk*, Neuhausen, 1978. For WEC-AUS, see: Stewart R. Dinnen, *When I Say Move . . .*, Ft Washington *et al.*, 1972. For the seventy-fifth anniversary of WEC, Helen Roseveare published a book giving a story from each year: Helen Roseveare, *Living Stones. Sacrifice, Faith, Holiness, Fellowship: 75 Years of WEC*, London *et al.*, 1988. Much valuable information can be gained from autobiographical books: Edith Buxton, *Reluctant Missionary*, London, 1969; *Reluctant No Longer. Address Given by Mrs Buxton at a Luncheon to Mark the Publication of the Paperback Edition of Reluctant Missionary, at the Westminster Theater*, London, [2]1974 (1973); Norman P. Grubb, *Once Caught, No Escape. My Life Story*, Ft. Washington, 1983 (London, 1969); Alfred W. Ruscoe, *The Lame Take the Prey. An Autobiography*, Ft Washington/Toronto, 1968. For biographies, see: Norman P. Grubb, *Successor to C. T. Studd. The Story of Jack Harrison*, London, 1949; *Mighty Through God. The Life of Edith Moules*, London, 1951; Betty Macindoe, *Going for God*, London, 1972 (Bessie Fricker-Brierley); Alan Burgess, *Daylight Must Come. The Story of a Courageous Woman Doctor in the Congo*, Minneapolis, n.d. (London, 1975; New York, 1977). The most recent Studd biography is: Eileen Vincent, *C. T. Studd and Priscilla. United to Fight for Jesus*, Bromley/Gerrards Cross/Eastbourne, 1988.

86  The talk was announced on billboards: 'Cannibals Want Missionaries' (V.

Cleverdon, *Pools on the Glowing Sand*, p. 96).

87 This time, only the doctors and his wife Priscilla tried to prevent him from travelling. For the whole trip, see: Vincent, *C. T. Studd and Priscilla*, pp. 142–149.

88 Departure was on 15 December 1910. In the Sudan, he travelled with Bishop Gwynne of Khartoum and Archdeacon Shaw, both CMS missionaries (Grubb, *C. T. Studd*, pp. 129ff.).

89 In 1927, together with Dr T. Lambie, he founded the Abyssinia Frontier Mission, which became the base for the SIM work in Ethiopia. He died in a German bomb attack on London.

90 On 16 October 1913, Studd and Buxton started their work at Niangara which, in 1950, was handed over to the AIM.

91 Elisabeth Schlansky and Alma Doering, *Die Kongo Inland Mission*, Brieg, n.d. (*ca.* 1913).

92 For the background, see Minutes Congo Inland Mission Field Conference 1925. For preceding tensions involving Alma Doering, see: Minutes Field Conference 1924. The Congo Inland Mission Home Board reacted sharply to the missionaries' demands, especially to the demand for full interdenominalization, and demanded an apology (Stan Nussbaum, *You Must be Born Again. A History of the Evangelical Mennonite Church*, Grand Rapids, 1973, p. 25).

93 'While Doering's early contribution to the Congo Inland Mission is unquestionable, it is also true that stable and consistant Congo Inland Mission development was not possible until she and her independent-minded friends resigned in 1926' (James C. Juhnke, *A People of Missions. A History of General Conference Mennonite Overseas Missions*, Newton, Kansas, 1979, p. 75). For later history, see also: *Die Saat geht auf. Fünfzig Jahre Missions- und Kirchengeschichte im Kwango-Zaire*, Basel, 1990. The first part of the book was written by Bakata Ibula, Maluku Mankatu Kubusa, Matonga Mvwamba and Bayaka Batutiaku; the second part by Traudel Witter.

94 UTM received most of its support from independent churches with fundamentalist tendencies. When Alma Doering became too old to work as UTM's Home Secretary, the decline of the UTM began, resulting in its dissolution in 1952 (James C. Juhnke, *A People of Missions*, p. 111).

95 This can easily be seen in the pages of *Heart of Africa* (1913–1931). Also: Jean Walker, *Fool and Fanatic? C. T. Studd. Quotations From His Letters*, Gerrards Cross, 1980.

96 This was not an organized faith mission, but more of a loosely connected group of independent missions, such as the Bassim Faith Mission, the Ellichpoor Faith Mission and so on. Most of these missions worked in India and later joined the CMA (see: *Sixth Annual Report International Missionary Alliance*, 11 October 1893, p. 21). For detailed information, turn to: A. T. Pierson's *The Missionary Review of the World*.

97 *AMZ*, 13 (1886), p. 243.

98 Its roots are in Albert Norton's independent mission 1874 (*EMCM*, p. 356). For Kurku Mission, see: Wiseman, *Elisabeth Baxter*, pp. 203ff. In 1890, the Council of the Missionary Training Home took over responsibility (p. 210).

99 Wiseman, *Elisabeth Baxter*.

100Wiseman, *Elisabeth Baxter*, pp. 181–201. By 1900, 336 women and men had been trained.

101Started by Anna Vansant in Pt Said (*EMCM*, p. 526); Jones, *Holiness Movement*, p. 243f. For work in Egypt, see: Laura Cammack Trachsel, *Kindled Fires in Africa*, Marion, 1960, pp. 107–121. For the whole history of Peniel Mission, see *EMCM*, p. 526. The only missionary activity of this small mission in Africa (Egypt) was taken over by the National Holiness Missionary Society in 1949, which later changed its name to World Gospel Mission.

102In 1951, the Hephzibah Faith Missionary Association joined the Church of the Nazarene. During 1895–1951, a total of thirty missionaries had been sent out (*EMCM*, pp. 315–316), some of them working in North Africa (Jones, *Holiness Movement*, pp. 224–227).

103James Gray Kallam, *A History of the Africa Evangelical Fellowship from its Inception to 1917*, PhD, New York University, 1978.

104Africa Evangelical Fellowship, *Guide for Daily Prayer for Personnel of the Fellowship and Associated Churches*, Reading, 1985, pp. 5–8.

105George E. Weeks, *W. Spencer Walton*, London/Edinburgh/New York, n.d. (World War 1). Contains many primary sources.

106Jooste, *Die Africa Evangelistic Band in Wese en Praktyk*, Bloemfontein, 1957.

1071910-26, Missionary Bureau of the National Association for the Promotion of Holiness, 1926–1947/54 National Holiness Missionary Society.

108The history of the Gospel Mission can be found in three books: Trachsel, *Kindled Fires in Africa*, with the companion volumes *Kindled Fires in Asia* (1960) and *Kindled Fires in Latin America* (1961). For further literature, see: Jones, *Holiness Movement*, pp. 413–415. The work in Egypt was started by taking over Peniel Missions.

109The Mission Philafricaine (CH) offered prospective missionaries eight-year contracts for industrial work in Angola (Minutes Mission Philafricaine 29 April 1899).

110David Livingstone received his call to become a missionary in 1834 through Gützlaff's 'Appeal to the Churches in Britain and America for Qualified Medical Missionaries' (George Seaver, *David Livingstone. His Life and Letters*, London, 1957, p. 21f. He had intended to go to China, but political circumstances hindered him.

111His autobiography: *Story of My Life*, New York, 1896. See also: *Taylor of California, Bishop of Africa*, London, 1897 (New York, 1896). For his principles, see: William Taylor, *Pauline Methods of Missionary Work*, Philadelphia, 1879. Further literature: Jones, *Holiness Movement*, pp. 761–763.

112William Taylor, *Four Years' Campaign in India*, London/New York, 1876; *Ten Years of Self-supporting Missions in India*, New York, 1882.

113Goodsil Filley Arms, *History of the William Taylor Self-supporting Missions in South America*, New York, 1921.

114This meant that he could establish his missionary work anywhere in Africa (excluding Liberia, where Methodist churches already existed).

115Regular reports in *MRW*. The US home base was 'The Transit and Building Fund Society of Bishop William Taylor's Self-supporting Missions'.

116*WWW*, 1884, pp. 142ff. ('Rev. Wm Taylor and his Work in Africa').

117David Langford, 'Joseph Boot', unpublished, n.d.

118By turning Seventh Day Baptist and starting denominational missionary work, Booth left the interdenominational faith mission movement in 1898 at the latest (William C. Hubbard, 'Sabbath Evangelizing and Industrial Association' in *Seventh Day Baptists in Europe and America*, Vol. I, pp. 577–583).

119Today, part of Africa Evangelical Fellowship.

120Fanny Guinness, *The New World of Central Africa*, pp. 189.

121Jean S. Corbett, *According to Plan. The Story of Samuel Alexander Bill, Founder of the Qua Iboe Mission, Nigeria*, Worthing, [2]1979 (1977), p. 45.

122Moline and Lawrence, the first two missionaries of the then Africa Industrial Mission were seconded to the Zambezi Industrial Mission to gain industrial mission experience (Minutes Africa Industrial Mission, 5 January 1899).

123In 1899, C. E. Hurlbert returned from his inspection tour of Kenya a convinced supporter of the industrial mission concept (Minutes Africa Industrial Mission, 19 September 1899).

124Irvine, *The Church of Christ in Zaire*, pp. 63–64.

125Minutes Africa Industrial Mission, 8 December 1899.

126In 1902, ZIM received £1500 in gifts and earned £8000 from the sale of agricultural products, for the NIM the figures were £529 and £1,369 respectively (James S. Dennis, *Centennial Survey of Foreign Missions*, New York/Chicago/Toronto, 1902).

127Alida Chatelin, *Héli Chatelin. L'Ami de l'Angola. Fondateur de la Mission Philafricaine. D'après sa correspondence*, Lausanne, 1918.

128In 1887–97, he was an independent missionary, which he combined in 1891–92 with the position of the US consul in Loanda.

129Héli Chatelin, a Swiss, went for missionary training to America, envisaging better possibilities there. In 1896, he founded the Philafrican Liberators' League. The new mission was not very successful. Gradually after 1899 the Swiss supporters of his work, under the leadership of his sister Alida Chatelin, took over (*Quatrième Rapport Mission Philafricaine* (1898)). In 1904, the 'Comité auxiliaire de la Mission Philafricaine' was officially organized (Minutes, 17 March 1904), which developed into the Mission Philafricaine, since 1952 part of the Alliance Missionaire Suisse/Schweizer Allianzmission, which goes back to Fredrik Franson.

130Rudolphe Bréchet, *J'ai ouvert une porte devant toi. Essai sur l'histoire de la Mission Philafricaine*, Lausanne, 1972.

131The first fugitive slave accepted into Lincoln (10 January 1902) was Catraio. He became an assistant evangelist and was baptized in 1912. (Alida Chatelin, *Héli*

*Chatelin*, p. 302). Twenty-two fugitive slaves lived in Lincoln in 1917 (p. 343).

132'Il désire aussi qu'on fasse un article sur les avantages des missions industrielles. M. Héli croit que c'est le meilleur moyen d'évangéliser' (Minutes Mission Philafricaine, 22 November 1906).

133Vereinbarung zwischen der Allianz-China-Mission und der Philafrikanischen Mission, valid as from 1 January 1952.

134The best source for his 'faith principles' is: George Müller, *A Narrative of Some of the Lord's Dealings with George Müller written by himself* (9th edn), London, 1895 (first edition, 1837).

135'At last, on December 12, 1829, I came to the conclusion to dissolve my connexion with the society… and to trust Him for the supply of my temporal wants' (George Müller, *A Narrative*, [9]1895, p. 52).

136A. T. Pierson, *George Müller of Bristol*, London, [6]1901.

137'M. Müller, of Bristol, in his narrative (p. 44) speaks of the example of Mr Groves, as making a great "impression" on him, and "delighting him much", and when he himself decided to look to the Lord alone, for the supply of his wants, he says, after alluding to the promises of God, as the "stay" of his soul; in addition to this, the example of Brother Groves was a great encouragement to me (p. 52)' (*Memoir of Anthony Norris Groves, Compiled Chiefly From His Journals and Letters, to Which is Added a Supplement, 'Containing Recollections of Miss Paget, and accounts of Missionary works in India, etc.'* By his widow, London, 1869).

138For its principles, see: F. Roy Coad, *A History of the Brethren Movement. Its Origins, its Worldwide Development and its Significance for the Present Day*, Exeter, 1968, pp. 46–47.

139See Moira McKay, *Faith and Facts*, p. 217f.

140For Doll's theology, see: Bernd Brandl, 'Ludwig Doll: Der Gründer der ersten deutschsprachigen Glaubensmission' in *Evangelikale Missiologie*, 1988, pp. 41–46.

141'Neukirchener Missions- und Heidenbote'. There are similarities between this magazine and Fanny Guinness' magazine *Regions Beyond* and A. B. Simpson's *The Gospel in All Lands* and *The Word, the Work and the World* (*WWW*).

142Opened on 27 August 1882. See: *Missions- und Heidenbote*, 1882, p. 74; *AMZ*, 9 (1882), p. 505 (with critical remarks on the 'faith principles').

143Ulrich Affeld, *Er mache uns im Glauben kühn. 100 Jahre Neukirchner Mission*, Wuppertal, 1978; Wilhelm Oehler, *Geschichte der deutschen Evangelischen Mission*, Band 2, Baden Baden, 1951, pp. 47–49.

144Warneck in *AMZ* 9(1882), p. 505; Affeld, *Er mache uns im Glauben kühn*, p. 21; For the Neukirchen understanding of 'faith principles', see: *AMZ*, 25 (1898), p. 125.

145Oehler, *Geschichte* 2, 46. Presently, Bernd Brandl is working on a dissertation on the history of Neukirchen Mission (ETF, Heverlee/Leuven).

146Two possible exceptions are the Zambezi Industrial Mission (Mitsidi, 1892) and the Nyassa Industrial Mission (Likhubula, 1893), both founded by Joseph Booth. But even they worked predominantly among non-Christians, although they started in the vicinity of the Church of Scotland Mission in Blantyre, about 10 km/ 6 miles away. Before starting at Mitsidi, Booth had been granted land by the Makolo chief Maseya in the Lower Shire area, but the colonial administration did not allow him to take up that offer because he was seen as too much of an anticolonialist.

# 3

# Not an easy endeavour: faith missions in Africa

By 1875, classical Protestant missions had managed to establish the church permanently in Africa south of the Sahara, and about one million Africans had been won to the Christian faith.[1] But their distribution was very uneven: Christianity was strongest in Southern Africa, Madagascar and Uganda. Even before colonial rule, some rulers had been baptized (Uganda and Madagascar) and folk churches[2] had come into existence. The main starting point for the evangelization of western Africa had been Sierra Leone, with its freed slave settlements. From there, missionary work had reached Nigeria, and Samuel Crowther had even established the Anglican mission diocese of Niger.[3] But missionary work only touched the southern third of present-day Nigeria. Various missions had managed to gain a foothold on the West African coast (Liberia, Ghana, Togo, Cameroon and Gabon), but they did not penetrate far inland.[4] Since the German pietist, Krapf, working for the CMS, had started Protestant missionary work in Kenya in 1844, other missions had started to work on the coast, but only very slowly penetrated inland.[5] The Muslim Maghreb was completely unreached. There were missionaries in Egypt, but they worked mainly among Copts. Similar attempts to infuse the Coptic Church of Ethiopia with new spiritual life had been made, but the attempt to reach the Oromo ('Galla') from there had failed.

When, in about 1875, the interior of Africa became gradually more accessible to European initiatives, the classical missions found it difficult to use these new opportunities. The most important reason was that they had more than enough to do simply to keep going the work which they had started and to expand it slowly. The situation was made even more difficult by the fact that the average life span of missionaries in West Africa was short[6] and because the home boards had trouble finding the required money.[7]

## Strategic concepts of the faith missions

The political developments which found their summary expression in the 1884–85 Berlin Conference ('Scramble for Africa'), and the great exploratory journeys of men such as Livingstone and Stanley, made the whole of the interior of Africa accessible (for missionaries as well) before the turn of the century. Before 1885, missionaries sometimes reached an area of Africa before the colonialists but later the reverse was true (with few exceptions). In their early decades, the classical missions had largely worked (with much sacrifice) at the fringe of a continent that was opening up slowly to European influences. Now that the whole continent had become accessible within a very short period, they were unable to meet the additional challenge, because their forces were already far too thinly spread out.

## THE PRIORITY OF THE UNREACHED

In 1875, there were, in missionary terms, four great unreached areas in Africa: Central Africa, the Congo Basin, the Sudan Belt and Muslim North Africa.

◇ Central Africa: it was Livingstone who first drew attention to Central Africa; the missions which responded were mainly classical missions. From 1881, however, through Frederick Stanley Arnot (1858–1914),[8] the non-church mission of the Brethren also started to work in the area, and this was to become the most important Brethren mission field in Africa.[9] Arnot also opened the way into Central Africa for other missions.[10]

◇ The Congo Basin: the largest part of the Congo Basin was made accessible to Europe by Stanley's famous 999-day-long journey from the East Coast to the mouth of the Congo.[11] Among the classical missions, only the English Baptists and the American Presbyterians felt able to take advantage of this opportunity.[12]

◇ The Sudan Belt: the largest unreached area and, in many respects, the most inaccessible one was the Sudan Belt. In those days, the term 'Sudan' comprised the whole area from Senegal to the borders of Ethiopia.[13] In its eastern section, the southern border was, at the same time, the northern border of the equally unreached Congo Basin. Lake Chad was considered to be the centre of the Sudan. Its inaccessability was due to climate and to political circumstances. Only the defeat of the Mahdi by the British in the battle of Omdurman had made the eastern part accessible, and the subjugation of the northern Nigerian Emirates to British rule had made travelling, if not

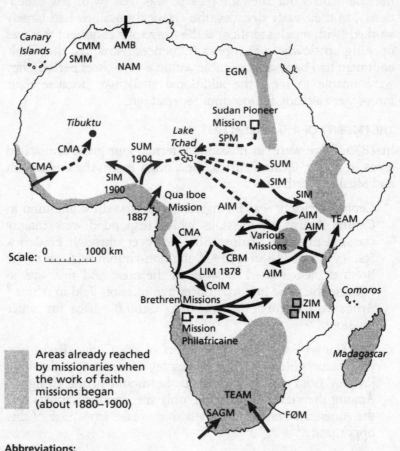

# THE ADVANCE OF FAITH MISSIONS AND THE BRETHREN MOVEMENT MISSIONS IN THE 'UNREACHED' PARTS OF AFRICA

Canary Islands

CMM
SMM
AMB
NAM

EGM

Tibuktu

Sudan Pioneer Mission
SPM

Lake Tchad

CMA
SUM 1904

CMA

SUM
SIM

SIM 1900

Qua Iboe Mission

SIM

1887
AIM

AIM
AIM
TEAM

Scale: 0 — 1000 km

CMA

Various Missions

CBM

LIM 1878
AIM

Comoros

CoIM

Brethren Missions

ZIM
NIM

Mission Philafricaine

Madagascar

TEAM

SAGM

FØM

Areas already reached by missionaries when the work of faith missions began (about 1880–1900)

## Abbreviations:

AIM:   Africa Inland Mission (1895)
AMB:   Algiers Mission Band
CBM:   Congo Balolo Mission
CMA:   Christian and Missionary Alliance
          (A. B. Simpson/USA)
CMM:   Central Morocco Mission
CoIM:  Congo Inland Mission
EGM:   Egypt General Mission
FØM:   Frie Østafrikanske Mission
LIM:    Livingstone Inland Mission (1878)
NAM:   North Africa Mission

NIM:    Nyasa Industrial Mission
SAGM:  South Africa General Mission
SIM:    Sudan Interior Mission (1900)
SMM:   Southern Morocco Mission
SPM:    Sudan Pioneer Mission
SUM:    Sudan United Mission (1904)
TEAM:  The Scandinavian Alliance
           Mission of North America
WEC:    Worldwide
           Evangelization Crusade
ZIM:    Zambezi Industrial Mission

missionary work, in that area much easier. It is not the case that colonial rule made missionary work that much easier everywhere: French colonial authorities quite arbitrarily prevented the Protestant missions from working in their domains.

◇ Muslim North Africa: hindrances to missionary work in North Africa were not due to the climate but were of a religious nature. The classical missions had attempted missionary work among Muslims in North Africa and had, indeed, reached some for Christ in Egypt, but they had not been able to establish a foothold in the Maghreb.

None of the early faith missions wanted to work where other missions were already working. They even avoided working close to them, because they saw missionary work in the remaining unreached areas of the globe as the only reason for their existence.[14] This made it comparatively easy for the classical missions to accept the newcomers. Often they were very welcome because they were trying to answer needs which the classical missionaries had perceived, but which they were not able to answer in addition to the work they were already doing.[15] The faith missions' priority for the unreached areas meant that they not only had to cope with their own inexperience, but also with the political, logistic and health problems which such an advance entailed.

A CHAIN OF MISSION STATIONS

As far as strategy was concerned, Paul, whose policy was always to preach where no one else had preached before him,[16] remained the shining example for faith missions everywhere. For the early faith mission strategists, the unreached areas of the interior of Africa seemed vast, and little was known about them. To make missionary work in this area feasible, they adopted the 'chain concept', a concept which seems to have been developed originally by Christian Friedrich Spittler (1782–1867), the founder of the Pilgermission St Chrischona, and propagated by Johann Ludwig Krapf (1810–81), who started Protestant missionary work in East Africa in 1844.

In the 1830s, Spittler had taken up the idea from Felician Count Zaremba (1794–1874),[17] who proposed a 'pilgrims' road' from Jerusalem to Ethiopia.[18] Laymen ('pilgrims') were to run the stations, to earn their living by their craft or trade and, by their 'simple testimony', to do missionary work. When, in 1846,

Samuel Gobat (1799–1879)[19] was made Bishop of Jerusalem, Spittler seized the opportunity to establish a 'Brüderhaus' there, as the base of the 'pilgrims' road'. In 1854, Chrischona sent the first 'missionary pilgrims'. From 1858 onwards, Spittler tried to establish the 'pilgrims' road' as the 'apostles' road'. At regular distances of fifty hours travelling time, twelve mission stations were to be established, each bearing the name of one of the apostles. The 'prophets' road' was then to continue from Ethiopia southwards, with another twelve mission stations. However, Spittler only managed to establish some of the stations and, because of the English-Ethiopian war of 1866–68 and financial difficulties, the idea was abandoned. [20]

Johann Ludwig Krapf was trained at the Basel Mission Seminary and joined the CMS to work in Ethiopia. In 1844, he established the Rabai Mission in Kenya. He considered this lonely station to be the first link in a chain of mission stations reaching from there to the Atlantic Coast.[21] Krapf never managed to establish more than that one station in his chain and, when the CMS entered Uganda in 1877, the mission at Mengo was not the final link in a long chain of mission stations, but the bridge-head of a 'daring leap forward'.[22]

When Peter Cameron Scott founded the AIM in 1895, he took up this vision, although he varied it somewhat: his aim was to establish a chain of mission stations from the coast to Lake Chad. Because the CMS already worked at Mombasa, he began his work at Nzawi, 400 km (250 miles) inland. In general, the idea of a chain of mission stations was difficult to realize, because cultural, linguistic, logistic and political arguments determined the position of each station, rather than the abstract 'chain idea'. In addition, secular means of transport soon became available, so that a chain of mission stations lost its logistic function.

After the AIM had survived its first great crisis, it continued to expand westwards.[23] Further westward lay Uganda which, according to Scott's understanding, was already evangelized by the CMS. This area was part of the Mombasa to Chad chain, but not an area for the AIM to work in. From 1910, the AIM tried to establish the next foothold in north-eastern Zaire.[24] Part of this endeavour was an agreement with C. T. Studd that he should start work there with what he conceived as an 'independent British branch' of the AIM. [25]

Soon, Studd felt his independence to be threatened[26] and he demanded independence for his 'branch'. Failing to achieve this independence, he and Alfred Buxton resigned from the AIM,[27] which agreed to divide up the area.[28] The AIM took the northern section, because it was directed towards Lake Chad and, in 1917, this 'last frontier' was envisaged. The title page of *Inland Africa*[29] was decorated with a map which set out the Mombasa-Chad vision. On it, the final 1,000 miles were marked.[30] In 1924, the AIM started work in the eastern corner of the Central African Republic. But, in spite of many reminders of the original vision of its founder, the AIM did not dare to advance further for decades.[31]

The other great vision was that of a chain of mission stations from the Nile to the Niger, or from the Niger to the Nile. Its promulgator was Karl Kumm. The first attempt to realize this vision was from Aswan, with the help of the Sudan-Pionier-Mission;[32] the attempt failed. Soon, the German mission supporters considered this to be incompatible; however, for logistical reasons, it would have been most difficult to reach the populated areas of Nigeria from the east, and the number of supporters of his mission in Germany would have been too small for such a far-flung advance.[33] In 1904, SUM started to work at the other end of the chain.

In 1909, Kumm once again took up the idea of a missionary advance beyond northern Nigeria[34] and travelled from the Niger to the Nile to further his vision.[35] C. T. Studd wanted to accompany him, but was prevented by a bout of malaria. When Kumm returned, he suggested that Studd should advance from the Anglo-Egyptian Sudan westwards,[36] whereas SUM was to advance from northern Nigeria eastwards.[37] With Bishop Gwynne, Khartoum, and the Rev. A. Shaw of the CMS, he made a reconnaissance trip into the Bahr-el-Ghazal. Because Studd found too few people living there, he did not start missionary work, although the CMS missionary work was extended.[38]

Because SUM was an international mission, Kumm suggested that each branch should take up one link in that chain: Australia and New Zealand were to work in the Anglo-Egyptian Sudan,[39] and Denmark was to work in Nigeria adjacent to the Cameroon border. The German branch was to work in Adamaua in northern Cameroon, [40] but the First World War made this impossible, so the Norwegian branch worked there instead.[41] The 'missing-link-country' was Chad, where SUM started work in 1926.[42]

Similarly to AIM, SUM never attempted to establish a chain of missions, and its branches acted quite independently. There was never any link between the SUM-AUS/NZ work in the Nuba

Mountains in the Sudan and the SUM activities in Chad. Each area had its own access to the coast or to Europe, and the branches had to deal with different colonial authorities. Nevertheless, for both AIM and SUM, the idea of a chain of mission stations was extremely important as a propelling vision. In the 1930s, this vision lost its compelling power in the wake of the religious and economic depression in the United States and Europe.

The work of the CMA was also propelled by a vision of a chain of mission stations, this time from the West Coast to Timbuktu, or even to Lake Chad.[43] Without much regard to the required sacrifices, and to effectiveness and continuity, the CMA quickly advanced from the coast of Sierra Leone to the frontier of Guinea.[44] The French colonial authorities refused permission to continue until 1917. Permission being granted, a quick advance to Timbuktu was made. Timbuktu seemed so desirable that the CMA relinquished its work in Sierra Leone. The chain of mission stations had no logistic use any more, because transport via the Guinean port of Conakry was much easier.[45] As in West Africa, the CMA's early work in the Congo was dominated by the chain concept: the chain of mission stations was to extend from the Lower Congo to the Great Lakes. The CMA stuck to this idea even after it had become clear that it might be possible to reach Zaire along the rivers rather than by a chain of stations overland.[46] Attempts were not made to establish more than the very first links in that chain, because the 'mission explosion'[47] had run its course and the CMA needed its resources for consolidation. When, after some time, new resources became available, the CMA expanded again, not along the intended chain but along the coast northwards into French colonial territory.[48]

Héli Chatelin combined the chain idea with the concept of an industrial mission.[49] He was convinced that each mission station could become self-supporting within a few years and then yield enough profit to establish another station further eastwards. Kalukembe (Lincoln) was envisaged as the first link in a chain reaching the Katanga.[50] But his economic ideas proved wrong,[51] and he failed to hold the co-workers which he would have needed for further expansion.[52] Later, the Mission Philafricaine concentrated its work in Angola, where it expanded, although not along an imaginary line.[53]

The chain idea was, to some extent, successful where there was a river to follow. The LIM pursued the aims of establishing a chain

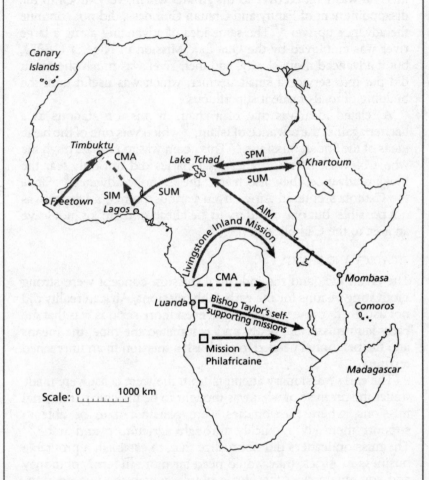

# THE CHAIN IN THE STRATEGY
# OF THE EARLY FAITH MISSIONS

Canary
Islands

Timbuktu
CMA
Lake Tchad
SPM
Khartoum
SUM
Freetown
SIM
Lagos
SUM
AIM
Livingstone Inland Mission
CMA
Mombasa
Luanda
Bishop Taylor's self-supporting missions
Comoros
Mission
Philafricaine
Madagascar

Scale: 0    1000 km

**Abbreviations:**
AIM:  Africa Inland Mission
CMA: Christian and Missionary Alliance
SIM:  Sudan Interior Mission
SPM:  Sudan Pioneer Mission
SUM:  Sudan United Mission

of mission stations to bypass the rapids of the Lower Congo, and then of progressing up river.[54] The LIM had achieved the first aim in 1883,[55] and it had started to achieve the second[56] when the mission was handed over to the ABMU which, very much to the disappointment of Fanny and Grattan Guinness, did not continue the advance upriver.[57] The same idea of advancing along a large river was employed by the Qua Iboe Mission in Nigeria (1887), but it advanced more slowly, and their river was much shorter. It did put into service a small steamer, which was useful until the building of roads made it superfluous.

A related idea was that of a chain of mission stations as a barrier against the advance of Islam,[58] which was one of the basic ideas of the Sudan missions.[59] This chain was to pass through the whole of West Africa.[60] The missionaries did not only fear the Muslim advance; they also feared the Catholic advance.[61] Since the Catholics entered Africa from various points, a barrier was not possible, but one could try to 'be ahead of them' or 'not leave an area to the Catholics alone'.[62]

STRATEGY AND REALITY

The chain idea and the industrial mission concept were strong motivating visions for the early faith missions. African reality did not usually fit these strategies, but even more serious was that the early faith missions greatly underestimated the time, the means and the personnel needed to establish a mission in an unreached territory.

The early missionary attempts from the west coast were made under the premise of what was thought to be the cheap industrial missions, where missionaries were considered to be able to support themselves quickly through agriculture and trade.[63] The mission leaders did not realize that, to establish a profitable business in Africa, they would need far more in terms of money and equipment than that, for example, which the five missionaries of the Missionary Union for the Evangelization of the World had had to start with. When A. B. Simpson's New York Gospel Tabernacle[64] learned of their plight, they immediately sent more money,[65] but John Condit, the leader of the group, had already died of fever, and Jensen, Pearson and Quayle had already sold their equipment for $600 to pay for the return tickets.[66]

Frank Garrish considered their action to be rash, and he joined the ABMU, which had just taken over the work of the LIM.[67] If A. B. Simpson and his fellow-workers had been able to learn from the experiences of Fanny Guinness' LIM as they had learned from the experiences of the East London Training Institute, they would never have conceived the idea of establishing an industrial mission on the Lower Congo. Fanny Guinness had already realized that such a concept could not succeed and that, for effective missionary work on the Lower Congo, far greater means were needed. She also recognized that Africans needed to be employed and that the necessary trade goods to pay them had to be transported.[68]

Despite these experiences, Fanny and Grattan Guinness planned a new industrial mission on the Qua Iboe in Eastern Nigeria. Samuel Bill was to support himself and the work of the mission, but less through agriculture than through trade.[69] Bill realized very quickly that he would have to compete with other traders and would have little time left for missionary work,[70] so he preferred to ask his friends in Northern Ireland to organize a faith mission for him.[71]

Rowland Bingham also failed with his industrial mission concepts. There are very few primary sources in existence on Bingham's 1893 attempt to establish a mission in northern Nigeria. Looking back on this attempt, Bingham recalled that, on arrival at Lagos, they realized that they were badly equipped and sold everything they could dispense with in order to be able to continue their work.[72] This allows the conclusion that they also had intended to establish a mission that was (at least partly) self-supporting. When Bingham made his second attempt, he expressed his concept through the name of the mission: not Sudan Interior Mission, but Africa Industrial Mission.[73] He even went so far as no longer insisting on the Sudan Belt as the field of service, thinking of smaller unreached areas in the vicinity of the Zambezi Industrial Mission in Malawi.[74] The first two missionaries were sent there to 'gain experience'.[75] After that, the mission decided for the Sudan Belt again,[76] but the industrial mission concept failed completely as a means of establishing a mission in unreached territory. The only cash crop available would have been cotton. In producing cotton, the mission would have had to compete with the local African farmers without any hope of being able to produce cotton as cheaply as they could. In 1905, the mission board in Toronto began to accept the facts and renamed the mission the Africa Evangelistic Mission, but it still felt obliged to emphasize that the industrial mission concept should not be abandoned completely.[77] In 1907, the name Sudan Interior Mission was adopted once again (today, SIM International).

On the western coast, it was Héli Chatelin who most strongly propagated the industrial mission idea. For him, too, it proved impossible to maintain the first station. In following his (and Simpson's) model, William Taylor did not fare much better. The American Episcopal Methodists had elevated him, in 1885, to 'Bishop of Africa'. In spite of this denominational tie (which permitted him to establish self-supporting missions with Methodists and non-Methodists alike, in the whole of Africa except Liberia) his missions looked far more like interdenominational faith missions than like classical denominational missions. William Taylor brought many missionaries with him. They had to earn their own support and often did so by teaching the children of white settlers. However, many of the missionaries were not happy and returned home, and many of the stations he founded were not viable.[78] After his retirement in 1896, the Missionary Society of the Methodist Episcopal Church took over the work he had started and transformed it into a regular classical mission.[79]

The only successful industrial missions were *not* established in *unreached territory*: the Zambezi Industrial Mission (1892) and the Nyassa Industrial Mission (1893). Booth had placed these missions in a largely non-Christian area, although not in completely unreached territory;[80] they were situated only miles away from the Scottish Presbyterian mission station at Blantyre, founded in 1876. Originally, Booth had wanted to start his mission further away from them, but he quickly realized that an industrial mission could only support itself if the area was already developed and had good transport connections. These missions did indeed manage to support themselves.[81] New money was needed only for expansion,[82] and the schools were partly paid for by British 'friends of the mission'.[83] However, the success which, in 1898, served as a model for Bingham's Africa Industrial Mission[84] did not last forever. In 1928, the earnings from agriculture declined dramatically, so that from 1930 onwards the English ZIM board, in a dramatic process of change, remodelled the ZIM into a faith mission like any other faith mission. In almost every case following the start of a faith mission, a severe crisis followed, in which the climate, insufficient equipment, lack of experience and personal peculiarities played a role. For LIM, the realization that the industrial mission idea was not viable was part of that crisis, but much more was the fact that many missionaries died during the first few years. The same applies to the Missionary Union for the Evangelization of

# Churches in Africa going back to faith missions: key

| AEF | Africa Evangelical Fellowship |
|------|-------------------------------|
| AIM | Africa Inland Mission |
| AMB | Algiers Mission Band |
| AEM | Angola Evangelical Mission |
| BTSSM | Bishop Taylor's Self-Supporting Missions |
| CBM | Congo Balolo Mission |
| CMA | Christian and Missionary Alliance |
| CMM | Central Morocco Mission |
| CoIM | Congo Inland Mission |
| GMU | Gospel Missionary Union |
| HF | Helgelseförbundet |
| LIM | Livingstone Inland Mission |
| MPH | Mission Philafricaine |
| NAM | North Africa Mission |
| NIM | Nyassa Industrial Mission |
| NM | Neukirchener Mission |
| PIM | Providence Industrial Mission |
| QIM | Qua Iboe Mission |
| SIM | Sudan Interior Mission |
| SMF | Svenska Missionsförbundet |
| SMM | Southern Morocco Mission |
| SUM | Sudan United Mission |
| SvAM | Svenska Alliansmissionen |
| TEAM | The Evangelical Alliance Mission |
| UMC | United Missionary Church |
| ZIM | Zambezi Industrial Mission |

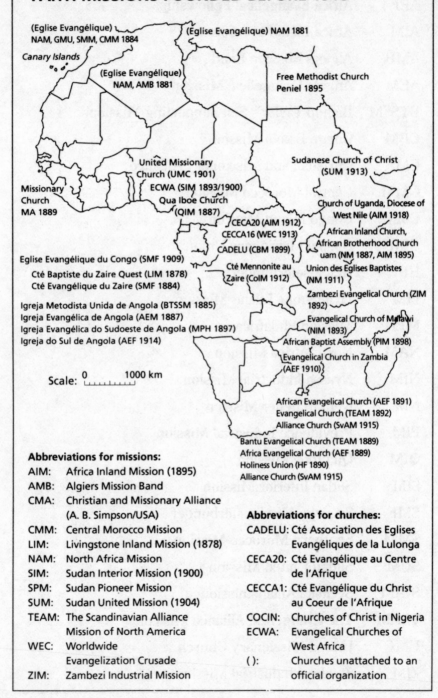

# AFRICAN CHURCHES ORIGINATING IN THE FAITH MISSIONS FOUNDED BEFORE 1918

(Eglise Evangélique) NAM, GMU, SMM, CMM 1884

Canary Islands

(Eglise Evangélique) NAM 1881

(Eglise Evangélique) NAM, AMB 1881

Free Methodist Church Peniel 1895

United Missionary Church (UMC 1901)

ECWA (SIM 1893/1900)

Qua Iboe Church (QIM 1887)

Missionary Church MA 1889

Sudanese Church of Christ (SUM 1913)

Church of Uganda, Diocese of West Nile (AIM 1918)

CECA20 (AIM 1912)
CECCA16 (WEC 1913)
CADELU (CBM 1899)

African Inland Church, African Brotherhood Church uam (NM 1887, AIM 1895)

Eglise Evangélique du Congo (SMF 1909)

Cté Mennonite au Zaire (CoIM 1912)

Union des Eglises Baptistes (NM 1911)

Cté Baptiste du Zaire Quest (LIM 1878)
Cté Evangélique du Zaire (SMF 1884)

Zambezi Evangelical Church (ZIM 1892)

Igreja Metodista Unida de Angola (BTSSM 1885)
Igreja Evangélica de Angola (AEM 1887)
Igreja Evangélica do Sudoeste de Angola (MPH 1897)
Igreja do Sul de Angola (AEF 1914)

Evangelical Church of Malawi (NIM 1893)

African Baptist Assembly (PIM 1898)

Evangelical Church in Zambia (AEF 1910)

Scale: 0 — 1000 km

African Evangelical Church (AEF 1891)
Evangelical Church (TEAM 1892)
Alliance Church (SvAM 1915)

Bantu Evangelical Church (TEAM 1889)
Africa Evangelical Church (AEF 1889)
Holiness Union (HF 1890)
Alliance Church (SvAM 1915)

**Abbreviations for missions:**
AIM:   Africa Inland Mission (1895)
AMB:   Algiers Mission Band
CMA:   Christian and Missionary Alliance
       (A. B. Simpson/USA)
CMM:   Central Morocco Mission
LIM:   Livingstone Inland Mission (1878)
NAM:   North Africa Mission
SIM:   Sudan Interior Mission (1900)
SPM:   Sudan Pioneer Mission
SUM:   Sudan United Mission (1904)
TEAM:  The Scandinavian Alliance
       Mission of North America
WEC:   Worldwide
       Evangelization Crusade
ZIM:   Zambezi Industrial Mission

**Abbreviations for churches:**
CADELU: Cté Association des Eglises
        Evangéliques de la Lulonga
CECA20: Cté Evangélique au Centre
        de l'Afrique
CECCA1: Cté Evangélique du Christ
        au Coeur de l'Afrique
COCIN:  Churches of Christ in Nigeria
ECWA:   Evangelical Churches of
        West Africa
( ):    Churches unattached to an
        official organization

the World (CMA) when it tried to work in the Lower Congo in 1885, and to the World's Gospel Union and the Evangelical Missionary Alliance (CMA) in 1890 in Sierra Leone.[85] With the AIM, the great initial crisis was not so much due to the death of the founder, Peter Cameron Scott,[86] but because the remaining missionaries all developed ideas of their own. All the members of his family who had joined the mission left it to become settlers.[87] The (holiness) Quaker, Hotchkiss, decided to start a mission of his own church[88] and Krieger left for doctrinal reasons.[89] The concept of a field-directed mission further contributed to the crisis. C. E. Hurlbert was, in the end, only able to solve the crisis by placing final authority with the Philadelphia Missionary Council.[90]

For the Scandinavian Alliance Mission, the crisis came when Lobengula, King of the Matabele, refused the missionaries permission to settle in his country.[91] After this refusal, they had no means of searching for another completely unreached territory, so they had to be content with a comparatively unreached area not far from Swaziland.[92] During this exploratory journey, Anders Haugerud, the leader of this first group, died.[93]

Despite all these difficulties, caused as often as not by external factors, nearly all the missions managed to establish themselves so that their work gave birth to churches which still exist today.

EARLY EXPANSION INTO NEW AREAS (UNTIL 1914)

Nearly all early faith missions had a vision of far-reaching advance but, until 1914, almost none of them managed to start work in more than one area *and* to establish itself thoroughly. From 1910, however, there were some very interesting steps toward new advances. In 1909, the AIM had taken over from the CMS a new field in northern Tanzania.[94] In 1910, the AIM made the first attempt to establish a mission among the 'Niam-Niam tribes' (Zande) in north-east Zaire;[95] in 1912, Karungu opened as the first AIM mission station in Zaire.[96] Contacts were also established with the West Nile Province of northern Uganda, where the CMS did not work, although a mission station was only established in 1918.[97] In addition, 1910 was the year in which Karl Kumm started to prepare his mission for a new advance.[98] In 1911, he travelled to Australia and New Zealand and got the SUM- AUS/NZ[99] to accept the work about to begin in the Anglo-Egyptian Sudan as its main responsibility.[100] The CMS left the Melut area in Sudan to the SUM, hoping that it could evangelize the area more effectively.[101] In 1909, the Svenska Missionsförbundet managed to start work as the first Protestant mission in the French Congo.[102] In 1911, the Neukirchen Mission began work in Burundi, also as the first Protestant mission there.[103] In 1911, the South African branch of the SUM began its own work among the Tiv in Nigeria[104] and, in 1913, the Danish branch started to work in the area of Numan.[105] In 1914, the South Africa General Mission opened its first station in southern Angola.

FAITH MISSIONS AND THE DEPRESSION

For all missions, the 1920s and 1930s were difficult years, because the war and its aftermath had eroded the economic base for missionary support. Worse than the economic depression, however, was the spiritual depression which ran parallel to the world economic crisis, but had started before it.[106] The spiritual depression affected the 'old-line denominations' hardest,[107] but it did not spare the evangelicals either.[108] America's declaration of war against Germany had triggered off at least some religious enthusiasm, but that dwindled away after the war had ended. Church attendance decreased, and home and foreign missions suffered from shortages of personnel and funds.[109] American Christianity was depressed,[110] and the aggressiveness of the liberals and fighting fundamentalists in those years seems to be evidence of that mood.[111] Between the two wars, no far-reaching spiritual renewal occurred in Europe or America, and any hope that the material depression would usher in a spiritual revival, as it had done in 1858–59, proved futile.

The time between 1918 and 1940 is characterized by slow expansion of faith missions in Africa. Some missions, which had started in English territories or in Zaire, managed to extend their work to French territories. During 1930–38, all the area of middle and northern Nigeria and of Zaire was finally divided up between the various missions which worked in comity with each other (in Nigeria, faith missions and classical missions; in Zaire, all Protestant missions). Often, the aims of a mission were reduced to consolidation.

Contrary to the general trend, WEC embarked on a programme of expansion, reviving the concept of reaching the unreached and, with it, the idea of 'inland mission'. Until WEC separated into the Unevangelized Fields Mission[112] and WEC in 1931,[113] and until the death of Studd the same year, north-

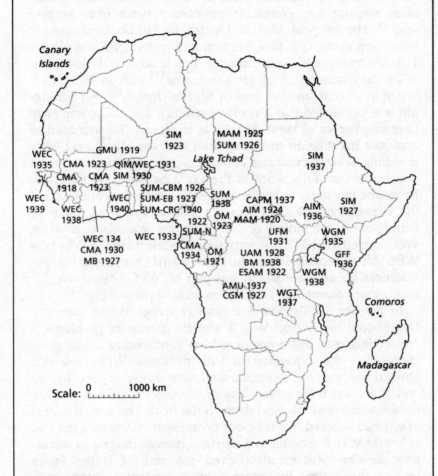

# NEW MISSION WORK
## 1918–1940

Canary
Islands

WEC
1935

GMU 1919

SIM
1923

MAM 1925
SUM 1926

Lake Tchad

SIM
1937

CMA 1923 QIM/WEC 1931
CMA
1918

CMA
1923

SIM 1930

SUM-CBM 1926

WEC
1939

WEC
1938

WEC
1940

SUM-EB 1923
SUM-CRC 1940

WEC
1922

SUM
1938

CAPM 1937
AIM 1924

SIM
1927

ÖM
1923

MAM 1920

AIM
1936

WEC 134
CMA 1930
MB 1927

WEC 1933

SUM-N

CMA
1934

ÖM
1921

UFM
1931

UAM 1928
BM 1938
ESAM 1922

WGM
1935

GFF
1936

AMU 1937
CGM 1927

WGT
1937

WGM
1938

Comoros

Scale: 0 — 1000 km

Madagascar

## Abbreviations:

AIM: Africa Inland Mission (1895)
AMB: Algiers Mission Band
CBM: Congo Balolo Mission
CMA: Christian and Missionary Alliance
(A. B. Simpson/USA)
CMM: Central Morocco Mission
CoIM: Congo Inland Mission
EGM: Egypt General Mission
FØM: Frie Østafrikanske Mission
LIM: Livingstone Inland Mission (1878)
NAM: North Africa Mission

NIM: Nyasa Industrial Mission
SAGM: South Africa General Mission
SIM: Sudan Interior Mission (1900)
SMM: Southern Morocco Mission
SPM: Sudan Pioneer Mission
SUM: Sudan United Mission (1904)
TEAM: The Scandinavian Alliance
Mission of North America
WEC: Worldwide
Evangelization Crusade
ZIM: Zambezi Industrial Mission

eastern Zaire was the only WEC mission field in Africa. Norman P. Grubb, Studd's son-in-law and successor, became convinced that the answer for the crisis of WEC should be a widespread advance into yet-unreached areas. Seven of the West African areas without any Protestant missionary work were singled out.[114] The original idea had come to Grubb from Stanley Benington of the Qua Iboe Mission in Nigeria. QIM was always a hardworking and solid mission, but it advanced slowly. In 1924, they started to look for a new area[115] and, in 1931, they began to work in another area of Nigeria (Igala),[116] but Benington was convinced that a resolute advance into still completely unreached areas of West Africa was necessary. He managed to convince his mission to entrust him with the job[117] and, after travelling several thousand kilometres investigating by car, he decided to start QIM work in French West Africa, at Bouroum Bouroum, in what is today Burkina Faso. Under the conditions of the Depression, the QIM was not able to invest as much as Benington had counted on, so everyone was content when WEC agreed, in 1937, to continue the work there.[118] Why was WEC able to expand during the Depression? One reason was the readiness for sacrifice which was part of 'WEC philosophy';[119] another was Norman P. Grubb's fascinating personality.[120]

In the late 1930s, the American churches awoke from the Depression, but World War 2 and the transport problems it created hindered this awakening from contributing in any great measure to the expansion of faith missions. When America entered the war, the situation was made worse so that by the end of the war there were many missionary candidates, but few means with which to send them to the field. The end of World War 1 had ushered in a religious depression in America; the end of World War 2 ushered in a religious revival. Interest in worldwide missions was greatly revived, too, and the United States became the leading Protestant-sending country. Growing missionary interest was concentrated in the more conservative churches and congregations, which led to a drastic change in the mission structures, with the 'ecumenical' missions declining and the 'evangelical' missions dramatically growing.

## AFRICAN CHURCHES

When Guinness, Simpson, Scott or Bingham developed their theology of mission before they began the actual work, the church on the mission field played hardly any role, simply

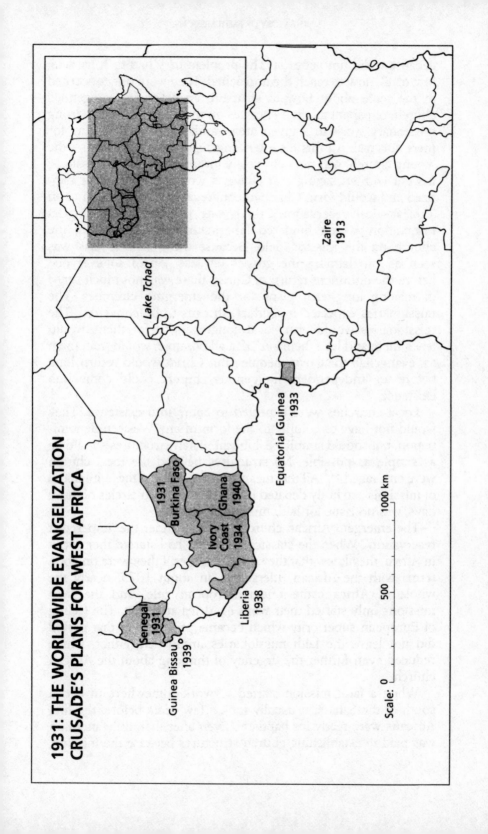

# 1931: THE WORLDWIDE EVANGELIZATION CRUSADE'S PLANS FOR WEST AFRICA

Senegal 1931

Guinea Bissau 1939

Burkina Faso 1931

Ivory Coast 1934

Ghana 1940

Liberia 1938

Equatorial Guinea 1933

Lake Tchad

Zaire 1913

Scale:

0    500    1000 km

because it did not yet exist. The problem they had to solve was, first of all, how to reach the unreached. They were not concerned in the main about how to structure an emergent indigenous church, but spent all their energies on the tough work of starting missionary work in a given area—and sometimes fighting for mere survival. All this meant: evangelism first. Nonetheless, the 'young church' was not completely forgotten. For faith missions, it went without saying that converts would eventually be baptized and would form Christian congregations. In addition to an 'ecclesiastical reservation', there was also an 'eschatological reservation' which hindered far-reaching thoughts about the church on the mission field. Because the mission's task was seen as proclaiming the gospel (at least once) to everyone before the imminent return of Christ, there was not much sense in making long-term plans for the emerging churches. The missionaries expected individual Africans to be converted. The missionaries would form local congregations for them, would teach them and lead them and, if at all possible, would train them to 'evangelize their own people'. But Christ would return long before an 'independent indigenous church' could come into existence.

Local churches were expected to come into existence. They would not have to comply to the form of any Western denomination, but should simply be 'biblical'. Their structures should be as simple as possible. No structures beyond the local church were envisaged.[121] All this meant that the issue of the 'euthanasia of missions', so hotly debated in classical mission circles of those days, was no issue for faith missions.

The emergent African church was also under the 'imperialist reservation'. When the classical missions had started their work in Africa, they knew that they could prosper if they were on good terms with the African rulers. But, in about 1875, nearly the whole of Africa came under European rule, and the faith missions only started their work in Africa after that. The feeling of European superiority which became prevalent in that period did not leave the faith missionaries untouched, either, which reduced even further the urgency of thinking about the African church.

When a faith mission started to work somewhere in Africa south of the Sahara, it usually took a few years before 'the first Africans were ready for baptism'. Even after that, little attention was paid to establishing church structures because the mission, with its centralized organization, already provided these structures. In the 1930s, faith missions started systematic discussions about what pattern the African church should follow. The answer was taken from the classical missions—not from their mainline thinking, but from a critical sideline, from Roland Allen and his 'indigenous church principles'. His strict separation (or how they understood it) between mission and church did not serve well the emergent African faith mission churches. Another reason for which faith missions invested little energy in developing African churches is that they themselves were quite weak in ecclesiology. They had, first of all, to find out if they even wanted to found 'proper' churches. Even if they agreed on that, they still had to decide what structures those churches should have.

All this meant that the 'wave of independence' which, after 1950, swept the continent caught the faith missions largely unawares. As a rule, they accepted the process to independence in state and church. Often this took place without serious problems, but sometimes serious frictions arose, as with the AIM in Kenya, which nearly resulted in a separation between the AIM and the church it had founded.[122]

On the whole, the process of independence did not differ in principle between faith mission churches and classical mission churches. Sometimes it was slower[123] and usually the leaders of faith mission churches were less qualified in academic terms. In most African countries, the full integration of mission and church is the rule, not only in Kenya, Zaire and Nigeria—the main 'faith mission countries'—but also in countries such as Guinea Bissau or the Congo. An example from Angola may serve as an illustration (see table: From mission to independent church[124]).

For African churches today, it is no longer a question of how to get rid of the missionaries, but of how to get enough of them. Also, in theology, the issue of mission is no longer as urgent for the African church as it was two decades ago. The most urgent issue for the church in Africa south of the Sahara in general (and for the great faith mission churches in particular) is how to cope with the tremendous numerical growth which they have experienced since the 1960s and which they are still experiencing today. The number of Christians in the AIM sphere in Kenya counted a few thousands in the 1950s; now there are more than one million Kenyans who claim some kind of allegiance to the Africa Inland Church.[125]

# From mission to independent church—the case of the Evangelical Church of South-east Angola

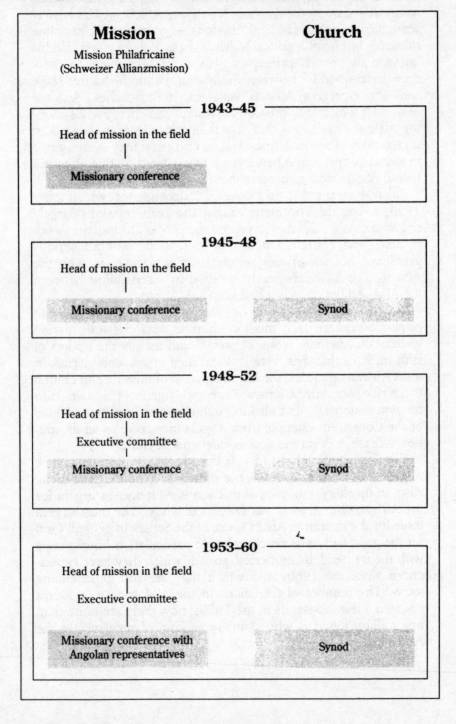

**Mission**

**Church**

Mission Philafricaine
(Schweizer Allianzmission)

**1943–45**

Head of mission in the field
|
Missionary conference

**1945–48**

Head of mission in the field
|
Missionary conference

Synod

**1948–52**

Head of mission in the field
|
Executive committee
|
Missionary conference

Synod

**1953–60**

Head of mission in the field
|
Executive committee
|
Missionary conference with
Angolan representatives

Synod

From mission to independent church (continued)

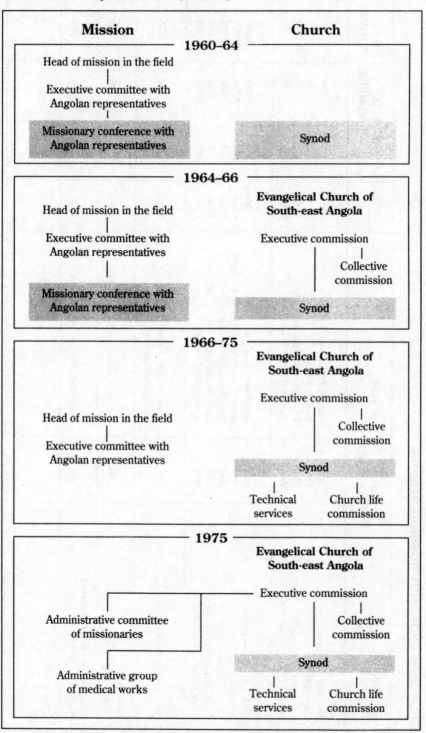

# Churches with faith mission origins

| MISSION | DATE FOUNDED | CHURCH | TYPE | CONGRE-GATIONS | FULL MEMBERS | TOTAL MEMBERS |
|---|---|---|---|---|---|---|
| **Algeria** | | | | | | |
| North Africa Mission | 1888 | Mission d'Afrique du Nord | Pint | 5 | 200 | 300 |
| Mission Rolland | 1908 | Mission Rolland | Pint | 2 | 30 | 200 |
| Emmanuel Mission Sahara Desert Mission | 1953 | Mission Évangélique au Sahara | Pint | 1 | 20 | 50 |
| Mission Biblique de Ghardaïa | 1956 | Mission Biblique de Ghardaïa | Pind | 1 | 20 | 50 |
| | | | | | | |
| **Angola** | | | | | | |
| [Bishop Taylor's Mission] | 1885 | [Igreja Metodista Unida de Angola] | [PMet] | 107 | 47,989 | 70,000 |
| Mission Philafricaine | 1897 | Igreja Evangélica do Sudoeste de Angola | PBap | 348 | 8,730 | 45,000 |
| Angola Evangelical Mission | 1887 | Igreja Evangélica de Angola[126] | PBap | ? | 1,000 | 2,000 |
| Angola Evangelical Mission | 1925 | Igreja Evangélica do Norte de Angola | PBap | 2 | 500 | 1,000 |
| Africa Evangelical Fellowship | 1914 | Igreja do Sul de Angola | Pint | 150 | 3,000 | 10,000 |
| | | | | | | |
| **Benin** | | | | | | |
| Sudan Interior Mission | 1946 | Association des Églises Évangéliques du Benin | Pint | 59 | 782 | 3,335 |
| | | | | | | |
| **Botswana** | | | | | | |
| Helgelseförbundet | c. 1960 | Holiness Union Church of Botswana[127] | PHol | | 300 | 500 |
| | | | | | | |
| **British Indian Ocean Territory** | | | | | | |
| World Wide Mission | 1961 | World Wide Missions of Cameroon | Pind | | 1,200 | 2,000 |
| | | | | | | |
| **Cape Verde** | | | | | | |

Churches with faith mission origins (continued)

| MISSION | DATE FOUNDED | CHURCH | TYPE | CONGRE-GATIONS | FULL MEMBERS | TOTAL MEMBERS |
|---|---|---|---|---|---|---|
| **Central African Republic** | | | | | | |
| Mid Africa Mission | 1920 | Églises Baptistes de la RCA | PBap | 375 | 60,000 | 150,000 |
| Africa Inland Mission | 1924 | Église Évangélique Centrafricaine | PInt | 100 | 1,000 | 5,000 |
| Central Africa Pioneer Mission | 1937 | Mission Évangélique (Americaine) | PInt | | 3,000 | 5,000 |
| Örebro Mission | 1923 | Union des Églises Baptistes | PPe2 | 29 | 26,595 | 5,000 |
| **Chad** | | | | | | |
| Mid Africa Mission | 1925 | Église Baptiste du Tchad | PBap | 150 | 20,000 | 30,000 |
| | | Église Dissidente du Tchad | Ipen | | 500 | 1,000 |
| Sudan United Mission[128] | 1926 | Églises Évangéliques au Tchad | PInt | 372 | 20,000 | 100,000 |
| **Comoros** | | | | | | |
| Africa Inland Mission | 1975 | [Église de Jésus-Christ aux Congo] | PInt | 1 | 20 | 40 |
| **Congo** | | | | | | |
| Svenska Missionsförbundet | 1909 | Église Évangélique du Congo | PCon | 90 | 68,800 | 120,000 |
| Örebro Mission | 1921 | Église Baptiste du Congo Populaire | PPe2 | 61 | 2,197 | 4,000 |
| United World Mission | 1946 | Église Évangélique de la Likouala | PInt | 9 | 1,000 | 3,000 |
| **Djibouti** | | | | | | |
| **Egypt** | | | | | | |
| Peniel Missionary Society | 1895 | Free Methodist Church | PHol | 92 | 4,250 | 15,250 |
| World Wide Mission | 1960 | Gospel Preaching Church | PInd | | 2,600 | 4,000 |
| Egypt General Mission[129] | | | | | | |
| Unevangelized Fields Mission | 1964 | | | | | |
| World Gospel Mission | 1949 | | | | | |

Churches with faith mission origins (continued)

| MISSION | DATE FOUNDED | CHURCH | TYPE | CONGRE-GATIONS | FULL MEMBERS | TOTAL MEMBERS |
|---|---|---|---|---|---|---|
| **Equatorial Guinea**<br>Worldwide Evangelization Crusade | 1933 | [Iglesia Evangélica en la Guinea Equatorial]<br>(Iglesia Evangélica Cruzada) | PRef | 30 | 1,300 | 4,000 |
| **Ethiopia**<br>Sudan Interior Mission<br>Red Sea Mission Team<br>World Wide Mission | 1927<br>1951<br>1966 | Word of Life Evangelical Church | PBap | 2,051 | 181,463 | 500,000 |
| **Gabon**<br>Christian and Missionary Alliance | 1934 | Église Évangélique du Sud Gabon | PHol | 188 | 6,854 | 15,000 |
| **Gambia**<br>Worldwide Evangelization Crusade | 1966 | Gambian Evangelical Fellowship | PInt | 3 | 50 | 200 |
| **Ghana**<br>Worldwide Evangelization Crusade<br>Mid Africa Mission<br>Evangelical Missionary Society<br>World Wide Mission | 1940<br>1946<br>1956 | Worldwide Evangelization Crusade<br>Baptist Mid Mission<br>Fellowship of Good News Churches<br>World Wide Missions of Ghana | PInt<br>PBap<br>PInt<br>PInd | 56<br>15<br>2 | 850<br>188<br>100<br>65,000 | 2,600<br>238<br>300<br>90,000 |
| **Guinea**<br>Christian and Missionary Alliance | 1918 | Église Évangélique Protestante[130] | PHol | 203 | 1,473 | 3,000 |
| **Guinea-Bissau**<br>Worldwide Evangelization Crusade | 1939 | Igreja Evangélica da Guiné | PInt | 24 | 1,252 | 2,500 |

Churches with faith mission origins (continued)

| MISSION | DATE FOUNDED | CHURCH | TYPE | CONGRE-GATIONS | FULL MEMBERS | TOTAL MEMBERS |
|---|---|---|---|---|---|---|
| **Ivory Coast** | | | | | | |
| Mission Biblique[131] | 1927 | Union des Églises Évangéliques du Sud Ouest | PBap | 192 | 2,772 | 15,000 |
| Christian and Missionary Alliance | 1930 | Église Protestante Évangélique du Centre | PHol | 392 | 9,326 | 20,583 |
| Worldwide Evangelization Crusade | 1934 | Église Protestante du Centre | PInt | 51 | 685 | 5,000 |
| World Wide Mission | 1967 | | | | | |
| Sudan Interior Mission | 1968 | [with ECWA] | | | | |
| **Kenya** | | | | | | |
| Africa Inland Mission | 1895 | Africa Inland Church[132] | PInt | 1,700 | 150,000 | 300,000 |
| | 1945 | African Brotherhood Church[133] | Iind | 342 | 30,869 | 64,030 |
| | 1947 | African Christian Churches and Schools | IBap | 33 | 8,000 | 30,500 |
| | | 1954 Voice of Salvation and Healing Church | Ipnt | 50 | 6,000 | 12,000 |
| | | 1961 African Church | IBap | 19 | 15,000 | 30,000 |
| Neukirchener Mission | 1878 | Africa Inland Church (s.o.) | | | | |
| World Gospel Mission | 1935 | Africa Gospel Church | PHol | 250 | 6,500 | 15,000 |
| | 1964 | Africa Gospel Unity Church | IHol | 19 | 1,000 | 1,500 |
| Gospel Missionary Society | c. 1940 | Bible Fellowship Church | PBap | 1 | 210 | 500 |
| Gospel Furthering Fellowship | 1936 | Gospel Furthering Bible Church | PBap | | 3,000 | 10,000 |
| | c. 1943 | Gospel Tabernacle Church | IBap | 15 | 2,650 | 8,000 |
| | | 1958 Good News Church of Africa | IBap | 120 | 11,050 | 30,000 |
| The Evangelical Alliance Mission | | | | | | |
| World Wide Mission | 1961 | | | | | |
| **Lesotho** | | | | | | |
| **Liberia** | | | | | | |
| Worldwide Evangelization Crusade | 1938 | United Liberia Inland Church | PInt | 35 | 3,000 | 5,000 |
| Sudan Interior Mission | 1951 | ELWA Chapels | PInt | 9 | 120 | 590 |
| Sudan Interior Mission | 1984 | Montserrado Evangelical Fellowship | PInt | 1 | | |
| | | c. 1968 Evangelical Church of Christ | Iind | 20 | 400 | 800 |

Churches with faith mission origins (continued)

| MISSION | DATE FOUNDED | CHURCH | TYPE | CONGRE-GATIONS | FULL MEMBERS | TOTAL MEMBERS |
|---|---|---|---|---|---|---|
| **Libya** | | | | | | |
| North Africa Mission | 1889 | | | | | |
| **Madagascar** | | | | | | |
| **Malawi** | | | | | | |
| Zambezi Industrial Mission | 1892 | Zambezi Evangelical Church | PInd | 258 | 10,000 | 30,000 |
| | | 1932 Congregation of the Lamb | IInd | 3 | 300 | 500 |
| | | c. 1953 African Church | | | | |
| Nyassa Industrial Mission[134] | 1893 | Evangelical Church of Malawi | PInt | 126 | 5,000 | 15,000 |
| Providence Industrial Mission | 1898 | 1946 African Nyasa Mission | | | | |
| | | African Baptist Assembly Malawi | IBap | 419 | 10,000 | 25,258 |
| | | 1920 Achewa Church | IInd | | 1,000 | 2,500 |
| Africa Evangelical Fellowship | 1900 | Africa Evangelical Church of Malawi | PInt | 63 | 2,000 | 5,000 |
| **Mali** | | | | | | |
| Gospel Missionary Union | 1919 | Église Évangélique Protestante au Mali | PHol | 70 | 3,000 | 5,000 |
| Christian and Missionary Alliance | 1923 | Église Chrétienne du Mali | PHol | 277 | 7,477 | 14,074 |
| United World Mission | 1953 | Église Protestante de Kayes | PHol | 8 | 350 | 1,000 |
| **Mauritania** | | | | | | |
| **Mauritius** | | | | | | |
| Africa Evangelical Fellowship | 1969 | Mauritius Mission | | | | |
| Indian Ocean Union Mission | | | | | | |
| **Mayotte** | | | | | | |

Churches with faith mission origins (continued)

| MISSION | DATE FOUNDED | CHURCH | TYPE | CONGRE-GATIONS | FULL MEMBERS | TOTAL MEMBERS |
|---|---|---|---|---|---|---|
| **Morocco** | | | | | | |
| North Africa Mission | 1884 | | PInt | 6 | 70 | 150 |
| Gospel Missionary Union | 1894 | | PHol | 5 | 30 | 50 |
| Southern Morocco Mission | | | | | | |
| Central Morocco Mission | | | | | | |
| Emmanuel Mission | | | | | | |
| Berean Mission | 1966 | | | | | |
| Morocco Evangelistic Mission[135] | | | | | | |
| Light of Africa Mission | | | | | | |
| **Mozambique** | | | | | | |
| Nyassa Industrial Mission [CSMI/NIM/ZIM/AEF] | 1921 | Igreja Evangélica Baptiste de Moçambique | PInt | 60 | 30,000 | 50,000 |
| **Namibia** | | | | | | |
| **Niger** | | | | | | |
| Sudan Interior Mission | 1923 | Églises Évangéliques du Niger | PInt | 90 | 1,000 | 2,000 |
| **Nigeria** | | | | | | |
| Qua Iboe Mission | 1887 | Qua Iboe Church | PInt | 800 | 45,000 | 90,000 |
| Sudan Interior Mission | 1893 | Evangelical Churches of West Africa | PInt | 1,330 | 60,000 | 500,000 |
| Sudan United Mission (GB) | 1904 | Church of Christ in Nigeria: Plateau+Bauchi | PInt | 1,003 | 22,104 | 220,000 |
| Sudan United Mission (CRC) | 1906 | Church of Christ in Nigeria: Benue | PRef | 232 | 9,259 | 150,000 |
| Sudan United Mission (RSA) | 1911 | Church of Christ in Nigeria: Mada Hills | PInt | 310 | 6,135 | 40,000 |
| Sudan United Mission (DRC/CRC) | 1911 | Church of Christ among the Tiv | PRef | 1,368 | 17,436 | 500,000 |
| Sudan United Mission (CBM) | 1923 | Church of Christ in Nigeria: Gabas | PDun | 302 | 18,955 | 70,000 |
| Sudan United Mission (EB/UM) | 1923 | Church of Christ in Nigeria: Muri | PMet | 220 | 7,839 | 60,000 |

Churches with faith mission origins (continued)

| MISSION | DATE FOUNDED | CHURCH | TYPE | CONGRE-GATIONS | FULL MEMBERS | TOTAL MEMBERS |
|---|---|---|---|---|---|---|
| Sudan United Mission (DK) | 1913 | Lutheran Church of Christ in Nigeria | PLut | 879 | 18,484 | 700,000 |
|  | 1940 | United Church of Christ in Nigeria | PInt | 10 | 341 | 6,000 |
| Missionary Church | 1901 | United Missionary Church of Africa | PHol | 191 | 7,000 | 15,000 |
| World Wide Mission | 1957 | World Wide Missions of Nigeria | PInd |  | 20,000 | 30,000 |
| New Testament Missionary Union |  |  |  |  |  |  |
| **Réunion** |  |  |  |  |  |  |
| Africa Evangelical Fellowship | 1970 | Église Évangélique de la Réunion |  |  |  |  |
| **Rwanda** |  |  |  |  |  |  |
| Africa Inland Mission | 1971 | Église Évangélique Calvaire d'Afrique | Ipe2 | 22 | 150 | 400 |
| **Sahara** |  |  |  |  |  |  |
| **St Helena** |  |  |  |  |  |  |
| **São Tomé and Principe** |  |  |  |  |  |  |
|  | 1935 | Igreja Evangélica | Iint | 3 | 1,000 | 2,000 |
| **Senegal** |  |  |  |  |  |  |
| Worldwide Evangelization Crusade | 1935 | Mission Évangélique | PInt | 6 | 50 | 200 |
| United World Mission | 1955 | Mission Mondiale Unie | PInt | 2 | 20 | 250 |
| New Tribes Mission | 1955 |  |  |  |  |  |
| World Wide Mission | 1965 |  |  |  |  |  |
| Calvary Ministries (CAPRO) |  |  |  |  |  |  |
| **Seychelles** |  |  |  |  |  |  |

Churches with faith mission origins (continued)

| MISSION | DATE FOUNDED | CHURCH | TYPE | CONGRE-GATIONS | FULL MEMBERS | TOTAL MEMBERS |
|---|---|---|---|---|---|---|
| **Sierra Leone** | | | | | | |
| Christian and Missionary Alliance[136] | 1965 | Sierra Leone Missionary Church | PHol | 35 | 320 | 1,350 |
| World Wide Mission | | | | | | |
| Christians in Action | | | | | | |
| **Somalia** | | | | | | |
| Sudan Interior Mission | 1954–74 | Somalia Believers Fellowship | PInt | 4 | 75 | 250 |
| **Spanish North Africa** | | | | | | |
| **South Africa** | | | | | | |
| The Evangelical Alliance Mission | 1889 | Bantu Evangelical Church | PInt | 309 | 9,581 | 17,000 |
| Hephzibah Faith Mission | | | | | | |
| Africa Evangelical Fellowship | 1890 | Indian Christian Fellowship | PInt | 22 | 727 | 1,590 |
| Helgelseförbundet | | Swedish Holiness Union Mission | PHol | 245 | 6,022 | 19,089 |
| East Africa Free Mission | | | | | | |
| Svenska Alliansmissionen | 1901 | Swedish Alliance Mission | | | 16,000 | 19,000 |
| Mahon Mission | | | | | | |
| Africa Evangelistic Mission | | | | | | |
| Dorothea Mission | | | | | | |
| **Sudan** | | | | | | |
| Sudan United Mission (AUS/NZ) | 1907 | Sudanese Church of Christ | PInd | 96 | 12,018 | 53,000 |
| Africa Inland Mission | 1936 | African Inland Church | PInt | 5 | 250 | 1,000 |
| Sudan Interior Mission | 1937 | Church in the East Central Sudan | PInt | 14 | 1,150 | 1,500 |
| **Swaziland** | | | | | | |
| Africa Evangelical Fellowship | 1891 | Africa Evangelical Church | PInt | 25 | 5,000 | 7,000 |
| Svenska Alliansmissionen | 1915 | Alliance Church of Sweden | PInd | 55 | 1,200 | 3,000 |
| | | 1950 Bantu Swedish Free Church | IInd | 8 | 2,500 | 4,000 |

Churches with faith mission origins (continued)

| MISSION | DATE FOUNDED | CHURCH | TYPE | CONGRE-GATIONS | FULL MEMBERS | TOTAL MEMBERS |
|---|---|---|---|---|---|---|
| **Tanzania** | | | | | | |
| Africa Inland Mission | 1908 | Africa Inland Church | PInt | 461 | 50,000 | 80,000 |
| Neukirchener Mission | 1960 | African Brotherhood Church | IInd | 4 | 200 | 340 |
| **Togo** | | | | | | |
| **Tunisia** | | | | | | |
| North Africa Mission | 1881 | Mission d'Afrique du Nord | PInt | 2 | 50 | 100 |
| **Uganda** | | | | | | |
| Africa Inland Mission | 1918 | Church of Uganda, Madi+West Nile Diocese | ALow | 420 | 12,500 | 30,000 |
| World Wide Mission | 1962 | World Wide Mission of Uganda | PInd | 150 | 300 | |
| **Zaire** | | | | | | |
| Christian and Missionary Alliance | 1884 | Communauté Évangélique de L'Alliance au Zaïre | PHol | 856 | 23,343 | 60,000 |
| Svenska Missionsförbundet | 1884 | Communauté Évangélique du Zaïre | PCon | 192 | 30,064 | 75,000 |
| Congo Balolo Mission = RBMU | 1889 | Communauté Association des Églises Évangéliques de la Lulonga (CADELU) | PInt | 468 | 33,450 | 75,000 |
| Congo Inland Mission | 1912 | Communauté Mennonite au Zaïre | PMen | 290 | 38,200 | 110,000 |
| | 1960 | Communauté Évangélique Mennonite du Sud-Kasai | PMen | 40 | 3,200 | 9,000 |
| Worldwide Evangelization Crusade | 1913 | Communauté Évangélique du Christ au Coeur d'Afrique | PInt | 550 | 52,201 | 110,000 |
| Evangelization Society ESAM | 1922 | Communauté Libre de Maniema-Kivu | PPen | 85 | 10,065 | 20,000 |
| Emmanuel Mission | 1923 | Communauté Assemblée des Frères au Zaïre | PCBr | 94 | 6,840 | 12,000 |

Churches with faith mission origins (continued)

| MISSION | DATE FOUNDED | CHURCH | TYPE | CONGRE-GATIONS | FULL MEMBERS | TOTAL MEMBERS |
|---|---|---|---|---|---|---|
| Unevangelized Africa Mission | 1928 | Communauté des Églises Baptistes du Kivu | PBap | 592 | 32,753 | 60,000 |
| Unevangelized Fields Mission | 1959 | Communauté Baptiste au Kivu | PBap | 370 | 21,600 | 40,000 |
|  | 1931 | Communauté Épiscopale Évangélique du Haut-Zaïre | PInt | 15 |  | 7,500 |
| Mid Africa Mission | 1949 | Communauté Baptiste Autonome entre Wamba-Bakali | IBap |  | 1,940 |  |
| Livingstone Inland Mission | 1878 | Communauté Baptiste du Zaïre-Ouest | PBap | 700 | 100,000 | 450,000 |
| Unevangelized Tribes Mission | 1961 | Communauté Baptiste du Sud-Kwango | PBap | 15 | 833 | 12,000 |
|  | 1952 | Communauté Évangélique du Kwango Pind | 206 | 6,700 | 20,000 |  |
|  | 1953 | Communauté Union des Églises Baptistes du Kwilu | IBap | 35 | 2,383 | 7,500 |
| Cooperation Évangélique Mondiale | 1965 | Communauté Cooperation Évangélique au Zaïre | Ipen | 10 | 2,663 | 8,000 |
| Congo Gospel Mission BMM | 1927 | Communauté Évangélique Zaïroise | PBap | 72 | 4,537 | 12,000 |
|  | 1932 | Communauté des Églises Baptistes Independantes | PBap | 226 | 10,592 | 25,000 |
| Worldwide Grace Testimony | 1939 | Communauté des Églises de Grace au Zaïre | PInt | 152 | 5,538 | 20,000 |
| Afrika MV, Peniel Mission ua | 1942 | Communauté des Églises Frères Mennonites au Zaïre | PMen | 140 | 10,180 | 16,000 |
| Africa Inland Mission | 1912 | Communauté Évangélique au Centre de l'Afrique | PInt | 1,140 | 63,047 | 300,000 |
| Berean Mission | 1938 | Communauté Évangélique Beréenne au Zaïre | PInt | 80 | 20,000 | 60,000 |
| **Zambia** |  |  |  |  |  |  |
| Africa Evangelical Fellowship | 1910 | Evangelical Church in Zambia | PInt | 340 | 7,000 | 20,000 |
| **Zimbabwe** |  |  |  |  |  |  |
| Svenska Alliansmissionen |  | Alliance Church in Zimbabwe | Pind | 6 | 200 | 500 |
| The Evangelical Alliance Mission | 1942 | Evangelical Church in Zimbabwe | PInt | 95 | 2,500 | 6,000 |

# Summary – 'faith mission Christians' in Africa according to countries

| | | | | |
|---|---:|---|---|---:|
| Algeria | 600 | | Mauritania | |
| Angola | 128,000 | | Mauritius | 0 |
| Benin | 3,335 | | Mayotte | |
| Botswana | 500 | | Morocco | 200 |
| British Indian Ocean Territories | | | Mozambique | 50,000 |
| Burkina Faso | 11,063 | | Namibia | |
| Burundi | 8,000 | | Niger | 2,000 |
| Cameroon | 77,398 | | Nigeria | 2,361,000 |
| Cape Verde | | | Réunion | 0 |
| Central African Republic | 165,000 | | Rwanda | 400 |
| Chad | 131,000 | | Sahara | |
| Comores | 40 | | São Tomé and Principe | 200 |
| Congo | 127,000 | | Senegal | 450 |
| Djibouti | | | Seychelles | |
| Egypt | 16,250 | | Sierra Leone | 1,350 |
| Equatorial Guinea | 4,000 | | Somalia | 250 |
| Ethiopia | 500,000 | | South Africa | 56,679 |
| Gabon | 15,000 | | Spanish North Africa | |
| Gambia | 200 | | St Helena | |
| Ghana | 93,138 | | Sudan | 55,500 |
| Guinea | 3,000 | | Swaziland | 14,000 |
| Guinea-Bissau | 2,500 | | Tanzania | 80,340 |
| Ivory Coast | 40,583 | | Togo | |
| Kenya | 501,530 | | Tunisia | 100 |
| Lesotho | | | Uganda | 30,300 |
| Liberia | 6,390 | | Zaire | 1,509,000 |
| Libya | | | Zambia | 20,000 |
| Madagascar | | | Zimbabwe | 6,500 |
| Malawi | 78,258 | | | |
| Mali | 20,074 | | Total: | 6,126,348 |

Summary:
2 countries with more than one million
5 countries with less than 100,000
14 countries with less than 10,000
18 countries with less than 1,000

Source: David Barrett (ed.), *World Christian Encyclopedia*.

Date: About 1975. Since 1975 most churches have grown considerably.

**Notes**

1    WCE, p. 782, gives a total of 3,108,450 Protestants and Anglicans for 1900 (total population: 1,078 million, of which 9.9 per cent are Christians). Warneck, Abriß, p. 310, gives 1,123,000 Protestants, not counting European immigrants. In Christian Alliance Foreign Missionary Weekly (3 July 1895), A. B. Simpson estimated that there were about one million Protestant Christians, half of them European immigrants. In 1882, Simpson mentioned 100,000 Protestant Africans as full church members and 300,000 hearers, and the same number for Madagascar (The Work and the World, June 1882). William Coppinger, secretary of the American Colonization Society, counted for 1880 506,966 Protestant Christians, including immigrants, with 122,700 full members (The Work and the World, 1882, p. 113).

2    I use this term to describe churches which, in theory or in fact, identify with the social entity they belong to (state, tribe, territory and so on), claiming authority in it and encompassing as its members a considerable section of that social entity. The German term would be 'Volkskirche'. This is often translated national church or territorial church ('Landeskirche'). Folk church has less of a political connotation. If the term alludes somewhat to folklore, that is its intention: the folk churches do indeed provide quite some folklore for the people (in the context of transition rites, festivals and public functions).

3    See: E. A. Ayandele, The Missionary Impact on Modern Nigeria 1842–1914. A Political and Social Analysis, London, 1966; J. F. Ade Ajayi, Christian Missions in Nigeria 1841–1891. The Making of a New Elite, London, 1965.

4    For early West African church history, see: Lamin Sanneh, West African Christianity: the Religious Impact, London, 1983.

5    For an overall view of East African church history, see: William B. Anderson, The Church in East Africa 1840–1974, Nairobi/Dodoma/Kampala, [2]1981 (1977). For the early years, see: Roland Oliver, The Missionary Factor in East Africa, London, [2]1965 (1952).

6    Discussed in detail in: Werner Ustorf, Die Missionsmethode Franz Michael Zahns und der Aufbau kirchlicher Strukturen in Westafrika (1862–1900), Erlangen, 1989, pp. 92–101.

7    A. T. Pierson reported, for example, in 1890 that the Presbyterian Board of Foreign Missions (United States) had an abiding deficit of $60.000 (MRW, 1890, p. 525).

8    Fredrick Stanley Arnot, Missionary Travels in Central Africa, London, 1914.

9    This area, called the 'Beloved Strip', comprised large sections of the highlands in Angola, Zambia and Zaire. The Brethren missions working in the Beloved Strip were: the Garangaze Evangelical Mission (1886) and the Luanza Mission (1894), both Open Brethren; and the Westcott Mission (1897) and the North Sankuru Mission (1930), both Exclusive Brethren, which joined in 1962 to form the North Kasai Mission.

10    Reinhard Henkel, Christian Missions in Africa. A Social Geographical Study of the Impact of Their Activities in Zambia, Berlin, 1989, p. 29.

11    Henry Morton Stanley, Through the Dark Continent (two volumes), London, 1899.

12  From 1878, the BMS tried to gain access to the navigable Congo River through northern Angola, and it reached Kinshasa in 1882. It extended its work speedily upriver, and reached Yakusu near Kisangani in 1896. The American Presbyterian Mission started in 1891 in Rom, but it was only in 1910 that a real extension of their activities became possible (Irvine, *The Church of Christ in Zaire*, p. 52f.).

13  Grattan Guinness, 'The Soudan' in *Faithful Witness*, 7 December 1889.

14  As a matter of fact, they were also proponents of new missionary principles, but the missions were not very conscious of this fact as a motivating force for missionary expansion.

15  This applies especially to the CMS, which, like faith missions, was strongly influenced by the Keswick movement.

16  'Thus making it my ambition to preach the gospel, not where Christ has already been named, lest I build on another man's foundation, but as it is written, "They shall see who have never been told of him, and they shall understand who have never heard of him"' (Romans 15:20–21).

17  A Russian Reformed missionary of German ancestry working for the Basel Mission which Spittler had founded in 1815.

18  Karl Rennstich, *Nicht jammern, sondern Hand anlegen! Christian Friedrich Spittler. Sein WerkLeben*, Metzingen 1987, p. 59.

19  Alfred Kober, *Samuel Gobat. Vom Juradorf nach Jerusalem*, Basel, 1968. Gobat, trained at the Basel Mission Seminary, became Bishop of Jerusalem on 1 January 1847 (p. 71).

20  Erich Schick and Klaus Haag, *Christian Friedrich Spittler. Handlanger Gottes*, Giessen/Basel, [2]1982, p. 80f.

21  In 1844, Krapf had developed the plan of a chain of nine or ten mission stations stretching from Mombasa to Gabon. Each station was to be occupied by four missionaries (*AMZ*, 9 (1882), p. 246).

22  Louise Pirouet, Makerere College, Kampala, Uganda, 1965.

23  When, in 1909, the AIM took over Nasa at the Southern end of Lake Victoria, this was more a step sideways.

24  In *HD*, August/September 1913, p. 17, northern Zaire and northern Uganda are depicted as steps towards Lake Chad.

25  He was accepted into AIM (having filled out his medical report himself) on 14 January 1913 and appointed 'Field Director' (Minutes First Meeting of the English Council, with Hurlbert present).

26  Minutes Executive Meeting, 22 January 1913. The Council accepted Studd's view that he 'should report in the first place to ... this Council', not to the General Director.

27  His proposed alterations to the constitution were submitted by Sutton, Buxton and Ingram (Minutes, 3 March 1913), after he had left for Zaire. When no agreement could be reached, they presented Studd's letter of resignation and resigned themselves, too, to form a body to represent Studd in Britain (Cable Buxton, Sutton, Coleman, Ingram—Studd, 4 March 1913).

28 Minutes, 3 March 1913; Cable Holden, Hurlbert—AIM-UK, 4 March 1913. See Alfred Buxton, *The First Ten Years*, London, 1923, p. 11f.

29 *Inland Africa* was the continuation of *Hearing and Doing (HD)*. Over the years, *HD* had become the magazine of the AIM only.

30 *Inland Africa* January/February 1917, p. 1. Along the western border of Sudan, another 1,000-mile advance was being charted. In 1936, AIM started to work in Sudan, but in a small area in the south-eastern corner that had not yet been assigned to any mission under the comity agreements.

31 In 1926 Hurlbert, who had been the guardian of the Chad vision, left the AIM, and his vision was no longer taken up. The AIM now (1993) has missionaries in Chad, working with Chadian missionaries of the Église Évange/lique au Tchad (Anderson–Fiedler, September 1993).

32 Minutes SPM, 25 October 1900; *Der Sudan Pionier* 1901, p. 47; *Der Sudan Pionier* 1901, p. 79 stresses that SPM is not to work among Muslims only.

33 In 1902, Kupfernagel suggested selling the house in Aswan and starting missionary work further south. His suggestion was first treated as not urgent (Minutes SPM, 10 April 1902) and was then rejected (Minutes SPM, 23 October 1902); *Der Sudan Pionier* 1902, p. 88 stresses that the mission still has all the Sudan in view, but maintains that the 300 km to Wadi Halfa will be sufficient for its limited resources for a long time to come. In 1928, the name was changed to 'Evangelische Muhammedaner-Mission' (Minutes, 3 October 1928); in 1953, to 'Evangelische Mission in Oberägypten'; in 1991, to 'Evangeliumsgemeinschaft Mittlerer Osten'. The meanwhile fully independent Swiss branch is named 'Evangelische Nillandmission'.

34 '[The SUM objective] is not merely to work in northern Nigeria but to establish a chain of missions across Africa from the Niger to the Nile and that an appeal be made to the Christian Public for at least 100 more men to further this great project' (Minutes SUM, 2 April 1909).

35 He started in northern Nigeria on 16 February 1909 and arrived in Khartoum on 3 December 1909. (Kumm, *From Hausaland to Egypt.*)

36 His intended mission was to bear the name 'Eastern Sudan Evangelical Mission' (Vincent, *C. T. Studd and Priscilla*, p. 152). The mission committee was most probably disbanded soon after, and Studd turned to the AIM.

37 Buxton, *The First Ten Years* p. 10.

38 Buxton, *The First Ten Years*, p. 10f. Missions were established in Yambio, Yei and Lau.

39 Peter J. Spartalis, *To the Nile and Beyond. The Birth and Growth of the Sudanese Church of Christ*, Homebush West, NSW, 1981.

40 Karl Kumm, 'Statement of Position of Sudan United Mission with Suggestions of Possible Future Developments to the Members of the Various S.U.M Councils', June 1910.

41 *Norske Missionstidende* 1921, p. 234f.; *Det Norske Missionsselskaps Aarbok*, 1927, Stavanger 1928, p. 75 ('Den Nye Mission i Kamerun'); *Det Norske Missionsselskaps årboken for 1928*.

42 See Florence Veary, *My Missionary Adventures... With Three V's*, Toronto, 1977, pp. 57ff.

43 *CMA Fourth Annual Report* (1900), p. 95. Sometimes the vision reached as far as Lake Chad (*International Missionary Alliance Seventh Annual Report* (13 October 1894), p. 18).

44 The annual reports show that the missions were too distant from each other and understaffed. In addition, the idea of itinerant evangelism, looking always to regions yet unreached, sidetracked the missionaries from establishing a church.

45 The CMA began to withdraw from Sierra Leone when, in 1917, it received the long-sought-for permission to work in French West Africa (Guinea). This permission made the long chain of mission stations stretching to the border of the Sudan useless, because access via Conakry was much easier. The missionary work in Sierra Leone was resumed in 1945 by the Missionary Church Association (in its origins related to CMA). The MCA history is described in: William Gerig, *Missionary Church Association*, unpublished, Fort Wayne Bible College, n.d. On pages 33–43, he describes the CMA's gradual abandonment of its Sierra Leone work. Gerig writes that, after the withdrawal of the Waites in 1935, there was no missionary for 10 years. He does mention Kate Driscoll, a CMA missionary who refused to be withdrawn and stayed in the Temne area until she died in 1941, aged 73. Together with the Temne pastor Ned Driscoll, she cared for the churches (p. 43). (When Ned married Elsa, a pupil of Kate Driscoll, they both assumed the name Driscoll because Kate Driscoll had helped both of them very much in spiritual matters.)

46 The plan was to establish a chain of mission stations from the mouth of the Congo to Lake Tanganyika (*Eighth Annual Report International Missionary Alliance 1895*, pp. 20–21).

47 Niklaus, Sawin, Stoesz, *All for Jesus*, p. 91f.

48 See: *CMA Annual Report 1899–1900*, p. 14.

49 'Notre oevre ne diffère que fort peu, en réalité, de certaines missions industrielles au Nyassa-Land et ailleurs' (Chatelin—Chamberlain, 11 November 1898 in *Quatrième rapport, Mission Philafricaine*).

50 'To establish self-supporting, self-propagating, native civilized Christian towns in Africa' (Chatelin—Chamberlain, 20 November 1897). Chatelin computed the amount he had used for establishing Lincoln (including the first year) as $6,000, expected that Lincoln would need a subsidy of $2,500 in the second year, almost nothing in the third year and that it would yield enough profit in the fourth year to start a new station (Philafrican Liberators' League (ed.), 'The First Expedition Successful', New York, 1897 in Alida Chatelin (ed.), *Les Rapports de la Mission Philafricaine 1898–1905*, Lausanne, n.d.)

51 *Le Philafricain*, July/August 1915.

52 Bréchet, *J'ai ouvert une porte*, pp. 12–15; Chatelin, *Héli Chatelin*, p. 323.

53 Map in Bréchet, *J'ai ouvert une porte*, second cover page.

54 The first aim was to reach the Equator across the Congo River (Fanny Guinness, *The New World of Central Africa*, p. 307).

55 The stations were: Palabala (1878), Banza Manteke (1879), Mukimvika (1881), Lukunga (1882), Mukimbungu (1882) and Kintambo/Kinshasa (1883).

56 In Kintambo/Kinshasa, the steamer *Henry Reed* was assembled and the upriver station Equator/Wangata (later Bolenge) was established. In 1897, the ABMU transferred Bolenge to the Disciples of Christ Congo Mission to begin its work there (Irvine, *The Church of Christ in Zaire*, p. 74).

57 In 1889, the Guinnesses took up the advance again by starting the Congo Balolo Mission.

58 'Islam is crouching in the Soudan as for a southward spring upon the eight tribes [Ossambur, Irondili, Il Mero, Njamus, Kamasia, Suk, Karamoja, Turkana, all in Kenya]' (C. E. Hurlbert in *HD*, July–October 1906).

59 For example, *Norske Missionstidende* 1921, p. 234f., in a report on plans for the norske Sudanmission. The founding of Melut, the first (Australian) SUM station in Sudan was seen as a further link in the growing chain of mission stations along the borderline with Islam all across Africa. (SUM Tenth Annual Report, 12 May 1914).

60 To make this possible, Kumm travelled from Nigeria to the Nile (*Daily Telegraph*, 30 December 1909: 'Dr Kumm's journey across Africa— Starving in Swamps—Remarkable Narrative'). The report of his journey: Kumm, *From Haussaland to Egypt.* For Livingstone as Kumm's hero see: John H. Boer, *The Last of the Livingstones: a Study of H. Karl W. Kumm's missiological conceptions of civilization*, Free Reformed University of Amsterdam, 1973.

61 Often, Muslim and Catholics advanced much faster in the various writers' imagination than they did in real life. Even in those days of Muslim advance, a statement such as this was plainly wrong: 'In very many parts of Africa, Catholic influence is advancing five times as fast as Protestant influence, but Muslim influence is spreading ten times as fast as Catholic influence' (*HD*, July–September 1909, p. 8). But even long after the Muslim advance had stopped, the dread of it was still there: 'Yet, out of every ten Africans who change their religion today, seven become Moslems and only three become Christians. In the past 30 years, Islam has advanced 1,000 miles down Africa' (H. S. Hillyer, *Being Sent Forth. The Story of Canadian Baptist Missionary Advance into Angola*, Toronto, n.d. (1959), p. 10).

62 This thought was also connected with the plan to start a German SUM branch to work in Adamaua (Ernst Lohmann (Orientmission)—Karl Kumm, 25 June 1912 and 8 July 1912).

63 For example, *WWW*, 1885, p. 220.

64 The Missionary Union for the Evangelization of the World was just a small department of the young New York Gospel Tabernacle Church.

65 Three hundred dollars , 'a considerable sum' (*WWW*, 1885, p. 220).

66 *WWW*, 1885, p. 220.

67 *WWW*, 1885, p. 220. See also: Irvine, *The Church of Christ in Zaire*, p. 63. Frank Gerrish worked until 1888 for the ABMU, being paid by the New York Gospel Tabernacle. He died a year after returning to the United States. (Niklaus, Sawin and Stoesz, *All for Jesus*, p. 60).

68  Fanny Guinness, *The New World of Central Africa*, pp. 258, 303, 347.

69  *Qua Iboe Mission Occasional Paper*, October 1893.

70  *Qua Iboe Mission Occasional Paper*, November 1890. First of all, he would have had to compete against the Christian trader Williams from Sierra Leone. Williams and his wife had done all they could to help Samuel Bill after his arrival (Robert L. M'Keown, *Twenty-five Years in Qua Iboe. The Story of A Missionary Effort in Nigeria*, London/Belfast, 1912, p. 55; Jean S. Corbett, *According to Plan. The Story of Samuel Alexander Bill, Founder of the Qua Iboe Mission, Nigeria*, Worthing, [2]1979 (1977), p. 19).

71  First Qua Iboe Mission Association Annual Report (31 December 1889). Fanny and Grattan Guinness had paid his fare and equipment from gifts of the Regions Beyond Helpers' Union (M'Keown, *Twenty-Five Years*, p. 55).

72  'Immediately, we saw that our resources were altogether inadequate for the long journey which lay before us through the unknown. We decided on a week of prayer and proposed to dispose of any keepsakes or non-essential articles' (Bingham, *Seven Sevens of Years*, p. 16).

73  Rowland V. Bingham, 'Modern Industrial Missions. A Plea for Self-supporting and Self-propagating Industrial Missions in Africa' in *The Faithful Witness*, 19 July 1898. 'Africa Industrial Mission. Our Field. Nyassaland ... Another reason for the choice of this district is its suitability for industrial operations.'

74  Bingham, 'Modern Industrial Missions' in *The Faithful Witness*, 19 July 1898.

75  Minutes Africa Industrial Mission, 30 January 1899.

76  Minutes Africa Industrial Mission, 21 February 1899.

77  Rowland V. Bingham, 'A New Name for an Established Mission' in *The Missionary Witness*, 17 October 1905.

78  *MRW* regularly reported on Bishop Taylor's activities, over the years becoming quite critical.

79  Irvine, *The Church of Christ in Zaire*, p. 62. In order to consolidate the work in Angola, the mission stations in Zaire (Vivi, Isangila and N'tombi with six missionaries) were given up.

80  In this, he met with the Presbyterian missionaries' strong disapproval: George Shepperson and Thomas Price, *Independent African. John Chilembwe and the Origins, Setting and Significance of the Nyasaland Native Rising of 1915*, Edinburgh, [2]1963 (1958), p. 32f.

81  Zambezi Industrial Mission, *Facts of Interest*, London, 1911; 1900–28, ZIM was largely self-supporting. Three of the missionaries were paid with money from Britain (*The Zambezi Industrial Mission*, 31 March 1930).

82  *The Christian*, 16 July 1925.

83  *The Zambezi Industrial Mission*, 31 March 1930; *List of Nyasa Mission Schools with Names of Supporters and Native Teachers* (n.d., copy in Yale University Day Missions Library).

84  Minutes Africa Industrial Mission, 27 May 1898.

85 'In A Strange Land. Two Topeka Missionaries Lose Their Lives' in *The Topeka Daily Capital*, 13 August 1890.

86 In addition to Scott, Jacob Toole and Thomas Allan also died.

87 Scott's sister Margaret belonged to the first missionary party, his parents and sister Ines followed in 1896. His parents were the first to leave the mission to become settlers, and they later even transferred his remains to the settler cemetery at Nairobi. Margaret Scott married Wilson, a member of the first missionary party, and they became settlers, too. The situation was worsened by the fact that the Scotts used $800 originally given for missionary work for themselves (with the consent of the donors, but without the knowledge of the other missionaries) (*HD*, December 1897).

88 Today, the East Africa Yearly Meeting of Friends, the largest Quaker church outside the United States (100,000 members according to *WCE*).

89 'Krieger will return home, being unwilling to continue on the doctrinal basis adopted at the founding of the mission' (*HD*, December 1897).

90 The AIM again became a field directed mission when Hurlbert decided to become a missionary himself. His resignation in 1926 was partly due to the fact that the American Home Council had increasingly taken control (Anderson—Fiedler, September 1993).

91 They could not accept his offer to return after a year because this trip had already severely strained their financial resources (Dawson, *History*, pp. 2–4).

92 They started their work thirty miles from the nearest SAGM station, but in good fellowship (Dawson, *History*, pp. 4ff).

93 Swanson, *Three Score Years*, p. 198.

94 *HD*, July-September 1909.

95 *Annual Report AIM 1910*.

96 *HD*, April–June 1912. This was part of the chain-vision of the AIM and developed into the church that is now CECA20.

97 John Dobson, *Daybreak in West Nile*, London, n.d. (1963), p. 5.

98 Karl Kumm, Statement of Position of Sudan United Mission, with Suggestions of Possible Future Developments to the Members of the Various S.U.M. Councils, June 1910.

99 SUM-AUS/NZ had already sent missionaries to Nigeria (William Fleming (New Zealand) in 1910 and C. T. Williams (Australia) in 1911).

100 A carefully researched history of SUM-AUS/NZ is: Spartalis, *To the Nile and Beyond*.

101 The CMS had no personnel in the area, but did have a certain claim to it. In 1913, Bishop Gwynne himself accompanied the first SUM party to Melut and helped them to get established there (Spartalis, *To the Nile and Beyond*, pp. 8–14).

102 Hilaire Nkounkou, *75e Anniversaire de la fondation de Madzia et de l'évangélisation du Congo par les missionaires protestants*, Brazzaville, 1984. The resulting church is the Eglise évangélique du Congo, with 120,000 members (*WCE*, 1975).

103The first station was Iruvura (Oehler, *Geschichte* 2, p. 175). After World War 1, the Neukirchener Mission (like the Bethel Mission in Rwanda) was not allowed back into the country. For how the work begun by Neukirchen was later continued, see: Donald Hohensee, *Church Growth in Burundi*, Pasadena, 1977.

104Eugene Rubingh, *Sons of Tiv*, Grand Rapids, 1969.

105Edmund Crampton, *Christianity in northern Nigeria*, London, [2]1979 (1975), p. 162.

106Robert T. Handy, *The American Religious Depression, 1925–1935* (Presidential address, American Society of Church History, 1959).

107This term is often now used to denote those churches which used to be called 'mainline churches', such as Anglicans, Presbyterians, American Baptists and Lutherans, but excluding more recent churches such as Conservative Baptists (see Handy, *The American Religious Depression*, p. 10).

108During 1928–33, CMA income dropped (only) by 35.2 per cent, whereas the 79 mainline and evangelical missions, which were members of the Foreign Missions Conference, experienced an average drop of 45.1 per cent. See Handy, *The American Religious Depression*, p. 10.

109During 1923–29, the number of Protestant American missionaries fell by 4.7 per cent (Handy, *The American Religious Depression*, p. 4).

110Handy, *The American Religious Depression*, p. 6, points out that, in 1927, Reinhold Niebuhr was already aware of the depression: 'A psychology of defeat, of which both fundamentalism and modernism are symptoms, has gripped the forces of religion' (Reinhold Niebuhr, *Does Civilization Need Religion? A Study in the Social Resources and Limitations of Religion in Modern Life*, New York, 1927, p. 2).

1111925 was the year of the so-called Monkey Trial against John T. Scopes, which was a victory for the fundamentalists only in the legal sense of the term (Louis Gasper, *The Fundamentalist Movement 1930–1956*, Grand Rapids,[2]1981 (1963), p. 14).

112The UFM (GB/US) has very little to offer on its history: Leonard F. Harris, *Our Days in His Hands. A Short History of the Unevangelized Fields Mission*, n.d. For the history of UFM-AUS/NZ (Asia Pacific Christian Mission), there is a solid book: John and Moyra Prince, *No Fading Vision. 50 Years of Adventure with God*, Melbourne, 1981.

113For the split, see: pp. 96–109; Harris, *Our Days in His Hands*, pp. 11–13; John and Moyra Prince, *No Fading Vision*, pp. 28–39. The archives are still closed.

114See many detailed reports in *Worldwide*, 1934–40.

115The work in Imo River District, begun in 1924, was soon abandoned because of a comity agreement. In 1928, the idea of taking up work in Cameroon was no longer pursued due to the return of the German missionaries (*Qua Iboe Mission Quarterly*, 8/1930; W. L. Wheatley, *Sunrise in Nigeria. A Record of Missionary Service from 1920 to 1952*, Belfast, 1977, pp. 68–74).

116J. W. Westgarth, *The Qua Iboe Mission Makes History*, 1946 (unpublished), pp. 20ff.; Wheatley, *Sunrise in Nigeria*, pp. 76–79. Four Qua Iboe evangelists helped to start the work in Igala (Qua Iboe Mission Annual Report 1933).

117*Qua Iboe Mission Quarterly* 8/1930, p. 185. Annual Report 1931.

118In spite of 'much publicity and prayer' no further missionaries volunteered. 'Station and converts' were handed over to WEC, and Benington returned to Nigeria in November 1938 (Qua Iboe Mission Annual Report 1938).

119The four pillars were sacrifice, faith, holiness and fellowship.

120His autobiography (Grubb, *Once Caught, No Escape. My Life Story*) shows an impressive personality. Norman P. Grubb, born 2 August 1895, joined WEC-UK in 1919, still (1988) lives at Ft. Washington, the American centre of the Christian Literature Crusade, a sister mission to WEC. His wife was Pauline Studd.

121Here, Brethren influences may be detected, because in their *theology* they admit no organizational unity beyond the local church.

122Gration, *The Relationship of the AIM and its National Church in Kenya Between 1895 and 1971*, pp. 306ff.

123Two reasons among others may be mentioned: the missions were younger and the number of career missionaries was usually higher.

124Based on a graph produced by Peter Mayer, Director of Beatenberg Bible School.

125*WCE* gives an inclusive membership of 300,000 for 1970 and of 630,000 for 1978 (p. 437). Since then, AIC has grown quickly; statistics are no longer kept. On inquiry, estimates between 1 million and 1.5 million were given.

126From 1957 onwards, Canadian Baptist Overseas Mission Board (CBOMB).

127Started by Zulu immigrants.

128Also TEAM, EMEK, WEC.

129At first, Egypt Mission Band; later, Middle East General Mission.

1301976: 2,300/12,700.

131With Unevangelized Fields Mission cooperating.

1321978: 630,000.

1331977: 78,622.

134Now, Africa Evangelical Fellowship.

135Later, Fellowship of Independent Missions.

1361945 Missionary Church.

## 4

# Born in revival: faith missions and the 1859/1873 revival

## Missions—children of revival

In German missiology it is commonplace to see classical missions as being a consequence of revival. This is true not only in Germany and Switzerland, and not only for classical missions. As they go back to the Great Awakening which was prevalent at the turn of the eighteenth century, and as pre-classical missions go back to the pietistic/puritan revival, so the origin of faith missions is in the revival of the second half of the nineteenth century.[1]

Faith mission theologians often see revivals as the most important events in church history—at least as its driving force. Therefore, they can speak of a 'succession of revivals' which help to unfold the drama of church history. They pay little attention to the early church, but all of them see mysticism as a kind of early revival,[2] followed by the revival led by John Wycliffe and Jan Hus, in turn, followed by the Reformation. When the fervour of the Reformation had hardened into Protestant orthodoxy, God sent pietism and its English/US counterpart, puritanism.[3] After pietism/puritanism came the Great Awakening, the beginning of which is usually dated with the revival in Jonathan Edwards' Congregationalist church in Northampton, Massachusetts, in 1735. Through his writings, Edwards strongly influenced William Carey and others.[4] Usually, the 1858–59 revival is seen as the one succeeding the Great Awakening, but there was another revival between the two, in the 1830s which, although less impressive and less widespread, produced three movements which would strongly influence the revival of 1858–59 and, with it, faith missions: the holiness movement, the Brethren movement and the prophetic movement. In faith mission circles, the succession of revivals is usually seen to have stopped with the 1858–59 revival and its second wave in 1873. Sometimes the 1904 Welsh revival is taken into account, but the next revival, that of pentecostalism (1900–06), is seen more as a deviation.[5]

112

Each revival is characterized by a new theological emphasis (or even by several new ones), and it always spreads across national and denominational borders. Every revival gives new opportunities to groups within the church which normally do not have much influence: laymen, women, less-educated people, minority groups. The renewed spiritual fervour tends to manifest itself in new activities, which lead to the establishment of new organizations. The revival's new theological emphasis is usually accepted by only a part of the church. This often produces splits: during the Reformation, political influences arranged the split geographically; otherwise, the splits crisscross the church(es). Sometimes these splits manifest themselves in theological variations, sometimes in the emergence of revival fellowship movements within or at the edge of the existing churches, and sometimes by the birth of new denominations or independent congregations.

This means that each revival decreases the uniformity of the church and, inevitably, increases its pluralism, as new spiritual truths and experiences express themselves in new initiatives and organizations. Prominent among these initiatives and organizations are evangelistic efforts, social activities and foreign missions.

The revival leaders usually (and mistakenly) claim to teach nothing new, but only to revive what always was the teaching of the church. Therefore, they do not expect a new revival (necessarily with new theological emphasis) to come after their own and, when it does come, they themselves or their successors are not usually happy about it. This was the case when the pietists challenged the heirs of the Reformation and when, in 1858–59, a new revival spread across Protestantism[6] close on the heels of the Great Awakening, most leaders of the classical missions, themselves born in revival, could only see the new movement as a danger or a nuisance. The leaders of the faith missions claimed their right to transform new experiences and old truths into new organizations, but when the pentecostal revival broke less than two generations later they, in turn, could only see these newcomers as a nuisance or as teachers of wrong doctrine.

Revivals start at a given point in church history and, after a time, fade out, but they do not disappear. Their teachings, their institutions and the fellowships they created continue to exist even after the revival fervour has waned. This means that one should not speak so much of a succession of revivals, as of a plurality of revivals: all revivals from the Reformation onwards are still with us, and every new revival increases the plurality of the church, so that unity must be sought beyond uniformity. It is to be expected that the next revival will also produce new organizations and will be greeted with mixed enthusiasm by the leaders of the preceding revival(s), and that it may, like the revivals which preceded it, add to the effectiveness of the missionary outreach of the church universal.

## THE REVIVAL OF THE SECOND HALF OF THE NINETEENTH CENTURY

Faith missions were new in their time, but are so no longer. They belong to the 1859/1873 revival, and the fact that they are still going strong shows that that revival may have lost its original cutting edge, but not its spiritual life. To understand faith missions, it is useful to know about the revival which produced them.

The revival first broke in the United States: there appeared extraordinary spiritual stirrings, such as a great urge for prayer and heavily attended evangelistic meetings, towards the end of 1857 on the east coast of the United States and, a little later, in Canada. In 1858, the revival was in full bloom. It was comparatively quiet, strongly emphasizing communal prayer. It was a lay movement, in which 'the laymen of all denominations gladly undertook ordinary and extraordinary responsibilities'.[7] The revival spread southwards, transformed Kentucky and Tennessee, was effective during the Civil War on both sides and affected whites and blacks equally. The churches gained more than one million new members.

In Europe, the revival broke first and strongest in Presbyterian Ulster. There, and equally in Scotland and Wales, about ten per cent of the population professed conversion; in the whole of Great Britain, another one million members were added to the churches. Spurgeon built his famous Metropolitan Tabernacle in London on the crest of this revival. The revival remained almost completely within the existing denominations. The British Free Churches fully supported it, but in the Anglican Church, there was opposition as well as support. It revitalized many Christian service agencies, and most early recruits to the CIM had been awakened in this revival.

Though the faith missions arose after this first (1858–59) wave of the revival, the second wave was far more important for them. This second wave is irreversibly bound to the name of Dwight Lyman Moody, who rose to worldwide fame not in his home country, but in Britain.[8] When he arrived there in 1873, he had trouble in finding a place in which to preach. When, more than two and a half years later, he finished his tour with a twenty-week campaign in London, about two and a half million people aggregate had heard him.[9] After his return to the United States, he worked there with equal success.

This revival spread to Germany in 1874 through the mediation of Robert Pearsall Smith. In Russia, two British gentlemen, Lord Radstock and Baedecker, were the evangelists, and I. S. Prokhanov, converted in 1886, became the founder of the All-Russian Evangelical Union, later to be united with the Baptists. In 1882, Moody preached at Cambridge University. One result of that effort was the famous Cambridge Seven who, under the leadership of C. T. Studd, joined CIM.[10] In Sweden, the revival brought new life to the Fosterlandsstiftelsen (a fellowship movement of the preceding revival) and, as an offshoot/split, the Svenska Missionsförbundet.

A third and final wave of this revival can be counted from 1902, the leader of which was Reuben Archer Torrey,[11] who Moody had made director of the Bible Institute in Chicago in 1889. His greatest impact was in Australia. Another crest of this third wave was the famous Welsh revival of 1904,[12] which already showed traits of the 1906 pentecostal revival.

Every revival has its special theological emphasis. The 1859/1873 revival drew this from three movements which had their roots in a smaller 'intermediate revival' in Britain in the 1830s.[13] That revival was not as widespread, but developed various distinctly new theologies, all of which seem to have had one thing in common: before the end of the age they wanted once more to return to pristine Christianity. Edward Irving developed the idea of the revived charismatic gifts before Christ's return. This pre-pentecostal teaching eventually led to the formation of the Catholic Apostolic Church (1832), which later gave birth to the New Apostolic Church (1863).[14]

Eventually, 'Irvingism' was excluded from the mainstream revival, 'but not so the prophetic movement, which arose in the same context and changed eschatology from being post-millennial to pre-millennial.[15] All the early faith mission leaders underwent that same theological change.

Another movement to arise in this revival was the adventist movement, which predicted Christ's return in 1844. After that event did not take place as expected, some formed the Seventh Day Adventist Church, which, like the successors of the Irvingites, had little fellowship with other Christian groups, but is now moving much closer to them.[16]

Closely connected with the prophetic movement (and, to some extent, even with Irving) was the Brethren movement, whose early major exponents were: John Nelson Darby, for the 'exclusive' variety;[17] and Anthony Norris Groves[18] and George Müller,[19] for the 'open' variety.[20] The Brethren tried to achieve Christian unity in spite of and beyond the denominations, a revolutionary concept considered by many as destructive.

Another movement which, like the Brethren, started as a non-church movement and, like them, became a *de facto* denomination, are the Churches of Christ/Christian Churches, which understood their fiercely congregational ecclesiology as a return to the tenets of the pristine church.

The third movement, and possibly the most important for the 1859/1873 revival, was the holiness movement. It originated in the United States in 1835, taking up the Wesleyan teaching on sanctification as a second crisis experience in the Christian life, distinct from and after conversion.[21] The holiness movement influenced the 1859 wave in Britain, but it really came into its own only during the second wave, when it was institutionalized in the Keswick Conventions (1875) and in many similar conventions all over the world.

The 1859/1873 revival was more than the sum total of these three movements, but much of the power of this revival was due to them and they greatly shaped the course of faith mission history.

THE SPIRIT OF REVIVAL

The revival managed to remain largely within the existing denominations. Nevertheless, its theology was often quite revolutionary because of its shifts in emphasis: the church was never felt to be without importance, but all emphasis was placed on evangelism. The same with baptism: it was never abolished, but what really counted was conversion, and it did not matter much whether baptism preceded or followed it. Traditional Christian doctrine was taken for granted, but emphasis was placed on practical Christianity. This led to many efforts to alleviate the suffering of the underprivileged, whether by charity or by social reform.[22]

116

For faith missions, the revival's most significant emphasis was on reaching the unreached for Christ. To achieve this, borders had to be crossed: class borders; the borders of crime and addiction; and national and geographical borders. The gospel was for all people and they were all to be presented with the gospel in a way they could understand.

## THE PENTECOSTAL REVIVAL[23]

The revival leaders were waiting and praying eagerly for a new revival, but they expected it to be one just like their own. They did register some slackening of Christian fervour around the turn of the century, but when the new revival broke, most of them were perturbed by its unexpected features such as speaking in tongues and other spiritual gifts mentioned in the New Testament.

Just as they had done, the new revivalists were out to discover the original power of the gospel message and, in this, they even shared some terminology. Moody and other revival leaders had taught the holiness experience under the term 'pentecostal blessing'. The fact that the exponents of the new revival interpreted 'pentecost' in a very different way soon led to a parting of ways, sometimes in a friendly manner, often less so.

The origins of the pentecostal revival are often traced to Topeka, Kansas, where Agnes Ozman was the first to experience the gift of tongues, influenced by her teacher Charles Fox Parham, whose Bible school she attended.[24] But, in those days, the pentecostal experience remained an isolated experience, and Parham never really integrated himself into the pentecostal movement that spread from Azusa Street in Los Angeles in 1906 under the leadership of William Seymour.

The Azusa Street pentecostal revival movement knew no colour bar, but it was nevertheless a revival movement with its roots in black American religiosity and under black leadership.[25] So there is some reason to call it an African Christian revival, which started in the United States and soon made its influence felt worldwide.

The pentecostal movement was missionary-minded from the very start. Charles Parham's Bible course in Topeka was intended to prepare prospective missionaries, and he was convinced that the gift of tongues meant *xenolalia*, the speaking of real foreign languages, which gift would enable missionaries to preach immediately and effectively in every foreign country. In spite of

117

these convictions, the Topeka revival produced no foreign missionaries. But the Azusa revival did: the first of them, Lillian and Alfred G. Garr of the Burning Bush Mission in Los Angeles, sailed for India and Hong Kong in June 1906. Soon, many others followed and, as is typical of revival times, women were prominent among them[26] and there was, as yet, no racial distinction.

The expectation of many of the early pentecostal missionaries that they would preach through *xenolalia* was soon to be disappointed, and a number of them did not complete even a year on the mission field. Another aspect that brought many disappointments was the 'faith principle' of support. This principle they shared with faith missions, but they did not share their pattern of organization. Thus, applying the typology used in this book, the early pentecostal missionaries were not faith missionaries, but independent missionaries. Up to 1920, the turnover (and failure) rate of pentecostal missionaries was high.

First attempts to reach a consolidation of this budding missionary fervour took their cue from the interdenominational faith missions. The leading early promotor of a pentecostal faith mission was Cecil Polhill, one of the famous Cambridge Seven, who had served with the China Inland Mission from 1885 until 1900. He received pentecostal baptism in 1908 in Los Angeles, and soon organized the pentecostal Missionary Union for Great Britain and Ireland.[27] A similar interdenominational attempt was the short-lived pentecostal Missionary Union (Levi Lupton, United States, 1909–10). The first *major* American mission of this type was the pentecostal Mission in South and Central Africa (1919), founded by a single congregation, the Bethel pentecostal Assembly, Newark, New Jersey, and directed by Minnie T. Draper.[28] Another mission, which clearly patterned itself after faith missions, although preaching a distinctively pentecostal message, was F. P. Burton's Congo Evangelistic Mission.[29]

On the whole, however, the pentecostal missionary movement did not develop along interdenominational faith mission lines; instead, the *denominational pentecostal mission* became the normal pattern. The first major mission of this type was the missionary work of the General Council of the Assemblies of God, organized in 1914 at Hot Springs, Arkansas.[30] In the beginning, the missionary work of the Assemblies of God was more of a collection of independent missionaries than a denominational mission but, over the years, clear denominational structures evolved, making it the largest pentecostal mission in the United States.[31]

In spite of the pentecostal missions' development along denominational lines, they kept close to their faith mission background in some ways. One aspect was the emphasis on field-directed missionary work; another was a generally lower level of support. Like the early faith missions, they gave considerable room to independent women, and, like faith missions, they reduced this room for independent women gradually but effectively over the years. But the most important remaining heritage goes back to A. B. Simpson. The whole pentecostal system of training for the ministry, abroad and at home, was patterned along the lines of Simpson's New York Missionary Training College[32] which, in turn, had been directly patterned on Fanny and Grattan Guinness' East London Training Institute.

In missiology, the pentecostal movement also shared many of the concerns of faith missions. If faith missions were strong on eschatology, the pentecostal missionaries were even stronger.[33] Both stressed the need to reach the unreached, but since the pentecostal missionaries also had an additional message ('full gospel'), they were often willing to work in areas already reached to some extent by other Protestant missions—something which the faith missions rarely did.

Though the pentecostal missions soon developed an identity of their own, it is interesting that in one aspect both pentecostal missions and faith missions went the same way—in their veneration of the High Anglican missiologist Roland Allen. Introduced by Alice E. Luce to the ideas of Allen, the Assemblies of God officially adopted them in 1921.[34] Many of the early Assemblies of God pioneers, especially in South America, used 'indigenous church principles', supported by Noel Perkins as director of the mission. These principles were given pentecostal literary form by Melvin L. Hodges, one of the foremost leaders in pentecostal missiological writing.[35]

Worldwide pentecostal missions and faith missions are quite separate entities but, over the past decades, contacts in various parts of the world have been growing. One common aspect was the rejection of fundamentalism by both the faith missions and the pentecostals in the 1940s. While in the 1920s and 1930s many pentecostals saw themselves as fundamentalists 'with a difference'.[36] The break had to come because fundamentalists, with their strong belief in Biblical miracles, could not go along with the pentecostals who believed that God was doing miracles even today.[37] Faith missions broke with fundamentalism about the priority of evangelism over 'right doctrine' and the concept of 'second grade separation' that was tied to it.

The common, though unrelated, break with fundamentalism by both the evangelicals (and faith missions with them) and the pentecostals opened the way for a closer cooperation between evangelicals and pentecostals. This found expression in the foundation of the National Association of Evangelicals, which included pentecostals but not fundamentalists, with pentecostals eventually even being in the majority.[38] There was never a major association of pentecostal missions, but, when the National Association of Evangelicals formed its missionary arm (Evangelical Foreign Missions Association, EFMA) in 1945, the major pentecostal missions joined. This brought organizational contact with faith missions in two ways: those interdenominational faith missions which, mainly due to their holiness emphasis (like WEC), were not welcome in IFMA (Interdenominational Foreign Missions Association, founded in 1917), also joined EFMA, and a few other faith missions hold double membership. The second and major point of contact between faith missions and pentecostal missions is the close ongoing cooperation between EFMA and IFMA and within the worldwide evangelical movement, as represented by the congresses on evangelism at Lausanne (1974) and Manila (1989).

## THE CHARISMATIC MOVEMENT

In spite of mutual acceptance and some cooperation, pentecostal theology and piety had little or no room in faith missions. This only changed with the coming of the charismatic movement, whose origins are usually dated in the 1960s, although its roots go back at least a dozen years further.[39] The charismatic movement had the 'full gospel' message in common with the pentecostal movement but, in contrast to the pentecostal movement, it originated deeply within the classical mainline churches (including various Baptist churches) and, to a large extent, has remained within them to date. As in the time of the holiness revival, the experience of the 'second blessing', or of the 'fullness', often made people feel the call to foreign mission work. Because faith missions never stopped accepting missionary candidates from mainline churches, in this way quite a number of 'charismatic' missionaries joined a faith mission, with great variations as to area and mission. This means that the 'pentecostal question' is once again before the faith missions. A few faith missions clearly dissociated themselves from the charismatic movement (such as the New Tribes Mission and the Unevangelized Fields Mission, both United States). Some missions, for example, the WEC, consciously attempted 'to straddle the charismatic divide'.[40] Most faith missions tried, in some pragmatic way, to come to terms with the influences of the charismatic movement.

Although the charismatic renewal largely remained within the various denominations, it did bring about some new denominations and independent churches. The best known of these movements is the British 'house church movement' with its strong Brethren influences,[41] which considers itself to be a 'network of non-denominational charismatic assemblies'. For this movement, there was the possibility of sending its missionaries into existing faith missions, and a number of missionaries actually joined WEC. There is a greater possibility that separate 'house church' missions will emerge.[42]

Together with the emergence of independent charismatic congregations and denominations, a charismatic missionary movement has gradually begun to form, the shape of which is not yet fully clear. There seems to be a growing tendency in some of the larger independent charismatic congregations for the local congregation to act as the sending mission agency as well.

## FAITH MISSIONS AND FURTHER REVIVALS

Faith missions were, and still are, clearly related to one definite revival. But although that revival has passed, neither the organizations it created nor the missions it gave birth to have vanished. The majority of faith missions have survived, and most of them have been able to accommodate to changes in the spiritual climate. New revivals have taken place, often bypassing existing faith missions. This means that faith missions are no longer the only alternative to the classical missions, but that various other post-classical missions are, in their turn, an alternative both to faith missions and to classical missions. But in this plural context, the faith missions still play an important role, which deserves a detailed study.

### Notes

1   Described in: J. Edwin Orr, *The Eager Feet. Evangelical Awakenings 1790–1830*, Chicago, 1975. This revival is sometimes called the 'Second Great Awakening'.

2   One of the 'saints' of the faith missions was Madame Guyon, a Catholic all her life, though admittedly not always in conformity with the hierarchy. Her life story

was printed in many editions, for example recently: Dorothy Gawne Coslet, *Madame Jeanne Guyon. Child of Another World*, Ft Washington (Christian Literature Crusade), [2]1985 (1984). For other names and details, see: Chapter 8, 'Power for service', on faith missions and the holiness movement.

3   It is not incidental that the great revival preacher Spurgeon did much to republish puritan theology. He is sometimes called 'the last of the puritans'.

4   In 1747, Edwards published in Boston: *An Humble Attempt to Promote Explicit Agreement and Visible Union Among God's People in Extraordinary Prayer, for the Revival of Religion and the Advancement of Christ's Kingdom on Earth, Pursuant to Scripture-Promises and Prophecies Concerning the Last Time*. This was republished in Northampton in 1789 by John Sutcliffe, one of the pastors in the Baptist Northhamptonshire Association, to which Carey belonged. It is the only book to which Carey in his *Enquiry* explicitly refers (p. 12).

5   Revival theologians tend to see the revival to which they belong as the final one.

6   J. Edwin Orr, *The Fervent Prayer. Evangelical Awakenings 1858–1899, Worldwide*, Chicago, 1974.

7   J. Edwin Orr, *The Flaming Tongue. Evangelical Awakenings, 1900*, Chicago, [2]1975 (1973), p. xv.

8   Two evangelists of the same second wave, important for the emerging CMA, were Major Whittle and Bliss.

9   Orr, *The Flaming Tongue*, p. xvii.

10   John Pollock, *The Cambridge Seven*, Basingstoke, [2]1985 (1955).

11   Roger Martin, *R. A. Torrey. Apostle of Certainty*, Murfreesboro, 1976. He was one of the editors of the 'fundamentals': Reuben Archer Torrey, Amie C. Dixon *et al.*, *The Fundamentals. A Testimony to the Truth*, Los Angeles (BIOLA), 1917, reprint edition, Grand Rapids (Baker), 1972.

12   Orr, *The Flaming Tongue*, pp. 1–28.

13   In the United States, this revival was stronger; its exponent was Charles Grandison Finney. He was still from the old revival stock, but by joining the holiness movement he became the link to the next great revival.

14   See: Jean Christie Root, *Edward Irving. Man, Preacher, Prophet*, Boston, 1912.

15   For a detailed discussion of this movement and its influence on faith missions, see: Chapter 9, 'A propelling vision'.

16   There is regular Christian fellowship between Seventh Day Adventists and other evangelical Christians in many places, but differences are still strong enough for SDA members not to join interdenominational faith missions. However, the Seventh Day Adventists are a strong missionary force of their own.

17   W. G. Turner, *John Nelson Darby*, London, [3]1944 (1901); H. E. Sturgeon, 'The Life of J. N. Darby', ThD, Southern Baptist Theological Seminary, 1957; J. H. Goddard, 'A Synthesis of the Bibliology, Theology, Angelology and Anthropology of J. N. Darby', dissertation, Dallas Theological Seminary, 1947.

18   H. Groves, *Memoir of the Late Anthony Norris Groves, Containing Extracts from*

*His Letters and Journals,* compiled by his widow, London, 1856; *Memoir of Anthony Norris Groves* (1869).

19  George Müller, *A Narrative of Some of the Lord's Dealings with George Müller Written by Himself,* London, [9]1895 ([1]1837); George Müller, *Autobiography,* Bristol/London, 1905; Arthur Tappan Pierson, *George Müller of Bristol,* London, [6]1901 (1899).

20  Coad, *Brethren Movement,* Exeter, 1968.

21  For a detailed discussion, see: Chapter 7.

22  These efforts later gave birth to the social gospel, whose later advocates cut it loose from the revival's emphasis on conversion and personal holiness.

23  For more information on the whole revival and many of its leading men and women, see the excellent: Stanley M. Burgess, Gary B. McGee and Patrick H. Alexander, *Dictionary of Pentecostal and Charismatic Movements,* Grand Rapids, [3]1989 *(DPCM).*

24  Her reminiscences are: Agnes O. LaBerge, *What God Hath Wrought* (n.p., n.d.). When she heard in 1906 about pentecostalism, she identified with it. She died in 1937 as an Assemblies of God evangelist.

25  Here I follow the argument of: Allan Anderson, *Bazalwane. African Pentecostals in South Africa,* Pretoria, 1992, pp. 17–32.

26  For example: Louise Condit, Lucy M. Leatherman and Lizzie Frazer (Gary B. McGee, 'Missions, Overseas (North American)' in *DPCM,* pp. 610–625 (p. 611).

27  Peter D. Hocken, 'Polhill, Cecil H.' in *DPCM,* p. 718.

28  When she died in 1921, her successor, as usual, was a man: Christian J. Lukas *(DPCM,* p. 614).

29  Harold Womersley, *William F. P. Burton, Congo Pioneer,* Eastbourne, 1973. Burton's spiritual kinship can be guessed from his book: *When God Makes a Missionary. The Life Story of Edgar Mahon,* London, 1936. For the history, see: David John Garrard, *The Congo Evangelistic Mission/Communauté Pentecôtiste au Zaire,* PhD, Aberdeen, 1983.

30  The development of the homeside of the missionary work of the Assemblies of God is well presented in: Gary B. McGee, *This Gospel Shall Be Preached,* Springfield, 1986.

31  It counts 1,530 US career missionaries abroad, which is more than the combined total of all other US pentecostal missions, W. Dayton Roberts and John A. Siewert (eds), *Mission Handbook. USA/Canada Protestant Ministries Overseas,* Monrovia/Grand Rapids, [14]1989.

32  L. F. Wilson, 'Bible Institutes, Colleges, Universities' in *DPCM,* pp. 57–65.

33  See: L. Grant McClung, 'Missiology' in *DPCM,* pp. 607–609.

34  *DPCM,* p. 621.

35  Melvin L. Hodges, *The Indigenous Church,* Springfield, 1953. As a book for 'national ministers and Bible School students in foreign lands' he published: *Build My Church,* Springfield, 1957.

36  H. Vinson Synan, 'Fundamentalism' in *DPCM*, pp. 324–327 (p. 325). One major common tie was the use of the Scofield Bible.

37  Fundamentalism is strongly super-rationalistic for the (Biblical) past; it is very rationalistic for the present. In spite of popular press usage, pentecostals cannot be classified as fundamentalists.

38  For the process of 'evangelicalization' of pentecostals, see: Cecil M. Robeck, 'National Association of Evangelicals' in *DPCM*, pp. 634–636 (p. 635).

39  For a detailed description, see: Peter D. Hocken, 'Charismatic Movement' in *DPCM*, pp. 130–160.

40  Interview Alastair M. Kennedy, 10 January 1987.

41  A penetrating study is: Andrew Walker, *Restoring the Kingdom. The Radical Christianity of the House Church Movement*, London, [2]1989 (1985).

42  (Dietrich Kuhl—Fiedler, 15 May 1988).

# 5

# Reaching the unreached: faith mission geography

It is often assumed that faith missions were started as a reaction against 'liberal theology', or as a reaction against the fact that the classical missions were beginning to absorb liberal concepts. This conception is unfounded in history[1] and has no basis in the early statements of faith missions.[2] These do differ from what was commonly held by the classical missions, but only in their ecclesiology—by assuming that varying and, at times, contradictory ecclesiologies can be rightly derived from the New Testament witness.[3] Faith missions came into existence primarily because there were millions of unreached people and no (classical) mission willing or able to evangelize them speedily. A secondary reason for the development of faith missions was their background in a different revival, which led to different concepts of evangelism, holiness and eschatology, and of the church and its offices. A third reason was new (or revived) methods such as faith support and itinerant evangelism.

This does not mean that faith mission leaders favoured a critical study of the Bible, but fighting 'liberalism' was not one of their main concerns. A. B. Simpson is typical: when he occasionally spoke of a captain on the Mississippi who used to say, when asked about the dangerous spots: 'I know where the river is *not* dangerous, and that's where I do my sailing'.[4] A. J. Gordon, founder of the Boston Missionary Training Institute, was claimed as a leading apologist of the Bible, but he defended it by expounding it.[5] When the AIM was founded, it stated that it wanted neither to criticize nor to fight any other organization, just to do what others were not doing.[6] What others were not doing sufficiently was trying to reach the unreached interior of Africa—hence the name: Africa *Inland* Mission.

## NEW MISSIONS TO REACH THE UNREACHED

Several founders of faith missions had tried, before they started a new mission, to make the classical missions advance into areas which they were convinced had become accessible, but which were still unreached. Hudson Taylor had travelled all over

England and Scotland to achieve this, but only one mission felt able to do any more than to advance slowly from the coast.[7] Rowland Bingham and Walter Gowans in 1893 did the same for the Sudan, although only for some weeks.[8] Dr Brønnum, the first Danish SUM missionary, had first applied officially to join the Danske Missionsselskab 'for work among black Mohammedans'[9]; and when Ernst Lohmann (Orientmission) wanted to begin a German SUM branch,[10] he first asked the Basel Mission if they would be willing to work in Adamaua,[11] but they felt unable to extend their coastal missionary work that far northwards.[12] In 1902, Lucy and Karl Kumm started the 'Lightbearers' League'—not, it soon turned out, as the nucleus of a new mission, but as a support for their effort to get the British Free churches moving to evangelize the unreached 60 million living in the Sudan, the largest still-unreached area in the world. Wherever they went, the echo was friendly and the answer the same: we cannot undertake new work without harming existing work. If any new work were to be undertaken, new resources would have to be found.[13]

However, new resources were difficult to come by, as there was little *new* revival among their supporters, who came from the classical revival.[14] They had their hands full with the work they had started earlier, and were usually sufficiently in debt to avoid new endeavours.[15] Sometimes they asked faith missions directly to take up opportunities which they could not use.[16]

The names of many of the faith missions illustrate very clearly their aim to reach the unreached: because the coastal areas were often already reached by the classical missions, and the faith missions did not want to compete with them, faith missions added to the geographical element in their names another element, indicating that they wanted to reach an unreached area: China *Inland* Mission, Africa *Inland* Mission, Congo *Inland* Mission, Sudan *Interior* Mission, *Unevangelized* Africa Mission, *Unevangelized* Tribes Mission, *New* Tribes Mission and Sudan-Pionier-Mission.[17] Some missions, such as the Southern Morocco Mission, the North Africa Mission, the Kurku and Central India Hill Mission and the Heart of Africa Mission, did not need to add such an element to their names, because the whole area was unreached.

An exception was the South Africa General Mission which, in its early years, also worked among the white population. In this work, however, they preached holiness and strictly avoided starting churches. Missions which very strongly endeavoured to reach the unreached but did not express this in their names were the Christian and Missionary Alliance and the Gospel Missionary Union, both of US origin.

This 'faith mission geography' was based on a distinct theology of salvation and lostness: Christ is the only saviour and everyone who does not believe in him is eternally lost. This makes all men equal.[18] James M. Gray, AIM missionary and later President of Moody Bible Institute, formulated what was then the general conviction:[19]

◇ The heathen are sinners like all mankind.

◇ Like everyone else, they are fully responsible to God (Romans 1:18–25).

◇ The hope of heathenism lies not in itself.[20]

◇ We have no right to assume that the heathen will be offered a chance of salvation after death.[21]

A. B. Simpson, when speaking at the 1892 Asbury Park Convention, used different words: 'There is another side to human life, not less real because less visible. Every fifteen minutes in yonder heavenly world the awful tidings are reported that a thousand souls have been lost forever.'[22]

The conviction that everyone who, for whatever reason, does not believe in Christ is eternally lost, did not draw faith mission leaders to speculation about the ways and means of God's eternal wisdom.[23] Their theology was an applied one, so they simply asked: What must we do? Henry W. Frost, the Canadian founder of the North American branch of the CIM, gave the typical answer during the Niagara Conference of 1885: 'I determined to alleviate the woes of the perishing millions.'[24] Prairie Bible Institute, the most important faith mission Bible school in Canada, formulated it thus: 'If we believe that all are lost without Christ, we'll give our lives for the perishing millions.'[25] Sometimes such a decision is very dramatic. Héli Chatelin was very often ill in his childhood. During a sickness, which brought him close to death, he 'finally found peace in Jesus, about whom he had known so much already'. He felt a deep longing to be with God, but he also longed 'to do something for God and mankind before his death'. In a vision he saw 'the black interior of Africa' and realized how many lives would have to be sacrificed, 'to bring the many heathen, poor and lost as they are,[26] to salvation'.[27] There and then, he decided to give his life to missionary work in the interior of Africa.

In faith mission publications, there are no hints that non-Christians might find a way to salvation within their own religions. Nor are there any hints that for those who never had a chance to hear the gospel there might exist some other way of salvation.[28] Because there is no other way, it is the Christians' duty to reach everyone with the gospel. This means priority for unreached areas.[29] Even in the countries of Christendom, those who 'really believe in Christ' are a minority, but everyone has a chance to hear the message or to read it. If someone in the 'reached countries' does not believe, that is his own decision, but in an unreached area no one can believe, since no one has the chance to hear.[30] Not to combat this state of affairs with an all-out effort[31] is Christianity's crime.[32]

## CATHOLIC IS UNREACHED

Faith missions had no intention of competing with other Protestant missions (see Romans 15:20) and, with few exceptions, they did not compete.[33] But their reluctance to avoid competition did not apply to Catholic areas. Following the lead of the Evangelical Alliance (1846), it was not doubted that it was possible for Catholics to attain to saving faith even within their church,[34] but neither the Roman Catholic Church nor the Orthodox churches were accepted as true churches.[35] Often the 'papacy' was identified with the Antichrist,[36] for example by A. B. Simpson[37] and by Grattan Guinness,[38] though clearly not by Fredrik Franson.[39]

This meant that the Catholic countries, for example France, counted as 'unreached'[40] and when the Guinnesses, after meeting Hudson Taylor, went to Paris for evangelistic service, that meant foreign mission work for them.[41] By means of her book *The Neglected Continent*, their daughter Lucy helped to establish that the whole of South America was to be regarded as an evangelical mission field.[42] One response to her book was that, in Toronto, a mission was founded for Peru, which came under the responsibility of the ELTI in 1897,[43] and from 1900 onwards under the name of Regions Beyond Missionary Union. It was only natural that the RBMU protested strongly when it was decided that missionary work among Catholics was not to be counted as foreign mission work.[44] This decision was one of several which caused faith missions and classical missions, which had been moving together somewhat, to begin definitely to move further apart again.[45]

In no way did faith missions regard Catholic missions as 'sister missions', but neither did they push hard to start work where Catholics had already started,[46] although they did sometimes attempt to reach an area before the Catholics could [47] or they tried to become the first Protestant mission in a 'Catholic country',[48] although there they did not work among the few Catholics.

## FAITH MISSIONS GO INTERNATIONAL

The idea of international cooperation in missionary work was not developed by the faith missions, but by the classical missions. German-speaking mission seminaries trained men for British and Dutch missions,[49] and even the Paris Mission did not want its own mission field in the beginning. The growing denominational consciousness sometimes made cooperation difficult but, more often, the simple wish to have a mission of one's own 'nationalized' the missionary work and, because the Protestant churches were usually territorial churches, international structures were strange to them.[50] Faith missions then took up the idea of international missionary work. Because they were not hampered by denominational borders (which were usually national borders, too), they could become far more international than the classical missions and, eventually, some (though by no means all) pushed the concept to its logical limits.[51] But the process was gradual.

The first faith mission was born in England, although Scotland and Ireland played an early and major role in it: some of the first CIM missionaries came from Scotland[52] and, through his trip to visit the Guinnesses in Dublin in 1866, Hudson Taylor won his first Irish missionaries.[53] The early development of the CIM is typical of many a faith mission. In whatever country of the United Kingdom they started, they tried to spread into the other countries: the Livingstone Inland Mission had strong roots in Wales;[54] the Qua Iboe Mission even today has its headquarters in Northern Ireland;[55] the Sudan United Mission found most of its early support in Scotland;[56] the North Africa Mission originated in London.[57] Typical was the endeavour of the SUM to establish as quickly as possible a council each in Scotland, Ireland and England.[58] Though the countries of the United Kingdom were politicaly united, they were organized separately in religious affairs. This British plurality was the first international step of faith missions, although later there developed a tendency to move offices to London and to dissolve the Scottish branch.

The first British mission to create a North American branch was the CIM (1888).[59] Grattan Guinness tried hard to spread faith mission ideas in the United States, but he did not try to start US branches for the ELTI-related missions. Instead, he encouraged the founding of US missions.[60] The Cape General Mission (later a constituent part of the SAGM) received US support as early as 1893[61] and, in 1906, the American branch became independent.[62] The SUM, founded in 1904, by 1906 had established a North American branch with a house of its own in Germantown, Philadelphia.[63] Later, the centre of gravity shifted to Canada.[64] In 1906, first Karl and then Lucy Kumm paid extensive visits to the United States,[65] and Lucy died there.[66] In 1906, SUM-USA already had four missionaries. The short-lived union with the Africa Industrial Mission (SIM) was another attempt to make the SUM even more international.

When a British mission took roots in the United States, there was usually an invitation or some previous contact. Both were lacking when Constance Brandon landed in 1920 to establish a WEC home base there.[67] In 1922, she had reached her aim of establishing an independent North American branch of WEC;[68] two years later, it had grown sufficiently that (led by the Rev. Roadhouse) the Canadian section became a home base of its own.[69] Because of problems with the autocratic leadership of C. T. Studd, nearly all the North American WEC missionaries joined the AIM.[70] The two North American branches ceased to exist after that because no agreement with C. T. Studd could be reached, in spite of Alfred Buxton's attempts to mediate.[71] In 1933,[72] Olive Ashton made a new start in Canada,[73] on which Alfred Ruscoe built.[74] In 1936, he re-established WEC-USA.[75]

For missions which had originated in the United States, it was obvious to look to Canada for international expansion; for Canadian missions, it was the other way round. A. B. Simpson's Missionary Alliance was renamed in 1889 the International Missionary Alliance, and included Canada.[76] The AIM tried very early to gain support from Canada,[77] but only in 1936 was a Canadian structure created.[78]

Like the British missions, US missions usually felt a strong urge to cross the Atlantic. The AIM was founded in Philadelphia in 1895.[79] It had a British Council in 1906,[80] from which an independent British branch developed.[81] The SIM, founded as the Africa Industrial Mission in Toronto in 1898,[82] soon had a Liverpool committee although, by 1920, it hardly existed any more. In 1922, Bingham visited Great Britain and organized a council each in Liverpool and in Glasgow.[83]

At about the same time, faith missions spread to the British dominions in Africa and Australia. For the SUM, this happened very quickly through a little leaflet[84] which a Scottish friend sent in 1905 to Dr Fallon in South Africa, after hearing Kumm speak.[85] He was so fascinated that he immediately organized an auxiliary,[86] which Kumm's visit in 1907 transformed into an independent council.[87]

Kumm's next great journey took him again to South Africa, but more important were Australia and New Zealand, where he organized SUM councils.[88] In 1913, the decision was taken that SUM-AUS/NZ should work in the Eastern section of the Sudan Belt, because their missionaries could reach the Anglo-Egyptian Sudan much easier than they could Nigeria.[89] Charles E. Hurlbert visited Australia in 1918, whereupon the Rev. and Mrs Stuart Bryson went to Kenya as AIM missionaries. When they had to leave Kenya for health reasons in 1938, Stuart Bryson became full-time secretary of the Australian Council.[90] In 1926, Bingham visited Australia and New Zealand and, over the following eleven years, twenty missionaries from these countries joined SIM.[91] In 1937, South Africans became interested in the SIM.[92]

WEC experienced a rapid worldwide expansion. Constance Brandon, who had started WEC in the United States in 1920, went to New Zealand and Australia in 1922 and began WEC work there.[93] Priscilla Studd followed up her contacts and established a permanent WEC home base there.[94] Priscilla went to South Africa as well.[95] After the WEC's big crisis, Hans von Staden,[96] missionary of the Africa Evangelistic Band (and, in 1942, the founder of the Dorothea Mission)[97], organized a South African WEC branch.[98]

A special role in this 'Commonwealth stage' of international faith mission expansion was played by the South Africa General Mission, which was organized in Capetown in 1894 by amalgamating the Cape General Mission (1889) and the South East Asia (1889) and South East Africa Evangelistic Mission (1891).[99] Some of its members were white South Africans. In spite of being founded in Capetown and the South African Andrew Murray being its president, the SAGM was not strictly a South African mission, but a field-directed British mission, expanded by sending branches in other English-speaking countries, of which South Africa was only one.[100]

The Zambezi Industrial Mission (1892)[101] and the Nyassa Industrial Mission (1893),[102] both founded by Joseph Booth from Australia,[103] were soon taken over by British Christians. A similar process took place with the Mission Philafricaine, which was founded by Héli Chatelin in 1896 in the United States as the 'Philafrican Liberators' League'.[104] In 1899, his sister Alida started a Swiss auxiliary.[105] The US committee transferred all reponsibility to it after the missionaries sent out could not agree with Chatelin and money had generally failed to come in.[106]

When Hudson Taylor visited Norway in 1889, this did not lead to a Norwegian branch, but rather to the establishment of an associated mission, the Kinamisjonsforbund.[107] That turned out to be a far-reaching decision. In 1888, Hudson Taylor had agreed to the establishment of a North American branch, but for non-English-speaking countries he choose the form of associated missions, which made them more independent and gave them a smaller share in common responsibility.[108] After a period of adjustment, these associated missions always received an area of their own in China within the overall structure of the CIM.[109] This pattern of associated missions came to an end, much to the dismay of some of them, when in 1950 the CIM decided to continue by opening work in several countries of East Asia, but to shed all the associated missions.[110] After 1950, no more associated missions were founded; their place was filled in some way by the 'National Mission Fellowships', such as Schweizerische Missions-Gemeinschaft (SMG) und Deutsche Missionsgemeinschaft (DMG), which do not have a mission field of their own but which send missionaries from their country into international missions.[111]

Fredrik Franson followed the same pattern. When he started the first missions in Europe, he could not create branches of a US mission because he had not yet founded the Scandinavian Alliance Mission (TEAM). The missions he founded, he associated closely to the CIM. When the SvAM, from 1892 onwards, worked in South Africa, members of the Scandinavian revival and mission movements which Franson had influenced so deeply joined the SvAM (Svenska Alliansmissionen,[112] Helgelseförbundet[113] or Norsk Misjonsforbundet).[114] After a time, all these groups received their own South African mission fields. Interesting, although not achieving the intended results, were Alma Doering's attempts to establish European branches of the Congo Inland Mission. When the Defenseless Mennonites (today Evangelical Mennonite Conference) and the Central Conference Mennonites had decided to begin the work of the CoIM, they had money, but no Mennonite missionaries.[115] So they agreed to Alma Doering's proposal that she try to find missionaries in Europe.[116] By 1915, she had found eleven missionary candidates from Great Britain, Holland, Germany, Norway and Sweden—financial support included.[117] A German branch of the CoIM was started,[118] and Elisabeth Schlansky, Alma Doering's colleague, published in her home town of Brieg in Silesia a booklet[119] promising independence to the nascent German branch.[120] The war prevented three of the eleven candidates from going, eight reached Zaire, but none of them felt at home in the CoIM[121] so, after 1925, the CoIM became a purely US mission.[122] This gave birth to two new missions: Oskar Anderson[123] began the Svenska Baptist Mission in Zaire; Henning and Elsa Karlson (Lundberg)[124] began the Mission Baptiste Suedoise of the Örebro Missionsförening in the Congo.

An important early exception to the rule of starting associated missions in non-English-speaking countries was the Danish SUM branch.[125] With the help of Ernst Lohmann, head of the Orientmission, Kumm also worked to establish a German branch.[126] Lohmann had a tract printed and some Germans applied to go to Adamaua,[127] although the war stopped them.

Eventually, the work in Adamaua was started by the Norwegian branch, whose beginnings dated back to 1917.[128] As the Danish SUM friends had done, so the Norwegians tried first of all to get their classical mission, the Norske Missionsselskap (NMS),[129] to start work in the Sudan Belt. When they failed to achieve this, a Norwegian mission for the Sudan was started and, after some time, the NMS became willing to enter into a kind of union with the new mission.[130] The Norwegian branch of the SUM started work in Ngaoundere in north Cameroon in 1925.[131] In 1927, it was almost completely integrated into the NMS,[132] though the NMS accepted full responsibility only in 1939.[133] Today, the NMS is still counted as one of the ten SUM branches. No other continental branches were started before 1938, though some attempts can be reported. In 1936, there were plans for Dr Pièrre de Benoit,[134] director of the first Swiss Bible school,[135] to start a Swiss SIM auxiliary.[136] In 1934, there had been plans to establish a Hungarian branch under the Rev. Zulauf in Budapest.[137]

The process of internationalization did not take place in all the major faith missions at the same speed. TEAM was quite slow;[138] a

Canadian office was only opened in 1946.[139] Even slower was the CMA. Their first foreign branch was in The Netherlands (CAMA-Zending).[140] The Gospel Missionary Union only recently opened a Canadian office, though support from there is much older. The World Gospel Mission established a Canadian branch in 1982.[141] In Great Britain, some of the missions did not go international—mostly smaller ones such as the Angola Evangelical Mission, the Southern Morocco Mission and the Central Morocco Mission.

Because Germany and the larger section of Switzerland share the same language, a mission started in one of the two countries tended to develop a branch in the other one but, after 1933, there was usually a split of some kind due to the political developments in Germany.

The faith missions experienced an internationalization far wider and far more permanent than that of the classical missions. This is understandable because they were not tied to a national church. Another reason is that faith missions were brought into existence at the crest of revival movements which were themselves intensely international. These movements, such as the holiness movement, usually did not separate from the churches they infiltrated, but they tended to claim the primary spiritual allegiance of those they influenced. Thus, a Swedish member of the Helgelseförbundet might feel much more akin in spirit to Alma Doering, herself strongly influenced by the holiness movement, than with the bishops of the Lutheran Church of Sweden, who had baptized him and whose church he would never leave. This led many people to attend holiness-influenced training institutions in Great Britain. Because these schools were bound to no church or mission (in this they differed from the classical mission seminaries) and were self-financing,[142] they could accept students from everywhere.[143] Others applied to international British missions because they would not, in any case, be acceptable to the missions of their own church, perhaps due to their lack of education or perhaps because they were women who wanted to evangelize, but could not provide a male missionary candidate who had promised marriage to them.[144] A cultural factor contributing strongly to the internationalization process was the English language, which was, and still is, *the* evangelical language worldwide. In addition to all cultural and spiritual factors, the process of internationalization relied, as did so much else in the development of faith missions, on personal relationships.

With growing internationalization, thought had to be given to the establishment of representative international structures. Few were created before 1950, and the original home base (usually in Great Britain or the United States) was accorded seniority. Karl Kumm did call an international meeting of the SUM (1912), but he himself had to represent all non-British branches except one.[145] Sometimes there were definite tensions between British and US branches, but 'amicable splits' to resolve these did not occur until more recently.[146]

After 1950, the process of internationalization went both ways. Some faith missions became more national. Sometimes this was simply because associated missions easily develop this tendency, but more often it was because theological tensions developed between the US and the British branch, with the US branch usually demanding a more detailed doctrinal statement.[147]

Up to 1950, the word 'international', even for faith missions, meant little more than English (Britain, US, Commonwealth) plus a few sprinkles from what the British in those days called the 'continent'. After 1950, quite a few strong branches were established on the continent, especially in Switzerland, the Netherlands, Germany and France.[148]

EMPLOYING NEGLECTED FORCES: FAITH MISSIONS' SOCIAL GEOGRAPHY

William Carey, the first of the classical missionaries, had made it clear that 'means' had to be used to convert the heathen. This effort met with success, but, since so many heathen remained unreached, obviously sufficient had not been done. The early faith mission leaders insisted, therefore, that the unreached must be reached not merely by 'means' but by *all* means. Hudson Taylor saw this as a justification for starting a new mission 'without interfering injuriously with any existing work'.[149]

After experiencing physical healing in 1881, A. B. Simpson paced up and down at the beach of the Old Orchard Convention Ground entreating God 'to raise up a great missionary movement that would reach the neglected fields of the world and utilize the neglected forces of the church at home, as was not then being done'.[150]

This vision was taken seriously by the early faith missions. Hudson Taylor decided that men and women from all walks of life would be acceptable as missionaries. Not intellectual ability (which he never despised) but spiritual power was decisive for a missionary. Whatever training she or he would need would be provided on the mission field 'by roughing it', and through senior missionaries.

With Fredrik Franson, the training of missionaries lasted usually two weeks. None of the seven original missionaries of Egypt General Mission felt that he needed any training, and neither Lilias Trotter nor her early co-workers[151] had any. Looking back, she wrote: 'None of us fit to pass a doctor for any society, not knowing a soul in the place, or a sentence of Arabic, or a clue for beginning a work on untouched ground: we only knew we had to come. Truely, if God needed weakness, He had it'.[152]

As Taylor's 1866 advice to the Guinnesses to remain in Britain and 'to train me the men and women'[153] shows, Hudson Taylor did not despise training, either: no one was to be barred from attending a training institute such as ELTI. Money was not to play a role, nor nationality and, if someone lacked previous education, ways would be found to get it. The length of stay depended not on the academic contents of the training, but on the needs of the mission field.[154] If someone lacked formal education, that was not the biggest problem, but if someone failed in street preaching, personal evangelism or practical outreach, that would put his stay at the institute and his intended missionary career in jeopardy.[155]

It is true that most of the early faith missionaries came from the 'neglected forces of Christianity'. Most of them would not have been acceptable to a classical mission: Hudson Taylor, Héli Chatelin, Peter Cameron Scott and C. T. Studd[156] (to name just a few) would never have passed the required medical tests, while very many had not had the necessary education. The majority of faith missionaries came from the lower strata of society: craftsmen, farmers or farm workers, shop assistants, clerical officers and so on. A typical example is Cuthbert Nairn, the founder of the Southern Morocco Mission, who came from a Scottish sheep farm.[157] Equally typical was Tommie Titcombe, the SIM pioneer missionary among the Yagba, who had been trained as a moulder for the Canadian Great Western Railway,[158] and Albert Victor Willcox, a draughtsman and one of the early QIM missionaries.[159]

Not many missionaries came from the lowest social classes. One who did was Malla Moe, a US farm worker, who became one of the most effective evangelists and by far the most famous missionary of the early Scandinavian Alliance Mission (TEAM) in South Africa.[160] Bessie Fricker, the WEC pioneer missionary, who founded the Igreja Evangélica da Guiné Bissau, came not only from very poor circumstances but also from an extremely difficult family situation.[161] Emile Rolland, founder of the Mission Rolland in Algeria, was a burnisher with Renault.[162]

Neither the fact that most faith missionaries came from the lower strata of society nor the certainty that a faith missionary's life was a simple one deterred a number of people from the middle class from casting in their lot with a faith mission. Quite early on, there were teachers, medical doctors (such as Hudson Taylor) or 'properly' trained theologians, who preferred faith missions for reasons of theology or spirituality. An important aspect of the social geography of faith missions was the fact that a small, but influential, group of their early leaders came from the upper class. Most famous were the 'Cambridge Seven', who joined the CIM in 1885. Their leader, C. T. Studd, was rich enough to give away, on 13 January 1887, £25,000 (a sum which today would make him a millionaire[163]), so that he could live by faith just as any other CIM missionary.[164] Grattan Guinness came from a less wealthy branch of the Guinness family so that, when he became twenty-one years old, he had only the £400 to give away that he had inherited from Arthur Guinness, the brewer.[165] A. B. Simpson was a well-to-do Presbyterian pastor in one of the wealthiest churches.[166] Lilias Trotter, who founded the Algiers Mission Band, had enough money to have devoted herself only to her artistic talents,[167] and Joseph Booth could start the Nyassa Industrial Mission primarily by selling what he owned.[168] The German Sudan-Pionier-Mission received strong support from the nobility. In its women's committee, there was not a single commoner.[169]

More successfully than the classical missions, faith missions managed to engage men and women from all strata of society in the world missionary effort. But, just as the pious often rise on the social ladder, so did the fellowship movements and mission halls from which many of the early faith missionaries came. After a while, faith missions began to demand more training[170] and sometimes felt obliged to turn down candidates because of their insufficient formal education—the most famous being Gladys Aylward, who went to China as an independent missionary, having first earned her own one-way fare.[171]

Today, faith missions require considerable training, usually several years of Bible school that may be in addition to specialized training. The number of those holding academic degrees is ever-growing. A process seems to repeat itself: those who are no longer qualified enough for the (old) faith missions are still acceptable to the new missions, be they evangelical, such as Operation Mobilization, or pentecostal, such as Youth With A Mission.

If the missionaries usually came from the lower strata of society (with important exceptions), this was true of their supporters (also with exceptions). Support did not usually come from the well-established congregations of the Established or Free Churches, but from mission halls, Sunday schools, YMCA groups and so on.[172] The mission halls usually consisted of recent converts from a revival, and usually these converts were working class people. They were part neither of the social establishment nor of the ecclesiatical establishment. The faith missions, in terms of their supporters as well as of their missionaries, definitely managed to 'utilize the neglected forces of Christianity' (A. B. Simpson) to reach the unreached. But this record was not without blemishes. Over the years, signs of conformity become visible—adaptations to 'what all the others do'.

BLACK MISSIONARIES NO LONGER?

When faith missions were born, Europe was still a white continent. Only in the United States was there a considerable Christian non-white minority, the descendants of former slaves, who had been deeply touched by various revivals. It is little wonder that some of them wanted to become missionaries, and they were acceptable to some classical missions[173] as they were also to the early faith missions.

When Fanny Guinness handed over the LIM to the American Baptist Missionary Union, one reason was that she hoped, though in vain, that from the many black congregations of the US Baptists missionaries for Zaire might be found. Her son Harry kept up that hope—also in vain.[174] A. B. Simpson had written in 1882: 'Africa wants that the Africans from America come to her aid'.[175] Héli Chatelin wanted first to go to Madagascar to find Malgache missionaries. When political circumstances made that plan falter, he turned to the United States to win black missionaries for his intended work in Africa.[176]

For Simpson, black missionaries were more than a hope. One of the first two missionaries to Sierra Leone in 1889 was the black American James A. Trice,[177] who worked there until 1900.[178] Trice did not come from the CMA, but from its related fellowship movement in Kansas, the Gospel Union (soon, World's Gospel Union; later, Gospel Missionary Union). Around the turn of the century, the CMA greatly emphasized their activities in black communities.[179] Because there was hope that the black CMA branches would produce missionary candidates, a special Bible institute was established for them, the Lovejoy Institute in Mills Spring, North Carolina.[180] The first missionary from the 'coloured work' of the CMA was Carrie Merriweather, but she was trained in Nyack where, in the meantime, the New York Missionary Training College had been moved.[181] She worked in Sierra Leone from 1913–17. During 1920–30, eight more black missionaries followed.[182] The last of them, Montrose and Anna Marie Waite, left the mission when the CMA finally abandoned its work in Sierra Leone in 1935 and could not (or was not willing to) find another place of service for them.[183]

The first missionary of the US branch of the SUM, the Rev. John Baker, was a black Jamaican, who had been converted in Sierra Leone as a British soldier and then had gone to the United States to study theology.[184] From 1907 to 1909, he was responsible for Ibi, the mission's supply station.[185] Then he left the US branch. The reasons are not quite clear, because he applied at the same time to join the British branch. The British branch refused, bowing to the intervention of Lowry Maxwell, the field director.[186] Kumm, at that time in Africa, regretted this, because Baker 'had done a good job', and tried in vain to overturn the decision.[187]

Already, in 1908, the British SUM home council had discussed the status of coloured missionaries, without coming to a conclusion. In January 1913, Falconer of the US branch reported that the Rev. Dr Ross, a black American, highly qualified as pastor and medical doctor, had applied.[188] Since the US branch was not independent, their acceptance of this candidate[189] had to be endorsed by the British committee, who turned the candidate down 'because of difficulties on the mission field about coloured missionaries'.[190] The minutes do not detail the difficulties. On 12 February 1913, it was decided that Redmayne enquire from US and British SUM missionaries in Nigeria, and that Kumm enquire from the CMS, about their experiences with black missionaries. Using today's insights, all this was obviously designed to cement racial prejudices. The result was 'that the British Committee cannot see their way to accept a coloured man for the present'.[191]

In 1904, the Africa Industrial Mission (SIM) received applications from a couple from Chicago 'occupying a good position in that city' and from two single women from Chicago and Cleveland.[192] They had good recommendations, but they never became missionaries of the Africa Industrial Mission.[193]

In the context of the other 'white' US missions, the CMA was a special case: there were more black missionaries in it than in any other mission. In spite of this, its racial policy ran the same course as had that of the other missions a decade or two earlier. In the 1930s, under Dr Shumann, even the CMA decided no longer to accept coloured missionaries.[194] In doing so, the CMA had decided to conform to the overall trend in church and society which fostered a growing apartheid.[195] In theory, all were still equal before God, faith missions still insisted on the need of the 'perishing millions' for missionaries and everyone who felt called could still apply to a mission—but if the person was black, she (the majority were women) or he could only apply to a black mission, and there were no black faith missions.

Because black missionaries obviously were not wanted in 'white' faith missions any more, Ernie Wilson,[196] supported by Norman P. Grubb and WEC-US, founded in Philadelphia the Afro-American Missionary Crusade[197] for missionary work in Liberia,[198] 'to provide a needed channel, whereby Christian young men and women of African extraction, may faithfully expend themselves, without constant frustration, in the missionary enterprise'.[199] The first AAMC missionaries were Anna Maria and Montrose Waite, for whom thirteen years before the CMA had not been able or willing to find a job, after closing its mission in Sierra Leone. They had applied before to 'white' missions, but were always refused.[200]

There is also at least one black independent mission of some importance to faith missions. When her black denominational mission could no longer support Eliza George, she decided to continue her work in Liberia as an independent missionary.[201] She founded what are today the Independent Churches of Africa, led by Guz Marwieh and supported by Christian Nationals Evangelism Commission (Partners International).

In about 1950, with growing missionary interest in the United States, the number of coloured applicants to the AIM rose. This bothered its Home Director, who first corresponded with, and then held a conference with, the leaders of other US faith missions.[202] All agreed that there was no objection to black missionaries in faith missions, but they agreed, too, that the time had not yet come to accept coloured missionaries. They should be kindly directed to apply to black missions. Only W. L. Thompson, of the Latin America Mission, disagreed. He saw no reason to turn down an applicant who was qualified and felt called, and he insisted that his views be put on record.[203]

In 1955, the CMA revised its decision against black missionaries, but could not find any.[204] Only in 1979 was Meysa J. Costa sent to Burkina Faso as the first black CMA missionary of the new era.[205] In 1957, the OMF (CIM) decided to transform itself into a fellowship of missionaries of all races and from all countries. Eventually, all the faith missions abolished racial barriers. However, the number of black missionaries remains comparatively small. This can be explained partly by the fact that, compared to the size of the 'black' denominations in the United States, the number of black missionaries was always comparatively small, whether in white or in black missions.[206] But there is another reason: faith missions have difficulty in adapting to the particular black subculture or the black missionaries have problems in adapting to the peculiar faith mission subculture.[207] That this is not necessarily so is shown by the California-based faith mission, Christians in Action. It was founded 'white' by Lee Shelley,[208] but one of the early missionaries, Elgin Taylor, was black.[209] Now nearly one-third of the missionaries are black Americans or black Britons, another one-third are either of Latin or Japanese descent, and Elgin Taylor is president.[210]

What made Christians in Action so successful in utilizing the neglected (coloured) forces of Christianity? The explanation may be found in that it was a new mission, using methods unorthodox for 'old' faith missions (such as house-to-house visitations or creating a home base through evangelism). New missions tend to appeal to the underprivileged in the ecclesiastical establishment. Will faith missions meet the challenge of utilizing the neglected coloured forces of Christianity or will that be done by 'ever new missions'?

THE WORLDWIDE CHALLENGE

When faith missions came into existence, they managed indeed to utilize 'neglected forces of Christianity'. Meanwhile, a century has passed, missionary work has been successful and the majority of Christians no longer live in the West. If God indeed does not mind what culture people belong to, there should be plenty of candidates for foreign missions among these now 'reached' millions, whether in Asia, Africa or Latin America. Will faith missions rise to this challenge and use these tremendous 'neglected forces' as well?[211]

Many faith missions have little chance of doing this because they

141

have remained or have become national missions, but it seems that most of the big international missions are rising to this worldwide challenge. Prominent among them is WEC International. Leslie Brierley was the first to conceive the idea of establishing non-Western WEC home bases, the first of which was established in Brazil. In 1971, the first Brazilian joined WEC; in 1978, WEC-Brazil became an independent sending base. Today (1987), WEC has 25 Brazilian members, seven of whom work in Africa. Due to the linguistic advantage, most of them work in Guinea Bissau.

In East Asia, WEC also is trying to establish an independent sending base, possibly in Singapore.[212] Until this process is finished, the Australian branch, at whose Missionary Training College in St Leonards, Tasmania, many of them have studied,[213] usually sends out missionaries from the Asian countries.[214] In order to challenge non-Western Christians for worldwide missions, WEC missionaries publish a magazine called *LOOK*, in various languages.

In Indonesia, they fostered a different development. Heini and Agnes German, a Swiss couple, started with conventional missionary work in unreached areas of West Kalimantan. The whole concept changed when WEC decided to start a Bible school in Batu in 1959[215] and to evangelize from there; this then also became the centre of the Indonesian Missionary Fellowship (IMF) founded in 1961 by Petrus Oktavianus, one of the leaders of the Indonesian revival. A pecularity of this mission is that the WEC missionaries working in Indonesia become full members. The IMF missionaries work mostly in Indonesia, but some work outside, sometimes in close cooperation with WEC.[216]

In Brazil, the New Tribes Mission followed a similar pattern to that of WEC in Indonesia. There is one difference: US NTM missionaries not only cooperate in the Brazilian NTM, but also share in its leadership.

A country with an increasing share in worldwide missions is South Korea.[217] There are associated missions, there is also a Korean Missionary Fellowship for sending missionaries into non-Korean missions (Korean Partnership Mission Fellowship, 1988) and the number of Korean missionaries in the big faith missions is growing fast. SIM has more than fifty Asian missionaries (the majority Koreans), with their own sending base in Singapore. One of the couples who teach at the Missionary Training College in Eldoret/Kenya is from Korea.[218]

## WORLDWIDE SHARING IN EVANGELISM, MONEY INCLUDED?

If race was once a barrier to the employment of the neglected forces of Christianity for world mission, that has been largely overcome. Another barrier, possibly more difficult to overcome, is finance. Among the southern half of the Christian church, many are definitely called for missionary work, whether abroad or in their own country (which often contains very different peoples and cultures), but the churches which support them are often very poor because the country is very poor. With the growing wealth of East Asia, it is comparatively easy to support foreign missionaries, but India presents a different picture, not to mention Zaire, where a pastor is well-paid if he receives $20 a month. Faith missions between the wars usually followed 'indigenous church principles', which meant that for them: white money is only for whites and the indigenous church must support its own workers. This rule was modified in quite a few cases, and often with a bad conscience—for example, by ruling that the *mission* might not support 'nationals', but the *individual missionary* could. In other cases, money was not paid for the work of individuals, but into the general church fund. Very often, money was paid for material investments, such as buildings, or to pay 'nationals' for secular work in the mission, such as medical work or school work. But faith missions were, and are, reluctant to pay 'nationals' for 'spiritual' work.

A conscious effort to overcome this racial and social barrier was initiated in China in the 1940s. In the 1930s, the situation in China, on the one hand, made the deployment of Western missionaries increasingly difficult because of political unrest and growing nationalism while, on the other hand, there was an increasing number of well-trained and highly motivated Chinese Christians who often lacked means for their support. A Washington state businessman, Dr N. A. Jepson, became convinced that a more effective evangelization of China could only be achieved by greatly adding to the number of Chinese evangelists.[219] In those years of the unquestioned rule of indigenous church principles, he found little support for his vision among US missionaries.[220]

In 1943, he met Duncan McRoberts of the CIM, who had a similar vision and suggested the young evangelist Calvin Chao as the leader of the Chinese side of the 'China Native Evangelistic Crusade'.[221] Chao could leave his small congregation and was able to use his organizational skills. Up to 1949, he had organized thirteen evangelistic 'preaching bands' in five Chinese provinces, and two Bible schools for training evangelists.[222] In 1951, when financial assistance to the preaching bands became impossible in Communist China, CNEC moved its activities to Hong Kong and worked among the Chinese in South East Asia. Over the years, the vision was widened and, following the usual faith mission pattern, the abbreviation was kept and the name changed: Christian Nationals Evangelism Commission.[223] Later, the name was changed to Partners International.[224]

The lasting contribution of CNEC to evangelical missiology was a *conscious* effort to overcome the narrowness and the racial prejudices that went with the indigenous church principle.[225] CNEC conceived all Christians as a unity, in whatever country they worked and lived.[226] In establishing the CNEC, Jepson took up one of Karl Gützlaff's principles: to evangelize China by Chinese. There were two differences, though: this time, there were many well-qualified Chinese evangelists available, and the CNEC took care to establish a way of having accountability with the evangelists without making them dependent.[227] During the past years, the British, Canadian and Australian branches of CNEC/Partners International have experienced considerable growth.[228] The development of a *theology* of worldwide sharing in reaching the unreached (and utilizing the neglected forces for that) is overdue, but very much needed, due to the simple fact that, with growing Western wealth, even faith missionaries become pretty expensive.[229]

# Employing neglected forces: Bible schools

The emphasis of faith missions of employing the neglected forces of Christianity created an institution which eventually strongly influenced not only faith missions, but also the whole of evangelical Christianity: that is, the Bible school. This term is not original and can be misleading. Bible schools were not created to compete with other institutions—the seminaries or universities—for the training of pastors. They were originally founded as missionary training institutes, as their early names clearly show. They were founded with a double edge: they were to provide the new (faith) missions with trained missionaries, and they were to provide missionary training for those who had no chance of receiving any theological training in the existing institutions, because they were not qualified and/or not wealthy enough to be accepted in them. Bible schools were uniquely intended for the training of missionaries/evangelists abroad *and* at home. Of course, it is difficult to draw a clear-cut dividing line between the evangelist and the pastor: once someone's evangelistic efforts were fruitful in a given locality, the missionary training institutes also got into the training of pastors for the new fellowship movements, for independent congregations, for missions and for mission halls.

For every new movement, it is difficult to give the date of its birth, because there are almost always forerunners. A. B. Simpson calls Chrischona the oldest Bible school.[230] It was started in 1840 by Christian Friedrich Spittler. The first student was a carpenter from Ravensburg, Joseph Mohr, who had left the Basel Mission Seminary because he had realized 'that his gifts lay elsewhere than in learning foreign languages'.[231] In 1859, Markus Spittler visited Great Britain.[232] It is imaginable that he exerted some influence there, but I could not find any sources to support this idea.[233] Another school which is sometimes seen as an early Bible school is Spurgeon's Pastors' College, which he founded as a private initiative in 1856[234] and which became the responsibility of his Tabernacle congregation in 1861. But its aim was to train pastors, and there were no women students.[235] One of the most prominent students of Spurgeon's College was Archibald Geikie Brown, who was pastor of the originally Baptist, then independent, Baptist East London Tabernacle, of which the Guinness family were members in the 1880s.[236] Putting the evidence in perspective, it can hardly be argued that either Spittler or Spurgeon started a Bible school, but perhaps their institutions were a kind of predecessor.

## THE EAST LONDON TRAINING INSTITUTE

The first missionary training institute in England (or, to use the later name, the first Bible school) was the East London Training Institute, which Fanny and Grattan Guinness opened in 1873 to multiply 'earnest and efficient missionaries at home and abroad'.[237] That was to be done by lessons, but also on the job: 'Mission work among the lapsed masses of the people; preaching in the open air, and in mission halls and rooms; teaching in schools; house-to-house visiting etc.'[238] Primary emphasis was neither academic nor practical learning, but spiritual development. How effective could an evangelist be if spiritually cold? How long the course was to last depended on the needs of the mission field, much as the amount of non-theological learning depended on actual needs. The school was financed by faith[239] and was, therefore, independent. The ELTI attracted many students, some of whom were converted through the Moody revival.[240] Soon the ELTI was enlarged. An extension which changed its character but made it a typical Bible school was the opening of Doric Lodge so that women, too, could be trained as evangelists for home and abroad.[241] This made ELTI differ very definitely from all the classical mission seminaries.

In the United States, too, some earlier schools may be found: the Rev. S. H. Tyng's 'Home of the Evangelists' for training city evangelists; the Rev. DeWitt Talmadge's 'Tabernacle Lay College' (1872); 'Bethany Institute' for women in Brooklyn. But they did not last long. Even if these were predecessors, A. B. Simpson still opened the first formal US Bible school.[242]

Early in 1882, Simpson published in his magazine a call to open a US school patterned on the East London Training Institute.[243] During the same year, he started to train missionaries within his Tabernacle church, then just about one year old.[244] On the 1 October 1883, A. B. Simpson, following the lead of the ELTI, opened the Missionary Training School for Christian Evangelists, soon to be named the New York Missionary Training College.[245] It became the pattern for many Bible schools in the United States and Canada, and also the pattern for pentecostal Bible schools.[246] Prairie Bible Institute, Three Hills, Alberta— today the most important Bible school in Canada—was founded by L. E. Maxwell, who had received his training at the Midlands Bible School in Kansas City, which goes back directly to the New York Missionary Training College.[247]

The second interdenominational training school was opened on Grattan Guinness' direct suggestion. In 1889, he visited the United States,[248] among other things intending to find out if the American Baptist Missionary Union could be in any way helped to fulfil its promise to advance further inland into Zaire. Because the ABMU had problems in finding the required candidates, Grattan Guinness suggested to A. J. Gordon that he train them in connection with his congregation. The same year, Gordon opened the Boston Missionary Training Institute.[249]

The most important Bible school in the history of faith missions is known as Moody Bible Institute,[250] founded in 1889.[251] Its origin is in the 'Bible work' which Moody had asked Emma Dryer to organize as a follow-up to his evangelistic efforts in 1873.[252] Moody had even promised to find her the necessary

house, immediately after his return from Great Britain in six
months. But Moody stayed more than two years in Great Britain
and lost interest in the idea, even after he had returned. In 1883,
Emma Dryer organized the first month-long Bible course, to
become known as the 'May Institute', which then took place
yearly. In 1886, Emma Dryer managed to interest Moody again
in the idea,[253] which later was felt to be a reason for dating the
birth of the school back to that year.[254] Because of the great
demand, Emma Dryer had to arrange for two month-long
courses in 1888. In 1889, Moody regained interest and bought
a plot to make a residential school, partly with the 5,000 C. T.
Studd had given him for missionary work in India. Emma Dryer
organized the school as the 'Bible Institute for Home and Foreign
Missions of the Chicago Evangelization Society', asking Grattan
Guinness to come to Chicago to advise her.[255] The intention of
the school was 'not to interfere with our theological seminaries,
but to supplement and complement their work by short practical
courses of study, mainly confined to the English Bible,[256]
practical theology, and Christian work by direct contact with
souls'.[257] After Emma Dryer had organized the school, Moody
made Reuben Archer Torrey its first director. After 1902, Torrey
became the leading evangelist of his time.[258] For Emma Dryer,
there was little room left in the set-up. The Moody Bible Institute
is still, today, the major faith mission Bible school.[259]

In Scandinavia, the connection between faith missions and
Bible schools was equally close. What became Örebro Missionsskola was started in about 1891 with annual evangelists'
courses[260] and, in 1908, the school became permanent.[261] Its
original aim was to train women and men as evangelists for
Sweden, but as soon as the Örebro Missionsförening opened up
to foreign missions, students of the school went abroad. At first,
the students joined a variety of missions,[262] then Örebro developed its own missionary work. The Bible school of the Helgelseförbundet in Götabro developed along similar lines.[263]

The oldest interdenominational French Bible school, the
Institut Biblique Nogent-sur-Marne near Paris, was started by
Ruben Saillens, who had attended the East London Training
Institute from 1873 to 1875.[264] To establish the institute, he
received considerable help from A. C. Dixon and C. E. Hurl-
bert.[265] The first Bible school of French-speaking Switzerland
was opened in 1926 by Pièrre de Benoit in Vennes,[266] near
Lausanne, as Institut Emmaüs.[267] The first Bible school in Ger-

man-speaking Switzerland was Beatenberg.[268] In 1934, Saturnin Wasserzug, a Swiss Jew and former missionary,[269] and his wife Gertrud held their first Bible courses there.[270] In 1945, Gertrud Wasserzug[271] began to train missionaries.[272]

In Africa, faith missions organized many schools which they called Bible schools. Using the terminology of this chapno, they were more like evangelists' and pastors' seminaries. Interdenominational Bible schools are still rare. In Africa, one example is the Christian Service College, Kumasi/Ghana, which was organized on the suggestion of WEC. A board in Ghana is responsible for it; a WEC couple (Myra and Bill Chapman) directs it.[273] In every year of its three-year course, missiology is taught. Even stronger is the missiological emphasis of the interdenominational missionary training institute of CAPRO, the Nigerian mission.

The Bible schools did not want to compete with seminaries or universities, but to supplement them,[274] thus using those people for ministry who elsewhere had little chance of using their gifts. Their aim was not to train pastors, but earnest and able missionaries for home and overseas.[275] In the beginning, Moody wanted to have only women trained in order not to compete with the seminaries.[276] Emma Dryer's Bible work developed in such a way that even men, though not qualified for a seminary, wanted to be trained.[277] Finally, Moody agreed and formulated as the aim of the school to train 'gap-men', men and women who were to fill the gap between the well-trained pastors and the people that they would not reach.[278]

Though the Bible schools did not want to train pastors, as a matter of fact they increasingly did. This was not due to a change in their intentions, but to a change in the Christian scene. As a result of the revival, more and more church-like groups emerged, such as mission halls, fellowships and so on. They needed personnel, and they did not usually turn to the established seminaries to find them. They looked for them where they could expect people with a revival theology similar to their own. Over the decades, some of the fellowship movements developed into Free churches, so their Bible schools became, in fact, seminaries, for example, Örebro and Chrischona.

**Notes**

1   Such reactions to liberalism occurred only in the twentieth century, but they did not usually take the form of a faith mission. The clearest example in the evangelical realm is probably the Conservative Baptist Foreign Mission Society (1987: 525 missionaries). It has some common features with faith missions, but it is a post-classical denominational mission. In the fundamentalist realm, the outstanding example is the Independent Board for Presbyterian Missions (1987: 40 missionaries), a classical fundamentalist mission.

2   They formulate what was common ground with the classical missions: 'Loyal to the fundamentals of the faith and the great basic doctrines of the Scripture' (Bingham, *Seven Sevens of Years*, p. 113).

3   The early LMS shared a similar opinion as far as church government was concerned. Using very different exegetical methods, the same result was reached by: Eduard Schweizer, *Church Order in the New Testament*, London, 1961, p. 13.

4   Thompson, *A. B. Simpson*, p. 156f.

5   Gordon, *How Christ Came to Church*, p. 102. Contradictions in the Bible he ascribed to his lack of understanding.

6   *HD*, No. 1, 1910.

7   Broomhall, *Survivors' Pact*, pp. 37–41. See Taylor, *Retrospect*, p. 113.

8   Bingham, *Seven Sevens of Years*, p. 15.

9   Niels Brønnum—Danske Missionsselskab (DMS), 4 September 1910. In so applying, he conformed to the wishes of his Sudan-Committee. This committee, on 10 January 1910, wrote to the DMS that should they reject Brønnum's application, they would find another way to send him to the Sudan. On 31 October 1910, the DMS wrote to Brønnum that they had accepted him for China (only). The same day, Brønnum suggested that his Sudan Committee cooperate with the SUM (Brønnum—Sudan Committee, 31 October 1910; he would not favour cooperation DMS/SUM, 27 November 1910). On 6 December 1910, SUM London wired that an independent Danish branch could be formed. The Danish Branch was officially recognized in June 1912. (SUM—Pedersen, 5 June 1912). Present name: Dansk Forenet Sudan Mission.

10   In spring 1914, the German Colonial Office finally granted permission for Protestant missionary work among the Laka in Northern Cameroon (Ernst Lohmann—Oettli, 31 March 1914).

11   Ernst Lohmann (Director, Deutscher Hilfsbund)—Kumm, 25 June 1912; Ernst Lohmann—Oettli, 31 May 1912 (mentioned in Oettli—Lohmann, 6 June 1912).

12   Oettli—Lohmann, 6 June 1912; 21 August 1913.

13   The Wesleyan Missionary Society's answer to the request of the Sudan Pioneer Mission to start work in the Sudan is representative of others: 'The Committee is impressed with the great need and the great opportunity presented at the present time in Eastern Nigeria, and with the special responsibility laid upon our Church by our position in West Africa. But in face of the overwhelming needs of our existing mission fields, and in view of prior calls of God to extension elsewhere,

the Committee does not feel justified in undertaking so large an enterprise as that proposed, unless means of carrying it on can be found independently of the Society's present resources' (Quoted in Minutes Sudan Pioneer Mission (date was lost in the process of photocopying), 1905).

14 The Kumms did not approach the CMS as they were preparing for an advance into what then became northern Nigeria. The CMS had, in contrast to the Free Churches, gained considerable support from the 1873 revival, especially through the Keswick movement.

15 Just one example: while Methodist membership was steadily growing, mission income decreased annually until 1893, reaching the 1875 level again only in 1902 (*Lightbearer*, May 1906, copied with permission from the *Wesleyan Mission Society Magazine*).

16 When Okut-Ibuno, the highest-ranking chief of Obarakan at the Qua Iboe River on the Calabar Coast, wrote to the United Free Church of Scotland missionaries asking for a white teacher; they felt unable to provide one and passed on the letter to Grattan Guinness, who read it to his students, asking them if someone would volunteer (Corbett, *According to Plan*).

17 The SUM also originally carried the name Sudan Pioneer Mission but, in order not to sound presumptuous, the name was changed to Sudan United Mission, because the SUM was not the very first mission in the whole of the Sudan, only in their area.

18 Grattan Guinness closes his article on the Sudan Belt with this plea: 'We plead for the neglected millions of the Soudan. We say to the Church of Jesus Christ, "Behold them! They are our own brothers and sisters in a common humanity. They are one with us in sin and ruin, let them be one with us in the knowledge of salvation"' (Grattan Guinness, 'The Soudan' in *The Faithful Witness*, 7 December 1889). This equality as a theological tenet was never questioned, but it was not always translated into everyday life and relationships, seen, for example, in the fact that, after about 1905, faith missions' attitude to black missionaries became increasingly negative.

19 James M. Gray, 'Are the Heathen Lost?' in *HD*, No 1, 1900. Similar: N. N., 'Are the Heathen Safe?' in *South African Pioneer*, 1891, p. 193. See also: the SIM tract 'Are The Heathen Lost?' or 'Will Those Who Have Never Heard The Gospel Go To Hell?' (Toronto, 5, n.d.).

20 This conception is based on verses such as John 14:6 or John 3:36. Matthew 25, where people who did not know Christ receive eternal life, was not taken into account.

21 At Andover Seminary, it was taught that those who had never heard of Christ would be given a chance of receiving eternal life after death. For an emphatic rebuttal of this 'Andover theory of probation', see: *MRW*, 1887, p. 296.

22 A. B. Simpson, 'Christianity's Crime' in A. B. Simpson, *Missionary Messages*, New York, n.d. (1925), p. 70. In his article 'Twenty-One Reasons' (1909), he combines the theme with one of his rare attacks against the 'new theology' of those who like to call themselves 'liberal Christians' (*Missionary Messages*, p. 86f.).

23 The issue of predestination was not discussed, because faith missions then were heavily influenced by Arminianism.

24  Delavan L. Pierson, *Arthur T. Pierson*, New York *et al.*, 1912, p. 61). See also: Alvyn J. Austin, 'Blessed Adversity: Henry W. Frost and the China Inland Mission' in Carpenter and Shenk, *Earthen Vessels*, pp. 47–70.

25  Junior Program 1953, Prairie Bible Institute.

26  Faith missions saw the heathen as suffering, but not primarily from poverty, ignorance and disease, but from not knowing Christ. The healing for this suffering is the proclamation of the Christian message. This did not and does not exclude endeavours to alleviate suffering from poverty, ignorance and disease.

27  Chatelin, *Héli Chatelin*, p. 13 (based on a handwritten autobiography of Chatelin which is no longer extant).

28  In the manifold primary sources, I could not find any other tendencies than those described here.

29  Studd formulated the aim of WEC: 'The speediest possible fulfilment of the command of Christ to evangelize the whole world by a definite attempt to evangelize the remaining unevangelized parts of the earth' (Studd, *Christ's Etceteras*, p. 6). For this effort 'We seek to evangelize only such portions of the world as are at present unevangelized' (p. 5).

30  *The Christian Alliance*, 1888, p. 79 (Helen Kinney) '. . . in America there is at least saving knowledge, if not saving faith, but in Africa even this knowledge is not yet known'.

31  A. T. Pierson states that it cannot be right to have 100 ministers for 70,000 Christians, but only three missionaries for 1 million heathen (A. T. Pierson, 'The World's Want and the Church's Neglect', in *WWW*, 1883, p. 29).

32  A. B. Simpson, 31 July 1892, sermon at Asbury Park Convention on Proverbs 24:1f., in Simpson, *Missionary Messages*, pp. 69–84.

33  An exception, already described, were the two industrial missions in Malawi (ZIM, NIM). A case of a somewhat uneasy nearness occurred in Kenya: the Neukirchen missionaries settled just across the Tana River from the Methodist missionaries. But the area was unreached insofar as the Methodists evangelized only among the 'Galla', whereas they had as yet done nothing for the majority Pokomo, who then reacted with great friendliness to the Neukirchen missionaries (Bernd Brandl, 'A Part of Kenyan Mission History: Observations on the Methodist Galla Mission at the Tana River', Report of a Research Journey, unpublished, ETF, Heverlee, 1992; David L. Miller, 'Problems and Possibilities in the Period of Colonial Consolidation: Christian Missions and Lower Pokomoni, c. 1900–1920' in Niels-Peter Moritzen and J. C. Winter, *Ostafrikanische Völker zwischen Mission und Regierung*, Erlangen, 1982, pp. 144–163 (p. 145). For the history of the Methodist Mission, see: E. S. Wakefield, *Thomas Wakefield. Missionary and Geographical Pioneer in East Africa*, London, 1904; Joseph Kirsop, *The Life of Robert Moss Ormerod*, London, 1901.

34  See: *Report of the Proceedings of the Conference, held at Freemasons' Hall, London, from August 19th to September 2nd inclusive, 1846*, London, 1847, for example pp. 263–270. Estimates about the percentage of 'saved' Catholics varied greatly.

35  In this, they were in accord with the official teaching of the Reformation churches.

36 For this view, too, they could call, for example, on Luther.

37 F. A. Pyles, 'The Missionary Eschatologie of A. B. Simpson' in Hartzfeld and Nienkirchen, *The Birth of a Vision*, pp. 29–48 (p. 33).

38 Grattan Guinness, never much pro-Catholic, had a disturbing experience when, on a visit from Paris to Spain in 1869, he visited the Quemadero, the burning place of the Spanish Inquisition, which was just under excavation, and found the ashes of the martyrs (Michele Guinness, *Guinness Legend*, p. 91). See also his: *Romanism and the Reformation from the Standpoint of Prophecy*, London, 1887.

39 Franson's talk during the Prophetical Conference, Chicago, 1881.

40 *MRW*, edited by A. T. Pierson, shows the significance of France as a faith mission field. The most important mission in France at that time was the McAll Mission, which also had ties to the ELTI, though no official ones. The McAll mission concentrated on evangelism; whenever a church sprang up, it was joined to an existing Protestant denomination. For details, see: Reuben Saillens, 'The Religious State of France and the McAll Mission' in *MRW*, 1888, pp. 896–902.

41 They started a 'chapel' in Rue Royal (Michele Guinness, *The Guinness Legend*, pp. 90–94).

42 The first major faith mission for Latin America was the Central America Mission, founded by Cyrus I. Scofield in 1890 (Charles G. Trumbull, *The Life Story of C. I. Scofield*, New York et al., 1920, pp. 66–74, 'Victory and Missions'). Through her book, Lucy Guinness and E. C. Millard, *South America. The Neglected Continent*, London, 1894, Lucy Guinness did much to establish Latin America as a Protestant mission field. Her book was instrumental in the start of a missionary work in Peru with a base in Toronto, which then, in 1897, came under the supervision of ELTI (Mackintosh, *Harry Guinness*, p. 55f., especially p. 56).

43 Mackintosh, *Harry Guinness*, p. 55f., especially p. 56.

44 The issue of whether missions working in a Catholic or Orthodox area were proper foreign missions was a major bone of contention in the preparations for Edinburgh 1910. RBMU protested officially against the decision not to include missionary work in Catholic countries (see also *MRW*, 1910, p. 561f.). After receiving a negative reply from the organizers, it was decided to hold a meeting with the view of possibly organizing a conference to find out if the Roman Catholic Church is a sister church or not (Minutes, 13 January 1910).

45 Some evangelical writers see Edinburgh 1910 as the summit of evangelicalism. Though Mott had been strongly influenced by A. T. Pierson in his formative years, seen from the standpoint of faith missions, this was definitely not the case. Many of them took part, but often with definite uneasiness. The whole conference rose when the news of Grattan Guinness' death was received and honoured him with a hymn, but Karl Kumm was allowed to present the case of the unreached Sudan only after protest and outside the main programme.

46 The early QIM, AIM, SIM, SUM, CBM, GMU and others had no Catholic competition.

47 Minutes SUM, 26 June 1912: 'If the CMS cannot start work in the Azande country (East Sudan) this year, the SUM is willing to start there next year... that

the country should be occupied by Protestants and not handed over to the Catholics, which would be a serious block to further work in the Central Sudan.'

48 The Livingstone Inland Mission (1878) was the first Protestant mission in Zaire, and Svenska Missionsförbundet was, in 1909, the first Protestant mission in Kongo (Brazzaville). Both countries could be considered 'Catholic countries' insofar as the Catholic mission was the first to enter the country, but neither LIM nor SMF worked among Catholics.

49 Two of them, who had some importance for faith missions, were Krapf (CMS) and Gützlaff (NZG).

50 This did not apply to the Moravians, one of the few international Protestant churches.

51 Some of the most international faith missions today are WEC, SIM, Wycliffe, OMF with branches in many countries and an ever-increasing share of non-Western missionaries.

52 Broomhall, *Survivors' Pact*, p. 150.

53 The trip to Ireland (19–28 February 1866) is described in Broomhall, *Survivors' Pact*, pp. 117–122; Michele Guinness, *Guinness Legend*, pp. 84–86.

54 The first initiative was taken by the Baptist pastor A. Tilly, of Cardiff, who solicited financial help from a Mr Cory, also from Cardiff. Another early supporter was James Irvine of Liverpool (Fanny Guinness, *The New World of Central Africa*, p. 179).

55 Today, the QIM receives half of its income from outside Ireland.

56 Minutes SUM 1904–06.

57 Steele, *Not in Vain*, pp. 14–19.

58 *Lightbearer*, July 1907 gives the complete list.

59 The North American CIM branch was initially almost exclusively a Canadian branch. It was founded by Henry W. Frost. His autobiography was never published; for a biography (which also contains much on Canadian CIM missionaries in China), see: Geraldine and Howard Taylor, *By Faith. Henry W. Frost and the China Inland Mission*, Singapore, [2]1988 (1938). For Frost's role in a new definition of CIM's doctrinal base, see: Alvyn J. Austin, 'Blessed Adversity: Henry W. Frost and the China Inland Mission' in Carpenter and Shenk, *Earthen Vessels*, pp. 47–70.

60 The most important lasting results were the Gospel Missionary Union in Kansas and the CMA missionary work in eastern Sierra Leone.

61 Walton travelled to the United States in 1893 with recommendations from Andrew Murray to A. T. Pierson and A. J. Gordon, fellow leaders in the holiness movement. At the SUM conference of 1894, Walton met Hudson Taylor (Weeks, *W. Spencer Walton*, p. 84f.). After 1940, the United States became more important as a home base than Britain (*AEF Guide*, p. 17).

62 *AEF Guide*, p. 7.

63 *Lightbearer*, July 1906. Much support came from the Rev. Stearn's Bible classes. The D. M. Stearn's Missionary Fund still exists today.

64 The first SUM-Canada Council met in 1924 (*The SUM 75th Jubilee 1904–1979*, Sidcup, 1979, p. 26). Not long after inauguration, the US branch became weak (Minutes SUM, 14 July 1909; 7 February 1911). Renewed interest from (holiness) Quakers prevented its dissolution (J. Gruhler, Builder, Germantown—Redmayne, 8 May 1911). In 1912, Kumm went to the United States to strengthen the US branch. When the war started in 1914, Kumm moved to the United States, feeling that with his former German citizenship he would do the mission a service by leaving Britain (Minutes SUM, 9 September 14, 'On the consideration of Home Expenses under the circumstances of the war, Dr Kumm suggested that it might be well for him to comply with the repeated invitations from the American Branch to help them develop their work'). Minutes, 20 February 1915, stated that it would be better for Kumm to remain in the United States.

65 *Lightbearer*, May 1906, p. 75.

66 She died of peritonitis on 11 August 1906 at Northfield after an untreated ectopic pregnancy in the fallopian tube which burst (Telegram Will Moody—Karl Kumm, 12 August 1906; Michele Guinness—Fiedler, 22 February 1993).

67 She was 'a single, unknown, lone Englishwomen, to represent the Heart of Africa Mission' (Rhoadhouse in the editorial of the first US issue of *The Worldwide Evangelization Crusade*, October/November 1923).I do *not* agree with Vincent, *C. T. Studd and Priscilla*, p. 217: 'The American council had been founded by the visits of Alfred Buxton, Priscilla, and the deputation secretary, Miss C. Brandon.'

68 Minutes First Meeting of the Council for North America, 24 January 1922, Constance Brandon Organizing Secretary.

69 Minutes WEC-US Council, 19 September 1924; *The Worldwide Evangelization Crusade*, US edn, December 1924. See Constance Brandon—Alfred Buxton, 9 August 1924.

70 HDC (AIM)—Grimwood, 7 January 1926; 18 January 1926; 26 January 1926; HDC—Field Council, 3 June 1926; HDC—Pierson, 28 June 1926.

71 The last information available to me on the US branch is that it would now work independently, as no agreement with C. T Studd could be reached (Alfred Buxton in 'Evangelization Now!', No. 64 (15 November 1926—15 January 1927)). There the sources at WEC-US end. But they must not be complete.

72 Perhaps already in 1932—the sources are ambiguous (*World Conquest* November/December 1933).

73 Olive Ashton had been as a WEC (HAM) missionary to Zaire, where she was given the name Ma Kanada. The correspondence relating to her work in Canada is at the WEC centre in Ft Washington. She left Canada in 1934 temporarily, handing her work over to Harry Spence. She did not return to Canada in 1935 because Norman P. Grubb wanted her to work with him in Britain (Ashton—Spence, 30 August 1935).

74 Ma Kanada (Ashton)—Rusiko (Ruscoe), 6 November 1936.

75 Alfred W. Ruscoe, *The Lame Take the Prey. An Autobiography*, Ft Washington/Toronto, 1968, tells the story. See, especially p. 75, pp. 95–97.

76 Niklaus, Sawin and Stoesz, *All for Jesus*, p. 85f., 'Canadian Cooperation'. In 1887, Dr William Cassidy became the first Canadian missionary and the first CMA

missionary to China, but he died on his way, in Japan, from smallpox, which he had contracted on board ship (steerage class) (Paul L. King, 'Early Alliance Missions in China' in Hartzfeld and Nienkirchen, *Birth of a Vision*, pp. 261–277 (p. 264f.)).

77 With the union of the Christian Alliance and the Missionary Alliance to form the Christian and Missionary Alliance, Canada lost its independence, which inaugurated a drastic decline of the CMA work there (Niklaus, Sawin and Stoesz, *All for Jesus*, p. 99). For the history of CMA-Canada and its founder John Salmon, see: Lindsay Reynolds, *Footprints. The Beginnings of The Christian and Missionary Alliance in Canada*, Toronto, 1982 (especially pp. 295ff.).

78 Oswald Smith, Pastor of the 'Peoples Church', a CMA congregation of the Tabernacle type, was president (see Wheaton Archives 81-7-4). In 1952, first steps were undertaken to make the Canadian branch independent (Minutes AIM, 17 December 1952). This was achieved in 1956 (Minutes AIM International Conference Meeting, 10–14 September 1956).

79 Scott was an immigrant from Scotland and, because one member was a Scotsman and the first party was to meet in Scotland, the AIM was constituted only there and Scott elected to lead it (*HD*, No. 1, p. 5 (1895)). But no Scottish or British home base was envisaged.

80 Mrs Elizabeth Parker-Brown was Organizing Secretary of the British Home Council. Two brief visits by Hurlbert and a letter by A. T. Pierson following them up laid the ground. The Rev. Stuart Holden headed the British Council. (*HD*, July/October 1906). The council became dormant after some time. It was re-established when Hurlbert met C. T. Studd and five Oxford students interested in working in Central Africa in 1912, and suggested they join the AIM (Anderson—Fiedler, September 1993).

81 For the development of the AIM, see: Wheaton Archives 81-7-4.

82 SIM and ECWA give 1893 as the year of foundation, but the enterprise of 1893 was an independent mission. There was personal continuity to the SIM, but no organizational continuity.

83 Minutes SIM First Council Meeting, 21 September 1922.

84 The leaflet was Karl Kumm's tract: *Crisis in Hausaland—Cross or Crescent.*

85 *Lightbearer*, 1908, p. 173.

86 *Lightbearer*, Christmas 1905. According to *Lightbearer*, 1908, p. 173, he first visited Andrew Murray, who advised him to start a South African auxiliary. The older source here seems to be more reliable.

87 *Lightbearer*, July 1907.

88 Karl Kumm, 'Report of a Visit to South Africa, Australia, New Zealand and the United States of America, Undertaken in the Interests of the United Mission'.

89 Minutes SUM, 23 April 1913. A similar development was the handing over of the CMS work in Central Tanzania by the CMS to the Australian branch. For an overview of SUM-AUS/NZ work, see: *The SUM 75th Jubilee 1904–1979*, p. 6.

90 Richardson, *Garden of Miracles*, p. 79f. In 1961, the council became fully independent.

91 Minutes SIM 1937 II-2.

92 The Rev. R. Wighton (Minutes SUM, 1937/II-2). In 1938, Isabella Graham became the first South African SIM missionary (Minutes SUM, 1938/II).

93 Constance Brandon— Priscilla Studd, 29 October 1925.

94 Eileen Vincent, *C. T. Studd and Priscilla*, p. 218. 'She covered over 31,000 miles in Australia and another 6,000 miles in New Zealand. Altogether, she took 272 meetings... 30 applied to the mission.'

95 Eileen Vincent, *C. T. Studd and Priscilla*, p. 218.

96 (1905–86). For his life story, see: *Dorothea Rundbrief*, p. 121.

97 See: '45 Jahre Dorothea Mission' in *Dorothea Rundbrief*, p. 123.

98 *The World of WEC*, Gerrards Cross, n.d. The relations between WEC and van Staden, who had a high appreciation of C. T Studd and visited north-eastern Zaire in 1935, remained close until his death. Patrick Johnstone, editor of *Operation World*, was a Dorothea missionary until, in 1979, on the suggestion of Leslie Brierley, he joined WEC to become its research secretary. The first *Operation World* was issued in 1974, the current is 1993.

99 Weeks, *Spencer Walton*, p. 90; *AEF Guide*, p. 6.

100 Meanwhile, AEF has a proper international structure with headquarters in Reading (Great Britain).

101 See also: Cairns (Mrs), *Pastor Charlie Bonongwe. Chosen, Called and Faithful*, Wroughton, n.d.; Brenda Hobrow, 'Malawi Revisited by Ruth Duncan, Mary Farquharson and Brenda Hobrow' in *News and Prayer Letter Brenda Hobrow*, June 1985.

102 Likhabula was founded in 1893 with Australian personnel and constituted a separate mission in 1896. Its Australian committee dissolved itself the same year for financial and other reasons (*The Jubilee of the Nyasa Mission 1893–1943*, p. 5). Richard Cory was NIM president until 1914 (p. 14).

103 Much valuable information on Booth is contained in George Shepperson and Thomas Price, *Independent African. John Chilembwe and the Origins, Setting and Significance of the Nyasaland Native Rising of 1915*, Edinburgh, 1958.

104 Héli Chatelin, 'The First Expedition Successful!' in *Les Rapports de la Mission Philafricaine 1898–1905*, Lausanne, 1905.

105 Already in 1896, Swiss ladies had organized a sale and sent Sfr 850 to New York ('Statement No. 3. Success of the Philafrican Liberators' League 7' in *Les Rapports de la Mission Philafricaine 1898–1905*, Lausanne, 1905).

106 Bréchet, *J'ai ouvert une porte*, pp. 12–14.

107 Today, Norsk Luthersk Misjonssamband. Oline Halvorson played an important role in this process (*Norsk Misjonsleksikon* Volume III, Stavanger, 1967, p. 227f.).

108 A German CIM branch was started in 1899, which soon developed into the associated Liebenzeller Mission (Andreas Franz, *Mission ohne Grenzen. Hudson Taylor und die deutschsprachigen Glaubensmissionen*, Giessen/Basel, 1993).

109For the associated missions, see: Marshall Broomhall, *The Jubilee Story of the China Inland Mission*, London, 1915, pp. 210–212, and Broomhall, *Assault on the Nine*, p. 614.

110CIM—Associate Missions, 28 December 1950. This did not apply to the Swiss Chrischona Mission which, despite its 'associated' name, was the regular Swiss branch of the CIM.

111Their role is discussed in the final section of: Andreas Franz, *Mission ohne Grenzen*.

112N. N., *Swedish Alliance Mission e South Africa 1901– 1951*, Piet Retief, 1951. K. A. Hjelm was the first missionary of the Svenska Alliansmissionen, and first worked for the Scandinavian Alliance Mission of America. In 1909, Hjelm informed the missionary conference that the Swedish Scandinavian Alliance Mission would now work independently, but keeping the old name (which was changed to Svenska Alliansmissionen in 1913 (Swedish Alliance Mission e South Africa 1901–1951, p. 167)) (Dawson, *History*, p. 155).

113Anna Matson was the first missionary (Dawson, *History*, p. 79). See: *Zulumissionären. Skildringar från Helgelseförbundets Missionsfält i Sydöstra Afrika*, Götabro, 1916.

114The first missionary was Knut Salvesen (Dawson, *History*, p. 79).

115Loewen, *Three Score*, p. 39. Alma Doering was, and remained, a Lutheran. The first Congo Inland Mission missionaries, Lawrence and Rose (Boehning) Haigh, were Baptists who had joined a Mennonite congregation.

116Juhnke, *A People of Mission*.

117To gain support, she published: Alma Doering, *Röster från Kongo*, Stockholm, n.d. For her visit to the conference of the Holiness Baptists at Örebro, see: Alma Doering, 'The Winning Side' in *The Christian Evangel*, December 1914, pp. 443–445, p. 480. For her activities in Europe in general, see the chapno: 'Missionary Interest in Europe' in Doering, *Leopard Spots*, Cleveland, Ohio, n.d. (1914).

118Doering, *Leopard Spots*, pp. 161–165.

119Elisabeth Schlansky and Alma Doering, *Die Kongo-Inland Mission*, Brieg, n.d. (1915).

120Juhnke, *A People of Mission*, p. 69.

121Lists of missionaries can be found in C. E. Rediger (ed.), *25 Years of Mission Work in Belgian Congo*, Chicago, 1938, p. 87f.; Loewen, *Three Score*, pp. 160–176. Brief information on the most important actors in the drama can be found in the extraordinary little handbook: Irvine, *The Church of Christ in Zaire*, pp. 67, 70, 104f., 125.

122Two missionaries (Tolefson und Edghard) joined the neighbouring Presbyterian mission (Rediger, *Twenty-five Years*, p. 87). Frederick Johnstone joined the Congo Evangelistic Mission, founded by Burton in 1915.

123He had received his call through a talk by Ebonne Sjöblom, the widow of E. V. Sjöblom, who was one of the first to publish the 'Congo atrocities'. For Anderson's time with the CoIM, see: 'Diary of Oskar Anderson August 14, 1914 through Nov. 4, 1916', typewritten from an original copy by Helen Neufeld Coon (for his separation from CoIM, see especially 15 October–4 November 1916). See also: by his wife Sarah (Kroeker), originally of CoIM: *The Congo Missionary Messenger* July/August 1953, pp. 14–21.

124See Elsa Karlson, *Med Gud i Kongo. Personliga minnen och upplevelser*, Örebro, 1956; Alma, 'The Winning Side' in *The Christian Evangel*, p. 445, for her call.

125Minutes SUM, 5 June 1912. Kumm would have preferred a Danish auxiliary (Kumm—Sir (Pedersen), 21 March 1911: 'I think the auxiliary idea is the better. It simplifies the work as control is self-centred'.) The SUM would then name two SUM directors of about sixteen.

126Minutes SUM, 17 July 1912; 11 September 1912.

127Minutes SUM, 8 January 1913.

128Fredrik Müller, director of the Norsk Indre Misjon (*Norsk Misjonsleksikon* 3, Stavanger, 1967).

129For its history, see: the four-volume *Det Norske Missionsselskaps Historie*, Stavanger, 1943–49.

130*Norsk Missionstidende*, 1921, p. 234f.

131Report of First Field Council, 8 July 1925.

132'Den Nye Mission i Kamerun' in *Det Norske Missionsselskaps Aarbok 1927*, Stavanger, 1928, p. 75. Although it is emphasized that the work in Cameroon is not a new mission but one joined to the NMS. But the Cameroon mission retained its own structures.

133*The SUM 75th Jubilee*, p. 20.

134René Pache (successor of de Benoit), *Dr Pièrre de Benoit 1884–1963. Notice biographic*, Vennes, 1965.

135Institut Emmaüs in Vennes near Lausanne, now in St Leger.

136Minutes SUM 1936/VIII-4.

137Zulauf was head of a house for deaconesses (Ziemendorf—Zulauf, 20 November 1934).

138From 1901 until 1909 there was something like a Scandinavian branch of the Scandinavian Alliance Mission of North America although, because of the loose organizational structure of the early SvAM, it should probably be referred to as an associated mission. In TEAM historiography (not highly developed), the 'Scandinavian branch' is not mentioned.

139Vernon Mortensen, *The Organizational Nature of TEAM*, n.d., p. 4. The immediate reason for establishing a Canadian office was the currency restrictions in effect. Because Chicago was so close to Canada, there had been otherwise little need felt for a Canadian branch.

140The official name is Stichting Alliance Zendingscentrum Parousia (1955). See: E. van Vollenhoven, 'Enkele grepen uit de vroege geschiedenis [1937–1953] van het CAMA-Werk in Ned. Oost-Indi' in *De Pionier*, May 1986, pp. 7f., 14. For details, see: Fiedler, *Ganz auf Vertrauen'*, p. 293.

14113NAPMO, p. 502.

142This does not mean that the fees, which the students or their friends paid, were sufficient. What was lacking, the school had to cover by free gifts from its circle of friends and supporters. But by choosing an interdenominational school, students kept their freedom to join the mission of their choice.

143The first ELTI student was Joshua Chowriappah from India; among his fellow students the same year were two Frenchmen, a Syrian and a Russian (Grattan Guinness, 'The East-End Training Institute for Home and Foreign Missions' in *The Illustrated Missionary News* 1874, pp. 96, 108, 120, 131 (p. 108)). Ruben Saillens of France and Karl Kumm of Germany were also trained at ELTI.

144In Germany, for example (later even with faith missions such as Liebenzell), women had little chance of being trained, or of reaching the mission field, unless they were willing to work as medical or educational missionaries or had someone to marry them.

145Minutes SUM First International Conference, Swanwick.

146There was indeed a British/US split in WEC in 1926, but that should not be seen primarily as being due to problems of nationality, but as part of the tensions which built up to the split between WEC and UFM in 1931. Dietrich Kuhl—Fiedler, 12 May 1988 agrees with this interpretation.

147Examples are RBMU (Interview Geoffrey Larcombe, 5 October 1985), Gospel Recordings and UFM. Usually some of the remaining branches opted for the British, some for the US variety. This meant that both new missions remained international to some extent.

148Bernd Schirrmacher, *Baumeister ist der Herr. Erfahrungen göttlicher Kleinarbeit in einem Missionswerk*, Neuhausen, 1978, tells the story.

149'Months of earnest prayers and not a few abortive efforts had resulted in a deep conviction that a special agency was essential for the evangelization of Inland China… The grave difficulty of possibly interfering with existing missionary operations at home was foreseen; but it was concluded that, by simple trust in God, a suitable agency might be raised up and sustained without interfering injuriously with any existing work. I had also a growing conviction that God would have me to seek from Him the needed workers, and to go forth with them. But for a long time unbelief hindered my taking the first step' (Taylor, *Retrospect*, p. 112).

150Samuel Stoesz, CMA Centennial Project (unpublished preparatory material for Niklaus, Sawin and Stoesz, *All for Jesus*), 1, p. 222.

151Blanche Haworth, Katie Stuart, Lucy Lewis-Pigott.

152Steele, *Not in Vain*, p. 123.

153Michele Guinness, *The Guinness Legend*, p. 86.

154Already by 1885, the training had been extended to last three years, although students could also opt for a one year's stay (*WWW*, 1885, p. 270).

155The following quotation is typical for many early Bible schools: 'During the coming winter, several new stations are to be opened, which will be connected with the college work; and the students will be engaged in these several evenings in each week, under the care of Rev. Robert Roden, and with the view not only of useful work, but also of practical training in conducting meetings, in exhortation, and in leading souls to accept Christ. The work will include also systematic visitation in the destitute fields of the city. This may be made an invaluable part of the course' (*WWW*, 1885, p. 270).

156He would not even have passed the medical test of the AIM in 1912. In the application form, he named Jesus Christ as his doctor and signed it as 'Member of College of the Great Physician, 30 years experience'.) (Application form, 6 November 1912, in the archives of AIM-UK)

157Steele, *Not in Vain*, p. 128.

158Sophie de la Haye, *Tread Upon the Lion*, p. 8.

159Qua Iboe Mission Archives D 3301/MA/17 (Albert Victor Willcox application).

160For her life, see: Nilsen and Sheetz, *Malla Moe*. For her leading position, see: Dawson, *History*. When the *Swaziland Post* issued, on 16 December 1992, a commemorative stamps issue for 100 years of TEAM's missionary work there, Malla Moe was honoured by a picture of her famous gospel wagon on the first-day covers.

161For her life, see: Betty Macindoe, *Going for God*, London, 1972.

162Jacques Blocher, 'Les Missions Périphériques', in René Blanc, Jacques Blocher, Etienne Kruger, *Histoire des Missions Protestantes Françaises*, Flavion, 1970, pp. 353–354.

163Interesting insights into Studd's spiritual affinities can be gleaned from the way he distributed his money: he gave £5,000 to Moody, asking him to start mission work in India where his father had earned the money. Moody spent the money on partially paying for the establishment of a school for missionaries, later to be known as the Moody Bible Institute. He gave George Müller £4,000 for his missionary society, the Scriptural Knowledge Institution, and £1,000 for his orphanages. £5,000 went to George Holland in Whitechapel for his activities among the London poor and £5,000 to Booth-Tucker to establish the Salvation Army in India. He gave £1,000 each to Annie McPherson (Home of Industry, London), Ellen Smyly in Dublin, General Booth (Salvation Army), the Rev. Archibald Brown, Pastor of the independent East London Tabernacle (and director of its social programmes), and to Dr Barnardo for his work among destitute children (Grubb, *Karl T. Studd*, p. 22f.). All recipients were strongly evangelistic, with a strong sense of social responsibility. See: Vincent, *C. T. Studd and Priscilla*, pp. 75–79. Later, he gave a few thousand pounds to the CIM.

164The remaining £3,400, Priscilla and C. T. Studd gave to the Salvation Army (from which Priscilla came) on their wedding day (Norman P. Grubb, *Karl T. Studd, Frontkämpfer Gottes*, Giessen, 1969, p. 22f.). How the children experienced this life of faith is brought out in Buxton, *Reluctant Missionary*—but see also her later booklet: *Reluctant No Longer*.

165He gave the money to his mother Jane Lucretia (née d'Esterre), so that she could live in some style, and continued to elicit temperance pledges from the people who crowded to hear him preach in Cheltenham (Michele Guinness, *The Guinness Legend*, p. 57).

166When he left 13th Street Presbyterian Church in 1881, his annual salary was

$5,000 (Niklaus, Sawin and Stoesz, *All for Jesus*, p. 45).

167The painter Ruskin supported her and tried to convince her to devote her talents to painting (Pigott, *Lilias Trotter*, pp. 9–15). For her family background, see pp. 3–6.

168For details, see: Shepperson and Price, *Independent African* p. 24.

169Baronesse von Hahn, Prinzessin Hohenlohe, Frau von Kiesewetter und Freiin von Massenbach (Minutes, 25 March 1915). SPM missionaries from the nobility were Gertrud von Massenbach (1883–1975) and Hedwig von Hahn. See: Dessien, *Wasser auf dürres Land*, pp. 13, 23; Gertrud von Massenbach, *Als Mohrenland noch christlich war*, Wiesbaden, 1930; *Mohrenland wird seine Hände ausstrecken zu Gott*, Wiesbaden, 1952; Margarete Unruh, *Hedwig von Hahn*, Wiesbaden, 1939.

170This issue is discussed in detail in Jacob P. Klassen, 'A. B. Simpson and the Tensions in the Preparation of Missionaries' in Hartzfeld and Nienkirchen, *The Birth of a Vision*, pp. 241–259. The tension becomes sometimes visible in one and the same issue of *WWW* (*p.* 249).

171Phyllis Thompson, *A London Sparrow. The Story of Gladys Aylward—The Small Woman*, London, ²1972 (1971), pp. 23–30).

172The early QIM Association may serve as an example. During its first year, the income was: £74 4s 1d, not counting the money Fanny Guinness contributed. Forty-six members contributed regularly (£39 4s 8d), there were thirty-one single gifts (£22 19s 5d) and four offerings from mission halls, and two from Sunday schools (a total of £11 19s 8d). See: *Qua Iboe Mission Mountpottinger Auxiliary, its Origin and Management.*

173Dr Sheppard, for example, the leading Presbyterian missionary in Zaire (Luebo), was black. When travelling on the same boat in 1906, Dr Sheppard suggested to Alma Doering that she start a new mission not far from his area. After the Mennonites, in 1910, had decided to start their own mission in close contact with the RBMU, Alma Doering took up his proposal at the very moment when the first group of missionaries reported after a stopover at ELTI about the crisis of the Institute, now under the leadership of Harry Guinness (Loewen, *Three Score*, p. 32f.).

174*The Christian Alliance*, 1888, p. 112.

175*WWW*, 1882, p. 100.

176Chatelin, *Héli Chatelin*, p. 25. The only black support that he won to my knowledge was that Booker T. Washington agreed to serve on the committee of the Philafrican Liberators' League, but the committee did not last long.

177He married during his first home leave. The CMA honoured them later by depicting them with their girls' school on the cover of *Christian Alliance*, 3 July 1895.

178He left the CMA in the context of a quarrel between several missionaries and their field leader, Eliphalet Kingmann, in 1900 (Samuel Stoesz, *Centennial Project*, p. 273). In 1906, Grattan Guinness recommended Kingmann to the SUM to head their work in Nigeria (Minutes SUM, 4 March 1906).

179Fourth annual report CMA 1900–01, p. 131f.: E. B. Nichols, 'Work Among the Colored People' in *Fifth Annual Report CMA 1901–02*, p. 11: 'The work among the colored people has become one of the brightest features of the Alliance work. A number of our most successful and liberal branches are founded among these beloved friends and fellow laborers. The work is strongly established in Pittsburg, Cleveland and in various parts of the South.'

180 For its history in the context of the growth and decline of black involvement in the Christian and Missionary Alliance, see: Niklaus, Sawin and Stoesz, *All for Jesus*, pp. 165–173.

181 Her life story: Georgie B. Minter, 'To Die Is Gain. An Appreciation of Carrie E. Merriweather' in *Alliance Weekly*, 25 April 1931. Lovejoy did not produce any CMA missionaries.

182 Sadie E. Moore Thornley (1922–26), Montrose A. Waite (1923–37), Eugene M. Thornley (1923–26), Raymond H. Wilson (1923–34), Ella May Scott Waite (1923–31) died of yellow fever (*Cahiers de l'Institut Biblique*, No. 1, 1932, p. 6), Anita Bolden (1923–28), Verna May Wilson (1929–34), Anna Marie Morris Waite (1930–37). Of these nine missionaries, six came from Cleveland and Pittsburgh and, with the exception of Anita Bolden (Guinea), all worked in Sierra Leone (Sawin—Fitts, 9 May 1980; Fitts—Sawin, 14 June 1980). Merriweather is often seen as the first black CMA missionary, but wrongly so.

183 Anna Maria Waite was convinced that the closure of the Sierra Leone field was also to serve the purpose of getting rid of the last black missionaries (transcript of an interview by Robert Cowles with Anna Maria and Montrose Waite, n.d., in the CMA archives).

184 Lucy Kumm in *Lightbearer*, 1906, p. 192; *Lightbearer*, July 1906, p. 124f.

185 Before his arrival, the British resident at Ibi had told the King of Ibi that he should receive him with all the respect due to a white man (*Lightbearer*, March 1907). He reported about his visit to the king: 'When I told him of the unity of the human race, and of other fundamental Biblical facts, he was delighted and told me to come again.' The European missionaries were glad that he taught them how to eat cassava, a Nigerian staple diet, which he was used to from Jamaica (*Lightbearer*, 1907, p. 64). In 1907 and 1908, the *Lightbearer* regularly reported on Baker's activities.

186 Minutes SUM, 10 November 1909.

187 Minutes SUM, 15 February 1910.

188 Minutes SUM, 8 January 1913.

189 Minutes SUM, 12 February 1913.

190 Minutes SUM, 8 January 1913.

191 Minutes SUM, 23 April 1913.

192 Minutes Africa Industrial Mission, 25 October 1904.

193 The couple in question probably were Mr and Mrs J. Ulysis Turner.

194 Niklaus, Sawin and Stoesz, *All for Jesus*, p. 171.

195 See also: Robert Gordon, 'Black Man's Burden. An Introduction to the Black Americans' Contribution to Protestant Foreign Missions', unpublished, Billy

Graham Center Archives and Wheaton College, pp. 5–7.

196Interview Dr Ernie Wilson, 12 April 1986.

197For important information about the composition of the Board of Directors (all black) and of the Advisory Board (including whites, among them Norman P. Grubb and A. Ruscoe of WEC) and the supporting circles (among others, Carver Bible Institute), see: *The Afro American Mission News* (first issue), spring 1948.

198The first (and up to now only) mission station was Baporo (Montrose Waite—friends, 9 November 1950).

199*The Afro American Mission News*, spring 1949.

200Montrose Waite—*Christianity Today* (n.d., ca. 1970).

201Lorry Lutz, *Born to Lose. Bound to Win. The Amazing Journey of Mother Eliza George*, Irvine, CA, 1980.

202E. L. Davis, 'Question of Accepting Colored Young People As Candidates for Foreign Missionary Service', unpublished, n.d. (1951).

203Minutes AIM, 17 January 1951.

204Niklaus, Sawin and Stoesz, *All for Jesus*, p. 291.

205Sawin—Fitts, 9 May 1980.

206For a partial survey of black American missionaries, see: Sylvia Jacobs (ed.), *Black Americans and the Missionary Movement in Africa*, Westport CT/London, 1982. Jacobs takes no account of black faith missionaries, though she corresponded with CMA while preparing her book. The distinction ascribed to Dr William J. Harvey ('veteran executive of black church missions') between black and white missions of his time that the black missions were industrial missions while the white missions were not (quoted approvingly in: S. Wilmore Gayraud, 'Black Americans in Mission: Setting the Record Straight' in *IBMR*, 1986, pp. 98–102 (p. 101)), is not consistent with the historical facts. At about the turn of the century, many white missions, classical and faith, were industrial missions—or tried to be. The SIM even started off with the name Africa Industrial Mission.

207This interpretation is supported by several answers to my enquiries about the participation of coloured missionaries. The answer often was: 'We have a few, but they often do not return to the field after their first term.'

208In about 1940, Lee Shelley had attended a CMA Bible school, then worked for about ten years as a missionary of the 'Soul Clinic' and became Vice President. He left the mission because the President divorced his wife and remarried (Interview James Marquardt, 6 March 1987). He then founded the Missionary and Soul Winning Fellowship, which later took its name from a local radio programme called 'Action Night'.

209He was to go to Nigeria but, because of the Biafra war, he went to Britain. He established a church there (Christians in Action Evangelical Church, Croydon) and a one-year missionary training school, which produced thirty missionaries (Interview Elgin Taylor, 6 March 1986).

210Interview Phil Blankenship, Vice President Christians in Action, 6 March 1987.

211Up to 1950, there were hardly any missionaries from non-Western countries in faith missions. A very early exception was Shao Mianzi Parker in CIM, but she got into the CIM by marriage. Hudson Taylor had strongly advised against this 'mixed' marriage, but then he accepted her fully as a CIM missionary, and she abundantly proved her worth among the CIM pioneers (Broomhall, *Assault on the Nine*, pp. 249–251, 389).

212WEC activities in Singapore were started by Ruth and Maurice Charman. Head of the Singapore Council is now the Rev. David Leah, pastor of the Tabernacle Church. Full independence of the Singapore Council is expected for 1995 (Dietrich Kuhl—Fiedler, 19 May 1988).

213For its history, see: Stewart R. Dinnen, *When I Say Move*, Ft Washington/ Pennant Hills/Auckland (CLC), n.d. At present, about one-third of the students are Asians (Dietrich Kuhl—Fiedler, 19 May 1988.

214Nan Pin and Eleonore Chee (Malaysia/New Zealand) established a WEC branch in Hong Kong, with eight missionaries (Dietrich Kuhl—Fiedler, 19 May 1988).

215Dietrich Kuhl, 'Prinzipien der theologischen Ausbildung am Institut Injil Indonesia in Batu (Indonesien)' in *Evangelische Mission, Jahrbuch 1985*, pp. 83–93.

216For an interview with one of them who works with WEC in Gambia, see: Veronika Elbers, 'Dritte Welt Missionare—Ein Interview mit Lotje Pelealu, Indonesische Missionsgemeinschaft' in *Evangelikale Missiologie*, 1992, p. 47f.

217Jin-Kuk Ju, 'Die evangelikale koreanische Missionsbewegung' in *Evangelikale Missiologie*, 1/1988, pp. 11–12.

218Interview Jin Ju, 14 December 1986.

219Allen Finley and Lorry Lutz, *The Family Tie. An Exciting Approach That Could Revolutionize World Missions*, Nashville/Camden/New York, 1983 (1981), p. 103.

220He did find support with the Native Preacher Company, a US mission (1924) which supported national preachers directly through missionaries. But Jepson felt that this policy would create dependency. The Native Preacher Company still existed in 1979, reporting to MARC an annual income of $4,000.

221Finley and Lutz, *The Family Tie*, pp. 105ff.

222Finley and Lutz, *The Family Tie*, pp. 106ff.

223There is as yet no CNEC history. Much information can be found in: Finley and Lutz, *The Family Tie*. Also published as: *Mission: A World-Family Affair. Sharing Resources in the Church around the World*, San Jose, n.d.

224Partners International today (1993) assists indigenous workers in fifty countries (CNEC—Fiedler, 4 January 1993).

225'Because of this attitude many missions yielded to the pressures of pride of race and culture and refused to support or to share the supplies available from the main part of the body with the "natives who could not be trusted". To justify this, the vague principles of "self supporting, self propagating" were put forth as the biblical norm, while the clear biblical principle of "sharing with our brothers in need" was often violated' (Finley and Lutz, *The Family Tie*, p. 54).

226Finley and Lutz, *Is Supporting Nationals Biblical?*, San Jose, n.d.

227Rather than directing the work in other countries, CNEC develops a working agreement with the supervising body of each ministry, usually a board of directors. These boards are made up of indigenous Christian leaders who are informed about the ministry and are responsible for it. The national missionaries are accountable to their board of directors. Each board of directors, assisted by the key staff members of their ministry, report back to CNEC on the progress of the work and the use of funds.

228For an expanded view of the CNEC concepts, see: Luis Bush and Lorry Lutz, *Partnering in Ministry*, Downers Grove, 1990.

229An IFMA study computed the direct costs of a North American missionary in 1990 as $29,526 and indirect costs as $43,000 (*MARC Newsletter*, 93-3).

230*WWW*, 1888, p. 76.

231Schick and Haag, *Christian Friedrich Spittler*, p. 49.

232Broomhall, *If I had a Thousand Lives*, p. 394.

233This is clearly supported by Grattan and Fanny Guinness' report on their first visit to St Chrischona in 1883: 'Last summer we paid a brief visit to the Pilgrim Mission House of St Chrischona... an Institution somewhat of the same nature as our own, save that it contemplates home mission work more than foreign... We felt much sympathy with Mr Rappard and his admirable wife... We commend this simple primitive evangelical school of the prophets to the warm sympathies of our readers' (*The Regions Beyond*, p. 101).

234In 1855, Spurgeon had accepted T. W. Medhurst as the first student; the second student was accepted in 1857; George Roger's principalship is reckoned from 1856 (see: *C. H. Spurgeon's Autobiography: Compiled from His Diary, Letters and Records* by his wife and his Private Secretary, London, 1899, Volume II, pp. 145, 148.

235There were very friendly relations between the two schools. Spurgeon brought his students to Harley for an athletics competition (Harry Guinness was an enthusiastic sportsman, even setting the world record for slow bicycling in the Crystal Palace on 10 June 1881) and the Harley students were invited to a pre-Christmas dinner. Michele Guinness reports from Lucy Guinness' diary: 'Mr Spurgeon had stipulated that Mama should be the only female member of the Harley party, but Mama, who was not daunted by anyone, even the most famous preacher in England, took five female friends with her including her two daughters. Never in her life, Lucy claimed, had she heard such a deafening noise as the sound of all those young men eating and talking!' (Michele Guinness, *The Guinness Legend*, p. 140)

236Members of this Tabernacle church who became missionaries did not join the Baptist Missionary Society but, almost exclusively, faith missions (Page, *A. G. B.*, p. 23ff.).

237Fanny Guinness, *Hulme Cliff College, Curbar, or, the Story of the Third Year of the East End Training Institute*, London, n.d.

238For a very good description of such evangelistic efforts, see: M. Wargenau-Saillens, *Ruben et Jeanne Saillens. Evangélistes*, Paris, 1947, p. 59.

239That was easier for Grattan Guinness, but Fanny (later, their daughter Geraldine) had to make ends meet.

240Rufus W. Clark, *The Work of God in Great Britain: Under Messrs Moody and Sankey, 1873 to 1875*, New York, 1875; John Hall and George H. Stuart, *The American Evangelists D. L. Moody and Ira Sankey in Great Britain and Ireland*, New York, 1875.

241Harry Guinness, *Not Unto Us. Record of Twenty One Years' Missionary Service*, London, n.d., p. 12.

242This is also the view of Sydney E. Ahlstrom, *A Religious History of the American People*, New Haven/London, [9]1979, (1972), p. 812.

243H. S., 'Lay Missionary Colleges' in *The Work, and the World* March 1882, p. 41.

244Niklaus, Sawin and Stoesz, *All For Jesus*, p. 58.

245*WWW*, 1883, pp. 154–157; Thompson, *A. B. Simpson*, p. 99.

246See: L. F. Wilson, 'Bible Institutes, Colleges, Universities' in Burgess, McGee and Alexander, *Dictionary of Pentecostal and Charismatic Movements*, pp. 57–65.

247The school was founded by W. C. Stevens, coworker of A. B. Simpson, and who had also taught at the New York Training Institute (Ted S. Rendall—Fiedler, 22 September 1988).

248Rowland V. Bingham (ed.), 'Rev. H. Grattan Guinness' in *Faithful Witness*, 3 August 1889 (title page with portrait).

249For its history, see: Dana L. Robert, *The Legacy of Adoniram Judson Gordon* in *IBMR*, October 1987, pp. 176–181 (p. 179f.).

250For history and context, see: Getz, *Moody Bible Institute*. This book is based on a dissertation. It has a tendency to overemphasize Moody's role, to the detriment of Emma Dryer's, in founding the Institute. But see p. 40. '

251From 1894 until 1905, this year was seen at MBI as the year of its birth (Getz, *Moody Bible Institute*, p. 34).

252The best source for the pre-history of MBI is: Emma Dryer—Blanchard, n.d. (1923).

253The process is well-presented in: Pollock, *Moody Without Sankey*, pp. 226–234, 'Slow Birth of the Bible Institute'. Pollock agrees with Emma Dryer's view of the origins of MBI.

254See: Getz, *Moody Bible Institute*, p. 34.

255Emma Dryer—Blanchard, n.d. (1923), p. 28. Getz ignores this when he writes: 'It is interesting to note that Moody Bible Institute, prior to Moody's death, was called the Bible Institute for Home and Foreign Missions of the Chicago Evangelization Society. Though this researcher could find no specific evidence, it may well be that D. L. Moody was influenced by the East London Institute for Home and Foreign Missions in attaching the same descriptive title to his own school' (p. 73). Most probably, it was not Moody who named the school thus, but Emma Dryer, who did all the organizing and who invited Grattan Guinness to advise her in 1889.

256It is possible that the Bible schools got their name from the fact that the students did not learn Greek and Hebrew, but studied the English Bible.

257J. M. Sherwood, 'Mr Moody's Training School' in MRW, 1889, p. 945f.

258The best biography is: Roger Martin, R. A. Torrey. Apostle of Certainty, Murfreesboro, 1976. For his time in MBI, see pp. 85–125.

259For today's doctrinal basis, see: Moody Bible Institute, Here We Stand, Chicago, 1986.

260Invitation to the first course: Banneret, 5 June 1891.

261For valuable primary material, see: Örebro Missionsförenings års- och revisionsberättelser. For histories, see: Örebro Missionsskola 1908–1933. Minneskrift med porträttsamling, Örebro, 1933; John Magnusson, Sven Lagerquist, and Samuel Sollerman (eds), Örebro Missionsskola 1908–1958, Örebro, 1958.

262In 1896, missionary work was supported in Denmark, Brazil and North Africa. In 1913, Alma Doering was able to win some Örebro missionaries for Zaire.

263Birger Davidsson, Det började med ett bönemöte... Missionssällskapet Helgelseförbundet. En presentation av Missionssällskapet Helgelseförbundets uppkomst, utveckling och verksamhet, Kumla, 1955, p. 11.

264M. Wargenau-Saillens, Ruben et Jeanne Saillens. Evangélistes, Paris, 1947, pp. 203–221 and pp. 57–72.

265Wargenan-Saillens, Reuben et Jeanne Saillens., pp. 206–210.

266His aim was: 'Former des saints, des prophètes, des sacrificateurs, des hommes et des femmes de prière' (Quoted in Frank Horton, Institut Emmaüs, Objectifs Généraux, 1968). The school is now at St Légier above Lausanne.

267Pache, Dr Pièrre de Benoit, pp. 34–47.

268Of all the years under Dr Wasserzug, there are only printed sources extant at Beatenberg (Interview Peter Mayer, 19 September 1986). For a short survey of the history, see: '50 Jahre Bibleheim Beatenberg' in Bible und Gebet, December 1984. A review of the history from her own point of view is: Gertrud Wasserzug, Wunder der Gnade Gottes. 50 Jahre Bibleheim Beatenberg, 30 Jahre Bibleheim Böblingen, Böblingen, 1984.

269Saturnin Wasserzug, 38 years older than his wife, died on 20 May 1950, aged 88. He was Jewish and had worked as a missionary among Jews.

270'Zum Gedächtnis an Saturnin Wasserzug' in Bible und Gebet, June 1950.

271Gertrud Wasserzug, 'By the Grace of God I Am What I Am', unpublished, n.d.

272Mitteilungen Bibleheim und Bibleschule Beatenberg, October 1944. Call for missionary trainees: Ibid., September 1943. In December 1946, eight women and eight men finished the first missionary course (Bible und Gebet, December 1946).

273Successful students can work for the University of Ghana External Diploma of Theology after their three-year course (Christian Service College Prospectus, (1987)).

274See: A. B. Simpson's programmatic article: 'A New Missionary Movement' (WWW, 1882, pp. 33ff.): 'Is there not room, is there not great need for such a class of foreign missionaries, humble men and women, fired with the love of Christ and souls, called of the Holy Ghost, dedicated to the work... who come from the plow and workshop and store with very ordinary education, but rich divine anointing, and who, receiving a simple specific missionary training of one or two years, can go forth, inexpensively, not as settled missionaries in all cases, but as pioneers, evangelists, itinerant heralds of the great salvation. They need not reason about Confucius, or teach philisophy to cannibal Africans, but they can tell the story of Jesus and pass it on.'

275Fanny Guinness, *Hulme Cliff College.*

276Emma Dryer—Blanchard, n.d. (1923), p. 8. Moody thought that deaconesses should be trained as at Mildmay. When Emma Dryer asked him what to to do with the young men, he answered: 'Let the theological seminaries take 'em. We'd find ourselves in hot water quick, if we undertook to educate young men.'

277Emma Dryer—Blanchard, n.d. (1923), p. 12.

278John Pollock, *Moody Without Sankey*, pp. 227, 232.

# 6

# Interdenominational missions and denominational churches: the concept of individual unity

If the unreached have priority, then evangelism has priority because only by evangelism can the unreached be reached. If evangelism has priority, the most effective way must be followed, and most probably, united effort will serve the best purpose. In giving their answers as to how best to unite the Christian efforts for worldwide evangelism, faith missions took many concepts from the Brethren movement.

## The Christian Brethren

The name makes it clear: the Christian Brethren wanted to be nothing in particular, and that is what made them so particular. They never wanted to start a new denomination and, though some today still claim not to be a denomination, they are quite a discernable entity (or several discernable entities) among the many Protestant denominations. Numbering about two and a half million, they are only a small denominational family,[1] but their size must not disguise the fact that, in the 1830s and later, they were an innovative revival movement whose influences reached far beyond their own ranks. One movement they strongly influenced was the faith mission movement.

The Brethren movement has no single source. Its most important early thinker was Anthony Norris Groves, a self-employed dentist who went to Baghdad in 1829 as an independent missionary, though originally he had intended to go as an ordained Anglican clergyman. He was an ardent student of the Bible, and he and his wife Mary put into practice the insights he gained, even when costly to themselves. They came to understand that their wealth was to be used in God's service, so Mary distributed 10 per cent of their income to the poor.[2] Later, they gave almost all their money for God's service, leading a very simple life themselves.

169

At Exeter, the Groves were influenced by two non-conformist ladies, the Misses Paget.[3] Their influence made Groves feel deeply the tragedy of Christian division. For his ordination course, Groves had to travel regularly to Dublin. There, he was influenced by and, in turn, influenced a number of evangelical Christians of varied denominational backgrounds. They all felt uneasy in their particular churches and were seeking a larger Christian unity.

Slowly, they gained the conviction that unity in Christ was not to be sought, but that it existed, regardless of denominational affiliation, just as it had existed in the primitive church when the believers met in simple obedience to break bread. They did what Groves suggested to them: they met on 'that simple principle of union, the love of Jesus, instead of *oneness* of judgment in minor things, things that may consist with a true love of Jesus'.[4] They had no intention of starting a new church. Their unity was not between denominations, but between *individuals* who loved the Lord. That was sufficient ground for the most intimate Christian fellowship, the breaking of bread. Differences in doctrine could coexist with that *individual* unity.

The Brethren movement continued to teach these principles but, by moving the meetings to Sunday morning, it soon became a new church. Faith missions used the same principles to define their unity: sincere love for the Lord; latitude in doctrinal views; aand acceptance of, but lack of concern about, the denominations. They differed in one important respect: they did not express their unity in Sunday morning worship (which would have made them a church), but in missionary work (which would make churches abroad).

Denominational structures could be left intact or disregarded. Groves chose to disregard them. He could not sign the thrity-nine articles, because in Article 37 he read that it 'is lawful for Christian men, at the commandment of the magistrate, to wear weapons and serve in the wars'. Also, he could see no reason why *one* denomination should ordain him. It came as a real relief to him when he realized that, according to the New Testament, there was no need at all for such an act. Eventually, he even repudiated his infant baptism.[5]

Among the Dublin group, an Irish clergyman, John Nelson Darby, quickly rose to prominence. It soon turned out that Darby held views quite different from those of Groves because, in spite of many principles they held in common, Darby introduced the principle of separation.[6]

From 1826 to 1828, Groves employed Henry Craik as a tutor. Craik accepted Groves' faith principles and, in 1829–30, passed them on to George Müller of Bristol, who married Grove's sister on 7 October 1830. In the early stages of the Brethren movement, there were two major centres: Plymouth and Bristol. Darby had links to Plymouth, but travelled widely and soon became the centre of much controversy within and beyond Brethren circles.[7] A leading preacher and teacher in the Plymouth assembly was Benjamin Wills Newton. In Bristol, the leaders were Craik and Müller.

From the beginning, Müller's (and Groves') concept of the church differed considerably from that of Darby. Müller was convinced that the local church was to have an organized structure and a recognized eldership, with each elder's personal call being confirmed by the possession of appropriate qualifications and by God's blessing upon his work.[8]

When Newton developed and published views about the incarnation to which Darby could not agree, Darby demanded, in 1845, that Newton retract them. Newton refused and the Plymouth assembly split. Darby broke off fellowship, and demanded that each assembly do the same.

Bristol was not involved in the controversy until Bethesda received into fellowship three members of Newton's assembly who had moved to Bristol, effectively challenging Darby's authority and his doctrine of separation.[9] This led to the permanent separation between Exclusive and Open Brethren. For faith missions, only the Open Brethren played a direct role, but their role was most important. In their formative years, Hudson Taylor, Fanny Guinness, Grattan Guinness and many others were strongly influenced by them. Hudson Taylor received the faith principle of support from Müller, who in turn had received it from Groves via Craik. Most of the early financial support for the CIM came from Brethren assemblies or through George Müller's 'Scriptural Knowledge Institution'.[10]

Of the Brethren's (non-)church concepts, several aspects became important for faith missions:

◇ The Brethren recognized neither ordination nor office. Those Brethren meetings, such as Bethesda, which recognized elders, expected them to be ordained by God, whose ordination would become visible in the fruits of their labours.

◇ The Brethren stressed direct reliance on God's call and independence from all human organizations.

◇ They believed in *existing* unity. Therefore, they could accept *and* ignore denominations at the same time, not feeling any need to work for organizational ('corporate') union of Christians.

◇ They were (at least in principle) willing to accept mutually exclusive views on minor issues of church order such as baptism: at Bristol, infants could not be baptized, but those who had been baptized as infants could be received into fellowship.[11]

Though these Brethren concepts all play a major role in faith mission ecclesiology, faith missions are not just Brethren. Most early faith mission leaders, although they profited greatly from the Brethren, could not stay with them, because some Brethren ideas tended to conflict with faith missions' priority for the unreached. Also, Brethren sometimes tended to become more narrow and exclusive, sometimes putting more emphasis on the right way of doing things than on finding the right ways to save the lost from perdition. This meant that almost all faith mission founders changed their denominational allegiance at least once.

# The interdenominational character of faith missions

In the personal lives of most faith mission founders, 'interdenominational' meant, first of all, a change of personal denominational allegiance and, at the same time, the decision not to take such a change too seriously. Both became constitutive for the concept of unity in faith missions.

## A FORMATIVE TRANSDENOMINATIONAL MOVEMENT

In this transdenominational movement, the Brethren, or similarly dependent congregations, usually played some part. Like his parents, Hudson Taylor was a Methodist and, when Barnsley Methodist Church split in 1849, he and his parents opted for the 'reformers', the later Methodist Free Church.[12] Soon after this, he was attracted by the Brethren meeting in Barnsley, because he was looking for a wider 'unity of all of God's children', not denominationally defined.[13] In 1851, he joined the Brethren assembly in Hull, which was led by Andrew Jukes and was in close contact with George Müller, the leader of the Open Brethren. There he was (re-)baptized.[14] While he studied medicine in London, he belonged to Brook Street Chapel Tottenham,[15] a Brethren meeting with Quaker background.[16] After his return from China, from 1860 to 1866, he was connected to the Twig Folly Mission in Bethnal Green,[17] but kept in close touch with the Brethren,[18] who helped him greatly in establishing the CIM.[19] Later, he became a Baptist, joining Westbourne Grove Baptist Church.[20]

Grattan Guinness came from a Free Church background.[21] After his conversion, he studied for a brief time at the Congregational New College in London[22] and preached wherever he could. Then the interdenominational Moorside Tabernacle gave him his credentials as a travelling interdenominational evangelist.[23] His wife Fanny Fitzgerald was Quaker,[24] but had strong leanings towards Brethren theology, as many Quakers had in those years.[25] They married in 1860, and Fanny brought Grattan into the Brethren movement,[26] whose 'historical eschatology' fascinated him.[27] When Grattan Guinness invited Hudson Taylor to Dublin in 1866, he was an elder of Merrion Hall Brethren Assembly there.[28] Because of a certain narrowness and lack of evangelistic vision, the Guinness family felt increasingly ill at ease among the Brethren.[29] In London, the Guinness family joined Archibald Brown's East London Tabernacle,[30] but kept in close contact with Thomas Barnardo's[31] Edinburgh Castle Mission Hall in Stepney Green.[32]

A. B. Simpson[33] had a strict Presbyterian upbringing. From 1865 to 1881, he was a Presbyterian pastor, first in Hamilton, Canada, then in Louisville, Kentucky, and finally in New York (13th Street Presbyterian). He left the Presbyterians because he wanted to 'reach the unreached masses of New York', but also because he had been (re-)baptized. He started his world mission endeavour as founder and pastor of the independent New York Gospel Tabernacle.[34] At the same time, he was the founder and leader of a fellowship movement for spiritual renewal, the Christian Alliance (later Christian and Missionary Alliance). Simpson had no intention of starting a new denomination, but also he had no objection if CMA members in a given place formed themselves into an independent congregation. He saw the local church as a means of reaching people, rather than as part of a denomination.

Fredrik Franson was born in Sweden to devout Lutheran parents who then emigrated to the United States. In 1874, two years after his conversion, he was baptized and joined Estina Swedish Baptist Church.[35] When Baptist ecclesiology became too narrow for him, he turned to Moody's interdenominational

Chicago Avenue Church,[36] which received him as a member on 4 August 1878. The next day, the church gave him his credentials as a travelling evangelist.[37] His ecclesiological studies helped considerably in the formation of the Evangelical Free Churches in the United States, but he remained a member of Chicago Avenue Church all his life.

Rowland V. Bingham, founder of the SIM, is usually taken to have been a Baptist. He came from Dissenter stock, then joined the Salvation Army, through which he experienced his conversion.[38] Before he first tried to reach the Sudan in 1893, he had come under Brethren influence[39] and worked as pastoral assistant to John Salmon,[40] pastor of the independent (CMA- aligned) Bethany Chapel in Toronto.[41] In attempting an independent mission, he may have followed Brethren missiology. After his return from Nigeria, he became interim pastor of a Baptist congregation in Newburgh, New York. His ministry prospered, so he was ordained.[42] First, he had the idea of starting a Baptist mission, but when a Presbyterian lady gave him a sum of money for the Sudan, he felt it wrong to accept Presbyterian money while refusing Presbyterian missionaries, so he decided that his Sudan mission was to be interdenominational.[43] Even while he was thinking of establishing a Baptist mission, he did this on his own initiative. He did not consult with the leaders of his denomination, in the same way that the leaders of Newburgh Baptist Church had not conferred with the leaders of their denomination when they ordained him.

Peter Cameron Scott, founder of the AIM, came from a devout Presbyterian family,[44] but before he went to Zaire as a CMA missionary, A. B. Simpson ordained him.[45] It was not the CMA which ordained him, since the CMA then was not yet a denomination, but the independent New York Gospel Tabernacle.

Charles E. Hurlbert, Scott's successor, came from a Congregationalist church close to Oberlin.[46] But his spiritual home was the YMCA, the Pennsylvania Bible Institute (full of holiness teaching and prophetic teaching) and the Bible classes around Philadelphia, which he taught at regular intervals.[47] He also acted without any reference to his denomination, but consulted the independent Presbyterian Arthur Tappan Pierson.[48] After leaving missionary service in old age, he joined the Church of the Open Door in Los Angeles, an interdenominational church patterned after Chicago Avenue Church,[49] from where he started the Unevangelized Africa Mission in 1928.[50]

Arthur Tappan Pierson (1837–1911)[51] came from 13th Street Presbyterian Church in New York,[52] where he was ordained in 1860.[53] During 1869–76, he was pastor of a Congregationalist church in Detroit;[54] in 1891–92 and 1892–93, he was pastor of Spurgeon's Metropolitan Tabernacle in London,[55] an independent Baptist church,[56] though Pierson himself had only been baptized as an infant. Only after leaving the Metropolitan Tabernacle was he baptized, on confession of his faith in 1896.[57] He did not become a Baptist,[58] but remained independent.[59] All his sympathies were with the Brethren. He wrote the first authoritative biography of George Müller,[60] whose Bethesda Chapel was for him one of the two 'really apostolic churches' which he knew.[61] In partnership with J. M. Sherwood, he continued *The Missionary Review of the World* (*MRW*), which the (somewhat dissenting) Presbyterian R. G. Wilder had begun in 1878.[62] In the *MRW*, he gave much prominence to independent and faith missions, because he saw them as important additional forces to supplement the still insufficient endeavours of the classical missions.[63]

George Pearse,[64] initiator of the Mission to the Kabyles (NAM), came from Hackney Brethren Assembly.[65] Edward Glenny, who took up Pearse's initiative and led the mission over a period of thirty-three years, also belonged to the Brethren.[66] Before joining the Brethren, Glenny had been an Anglican. Pearse had joined the Brethren in his youth.[67] Carl Polnick, leader of the Deutsche China-Allianz-Mission, was, at the same time, founder and leader of an independent-mission-hall type of fellowship, Pannewiese in Wuppertal.[68]

A few of the founders of the early faith missions remained more or less true to their original church, though often less than more. None of them played a major role in his or her denomination, while most were not even ordained. Spencer Walton, who founded the Cape General Mission (SAGM/AEF), was an Anglican strongly influenced by the Brethren, whom he joined on 19 January 1872, a day after his conversion.[69] After some time, he returned to the Anglican church, 'due to increased knowledge and clearer light',[70] and worked, from 1882 to 1884, for the Parochial Missionary Society, which had been founded on the suggestion of Moody. He then left the Parochial Missionary Society to regain his independence and to work without regard to denominational boundaries.[71]

C. T. Studd joined the CIM as an Anglican but, although the CIM in China had an 'Anglican section', he did not care to be sent there. Priscilla was from the Salvation Army. After some time, he left the Anglican church and, much to the dismay of his family, refused to have his children baptized. In India, he was pastor of an interdenominational church and in his garden, he baptized his four daughters (aged 12–18 years) as believers.[72] There is no information available that he ever joined a denomination. When asked in 1912 to state his denominational allegiance on the AIM-UK application form, he wrote: 'The Church of Christ'.[73]

Information about Karl Kumm's denominational affiliation is scarce. He is said to have remained a Lutheran all his life, but he married the independent Baptist Lucy Guinness and, during his years in Britain, when he and Lucy founded the SUM, he lived far away from the nearest Lutheran church—after all, he was far too much of a traveller to attend any one church regularly.[74] The two children born of his marriage to Gertrude Cato (Lucy[75] and John) were baptized as infants, probably in an Anglican church.[76]

Alma Doering's case is similar. From German Lutheran stock, she was baptized as an infant and is said never to have changed her denominational allegiance. But she worked most closely with the Defenseless Mennonites, who sent her to work on their Mennonite AIM mission station Matara/Kenya.[77] She was never re-baptized,[78] not because she was a convinced Lutheran holding fast to the prevenient grace of her infant baptism, but simply because she did not care about denominations.[79]

Héli Chatelin, who founded the Mission Philafricaine, came from the Église Réformée du Vaud (Switzerland). Living almost always abroad, he could hardly be an active member of his church. For a time, he became a Methodist. When he was a member of Bishop Taylor's Self Supporting Mission and the bishop arrived with the first group of twenty-three missionaries in Luanda, Angola, the bishop's first official action was to start a Methodist church, and he made all the missionaries and their children members—although only a minority of the missionaries had been Methodists when they left the United States.[80] By 1887, Chatelin felt decidedly unhappy about being a Methodist, because he no longer wanted to be tied to any one denomination.[81] It was only logical, then, that he became an independent missionary in 1888[82] and, in 1896, founded an interdenominational faith mission. During the closing years of his life, he revived his interest in his home church and tried to 'bequeath' his mission to it.[83]

The only founder of a faith mission who was an ordained minister of a classical church was Ludwig Doll (1846–83). He was most impressed by George Müller of the Brethren[84] and, following Müller's example, he first founded an orphanage; then, following Grattan Guinness' example, he founded a missionary training school (Missionsseminar Neukirchen); and, finally, he founded the interdenominational Neukirchener Mission.[85] Even as a regular Reformed pastor, his personal concept of the church was Free Evangelical.[86] Doll died early; his successor Stursberg was Reformed, as Doll was, but twice baptized.

To sum up: the initiative for starting a faith mission usually came from men and women who belonged to the Brethren, who were influenced by them or who belonged to independent congregations. Even if the founders belonged to a 'regular' denomination, they still acted very independently. The role of the Brethren is conspicious,[87] but most faith mission leaders could not accept narrow Brethrenism. Their evangelistic impulse was too strong for that.[88] The Brethren and independent missionaries had provided the nascent faith missions with innovative patterns to follow. The missiological achievement of faith missions lies in the fact that they managed both to use these new patterns and to surpass them.[89] Like their predecessors, they based their concepts on individuality and independence, while avoiding the logical extreme of complete independence, whether of the individual missionary or the individual congregation, thus making possible a more effective organization.

## DENOMINATIONAL BACKGROUND OF THE FAITH MISSIONARIES

For faith missions, unity is basically individual, not corporate.[91] Christian unity always means cooperation not of churches, but of *individuals* belonging to different churches.[92] The agreement of a church for one of its members to join a faith mission is not required although, if freely granted, is gladly accepted. Every faith missionary is expected to have a positive relationship to his or her church (whichever Protestant church it may be).[93] If a missionary wants to change his denomination, no objections are raised. It is a matter of individual concern.[94] Faith missions accept the existing churches,[95] but insist that their own place is outside of all ecclesiastical structures, an insistence which they back up by financing themselves.[96]

The idea not to transplant denominational divisions to the mission field dates back at least to William Carey, although he felt

# The denominational development of the early faith mission leaders[90]

| Name | Abbr. | Denominational development |
|---|---|---|
| Hudson Taylor | CIM | Methodist—Free Methodist—Brethren—Mission Hall—Baptist |
| Grattan Guinness | ELTI | Dissenter—Brethren—Mission Hall—Independent Baptist—Anglican |
| Fanny Guinness | LIM | Quaker—Brethren—Mission Hall—Independent Baptist |
| Lucy Guinness | SUM | Brethren—Mission Hall—Independent Baptist |
| A. B. Simpson | CMA | Presbyterian—Independent |
| Fredrik Franson | TEAM | Lutheran—Baptist—Independent |
| Rowland Bingham | SIM | Dissenter—Salvation Army—Independent/Brethren—Baptist |
| Peter C. Scott | AIM | Presbyterian—Independent (CMA) |
| Charles Hurlbert | AIM | Congregationalist—Independent |
| Arthur T. Pierson | | Presbyterian—Congregationalist—(Brethren/Baptist)—Independent |
| George Pearse | NAM | Anglican—Brethren |
| Edward Glenny | NAM | Anglican—Brethren |
| Carl Polnick | ACM | Protestant—Independent |
| Spencer Walton | SAGM | Anglican—Brethren—Anglican |
| Karl Kumm | SUM | Lutheran—(Mission Hall) |
| Alma Doering | ColM | Lutheran—(Mennonite)—Independent |
| Héli Chatelin | MPh | Reformed—Methodist—no official church membership, reformed tendency |
| Ludwig Doll | Neuk | Reformed—(Free evangelical leanings) |
| John Ongman | Örebro | Lutheran—Baptist—(Örebro Missionsforening) |
| C. T. Studd | WEC | Anglican—Independent (India: Interdenominational)—no formal membership |
| Priscilla Studd | WEC | Salvation Army—(India: Interdenominational)—? |

that for practical reasons every denomination should work separately.[97] Three years later, the (London) Missionary Society put Carey's ideal into practice, making it is 'fundamental principle... not to send Presbyterianism, Independency, Episcopacy, or any other form of Church Order or Government (about which there may be differences of opinion among serious Persons), but the Glorious Gospel of the blessed God to the Heathen'.[98]

The various churches which the LMS envisaged in its 'fundamental principle' differed greatly on the form of church government but all agreed on infant baptism.[99] The same applies to all the early interdenominational classical missions: Baptists were not welcome. When Reuben Saillens, later student of ELTI and founder of the first French interdenominational missionary training institute (Nogent-sur-Marne), informed the Paris Mission that his views on baptism had changed, the Paris Mission's approval of his candidacy was immediately withdrawn.[100] Equally, Adoniram Judson immediately left the American Board of Commissioners for Foreign Missions, when he accepted believers' baptism.[101] Faith missions' concept of interdenominationalism was similar to that of the classical missions, but much wider: faith missions accept both modes of baptism, thus accepting two mutually exclusive doctrines as both being right. For faith missions, interdenominational did not mean just cooperation between Christians from similar churches, but from churches with mutually exclusive doctrines, such as Baptists and Anglicans.

The early CIM did not care much about to which denomination a missionary candidate belonged; it was not even officially registered.[102] Nevertheless, Hudson Taylor was personally informed enough to say: 'Those already associated with me represent all the leading denominations of our native land—Episcopal, Presbyterian, Congregational, Methodist, Baptist and Paedobaptist. Besides these, two are or have been connected with the 'Brethren' so-called.'[103] Hudson Taylor's description of his early missionary company could be applied to almost all the early faith missions. Understandably, the denominational mixture of the members of a smaller mission might be less varied: the early QIM missionaries were mostly Presbyterians, the early Sudan-Pionier-Mission members were all from the German territorial churches, but the three missionaries who formed an independent mission to reach the Sudan in 1893 were of three different denominations.[104]

The above-quoted words of Hudson Taylor also illustrate the limits of 'interdenominational': all Protestants were acceptable. He had no need to say that Catholics were not. The Catholic church ('Romanism') was not considered a true church, but an apostate heretical body, and Catholic areas were seen as possible mission fields.

More important than merely being Protestant, a prospective missionary had to subscribe to the 'doctrinal base' or 'statement of faith' of the mission.[105] These he could usually find in a little booklet with some such title as 'Principles and Practice'. The first 'Principles and Practice' of the CIM did not contain a statement of faith: what was 'generally held among evangelical Christians' could be assumed to be known.[106] In the 'Principles and Practice' of 1885 what was generally held was explicitly stated: 'Candidates are expected to satisfy the Directors and the Council as to their soundness in the faith in all fundamental truths, especially as to the inspiration of the Scriptures, the Trinity, the fall of man, and his state by nature, the atonement, the eternal salvation of the redeemed and the everlasting punishment of the lost.'[107] This list of basic evangelical ('fundamental') truths is similar to the 'basis' of the Evangelical Alliance of 1846,[108] except that Taylor's list was one item short (Article 9): 'The Divine institution of the Christian Ministry, and the obligation and perpetuity of the ordinances of Baptism and the Lord's Supper'. Taylor felt these things not to be so important, though he opposed none of them.[109] Some early faith missions adopted the 'basis' of the Evangelical Alliance as their doctrinal base, including Article 9.[110] Other missions used their own words to the same effect.[111]

These early enumerations of the fundamental doctrines of the Christian faith did not serve the purpose of delineation against the denominational missions, since they did not differ on the fundamentals. Statements of faith did not serve the purpose of separation, but of defining unity. The classical missions demanded in addition agreement in the field of ecclesiology, which faith missions (following Groves) considered to be minor matters. Faith missions were not in conflict with liberal theology, not because they were in sympathy with liberal views, but because there were no liberal missions. Though there was no direct controversy with liberal theology, the doctrinal statements, basic as they were, would have frightened off any liberal applicants.[112]

Issues of church order were minor matters for faith missions. They were not dealt with in their statements of faith or, at most, only in a negative way. The SAGM stated that neither workers nor converts would be tied to any special form of church order.[113] The AIM left it to the individual missionary to decide on church order. In the SIM, the field conference was to decide. As much as faith missions did not insist on a given form of church order, so they did not choose, with few exceptions, between Arminian and Calvinist theology.[114] There was a saying attributed to Moody: 'I am an Arminian up to the cross, but a Calvinist beyond.'[115]

In defining interdenominational, it was easy to establish limits against Catholics and Liberals. It was much more difficult to find the limits of what was interdenominationally bearable *within* the evangelical camp, since many of those who held extreme views could honestly sign the required statement of doctrine. The early SUM provides two interesting cases which point out these limits and how they were stated in actual life.[116] One of the first candidates of the SUM (then still the Sudan Pioneer Mission) was Hermann Harris, who had previously been a missionary with the failed Central Soudan Mission.[117] Kumm was glad to have him because he spoke Haussa and French, and had been to the Sudan Belt. But since he and his wife had been followers of John Alexander Dowie of Zion, Illinois,[118] who taught that for Christians, faith and prayer would be the only necessary medicines,[119] doubts arose as to his suitability. Kumm was willing to accept him, but Harris was not willing to work with 'missionaries who are not faith healers'.[120]

Among the first group which learned Haussa in Tripolis were Forrest and Shand, both members of Gordon Hall Mission in Aberdeen. Influenced by his mother, Shand began to attend Exclusive Brethren meetings. With great reservation, he signed the 'Principles and Practice' before going to Tripolis.[121] After returning from Tripolis, he formally joined the Exclusive Brethren and ended his career as an SUM missionary.[122]

A similar case can be reported from the British SIM in 1926. Heenan was an adherent of eradicationism, the radical variety of holiness teaching.[123] Because he held the radical version of an otherwise acceptable doctrine, and because of his insistence that he would teach this doctrine, he was rejected by the council.[124]

These three cases are typical: Shand, Harris and Heenan rejected none of the points in the doctrinal statements, and less-extreme varieties of their views were very acceptable in the respective missions. A. B. Simpson taught faith healing, and faith missions had received much of their interdenominationalism from the 'non-church ecclesiology' of the Brethren; also, to see sanctification as the second crisis experience after conversion was common in many a mission. But the missions could not accept the extreme varieties of these teachings. The yardstick to decide what where an extreme was less dogmatic than practical: if a candidate was unable to agree that differing views might be equally true as those he currently held, he was rejected as an extremist who would endanger the unity of the mission.

For faith missions, 'interdenominational' means cooperation of individuals. There are two exceptions:

◇ TEAM, started as 'The Scandinavian Alliance Mission of North America' by Fredrik Franson, sees itself foremost not as coordinating the mission effort of individuals, but of individual congregations, which therefore are represented on the board of TEAM.[125]

◇ Lucy and Karl Kumm intended the SUM to be something like a cooperative effort of the British Free Churches. That effort had limited success, but several churches agreed to nominate one of the sixteen honorary Directors of the SUM.[126] In another aspect, the SUM succeeded: five of its ten branches are denominational branches.[127] Such branches, representing the concept of *corporate* unity, are unique among faith missions.

Early faith missionaries came from very different denominations indeed, but their differences were smaller than the differences between their denominations might suggest, because they all had a common background in the same revival and, very often, belonged to a fellowship of some kind which had arisen from it. Typical of this are Samuel Alexander Bill (Qua Iboe Mission) and John McKittrick (Congo Balolo Mission). Both were, and remained, Presbyterians, but their spiritual home was the (interdenominational) YMCA in Mountpottinger and the (interdenominational) Island Street Mission Hall in Belfast. John Anderson, founder of the Southern Morocco Mission, and its first missionaries, Jessie Nairn and her brother Cuthbert, all came from the Scottish revival and fellowship movement, MRW 'Ayreshire Christian Union'.[128] The Gospel Missionary Union, founded in 1892 as World's Gospel Union for the Evangelization of Neglected Fields,[129] has its roots far more in a revival and fellowship movement, the World's Gospel Union in Kansas, than in the YMCA.[130] Fellowship movements were one result of the revival; other results were 'mission halls' (in Britain), 'missions' (their US equivalent) or 'the Indre Mission' in Scandinavia.[131] All this means that it was not the minimal 'statement of doctrine' which held the faith missionaries together, but a common revival experience and a common piety deriving from that. And, because revivals usually run across denominational boundaries, it is no wonder that faith missions did so, too.

# Interdenominational concepts

faith missions developed an intriguing attitude towards the churches. They avoided all non-denominational concepts, which the Brethren offered. Equally, they refused all offers of integration, whether from denominations or from supra-denominational organizations. They had to do this if they wanted to survive. Non-denominational concepts would have made a faith mission into a new denomination. And integration would have destroyed the concept of individual unity on which faith missions are based. What were the resulting attitudes towards the sacraments and the offices of the church?

## THE DOUBLE CONCEPT OF BAPTISM

Faith missions accepted and ignored the churches at the same time. For faith missions, the limits of the (true) church are not defined by baptism, but by individual faith. Baptism was therefore of secondary importance. By accepting both infant baptism and believers' baptism, they chose to ignore, for example, as much the Anglican concept that baptism can never be repeated as the Baptist conviction that infant baptism is no baptism at all. In addition, they accepted the individual's freedom to change from one position to the other: re-baptism (or believers' baptism of people previously 'baptized' as infants, as others would call it) was a matter of individual spiritual development.[132]

This was the option which many of the early faith mission founders had accepted for themselves: Hudson Taylor was (re-) baptized by the Brethren in Hull.[133] In the early years of the CIM, he may have had some problems reconciling the interdenominational character of the mission with his own views on baptism.[134] After five years' consideration of the issue,[135] Grattan Guinness was baptized as a believer.[136] Although he was baptized in a

183

Baptist chapel,[137] he did not consider that this step made him a Baptist. It was simply a matter of personal obedience in faith.[138] Their children were not baptized as infants.[139] Both founders of the NAM, George Pearse and Edward Glenny, had accepted believers' baptism beforehand.[140] A. B. Simpson who, as a student of Knox College (Canadian Presbyterian Church) had received the John Knox Bursary prize for an essay on infant baptism,[141] was baptized again in 1881. The way his baptism took place was typical of such re-baptisms: the pastor of a little Italian mission church baptized him, but no congregation was present, the only witness being the pastor's wife.[142] In arranging his baptism in this way, he defined the act as being personal and as having no ecclesiological relevance. Though a Baptist baptized him, he did not become a Baptist either in membership or in thinking. In the New York Gospel Tabernacle, which he started the same year, no children would be baptized, but believers' baptism was no more a prerequisite for membership than infant baptism was a hindrance to the subsequent believer's baptism of a member of his church.[143] As Grattan Guinness had done, so did Simpson: he privatized baptism. A. T. Pierson did the same in 1896: he arranged for his baptism by Dr James A. Spurgeon (brother to the 'prince of preachers') in West Croydon Chapel, London, on a Saturday evening, in the presence of a few friends.[144] He remained a Presbyterian, though his presbytery excluded him.[145]

When Fredrik Franson was baptized, he became a real Baptist,[146] although not for long. Meeting Moody and/or his church,[147] made him divest baptism of much of its ecclesiological importance.[148] The Rev. and Mrs Blocher, the pastors of the independent Tabernacle Church in Paris, went less far. In their church baptism was only believers' baptism, but they did not stipulate this for the Mission Biblique (Côte d'Ivoire) which they founded.[149] Edgar Mahon, founder of the Mahon Mission in Zion, Illinois, discussed the issue of baptism during a ride on horseback with his wife's stepbrother. Being convinced, he was baptized as soon as they found enough water at the roadside.[150]

Very few of the faith mission leaders practised infant baptism. Alma Doering was not re-baptized (at least, not during her active missionary carreer),[151] but she cooperated most closely with Mennonites and the Baptist type of 'fundamentalists'.[152] Spencer Walton (SAGM) remained an Anglican, but was never ordained.[153] Héli Chatelin. Ludwig Doll, Neukirchen, did baptize infants, but fervently preached that without conversion baptism was useless.[154]

In theory, believers' baptism and infant baptism were accepted by faith missions as equal. Though there are no statistics available to me, my impression is that the majority of the early faith missionaries were only baptized as children and never re-baptized. This was definitely not true of their leaders. which makes it understandable that, on the mission field, faith missions showed a clear tendency towards believers' baptism. Even in the ranks of the missionaries, there seems to have been a growing prominence, although by no means dominance, of believers' baptism. In many countries, the 'old-line' denominations were in decline while, at the same time, in other countries some fellowship movements turn themselves into Free Churches with a tendency to believers' baptism—a typical case was the Svenska Alliansmissionen.[155] Another reason for this shift was the increasing role of independent congregations, most of which practise believers' baptism.[156]

## THE CONCEPT OF THE DELEGATED LORD'S TABLE

That the Lord's Table can equally well be the expression of Christian unity as of Christian disunity, faith missions may have learned from the history of the Brethren. According to Darby (and in this he held a position shared by the Catholic church and the Anglican church of his time), those who (corporately) agreed in doctrine could share in the Lord's Table, whereas for Müller and, with him, the Independent (Open) Brethren (individual) faith in Christ was the only precondition.[157] Because of their interdenominational character, faith missions placed little practical emphasis on the Lord's Table but, for the same reason, neither could they ignore it. Therefore, they did what so many revival and fellowship movements had done before: they delegated holy communion to the churches. The fellowship movements had done this. Although they often severely criticized these same churches, counting many of their pastors as unbelievers, they still entrusted those pastors with the administration of the sacrament.

In delegating the Lord's Table to the churches, faith missions preserved their unity and effectiveness but, at the same time, accepted (and ignored) doctrines which they were not party to. They were not convinced of the Anglican insistence on apostolic succession, nor of the, then still commonly held, Baptist conviction that only those baptized as believers may share the Lord's

185

Table, nor did they agree to the Lutheran practice of admitting all confirmed Christians to communion, irrespective of their individual faith. Because faith missions were convinced that baptism and confirmation without personal faith do not make a Christian, it would have been logical for them to admit only believers to communion, but the strength of faith missions is that their ecclesiology is *not* logical. They felt it to be more important to put all their efforts into the main job of the church—to reach those without the gospel—rather than to define minor dogmatic points like the sacraments.

## ORDINATION OF THE PIERCED HANDS

None of the early CIM missionaries was ordained. That was typical for the first phase of faith missions. There were several reasons. For someone who had studied so long for the ministry, faith missions seemed to offer little reward, compared to a British benefice. Perhaps more important was the fact that they usually recruited their personnel from groups in which ordination was not as important. Brethren and Quaker did not recognize ordination. Baptists practised ordination but, with them, it conveyed no rights which a 'lay' Baptist did not also have. Moreover, because faith missions tried to utilize neglected forces, it may be assumed that these were usually not ordained.[158] In addition, some of the great evangelists, the shining lights of the revival were never ordained: neither Radcliffe nor Spurgeon, nor Müller nor Moody, nor Major Whittle, who so strongly influenced Pierson and Simpson.

C. T. Studd, who usually did not mince his words, expressed the faith mission attitude thus: 'I have not much faith in any but God's ordination which comes through such channels as He pleases.'[159] A. B. Simpson stated: 'We need no ordination. Ordination by the Holy Spirit is sufficient.'[160] This he said, himself being ordained and also having ordained missionaries.[161] The Southern Morocco Mission, having no ordained missionary, argued from the supremacy of conversion: 'Will those whom God honours in the conversion of souls not be warranted to receiving them into church fellowship? Or would it be better that they should remain in their sins, rather than plan admission into the church of Christ by the hands of unauthorized laymen?'[162]

With all this, it is clear that the missionaries were convinced of having a kind of ordination. One of the favourite hymn verses of one of the founders of the Egypt General Mission read:[163]

> Christ, the Son of God, hath sent me
> Through the midnight lands;
> Mine the mighty ordination
> Of the pierced hands.

The biographer of Spencer Walton uses the same image when he writes of Spencer Walton that he had no ordination except 'the mighty ordination of the pierced hands'.[164]

The verse quoted and alluded to is from a poem on Paul in a volume of poetry featuring mainly German mystical poems.[165] As faith missionaries usually appreciated mysticism, it can be assumed that they appreciated this poem, too. But the poem, signed C.P.C. was written not by a German mystic, but by the editor of the book herself, Frances Bevan.[166] This is perhaps another reason for the appreciation of this poem: Frances Bevan belonged to the Brethren. Through the use of mystical language, she formulates how the Brethren understood ordination: being called by Christ needs no human confirmation, only divine.

Faith missions did not feel human ordination (by men) to be important, but neither did they oppose it, as long a those ordained did not require special treatment. To make sure of this, Hudson Taylor forbade mentioning titles when giving the names of missionaries.[167] Other missions were less reluctant about titles. At times, some may have been glad to gain some respectability by publishing titles. Beyond any need for publicity, however, it was difficult to convince a US railway ticket agent that a missionary who needed no ordination was still entitled to the greatly reduced pastors' fare. Even greater problems arose in certain countries when a missionary was to conduct a wedding. In such a case, even C. T. Studd realized that he was ordained indeed, namely by Moody and Torrey during a Northfield Convention before returning to China.[168] It did not matter to him (nor to the Belgian colonial officers) that Moody himself had repeatedly refused to be ordained [169] nor that Torrey had had a congregational ordination.[170]. When necessary, he even provided two ordinations,[171] the first by Reginald Radcliffe[172], one of the evangelists of the 1859 revival, who also consistantly refused to be ordained.[173]

# A different concept of unity in Africa

In Africa, faith missions could not employ the same concept of the church as they did in Europe or in the United States. Where faith missionaries started their work, there were no denominations for them to accept and to ignore, as was their practice in the West; but neither were there churches to whom they could delegate baptisms, communion and marriages. This meant that faith missions had to develop new concepts of Christian unity. They had to define their unity with neighbouring missions, be they classical or not. This they did by accepting the concept of 'mission comity': unity not by accepting competing ecclesiologies, but by territorial delineation. Every mission, classical or post-classical, had its own area. Whenever work in separate territories approached each other, borders were agreed upon. This was usually done with the support of the colonial administration and sometimes even on its demand.

## UNITY THROUGH GEOGRAPHICAL SEPARATION: COMITY

Comity means mutual acceptance on the condition of organizational separation, which primarily meant geographic separation.[174] Comity was devised to avoid duplication and, by doing so, to evangelize more effectively the many unreached areas of the globe.[175] As soon as the missions had spread into more or less all areas that could be reached, comity served mainly to avoid competition.[176]

Another, but far less important, aspect of comity was unification. Neighbouring missions agreed to employ the same standards for admission to holy communion or for employment as evangelists. Sometimes they agreed to use a common catechism.[177] In Zaire, they even created a common transferable church membership.[178] Often, all this did not happen; comity meant accepting each other's members and not employing any other mission's employee[179] without first receiving that mission's agreement.[180] Sometimes comity also meant cooperation in areas such as Bible translation, education or publishing. Of the three aspects—separation, unification and cooperation—the first was the most important.

For all missions, comity provided many advantages: there was no need to settle theological differences. Each mission could accord equality to the others, but with no need to practise it. Anglicans could recognize the Disciples of Christ's 'sphere of influence' without needing either to accept or to deny the validity of their ordinations. Baptists could admit travelling Anglicans to the Lord's Table, without needing to decide if believers' baptism was really the necessary precondition. Comity made it possible for the various missions to accept theological pluralism, without

# Comity agreements in northern Nigeria

The areas of influence of the Protestant missions in northern Nigeria

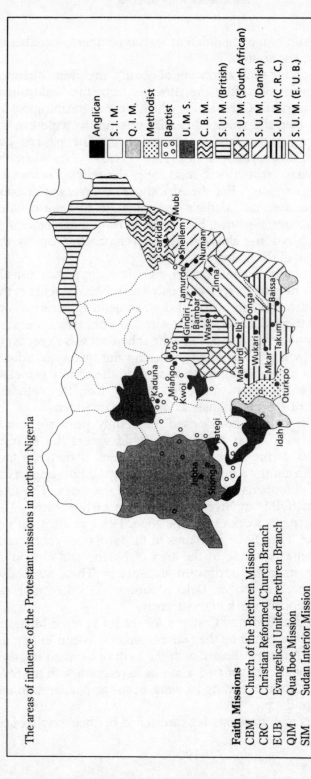

| | |
|---|---|
| ■ | Anglican |
| ☐ | S. I. M. |
| ▨ | Q. I. M. |
| ▨ | Methodist |
| ∘∘∘ | Baptist |
| ● | U. M. S. |
| ⩗ | C. B. M. |
| ‖ | S. U. M. (British) |
| ⊠ | S. U. M. (South African) |
| ⫽ | S. U. M. (Danish) |
| ‖‖ | S. U. M. (C. R. C.) |
| ╱ | S. U. M. (E. U. B.) |

**Faith Missions**

| | |
|---|---|
| CBM | Church of the Brethren Mission |
| CRC | Christian Reformed Church Branch |
| EUB | Evangelical United Brethren Branch |
| QIM | Qua Iboe Mission |
| SIM | Sudan Interior Mission |
| SUM | Sudan United Mission |
| UMS | United Missionary Society |

(The United Missionary Society is a denominational evangelical mission which started as a faith mission.)

Source: Edmund P. T. Crampton, *Christianity in Northern Nigeria*, London, ? 1979 (1975), p. 148.

feeling the pain of having different and sometimes contradictory theologies in *one* church.

As a reason for such a concept of comity, the pious intention was often given of saving the Africans from the 'unfortunate divisions' of western Christianity, which were so meaningless for Africans. In fact, the result of comity was not to wipe out the divisions for Africans but to cement them. The pattern had already been employed after the Thirty Years' War, when the Augsburg Peace Treaty ruled: *cuius regio, eius religio* ('whose the land, his the religion'). For the Africans, of course, the division was not quite absolute, as their denomination was not decided upon by a territorial prince, but by the territorial agreements of the various missions, although these were backed up by the worldly rulers of the country.

For the colonial administrators, mission comity was usually convenient—helping to spread evenly such social benefits of the missions as schools and hospitals. But, sometimes, it turned out to be counter-productive for the Africans concerned, because when a mission refused to provide the schools it was expected to establish or when it was slack in raising the quality of education.[181] Sometimes the administration used the comity principle in a way the Protestant missions did not like, by including Catholics[182] or even Muslims—as happened in Sudan.[183]

Faith missions had not devised the comity principle, but it suited them well. As at home, they could accept the existing churches and, at the same time, ignore them. If they ran into problems with comity it was not because they did not support the principle.[184] Problems with comity were local ones. The Qua Iboe Mission (QIM) in Nigeria provides an early example. The QIM had started its work east of the Niger Delta, at the mouth of the Qua Iboe. The QIM saw claims of Bishop James Johnson of the Niger Delta Pastorate to the area of Essene and Opobo as endangering its own northward expansion. They were also convinced that the Niger Delta Pastorate[185] would not do effective missionary work in those areas.[186]

The American Board of Commissioners for Foreign Missions in Egypt felt threatened by the Sudan-Pionier-Mission in Aswan. In 1913, the American Board, with the help of German missiologist Julius Richter, negotiated a comity agreement with the SPM which kept it from extending its work from the Nubian into the Arabic area of Egypt.[187]

Sometimes faith missions felt threatened by their neighbours.

# Comity borders prescribed by the colonial government

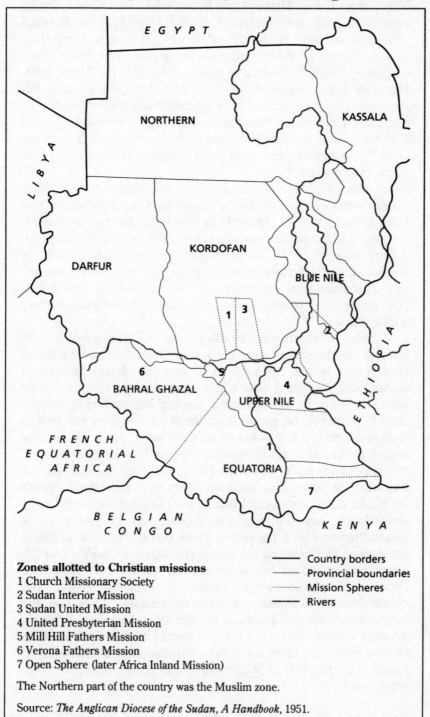

**Zones allotted to Christian missions**
1 Church Missionary Society
2 Sudan Interior Mission
3 Sudan United Mission
4 United Presbyterian Mission
5 Mill Hill Fathers Mission
6 Verona Fathers Mission
7 Open Sphere (later Africa Inland Mission)

The Northern part of the country was the Muslim zone.

Source: *The Anglican Diocese of the Sudan, A Handbook*, 1951.

The Congo Balolo Mission had little problem signing a comity agreement with the similar Mission Évangélique de l'Ubangi (Evangelical Free Church of America),[188] but it had problems in reaching an agreement with the less similar Disciples of Christ Congo Mission.[189] The same year, 1893, that the Niger Delta Pastorate felt threatened by the QIM, the QIM in turn felt threatened by a newcomer, the Primitive Methodist Mission. It had started its work on the coast between the QIM and the United Free Church of Scotland, and had spread northwards faster then QIM,[190] thus effectively limiting the Qua Iboe Mission to the area south of Umuahia.[191]

In spite of local problems here and there, neither faith missions nor classical missions questioned the comity principle before World War 2. Unlike faith missions, some non-denominational and pentecostal missions were not willing to enter into comity agreements (for example, in Burundi—see map). Zaire, in particular, with its plurality of classical missions, faith missions, non-denominational missions and denominational evangelical and pentecostal missions, had an extremely well-functioning comity system.[192]

Comity, although well-meaning, was full of paternalism. It divided people into two groups: one for whom centuries of church history had not sufficed to sort out certain theological issues, and another group which must be spared these same problems—not by the missions solving the problems, but by shielding the second group from them. The African reaction to the comity principle was not always the same, but it was usually negative. Africans gladly availed themselves of the positive aspects, for example, when travelling. But they did not like the idea that, in any given location, only one Protestant church should be allowed to exist. Equally, the missions were not happy about losing any followers who moved into the towns to the denomination which happened to be there first. This problem was solved by declaring the big towns 'open territory' in which every mission could follow its church members to look after them.[193] The missionaries believed in religious freedom, but comity denied complete freedom to Africans. They had the freedom to become Christians or not. Often they could choose between Catholic or Protestant. But comity made it impossible to choose between Protestant denominations—unless they moved house to the territory of the church of their choice or moved into a big town.

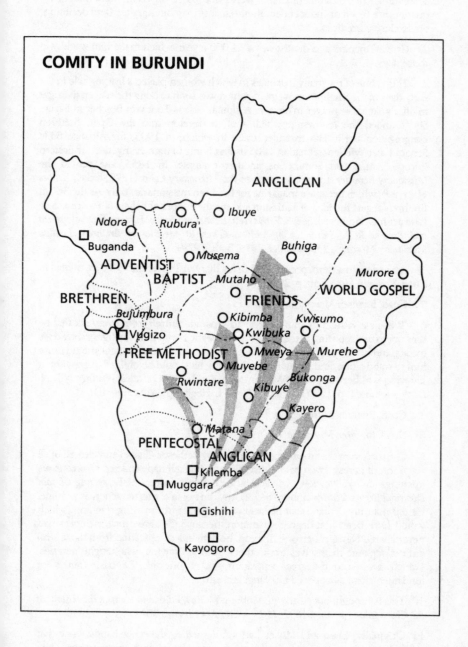

## COMITY IN BURUNDI

ANGLICAN

Ndora
Rubura
Ibuye

Buganda

Buhiga

ADVENTIST

Musema

BAPTIST

Mutaho

Murore

BRETHREN

WORLD GOSPEL

FRIENDS

Bujumbura

Kibimba

Kwisumo

Vugizo

Kwibuka

FREE METHODIST

Murehe

Mweya

Muyebe

Bukonga

Rwintare

Kibuye

Kayero

Matana

PENTECOSTAL

ANGLICAN

Kilemba

Muggara

Gishihi

Kayogoro

**Notes**

1 Estimate of overall membership worldwide, based on WCE. More than three-quarters are Open or Independent Brethren, less than one-quarter (and declining) are Exclusive Brethren.

2 Groves' income as a dentist was a £1,000 a year, which made him wealthy in those days.

3 This is one of the many instances in which women played a leading role in the early days of the Brethren movement, which was soon to deny them even the right to offer an audible prayer in church. A similar case is Toni von Blücher in Berlin. She founded the fellowship which was to develop into the Open Brethren congregation Berlin-Hohenstaufenstraße in which, in 1905, the Alliance Bible School (later Wiedenest) had in 1905 its first home to train evangelists for Eastern Europe. Annie van Sommer is another example. In 1853, she started the *Missionary Reporter*, the predecessor of the *Missionary Echo* (1872; today, *Echoes of Service*), which became a magazine for Brethren missionaries only. As the British Brethren negate the idea of a mission society, the editors of *Echoes of Service* as a *de facto* act mission board. See: S. F. Warren, *Echoes of Service. Historical Development and Present Role. Substance of Address Given at Meeting of Brethren, London Missionary Meetings, 25th October, 1979*, Bath, 1979.

4 According to a retrospective note in his diary of 14 December 1833, quoted in Coad, *Brethren Movement*, p. 20.

5 Coad, *Brethren Movement*, p. 23.

6 'It is clearly the duty of a believer to separate himself from every act that he sees not to be according to the word though bearing with him who ignorantly does the act, and his duty requires this of him, even though his faithfulness should cause him to stand alone, and though, like Abraham, he should be obliged to go without knowing whither he goes.' (William Kelly (ed.), *The Collected Writings of J. N. Darby*, volume I, p. 153 (Reprint 1971, H. L. Heijkoop, Winschoten)).

7 Coad, *Brethren Movement*, p. 140.

8 Coad, *Brethren Movement*, p. 154f.

9 The three new members were examined by Bethesda Chapel and cleared of all suspicion of heresy. Even before that, Newton himself had retracted all erroneous teachings: B. W. Newton, *A Statement and Acknowledgement Respecting Certain Doctrinal Errors*, 26 November 1847. Darby did not take this retraction as genuine. He did not only demand that Bethesda not separate from wrong teaching (which would have been first-degree separation, because the three new members had never shared Newton's errors). Instead, he demanded separation from those who did not separate themselves from others, such as Newton, who taught 'heresies' (which was second-degree separation, today one of the basic tenets of fundamentalism as opposed to evangelicalism).

10 This is brought out clearly in: Mohra J. McKay, *Faith and Facts in the History of the China Inland Mission 1832–1905*, MLitt, Aberdeen, 1981.

11 Originally, Craik and Müller had subscribed to the strict Baptist view that infant baptism can never be sufficient grounds for church membership. They changed their practice in 1837, basing their decision on 2 Thessalonians 3:6. The

example of the apostles 'would be an unsurmountable difficulty had not the truth been mingled with error for so long a time, so that it does not prove wilful disobedience if any in our day should refuse to be baptized after believing' (Coad, *Brethren Movement*, p. 123).

12 'With regard to my denominational views: at first I joined the Wesleyan Methodists, as my parents and friends were members of that body. But not being able to reconcile the late proceedings with the doctrines and precepts of Holy Scripture, I withdrew, and am at present united to the branch Society' (Hudson Taylor—George Pearse, 25 April 1851. The full text in: Geraldine and Howard Taylor, *Hudson Taylor in Early Years. The Growth of a Soul*, London, 1911, pp. 101–104 (especially p. 104) ).

13 Geraldine and Howard Taylor, *Hudson Taylor in Early Years*, p. 112. In those days, the Brethren met in York Street, then in Foundry Hall, then in Heelis Street, today in Mottram Hall (Mottram Hall, *25th Anniversary 1963*; James Marshall—Fiedler, 9 November 1990).

14 Broomhall, *Over the Treaty Wall*, p. 42.

15 Geraldine and Howard Taylor, *Hudson Taylor in Early Years*, pp. 115–118. For the history of the congregation, see: *Brook Street Chapel Tottenham, N17 1839–1989*. Sometimes it is argued that Hudson Taylor was in contact with the Brethren but never joined them. This misunderstanding is due to the fact that the Brethren as a non-church movement know no official church membership. Membership in a local assembly is defined by living in a given locality and being admitted to the breaking of bread. Both applied to Taylor (Coad, *Brethren Movement*, p. 76). Hudson Taylor shared in the Lord's Table in Brook Street Chapel, although his name was not entered into the list of 'Members in Communion at Brook Street Tottenham' (J. E. Frost, Tottenham—Fiedler, 1 November 1990).

16 For the origins of that assembly and for its Quaker background, see: Coad, *Brethren Movement*, p. 76.

17 McKay, *Faith and Facts*, p. 105. Reports in the journal *Revival*. See: Broomhall, *Survivors' Pact*, p. 76.

18 The Brethren usually did not accept mission societies, but the CIM was an exception (Cecil P. Williams, *The Recruitment and Training of Overseas Missionaries in England Between 1850 and 1900*, MLitt, Bristol, 1977, p. 185).

19 Decisive financial support again and again came from George Müller through his Scriptural Knowledge Institution. Berger, Barnardo, Lord Radstock, Pearse and the Soltaus were Brethren. McKay, *Faith and Facts*, pp. 259–295 checks on the denominational background of early CIM supporters and comes to the conclusion that Brethren, Anglicans and Baptists (in this order) provided the lion's share of support (p. 290f.).

20 He kept his membership there even when he later lived in other parts of London (A. J. Broomhall—Moira McKay, 31 July 1988; Broomhall, *If I Had a Thousand Lives*, p. 248f.).

21 Arthur Guinness, Grattan Guinness' grandfather and founder of the famous brewery, was influenced by Methodism but remained a faithful member of the Anglican Church. Grattan's father, Captain John Guinness, was converted in India and met his second wife, Jane Lucretia d'Esterre, in the Methodist York Street

Chapel in Dublin, where their son Grattan was baptized as an infant (Michele Guinness—Fiedler, 29 February 1988).

22  He was no success there (Michele Guinness, *The Guinness Legend*, p. 55f.).

23  Holmes, *The Cloud Moves*, p. 10.

24  As a young child, she had been adopted by Mary and Arthur West, who were Quakers (Lucy Guinness, *Enter Thou*, p. 8f.).

25  In those years, many Quakers became Brethren (Timothy C. F. Stunt, *Early Brethren and the Society of Friends*, Pinner, 1970, Christian Brethren Research Fellowship Occasional Paper No. 3).

26  They married in the Quaker Meeting House in Bath, but soon joined a Brethren assembly (Michele Guinness—Fiedler, 29 February 1988).

27  Michele Guinness—Fiedler, 29 February 1988.

28  Michele Guinness, *The Guinness Legend*, p. 83.

29  By 1880 at the latest, in his inner struggle with Brethren concepts, he came to a conclusion, which he formulated as an entry in his study Bible. I thank Michele Guinness for this information and for a copy of that entry.

30  Annie Reed and Harry Guinness were married there in 1887 (Mackintosh, *Harry Guinness*, p. 29). Dana L. Robert's statement, that Fanny and Grattan Guinness were 'prominent English Baptists' ('The Legacy of Adoniram Judson Gordon' in *IBMR*, October 1987, pp. 176–181 (p. 177), is, at least, misleading. The East London Tabernacle left the Baptist Union on 28 October 1887, the same day as Spurgeon's Metropolitan Tabernacle.

31  Grattan Guinness had met Thomas Barnardo for the first time in Merrion Street Brethren Assembly in Dublin (Michele Guinness—Fiedler, 29 February 1988).

32  Harry, Lucy and Geraldine were baptized there in 1873 (Kenneth Holmes, *The Cloud Moves*, p. 21). Harry (born 2 October 1861) was twelve years old, Lucy was nine and Geraldine was seven (Wargenau-Saillens, *Ruben et Jeanne Saillens*, p. 66).

33  The standard biographies, Thompson, *The Life of A. B. Simpson* and Tozer, *Wingspread*, (a kind of hagiography) which, over the years, were increasingly felt to be insufficient, have now been superseded by the reliable and well-written: Niklaus, Sawin and Stoesz, *All For Jesus*. For a thorough and scholarly treatment of his theology, see: David F. Hartzfeld and Charles Nienkirchen, *The Birth of a Vision. Essays by Members of the Faculty of Canadian Bible College and the Faculty of Canadian Theological Seminary Regina, Saskatchewan, the Official College and Seminary of The Christian and Missionary Alliance in Canada on the Occasion of the Centennial of the Christian and Missionary Alliance 1887–1987*, Regina, 1986.

34  Niklaus, Sawin and Stoesz, *All for Jesus*, pp. 52ff. Earlier, he had already worked for world mission by publishing the illustrated missionary magazine *The Gospel in All Lands* (*All for Jesus*, pp. 36–39).

35  Sheetz, *The Sovereign Hand*, p. 17.

36  For a study of Moody's concept of the church, see: Stan Nussbaum, 'D. L. Moody and the Church: a Study of the Ecclesiological Implications of Extra-Ecclesiastical Evangelism', MA, Deerfield, 1973. It is very likely that the Chicago

Avenue Church was the first independent and interdenominational church in the United States (Edvard Torjesen—Fiedler, 11 March 1988). For its history, see: Flood, *The Story of Moody Church.*. This informative book shows harmonizing tendencies. So the drastic change from holiness movement (Rader) to the Brethren movement and historic fundamentalism (Ironside) is not noted clearly enough.

37  Torjesen, *A Study of Fredrik Franson*, p. 79f.

38  Hunter, *A Flame of Fire*, p. 39; pp. 43ff.

39  Bingham, *Seven Sevens of Years*, p. 106.

40  John Salmon, neglected by historians, was the founder of the CMA in Canada (Lindsay Reynolds, *Footprints. The Beginnings of The Christian and Missionary Alliance in Canada*, Toronto, 1981).

41  Lindsay Reynolds, *Footprints*, pp. 179–182.

42  Lindsay Reynolds, *Footprints*, p. 106.

43  Bingham, *Seven Sevens of Years*, p. 109. He became convinced 'that minor differences of denominations afforded no basis for separation in our work'.

44  Richardson, *Garden of Miracles*, pp. 21, 23.

45  Richardson, *Garden of Miracles*, p. 24. It was the exception that Simpson ordained a missionary before he left. This ordination must mean that Scott either joined the independent New York Gospel Tabernacle, or at least shared its convictions. There are no documents available about his ordination in the CMA. On the side effects of ordinations within the interdenominational fellowship movement CMA, see: Reynolds, *Footprints*, pp. 164–167.

46  Richardson, *Garden of Miracles*, p. 43.

47  This is brought out very clearly by *Hearing and Doing*, 1896– 1900.

48  On 14 June 1900, he wrote this letter of recommendation for Hurlbert: 'Mr Charles E. Hurlbert, who is connected with the Africa Inland Mission and intimately known by me, and has my entire confidence. The mission he superintends is in my judgment based on sound scriptural and apostolic principles. Its foundations are laid in Holy Scripture, the atonement, and the work of the blessed Spirit. It is a work of faith and prayer. I can heartily commend it to all friends of mission, and believers in Christ our Lord, as worthy to enlist sympathy and prayer, and as offering a fit opportunity to invest consecrated gifts for the purpose of carrying out our Lord's great command.' (Reprinted in facsimile on the cover of *Hearing and Doing*, July–September 1911, commemorating Pierson's death). Pierson advised Hurlbert when he reorganized the AIM after Scott's death and drafted the AIM's doctrinal statement (p. 7).

49  In the official history of the Church of the Open Door (Michael Cocoris, *70 Years on Hope Street. A History of the Church of the Open Door 1915–1985*, Los Angeles, Glendora, 1985) Hurlbert is not mentioned, but he was indeed a member of this church: Church of the Open Door (Dianne Elyse Enderby)—Fiedler, 5 October 1987.

50  The work of the UAM was overshadowed by severe personality problems throughout all the years of its existence. In 1945, it became the first field of the Conservative Baptist Foreign Mission Society which had been founded the

previous year (N. N., *Founded on the Word, Focused on the World. The Story of the Conservative Baptist Foreign Mission Society*, Wheaton, 1978, p. 77).

51 His biographies are: J. Kennedy Maclean, *Dr Pierson and His Message*, London, n.d. (1911); Delavan Leonard Pierson, *Arthur T. Pierson. A Biography by His Son*, London, 1912. See: Dana L. Robert, ' "The Crisis of Missions": Premillennial Missions Theory and the Origins of Independent Evangelical Missions' in Carpenter and Shenk, *Earthen Vessels*, pp. 29–46.

52 From 1879 to 1881, A. B. Simpson was pastor of this congregation, which he left to start an evangelistic Tabernacle congregation.

53 Pierson, *Arthur T. Pierson*, p. 72f.

54 Pierson, *Arthur T. Pierson*, pp. 127ff.

55 Maclean, *Dr Pierson and His Message*, pp. 13–21; Pierson, *Arthur T. Pierson* pp. 226–251.

56 The Metropolitan Tabernacle had its origins in the Baptist Union. But even while still a member, it acted quite independently, for example, by starting its own pastors' seminary. On 28 October 1887, the Tabernacle left the Baptist Union in the wake of the 'down-grade controversy'. See: *C. H. Spurgeon's Autobiography*, Volume IV, pp. 253–264.

57 He had intended to be baptized by his Brethren friend George Müller, but was baptized on 1 February 1896 by Dr James Spurgeon, Charles Haddon Spurgeon's brother, in West Croydon Chapel, because he felt that he should not delay any longer this act of obedience. He was baptized on a Saturday in the presence of a few friends (Pierson, *Arthur T. Pierson*, p. 263).

58 He could not agree to the then standard Baptist position that believers' baptism was a precondition for being admitted to the Lord's table (Pierson, *Arthur T. Pierson*, p. 269).

59 This was also the case with A. B. Simpson, who was baptized by a Baptist, but never became one. Pierson also was not baptized in a Sunday service, contrary to normal Baptist practice.

60 Arthur T. Pierson, *George Müller of Bristol*, London, 61901.

61 Roger Steer, *George Müller. Delighted in God*, London, 1975, p. 101.

62 *MRW* editorial, No. 1, 1888. Wilder had been a missionary to India who had to retire for health reasons.

63 Starting in January 1884, p. 52, *MRW* regularly reports about 'Independent Foreign Missions and Missionaries'. Roberts, 'The Crisis of Missions', p. 32f.

64 In 1850, George Pearse was one of the founders of the Chinese Evangelization Society, which sent Hudson Taylor to China in 1854. The CIM still keeps the CES archives.

65 Coad, *Brethren Movement*, p. 166.

66 Steele, *Not in Vain*, p. 18.

67 Steele, *Not in Vain*, p. 15.

68 Bertha Polnick, *Carl Polnick. Ein Lebensbild*, Barmen, 1920, pp. 17–19; *50*

*Jahre Allianz-China-Mission*, Barmen, p. 11. The fellowship (then called Christlicher Missionsverein, Seifenstraße) joined the Bund Freier evangelischer Gemeinden in 1924 (Gärtner, 1924, p. 429 (Dirk Stechulat—Fiedler)).

69 Diary entry 19 January 1872 (the context shows that it was 19 February 1872) in Weeks, *W. Spencer Walton*, p. 7. He most probably joined the Brixton Hall Assembly, where he followed the Bible teaching of the famous Dr Cronin.

70 Weeks, *W. Spencer Walton*, p. 7.

71 Weeks, *W. Spencer Walton*, p. 23. A contemporary announcement reads: 'Among other reasons he desires not to confine himself to one branch of Christ's Church, but to take up general and undenominational mission work.'

72 Vincent, *C. T. Studd and Priscilla*, p. 123f. Amy Carmichael and the local Anglican vicar were present.

73 Application form in the AIM-UK archives.

74 Lucy Kumm, while living in Castleton, most probably attended free church worship (Michele Guinness—Fiedler, 22 April 1989).

75 Lucy died from diabetes at the age of fourteen.

76 Cleverdon, *Pools on the Glowing Sand*, pp. 152, 156.

77 In 1906, the Defenseless Mennonites agreed to staff Matara as an AIM station for five years. In 1911, the Defenseless Mennonites sold their station to the AIM (*HD* April–December 1910, p. 14).

78 This information is not necessarily correct. When she had become too old to be UTM's travelling secretary, she retired and started the D + D (Doering and Dunkelberger) Missionary Home in St Petersburg, FL, 1955–57. She regularly attended the Gospel Tabernacle, whose pastor was Edwin Drew, founder of the interdenominational China Boat Mission. Then she was a member of the independent Community Baptist Church. She died a member of Elyria Independent Baptist Church in Elyria OH. This may imply that later in her life she was (re-)baptized (Louisa Howard—Fiedler, 30 September 1988). Pastor of Elyria Baptist Church for many years was Dr Ralph Neighbor, whose widow then worked for the publishing house of Beatenberg Bible School in Switzerland.

79 Interview Louise Howard, 21 February 1986.

80 Chatelin's letter of 23 March 1885 in Chatelin, *Héli Chatelin*, p. 67.

81 'Je vois clairement que je ne puis, sans grand sacrifice, être membre actif d'aucune dénomination, et que mon influence doit se faire valoir surtout en faveur de l'évangélisation non-confessionelle' ['I see clearly that I cannot, without great sacrifice, be an active member of any denomination, and that my influence must tend above all to the support of non-confessional evangelism.'] (Héli Chatelin— Chatelin, 8 October 1887, in Chatelin, *Héli Chatelin*).

82 Chatelin, *Héli Chatelin*, p. 137.

83 The church as such did not take him up on the offer, but Reformed Christians largely took responsibility for the Swiss side of the mission, though the mission remained interdenominational.

84 Doll had met George Müller in spring 1877 during his visit to Rhenania

(Affeld, *Er mache uns im Glauben kühn*, p. 9). On 27 August 1882, Müller preached the sermon in the parish church at the opening of the mission seminary, and in the afternoon he gave a lecture (p. 11).

85 For his life, see: Brandl, 'Ludwig Doll. Der Gründer der ersten deutschsprachigen Glaubensmission' in *Evangelikale Missiologie*, 1988, pp. 41–46. Bernd Brandl is presently working on a dissertation on the history of Neukirchen Mission for ETF Heverlee/Leuven.

86 This is shown by the fact that he counselled the leaders of a revival in the Biedenkopf area to attempt to conserve the fruits of the revival by aiming at the establishment of Free Evangelical Churches (*Missions- und Heidenbote*, 1928, p. 269f.).

87 'Many of those who joined the society lived in a sort of spiritual no-man's land. Their spiritual inspiration came less from the orthodox churches than from the experiences of the revival and, later, of the Holiness movement. Denominational membership... often involved a transdenominational movement, with membership of the Brethren playing some part' (Williams, *Recruitment and Training*, p. 185).

88 Lucy Guinness married the Lutheran Karl Kumm. The Brethren were too narrow for her (Lucy Guinness, 1883 diary). Harry and Annie Guinness joined the Church of England after their marriage. In 1903, Grattan Guinness married Grace Hurditch, his junior by forty-one years, daughter of Charles Russel Hurditch, one of the Brethren leaders (Michele Guinness, *The Guinness Legend* pp. 247ff.; see: Coad, *Brethren Movement*, pp. 169–181). After a trip around the world to visit former ELTI students, they joined the Church of England in Bath, where their two sons, John Christopher (20 July 1906) and Paul (8 May 1908) were baptized as infants (Michele Guinness—Fiedler 29 Feb,ruary 1988).

89 In this context, it should be recalled that Hudson Taylor was an independent missionary before he founded CIM. Likewise, Héli Chatelin, Rowland Bingham and others were independent missionaries earlier in their careers. Several faith missions started as independent missions, for example, the Qua Iboe Mission and the Angola Evangelical Mission. Others, such as the early CMA, had independent tendencies.

90 Information in brackets denote influences, often coupled with active participation but without formal membership, the original denominational affiliation being retained.

91 This basic *concept* of unity does not exclude, but includes organizational cooperation where it is deemed useful.

92 Possible formulas are: 'A union effort of Christians of all denominations' (*The Missionary Witness*, March 1914); or: 'The basis of the Congo Balolo Mission is interdenominational, simply Christian and thoroughly evangelical. Members of any of the evangelical churches are welcomed as workers in it' (Fanny Guinness, *The New World of Central Africa*, p. 483).

93 A typical statement of this can be found in the 1973–74 *Catalogue of the Canadian Prairie Bible Institute* (p. 11): 'The School is denominationally unrelated, yet it is definitely not antidenominational... [The students] prefer the whole undivided body to any one division thereof, while yet remaining warmhearted

members of their particular denomination.'

94 Gary R. Corwin, 'Evangelical Separatism and the Growth of Independent Mission Boards 1920–1945. Some Preliminary Observations From the History of the Sudan Interior Mission', Preliminary Paper, 1986, p. 9f. (based on questionnaires sent to retired SIM missionaries) indicates that sixteen out of 121 SIM missionaries who responded to the questionnaire had left a classical church and joined Baptist or independent congregations while being members of SIM. Corwin did not look into the important question if the missionaries changed their denominational allegiance while in active service or after retirement. His findings seem to be representative for the United States, but the rate for Europe is probably lower.

95 Norman P. Grubb—Alfred Ruscoe, 22 November 1940: '. . . that we boldly stand with all denominations as a unifying force and up-to-date attempt to complete the task of worldwide evangelization'.

96 There is no detailed study yet on the financing of faith missions. For some historical information, see: Moira J. McKay, 'Faith and Facts. Mainly Based on Questionnaires Sent to American Faith Missions' in Eileen Sauer, *The Dynamics Affecting Faith Mission Finance*, MA, Columbia Bible College, 1969.

97 'I wish with all my heart, that every one who loves our Lord Jesus Christ in sincerity, would in some way or other engage in it. But in the present divided state of Christendom, it would be more likely for good to be done by each denomination engaging separately in the work, than if they were to embark in it conjointly' (Carey, *An Enquiry*, p. 84).

98 'As the union of God's People of various Denominations, in carrying on this great Work, is a most desirable Object, so, to prevent, if possible, any cause of future dissention, it is declared to be a fundamental principle of the Missionary Society, that our design is not to send Presbyterianism, Independency, Episcopacy, or any other form of Church Order or Government (about which there may be differences of opinion among serious Persons), but the Glorious Gospel of the blessed God to the Heathen: and that it shall be left (as it ever ought to be left) to the minds of the Persons whom God may call into the fellowship of His Son from among them to assume for themselves such form of Church Government, as to them shall appear most agreeable to the Word of God' (Minutes LMS, 9 May 1796, in Richard Lovett, *The History of the London Missionary Society 1795–1895*, London, 1899, p. 49f.).

99 See: W. H. Willis—Lovett, 12 February 1895 in Lovett, *The History of the London Missionary Society*, volume I, p. 802.

100 Casalis—A. Saillens, 18 October 1870; A. Saillens—Casalis, 20 October 1872; Wargenau-Saillens, *Ruben et Jeanne Saillens*, p. 57.

101 Stacy R. Warburton, Ostwärts! Die Lebensgeschichte von Adoniram Judson, St Gallen, 1947, p. 84f.

102 Williams, *Recruitment and Training*, p. 154.

103 Geraldine and Howard Taylor, *Hudson Taylor*, p. 416. See: Bacon, *From Faith to Faith*, p. 54.

104 Walter Gowans was a Presbyterian (his sister was a CMA missionary in Beijing

(*Sixth Annual Report International Missionary Alliance*, 11 October 1893)), Tom Kent was a Congregationalist. Bingham himself was a former Salvation Army member, who felt strongly attracted by the teachings of the Brethren (Bingham, *Seven Sevens of Years*, p. 106), presently working as 'pastoral assistant' in the independent (CMA related) Bethany Chapel in Toronto.

105 For some representative statements of faith, see Appendix.

106 The first CIM 'Principles and Practice' were written 2 February 1866 on board the *Lammermuir* by three of the male members of the party. They became valid in May 1867 after being signed by all (McKay, *Faith and Facts*, p. 140).

107 CIM, *Principles and Practice*, 1885.

108 Evangelical Alliance, *Minutes of the Proceedings of the Conference, held at Freemasons' Hall, London, August 19th, and following days*, London, n.d. (1846), pp. 122, 125, 128, 152, 169, 183ff.

109 'We many of us hold the view so strongly advocated by Dr Pierson "that the distinction of clerical and lay is Anti-Scriptural, Romish and from the Devil". Nevertheless, most of us believe in ordination, and not a few are ordained.' (CIM archives K 128 quoted by McKay, p. 121).

110 The largest of these missions is SUM.

111 For example, Mortenson, *This is TEAM*, p. 47).

112 In the many primary sources, I have not come across a rejection of a missionary candidate because of too liberal views.

113 South Africa General Mission, *Statement of Position*, February 1903.

114 A fair treatment of both positions, written from a Calvinist point of view, is: David N. Steele and Curtis C. Thomas, *The Five Points of Calvinism Defined, Defended, Documented*, Philadelphia, 1963. On pp. 16–19, both positions are contrasted point by point.

115 Gundry, *Love Them In*, p. 143. This statement fits Moody's theology well, but up to now no primary source has been found to prove its authenticity. L. E. Maxwell, founder of Prairie Bible Institute, taught that the 'Arminian' and the 'Calvinist' texts expressed different aspects of the same truth, conditioned by the fact that the various letters of the New Testament were written to answer concrete problems (L. E. Maxwell, *Prairie Pillars*, Three Hills, 1971, p. 54). Even the Africa Evangelistic Band, with its strong roots in the holiness movement, did not make Arminianism obligatory: 'In any case, young people preaching all over the country having had only two years in a Bible College are not expected to be theologians. Their desire is that souls get saved—be it Calvinistically or Methodistically' (Colin N. Peckham, *The Africa Evangelistic Band. An Historical and Doctrinal Appraisal*, Dipl.Th., Johannesburg, 1973, p. 176).

116 Minutes SUM, 2 November 1903.

117 The Central Soudan Mission was supported by the (holiness) pentecostal League. Kumm derided their attempt to reach the Sudan from Tripolis and across the Sahara as dreamy ['schwärmerisch und phantastisch'] (Minutes Sudan-Pionier-Mission, 25 October 1900).

118 His biography, written from a charismatic point of view, is: Gordon Lindsay,

*John Alexander Dowie. A Life Story of Trials, Tragedies and Triumphs*, Dallas, 1980. See: Hollenweger, *Enthusiastisches Christentum*, pp. 124–130. Lindsay also published Dowie's sermons: *Champion of Faith. The Sermons of John Alexander Dowie*, compiled and edited by Gordon Lindsay, Dallas, n.d. The most important primary sources are the relevant volumes of 'Leaves of Healing'.

119 Members of congregations going back to Dowie frequently report that their parents or other members of that generation moved to Zion after experiencing extraordinary healings in answer to prayer (Interview Grant Sisson, 30 March 1986).

120 Minutes SUM, 2 November 1903 and additional note. Harries applied to the Colonial Service for work in Nigeria; later, he applied again to the SUM, but was rejected.

121 He was afraid that his signature would bind him to men instead of to Christ alone, who had called him to the Sudan (Minutes, 17 March 1904).

122 Minutes Seventh English Council of SUM, 17 June 1904.

123 The holiness movement is discussed in detail in the next chapter.

124 '... he said he believed in the complete eradication of the old nature, and that this had taken place in his own experience, and further, if accepted he would teach this' (Minutes SIM-UK 1926, p. 39). It is interesting that the rejection was not unanimous (p. 40). Bingham, present on a visit from Canada, agreed to the rejection, but pressed the point that such a rejection must not be automatic (p. 41). Heenan had been trained at Birkenhead, the Bible school founded by the holiness evangelist Drysdale, which trained numerous WEC missionaries during those years.

125 Mortenson, *This is TEAM*, p. 22. Thus, TEAM is one of the very few faith missions in which local churches have a *legal* position. See: Article II of the constitution: '... to form a missionary agency representing [local] churches, societies, and individuals'.

126 The Anglican Church, having through the CMS its own mission in the Sudan, was not asked to nominate an honorary director. But Anglicans played their part in SUM leadership, most notably Prebendary Webb-Peploe, a Keswick leader.

127 The interdenominational branches are: Great Britain, South Africa, Australia/ New Zealand, Switzerland and France. The denominational branches are: Denmark, Norway (part of Norske Missionsselskab), Christian Reformed Church (United States), Netherlands Reformed Congregations and United Methodists (United States) (*The S.U.M. 75th Jubilee 1904–1979*, London, 1979).

128 Steele, *Not in Vain*, 1981, p. 126. Anderson was ACU's first president. In 1892–1914, he was Principal of Glasgow Bible Training Institute (p. 127). For the history of BTI, there is only: Glasgow United Evangelistic Association, *Christ in the City 1871–1974*, Glasgow, 1974, pp. 6–11.

129 R. J. Reinmiller, 'Gospel Missionary Union, Smithville, Missouri. Early History', unpublished, 1964. (1) The WGU's magazine was *The Gospel Message*. George S. Fisher was secretary until he died in 1920. In 1901, the name was changed to Gospel Missionary Union. (2) A. E. Bishop was president. R. A. Torrey of Moody Bible Institute was vice-president. For a full list of office bearers, see: *The Gospel Message*, 1893, p. 2.

130'The movement was the outcome of the special work of grace in gospel and missionary lines carried on by the YMCA in Kansas and the West from 1888 to 1891, and which was so strongly condemned and fought by the International Committee and other prominent leaders in the association work' (*The Gospel Union' in The Gospel Message* October 1893, p. 910 (9)).

131See: Joel A. Carpenter, 'Propagating the Faith Once Delivered: The Fundamentalist Mission Enterprise, 1920–1945' in Carpenter and Schenk, *Earthen Vessels*, pp. 92–132 (pp. 117–122).

132A most impressive example of such a (re-)baptism may have been that of Malla Moe, who was baptized together with her first convert, John (Mapelepele) Gamede. She changed her theology of baptism after leaving the United States. But this had no ecclesiologial consequences for her and she worked all the years happily with missionaries who held their infant baptism to be valid (Nilsen and Sheetz, *Malla Moe*, p. 67).

133Instrumental in Taylor's change of conviction was Andrew Jukes, a former Anglican deacon who had joined the Brethren in Hull, but who later left them to form his own congregation there. Hudson Taylor was baptized in the Hull Brethren Assembly in 1852. He convinced his sister Amelia of the need for believers' baptism and actually baptized her, a step which she very soon came to regret (Broomhall, *Over the Treaty Wall*, p. 42).

134While on the *Lammermuir*, Mary Bowyer, Jane McLean and Elizabeth Rose felt their infant baptisms to be no longer sufficient, and Hudson Taylor, on their request, baptized them in August 1866 in Anjer/Java (Broomhall, *Survivors' Pact*, p. 192f.). John Pollock, *Hudson Taylor and Maria. Pioneers in China*, London, 1962, p. 157 puts it that this was due to Taylor's initiative. He 'encouraged the Misses McLean and Bowyer'. This seems unlikely because Maria Taylor was a Presbyterian who never doubted the validity of her infant baptism. Pollock also mistakenly mentions that Taylor held the Baptist view on baptism and that members of the crew were also baptized at Anjer. Taylor's report of this day simply reads: 'We had to put in at Anjer for water, and having permission from Captain Bell to go ashore, we spend a pleasant day among the tropical beauties of the island; our hearts glad at the prospect of speedily setting our feet on the shores of China' (J. Hudson Taylor, *Brief Account of the Progress of The China Inland Mission, From May 1866 to May 1868*, London, 1868).

135During those years, he baptized neither infants (doubting the validity) nor believers (himself being not baptized as a believer). See: Grattan Guinness, *A Plea for Believers' Baptism. An Address Delivered in Somerset-Street Chapel, Bath, Sept. 29, 1860, Previous to his Baptism*, London, 1860; Sydney, 1861; Dublin, 1863 (revised and expanded), pp. 4–5, 29.

136'... and, never having been baptized, as I consider, aright, I desire this night to conform to the commandment of the Lord Jesus in this matter' (Grattan Guinness, *A Plea for Believers' Baptism*).

137He preached his own baptismal sermon and had it printed as: *A Plea for Believers' Baptism*, by the Rev. H. Grattan Guinness of New College, St. John's Wood, London, 1860; Sydney, 1861; Dublin, 1863 (revised and expanded) .

138'My baptism, which was performed by one of the ministers of your body (Brethren) in a Baptist Chapel, I never intended or regarded the step, as leaving any one denomination or joining any other, but as an act of simple obedience to Christ' (Grattan Guinness, *A Letter to the 'Plymouth Brethren' on the Recognition of Pastors*, London, 1863, p. 5).

139When their first children were born, Fanny and Grattan Guinness were still Brethren. Harry, Lucy and Geraldine Guinness were baptized on 29 August 1873 in Edinburgh Castle Mission Hall in Stepney Green by Dr Barnardo (Holmes, *The Cloud Moves*, p. 21).

140Glenny was originally an Anglican (Steele, *Not in Vain*, p. 18).

141Thompson, *A. B. Simpson*, p. 34. See p. 37 for Simpson's later views on this matter.

142Later, he described his experience in the third person like this: 'It was a bitter autumn day when even the water was cold as ice. No audience present but the wife of the humble evangelist who baptized him, no sympathy from a single human friend, but a consciousness of being utterly alone, misunderstood and condemned even by his dearest friends for an act of eccentric fanaticism that must surely separate him from all the associations of his Christian life and work... After it was over, he hastily robed himself and threw himself upon his knees and thanked the Lord for the unspeakable privilege of following Him in full obedience into death. No language can ever express the unutterable joy that came sweeping into his soul and spirit as the Master seemed to say, "You have gone with Me into the death, now you shall come with Me into resurrection"' (A. B. Simpson, *Baptism and the Baptism of the Holy Spirit*, New York, 1902, p. 286, quoted in: Niklaus, Sawin and Stoesz, *All for Jesus*, p. 43).

143During CMA conventions, many were baptized, but that did not involve a change of denominational allegiance.

144Pierson, *Arthur T. Pierson*, p. 263.

145On 6 April 1896, his presbytery informed him that, because of his changed views on baptism, he could no longer be its member. But Pierson never joined any other denomination (Pierson, *Arthur T. Pierson*, p. 268f.).

146His baptism joined him to Estina Swedish Baptist Church. Sheetz, *The Sovereign Hand*, p. 17; Torjesen, *A Study of Fredrik Franson*, pp. 42–44.

147There are no sources available to show what exactly caused his views on baptism to change (Torjesen, *A Study of Fredrik Franson*, pp. 47ff.).

148This position is held by the Free Evangelical Churches.

149Interview M. Maré, 28 August 1986.

150William Burton, *When God Makes a Missionary. The Life Story of Edgar Mahon*, Zion, [2]1961 (1936), p. 22. This happened after he had been healed from tuberculosis.

151Interview Louisa Howard, 21 February 1986.

152The early centre of this kind of fundamentalist group was the Grand Rapids Auxiliary of the Congo Inland Mission. When the UTM dissolved itself in the United States, the Congo Inland Mission was willing to take over all stations but, for the majority of the UTM missionaries, the CoIM was not fundamentalist enough, and so they joined the Baptist Mid Mission, which had started as a faith missions in the 1920s (Mid-Africa Mission), but meanwhile had turned itself into a Baptist fundamentalist mission.

153After his conversion, he had joined the Brethren, but most probably was never baptized by them.

154Affeld, *Er mache uns im Glauben kühn*, p. 7.

155Interview N. N., Svenska Alliansmissionen, 16 June 1986.

156Somewhat unusual is Bethany Church in Minneapolis, a Lutheran type of church and base of the Bethany Fellowship, with infant baptism as the norm (Interview, 14 March 1986). Independent congregations which practise both types of baptism side by side are rare, Wheaton College Bible Church being an example (Interview John Gration, 20 March 1986).

157This policy of basing admission to fellowship only on faith in Christ was formulated in connection with the Plymouth/Bethesda controversy as 'The Tottenham Statement' (Coad, *History of the Brethren*, p. 301). It reads in part: '3. We welcome to the table, on individual grounds, each saint, not because he or she is a member of this or that gathering or denomination of Christians nor because they are followers of any particular Christian leader, but on such testimony as commends itself to us as being sufficient. 4. We distinctly refuse to be parties to any exclusion of those who, we are satisfied, are believers—except on grounds personally applying to their individual faith and conduct. Adopted by Brethren at Tottenham the 4th of March 1849.' (Quoted in Coad, *History of the Brethren*, p. 301.)

158Classical missions also trained men who would not have become pastors in their churches, but this training led to ordination, although sometimes to an ordination which was only valid on the mission field.

159Walker, *Fool and Fanatic?*, p. 114. (The letter is undated, probably 1913).

160A. B. Simpson, 'New Testament Missionary Types', sermon on Philemon 17 during a Nyack Convention on 29 July 1906, in Simpson, *Missionary Messages*, p. 48.

161The first to be ordained by the CMA was the Canadian William Cassidy (Reynolds, *Footprints*, p. 458).

162*The Reaper*, 1888, quoted in: Steele, *Not in Vain*, p. 129.

163Douglas D. Porter, *At Thy Disposal. The Beginnings of the Egypt General Mission*, London, 1934, p. 2.

164Weeks, *W. Spencer Walton*, p. 41.

165Frances Bevan, *Hymns of Ter Steegen, Suso and Others*, London, 1894.

166Frances Bevan followed the custom of the early Brethren authors in signing with initials only. However, she did not use the initials of her name but those of the place where she wrote the poem—Chalet Passiflora, Cannes (C.P.C.) (John S. Andrews, 'Frances Bevan: Translator of German Hymns' in *Evangelical Quarterly*, 1962, pp. 206–213; 1963, pp. 30–38 (p. 208); Andrew Walls—Fiedler, 4 February 1988).

167McKay, *Faith and Facts*, p. 121.

168He reports on the wedding of his daughter Edith to Alfred Buxton: 'The service was sweet, and not over long. My ordination—that of D. L. Moody and Dr Torrey—was the authority for the performance of the religious ceremony' (Grubb, *C. T. Studd*).

169He refused to be ordained because he wanted to remain free from all denominations (Flood, *The Story of Moody Church*, p. 9).

170Roger Martin, *R. A. Torrey*, Murfreesboro, 1976, p. 47.

171Walker, *Fool and Fanatic?*, p. 114.

172(1825–1890). See: Jane Radcliffe, *Recollections of Reginald Radcliffe*. By his wife, London, n.d. (*ca.* 1896).

173Walker, *Fool and Fanatic?* (undated letter, after 1913, answering a Mr C. who did not doubt the success of his work, but had doubts whether Studd was entitled to ordain deacons and elders. When someone suggested to Reginald Radcliffe that he become ordained, '... his curt and emphatic reference in his correspondence to this proposal was, "I hope, never!"' (Jane Radcliffe, *Recollections*, p. 49). He never abandoned this position).

174The standard book on the comity principle is R. Pierce Beaver, *Ecumenical Beginnings in Protestant World Mission. A History of Comity*, New York/Edinburgh/Toronto, 1962.

175With this purpose in mind, A. T. Pierson supported worldwide comity (*MRW*, 1885, pp. 368ff., 464ff.).

176See: William R. Hogg, *Ecumenical Foundations. A History of the International Missionary Council And Its Nineteenth Century Background*, New York, 1952, p. 33f. By 1898, this already met with criticism: 'While the old denominations have much to say about missionary 'comity' and resent infringement on each other's territory, these informal evangelizers have little to say about mine and thine, but rather rejoice in whoever may spread the glad tidings' (Chapell, *The Eleventh-Hour Laborers*, p. 56).

177In northern Nigeria, this was done by the SUM deciding to use the CMS catechism (Minutes SUM, 5 October 1911).

178In Zaire, all Protestant missions even created a unified and transferable church membership within the 'Église du Christ au Congo', which legally did not even exist (R. Pierce Beaver, *Ecumenical Beginnings*, p. 187). When the Zaire government forced all Protestant churches to unite to form the Église du Christ au Zaire, it looked—though it was not—simply a continuation of the former 'Église du Christ au Congo'.

179Here, financial considerations played a major role. Competition might cause salaries to go up. This was the complaint of the Church of Scotland Mission against Booth and his Zambezi Industrial Mission: 'He is enticing our Mission boys to join his mission by the offer of enormously increased wages... He sent our printing boys a circular showing his increased rates of pay... Two have gone to him who were our church members and were asked by him to be re-baptized. You can imagine what all this means in a small community such as ours... There is a great and immense indignation among the European community at Booth's attitude. He is ruining the labour question by his preposterous wages (Alexander Hetherwick in Church of Scotland Mission Board Record xix, p. 27 (quoted in John Selfridge, *Booth*, p. 38)). This principle was also applied to missionaries changing their allegiance. When almost all American WEC missionaries decided to join AIM, they were only accepted after WEC had agreed (DHC—Pierson, 28 June 1926).

180'Care should be taken for better cooperation in church discipline between neighbouring missions. When members or teachers apply to be received into another communion information should always be sought from the communion from which they have come, with a view to the maintenance of discipline' ('Recommendations and Resolutions, Le Zoute Conference' in Edwin W. Smith, *The Christian Mission in Africa. A Study Based on the Proceedings of the International Conference at Le Zoute, Belgium, September 14th to 21st, 1926*, p. 109).

181It was for this reason that the people of Wamba Luemba in Eastern Zaire forced the fundamentalist BMM missionaries to leave.

182An instance of this concerns the slopes of Mt Kilimanjaro, where neighbouring ridges are either Lutheran or Catholic. The Chagga had their share in this process, too: J. C. Winter, 'The Chagga Contribution to the Denominational Partition of Kilimanjaro' in Niels Peter Moritzen and J. C. Winter (eds), *Ostafrikanische Völker zwischen Mission und Regierung*, Erlangen, 1982. In Zaire, the Belgians allowed a choice between Catholic and Protestant, only caring that their missions were not too close to each other.

183According to this application of comity, Christians were not to evangelize in the Muslim zone, although they were allowed to follow up Christians who had moved into it. In 1900, when Samuel Ali Hussein started the work of the Sudan-Pionier-Mission, the colonial government had still allowed him to work among Muslim (Minutes SPM, 25 October 1900).

184A typical case was Gabon. Since 1843, the Paris Mission was working on the banks and north of the Ogowe. In the 1920s, the CMA wanted to evangelize the unreached areas of Southern Gabon. They enquired from the Paris Mission, whose secretary recommended that the CMA should wait a few years and first expand in West Africa. When, after some years, the Paris Mission felt unable to expand southwards, they 'handed over' the area to the CMA (*CMA Missionary Atlas*, 1960, pp. 44–51, with detailed map; Etienne Kruger, 'Histoire de la Société des Missions Évangéliques de Paris' in Blanc, Blocher and Kruger, *Histoire des Missions Protestantes Françaises*, Flavion, 1970, pp. 157–169, with sketch map).

185For the history of the Niger Delta Pastorates, see: E. A. Ayandele, *The Missionary Impact on Modern Nigeria 1842–1914. A Political and Social Analysis*, London, 1966, pp. 221–238. Bishop Johnson's picture is on pp. 236–237. (Ayandele wrongly classifies QIM as a Congregationalist mission (p. 115]).

186'Private Notes by R. L. McKeown on Visit to Qua !boe', March 1909, (D 3301/CC/1).

187Edfu was to be the northern limit of SPM territory; in Cairo, they were to work only among Nubians (Minutes SPM, 17 October 1913).

188Minutes Congo Balolo Mission Field Conference at Ikau 9– 18 October 1930, No. 34. Titus M. Johnson went from Sweden to the United States to study medicine. In 1918, he joined AIM, which he left in 1922 to find a mission field for his denomination where no Protestant mission had yet worked (Irvine, *The*

*Church of Christ in Zaire*, p. 95).

189Irvine, *The Church of Christ in Zaire*. The minutes express the necessity; the 'accompanying letter' (field council—London HQ) reports DCCM (Disciples of Christ Congo Mission) incursions into Congo Balolo Mission territory: 'They have come into CBM villages, in some cases placing teachers and in other cases baptizing large numbers of natives without any reference to us.') The Yuli elders reported that eight villages from DCCM territory had applied to them for a teacher as they would not get one from DCCM (Report of two elders from Yuli, enclosure to Minutes Field Conference at Ikau 9–18 October 1930).

190E. A. Udo,'The missionary scramble for spheres of influence in South-eastern Nigeria 1900–52' in Ogbu U. Kalu (ed.), *The History of Christianity in West Africa*, Harlow, [2]1981(1980), pp. 159–181. The presentation is very detailed. Although no QIM primary sources were used, very many Methodist primary sources also contain QIM letters.

191Only in 1930 did QIM dare to start a new field further north, in Igala (Edmund P.T. Crampton, 'Christianity in Northern Nigeria' in Ogbu Kalu, *Christianity in West Africa. The Nigerian Story*, Ibadan, 1978, pp. 141, 161).

192'Probably no field demonstrates better than Congo that comity in spirit and practice has been a fundamental part of the Protestant mission system and that it is the basis on which active cooperation developed' (Beaver, *Ecumenical Beginnings*, p. 187).

193Today, twenty-seven of the sixty-two Communautés of the Église du Christ au Zaire (ECZ) work in Kinshasa (Nsafu Mbodo, *La Communauté Évangélique de l'Alliance au Zaire*, grad. theol., Kinshasa, 1984, p. 10).

# 7

# Power for service: faith missions and the holiness movement[1]

The doctrinal statements of faith missions formulate the minimum consensus on central theological issues and are therefore insufficient to describe the theology of a given mission. As a minimum consensus these statements of faith show that, in faith missions, very different concepts of holiness may be accommodated.

The first *Principles and Practice* of the China Inland Mission (1867) contain no statement of faith. Even the 'principles and practice' of 1885—in which 'fundamental truths' are described as 'the inspiration of the scriptures, the trinity, the fall of man and his state by nature, the atonement, the eternal salvation of the redeemed and the everlasting punishment of the lost'—contain no hint of the doctrine of holiness.[2] Only the 'principles and practice' of the Overseas Missionary Fellowship (successor to CIM) of 1966 demand that candidates describe their concept of holiness. As with all other major issues, candidates are to note if they are 'conscious that their views differ in any important respect from those usually held by evangelical Christians'.[3]

In the doctrinal statements of other faith missions we find, equally, only very general statements of the doctrine of holiness. The Regions Beyond Missionary Union demands faith in 'the work of the Holy Spirit in the conversion and sanctification of the sinner'.[4] The constitution of the Unevangelized Fields Mission speaks of 'faith in the imperative necessity and full sufficiency of the atoning sacrifice of Christ, and the regenerating and sanctifying work of the Holy Spirit'.[5] The Zambezi Mission teaches 'that the evidence of the new life should be manifested by a daily walk in the Spirit'.[6] The Gospel Missionary Union stresses that 'we believe in the sonship of all born-again believers in the family of God, their justification, sanctification, and eternal redemption being fully provided for and assured in the finished work of Christ on Calvary and in his continued intercession above'.[7] TEAM teaches that the Holy Spirit will 'indwell, guide, instruct, fill, and empower the believer for godly living and service'.[8]

Some faith missions did not formulate a doctrinal statement of their own, but accepted the basis of the Evangelical Alliance as the expression of their understanding of the faith.[9] Its statement on holiness reads: '[We believe in] the work of the Holy Spirit in the conversion and sanctification of the sinner'. This accommodates both views of holiness, seeing it as a process of growth and as a crisis experience. Because many of the founders of the Evangelical Alliance were influenced by the early holiness movement, this ambivalence of expression was probably intentional.[10]

Only very few faith missions explicitly demanded adherence to the concept of holiness propagated by the holiness movement. The best example is the World Gospel Mission which, in 1910, the year of its foundation, defined sanctification clearly as a definite and sudden work of the Spirit.[11] In a similar fashion, the Christian and Missionary Alliance defines sanctification as a crisis experience followed by a process of growth.[12] These detailed definitions of holiness limit the membership of these missions to those who can subscribe to 'Wesleyan' concepts: as a result, they are somewhat on the fringe of the American faith missions community. They cannot be members of the more Calvinist IFMA (Interdenominational Foreign Missions Association) but only of EFMA (Evangelical Foreign Missions Association), which has a broader theological base and is home mainly to denominational evangelical missions.

The Africa Evangelistic Band speaks in its doctrinal statement of the 'victorious life'. The term makes clear the close relation to the holiness movement.[13] In the doctrinal statement of the Africa Evangelical Fellowship we find the general statement that the work of the Holy Spirit is the only way to regeneration and sanctification and that there is 'full provision for holiness in Christ Jesus'.[14] More openly, 'holiness' is the aim of the mission: 'to preach the gospel to every creature and to teach scriptural holiness'.[15]

Since faith missions' statements of faith represent a minimal theological consensus, the results of this investigation are misleading. More specific results can be expected from an analysis and historical survey of the relationship of the various faith missions to the various strands of the holiness movement. Before this, the history and theology of the holiness movement and its component parts must be described briefly.

# The holiness movement[16]

At the base of the holiness movement is the concept of sanctification of John Wesley (1703–91) He saw sanctification as a work of divine grace, following after conversion and being clearly distinct from it.[17] As with conversion, sanctification is a clearly datable crisis experience, though the experience may be the culmination of a long development. This crisis experience is open to all Christians, but most do not reach it.[18] Wesley used different names to describe this crisis experience: 'entire sanctification'; 'being made perfect in love'; 'Christian perfection'; even 'sinless perfection'[19], a term by which he took up again the concept of 'pure love'.[20] To understand better Wesley's concept of holiness, it must be clear that, theologically, he was not a Calvinist, but an Arminian. In classical Calvinism, justification of the sinner is due only to the action of God's grace,[21] with humankind having no free will, and holiness is a gradual process with human will playing the major role. Arminianism, on the other hand, understands justification as a process in which divine grace and the human will 'cooperate', and sanctification is a sudden gift of divine grace for which people can prepare themselves.[22]

## THE ORIGINS OF THE HOLINESS MOVEMENT

The holiness movement[23] of the nineteenth century can be seen as a reaction against the decline of the teaching of holiness after Wesley's death. It is not possible to date precisely the beginning, but we may take the holiness experiences (in Boston in 1835) of the sisters Sarah Lankford (1806–96)[24] and Phoebe Palmer (1807–75)[25] as the starting point of this spiritual renewal movement. Although Sarah Lankford's holiness experience took place somewhat earlier,[26] her sister Phoebe Palmer became the leading personality of the early holiness movement. Together with her husband, Dr Walter Palmer (1804–83),[27] she instituted the interdenominational 'Tuesday meetings', through which she attempted to make holiness teaching and experience accessible to others.[28] Many who participated in these 'Tuesday meetings' were not Methodists, but belonged to churches with Calvinist concepts of holiness.[29] The movement spread quickly. A few names may suffice here: Charles Grandison Finney (1792–1875),[30] Asa Mahan (1799–1889),[31] Thomas Upham (1799–

1872).[32] Finney and Mahan date their holiness experience to 1836,[33] and Upham to 1839 after a Tuesday meeting.[34] None of them left their own church, so a far-reaching process of 'Arminianization of Calvinism' took place.[35] The theological concepts of Calvinism were largely retained but, in the Calvinist churches, 'Arminian' ways of behaviour spread, for example, in evangelism[36] and missionary work. Faith missions took an active part in this process of 'Arminianization'.

## THEOLOGICAL TENDENCIES IN THE HOLINESS MOVEMENT

All sections of the holiness movement agree that sanctification is an act of divine grace and, at the same time, a human crisis experience which follows conversion but is definitely different from it. But beyond this basic consensus, disagreement begins. The most extreme view is that of the 'eradicationist school'. It contends that sanctification eradicates the root of sin and, by it, sinful nature itself. Today, these views can be found in the 'holiness denominations' of the United States,[37] and with individuals and groups there connected to the Christian (formerly: National) Holiness Association.[38] Less extreme is the 'suppressionist school', which teaches that the sinful nature is not eradicated, but suppressed. This concept was widespread in the Keswick Movement, sometimes called the 'moderate holiness movement'.[39] Keswick was initiated by US holiness evangelists, among whom Hannah Whitall Smith[40] and Robert Pearsall Smith[41] played the leading roles.[42] This British holiness movement experienced an early culmination in the conferences of Oxford (1874)[43] and Brighton (1875).[44] Its name was taken from the little town of Keswick,[45] where this most important holiness conference of Great Britain has been meeting annually since 1875.[46] The 'eradicationist school' and the 'suppressionist school' have many things in common, and an intermediate position was maintained by A. B. Simpson and his Christian and Missionary Alliance.[47]

Widely used terminology, which cannot clearly be identified with one of the schools, occurs in three variants: 'higher Christian life'; 'deeper Christian life'; and 'victorious Christian life'. This terminology stresses not so much suppression or eradication of sinful nature, but the possibility of an 'exchanged life' with 'victory over sin' and 'power for service'.[48]

One theological 'holiness term', which today is hardly recognizable as such, is the 'baptism of the Holy Spirit'. The meaning of this term was later changed by the pentecostal movement, which identified the baptism of the Spirit with speaking in tongues. Originally, the term 'baptism of the Holy Spirit'[49] was mainly used by the great evangelists to challenge those who were already converted, but who were longing for a deeper spiritual life. Typical of this was the famous evangelist Dwight Lyman Moody (1837–99).[50] He was not a holiness preacher in the narrow sense of the word. In his preaching, he did not try only to convert the unconverted, but challenged the 'believers' to take a second step of faith, for which he often used the term 'baptism in the Spirit'.[51] Moody's message was rooted in his own dramatic holiness experience of 1871.[52] This happened after two women from the holiness movement (Mrs Sarah Anne Cooke, a Free Methodist,[53] and Mrs Hawxhurst) had made him long for this experience. It happened less than two years before Moody's evangelistic campaigns in Great Britain which were to make him famous. Though he did not directly propagate foreign missions, many who later joined a faith mission had received their call in his campaigns.

All these holiness doctrines can be traced back to Wesley's 'two-crisis' teaching.[54] The first crisis, the conversion, brings full salvation, but only the second experience, sanctification, allows access to all the riches of God's grace and God's power. The holiness movement met the longing of many Christians to receive not only forensic forgiveness of sin, but also to *experience* victory over sin, courage for discipleship, power for service and a fulfilled life. To this longing, it provided spiritual, ritual and institutional answers.

## THE HOLINESS MOVEMENT AND MYSTICISM

Beyond Wesley, the roots of the holiness movement reach back to mysticism. Wesley's most important link to it was William Law (1686–1761)[55] and his book *Serious Call to a Devout and Holy Life*.[56] Of major importance to the spirituality of faith missions were authors such as François Fénelon (1651–1715),[57] Jeanne de la Motte Guyon (1648–1717),[58] Miguel de Molinos (1640–97),[59] Heinrich Seuse (Suso) (*ca.* 1300–65)[60] and Gerhard Tersteegen (1697–1767).[61] Common ground between mysticism and the holiness movement is the idea of two levels of Christian life and the concept of direct divine guidance of the believer. But, in contrast to many branches of mysticism, the holiness movement showed more active characteristics: evangelism, foreign missions, social service and criticism of society.

## THE KESWICK TEACHING

For faith missions, the most important branch of the holiness movement was Keswick, at which were taught three basic steps to spiritual fulfilment and power:

◇ full surrender to Christ (consecration);

◇ being filled with the Spirit; and

◇ power for service.[62]

Full surrender to Christ: this first step is not really concerned with sin, because that was dealt with in the conversion experience, although it includes as a precondition the giving up of all *known* sins, if there are any. Full surrender does not mean to surrender sin, but to surrender one's own self. One's own will must be replaced by the Spirit's will. Through conversion, Christ became one's Lord in principle—but full surrender puts all areas of one's life under his direct command. If the Holy Spirit is to live in a body, there is only room for one will: the Spirit's. A Christian must abdicate his own will.[63] A Christian loses his freedom, but because now divine will rules, gains the utmost freedom.[64]

Being filled with the Spirit (baptism of the Holy Spirit): in good Arminian tradition, full surrender, as well as being filled with the Spirit, is a process in which divine grace and man's free will cooperate. But, finally, it is the Holy Spirit which makes a person–whose will is always insufficient–'willing to be made willing'.[65] In the act of full surrender, the baptism of the Holy Spirit is claimed by faith, irrespective of one's feelings. Usually the consciousness or the sense of the indwelling of the Holy Spirit follows soon after.[66]

Power for service: the sanctification experience is not quietistic. It is an active experience which leads to serious activity, although this activity has quietist roots, as much as the holiness experience contains quietist elements. The Spirit-filled life is marked by the 'rest of faith', power over sin, consciousness of communion with God and habitual prayer. Out of this rest and power, the sanctified Christian experiences a deep longing to help others in things material and eternal. He or she receives this 'power for service' from God, so that his or her efforts are not a burden but a privilege.

For the Keswick movement, 'full surrender' is the decisive crisis experience after conversion. This is not the aim of lifelong striving, but the start of a Christian life on a different ('higher/

deeper/victorious') level. This avoids (at least in theory) all perfectionism.

The early Keswick conferences were not concerned about missions. Therefore, Hudson Taylor gave his first Keswick address not as a missionary, but as a holiness preacher.[67] In 1886, Reginald Radcliffe gave the first missionary address, although outside the official programme.[68] In time, mission became one of the major issues at Keswick.

# Faith missions and the holiness movement

### BRITISH FAITH MISSIONS AND THE HOLINESS MOVEMENT

After this brief overview, we will look into the relationship between the holiness movement and faith missions. In this respect, Hudson Taylor is typical for faith missions. His parents were active Methodists. His conversion in 1849 at the age of fifteen took place in the context of that church and its theology.[69] In the same year, his congregation split, and he and his parents sided with the 'reformers' whose aim was to restore the original holiness teaching of John Wesley.[70] This 'reform' resulted in the formation of the Methodist Free Church.[71] His Methodist (and Methodist Free) origin is Taylor's first link to holiness teaching, but he was also in contact with the modern holiness movement of his day. In 1849, he was so impressed by the article: *The Beauty of Holiness*[72] that he began to 'strive for entire sanctification'.[73] One afternoon in December 1849, he had an experience of divine presence.[74] He did not call it 'sanctification', but it had all the typical marks of a holiness experience.[75] In 1869 in China, he had a similar experience, which saved him from a serious crisis. This experience was again connected with reading an article from the holiness movement, this time one by Robert Pearsall Smith.[76] Taylor had two holiness experiences, though he did not call them that. This is typical of faith missions: they use holiness theology in a non-dogmatic way.[77]

The connections of the Guinness family with the holiness movement were quite strong, although not as strong as Hudson Taylor's. Nevertheless, the young Grattan Guinness, two years after his conversion, experienced 'a deep consciousness of sin, and the longing for holiness and for a life in the Lord's service'.[78] In 1896, Lucy Guinness, writing about the unreached areas of North East Zaire, takes the holiness movement fully for granted.[79]

F. B. Meyer (1847–1929),[80] a close friend of the Guinness family who later became director of the Regions Beyond Missionary Union, was a major Keswick speaker.[81] In 1882, through a visit to his university of C. T. Studd, another member of the Cambridge Seven, he broke through to a new (holiness) piety. In spite of these holiness connections, and in spite of the fact that the East London Training Institute provided many missionaries for the China Inland Mission, the Guinness family and its circle[82] seem somewhat closer, first, to the Brethren movement and then to the prophetic movement. Still, it should not be forgotten that the prophetic movement was closely related to the holiness movement,[83] and that there were in those days many Brethren who also belonged to the holiness movement.

With those missions related to the Guinness family, connections to the holiness movement are easily recognizable. Many of their early missionaries were influenced directly or indirectly by Moody. In Great Britain, Moody strongly influenced the YMCA. Many of his converts, or those 'revived' by him, started 'mission halls'. Bill and Bailie, the first missionaries of the Qua Iboe Mission, and McKittrick, the first missionary of the Congo Balolo Mission, came from the mission hall in Island Street, Mountpottinger, near Belfast.[84] The members of Island Street Mission Hall were, at first, solely responsible for the newly founded Qua Iboe Mission, after Bill had written to Ferguson, a member of that mission hall and asked him to start 'a kind of mission society'.[85] The receipt books of the young mission show who supported it: about seventy people paid regularly, and about the same number of collection boxes were in use. In addition, gifts had been received from fourteen Sunday schools and mission halls in the dstrict. No church congregation participated, which was typical for the first decades of the faith missions in Great Britain. Bill and Bailie were not only members of Island Street Mission Hall, but also of Mountpottinger YMCA, where they met with McKittrick every Saturday for prayer, mainly to gain clarity as to their future.[86] Other YMCA groups also supported the Qua Iboe Mission.[87] Lowry Maxwell, one of the early leading missionaries of the Sudan United Mission, came from Dublin City YMCA.[88] And it was no accident that the meetings of the SUM Committee in Sheffield often met in the rooms of the Sheffield YMCA.[89]

Faith missions not only received many of their early missionaries from mission halls: they sometimes established such halls themselves. For many years, Glenny was the home director of the North Africa Mission; he also supervised the work in four mission halls. They were also used to train the missionary candidates, who had to stay for one year at headquarters in Barking, for evangelistic work.[90] This close connection between training institute and evangelistic work was most probably modelled after the East London Training Institute, with its 'Berger Hall'.[91] Similarly, the New York Missionary Training College established four 'missions'.

In a different way from the 'Guinness missions', there were some missions in Great Britain which were very strongly related to the holiness movement. The group of young men who later formed the Egypt Mission Band (Egypt General Mission), had their spiritual home in a Methodist manse.[92] Martin Cleaver, one of the leaders of that group, had been led by a fellow student to a life of 'full surrender to the Lord Jesus Christ',[93] and one of the early missionaries had experienced his call through a booklet by Lilias Trotter (founder of the Algiers Mission Band), who was in turn strongly influenced by the holiness movement.[94]

Among early British missions, the Cape General Mission/ South Africa General Mission had the strongest connection to the holiness movement. Spencer Walton, founder of the Cape General Mission, worked in 1882 as evangelist for the Church Parochial Mission Society,[95] which had been founded on Moody's suggestion. In the same year, Walton was the guest of Canon Battersby, who brought the holiness conferences to Keswick[96] in 1875 (after Oxford, 1874, and Brighton, 1857). In Canon Battersby's[97] house, he met the Reformed pastor Andrew Murray, the leading holiness theologian of South Africa,[98] who suggested that Walton should visit South Africa as an evangelist. When, after some years, Walton was willing to take up that invitation, it was Andrew Murray who formed a committee and organized the trip.[99] Some time later Walton, 'in the quiet of the woods of Mrs Elizabeth Hanbury', received his call to become a missionary.[100] On 17 October of that same year, after hearing a man whom he calls in his diary Mr H., he had a deep holiness experience which, for him, meant mainly 'receiving [divine] power'.[101] When Walton finally decided to start a mission in South Africa in 1885, one of its major aims was to proclaim the holiness message among the white Christians of South Africa.[102] For this, the mission instituted the annual Wellington Convention,[103] a holiness conference of the Keswick type.[104] The president of the mission, whose headquarters were in South Africa, was Andrew Murray.

Andrew Murray had made his Dutch Reformed Church (Nederduitse Gereformeerde Kerk) start missionary work among the black Africans of their country and had started a seminary for training missionaries.[105] After being sick for two years and having lost his voice, he went to Europe to contact the leaders of the holiness movement and the healing movement.[106] In London, he stayed at Bethshan Healing Home,[107] which was founded on William E. Boardman's (1810–86)[108] initiative, and led by Elizabeth Baxter.[109] At Bethshan, Murray regained his voice, a healing which proved to be permanent.[110] Returning to South Africa, he became the leading holiness preacher there. His holiness books and conference talks in South Africa, England and the United States made him one of the best-known holiness leaders.[111] When Murray turned to the interdenominational holiness movement, he also began to support interdenominational faith missions (Cape General Mission/SAGM, Sudan United Mission)[112], although for him, as for A. J. Gordon (Boston), this did not mean stopping support for the missionary work of his own denomination.[113]

Even more closely tied to the holiness movement was the Africa Evangelistic Band. The stages of the spiritual development of its founder Helene Garrath is typical for holiness theology: her mother Harriette, a Quaker, was a convert of the 1859 revival. Helene was converted at the age of nine years and was led to 'full surrender' by Moody in 1882. In 1885, her twin brothers attended Keswick and were highly impressed by the CIM missionary Charlotte Kerr. Like her brothers, she began, with her sisters May and Emma, 'to seek God, and experienced him'.[114] During a conference of the International Police Association in Belfast in 1891, she met John George Govan,[115] who had given up his business to start an Inland Mission for Scotland: The Faith Mission (1886), taking the CIM as his pattern. Its 'pilgrims' were to take the Gospel to the 'needy villages of Scotland'.[116] As Govan preached the same 'full salvation'[117] as the Garratt sisters, they asked the Faith Mission to come to Ireland.[118] When they later became convinced that a 'pilgrims' mission' for South Africa should be started, Govan told them that they should do it themselves.[119]

Priscilla and C. T. Studd were strongly connected to the holiness movement. Priscilla was a member of the Salvation

Army when she joined the CIM, and Charles was strongly influenced by Moody, as were all the Cambridge Seven. In 1913, C. T. Studd formulated—in addition to the 'five smooth stones'[120]—a kind of WEC basis of faith: the programmatic 'four pillars'. Together with sacrifice, faith and fellowship, the third pillar is holiness. In 1927, Priscilla Studd was in close contact with J. D. Drysdale[121] and his Emmanuel Missionary Training Home[122] in Birkenhead, Liverpool.[123] Drysdale was one of the leading British interdenominational holiness evangelists.[124] Over many years, a great portion of WEC missionaries came from Birkenhead[125] or from the Bible College of Wales in Swansea, another holiness school, which emphasized worldwide intercession and the 'life of faith'.[126] Its founder, Rees Howells, was a leader in the 1904 Wales holiness revival[127] and, at the 1906 Llandrindod Wells Convention ('Keswick of Wales'), he went through a protracted holiness experience.[128]

Lilias Trotter, the founder of the Algiers Mission Band (1888),[129] was won for the holiness movement in 1872 at a conference organized by Lady Mount Temple in Broadlands for Hannah Whitall and Robert Pearsall Smith.[130] She also participated in the Oxford and Brighton conferences of 1874 and 1875.[131] Matthew Z. Stober, founder of the Angola Evangelical Mission (later taken over by the Canadian Baptist Overseas Mission Board) taught to its converts the baptism of the Holy Spirit as the second crisis experience of the life of faith.[132] The Zambezi Mission (originally Zambezi Industrial Mission) created the 'Malawi Keswick'.[133]

## US MISSIONS AND THE HOLINESS MOVEMENT

The CMA,[134] as a US fellowship movement, was first of all a holiness movement. A. B. Simpson preached and taught the *fourfold gospel*[135] ('Christ our Saviour, Sanctifier; Healer and Coming King').[136] Simpson had started the Christian Alliance as pastor of an independent Tabernacle.[137] What had affected him sufficiently to do this? There were three major changes in his life. While he was a pastor in Louisville, he invited the (holiness) evangelists Whittle and Bliss to his church. From them, he received a longing for a deep and new spiritual experience; he also learned that it was the job of the church to reach the masses.[138] This made him transform his traditional presbyterian congregation into a Tabernacle church, accessible to people from all walks of life. Simpson went to Chicago to ask Moody for help in satisfying his spiritual hunger, but he heard only the simple testimony of a man unknown to him and returned home. He found what he was searching for in the quietness of his study[139] while reading a book with extracts from seventeenth-century mystics. The third decisive experience was his meeting the Episcopalian physician Charles Cullis (1833–92)[140] in Old Orchard.[141] Cullis practised healing by faith ('divine healing'),[142] and A. B. Simpson was thoroughly healed. Simpson soon became a leader of the healing movement, which often overlapped with the holiness movement.[143]

In his sermons and publications, he taught the possibility and necessity of divine healing. The institutions that he created became well known. Following Phoebe Palmer's example, he started a 'Friday meeting' in his tabernacle.[144] Wherever he was given a chance, he held 'conventions'—with holiness, healing and mission as major themes.[145] Beyond his own sphere, he cooperated closely with A. T. Pierson (1837–1911),[146] editor of the *Missionary Review of the World*, who in turn taught at the New York Missionary Training College, and with Adoniram Judson Gordon (1836–95),[147] pastor of Clarendon Street Baptist Church in Boston and founder of the interdenominational Boston Missionary Training Institute. Both were important holiness preachers.[148]

Peter Cameron Scott had attended the New York Missionary Training College and then worked as a CMA missionary on the Lower Congo, so he came from the hotbed of holiness teaching.[149] Support for the early AIM came largely through the Philadelphia Bible College and its missionary council, with the college paper (*Hearing and Doing*) doubling as the AIM paper. An important teacher there was James H. McConkey.[150] During the first decade, nearly every issue of *Hearing and Doing* featured one of McConkey's articles on issues of holiness teaching. Charles E. Hurlbert, who also was a teacher at the Philadelphia Bible College before he took over the leadership of AIM, concentrated more on eschatology but, when on deputation, he called not only for support of missionary work, but for a deeper walk with God.[151] Among the early members of the AIM, Willis Hotchkiss (1873–1948) was a strong supporter of the holiness teaching.[152] In 1899, he left the AIM,[153]; in 1902, together with Arthur Chilson and Edgar Hole, he started a mission of his own denomination at Kaimosi.[154] In 1905, he founded the Lumbwa Industrial Mission as an independent mission in Chagaik, near Kericho[155] which, in

1932, served as the stepping stone for the first African field of the World Gospel Mission, founded in 1910.[156]

Alma Doering, first a missionary of CMA and Svenska Missionsförbundet[157] and later founder of the Congo Inland Mission and the Unevangelized Tribes Mission, came from the same milieu. She had a holiness experience at the age of twenty.[158] After this, she spent some time in a 'faith home' in Chicago, then worked as an evangelist among miners and wood cutters in North Wisconsin.[159] In Europe, she had contact with the Swiss pastor Otto Stockmayer (1838–1917).[160] In his healing home (which had been founded in 1878), she sought and found healing for body and soul on her way to join the AIM work in Kenya in 1906.[161]

Rowland Bingham (1882–1942),[162] founder of the SIM, was originally a member of the Salvation Army.[163] He left it in the autumn of 1892,[164] but did not give up holiness teaching, although he followed the 'milder' Keswick variety—similar to CMA teaching—to whose Canadian leader John Salmon[165] he was 1892–93 pastoral assistant before going to Nigeria for the first time.[166] To give prominence to 'victorious life teaching' in Canada, he started the 'Canadian Keswick' in 1924, and remained its director until his death.[167] Bingham was also directly influenced by A. B. Simpson, whose New York Missionary Training College he attended in 1895–96.[168] In spite of later differences with Simpson over divine healing,[169] he never criticized Simpson's holiness teaching.[170]

Fredrik Franson was less directly involved in the holiness movement. But because he was influenced by Moody, he would have absorbed at least some holiness teaching. Before going to Scandinavia for the first time, he attended the Scandinavian Baptist Deeper Life Conference in Altamont (11–13 October 1878).[171] While in Denmark (and only there), he strongly emphasized divine healing.[172] During his visit to London, he was greatly influenced by Elizabeth Baxter of Bethshan Healing Home.[173] In Sweden, he was a regular speaker at the camp meetings of the Helgelseförbundet in Torp,[174] side-by-side with the holiness evangelist Nelli Hall.[175] Franson shared similar holiness views to those of Keswick, but he never joined the movement.[176]

Looking at some faith missions today, the early involvement in the holiness movement is somewhat surprising. The AIM has been mentioned, the Gospel Missionary Union is another example.[177] Some missions were direct offshoots of US holiness groups: the Peniel Mission working in Egypt and the Hephzibah Mission in South Africa. In 1910, the World Gospel Mission was founded as the foreign missions arm of the National Holiness Association.[178]

## ARMINIANIZING OF CALVINISM

The close relationship of the early British and US faith missions to the holiness movement must be seen as part of a process of the Arminianizing of Calvinism. The faith missionaries came largely from churches with a Calvinist theology but, in their revival (1859/1873), the major driving force was a holiness teaching which was quite contrary to the Calvinist concept of sanctification. Those Calvinists who accepted the holiness teaching did not leave their churches, but accommodated the new teaching within a Calvinist framework. The holiness movement was the major innovative force in evangelical circles for about two generations, so it is no wonder that the innovative faith missions played a prominent part in this process of the Arminianizing of Calvinism. Since this process took place *within* the framework of Calvinism, it meant that Calvinism could assert itself again as soon as the innovative forces subsided. This happened when the holiness movement began to decline towards the end of the century. The process of re-Calvinization was speeded up by the birth of the pentecostal movement out of the holiness movement after the turn of the century, and the removal of much of the holiness impetus from faith missions (and from the circles which supported them) to the pentecostal missions and the pentecostal churches.

Among the three movements which very strongly influenced faith missions, the Arminian holiness movement was by far the strongest but, with its decline, the other two movements—both from a Calvinistic background—could come more into their own: both the Brethren movement and the prophetic movement shared Calvinistic concepts of dispensationalism. This means that, to date, there has been a tendency to ignore and neglect, and sometimes even to deny, the holiness roots of faith missions.[179]

Today, strict dispensationalism as seen, for example, in American fighting fundamentalism is regularly anti-charismatic (which includes being anti-holiness).[180] At the time of the early faith missions, this was definitely not so. The Congregationalist pastor Cyrus Ingersoll Scofield (1843–1921),[181] editor of the well-known *Scofield Bible*, may serve as an example.[182] He was, equally, an exponent of dispensationalism *and* holiness teaching. He was the Christian and Missionary Alliance representative for the West and, in 1890, founded the Central America Mission as the first US faith mission for Latin America. The background of the AIM is very similar: *Hearing and Doing*, the AIM mission magazine, shows that holiness teaching and dispensationalism went hand-in-hand, but holiness teaching was the more basic layer. Within less than two decades, the AIM had largely cut itself off from its holiness base[183] but had kept its prophetic and dispensational emphasis. Because the prophetic movement and the holiness movement had largely touched the same groups, where the holiness movement receded, it was often the prophetic movement alone that held sway.[184]

What applies to the relationship between the holiness movement and prophetic movement applies to some extent to the relationship between the holiness movement and Brethren movement. Today, they have a very different *doctrine* of sanctification: the Brethren stress its forensic aspects, and the holiness people stress its experiential aspect. In the early stages, there was much overlapping between the two movements. Quite a number of Brethren assemblies had originally been fellowships of the holiness movement, such as Berlin-Hohenstaufenstraße, the original home of the Allianz Bibelschule Berlin (now Bibelschule Wiedenest).[185] Baedeker, the famous Brethren evangelist to Russia, was a holiness teacher, and at the Blankenburg conferences in Germany, holiness and Brethren teaching merged.[186] Another sign of closeness between the two movements was the close friendship between A. T. Pierson and George Müller. Andrew Murray even counted George Müller as belonging to the holiness movement.[187] That the holiness movement influenced the Brethren can also be assumed from Frances Bevan, who published books on the German mystics for the Brethren,[188] supported by the (today quite astonishing) fact that, among the early Brethren, the sisters did not have to keep as quiet as later on.[189]

CONTINENTAL FAITH MISSIONS AND THE HOLINESS MOVEMENT

The leading figure in French faith mission circles was Ruben Saillens, former ELTI student and founder of the first Bible school in France, the Institute Biblique in Nogent-sur-Marne.[190] His wife, Jeanne Crétin, had been led to the sanctification experience before her marriage by the French preacher Paul Besson. Later, Ruben Saillens organized the Swiss Keswick at Morges.[191]

Saillens strongly influenced both the Mission Rolland[192] and the Mission Biblique en Côte d'Ivoire.

In the development of the Bibelschule Beatenberg, the first Bible School in German-speaking Switzerland, the same mixture can be found as with Scofield: a predominant interest in evangelism and missions, combined with dispensationalism and holiness teaching.[193] Gertrud Wasserzug learned the holiness teaching from the CIM Missionary Ruth Paxson,[194] whose books were published in 1932 by one of the leading German holiness publishing houses.[195]

The students from Beatenberg were not acceptable to the Chrischona Mission, the CIM branch in Switzerland. This may have been caused by two things: first, that Chrischona did not share the dispensationalist theology of Beatenberg; and secondly, that it had put aside early holiness influences. Chrischona had started as a specialized classical mission with a seminary (for men only). After the death of Spittler (1867), Chrischona faced a severe crisis, which included a debt of Sfr.73,500. The task of solving this crisis was entrusted to Carl Heinrich (1837–1909)[196] and Dora Rappard[197] in 1868. Heinrich was primarily an evangelist, and he transformed Chrischona into a fellowship movement.[198] In 1874, he attended the Oxford holiness conference and joined the holiness movement, starting both a magazine (Glaubensbote) to promote holiness teaching and an annual holiness conference. When Chrischona founded its CIM branch in 1895, it was no longer a specialized classical mission,[199] but an ordinary faith mission strongly influenced, as usual, by the holiness movement.[200]

Although the German-speaking fellowship movement, which originated in Germany from the (holiness) fellowship movement, rejected its early holiness origins when conflict arose over the pentecostal movement, it is clear, historically, that almost all German faith missions were strongly rooted in the holiness movement. This has been shown in detail for all the missions related to Hudson Taylor.[201] The Alliance Bible School in Berlin (established for students from Eastern Europe) had similar roots, as its connections to Toni von Blücher and Baedecker show, and other missions were strongly rooted in the Gemeinschaftsbewegung (fellowship movement) with its undeniable holiness roots (such as Süd-Ost-Europa Mission, 1905). For Neukirchen, little direct influence can be traced; the Sudan-Pionier-Mission is related to the holiness movement through its founders, Lucy and Karl Kumm.[202]

In Scandinavia, the situation is clear: the three early faith missions were all based in a holiness fellowship movement. One of them (Helgelseförbundet) even carried the tag in its name. Helgelseförbundet and Svenska Alliansmissionen were fellowship movements within the Lutheran church. The Örebro Missionsförening was a holiness movement within the Baptist Union of Sweden, started by John Ongman, who had come under the influence of A. B. Simpson while in the United States.[203]

## ETHICAL ASPECTS OF HOLINESS THEOLOGY

For the early faith missionaries, the search for holiness did not mean primarily the search for private perfection, but for power to serve. The holiness experience had led them to *full surrender*. They wanted to be effective evangelists and were willing to live a sacrificial life. Sometimes their sacrificial spirit even tended towards carelessness, and led them to take medical and logistic precautions lightly.[204]

Holiness as 'power for service' was applied to evangelistic and social service at the same time. The later opposition in some evangelical circles to social service ('the great reversal'), as a reaction against the social gospel, was unknown to the 1859/1873 revival. They were engaged in all kinds of social services: help for the destitute; rescue missions; self-help schemes; orphanages. These activities were never divorced from evangelism and, in most cases, did not offer just help, but also offered opportunities for people to redefine their role in life—for example, to take the church into their own hands, as they did in mission halls, fellowships and missions. Due to space limitations, only a few aspects of this, relating to the early faith missionaries, will be described here.

For Lilias Trotter (Algiers Mission Band), 'power for service' meant both practical help and evangelism. In 1872, she was strongly influenced by the holiness movement; in 1875, she helped as a counsellor during Moody's London evangelistic campaign and sang in the choir. Soon, she started evangelistic and social activities among London sales girls, and then among prostitutes.[205] Geraldine and Lucy Guinness worked among the population of the East End both as evangelists and educators. Lucy cared especially for the factory girls. In order to identify more closely with them, she herself worked in a factory for a time.[206] There are many examples of such activities.

The same applies to missionary work: there was no missionary without a medicine box, and hardly ever a mission station in

Africa without a school. Only in ignorance or prejudice can it be said that the evangelical missions did nothing but evangelistic work. Throughout Africa, wherever allowed by the government, missions support a regular school system, hospitals and, more recently, many development projects, including youth clubs, chicken farms and re-afforestation projects.[207]

One case in which social concern, so common in the holiness movement, was translated into political activity is connected to Harry Guinness. As taught at Keswick, he had accepted for himself the 'rest of faith', and was convinced that he should do all in his power to ensure that as many as possible could find this same rest. The first precondition for this was to be alive. His, and his family's, convictions were put to the test by the 'Congo atrocities',[208] perpetrated by the Congo Free State ruled by Leopold II, in which whole villages were depopulated to get more rubber.[209] The very first agitation against the atrocities was connected to the Guinness family. The first to make the atrocities public, in 1895, was J. B. Murphy of ABMU,[210] which had taken over the ELTI-related Livingstone Inland Mission in 1884. In 1896, two other ABMU missionaries (Banks and Sjöblom) once again made the atrocities public. Sjöblom, working at Bolenge,[211] who had been trained at ELTI, joined the Congo Balolo Mission in 1892 and moved to ABMU in 1893.[212] In May 1896, Harry Guinness travelled to Brussels to intervene with Leopold II. He told the king what he had learned from Bolenge. Among other things he reported:

> On December 14th, 1895, my friend, Mrs Banks, had been crossing the station compound at Bolengi when she saw a poor woman being beaten by a native sentry, and on enquiring what was the matter, the sentry replied 'She has lost one!' 'One what?' enquired Mrs Banks. 'Why, one of the hands,' said the sentry. And then Mrs Banks noticed that the basket on the back of the woman was filled with human hands. She immediately called her husband and Mr Sjöblom, who happened to be on the station at the time, and the hands were counted in their presence. There were eighteen in all, and the angry sentry still asserted that there ought to have been nineteen! Some of these smoked hands were those of children, some of women, and some of men. And undoubtedly most of them had

belonged to relatives of the unfortunate woman who was carrying them. 'Where are you taking these?' asked one of the missionaries. 'To the White man' (the State man), 'to whom I have to prove that I have been diligent in pushing the rubber business, and who would punish me, if I did not compel the people to bring in a sufficient quantity'.[213]

The king promised to investigate. He asked for the names of the guilty officers and had them removed. For the missionaries, things definitely improved, but later they learned that the guilty officers only had been removed to posts further removed from 'missionary control' to carry on as usual.[214] In 1904, Harry Guinness decided for public agitation[215] and, during the winter months of 1904, 1905 and 1906, he gave many talks for the Congo Reform Association, illustrated with magic lantern pictures and a hippo hide whip which had been used to beat people to death for not collecting enough rubber.[216] Lucy Kumm shared her brother's concern and, during the final weeks of her life in Northfield,[217] she put all her energy into writing a booklet on the issue, *Our Slave State*.[218] Harry Guinness had two more audiences with Leopold II and, on his way to visit RBMU missionaries in Peru, he went out of his way to see President Roosevelt in Washington.[219] In 1908, Grattan Guinness published a final appeal, *The Congo Crisis*.[220] He was convinced that others now had to put all their weight into the protest.[221] That same year, the crisis began which led to the closure of ELTI in 1910. Grattan Guinness died in the same year; Harry Guinness died in 1915.

As a whole, holiness theology had strong emancipatory results. This was especially visible in the impact of holiness theology on the process of the emancipation of women, which will be discussed in a later chapno. It should be mentioned here, however, that Oberlin College, founded by Finney, was the first to introduce co-education and, also, that it offered the same education to black and white students. Co-education became the general pattern of all the Bible schools. A similar process of emancipation took place for lay people relative to the clergy, with many of the faith mission founders seeing no need for ordination.

Holiness theology raised the question as to the power of justification by faith. Was justification only a forensic act or was it the first step in an effective life of service? Was it sufficient to experience forgiveness of sin or was it also possible and neccessary, in addition, to have victory over sin? The holiness movement gave a clear answer. Two steps are necessary: justification and sanctification. Because the holiness movement accepted all denominations, this meant that, for them, there were three groups in the church: the unconverted, the converted and those who had also experienced sanctification. All this was Arminian theology, which most faith missions never *explicitly* embraced. By not doing so, they were most open to influences from the holiness movement, but they were also open the other way round, so that when the holiness influences subsided, Calvinistic concepts of holiness could reassert themselves. The holiness theology of the African faith mission churches can be seen as a result of this process.

**Notes**

1   In this book, the holiness movement is treated only insofar as it was connected to faith missions. The standard bibliographies are: Charles Edwin Jones, *A Guide to the Study of the Holiness Movement*, Metuchen, NJ, 1974; Melvin E. Dieter, *The Holiness Revival of the Nineteenth Century*, Metuchen, 1980; and Charles Edwin Jones, *Perfectionist Persuasion: the Holiness Movement and American Methodism, 1867–1936*, Metuchen, 1974. All three books also contain much valuable historical information.

2   CIM, *Principles and Practice*, London, 1885.

3   Overseas Missionary Fellowship, *Principles and Practice*, 1966, Section 6B, 'Doctrinal Belief'.

4   *Principles and Practice of the Regions Beyond Missionary Union*, revised edition, May 1956.

5   *UFM Constitution*, n.d. (valid in the 1930s).

6   Zambezi Mission, *Principles and Practice*, revised edition, 1946.

7   *Gospel Missionary Union Handbook*, n.d. (valid 1987).

8   TEAM, *Principles and Practice*, n.d. (valid 1987), p. 5.

9   For example, the Africa Industrial Mission—even today's doctrinal statement of SIM does not deal with holiness: *SIM Manual*, 1986 (1984), p. 4) The Dorothea Mission (South Africa) uses, instead, the similar doctrinal statement of the Intervarsity Fellowship. On holiness, it demands faith in 'the indwelling and work of the Holy Spirit in the believer' (*Some Vital Facts About The Dorothea*

*Mission,* Rosslyn, n.d. (valid 1987), p. 8).

10 Dieter, *Holiness Revival,* p. 38.

11 'Relative to the doctrine and experience of entire sanctification: entire sanctification is that act of divine grace, through the baptism with the Holy Ghost, by which the heart is cleansed from all sin and filled with the pure love of God. It is a definite and sudden work wrought in the believer, through faith, subsequent to regeneration, and is attested by the Holy Ghost' (World Gospel Mission, Statement of Doctrine, 1910). Today's formula is: 'We believe in the salvation of the human soul, including the new birth, and in a subsequent work of God in the soul, a crisis, wrought by faith, whereby the heart is cleansed from all sin and filled with the Holy Spirit. This gracious experience is retained by faith as expressed in a constant obedience to God's revealed will, thus giving us perfect cleansing moment by moment (1 John 1:7–9). We stand for the Wesleyan position.' (World Gospel Mission, *Reaching the Unreached Now,* information sheet.).

12 'It is the will of God that each believer should be filled with the Holy Spirit and be sanctified wholly, being separated from sin and the world and fully dedicated to the will of God, thereby receiving power for holy living and effective service. This is both a crisis and a progressive experience in the life of the believer subsequent to conversion' (Statement of Faith adopted by the 68th General Council of the Christian and Missionary Alliance).

13 '[AEB believes] in deliverance from sin's power, heart cleansing, and the fulness of the Holy Spirit as a definite experience by faith, resulting in a life of victory and fruitfulness through the indwelling Christ' (Africa Evangelistic Band, *Prayer Fellowship,* 1987, p. 3). For AEB in general, see: Jones, *Holiness Movement,* p. 388f.

14 AEF, *Fellowship, Organisation and Administration,* Reading, 1985, p. 5f. The formula can be interpreted differently, but is definitely a formula of the holiness movement.

15 'Scriptural holiness' is also the defined aim of the Keswick conferences.

16 The development of separate 'holiness denominations' in the United States and the conflict with the pentecostal movement (originating in the holiness movement) in 1906, which has not yet fully subsided, brought about a change in terminology: 'holiness movement' is used by some to describe only the more extreme varieties, but in the second half of the nineteenth century this was not so. The striving for sanctification as more or less a crisis experience, as distinct from justification and conversion, took on different forms, and there were different tendencies—some more Calvinistic, some less. One could speak of different varieties of the holiness movement, but between these different strands there were no clear boundaries. In this book, the term 'holiness movement' always denotehead the broader movement.

17 The best source for his teaching on sanctification is: John Wesley, 'A Plain Account of Christian Perfection, as Believed and Taught by the Reverend Mr John Wesley' in John Wesley (ed. Wesleyan Conference Office), *The Works of Rev. John Wesley. With the Last Corrections of the Author,* London, [3]1872, Volume 11, pp. 366–446.

18  See: Salvation Army, *Heritage of Holiness*, p. 66.

19  In order not to misunderstand Wesley's term 'perfection', it is important to be aware of his definition of sin: sin is the *conscious* transgression of a known divine law. For Wesley's concept of sin, see: Salvation Army, *Heritage of Holiness*, p. 65.

20  'Entire sanctification or Christian perfection is neither more nor less than pure love; love expelling sin, and governing both the heart and life of a child of God. The Refiner's fire purges out all that is contrary to love' (Thomas Jackson (ed.), *The Works of John Wesley*, Grand Rapids, 1959, XII, p. 432).

21  For a modern version of the doctrine of predestination from a section of Presbyterianism close to faith missions, see: Paul K. Jewett, *Election and Predestination*, Grand Rapids/Exeter, 1985. Jewett was professor at Fuller School of Theology in Pasadena, closely related to the Fuller School of World Missions.

22  In the seventeenth century, Arminianism was a Dutch theological protest movement against the rigorous Calvinistic doctrine of predestination. It found expression in the 'Remonstrantie' of 1610. The Synod of Dordrecht (1618–19) rejected all five points of the 'Remonstrantie'. Anglo-Saxon Arminianism does not stand in direct historical continuity to Dutch Arminianism, but shares its rejection of predestination. The classical teaching of Calvinism is formulated in the acronym 'tulip': total depravity; unconditional election; limited atonement; irresistible grace; perseverance of the saints. To the contrary, Arminianism believes in: human ability, conditional election, general atonement, resistible grace, possible falling from grace. A brief overview of Arminianism can be found in: F. L. Cross (ed.), *The Oxford Dictionary of the Christian Church*. The doctrines of classical Arminianism are described in: Matthias Schneckenburger, *Vorlesungen über die Lehrbegriffe der kleineren protestantischen Kirchenparteien*, Frankfurt, 1863, pp. 5–26. A systematic presentation of the current Arminian position is: Randy L. Maddox, *Responsible Grace' in Wesleyan Theological Journal*, bulletin of the Wesleyan Theological Society, Asbury Theological Seminary, 1984, pp. 7ff. A defence of the classical Calvinist position (with a fair description of the Arminian position) is: David N. Steele and Curtis C. Thomas, *The Five Points of Calvinism Defined, Defended, Documented*, Philadelphia, 1963. For an overview of the historical development in Great Britain up to 1900, see: Alan P. F. Sell, *The Great Debate. Calvinism, Arminianism and Salvation*, Worthing, 1982/Grand Rapids, 1983. Sell adheres to a moderate Calvinist position. He summarizes his arguments, pp. 89–98.

23  The most important publications of the holiness movement are made accessible once again by Garland Publishing (136 Madison Ave, New York, NY 10016) in the 48-volume series: Donald W. Dayton (ed.), *The Higher Christian Life. Sources for the Study of the Holiness, Pentecostal and Keswick Movements*. For bibliography, see: Donald W. Dayton (ed.), *The Higher Christian Life. A Bibliographical Overview*, New York, 1984.

24  Her biography is: John Alexander Roche, *The Life of Mrs Sarah A. Lankford Palmer, Who for Sixty Years was the Able Teacher of Entire Holiness*, New York, 1898.

25  The best source for Phoebe Palmer, born Worall, is: Richard Wheatley, *Life and Letters of Mrs Phoebe Palmer*, New York, 1876. A modern biography, although highly desirable because of her contribution to the feminist movement, does not exist. See: Ernest Wall, 'I Commend unto you Phoebe' in *Religion in Life*, 1957, pp. 396–408.

26  21 May 1835, 2.30pm. She describes her experience thus: 'All was calm and stillness; I had none of the expected emotions. I arose from my knees fully determined to rest in God... if I had not a joyous emotion in forty years. Since that... May 21st, 1835, I think there has not been a day... [without] resting in the... atonement (Roche, *The Life of Mrs Sarah A. Lankford Palmer*, p. 32f.).

27  George Hughes, *The Beloved Physician, Walter C. Palmer, MD. His Sun-Lit Journey to the Celestial City*, New York, 1884.

28  George Hughes, *Fragrant Memories of the Tuesday Meetings and The Guide to Holiness, and their Fifty Years' Work for Jesus*, New York, n.d. (1886).

29  Dieter, *Holiness Revival*, p. 34.

30  Charles Grandison Finney, *Views of Sanctification*, Oberlin, Ohio, 1840, 206 pages.

31  Barbara B. Zikmund, *Asa Mahan and Oberlin Perfectionism*, PhD, Duke University, 1969 (UMI). His autobiography is: Asa Mahan. *Autobiography. Intellectual, Moral, and Spiritual*, London, 1882.

32  Thomas Cogswell Upham, *Principles of the Interior or Hidden Life*, Boston, 1846.

33  Charles G. Finney, *Memoirs*, New York, 1876, pp. 336–341, 349–351; Asa Mahan, *Out of Darkness into Light or The Hidden Life made manifest*, Louisville, n.d. (1876), p. 42.

34  Dieter, *Holiness Revival*, p. 34. Upham was Congregationalist.

35  Dieter, *Holiness Revival*, p. 19; Phoebe Palmer (ed.), *Pioneer Experiences*, New York, 1868, contains 'testimonies of eighty living ministers' on their sanctification experience.

36  An example for this is C. H. Spurgeon. He was a convinced Calvinist but, because of his practice of evangelism, he had to contend with many a rebuke from those whom he called 'Hypercalvinists'. For his life, see: M. K. Nicholls, *C. H. Spurgeon: The Pastor Evangelist*, Baptist Historical Society, 1992.

37  For example, Church of the Nazarene, Wesleyan Methodist Church (United States) and Pilgrim Holiness Church (united since 1968 as the Wesleyan Church).

38  History and literature in: Jones, *Holiness Movement*, pp. 9ff.

39  For literature, see: Jones, *Holiness Movement*, pp. 485–512.

40  Her most famous book (with millions sold) is: *The Christian's Secret of a Happy Life*, 1875. Her autobiography is: *The Unselfishness of God. A Spiritual Autobiography*, New York, 1903. The current biography is: Marie Henry, *The Secret Life of Hannah Whitall Smith*, Grand Rapids, 1984.

41  His most important book is: *Holiness Through Faith*, London, [2]1875 (1870).

42  See: Henry, *The Secret Life*, pp. 62–88. Another important factor in the crossing of the Atlantic of the holiness movement was an article published by Hannah Whitall Smith in the magazine *Revival*: 'The Way to be Holy' (November 1867). Former visits of Phoebe Palmer had prepared the soil, but had not started a lasting movement.

43 *Account of the Union Meeting for the Promotion of Scriptural Holiness, Held at Oxford, Aug. 29 to Sept 7, 1874*, London, 1874, Boston/New York, 1874. Hannah Whitall Smith's memories: *The Unselfishness of God*, pp. 221–227.

44 The conference had 6,000 participants. One thousand pastors participated in the 1874 conference (Samuel J. Stoesz, 'The Doctrine of Sanctification in the Thought of A. B. Simpson' in Hartzfeld and Nienkirchen, *The Birth of a Vision*, pp. 107–123 (p. 110)). The extraordinary atmosphere of this conference can be best seen from: J. B. Figgis, *Keswick from Within*, London/Edinburgh/New York, n.d. (1914), pp. 21–47.

45 Now there are also conferences such as 'Malawi Keswick' or 'Canadian Keswick'.

46 The writing of one of the very first Keswick histories was suggested by Hannah Whitall Smith: Figgis, *Keswick from Within*. The official history is: J. C. Pollock, *The Keswick Story. The Authorized History of the Keswick Convention*, London, 1964.

47 For Simpson's concept of holiness, see: Stoesz, 'The Doctrine of Sanctification in the Thought of A. B. Simpson' in Hartzfeld and Nienkirchen, *Birth of a Vision*, pp. 107–123 (pp. 116–119). The best source is: A. B. Simpson, *Wholly Sanctified*, New York, 1890. This book is based on his sermons.

48 Among faith missions, the Christian Literature Crusade (born out of WEC) did much to spread 'deeper life' literature, in the United States and elsewhere, by being publishers of such literature. See: Norman P. Grubb, *Leap of Faith. The Story of the Christian Literature Crusade*, Ft Washington, [3]1984 (1962), p. 131. Bethany Fellowship, Minneapolis (see Jones, *Holiness Movement*, p. 390), also publishes much holiness literature. Both CLC and Bethany started to do this in the 1950s, when this type of literature had virtually disappeared from the US book market.

49 The term was coined by William Edwin Boardman (1810–86) in his book *In the Power of the Spirit, or Christian Experience in the Light of the Bible*, Boston 1875/ London, 1879, to describe the 'second blessing experience' (Zikmund, Asa Mahan and Oberlin, *Perfectionism*, p. 264). The origins can also be traced to: Asa Mahan (1799–1889), *The Baptism of the Holy Ghost*, New York, 1870.

50 For his theology and for further literature, see: Gundry, *Love Them In*.

51 See: D. L. Moody, *Secret Power; or, the Secret of Success in Christian Life and Christian Work*, Chicago 1881; *Power from on High*, London, n.d.

52 Some biographies of Moody pay little or no attention to this event. The popular biography by Faith Coxe Bailey (*Dwight L. Moody*, Chicago, Moody Bible Institute, 1959) moves Moody's transformation to his 1867 visit to England, where men such as George Müller, Charles Haddon Spurgeon and Henry Varley impressed him. His 'baptism by the Holy Spirit' is not mentioned at all. Bailey is typical for the tendency to make the great evangelist Moody suitable for the post-1906 period. The best current biography, *Moody Without Sankey*, is by John Pollock, who does not make that mistake (pp. 82–87): 'Moody locked the door and sat on the sofa. The room seemed ablaze with God. He dropped to the floor and lay bathing his soul in the Divine... "I can only say that God revealed himself to me, and I had such an experience of His love that I had to ask Him to stay His hand... I was all the time tugging and carrying water. But now I have a river that carries me"... Crazy Moody became Moody the man of God' (p. 87). As with

Hudson Taylor, this experience was preceded by a surrender of the will for God's service.

53 Pollock, *Moody Without Sankey*, p. 83.

54 Wesley, 'A Plain Account of Christian Perfection' in John Wesley (ed.), *The Works of Rev. John Wesley*, Volume 11, pp. 366–446.

55 A detailed analysis of Wesley's relation to Law is: Eric Baker, *A Herald of the Evangelical Revival. A Critical Inquiry into the Relation of William Law to John Wesley and the Beginnings of Methodism*, London, 1948. For a recent study of Law, see: George E. Clarkson, *The Mysticism of William Law*, New York/Bern/Frankfurt/ Paris, 1992. Today, still available from Christian Literature Crusade (Ft Washington), edited by Dave Hunt: William Law, *The Power of the Spirit*. In South Africa, Andrew Murray published Law anew (William Law, *The Power of the Spirit. With Additional Extracts From the Writings of W. Law. Selected and With an Introduction by A. Murray*, London, 1896).

56 William Law, *A Serious Call to a Devout and Holy Life, Adapted to the State and Condition of all Orders of Christians*, London, 1729, [2]1732, [6]1753, [10]1772. Also Philadelphia, 1948, (Westminster Press) and elsewhere.

57 François de Salignac de la Mothe Fénelon (ascribed?), *The Archbishop of Cambray's Dissertation on Pure Love, With an Account of the Life and Writings of the Lady For Whose Sake the Archbishop was Banish'd From Court*, n.p., 3, 1750.

58 Phoebe and Walter Palmer published, in their own publishing house: *Letters of Madame Guyon: Being Selections of her Religious Thoughts and Experiences, Translated and Re-arranged From Her Private Correspondence; Including Her Correspondence with Fénelon*, abridged by Mrs P. L. Upham, New York, 1870. Today, available from a faith mission: Dorothy Gawne Coslet, *Madame Jeanne Guyon. Child of Another World*, Ft Washington (Christian Literature Crusade), [2]1985 (1984).

59 The final impulse for Simpson's holiness experience came from an anonymous book published by the Quakers William Backhouse and James Janson: *A Guide to True Peace; or, a Method of Attaining to Inward and Spiritual Prayer. Compiled Chiefly From the Writings of Fénelon, Archbishop of Cambray, Lady Guion and Michael de Molinos*. Second edition, corrected and enlarged, York/ London, 1815 (also York/London/Derby, 1847), which mainly consists of extracts of Madame Guyon's *Short Method of Prayer*, Fénelon's *Maxims of the Saints* and Molinos' *Spiritual Guide* (1675) (Dwayne Ratzlaff, 'An Old Mediaeval Message. A Turning Point in the Life of A. B. Simpson', in Hartzfeld and Nienkirchen, *Birth of a Vision*, p. 172). Simpson learned from it 'that God was waiting in the depth of my being to talk to me if I would only get still enough to hear His voice' (p. 168). The final impulse for A. B. Simpson's conversion was also a book of mysticism: Walter Marshall (1628–80), *The Gospel-Mystery of Sanctification Opened in Sundry Practical Directions, Suited especially to the Case of those who Labour Under the Guilt and Power of Indwelling Sin. To Which is Added a Sermon of Justification*, London, 1692; New York, 1811 (From the 12th European edition (most probably of 1788). (See: A. E. Thompson, *A. B. Simpson, His Life and Work*, p. 16). It is not sure whether A. B. Simpson read this edition or another.

60 See: Wilhelm Preger, *Geschichte der deutschen Mystik im Mittelalter. Nach den Quellen untersucht und dargestellt*, Leipzig, 1881, pp. 309–347. His writings:

Heinrich Seuse, *Deutsche mystische Schriften*. Aus dem Mittelhochdeutschen übertragen und herausgegeben von Georg Hofmann, Düsseldorf, 1966.

61 Tersteegen, a major exponent of pietism, was strongly influenced by quietist mysticism. He published three volumes: *Auserlesene Lebensbeschreibungen heiliger Seelen* (1733–53), containing the lives of Catholic saints.

62 In *MRW*, XX (February 1897), p. 87, A. T. Pierson describes the holiness concept of Keswick in five steps: the definite and immediate abandonment of every known sin or hindrance to holy living; the abandonment and renunciation by faith of the self-life, or the life that centres in self-indulgence and self-dependence; the immediate surrender of the will in loving and complete obedience to the will of God, separation in order to consecration; the infilling of the Holy Spirit, or the claiming of the believer's share in the Spirit's pentecostal gift of power for service; and the revelation of Christ as an indwelling presence in the believer's soul and daily life, and as his actual Master and Lord. Pierson, *A. T. Pierson*, p. 288, describes the holiness experience in six steps. See also: A. T. Pierson, *The Keswick Movement in Precept and Practice*, New York/London, 1903.

63 In many cases, the decisive point was the willingness (or not) to become a missionary. With Moody, the final point of (not yet) surrender in 1871 was 'to go out and preach the Gospel all over the land' (Pollock, *Moody Without Sankey*, p. 84).

64 A typical example of this experience is Norman P. Grubb's description of Rees Howells' full surrender (Norman P. Grubb, *Rees Howells. Intercessor*, Guildford/London, [8]1983, pp. 37–43). His struggle lasted five days; every day he surrendered another area of his life: money, selection of a marriage partner, ambition, property, reputation.

65 See, for example: Grubb, *Rees Howells*, p. 43.

66 For this and for the experience of sanctification in general, see Pierson's description in his biography of his father: *A. T. Pierson*, p. 287f. This description represents Keswick theology well. Every Keswick speaker had to testify to this experience.

67 McKay, *Faith and Facts*, p. 159.

68 Figgis, *Keswick from Within*, p. 94. Radcliffe was a travelling evangelist in the Brethren movement, but also belonged to the holiness movement.

69 His account: Hudson Taylor, *Retrospect*, pp. 11–13.

70 Later histories of the Methodist Free Church cite quarrels over the role of laymen in the church as the decisive point for the split. Sources closer to CIM stress the attempted renewal of holiness teaching as the major factor.

71 Geraldine and Howard Taylor, *Hudson Taylor in Early Years*, p. 112.

72 'The Beauty of Holiness. A Letter to the Newark Presbytery', by a Pastor of the Free Presbyterian Church, Newark, NJ, in *Wesleyan Methodist Magazine*, (November) 1849, pp. 1144–1150, 1270–1274.

73 Hudson Taylor—Amelia Taylor, 2 December 1849 in Broomhall, *Barbarians at the Gates*, p. 354.

74 'Well do I remember, as in unreserved consecration I put myself, my life, my

friends, my all, upon the altar, the deep solemnity that came over my soul with the assurance that my offering was accepted. The presence of God became unutterably real and blessed; and though but a child under sixteen, I remember stretching myself on the ground, and lying there silent before Him with unspeakable awe and unspeakable joy' (Hudson Taylor, *Retrospect*, p. 15).

75  He surrendered his whole life to God and experienced a deep stillness. He felt that God had accepted his surrender and 'heard' as if a human voice had spoken: 'Then go for me to China'. Hudson Taylor rarely spoke of this experience. This explains the fact that accounts vary in details. (See: Geraldine and Howard Taylor, *Hudson Taylor in Early Years*, p. 78f.; Hudson Taylor, *Retrospect*, pp. 15ff.; Broomhall, *Barbarians at the Gates*, pp. 353–355).

76  McKay, *Faith and Facts*, p. 154. The essay in the magazine *The Revival* was: 'If we believe not; He abideth faithful'. See: Broomhall, *Refiner's Fire*, pp. 210–215, where the event is described in the context of CIM and the holiness movement.

77  Classical holiness teaching knows only one holiness experience. In CIM, terms were used such as: life on a higher plane; exchanged life; or to be one with Christ.

78  Holmes, *The Cloud Moves*, p. 9. Then he began evangelistic work among Catholics in Ireland. On 29 July 1857, the Moorfield Tabernacle in London made him a travelling evangelist (p. 10).

79  'This is July, 1896. At Mildmay, Northfield, Keswick, and a hundred other conferences in England and America, thousands are meeting this summer to sing and pray, and listen to the Scriptures, and talk of holiness... Think of it for a moment. Stand here in this Keswick tent with the three thousand Christians gathered at the closing consecration meeting. The men and women sitting in these crowded seats possess money enough to float a steamer carrying the gospel on that far Upper Congo, and to open a dozen mission stations beyond Stanley Falls within the next six months without diminishing their ordinary gifts to Christian work. Scores of young men and women, student volunteers and others, are here with bent heads among this praying multitude, young lives washed by the blood of Jesus Christ, lived in the shadow of the Cross, young lives just fitted 'to help heal this open sore of the world'. But this Keswick will close as so many other Conferences have closed—Will it?' (Lucy Guinness, *To Help to Heal. A Missionary Study and an Appeal for Prayer*, London, n.d. (1896), p. 19f.).

80  Frederick Brotherton Meyer, *The Soul's Pure Intention*, London, 1906; *The Call and Challenge of the Unseen*, London, 1928.

81  Grattan Guinness and Karl Kumm were not Keswick speakers, but Lucy Guinness and Karl Kumm spoke during missionary meetings there. Karl Kumm's talk of 1903 was very important for the nascent SUM (*Lightbearer*, August/September 1906).

82  This 'circle' includes: Livingstone Inland Mission, Congo Balolo Mission, Qua Iboe Mission, NAM and SUM. But there were also relations to Keswick. (See: 'Memoirs of Keswick 1893. By a First Attender' in *Qua Iboe Mission Occasional Papers*, October 1893).

83  The most prominent case is that of Cyrus Ingersoll Scofield (1843–1921), who produced the Scofield Bible. His biography is: Trumbull, *The Life Story of C. I.*

*Scofield*. C. E. Hurlbert held a similar position (*Inland Africa*, November 1917, pp. 3–4).

84 *Qua Iboe Mission Mountpottinger Auxiliary—Its Origin and Management.*

85 *Ibid.*

86 Corbett, *According to Plan*, p. 13.

87 In 1890, three YMCA secretaries (Black, Miller, M'Cann) issued the first *Qua Iboe Mission Occasional Paper*; in January 1891, there were two YMCA auxiliaries. M'Keown, for many years QIM's home director, was earlier YMCA secretary in Londonderry (*QIM Occasional Paper*, March 1896).

88 *Lightbearer*, October 1908.

89 SUM minutes book. The 'branches' in Aberdeen and Dublin were directly related to YMCA/YWCA (*Lightbearer*, February 1904).

90 Steele, *Not in Vain*, p. 20.

91 So-called after William Thomas Berger (*ca.* 1812–99), the first CIM Home Director, who also supported Grattan Guinness who, in turn, was a CIM 'referee'. Later, more mission halls were added; also, literacy classes and a factory girls' club.

92 Swan, *Lacked Ye*, p. 11.

93 Swan, *Lacked Ye*, p. 9.

94 Swan, *Lacked Ye*, p. 17. In addition, the EGM had strong ties to the YMCA (p. 10).

95 Weeks, *W. Spencer Walton*, p. 11.

96 Figgis, *Keswick from Within* p. 50f.

97 Thomas D. H. Battersby, *Memoir of T. D. Harford-Battersby. Together With Some Account of the Keswick Convention By Two of His Sons*, London, 1890.

98 The present biography, published by a faith mission, is: Leona Choy, *Andrew Murray. Apostle of Abiding Love*, Ft Washington, CLC, 1978. Older biographies are: J. Du Plessis, *The Life of Andrew Murray of South Africa*, London/Edinburgh/New York, 1919; W. M. Douglas, *Andrew Murray and His Message—One of God's Choice Saints*, London/Edinburgh, 1926 (Ft Washington, 1957). '

99 Weeks, *W. Spencer Walton*, p. 43f.

100 Weeks, *W. Spencer Walton*, p. 36.

101 Weeks, *W. Spencer Walton*, pp. 21f; 28.

102 'The object of the Mission is: 1st To fulfil Christ's Command to "Preach the Gospel to every creature" and 2nd, To help to promote and deepen the spiritual life of Christians' (South Africa General Mission, *Statement of Position*, February 1903).

103 *South African Pioneer*, 1891, p. 250f.

104 Weeks, *W. Spencer Walton*, p. 99.

105 Choy, *Murray*, pp. 187–204. His most important mission publication is: Andrew Murray, *The Key to the Missionary Problem*, London, 1901. The book was

written in connection with the Ecumenical Missionary Conference, New York 1900. See Choy, *Andrew Murray*, pp. 195–204. For Murray, mission was 'the chief end of the church' (Per Hassing).

106Choy, *Andrew Murray*, p. 146. He had been influenced, among others, by Stockmayer's writin'·s, and had also met him personally (p. 144).

107In Bethshan, influences from the Swiss and the US healing movement converged. Mrs Baxter had been influenced by Stockmayer and his work in Männedorf (Switzerland). Boardman, like A. B. Simpson, was influenced by Dr Cullis of Boston: 'Fullness of life is fullness of health. Disease is incompatible with fullness of life. His presence in us learned by faith as our fullness of life, and so of health, is really the expulsive force that rebukes and expells disease' (Wiseman, *Elizabeth Baxter*, p. 132).

108With his famous book *Higher Christian Life* (London, 1859) he created one of the most important holiness terms. His biography: Mary M. Boardman, *Life and Labours of Rev. W. E. Boardman*, New York, 1886.

109Wiseman, *Elizabeth Baxter*. For Bethshan: see, pp. 129–178.

110Choy, *Andrew Murray*, p. 147; Wiseman, *Elizabeth Baxter*, p. 134.

111For an overview of his many books, see: Choy, *Andrew Murray*, pp. 253–274. Important ones are: *Abide in Christ (1864); Be Perfect* (1893); *Divine Healing* (1900); *The Full Blessing of Pentecost* (1907); and *The State of the Church* (written for Edinburgh 1910) (1911).

112N. J. Brümmer, 'Dr Kumm' in *De Kerkbode*, 1907, p. 306; 'Correspondentie' in *De Kerkbode*, 1907, p. 370; Andrew Murray, 'De Soedan' in *De Kerkbode*, 1907, p. 443f.; p. 481f. (See: Torjesen, *A Study of Fredrik Franson*, p. 775f.). When Kumm revisited South Africa in 1911, Andrew Murray presided on 9 August 1911 over an important conference (Report of a visit to South Africa, Australia, New Zealand and the United States of America, undertaken in the interests of the United Mission by H. K. W. Kumm, 1912).

113A parallel case is that of Adoniram Judson Gordon, who was at the same time president of the executive committee of the American Baptist Missionary Union, and an ardent supporter and propagator of the new faith missions (Robert, 'The Legacy of Adoniram Judson Gordon' in *IBMR*, October 1987, pp. 176–181 (p. 179)). For his view on faith missions, see: A. J. Gordon, 'The Overflow of Missions' in *MRW*, March 1893.

114Colin N. Peckham, *The Africa Evangelistic Band. An Historical and Doctrinal Appraisal*, Diploma of Theology, Theological College, Johannesburg, 1973, p. 3f. Here there are three levels of Christian living, not two, as usual: childhood piety, 'inherited' from the parents, but consciously accepted in a conversion experience; the conscious decision to live for Christ (her house in Glenvar very soon became a centre of Christian activity); and reaching the higher plane of Christian living. Of Keswick, it was said, 'there was dynamite indeed' (p. 4).

115I. R. Govan, *Spirit of Revival. The Story of J. G. Govan and the Faith Mission*, Edinburgh, [4]1978 (1938), pp. 91ff.

116Govan, *Spirit of Revival*, p. 36f.

117'Full salvation' is another term for the second level in holiness doctrine. In the pentecostal movement this was changed to 'full gospel'. The Africa Evangelistic Band, even in its statistics, distinguishes between conversion and 'full salvation' (Govan, *Spirit of Revival*, p. 211).

118'We had recently entered into the experience of holiness ourselves, and had suffered somewhat for it, so we felt drawn to this man who had been passing through the fire for this same truth that had transformed our Christian lives' (Govan, *Spirit of Revival*, p. 99).

119Peckham, *Africa Evangelistic Band*, p. 15f.

120See: 1 Samuel 17:40. Printed the first time in: C. T. Studd, *Christ's Etceteras*, p. 9f. *Christ's Etceteras* was written by Studd in Zaire before he started his work there.

121His autobiography: Norman P. Grubb, *J. D. Drysdale, Prophet of Holiness*, London, 1955, pp. 1–184.

122The school was especially designed to train missionaries, teach them to live by faith and in close fellowship. The fees were very low and the students were taught 'to receive a clean heart by the baptism with the Holy Ghost and fire' (Grubb, *Drysdale, p. 101*).

123Grubb, *Drysdale*, pp. 10, 101f., 118ff.

124Grubb, *Drysdale*, p. 144. He also started a holiness denomination in 1916, only as a sideline: today, there are six congregations. The Emmanuel Holiness Church combined a number of formerly independent evangelistic congregations in and around Birkenhead.

125Looking back, those years were considered as 'spiritually red hot' (N. N.). The quest for holiness was intense, patterned on Acts 1:4: there were 'tarrying meetings' to wait for the Holy Spirit. Today, the school has lost its importance among English Bible schools and is no longer one of the schools with a special WEC recommendation.

126The close contacts of the school to Ethiopia are fascinating. On the suggestion of Alfred Buxton (then Bible Churchmen's Missionary Society), Asrate Kassa, son of the Ras Kassa, became a student at the school. The emperor visited the school and his son-in-law, Abye Abebe, married to Princess Tshai, became a student there; later, other members of the emperor's family did so, too (Doris M. Ruscoe, *The Intercession of Rees Howells*, Guildford/Ft Washington, 1983, pp. 22–23). See also: Norman P. Grubb, *Rees Howells*. The school no longer carries a special WEC recommendation.

127See: Vyrnwy Morgan, *The Welsh Religious Revival 1904–05. A Retrospect and a Criticism*, London, 1909.

128Grubb, *Rees Howells*, pp. 36ff. In contrast to the 'eradicationist school', Howells understood the replacement of 'self nature' by 'divine nature' as a gradual process, for which the crisis experience of sanctification is the precondition (Grubb, *Rees Howells*, p. 100f.).

129For ABM history, see: Steele, *Not in Vain*, pp. 121–126.

130Pigott, *I. Lilias Trotter*, p. 4: 'In 1872, her mother took her to the conference at Broadlands, where Lady Mount Templei collected from far and near those who came to welcome the Quaker preachers, Mr and Mrs Pearsall Smith of

Philadelphia, and to listen to their teaching on the Life of Consecration. Of the great spiritual emancipation here given her, Lily's whole life was an illustration.'

131 Pigott, *I. Lilias Trotter*, p. 4. Today, the emancipating aspect of the holiness movement is often neglected. Equal spiritual and ecclesiastical rights for women, co-education, independence from ecclesiastical hierarchies are prominent examples.

132 Angola (circular letter), 21 June 1927 (Yale). In *Angola Evangelical Mission*, 16 February 1928, Stober uses typical holiness terms such as 'spirit of consecration'. Also, there was an 'Angola Party', a daily prayer meeting at Keswick in 1927 (*Angola*, 21 June 1927).

133 Interview D. L. Evans, 18 October 1985.

134 This includes the earlier Missionary Union for the Evangelization of the World, Christian Alliance, Missionary Alliance and International Missionary Alliance. For a bibliography, see: Jones, *Holiness Movement*, pp. 498–509.

135 This 'fourfold gospel' became the pentecostal 'foursquare gospel' (Aimee Semple McPherson (1890–1944)), sanctification being replaced by baptism in the Holy Spirit.

136 For A. B. Simpson's holiness doctrine, see: A. B. Simpson, *The Fourfold Gospel. Jesus Christ: Saviour, Sanctifier, Healer, Coming Lord*, Camp Hill, PA, 1984 (updated and edited edition). For a scholarly review, see: Sawin, 'The Fourfold Gospel' in Hartzfeld and Nienkirchen, *The Birth of a Vision*, pp. 1–28; Stoesz, 'The Doctrine of Sanctification in the Thought of A. B. Simpson' in Hartzfeld and Nienkirchen, *The Birth of a Vision*, pp. 107–124.

137 The word 'tabernacle' alludes to Israel's tabernacle in the wilderness, which was put up wherever the people were. In the days of Whitefield and Wesley, tabernacles were temporary structures erected for evangelistic campaigns. Later, the term came to be used for non-conventional 'churches' in the urban areas, built for the masses such as Spurgeon's Metropolitan Tabernacle. When tenders were invited for the Tabernacle, it was made clear that a Gothic (church like) building was not at all what was wanted.

138 Thompson, *A. B. Simpson*, pp. 72–81; pp. 138–149; Niklaus, Sawin and Stoesz, *All for Jesus*, pp. 7–16. In 1874, A. T. Pierson was strongly influenced by Whittle and Bliss (Pierson, *Arthur T. Pierson*, pp. 128ff.). For Whittle, see: Ernest O. Sellers, *Evangelism in Sermon and Song*, Chicago, 1946, pp. 37–41.

139 Ratzlaff, 'An Old Mediaeval Message' in Hartzfeld and Nienkirchen, *The Birth of a Vision*, pp. 165–194, deals in detail with Simpson's sanctification experience and relates it to the broad realm of mysticism. A very rare experience in the faith mission context was the vision of Christ which Amelia, Hudson Taylor's sister, experienced: 'It happened when she was asleep, in a dream. She was standing in a cornfield that had just been reaped, and the winnowing process was going on. The wheat was being separated from the chaff. Then, as she looked, she saw a cloud in the sky, bright and gleaming, and she saw it was coming down, down to where she stood, and in it she saw a Figure. Beside her on one side was her husband, and on the other side Harriet the cook, and catching their hands in hers she felt herself lifted up in an ecstasy towards the Figure in the cloud, and then she saw His face ... She very rarely spoke of it, and could never describe that blessed face. She

only knew that more than anything else she longed to see it again' (Phyllis Thompson, *Each to Her Post*, London/Sevenoaks, 1982, p. 30).

140Charles Cullis, *Faith Cures or Answers to Prayer in the Healing of the Sick*, Boston, 1879; *Tuesday Afternoon Talks*, Boston, 1892. W. H. Daniels, *Dr Cullis and his Work*, Boston, 1885. For Bingham's positive attitude to Dr Cullis, see: Rowland V. Bingham, *The Bible and the Body. Healing in the Scriptures*, London/Edinburgh, [4]1952 (1921), pp. 15–17.

141 A 'convention ground' at the shore used by various groups. Later, 'Old Orchard Convention' became perhaps the most important of the many CMA conventions.

142See: Niklaus, Sawin and Stoesz, *All for Jesus*, VI and VII, pp. 39–42; and McKenzie, 'My Memories of Dr Simpson', 5 June 1937, unpublished.

143Sawin, 'The Fourfold Gospel' in Hartzfeld and Nienkirchen, *The Birth of a Vision*, pp. 1–28 (see pp. 11–15); A. B. Simpson, *The Gospel of Healing*, New York, 1887 (and further editions until today). For Bingham's criticism of Simpson's healing doctrine, see: Bingham, *The Bible and the Body*, pp. 96–104. For counter-critisism, see: Reynolds, *Footprints*, p. 387.

144Niklaus, Sawin and Stoesz, *All for Jesus*, p. 55f. These brought about the establishment of Berachah Home (p. 56f.), a healing home similar to Mrs Baxter's Bethshan.

145Niklaus, Sawin and Stoesz, *All for Jesus*, pp. 73–79.

146J. Kennedy Maclean, *Dr Pierson and his Message. A Sketch of the Life and Work of a Great Preacher, Together With a Varied Selection From His Unpublished Manuscripts*, New York, 1911. His biography is: Pierson, *A. T Pierson* Important publications: *The Crisis of Missions or The Voice out of the Cloud*, London, 4 n.d. (1886); *The Divine Enterprise of Missions. A Series of Lectures*, London, 1902; *Forward Movements of the Last Half Century Being a Glance at the More Marked Philanthropic, Missionary and Spiritual Movements Characteristic of Our Time*, New York, 1905 (Garland reprint, New York/London, 1984).

147Robert, 'The Legacy of Adoniram Judson Gordon' in *IBMR*, 1987, pp. 176–181; Ernest B. Gordon, *Adoniram Judson Gordon. A Biography*, New York, 1896; George G. Houghton, *The Contributions of Adoniram Judson Gordon to American Christianity*, ThD, Dallas Theological Seminary, 1970. Gordon's best known book is: *The Holy Spirit in Missions*, New York, 1893. See also: 'The Holy Spirit in Missions', report of the First International Convention of the Student Volunteer Movement for Foreign Missions, Cleveland/Boston, 1891.

148For A. T. Pierson's view of the holiness movement, see: Arthur T. Pierson, *Forward Movements*, ('The Increase of Personal Holiness', pp. 1–13; 'The Oxford Movement Toward Holiness', pp. 14–23; 'Keswick Teaching', pp. 24–38; 'Keswick Method', pp. 39–50).

149The 'in memoriam' of *HD*, No. 3, February 1897 dates his 'consecration' in about 1888. This must be understood as a sanctification experience. Jones, *Holiness Movement*, p. 739f., classifies him as an important personality of the holiness movement.

150See: James Henry McConkey, *The Three-Fold Secret of the Holy Spirit*, Harrisburg, 1908.

151 Robert C. McQuilkin, 'Carrying the Victory Message' in *Inland Africa*, November 1917, pp. 3–4.

152 He was a Quaker, but belonged to the group which was strongly influenced by the holiness movement (Willis Ray Hotchkiss, *Then and Now in Kenya Colony. Forty Adventurous Years in East Africa*, New York, n.d. (*ca.* 1937)).

153 *HD*, August/September 1899.

154 Hurlbert negotiated with the (holiness) Quakers in Ohio, and the conclusion was reached that the founding of a new mission would not be advisable (*HD*, August/September 1899). The East Africa Yearly Meeting of Friends today (*ca.* 1975, *ca.* 100,000 members) is the largest outside the United States.

155 Burnette and Gerald Fish, *The Place of Songs*, Nairobi, 1989.

156 Burnette and Gerald Fish, *The Call to Battle*, Kericho, 1982, p. 10f. The WGM started in 1935 in the area of Tenweck. The link between the Lumbwa Industrial Mission and WGM was Johana Ng'etich (p. 12). For the work of WGM in Kenya, see: Trachsel, *Kindled Fires in Africa*.

157 Loewen, *Three Score*, p. 32.

158 Before she travelled to Kenya, the AIM wrote about her: 'Until finally there came an unquenchable thirst for the power of the Holy Spirit for Christ-likeness and power in soulwinning. It was in this hallowed hour of consecration, Miss Doering says, that God spoke Africa to her soul' (*HD*, April/June 1906, p. 8).

159 *HD*, April/June 1906, p. 8.

160 Alfred Roth, *Otto Stockmayer. Ein Zeuge und Nachfolger Jesu Christi*, Gotha, 1925 ([2]1938).

161 *HD*, July/October 1906.

162 His current biography is still: J. H. Hunter, *A Flame of Fire. The Life and Work of R. V. Bingham*, Toronto, 1961. His autobiography is: Bingham, *Seven Sevens of Years*.

163 He was converted in a Salvation Army meeting by the preaching of a converted Jew (Hunter, *Flame of Fire*, pp. 43ff.).

164 Reynolds, *Footprints*, p. 179.

165 The best source is: Reynolds, *Footprints*, pp. 1–320. Salmon has been undeservedly forgotten. In Jones, *Holiness Movement*, he is not even mentioned.

166 Reynolds, *Footprints*, p. 179. There, he met Helen Blair, daughter of the CMA branch president of Aberfoyle near Toronto, whom he married five years later (p. 182). In 1893, Bethany Chapel ('an independent church affiliated with the CMA') sent him to the Sudan as an independent missionary (p. 184). Salmon later became the most important member of the SIM home board (Minutes Africa Industrial Mission 1898ff.). He held this position in spite of the fact that the CMA had its own far-reaching missionary programme.

167 Hunter, *Flame of Fire*, pp. 268–274.

168 Hunter, *Flame of Fire*, p. 65.

169 A comprehensive exposition of Bingham's views on healing is: Bingham, *The*

*Bible and the Body*. In 1886, Bingham distanced himself from Simpson's position 'that healing is in the atonement' (p. 91).

170 Hunter, *Flame of Fire*, pp. 85; 298.

171 Torjesen, *A Study of Fredrik Franson*, p. 80.

172 Torjesen, *A Study of Fredrik Franson*, pp. 321–358. Soon he could not control the healing meetings, so he stopped them. But he continued to pray individually over the sick.

173 Spoken communication Edvard Torjesen, 13 November 1987.

174 See the news in *Trons Segrar*.

175 Franson wanted to marry her, but she refused him.

176 Spoken communication Edvard Torjesen, 13 November 1987. During his first evangelists' course, he had still taught: 'Present sanctification as a normal walk or growth in grace, not as some new experience or some new status' (Torjesen, *A Study of Fredrik Franson*, p. 317). But this course had taken place before his visit to England, where he was strongly influenced by the holiness movement.

177 The answer to my letter of inquiry to the GMU was that there had never been any influences of the holiness movement. This reply does not match with the fact that the first GMU missionaries were sent out by the CMA, and that Fisher was the CMA representative for the middle West and member of the CMA general council. The early GMU magazines show clearly the prevalence of holiness teaching. Like the Central America Mission started by C. I. Scofield in 1890, it belonged to that branch of the holiness movement which was equally strongly influenced by the prophetic movement.

178 Bibliography and overview: Jones, *Holiness Movement*, pp. 9– 95.

179 Especially so in Germany: Andreas Franz, 'Der Einfluß der Heiligungsbewegung auf die deutschsprachigen Glaubensmissionen' in *Evangelikale Missiologie*, 1992, pp. 67–71.

180 Clearly visible from Carl McIntire's sermons (Collingswood Bible Presbyterian Church, 15 and 22 March 1986).

181 His biography is: Trumbull, *The Life Story of C. I. Scofield*.

182 See also: Sydney E. Ahlstrom, *A Religious History of the American People*, New Haven/London, [9]1979 (1972), pp. 808ff.

183 In the first decade, AIM still recommended holiness Bible schools such as Peniel (*HD*, May 1900) and Hephzibah House (*HD*, December 1905) for missionary training.

184 Stoesz, 'The Doctrine of Sanctification in the Thought of A. B. Simpson', pp. 107–123 (p. 115).

185 Ernst Schrupp (ed.), *Im Dienst von Gemeinde und Mission. 75 Jahre Bibelschule und Mission*, Bergneustadt, 1980.

186 At the 1896 Blankenburg Conference in Thuringia, Hudson Taylor was a major speaker.

187 Andrew Murray, *The Two Covenants and the Second Blessing*, London, 1899,

Appendix: 'George Müller and His Second Conversion'.

188Bevan, *Hymns of Ter Steegen, Suso and Others*; John S. Andrews, 'Frances Bevan' in *Evangelical Quarterly*, 1962, pp. 206–213; 1963, pp. 30–38.

189Coad, *Brethren Movement*, p. 66.

190Jeanne Saillens, *L'Institut Biblique de Nogent-sur-Marne. Coup-d'oeil rétrospectif*, n.p., n.d.

191Wargenau-Saillens, *Ruben et Jeanne Saillens*, pp. 145ff.

192Saillens suggested that Rolland, a worker with Renault, go to Algiers as a missionary.

193This led to the astonishing fact that those students who wanted to join the CIM were acceptable neither to the Swiss (Chrischona) branch of the CIM nor to the two associated missions (Schweizer Allianz-China-Mission and Diakonissen-Mutterhaus Ländli (Yünnanmission)). See: Andreas Franz, *Hudson Taylor und die deutschsprachigen Glaubensmissionen*, p. 127f.

194'Before we began our work in Switzerland, the home country of my husband, the Lord in His grace gave me a new great gift in meeting Ruth Paxson who pointed out so clearly: you must be filled with the Holy Spirit. I knew it was the power I needed to enter the great task the Lord had placed before us. It was again a day of grace when I accepted by faith the fullness of the Holy Spirit. Since that time, it is now more than 30 years ago, the power of the Holy Spirit is the promise of God in my life to strengthen me and give me the courage to work, to stand alone in the confession of the full inspiration of the Bible, to win souls and to overcome all difficulties of life' (Gertrud Wasserzug, 'By the Grace of God I Am What I Am', n.d., unpublished).

195Ruth Paxson, *Life On the Highest Plane*, three volumes in one, Chicago, 1928; German edition: Ruth Paxson, *Das Leben im Geist*; Christus und die Gläubigen; Der Heilige Geist und die Gläubigen, all Dinglingen, 1932. 1944: *Ströme lebendigen Wassers*.

196Dora Rappard, *Carl Heinrich Rappard. Ein Lebensbild*, 1910 (reprint Giessen/ Basel, 1983).

197She became famous as an author.

198Edgar Schmid (ed.), *Wenn Gottes Liebe Kreise zieht. 150 Jahre Pilgermission St Chrischona (1840–1990)*, Giessen/Basel, 1990, p. 13.

199A very good overview of the varied *foreign* mission history of Chrischona is: Lutz Behrens, 'Gottes Werkzeuge in aller Welt. Die Pilgermission und die äußere Mission' in Edgar Schmid (ed.), *Wenn Gottes Liebe*, pp. 106–117.

200Franz, *Hudson Taylor*, pp. 114ff.

201Andreas Franz, 'Der Einfluß der Heiligungsbewegung auf die deutschsprachigen Glaubensmissionen' in *Evangelikale Missiologie*, 1992, pp. 67–71.

202The leadership was then taken over by Ziemendorf, a leader of the Hessian fellowship movement. How far he *directly* contributed to the holiness movement remains still to be assessed.

203J. Magnusson, *50 år i ord och bild 1892–1942. Jubileumskrift för Örebro Missionsförening*, Örebro, 1942, p.12f.

204Fanny Guinness sums up the experience when she writes that the early LIM missionaries should have been better equipped: 'It would not do to risk the lives of missionaries for lack of Kroo-boy help' (Fanny Guinness, *The New World of Central Africa*, p. 203, similarly p. 187).

205Pigott, I. *Lilias Trotter*, p. 4f; Steele, *Not in Vain*, p. 122.

206About her experiences, she wrote: *Only a Factory Girl*, London, 1896. See: Grattan Guinness, *Lucy Guinness Kumm. Her Life Story. With Extracts From Her Writings*, London, 1907, p. 9; Michele Guinness, *Guinness Legend*, pp. 178–182.

207There are occasional exceptions: the Gospel Furthering Fellowship in Kenya does only spiritual work (Interview George L. Machamer, Nairobi, 29 December 1986).

208See also: W. D. Armstrong, 'Sunrise on the Congo. A Record of the Earlier Years of the Congo Balolo Mission', unpublished (283 pages), n.d., pp. 204, 239ff.

209The Congo question is treated in detail in: S. J. S. Cookey, *Britain and the Congo Question 1885–1913*, London, 1968. Harry Guinness is mentioned six times (pp. 109–111, 143f.) but, because Cookey did not choose to use RBMU documents or books, Guinness is only seen from the viewpoint of the Aborigines Protection Society (to Fox Bourne he was a 'slippery customer' (p. 111)) and the Congo Reform Association for which he only started to work in 1904.

210Cookey, *Congo Question*, p. 40; Mackintosh, *Harry Guinness*, p. 70.

211In 1883, Equator/Bolenge was the last station founded by LIM close to what is today Mbandaka. It was handed over to the ABMU in 1884, which passed it on to the Disciples of Christ in 1889.

212The Swedish Baptist, Sjöblom, had gone to Britain in 1891 to work there; he attended ELTI; in 1892, he became a missionary of the Congo Balolo Mission; and he joined the ABMU in 1893 (but continued to be supported by Swedish Baptists). He worked first in Bolenge, then in Ikoko, where he died in 1903 (*Baptistmissionens årstryk, 1911, p. 31; Irvine, The Church of Christ in Zaire*, p. 104). See also: David Lagergren, 'En ringa begynnelse—en historisk insats' in David Lagergren (ed.), *I Kongo. Svensk baptistmissionen under 50 år i ord och bild*, n.p., 1969, pp. 22ff.; David Lagergren, *Mission and State in the Congo. A Study of the Relations Between Protestant Missions and the Congo Independent State Authorities with Special Reference to the Equator District, 1885–1903* (Studia Missionalia Uppsaliensia XIII, 1970).

213Grattan Guinness, *The Congo Crisis*, London, 1908, p. 17f., italics in the original.

214Mackintosh, *Harry Guinness*, p. 71.

215See: Harry Grattan Guinness, *Congo Slavery. A Brief Survey of the Congo Question From the humanitarian Point of View*, London, n.d. 'Just because the missionaries know the possibilities of the Congo natives, they stand in the front row of those who demand that they shall be freed from their present oppression' (p. 31). This book also contains detailed eyewitness accounts by CBM missionaries.

216Mackintosh, *Harry Guinness*, pp. 72–74.

217Her husband Karl Kumm had asked her to join him in the United States to help in establishing the US branch of SUM and to stay on after he had to return to Britain. Northfield was Moody's home and, after his death, a Christian conference centre remained, with special emphasis on holiness teaching.

218It has not been possible to trace a copy of this manuscript. It was to be published under the title 'Our Slave State' but was never printed (Michele Guinness—Fiedler, 29 February 1988).

219He reminded the President of his duty, because the United States was a signatory power of the Berlin Act. It is not known what impression Harry Guinness made on Roosevelt (Michele Guinness, *The Guinness Legend*, p. 275). No record of the conversation could be traced in the Roosevelt archive.

220Grattan Guinness, *The Congo Crisis* (Special Issue in Regions Beyond, January/ February 1908).

221His impression was right. After 1907, the Congo question was a major diplomatic issue between Britain and Belgium (Cookey, *Congo Question*, pp. 208ff.). About 1908, a severe financial crisis began to hit ELTI, which led to its closure in 1910 (Minutes RBMU, 4 March 1910). Grattan Guinness died in 1910, and Harry Guinness in 1915.

# 8
# The rigorous Christian life: faith missions and African holiness

Holiness preaching in the United States and Europe, so dear to almost all the early faith missionaries, was essentially revival preaching. The holiness preachers and evangelists preached their message to people who had long been converted and yearned for a higher or deeper Christian life. This preaching often did not take place within the context of the established churches of the various denominations, but within movements which organized and financed themselves and, thus, in some way competed with the church establishment. The holiness movement did not reject the churches, but by teaching a message which the churches usually did not have, it was nevertheless critical of them.

When faith mission missionaries came to Africa they could not preach holiness, because where they started their work there were as yet no Christians. Even those missionaries who at home had been quite critical of the churches had, in Africa, first of all to establish such churches. This they had to do not by means of holiness preaching, but by preaching conversion (along with such auxiliary means as educational, technical or medical services).

Because the process of conversion was, in the beginning, a very slow one, it is understandable that not much time or energy was left for holiness preaching. Even after churches had been established, the sources indicate very little holiness preaching. It is very difficult to know in detail what the missionaries preached, but in Africa they definitely did not try to build the holiness structures they were used to, such as conferences, camp meetings and fellowship groups. They did not translate holiness literature into African languages, nor did they write their own holiness literature in such languages. The observation that the missionaries worked in a situation which was very different from what they were used to at home is only part of the answer. The other factor that must be taken into account is that in Africa the missionaries had changed roles. They could no longer be critical of the church establishment, for they had become the church establishment. So it is understandable that they were not interested in erecting structures which would compete with their own establishment.

Some exceptions, however, should be noted. In 1906 in Wellington, north-east of Cape Town, the SAGM instituted an annual conference on the Keswick pattern.[1] But that conference was for whites. The SAGM's pioneer work among black Africans did not differ much from that of other missions. The World Gospel Mission in Kenya, with its strong holiness roots, consciously tried, and still tries, to pass on its holiness heritage to the Africa Gospel Church, but felt it often difficult to do so.[2] The early WEC missionaries in north-eastern Zaire also tried to lead the people not only to faith in Christ, but also to a 'victorious life'.[3] The same is reported from the Angola Evangelical Mission. There may have been other cases; even in the early faith missions, there was very little holiness preaching in the terms of the holiness movement.

## It is not easy to become a church member

This does not mean that faith missions did not preach holiness in Africa, but that their holiness preaching there underwent a clear process of 'recalvinization'. The focus of holiness preaching was no longer the 'Arminian' second blessing experience but the 'Calvinist' striving to live a godly live. This striving to live a holy life frequently expressed itself in strict ethical rigorism which, even for the 'Arminian' missionaries, was not at all a strange thing,[4] because almost all missionaries, irrespective of their more Arminian or more Calvinist leanings, came from new spiritual movements which were quite critical of society and of established churches.[5] Ethical rigorism tends to turn itself into legalism when the spiritual impulses which supported that rigorism diminish.[6] Also, when a 'rigorous' group grows in numbers and comes more to terms with society, its ethical rigorism is reduced.[7]

When faith missionaries started their work in Africa, a situation developed which was similar to their own at home. With the small number of their converts, they were a minority in conflict with the 'church' of the majority of society, the African traditional religion. They continued to teach and practise their ethical rigorism.[8] because they were as willing to clash with African culture in their attempt to live a holy life as they had been prepared to clash with Western culture. These issues have received sufficient attention from missionaries, missiologists and historians alike, so there is no need to review the whole issue of 'church and African culture' here.[9] Only a limited number of aspects will be treated, which shed some special light on some or all of the faith missions.

## DELAYED BAPTISM

One observation is that, in many of the early faith missions, it was not easy to be admitted to baptism, and in some faith mission churches this is still the case.[10] Lakan, the first elder of Langtang congregation (SUM, now COCIN) was converted in 1914 and only baptized in 1919.[11] In the Lupwa congregation (SUM-US), two adults were baptized after being 'faithful enquirers for at least six years'.[12] For Benvinda Vaz Martins, the only woman in full-time service of the Igreja Evangélica da Guiné Bissau (WEC), there was a period of five years between conversion and baptism,[13] and Johana Ng'etich, the first pastor of the Africa Gospel Church (WGM), was even accepted into the church before his baptism.[14]

Because most faith missionaries took the reports in the book of Acts not only as historic, but also as normative, they should have developed a pattern of baptism following soon on conversion. And, indeed, there often have been tendencies in this direction. According to later conviction, the early CMA baptized too early in Zaire.[15] The same is reported about WEC missionaries in Burkina Faso.[16] Most marked was C. T. Studd's change of attitude towards baptism. In the early days of the Heart of Africa Mission (WEC), baptism was administered very soon after professed conversion.[17] However, when, after some time, some of the newly baptized 'disappointed' the missionaries, Studd suspended not only baptism,[18] but even the celebration of the Lord's table. Only in 1938, seven years after Studd's death, was baptism reintroduced into the church.[19] Studd based his action on the tenet that 'without holiness no man shall see the Lord' (Hebrews 12:4).[20] Studd never tried to work out a doctrine of a church without sacraments. His decision simply to abolish them for a certain time must be understood in terms of his radical personality, supported by the general conviction of faith missions that it was finally faith that was decisive for salvation, and not the sacraments. Though most probably this is the sole case of the temporary abolition of the sacraments in faith missions, it must nevertheless be seen only as a most extreme variation of a general attitude. In the present-day churches which have their origin in WEC, only a small proportion of the believers (who confess their faith and try to live accordingly) has ever been baptized.[21] A similar attitude is on record for the early Neukirchen Mission.[22] Héli Chatelin reported from Lincoln a good church attendance, conversions and the employment of evangelists, but as long as he lived no baptism took place.

A most extreme case still exists at the borderline between faith missions and classical missions. The Reformed Church among the Tiv in Nigeria[23] is famous for its strict church discipline and for the immense difficulty in becoming a church member,[24] so that the ratio of regular attenders to church members stands now at 17:1.[25]

Relative to the time of baptism, three tendencies can be distinguished: immediate baptism, conversion being—as in Acts—the only precondition; suspended baptism, which takes place after the convert has shown her or his worth over a period of several years; and baptism after a prolonged period of learning. In the long run, this became the pattern mostly adhered to among faith missions, who adapted their earlier practice and theology to that of the classical missions.

Faith missions did not try to come to *theological* terms with their policy of delaying baptism in one way or another. Because for a faith mission the basic mark of the church was conversion, a new definition of what conversion meant in an African context should have been attempted. When someone in the revival climate of Europe of those days professed 'to believe in Christ', he or she knew what that meant and what was expected. For an African, to whom Christianity presented itself as a new and attractive religious and cultural force, to profess belief in Christ first of all meant to join that religion and culture. Perhaps the redefinition of conversion in an African context should have taken this into account, defining conversion not as an momentous event but as a process (learning included) culminating in a deep inner commitment.

# A new definition of conversion or the chronological approach

One faith mission, the New Tribes Mission, did indeed redefine conversion. This did not happen through theological reflection, but by introducing a new way to preach conversion: the 'chronological approach'. Paul Fleming and Paul Lin, with whom the NTM originated in Malaysia, used the conventional approach of conversion preaching, sometimes even using a tent, and more than 3,000 conversions were reported over a period of two years. The chronological approach does not start with preaching the necessity of conversion, but with teaching very gradually (and with lively narrative) the history of salvation, starting with creation, and culminating, after a year or so of weekly meetings, in the 'giving of the gospel'. This method was first developed by Trevor McIlwain among the North Palawan in the Philippines.[26] His method caught on very quickly in almost all NTM fields, because the missionaries were frustrated by the easy-going conversion preaching of their earlier days.[27] Also, many felt that narrative evangelism was better adapted to the culture of their listeners than the often cumbersome systematic teaching of the truths of the Christian faith.[28]

In Senegal—where NTM had started to work in 1954 in co-operation with WEC, but with few results to show for much effort—the chronological approach was introduced in recent years in all areas. Now missionary work is seen as going through three phases:

◇ The first phase is that of cultural and linguistic learning, lasting at least two years, but usually three or more.[29] During this phase of 'pre-evangelism', there is neither preaching nor teaching.[30]

◇ The second phase is that of 'chronological evangelism'. In about seventy units, usually spread evenly over a year or more, the story of salvation, from creation to ascension, is taught as vividly as possible. During all the teaching of the Old Testament stories,[31] the name of Christ is never mentioned, but the missionary speaks of God's order, holiness and wrath, about the various offerings and the need for redemption and, if possible, even enacts the stories.[32] There is no singing, there are no prayers, no church building is erected, not even a school.[33] Only after at least a year, usually in connection with the story of Christ's passion, is the gospel presented to the group,[34] and the missionary (or whoever 'teaches' the 'course') asks his listeners politely, but in clear terms, to decide for the gospel of Christ.[35]

◇ The third phase is that of spiritual growth. It starts with a repetition of the stories told in the previous phase, but this

251

time each story is related to the New Testament, with special emphasis upon God's grace. After that, the teaching is conducted through five additional further levels.[36] Ideally, all this instruction is given in meetings for believers only, while the missionary (or even one or more of the new believers) tries to win other people, or people in other places, by way of 'chronological evangelism'.[37] It is hoped that the group of believers will then decide to build a meeting house, to organize itself as a church and so on[38] but, most of all, that it will evangelize elsewhere, using the same approach.[39]

The chronological approach has, up to now, been most effectively used in Papua New Guinea among the Bisario, where several churches have been started in this way. As hoped for, Bisario Christians used the chronological approach for their own evangelism, and people won in this way have been baptized by now. In Senegal, to date the only NTM field in Africa, this method has still to prove its worth, but it seems to present a serious alternative to the usual practice of fast conversion and slow baptism.

## A rigorous church

Two aspects of African culture toward which the classical missions usually reacted more generously were the consumption of alcoholic beverages and dancing.[40] Most faith missions either forbade the drinking of alcohol[41] or helped their converts to come to such a decision.[42] Some even forbade the brewing of beer and, because this was exclusively a woman's job, that rule created a host of problems for Christian wives whose husbands were not Christians.[43]

Whereas some classical missions tolerated dancing, or even tried to integrate it into the life of a congregation, faith missions could not see the point in accepting in Africa what was not acceptable to them in the culture they came from. For the missionaries, both decisions were comparatively easy to make, because they had dealt with the matter in their own culture. But how were they to deal with circumcision and related initiation rites, which they had never had to deal with in their own (sub)cultures? The issue became even more complicated by the fact that in the Old Testament one form of circumcision (that of male infants) was a divine command, and in the New Testament an accepted fact. Nevertheless, much of it was repugnant to the

Western faith missionary and, even if the operations were accepted, what about the heathen practices inextricably connected to them? The response of the faith missions varied, although wholesale rejection was more frequent than conscious Christianization.[44]

The most drastic case in this respect was probably the controversy over the circumcision of girls in Kenya[45] in which—after the Church of Scotland Mission—the AIM played the leading role. The controversy has been described several times,[46] so that it will suffice here to add some information on AIM's role in the conflict[47] and to bring out what this conflict meant for faith missions' concept of the church. The controversy was started by the Church of Scotland Mission at Kikuyu under the leadership of Dr Arthur,[48] but the two faith missions, AIM and Gospel Missionary Society (GMS), resolutely joined the CSM. Four factors made the controversy what it was:

◇ Among a progressive educated minority of the (Christian) Kikuyu, there developed a tendency to get rid of such a useless custom as circumcision, especially of girls.[49]

◇ With the growing establishment of the mission (and the diminution of contact to the people resulting from it),[50], the missionaries saw a realistic chance of confronting and abolishing a custom which they saw as meaningless and as positively dangerous from the medical point of view.

◇ However, the great majority of the Kikuyu, Christians included, saw circumcision as an integral and most important element of their culture.

◇ The missions' fight against clitoridectomy was seen by the Kikuyu nationalist movement as yet another attempt to subjugate the Kikuyu.[51]

The original attitude of the AIM with respect to circumcision was quite acceptable to the Kikuyu: the AIM saw circumcision as a heathen practice which it could not accept, but it did nothing to enforce this view.[52] The Kikuyu Christians could follow the mission's ruling or could take it just as an opinion expressed.[53] If parents wanted circumcision for their children and still 'avoid everything pagan', the AIM arranged for circumcision, even for girls, at Kijabe Hospital.[54] By doing so, circumcision was divested of its communal character, but girls and boys so circumcised were nevertheless accepted as adult members of Kikuyu society.[55]

In 1926, feeling backed by medical opinion in the mission, the AIM started openly to fight clitoridectomy.[56] In 1929 in Kambui, a girl was forcibly circumcised, and the GMS missionaries took the case to court,[57] but the circumcisors received only meaningless punishments.[58] This made the missions enhance their pressure. Following the lead of the CSM, the AIM now demanded a clear denunciation of clitoridectomy, first from church employees only, but then from every church member, from every pupil attending a mission school and from the pupils' parents, whether Christian or not.[59] This was usually understood as an oath.[60] About 90 per cent of all AIM members and adherents refused to sign,[61] and the few 'loyalists' who did sign came under heavy social pressure. The dramatic culmination of the confrontation was the murder of Hilda Stumpf on 3 January 1930.[62] On the last Sunday of 1929, acting as secretary of the mission in Kijabe church, she had composed a brief list of those who had signed the oath.[63] In 1932, under the combined pressure of events and the colonial administration, the AIM gave in. In the end, only office bearers of the church were required to sign the oath—pupils could attend school without any restrictions and soon one could even become an ordinary lay Christian without the oath.[64]

The circumcision controversy has often been interpreted as a quarrel between 'the missionaries' and 'the Kikuyu'. This view of things assumes that all missionaries were of the same opinion[65] and that Africans, who shared the missionaries' opinion, did so only under pressure from the missionaries.[66] In order to reach a fair assessment, it may be useful to take into account the circumcision controversy which shattered the Lutheran church on the slopes of Mt Kilimanjaro between 1923 and 1926, but in which the missionaries took the opposite side.

Leipzig Mission's medical opinion was, understandably, not very favourable towards clitoridectomy. But the mission, which held the view that the mission should not interfere with the church's attitude to the *adiaphora* (things that are neither intrinsically good nor bad), could do very little to combat clitoridectomy, since that was obviously an adiaphora. Because of the Versailles Treaty, all Leipzig missionaries had to leave Tanzania in 1920,[67] and the annual conference of teachers (who acted as pastors)[68] and elders was given the leadership. This conference discussed the issue of male and female circumcision in 1922 and decided, in January 1923, to forbid circumcision 'as

being contrary to the Bible'.[69] The parallel missionary conference, composed of recently arrived American Augustana Synod
(Lutheran) missionaries, ratified the decision, because the indigenous church could regulate on adiaphora.[70] After this ratifica-
tion, the 'teachers' began rigorously to implement the new
regulation. Exercise books were distributed, and everyone had
to sign that he or she would have nothing to do with circumcision, male or female. Anyone accepting circumcision or in any
way conniving in it was expelled from the church. The conference of teachers and elders explicitly endorsed the punishments,
and it was only in 1926, when the Leipzig missionaries were
allowed to return, that Bruno Gutmann of Old Moshi was able to
quell the initiative. Being correctly convinced that he knew the
mind of the Chagga congregations better than their elected
leaders, and with the help of some other missionaries, he forced
the Chagga leaders to withdraw the regulation.[71] They resisted as
long as they could, but stood no chance against the returned
Leipzig missionaries, who had the support of the vast majority of
the Chagga Christians [72]

Although this controversy had shattered the congregations,
the missionary world took no notice. There is no hint that the
Kenya missionaries knew anything about the controversy, which
might have been a warning for them, although at least some were
aware of Vincent Lucas' attempts to Christianize circumcision
among the Yao in southern Tanzania.[73] The Chagga circumcision controversy may help to shed some light on the controversy
among the Kikuyu, because the Chagga circumcision controversy cannot be seen as a conflict between Africans and European missionaries. It must be seen as a conflict pertaining to
issues of Christian ethics, in which the dividing lines did not
follow the cultural divide. This implies that the Kikuyu who
opposed clitoridectomy were not just loyalists but, like the
Chagga teachers, were a progressive minority, which failed to
understand that, although they could lead their fellow Christians
in many things, their leadership was not acceptable in all matters.

The various groups acting in the controversies displayed
considerable spirit. Filipo Njau, who led the fight against circumcision at Old Moshi, had done nothing to combat circumcision
before the teachers' conference in 1922–23 had decided to
abolish it. Then he suddenly put all his weight behind the issue;
in 1926, when the missionaries' conference rescinded the
teachers' conference's laws, he did not even inform the church.

When the resident Augustana missionary enquired about the congregation's reaction, Filipo Njau gave the impression that the congregation had refused to accept the new ruling[74] when, in fact, the congregation had never been told about it.

The AIM missionaries displayed the same spirit. Hilda Stumpf had grave doubts about how the fight against female circumcision was conducted.[75] When the virtual boycott of the mission school had not ended after several months, other missionaries quietly voiced the doubts which they had had before. John Stauffacher, the only AIM missionary among the Masai, complied—albeit very reluctantly—with the group decision of the missionaries in demanding the oath from his congregation. The result was that only three boys were left in it.[76] Among the Chagga teachers as among the AIM missionaries, a small, but very vocal, minority carried the day with their argument, perhaps because those who were not so vocal were not so sure of their position.

There is one difference between the two controversies: the Chagga did not differentiate between male and female circumcision. Most of the Kikuyu saw it the same way; even the AIM missionaries did not want to differentiate in the early stages, but accepted that the New Testament permitted male circumcision 'without heathen rites'.[77] For the interdiction on female circumcision, only medical reasons remained.[78]

Although quite a few AIM missionaries were horrified over the loss of 90 per cent of their church members,[79] many felt the controversy to be a painful, but necessary, means to ensure 'high standards' among the African Christians.[80] For the time being at least, the mission had opted for achieving holiness in the church by adopting a rigorous ethical code suited only to a minority. Stauffacher, like much of his congregation at Narok, clearly recognized the problem. In a sermon on Revelation 21:27, he emphasized that the oath (written down as it was in an exercise book) did not mean that one's name was entered into the book of life but that, for this, only faith in the blood of Christ would be sufficient. In response, his listeners asked him: if it were so, why should female circumcision be such a terrible sin that it would exclude from the church those who believe in Jesus?[81] Although the AIM compromised after a time, there was no general move back to the AIM but, instead, there was a move into the African Independent Churches.[82] The AIM's original raison d'être had been to reach the unreached for Christ, but this had been changed into keeping the rigorous for Christ.

In refusing to allow polygamy, faith missions did not differ very much from the classical missions, but they had to come to terms with the thorny issue of what to do with polygamists who sincerely confessed their faith in Christ. Was not faith in Christ the only condition for baptism? In the early years, some faith missions saw things exactly that way. They opposed polygamy, but opposed divorce even more so. How then could one combat the evil of polygamy (practised in the Old Testament and not too explicitly forbidden in the New) by the sin of divorce when divorce was explicitly forbidden by the Lord and the apostles? Church membership and baptism must be possible to those who had entered a polygamous union before being converted, though 'bishops and deacons' (1 Timothy 3:2, 12) must have one wife only.[83]

In baptizing polygamists under these conditions, faith missions in Africa followed the example of the CIM: the difference was that, in China, polygamous marriages were rare, whereas in Africa they were common. Studd, Buxton and the early WEC missionaries in Zaire readily baptized polygamists,[84] but after 'disappointments' Studd stopped baptisms altogether, and when they were resumed in 1938 there was no thought of baptizing polygamous believers.[85] In a similar way, in the early Mid Africa Mission, polygamous men were baptized.[86]

In South Africa, the SAGM came to the conclusion that it would be more consonant with scripture to baptize polygamous men than to refuse baptism to them.[87] The Livingstone Inland Mission also felt it unjust for a wife to be divorced in order to allow her husband to be baptized.[88] The early SUM ruled that only an elder must not be polygamous.[89]

To baptize all polygamists who sincerely confessed their faith in Christ would have been consonant with the understanding of faith missions that conversion (and the faith and life resulting from it) is the basic constituent element of the church. But although many held this position in their early days, the faith missions soon gave it up and practically all of them made polygamy an absolute hindrance to baptism.[90] In this they conformed to the practice of the classical missions, which had accepted an occasional polygamist into the church in India and China but refused to do the same in Africa.[91]

Like the classical missions, faith missions also had to decide whether polygamy was the same obstacle to baptism for women as for men. The early Congo Balolo Mission made no distinction and baptized only a man's first wife. The Balolo did not appreciate this attitude, since the Catholics and the nearby Disciples of Christ baptized all wives of a polygamous marriage.[92] In refusing baptism to polygamous women, some early faith missions were more rigorous than the classical missions. Over the years, practically all faith missions conformed to the practice of the classical missions in refusing baptism to polygamous men, at the same time admitting all polygamous women to it.[93] The rationale for this rule was provided by the juridical fiction that in Africa women had no legal possibility of dissolving a marriage.[94] In reality, this decision meant that the missions were willing to accommodate polygamy in practice, while at the same time fighting it in theory.

CHURCH DISCIPLINE

The rigorous Christian life was to be safeguarded in faith missions not only by delay of, and strict conditions for, admission to baptism, but also by church discipline. This was in keeping with their concept that faith must become visible in Christian commitment and ethics, and that only those who had experienced salvation could belong to the church.

In the early years, church discipline was often handled very individually as a means of safeguarding a rigorous Christian commitment. With growing numbers of church members, discipline in faith missions, as in the classical missions, has tended to become ever more summary and legalistic, taking as its basic first commandment: 'Thou shalt have only one wife'. To marry a second wife means expulsion from the church until this second wife is dismissed again or the first wife dies. Premarital pregnancies are also rewarded with automatic church discipline and, in many faith mission churches, also 'marriage by eloping'.[95] As a whole, sexual sins are quite stringently punished, whereas other sins such as embezzlement of church funds, drunkenness[96] or accusing someone of being a witch are treated lightly or are even overlooked.[97] The standardized legalistic pattern of church discipline proves that faith mission churches have not been able to cope well with rapid numerical growth and the growing up of third and fourth generation Christians.[98] Church discipline is no longer a means of pastoral care, but a means of safeguarding dwindling ethical values in a changing society.

# Can one learn to be a Christian?

Conversion is central to faith missions' understanding of the church. When the missionaries started to preach conversion in their respective areas, they usually had plenty of time to explain what conversion and the Christian life meant, because conversions were few in the early years, when to become a Christian usually meant to lose one's standing in society. But it was usually not too long before conversion to Christianity began to equate with identification with social progress and even an enhancement of social prestige. This made people much more easily willing to become converted, long before they had undergone the long period of Christian preaching that was usual for the early converts. 'Faster' conversions led to the introduction of pre-baptismal instruction, again following the pattern set by the classical missions. 'Profession of conversion' was—at least in theory—a precondition for admission to baptismal instruction, but admission to baptism depended on faithfully and successfully completing the course of baptismal instruction, usually lasting one or two years.

This created the strong impression that Christianity was something to be learned, like the things one learned in school. The situation today is that the larger faith mission churches, in spite of constant conversion preaching,[99] must be classified as churches in which being a Christian is something that can be learned. They have, to quite some extent, conformed to the pattern of the folk church, so prevalent in the classical missions. One difference remained: in classical folk churches being a Christian is 'learned' *after* infant baptism whereas in faith mission folk churches, it is 'learned' *before* teenager baptism. In both types of church, the real condition for full membership is not conversion (though faith mission churches claim that it is), but successful learning, or at least a serious attempt at it.

Holiness preaching has often undergone a drastic process of change. Whereas for the missionaries, holiness meant spiritual power for service, for their converts it tended more to mean striving for a rigorous Christian commitment. Today, in third- and fourth-generation faith mission churches, holiness preaching is often little more than an exhortation to behave well.

## BACK TO REVIVAL

Faith missions were born in revival, and revival usually meant 'a profound sense of sinfulness, confession, the assurance of forgiveness and a strong missionary urge'.[100] Such a revival cannot be taught or organized, but occurs as a work of the Holy Spirit. If a revival breaks out this always creates tension in the churches so-blessed, and often results in denominational splits.[101] In every case, revival is critical of 'nominal Christianity' and low Christian commitment. The revival preaches holiness (often in very strict terms), but also makes accessible the power to lead such a committed life. Second- and third-generation faith mission churches, with all their tendencies towards becoming folk churches, were therefore ripe for revival. How would these churches and missionaries react if such a revival broke in their area, where they had come to represent the church establishment?

The most dramatic revival occurred in 1928 in the Qua Iboe Mission in Nigeria.[102] It started among the mission's teachers. Exactly where it originated could not be ascertained.[103] The revival seems to have developed inconspicuously for some time, but then came into the open with many enthusiastic manifestations. Suddenly, prayer meetings were more intense, the regular teacher training sessions were transformed into fellowship meetings, regular evening meetings suddenly lasted until daybreak and so on. Many repented of sins that had remained hidden for years, others returned money that had been 'forgotten' over a long time, others suddenly became reconciled. Sometimes non-Christians were gripped by an unexplainable power, and brought their cult objects to the church to have them burnt. All these things, though clothed in a different cultural guise, had occurred in the 1859/1873 holiness revival. What is interesting to note, but difficult to explain, is the fact that the revival only spread to some parts of the church. Westgarth, one of the leading missionaries, understood the movement as a graceful visitation by the Spirit,[104] and he only tried to curb what was obviously excessive.[105] Where a congregation explicitly refused entry to the revival, it could achieve only little.[106] Like all revivals, this one also declined after a time. No fellowship movement formed itself to carry on the revival tradition but, through it, the Qua Iboe Church gained many new members and some of its future leaders.

The revival which started in 1947 from Ngouédi in (French) Congo took a similar course. The Svenska Missionsförbundet's missionaries did not try, despite some 'pentecostal' characteristics, to suppress the movement. It remained within the church, and the church today still benefits from it. [107]

# THE WORLDWIDE STRUCTURE OF WEC INTERNATIONAL

The WEC operates in six regions (designated by circles on the map)
The branches of the WEC which send missionaries out are listed around the map

**Independent Branches**
USA
Canada

**Independent Branch**
Brazil

In addition, individual missionaries from:

Argentina
Costa Rica
Jamaica
Colombia
Puerto Rico

Belgium
Denmark
Italy
Portugal
Spain
Sweden

India
Jordan
Turkey
Mauritius
Zimbabwe

**Independent Branches**
Britain
Switzerland
Netherlands
Germany

**Cooperation with National
Mission Organizations**
Finland
Korea

**Non-independent Branches**
France
Singapore/Malaysia
Hong Kong

**Independent Sister Mission**
Indonesian Missionary
Fellowship

**Independent Branches**
South Africa
New Zealand
Australia

EUROPE

MIDDLE EAST

SOUTH ASIA

EAST ASIA

AFRICA

SOUTH AMERICA

In the WEC area of North Eastern Zaire, it was Edith Moules who, through the severe illness of her husband Percy, came into contact with the East African Revival in Rwanda. She invited Rwandese evangelistic teams, and a revival spread all over the area of what is now CECCA16.[108]

In the revival movements described here, faith missionaries were confronted with their own spiritual heritage. They lived up to their heritage, accepted the revival and did not attempt to drive it out of the church, although these revivals also challenged the establishment. In churches which more and more become folk churches, revival movements are guardians of much of the holiness tradition of the church. If a church takes Christian teaching on holiness seriously, it does well to accept movements which help to safeguard this important aspect of the church ('One, Catholic, Apostolic and Holy', as the creed maintains), even though those movements pose a serious challenge to the establishment.

What should be the role of faith missions in the present day faith mission 'folk churches'? The missions, which represented revival movements critical of the established churches, had switched sides in Africa, establishing churches there which now, after three generations or so, are being challenged by new revival and renewal movements. If faith missions want to be true to their own revival heritage, they might once again switch sides here and there, encouraging revival movements and perhaps even trying to bring revival about, even if that means dissociating themselves to some extent from the structures of those very churches which they helped to establish.

## Notes

1   The dominant personality of these conferences was Andrew Murray (Choy, *Andrew Murray*, p. 218).

2   This endeavour was clearly visible during the youth conference which I attended on 17 December 1986. Opinions differ on how far the WGM succeeded in passing on the holiness message (Interview Bill Reincheld, 18 December 1986; Interview N. N., 16–18 December 1986, Kericho).

3   *Congo Mission News* (Congo Protestant Council), 1946, p. 12.

4   Their ethical rigorism even made some of them conscientious objectors against military service. An example of this attitude is Drysdale, holiness evangelist and founder of the missionary training school in Birkenhead, which

was very important for the early WEC (Grubb, J. D. Drysdale). Grubb describes his own change of attitude from 'thoughtless enthusiasm' to a much more critical position in his: Once Caught, pp. 184–187.

5   For the role of ethical rigorism in religious group identity, see: Ernst Troeltsch, Die Soziallehren der christlichen Kirchen und Gruppen, [2]1919 (1912), pp. 967ff.; Hollenweger, Enthusiastisches Christentum, pp. 461ff.

6   In some groups with strong fundamentalist leanings, rigorism seems to have shifted to theology (with fights against new Bible translations, against the World Council of Churches, against compromise and Communism, and so on). A case in point is the Northern Ireland fundamentalist leader (Ian Paisley), who is in no way connected to faith missions. See, for example: Ian R. K. Paisley, The New English Bible, Version or Perversion, Belfast, 6n.d.; Messages from the Prison Cell, Belfast, 1966.

7   This applies definitely to ECWA (E. T. P. Crampton in Ogbu Kalu, Christianity in West Africa. The Nigerian Story, p. 175).

8   In many respects, classical missionaries had been in a similar situation because they also came from revival movements, but because the revival they came from was half a century older and less critical of the established churches, their ethical rigorism had usually somewhat quietened down.

9   My own contribution to this issue is a book on classical missionaries who professed an explicitly positive attitude to African culture: Christentum und afrikanische Kultur. Konservative deutsche Missionare in Tanzania 1900–1940, Gütersloh, 1983 (reprint, Bonn, 1993). For an example of decreasing rigorism (Moravians), see pp. 53–58; for an example of a less critical attitude among the established churches (Bruno Gutmann), see pp. 33–52. The English version of the book is expected for 1994.

10   See also: Smith, Nigerian Harvest, p. 45.

11   Peter Spartalis et al., The History of COCIN (publication expected, Bonn, 1994). He had to wait, although his conversion was 'visible'. He had burnt his cult objects and both his wives had left him, taking the children. He even had to fetch water himself.

12   Smith, Nigerian Harvest, p. 45.

13   Interview Benvinda Vaz Martins, Bissau, 5 August 1986.

14   He first came into contact with Christianity in December 1911, his conversion dates from 1913 at the latest; he was accepted into the church on 5 August 1917 and, together with his wife whom he had married in about 1912, he was baptized in 1919. In 1920, they were married in church (Burnette and Gerald Fish, the Rev. and Mrs Richard Adkins, The Call to Battle, Kericho, 1982).

15   CMA, Fifth Annual Report (1901–02), p. 27. They were now convinced that 'waiting is a test which often manifests the spurious converts, and so saves future trouble'. In this, they now conformed to the practice of the classical missions.

16   Interview the Rev. Jean Kambou, Président d'Église Protestante Évangélique de Burkina Faso, 13 January 1987. Of those baptized in the beginning, not one is still a church member. In a general report about WEC's work in West Africa, it is stressed that caution is being exercised not to baptize too quickly (Weltweit (Switzerland), May 1952).

17 In the Welle area where the mission started, the missionaries, basing their argument on the book of Acts, baptized not long after conversion. When the mission started to work in the Ituri, a mass movement soon developed, and baptisms were more numerous and even speedier. The theological principles behind this practice are described in detail in: Alfred Buxton, *Nala Methods*, London, 1916. The oldest pastor still living, who remembers those days, is of the opinion that only later were people baptized 'according to good order' (Interview Pastor Ndugu, 9 January 1987).

18 Today, this suspension of baptism is interpreted as a reaction against the Catholic practice, 'just demanding to have one wife only, but the old life could continue unchanged' (Interview with six CECCA16 representatives 12 January 1987). It can also be seen as 'a hard measure to combat the idea, prevalent in an animistic people, that the rites and ceremonies were the important thing' (Margaret White—Fiedler, 22 February 1993).

19 Interview with six CECCA16 representatives, 12 January 1987.

20 N. P. Grubb, *Mit Studd im Kongo*, p. 75.

21 Interview Alastair M. Kennedy, WEC Regional Secretary for Africa (Abidjan), 10 January 1987. This applies especially to Ivory Coast and Ghana, but also to Guinea Bissau, although the church there is more than fifty years old. But even in Zaire, most of those who attend church have never been baptized (Interview Douglas Craig, 10 January 1987).

22 David L. Miller, 'Problems and Possibilities in the Period of Colonial Consolidation: Christian Missions and Lower Pokomoni, Circa 1900– 1920' in *Ostafrikanische Völker zwischen Mission und Regierung. Referate einer Arbeitskonferenz in Erlangen 16–18 June 1982*, pp. 143–163 (p. 147f.).

23 1911–16, part of SUM-RSA. The missionaries then joined their work to the Dutch Reformed Church they came from, which in 1950 handed a part and, in 1961, all back to the SUM, Christian Reformed Church Branch (United States).

24 For a thorough treatment of its history, see: Eugene Rubingh, *Sons of Tiv. A Study of the Rise of the Church Among the Tiv of Central Nigeria*, Grand Rapids, 1969. See also: Crampton in Kalu, *Christianity in West Africa*, pp. 168–173.

25 See: Crampton in Kalu, *Christianity in West Africa*, pp. 169, 198–200.

26 Trevor McIlwain, *The Chronological Approach to Evangelism and Church Planting*, Sanford, 1985 (provisional edition).

27 'The early missionaries were imbued with dedication and zeal, which sterling qualities were surpassed only by monumental naivete. Perhaps it is always so where the young and exuberant throw themselves headlong into the conflict of the ages. Hundreds ... [were] hastily baptized on the profession of 'faith', when a large percentage of them had not the foggiest notion of what was implied either in salvation or baptism. In those heady days, the least sign of assent on the part of any was joyfully seized upon as evidence of yet another 'convert'. Unfortunately, the distilled darkness of centuries is not always dissolved in a blinding flash by the first recitation of Four Things God Wants You To Know, and even less so when the first declaration is given in a trade language only partially understood by the listeners' (Tom Steffen, 'Pre-Evangelism: Part II' in *Outreach* (NTM Research and Planning) December 1981, p. 2).

28  Interview John Mikitson, 27 July 1986.

29  In Madina Bafe, the pre-evangelism phase is, after two years with five missionaries, nearing its end. Chronological teaching was to start on 1 January 1987 (Interview Frank Lyttleton, 28 July 1986).

30  See: Steffen, 'Pre-Evangelism' in *Outreach*, September and December 1981.

31  The importance put on Old Testament salvation history necessitated the early translation of certain sections of the Old Testament (Dick Sollis, 'Scripture Translation and the Chronological Approach' in *Outreach*, April 1985, pp.1–2). Trevor McIlwain, 'Old Testament Teaching for New Testament Saints' in *Outreach*, September 1984, pp. 1–3, stresses the necessity for the young churches. For a list of texts recommended for translation see: Trevor McIlwain, 'Key Old Testament Passages for Translation' in *Outreach*, December 1983, p. 1.

32  It is highly appreciated when this narrative approach is accompanied by some drama (see: Bob Kennell and George Walker, 'The Bisorio Work in Papua New Guinea' in *Outreach*, September 1983, pp. 1–9).

33  The New Tribes Mission sees the provision of social services as not being a major part of its job. But this does not exclude informal assistance, such as helping with medical problems. Literacy work is seen as part of the mission's job.

34  When an individual participant in such a course has obviously already developed the ability to understand the gospel, the missionary may present it to him individually before its being due according to the chronological approach (Interview various missionaries, NTM Senegal, 26–28 March 1987).

35  After having presented the gospel in this way, the missionary tells his listeners that those who do believe should come to see him. In Chobo, where this decisive moment was first reached in Senegal, the next day five of the twelve participants contacted the missionary. Two from outside Chobo also came. The aged mother of one of the converts never came to see the missionary but participates in all believers' meetings (Interview John Mikitson, 27 July 1986). See also: John Mikitson, 'Breakthrough in Chobo' in *Under the Sun*, West African Field Paper, NTM, February 1986, p. 1f.

36  In Africa, no missionary has yet reached further than level 2. The plan thereafter is: 3. Acts of the Apostles for new converts; 4. Romans to Revelation for new converts 5–7. The texts of levels 2–4 applied to more mature Christians (McIlwain, *The Chronological Approach*, pp. 39–50).

37  One of the five original Chobo converts, now (1986) teaches level 1 in Ténkoto (Interview John Mikitson, 27 July 1986).

38  Up to mid-1986, no wish to build a meeting house had been expressed. Communion has been celebrated twice. As soon as the rains start, there is to be a baptism (Interview John Mikitson, 27 July 1986).

39  Trevor McIlwain uses many of Roland Allan's ideas, though without directly referring to him. In the early NTM, Roland Allan's books were required standard reading.

40  Not every classical mission reacted more generously. See, for Malawi: Kenneth R. Ross, *You Did Not Dance: Christianity and Recreation in the African Context* (Faith and Knowledge Seminar No. 13, Chancellor College Chaplaincy, University of Malawi, 1992).

41 For example, AIM and GMS in Kenya (Sandgren, *The Kikuyu*, p. 285). Some among the classical missions also did so, for example, the Dutch Reformed Church Mission in Malawi (Heleman A. Kamnkhwani, 'A Brief History of Mvera Congregation', BD University of the North, 1981, pp. 91, 106).

42 For a good example, see: Dawson, *History*, p. 47.

43 For example, the Mahon Mission in South Africa (William Burton, *When God Makes a Missionary. The Life Story of Edgar Mahon* (revised by Alfred J. and Margaret Mahon), Zion, [2]1961 (1936), p. 69).

44 The World Gospel Mission among others organized Christian initiation camps for boys (Interview Loren Clark, Kericho, 17 December 1986).

45 The best source for the traditional custom is: Jomo Kenyatta, *Facing Mount Kenya*, London, [2]1968 (1938). His description refers to the AIM area.

46 See: Sandgren, *The Kikuyu*; Robert W. Strayer, *The Making of Mission Communities in East Africa. Anglicans and Africans in Colonial Kenya 1875–1935*, Nairobi *et al.*, 1986 (Chapter VIII, written in conjunction with Jocelyn Murray); Jocelyn Murray, *The Kikuyu Female Circumcision Controversy, With Special Reference to the Church Missionary Society's Sphere of Influence*, PhD, UCLA, 1974. Much information is also found in: John A. Gration, *The Relationship of the Africa Inland Mission and its National Church in Kenya Between 1895 and 1971*, PhD, New York University, 1973 (UMI).

47 The brief presentation of the controversy in the mission's standard history is pious fiction: 'Slowly the church recovered from its setback. Members who had fallen away because of the high standards adopted, gradually found their way back, and numbers built up again. But the standards were never relaxed and those who returned had to accept them' (Richardson, *Garden of Miracles*, p. 78).

48 He had started his career as a physician and had then been ordained.

49 A. J. Temu, *British Protestant Missions*, London, 1972, p. 157 contradicts this idea: 'There is little doubt, now, that reports of the missions stating that the African church leaders agreed that laws should be passed against female circumcision, is not correct'. Although he uses no primary sources, he categorically states that the missionaries simply forced the decisions upon the Africans (p. 155f.). But by 1920, there had already been an African initiative in the Githumu area to forbid clitoridectomy (Gration, *AIM and its National Church*, p. 139).

50 Sandgren, *The Kikuyu*, pp. 198–200.

51 See: Kenyatta, *Facing Mount Kenya*, p. 135.

52 Sandgren, *The Kikuyu*, p. 216.

53 Sandgren, *The Kikuyu*, p. 207.

54 Sandgren, *The Kikuyu*, p. 206 (based on Interview Johanna Nyerjeri, 25 October 1970, NCCK Limuru Archives).

55 This was also the case among the Tiriki in Kenya (Walter Sangree, *Age, Prayer and Politics in Tiriki, Kenya*, London 1966). All over East Africa, the initiation rites tend to lose their communal character and to become family rituals. Even where there is no mission influence, the duration of initiation has been reduced, often drastically so (Marja-Liisa Swantz, *Ritual and Symbol in Transitional Zaramo Society*

*With Special Reference to Women*, Gleerup, 1970, especially pp. 151–162).

56 Sandgren, *The Kikuyu*, p. 208. Even in the UMCA, where Bishop Vincent Lucas Christianized circumcision, medical opinion did not agree (Leader Stirling, *Ritual Circumcision in Southern Tanganyika' in East African Medical Journal*, June 1941, p. 35f.).

57 Church of Scotland, 'Confidential Memorandum Prepared by the Kikuyu Mission Council on Female Circumcision', Kikuyu 1 December 1931 (National Archives of Scotland, ACC 7548 D64), pp. 35–39. The AIM had shared in the preparation of this 104-page memorandum, and supported it fully.

58 The women were not fined because they circumcised the girl but because they performed the 'big' operation instead of the small one (for definitions see 'Memorandum', p. 1f.). The Local Native Council Kiambu had outlawed only the 'big' operation ('Memorandum', p. 37f.).

59 Gration, *Africa Inland Mission*, p. 139.

60 This 'oath' was taken by signing a document, if necessary by finger print ('kirore'). Those who signed were therefore termed 'kirore' in Kikuyu usage. Stauffacher—Campbell, 17 September 1930, uses the term 'vow', which he also uses in the same letter in 'baptismal vow'.

61 Lee Downing (field leader) in *Inland Africa* XV, p. 3 (1931). Sandgren, *The Kikuyu*, p. 252 estimates 95 per cent.

62 Parts of today's oral tradition assumes that an attempt had been made to circumcise her by force. The extant AIM correspondence relating to the event does not support this idea, though it supports the idea that the murder had something to do with the controversy. (See also: *New York Times*, 6 January 1930). The Chief Justice agreed to the opinion of the prosecution that there was no relationship between the murder and the controversy (*East African Standard*, November 1930). The accused was acquitted by the court. Though there is no proof that the murder had anything to do with the controversy, it is clear that it was largely assumed that it had. See: Downing—Grimwood, 31 January 1930; Grimwood—Downing, 3 March 1930. See also: Gration, *Africa Inland Mission*, pp. 145–148.

63 Virginia Blakeslee, *Beyond the Kikuyu Curtain*, Chicago, 1956, p. 191.

64 Sandgren, *The Kikuyu*, p. 253, based on District Commissioner, Kiambu—Provincial Commissioner, Nyeri, 27 January 1932 (Kenya National Archives PC/CP 8/1/2). Kenyatta calls this a 'gentlemen's agreement' (*Facing Mount Kenya*, p. 131).

65 At least, in CSM, AIM and GMS. The CMS was divided, Methodists and Catholics refused to join the fight against clitoridectomy.

66 Temu, *British Protestant Missions*, p. 157 (no sources given).

67 Only Eisenschmidt, a German from the Baltic States, was allowed to stay, because he was classified as a Russian. But he played no role in the controversy.

68 In the Lutheran Church on Kilimanjaro the first Africans were only ordained in 1934.

69 Minutes Missionary Conference, 6–13 September 1927; *Evangelisches Missionsblatt*, 1926, p. 29. The Leipzig sources do not record why circumcision

was held to be contrary to the Bible, and oral tradition at Kidia equally does not know the reason given.

70 Minutes Missionary Conference, 6–13 September 1927.

71 The teachers and elders resisted two full days, but finally had to admit defeat. 'Finally complete understanding was reached between the missionaries and the Christians, and the natives thanked the missionaries, especially B. Gutmann.' The decision read: 'For the Chagga congregations, circumcision shall not be forbidden, but it shall also not be seen as permitted by the church. If a Christian wants to undergo circumcision, he must be informed that this is a custom which the church wants to abolish. He is alone responsible for his action (Minutes Missionary Conference 3.7.9. 1925 (translations, K. F.)).

72 See: Klaus Fiedler, 'Bishop Lucas' Christianization of Traditional Rites, the Kikuyu Female Circumcision Controversy and the "Cultural Approach" of Conservative German Missionaries in Tanzania' in Noel Q. King, Klaus Fiedler (eds), *Robin Lamburn—From a Missionary's Notebook: The Yao of Tunduru and other Essays*, Saarbrücken/Ft Lauderdale, 1991, pp. 207–217.

73 Sandgren, *The Kikuyu*, p. 255. For his approach, see: Vincent Lucas, The Educational Value of Initiatory Rites' in *IRM*, 1927, pp. 192–198; 'The Christian Approach to Non-Christian Customs' in E. R. Morgan, *Essays Catholic and Missionary*, London, 1928 (pp. 114–151), also: *Christianity and Native Rites*, London, 1950. For interesting details, see: Robin Lamburn, 'The Yao of Tunduru', pp. 28–68 in King and Fiedler, *Robin Lamburn*. The analysis of a historian is: Terence O. Ranger, 'Missionary Adaptation of African Religious Institutions: The Masasi Case' in T. O. Ranger and I. N. Kimambo, *The Historical Study of African Religion*, London/Ibadan/Nairobi, 1972, pp. 221–251.

74 Minutes elders' council, Kidia congregation, Kidia, 19 May 1926.

75 Gration, *Africa Inland Mission*, p. 147f.

76 Stauffacher—Campbell, 17 September 1930.

77 Sandgren, *The Kikuyu*, p. 203.

78 A number of missionaries seem to have held the idea that this argument was not sufficient. They demanded that the 'justified interdiction' of female circumcision should be extended to include male circumcision as well (Stauffacher—Campbell, 17 October 1930).

79 In mid-1930, some were already no longer demanding the oath (Stauffacher—Campbell, 17 September 1930). See: Sandgren, *The Kikuyu*, p. 252.

80 Richardson, *Garden of Miracles*, p. 78.

81 'They wanted to know why female circumcision was such a deadly sin that it had to be separated from all the other sins enumerated in the Baptismal vow, and that this should have a special vow. Many of them do not raise the question at all as to whether circumcision is right or wrong, but they object to the vow as being unfair, and in their own minds I am certain it is confusing and endangering the Solid Rock of Salvation by Faith' (Stauffacher—Campbell, 17 November 1930).

82 Sandgren, *The Kikuyu*, p. 257. The churches resulting from these controversies (but not from AIM/GMS only) are the African Independent

pentecostal Church of Africa and the African Orthodox Church (Sandgren, *The Kikuyu*, pp. 267–312. See: Barrett, *Kenya Churches Handbook*, p. 231f.).

83  One example of this position was the SIM: 'We believe that the Scriptures teach that any believer who has entered into union with more than one wife while in unbelief must be excluded from all office and leadership in the Church (Titus 1:6; 1 Timothy 3:2, 12) until such time as the union has been dissolved in a manner approved by the Church, and that all received as members shall be expected to give evidence of repentance for the sinful life which has entangled them in unholy unions, and a willingness and desire to separate from these entanglements as speedily as possible and in such manner as shall be honorable alike to the individual, the Church and the State' (Minutes SIM, 7 April 1913).

84  Described in detail, including the argument from scripture, in: Alfred Buxton, *Nala Missionary Methods*, London, 1916, pp. 5–7.

85  To the CECCA16 of today these polygamous baptisms make no sense (Interview Pastor Ndugu, 9 January 1987).

86  Among the 150 converts baptized in the first baptism, there were many polygamists, including a man who had six wives (Margaret N. Laird, *They Called Me Mama*, Chicago, 1975, p. 91f.). The founder of the Mid Africa Mission had earlier served with WEC. The Mid Africa Mission later became the fundamentalist Baptist Mid Missions.

87  South Africa General Mission, Memorandum on Polygamy, n.d. (*ca.* 1905?).

88  'If a man is a polygamist when converted we do not make him put away any of his wives. To do so in Africa would be very wrong' (Henry Richards, 'Banza Manteka', quoted in: Fanny Guinness, *The New World of Central Africa*, p. 429). The early Qua Iboe Mission, also connected to Fanny Guinness, saw things differently. When Chief Egbo Egbo (who had arranged for the letter asking the Presbyterian Mission at Calabar for a white teacher to be written and which the United Presbyterian Mission then had passed on to Grattan Guinness) wanted to become a Christian, he had no doubts that he had to dismiss eleven of his twelve wives (Gracie Bill, *David Ekong. Called. Chosen. Faithful. The Story of the First Convert and Pastor of the Qua Iboe Mission*, n.p., n.d., p. 14). A reason for this may have been that the first Christian preachers at Qua Iboe were not the QIM missionaries, but Presbyterian Christians from Calabar (p. 11).

89  *Constitution of the Sudan United Mission (revised)*, 11 September 1912.

90  For example, *Constitution and Policy of the Africa Inland Mission*, Philadelphia, 1912, p. 20. Others see this differently: 'The biggest single error of all Christian missions in Africa has been to declare monogamy a non-negotiable condition of baptism' (Harry R. Boer, 'My Pilgrimage in Mission' in *IBMR*, 1987, pp. 172–175).

91  For the discussion of this development see: Fiedler, *Christentum und afrikanische Kultur*, pp. 59–65. In the early Basel missionary work in South Cameroon, at least one polygamist was baptized.

92  The Yuli elders declared: 'We are greatly exercised over the matter of polygamy, but our people are beginning now to understand the mind of God concerning it. If we go over to the DCCM our people will again return to the old practice, and then, when will they learn the truth?' (Accompanying letter, Minutes Field Conference at Ikau, 9–18 October 1930).

93  Polygamous men could be baptized after dismissing the additional wives. But that presented problems, too: Chief Pedro of Akurenan in Equatorial Guinea also used the occasion of his attending the monthly court session to visit the WEC missionary Alec Thorne (Kiwi). In the course of a longer conversation, he told Kiwi that God had dealt with him in the matter of his three wives. He would dismiss the first two wives and keep the youngest. Kiwi did not accept this as what God wanted of Chief Pedro and told him that he had to keep his first wife, the mother of his two daughters (Prayer letter, Alec Thorne No. 36, June 1940).

94  The legal position of wives in African societies varies greatly, but usually they have legal access to divorce. Even in those societies where women had easy access to divorce, the practice of baptism was not changed accordingly.

95  See Chapter 11 for details.

96  In many cases, where the use of alcohol is not permitted, even its abuse is not subjected to church discipline. It does happen that church elders are known as 'drinkers' (walevi), which may also mean drunkards (Interview N. N.).

97  For example, Interview Alastair M. Kennedy, 10 January 1987.

98  For example, Interview Alastair M. Kennedy, 10 January 1987 (general assessment of the WEC-related churches all of which he knows). From a journey to further the CECCA16 foreign mission programme Mission CECCA Zaire, the WEC missionary Margaret White reports: 'I just can't describe the hordes of young people who came for the slides in the evenings, but the churches have virtually nobody who knows how to relate to them and reach them for the Lord. The church leaders recognize that they are getting old and hardly any young people are coming forward to take their place' (Circular letter, 20 February 1988). These two assessments are supported in varying degrees by Interview N. N.

99  'Every Sunday in church we hear an evangelistic sermon' (Interview Mrs Downing, 13 December 1986). 'Every Sunday the Sunday School teacher asks "Who wants to believe?" Many lift up their hands, not only once' (Interview Alice Ndolo, 28 December 1986).

100 Stephen Neill, Christian Missions, Harmondsworth, [2]1966 (1964), p. 501.

101 David Barrett has drawn attention convincingly to the fact that the so-called African Independent Churches were born not only in schism, but also in revival. See the title of his book: Schism and Renewal in Africa. An Analysis of Six Thousand Contemporary Movements, Nairobi/Addis Ababa/Lusaka, 1968.

102 For a reflective description of this revival, see: J. W. Westgarth, 'The Holy Spirit and the Primitive Mind', n.d. (unpublished). Typed copies are available at QIM (Belfast) and at CENERM (Selly Oaks, Birmingham).

103 Westgarth, 'The Holy Spirit', p. 1.

104 Westgarth had some previous experience. While at the Bible Training Institute in Glasgow, he had witnessed the 1904 Welsh Revival. For a critical review of this revival, written by a participant, see: J. Vyrnwy Morgan, The Welsh Religious Revival 1904–5. A Retrospect and a Criticism, London, 1909.

105 It is surprising that he took the speaking in tongues that occurred as genuine, in spite of his 'terrible experiences with the tongues movement' (Westgarth, 'The Holy Spirit', p. 10).

106Westgarth, 'The Holy Spirit', p. 14.

107Hilaire Nkounkou *et al.*, *75e anniversaire de la fondation de Madzia et de l'évangelisation du Congo par les missionaires protestants*, Brazzaville 1984, p. 16; Interview Curt Olofson, 29 January 1987; Johan Gustafson, *Kongo Vaknar*, Stockholm, [2]1947.

108Interview Evangeliste Bamata-Ambenese, 9 January 1987; Réport du Président de CECCA16 au Assemblée Generale 1987; interview with six CECCA16 representatives, 12 January 1987. For an earlier revival, see: Eva Stuart Watt, *Floods on Dry Ground*, London, 1940.

# 9
# A propelling vision: faith missions and the prophetic movement

Of the three movements which contributed to faith mission theology, the prophetic movement remains to be considered. As with the holiness movement, the prophetic movement cannot be treated as a whole, but only with regards to its impact on faith missions. To assess its impact, two things must be highlighted: it brought a drastic change in eschatology; and today's faith mission eschatology is not necessarily the same as that of the early years of the faith mission.

## CLASSICAL MISSION ESCHATOLOGY: POSTMILLENNIALISM

The classical missions and the revival which had brought them into existence followed a postmillennial eschatology.[1] This post-millennial eschatology was most forcefully propagated by Jonathan Edwards (1703–58), the leading theologian of the Great Awakening in the United States (*ca.* 1726–60).[2] Edwards expected Christ's return *after* the millennium. This would come about in a gradual process of revivals and social reform.[3] Part of this process would be worldwide missionary work: 'And doubtless one nation shall be enlightened and converted after another, one false religion and false way of worship exploded after another'.[4] Equally, Christian (Western) civilization would play its part in that process: 'The most barbarous nations shall become as bright as England.'[5] This means that worldwide missions play a role in the process of bringing about the millennium, a role which is shared by 'Christian culture' (that is, Western culture, but only its best aspects).

Postmillennialism was born from an optimistic world-view, which counted on an evolution of world history into the fullness of God's kingdom. Christian nations were seen as major elements in this process.[6] Originally, postmillennialism expected a great worldwide revival to crown the gradual process whereas, later, more stress was laid on the gradual process so that postmillennial hope came somewhat close to a Christian evolution.

272

# The prophetic movement

Beginning with the second decade of the nineteenth century starting in circles critical to established theology and church structures, a dramatic change in eschatological expectations took place.[7] Leading figures in Britain were: Edward Irving (presbyterian);[8] John Nelson Darby, Dr Tregelles and B. W. Newton (all Brethren); Michael Baxter (Anglican, married to Elizabeth Baxter); and, in the United States, Joseph A. Seiss, James H. Brooks, Nathanael West and William Blackstone.[9] They expected Christ's return not after, but before, the millennium. During the millennium, Christ would rule as king. They accused postmillennialism of propagating a 'kingdom without a king'. In Britain, the major force in this movement were the Brethren,[10] in the United States, it found its most vivid expression in prophetic conferences (New York, 1878; Chicago, 1886; Allegheny, 1895; Boston, 1901; Chicago, 1914; Philadelphia and New York, 1918).[11]

This change to premillennialism was not brought about by faith missions, but took place in groups which were quite close to them. Typical of this process is Moody. Meeting Harry Moorhouse, the 'boy evangelist' of the English Brethren,[12] not only changed his preaching style, but also his eschatology. He no longer expected Christ to come to crown human efforts, but expected the millennium to break in as the result of Christ's coming.[13] How important this new vision was for him is shown by one of his first conversations with Emma Dryer, who later founded the Missionary Training Institute of the Chicago Evangelization Society.[14] He asked her if she understood 'the doctrine of the Coming and Kingdom of Christ?' She answered in the affirmative. He replied emphatically: 'I am mighty glad you know that doctrine. Why! It is the key to the Scriptures. Do you know Mrs Goodwin?' He ended the ensuing conversation on the topic he ended with the words: 'Mrs Goodwin understands that doctrine, and you understand it and I understand it. That makes three in Chicago!'[15]

Influenced by George Müller, A. T. Pierson underwent the same change,[16] as did A. J. Gordon. During his training as a Baptist pastor, he had been taught postmillennialism. He heard premillennial eschatology from two unnamed laymen and accepted it for himself after a careful study of the Bible. That was for him a crisis experience, which he put on an equal footing with his holiness experience.[17]

The change from post- to premillennialism was more than just a change of date when to expect Christ's return. It signified a drastic change in world-view and the interpretation of history. Postmillennialism was characterized by an optimistic world-view, which premillennialists conceived as unrealistic. And were they not right? Who, for example, could see the American Civil War as a sign of progressing Christian civilization?[18] A. B. Simpson accused postmillennialism of 'having no consequences'.[19] Postmillennialists saw it exactly the other way round. Had postmillennial eschatology not been a driving force behind so many efforts in revival, reform and mission?[20] But over the decades the time factor was lengthened. Emphasis was no longer laid as much on the idea that efforts in reform and mission would bring about the millennium, but more on the idea that such a process would be slow.[21] This change of emphasis meant that postmillennialism ceased to be a driving force for missions.

## VARIETIES OF FAITH MISSION PREMILLENNIALISM

Grattan Guinness had been introduced to prophetic thinking when he married Fanny in 1860. After Grattan Guinness' not too successful training course at Dublin, they moved to Paris to start evangelistic work there.[22] When the turmoil preceeding the Franco-Prussian war of 1870 had become too great, Fanny decided that they move back to Bath,[23] and Grattan started to research current events to see if they might not be the fulfilment of biblical prophecies. He became convinced that the return of Christ before the millennium was clearly predicted in scripture.[24] In 1873, Fanny and Grattan Guinness started the East London Training Institute.[25] Besides missions, Grattan Guinness' major interest was prophecy.[26] Both subjects were so closely interrelated in his thinking that they almost melted into one. In 1887, Grattan and Fanny Guinness handed over responsibility for the Institute to their son Harry and his Australian wife Annie Reed, so that Grattan could concentrate on his prophetic studies.[27]

During his Louisville pastorate, at about the same time as his holiness experience, A. B. Simpson became convinced of the premillennial return of Christ.[28] Before long, the premillennial return of Christ became the fourth aspect of his 'fourfold Gospel': Christ the coming king.[29] During the millennium, Christ will rule in person, because there will be no kingdom without a king!

The return of Christ is dependent on mission. He himself made the preaching of the gospel to the *whole* world the precondition for his return.[30] If the church does its duty, it can speed up the coming of its Lord.[31] This means that Christ's return is *imminent*, not that it is to be expected any moment. For Simpson, *imminent* means a time *span*, imminently important for all Christians. They are not to expect Christ any moment, but they are, at *any moment*, to put all effort in fulfilling the preconditions for his return.[32] This made eschatology a propelling force for missions.

There are no sources available as to how Fredrik Franson became a premillennialist.[33] When he evangelized in the Mid-West around 1880, his position was already clear.[34] Unlike Simpson, he expected Christ's coming at 'any moment'[35] and originally preached this eschatology, not in the context of world mission but of evangelism (in Christian countries). He was interested in foreign missions, too, but foreign missions were not a motivating force.[36] It was his journey to London in 1882 which changed this. His first journey to Scandinavia had the theme 'Christ's return and revival', his second journey had the theme 'Christ's return and missions'.[37] Like Hudson Taylor, he was convinced that before Christ's return everyone must get a chance to hear the gospel.[38]

## HISTORICAL AND FUTURIST PREMILLENNIAL ESCHATOLOGY

Both Guinness and Simpson interpreted their premillennial eschatology historically. The prophecies of the Bible for the 'last days' include certain predicted events. Some of them are already past, some (few) are still to happen.[39] Simpson saw two signs as being fulfilled: the antichrist and the false prophet. The papacy was the antichrist and Muhammad was the false prophet,[40] and both had passed their eclipse: the French troops had humbled the papacy and the Muhammadan lands were almost all subject to Western powers. Grattan Guinness saw 'Romanism' predicted by Paul and John,[41] and he could claim that his interpretation was shared by the theologians of the Reformation.[42] A sign which he saw in the process of being fulfilled was the Jews' return to Israel.[43] The one remaining unfulfilled sign was the preaching of the gospel among all nations. Now, when in God's providence the whole world had become accessible, it was the church's duty—with a tremendous missionary effort—to work for the fulfilment of this last sign and 'to bring the king back'.

Grattan Guinness, A. B. Simpson and others, such as A. J.

Gordon,[44] were representatives of a clearly historicist premillennialism. This kind of eschatology creates the closest interconnection between eschatology and missiology. Different from historical premillennialism is futurist premillennialism. Its basic assumption is that all the events predicted in the Bible for the 'last days' are still to happen, all in a relatively short time before Christ's return. (This futurist version of premillennialism usually replaced the historicist variety.)

An exponent of futurist premillennarianism was Fredrik Franson, who stated explicitly during the Chicago 1881 prophetic conference that the Pope was not the antichrist.[45] For Franson, too, the worldwide preaching of the gospel was one of the signs of Christ's coming, but possibly it was already fulfilled. Perhaps what was still lacking was the full readiness of the church to receive her Lord.[46] But unlike Darby's, Franson's futurist premillennialism was not exclusive. Franson held the view that many prophecies have a threefold fulfilment: they have been fulfilled, are being fulfilled and will be fulfilled in the future. Therefore, his eschatology can be called 'inclusive futurist premillennialism'.[47] Franson was aware of the tensions between the different eschatological interpretations. He is convinced that truth may comprise both extremes, even if we are not able to see how they are connected.[48] There is a fascinating parallel between Fredrik Franson's attitude to contradictions in eschatology and faith missions' general attitude towards contradictions in ecclesiology.

APPLIED ESCHATOLOGY

The men described so far are representative for all faith missions. A few examples may suffice: for C. E. Hurlbert and the Pennsylvania Bible Institute, where he taught and which formed a base for the AIM, eschatology was the other major emphasis besides holiness.[49] Rowland Bingham not only lectured about missions, but also about 'fulfilled prophecy', using slides from Palestine.[50] One of the leading figures in US premillennialism was Scofield, the author of the dispensationalist 'Scofield Bible' and also the founder of the Central America Mission.[51] Another leading premillennial Bible expositor, who played an important role in the birth of the Gospel Missionary Union, was James Hall Brookes (1830–97).[52]

Contrary to some of their contemporaries in the prophetic movement, for faith mission leaders, eschatology was not *spec-*

*ulative*, but *applied*. Here again, Hudson Taylor gave the lead. In Hull, he attended Brethren meetings the leader of which, Andrew Jukes, a former Anglican priest, held a very speculative eschatology.[53] 'From a friend', Hudson Taylor received a list of Bible references, which convinced him, like Jukes, that Christ would return before the millennium. With Hudson Taylor, however, the results were not speculative, but very practical: he checked through his books and clothes and gave away all that he did not really need.[54] This was applied eschatology. Later he applied eschatology in a very practical way to missionary work in China, asking for ever more missionaries. A. B. Simpson formulated it vividly: 'There is no mockery more sad and inconsistent than that of believing and speaking of the Blessed Hope [Titus 2:12f.] with folded hands and selfish heart. No man can rightly believe in the coming of Jesus without expending all the strength of his being in preparing for it by sending the Gospel to all nations'.[55] Since Jesus has bound his command to evangelize the world to the promise of his return, world mission is the first eschatological command. C. T Studd: 'To evangelize the world and have Christ back'.[56]

For Simpson, the evangelization of the world was the one still outstanding sign, and he did all he could to change that.[57] Oswald Smith (People's Church, Toronto) saw this last sign as fulfilled as soon as the gospel had entered the last nation still unreached.[58]

In Zaire, C. T Studd received a letter enquiring how $9,000 could be used best 'to hasten the return of the Lord by evangelizing Central Africa'.[59] A. B. Simpson expressed the same idea in 1892, saying that God may have given to the church the key for the future. By fulfilling the great commission, the bride may fix the date for the wedding of the Lamb.[60]

This way of thinking is based on 2 Peter 3:12: 'looking for and *hasting* the coming of the day of God' (AV). The idea that it is possible to speed the coming of Christ is based not only on this verse, which is open to varying interpretations, because missions are not mentioned in it, but on historicist eschatology in general. During 1891–1900, CMA experienced an unparalleled 'missionary explosion', and Simpson's eschatology of expecting Christ not any moment but when the church has done her duty, is one of the explanations as to why it took place.[61]

The conviction that it was possible to evangelize the world before Christ's return, or even to speed it, was a major reason why faith missions gave top priority to the unreached areas of the world.[62] It influenced their methods further: because there was great urgency, great numbers of evangelists had to be employed. To find them, one was not to rely on ordained pastors. Women must be employed as evangelists, not just as missionary wives. Sometimes it even led to the conviction that in the mission field there was no need for mission stations, just travellers who presented the saving gospel to as many persons as possible.[63] Necessity soon modified this concept.

The eschatological concepts of faith missions had several further repercussions. In Acts 2:17f. the prophet Joel is quoted, predicting that *in the last days* the Spirit will be poured out and signs will happen. Since the premillennialists, different from Peter, took the last days not as a period that began with Pentecost but as referring to their own days, this verse offered a good reason for allow womening to preach: prophesying daughters![64] In this, they employed a concept that may go back to Edward Irving, founder of the Catholic Apostolic Church, who expected, in the end times, the renewal of the gifts of the Spirit such as speaking in tongues, healing and prophecy which, indeed, happened in his church in 1831.[65] But the faith missions rejected this except, to some extent, healing, and the pentecostal revival took up the idea again later.

One problematic effect of faith missions' eschatology was that the expectation of Christ's imminent return left little room for an explicit ecclesiology. Thus, faith mission ecclesiology was doubly weakened: by their interdenominational character and by their eschatology.

Another side effect of premillennialism was its negative world-view. It was in some ways more realistic than postmillennialism's optimism, but was it really realistic? If the world is in hopeless decline anyhow, efforts to improve it (or even parts of it) may not be very worthwhile.

A DECLINE OF THE VISION

Today's faith mission eschatology is not the same as in its early days. The doctrinal side has not changed very much: Christ's return is still expected, and it is expected before the millennium. But eschatology is no longer the driving force for mission that it was in the beginning.

One change took place quite early in the CMA.[66] For Simpson, Christ's return was imminent, so Christians had to *work* for it.

Soon, Christ's return was expected at any moment, so Christians had to *wait* for it. This simplifies the issue, but giving up historical premillennialism in favour of any-moment premillennialism loosened the ties between eschatology and the missionary effort.

This decline of eschatology in the CMA was not an isolated phenomenon. It can be generally observed that the role played by eschatology in faith missions and in the circles of their supporters has declined, so that one writer even speaks of a 'forgotten doctrine'.[67] One reason is that speculative eschatology has to some extent discredited itself by repeatedly changing its world scenarios and by always defining the end-times as being about the time of the author's writing.[68]

If speculative eschatology has lost its motivating power for missions, it has definitely not lost its *frightening* power and the threat, perceived or real, of worldwide communist expansion has served as a poor missionary motivation.[69] It motivated not world missions, but national defence (if necessary, even nuclear war).[70] How the demise of Communism, unforeseen by speculative premillennialism, will influence this kind of eschatology must be awaited. One thing, however, seems sure: after the quiet death of Communism, there is available to speculation a new super-enemy of Christianity, the West and all that is good: that new enemy is Islam. This concept has the power to frighten and to demotivate missions.

Among evangelicals, premillennialism is still the dominant eschatology, more so in the United States than in Europe. One attempt at a new thinking should be noted, however, as it can be traced very indirectly back to Grattan Guinness. John Jefferson Davis of Gordon-Conwell University (going back, in one of its roots, to A. J. Gordon's Boston Missionary Training Institute, which Grattan Guinness had suggested in 1889) is convinced that postmillennialism is consistent with Christ's greatness and therefore needs to be reconsidered.[71] It is not yet clear how much support he will find and how, if at all, his concept will influence evangelical missionary motivation.

# New efforts

I have mainly described the effects of premillennial eschatology on missionary work in the first generation of faith missions. In this section, some additional efforts, more or less directly related to the prophetic movement and the premillennialist eschatology it produced, will be briefly described.

## REACHING THE LAST TRIBE: THE NEW TRIBES MISSION

The New Tribes Mission[72] is a comparative latecomer among the big faith missions, but its eschatological motivation is obvious. It can be traced back to Moody. Paul Fleming, founder of NTM, was strongly influenced by the evangelist Paul Rader of Chicago,[73] through whom he received his missionary vision and for whom he worked for some time. Certain events made him leave Rader.[74] After his marriage to Cherrill Harter in 1936, the couple expected that the independent Country Church in Hollywood would provide a base for their intended missionary work. When that prospect failed, they sailed for Sumatra in 1937 as independent missionaries, but could not get permission to work there because of Muslim resistance. In Singapore, they heard about the unreached Arang Asli in Malaysia, and the Flemings felt called to reach them. Also in Singapore, they met the CMA missionary leader Dr Jaffray (1873–1945),[75] who shared their vision and accepted them as CMA missionaries, because the Flemings would not have received a permit as independent missionaries.[76] Jaffray directed him to Paul Lin (Kwang Lin),[77] a Chinese missionary to Malaysia, and together they evangelized among the Sakai. Severe ill health, made worse by incorrect malaria medication, forced the Flemings to return to the United States.[78] Paul Lin continued the work among the Sakai.[79]

Though barely recovered, Paul Fleming travelled the length and breadth of the United States to promote his vision 'to reach the last tribe with the Gospel, so that Christ can return'.[80] The result was that a group of men were formed to further this aim, most of them influenced by Rader.[81] In 1942, they came to the conviction that they would have to start a new mission if they wanted to fulfil their vision.[82] Fleming wanted the early NTM to start in Eastern Asia,[83] but the war turned their attention to Latin America.[84] There, they attempted first of all to reach the completely unreached Ayoré, an attempt for which they received help from the Bolivian Indian Mission. Five missionaries were killed before the NTM succeeded in reaching the Ayoré.[85]

Fleming was convinced that in order to reach the last tribe before the return of Christ, innovative methods had to be used: the mission had to be interdenominational (which was the norm for faith missions), but even including pentecostals (which was very unusual at that time). Those who were or would have been rejected by other missions, due to lack of education, lack of spouse, too many children or insufficient education, would be acceptable to NTM, as long as they were called by the Lord and could survive the boot camp, where they were prepared for work among the 'last tribes'. Because transporting the missionaries to their fields was a problem, the NTM once bought a ship (the M. V. Tribesman)[86] and two plans (Tribesman and Tribesman II). Both planes crashed, and Paul Fleming died in the second crash.[87]

Paul Fleming's applied eschatology found most of its early support in what one might call today 'independent Bible churches' around Chicago.[88] Most of them can be designated as 'tabernacle churches', meaning independent churches reaching the unchurched bby employing innovative means. This was the case with Paul Rader, who was behind much of NTM's early history. From 1915 to 1922 he was pastor of Moody Memorial Church, which he tried so much to transform into a tabernacle church that those years are called the 'sawdust years'.[89] In 1919 he succeeded A. B. Simpson as President of the CMA. It soon turned out that another organization was not happy with him.[90] He left Moody Memorial Church and began the Chicago Gospel Tabernacle.[91] He differed from Moody not in his attempts to reach the unchurched with innovative methods, but in his concept of the church. For Moody the independent congregation was a useful means of helping converts from the lower classes who did not feel at home in the existing churches—but it should be in good fellowship with all the other churches around. Rader, to the contrary, conceived the denominations as decadent and irrelevant.[92] Rader strongly influenced Lance Latham, one of the early NTM leaders. Fleming had a wider vision, even members of denominations were welcome to him in helping to fulfill the remaining task. After his death, the vision was narrowed,and the NTM confined its home base more or less to the independent Bible churches, defining itself as non-ecumenical and non-charismatic.[93]

In order to fulfil its commission to reach the last tribe as quickly as possible, the early NTM wholeheartedly embraced the then innovative principle of the indigenous church. Those whom the mission won for the gospel should carry it further as soon as possible by themselves.[94] In the early training camps of the NTM, the name Roland Allen became a household word, and his ideas were made the basis of NTM missiology.[95] It can be questioned whether these principles really achieved what they were designed for, namely to speed up the evangelization of the last remaining tribes, because of its rule (quite convenient after the Depression): 'Foreign money should be used only in doing the work which leads up *to* the church and not on the work *of* the church. Foreign money for the foreign missionary—native money for the native workers.'[96]

The NTM not only followed the lead given by Roland Allen but, even more, the lead given by Alexander Hay, who had transformed the Inland South America Missionary Union into the New Testament Missionary Union.[97] He had incorporated the principle of the independent local congregation into Roland Allen's concepts, and that made him very attractive to the NTM leaders with their independent church background.[98] Alexander Hay insisted that the congregations were to be fully independent, even in their very first stages. Whereas Hay's NTMU developed into a worldwide denomination, being the only interdenominational mission ever to do so,[99] the NTM stuck to its principle of the absolute independence of the congregations it had founded.[100] All this was designed to effect the speediest possible evangelization before Christ's return, but it is an open question as to how well principle produces effect.[101]

Today, the New Tribes Mission is one of the largest US faith missions. In addition, there are non-US branches and missionaries, and also non-Western sister missions, all devoted to the same aim: to reach those who are not reached yet, wherever they live and however small a 'tribe' may be.

GOD DOES SPEAK EVERY LANGUAGE—EVEN THE REMOTEST

Another mission, which originated between the two wars and was equally innovative in its concepts, were the Wycliffe Bible Translators, founded by William Cameron Townsend (1896–1982).[102] In 1917, he left Los Angeles to work as an independent missionary in Guatemala in Bible colportage work. After travelling a couple of months in the Cakchiqel Highlands, his companion asked him why God only spoke Spanish and not Cakchiqel.[103] He decided to work among the Cakchiqel as a missionary, and joined the Central America Mission, which Scofield had founded in 1890. In 1931, he had the New Testement translated into Cakchiqel.[104] In the process of translation he not only mastered the language but also acquired some mastery of linguistics. He had also done some theological thinking and had reached the conclusion that everyone (irrespective of how many or how few spoke the same language) had the right to read God's word in his or her mother tongue, 'the only language that talks to the heart'. In 1933, he went to Mexico; in 1934, he organized (for two participants) his first 'Camp Wycliffe' in Sulphur Springs, Arkansas. In 1935, the first Camp Wycliffe students started translation work in Mexico. In 1935, he started the Summer Institute of Linguistics (SIL) to institutionalize the linguistic courses. In 1942, he founded the Wycliffe Bible Translators to represent the work of the SIL in America and to provide the necessary support.

Wycliffe Bible Translators is now one of the largest faith missions worldwide. Its innovative concept was to start churches[105] through the translation of the New Testament[106] and, in this way, to reach the marginal peoples of the world to fulfil the Lord's commission.

## A RENEWED ESCHATOLOGICAL VISION

Another mission, which must stand for a number of others, which is recent and has a strong emphasis on applied eschatology is the Christian Outreach Fellowship. It originated when a number of young Ghanaians attending an 'Easter House Party' in 1974 realized that many Ghanaians had never heard the gospel and that, if missionary work continued to progress at its the current rate, most of them would have little chance of hearing the gospel even by the year 2000. So they started the Christian Outreach Fellowship. Its aim is to identify the unreached villages and areas in Ghana and either to start missionary work there or to get others to do so.[107] They embodied heir applied eschatological vision in a poem, a custom well known from the early faith missions in Europe and America:

> Three things the Master asks of US
> And we who serve Him here below,
> And long to see His Kingdom come
> May PRAY and GIVE or GO.
> He needs them all—the open hand
> The willing feet, the praying heart.[108]

A new Nigerian interdenominational mission, which expressly identifies itself with the eschatological motive of Matthew 24:14 is the Christian Missionary Foundation. Its aim is to reach the unreached and to bring the king back.[109]

## Notes

1   See Iain H. Murray, *The Puritan Hope. Revival and the Interpretation of Prophecy*, Edinburgh/Carlisle, PA, 1984 (1971), especially pp. 107–183 and p. 187.

2   C. C. Goen, 'Jonathan Edwards: A New Departure in Eschatology' in *Church History*, XXVII (March 1959), pp. 25–40. A predecessor of Edwards was Daniel Whitby (1638–1725): 'A Treatise of the Millennium: Shewing That It Is Not a Reign of Persons Raised from the Dead, but of the Church Flourishing Gloriously for a Thousand Years after the Conversion of the Jews, and the Flowing-in of All Nations to Them Thus Converted to the Christian Faith' in *Paraphrase and Commentary on the New Testament* (1703).

3   For some leaders of the Great Awakening, this process had already advanced far. For Lyman Beecher, the millennium was at the doorstep, and Charles G. Finney was convinced that the millennium would surely come within three years if the church did her duty (William G. McLoughlin, *Modern Revivalism*, New York, 1959, p. 105).

4   Jonathan Edwards, *Works*, New York, 1881, I, p. 482.

5   Harvey G. Townsend (ed.), *The Philosophy of Jonathan Edwards From His Private Notebooks*, Eugene, OR, 1955, p. 207, quoted in Goen, 'Jonathan Edwards' in *Church History*, XXVII (March 1959), p. 28).

6   There is good reason for assuming that postmillennial eschatology tends to run parallel with an optimistic *Zeitgeist*, and premillennial eschatology with a pessimistic *Zeitgeist* (Stanley N. Gundry, 'Hermeneutics or Zeitgeist as the Determining Factor in the History of Eschatologies?' in *Journal of the Evangelical Theological Society*, 1970, p. 50).

7   For a critical assessment, see: Murray, *The Puritan Hope*, pp. 187–206.

8   He made known his views in 1825. In 1827, he published his translation of the South American Jesuit Manuel De Lacunza's *The Coming of Messiah in Glory and Majesty* (1812), prefaced by 200 pages of his own, in which he also describes the development of his views (Murray, *The Puritan Hope*, pp. 188–190). For his life, see: Root, *Edward Irving*.

9   Edvard Torjesen, *In the Expectation of Christ's Return. A Study of Premillennialism In the Perspective of Church History and the Writings of Fredrik Franson* (Prepared for the Second Consultation of Organizations with a Franson Heritage, Ewersbach, 29.8.2.9. 1983), pp. 7–17.

10  See: F. Roy Coad, *Prophetic Developments. With Particular Reference to the Early Brethren Movement*, Pinner, Middlesex, 1966 (Christian Brethren Research Fellowship Occasional Paper No. 2). Another centre of premillennialism was Mildmay (*WWW*, 1885, p. 48). The earliest premillennial publication of this period is probably: W. Cuninghame, *Pre- Millennial Advent of Christ Demonstrated From the Scriptures* (1813).

11  Timothy P. Weber, *Living in the Shadow of the Second Coming. American Premillennialism 1875–1982* (enlarged edition), Grand Rapids 1983 (1979). For where to find the records of these conferences, see p. 250.

12  Moorhouse was converted in a revival meeting in December 1861 (Coad, *Brethren Movement*, p. 171). For his meeting with Moody, see p. 187f.

13 For Moody meeting Moorhouse, see: Pollock, *Moody Without Sankey*, pp. 69–74. For his eschatology, see Gundry, *Love Them In*, pp. 175–193.

14 Later, Moody Bible Institute (MBI).

15 Emma Dryer—Blanchard n.d. (1923). This 33-page letter, containing her memories of Moody, is a most important source for her often neglected role in the founding of the Institute.

16 Pierson, *A. T. Pierson*, pp. 142–144.

17 Gordon, *How Christ Came to Church*, especially p. 24f.

18 See: Coad, *Prophetic Developments*.

19 A. B. Simpson, 'Looking For and Hasting Forward' in *The Christian and Missionary Alliance*, 8 June 1898, p. 533.

20 Weber, *Living in the Shadow*, p. 13f.

21 Franklin Arthur Pyles, 'The Missionary Eschatology of A. Simpson' in Hartzfeld and Nienkirchen, *The Birth of a Vision*, pp. 29–47 (p. 37).

22 When Hudson Taylor sent the children to Britain after Maria's death, they stayed in Paris for an extended period with Fanny Guinness and her family.

23 Michele Guinness, *The Guinness Legend*, p. 93.

24 Grattan Guinness, *The Approaching End of the Age*, New York, [2]1881 (1878). Guinness first read the postmillennial David Brown, *Christ's Second Coming: Will it be Pre-Millennial?* (probably the enlarged version Edinburgh/London, [2]1849), but that did not satisfy him. See: Iain H. Murray, *The Puritan Hope*, p. 198f.

25 The building was ready in 1872; Joshua Chowriappah, the first student, began early in 1873 (Michele Guinness, *Guinness Legend*, p. 99).

26 The most important books of his on this subject were: *The Approaching End of the Age* (London, 1878); *Light for the Last Days. A Study Historical and Prophetical* (London, 1886; [2]1917); *Romanism and the Reformation* (London, 1887).

27 Holmes, *The Cloud Moves*, p. 21f. Fanny Guinness died in 1898; Grattan Guinness died in 1910.

28 A. B. Simpson, 'How I Was Led to Believe in Pre-Millennarianism' in *CMA Weekly*, 13 November 1891. For a detailed study of his eschatology, see: Pyles, 'The Missionary Eschatology of A. B. Simpson' in Hartzfeld and Nienkirchen, *The Birth of a Vision*, pp. 29–48.

29 Sawin, 'The Fourfold Gospel' in Hartzfeld and Nienkirchen, *The Birth of a Vision*, pp. 29–48, is a scholarly presentation of the 'fourfold gospel'.

30 'On the great missionary movement hangs the appointed hour of the millennial dawn, of the marriage of the Lamb, of the glory of the resurrection, of the time of the restitution of all things' (*Annual Report International Missionary Alliance*, 1892, p. 62).

31 *Annual Report CMA*, 1897, 26.

32 For the meaning of 'imminency', see: Pyles, 'The Missionary Eschatology of A. B. Simpson' in Hartzfeld and Nienkirchen, *The Birth of a Vision*, p. 35f.

33  For a booklet delineating Franson's eschatology and showing its context see: Torjesen, *In the Expectation*.

34  Torjesen, *In the Expectation*, p. 19; see: Torjesen, *A Study of Fredrik Franson*, p. 109.

35  Torjesen, *In the Expectation*, p. 19; see: Torjesen, *A Study of Fredrik Franson*, p. 109.

36  Torjesen, *A Study of Fredrik Franson*, p. 226.

37  Torjesen, *In the Expectation*, p. 43, based on: Fredrik Franson, 'Några afskedsord' in *Trosvittnet*, 1 October 1898, and Missionaeren 29 September 1898.

38  'Soon your Saviour will come. If you keep this hope in mind, it will help you to use your time to win souls for heaven' (Torjesen, *A Study of Fredrik Franson*, p. 282, translated from: Franson, 'Arv og Løn' in *Morgenrøden*, summer 1883).

39  Jonathan Edwards, with whom postmillennialism originated, was also a historicist, but used historicism to support his postmillennialism (Goen, 'Jonathan Edwards' in *Church History*, XXVII (March 1959), pp. 25–40; 26f.).

40  Pyles, 'The Missionary Eschatology of A. B. Simpson' in Hartzfeld and Nienkirchen, *The Birth of a Vision*, p. 33. (That he saw the Papacy as the antichrist may be due to his strong Presbyterian conviction. The Westminster Confession (25, 6) demands this view.)

41  Grattan Guinness, *Romanism and the Reformation*, London, 1887, pp. 73–178.

42  Guinness, *Romanism*, pp. 179–260.

43  This led to a positive appreciation of Zionism. See: Weber, *Living in the Shadow*, pp. 131–141. Five years before Herzl published his book *Der Judenstaat*, W. E. Blackstone had proclaimed the right of the Jews to have their own state in Israel (Memorial Blackstone to President Benjamin Harrison and Secretary of State James Blaine, 5 March 1891).

44  Others too, for example, A. J. Gordon (Pyles, 'The Missionary Eschatology of A. B. Simpson' in Hartzfeld and Nienkirchen, *The Birth of a Vision*, p. 30).

45  Torjesen, *In the Expectation*, p. 31.

46  Fredrik Franson, *Himlauret*, Stockholm, [2]1898, p. 263f.

47  Torjesen, *In the Expectation*, p. 19f.

48  Fredrik Franson, 'Uppenbarelseboken' in *Morgonstjernan*, 29 November 1883 quoted in Torjesen, *In the Expectation of Christ's Return*, p. 19.

49  This can be seen clearly from the early volumes of *Hearing and Doing*.

50  Bingham, *Seven Sevens of Years*, p. 66.

51  For history and criticism, see: Douglas W. Frank, *Less Than Conquerors. How Evangelicals Entered the Twentieth Century*, Grand Rapids, 1986, pp. 73–75.

52  See: Torjesen, *In the Expectation*, p. 13f; see also: James H. Brookes, 'How I became a Premillennialist' in *HD*, July 1899.

53  Coad, *Brethren movement*, p. 78.

54 Taylor, *Retrospect*, p. 18f.

55 Simpson, *Missionary Messages*, p. 37. See also: *WWW*, 1882, p. 34.

56 Walker, *Fool and Fanatic?*, p. 18 (From an undated letter, possibly written 1913–14. The originals are not yet accessible. Jean Walker died July 1987). In another letter, he writes: 'It has been suggested that our Lord's return does not demand the previous evangelization of the world. Whether such be the case or not, our honour demands it' (Walker, *Fool and Fanatic?*, p. 119).

57 Hartzfeld and Nienkirchen, *The Birth of a Vision*, p. 32.

58 His book *The Challenge of Missions*, originally written in 1959 as *The Cry of the World*, starts with a dramatic scene in Satan's realm, wherein he realizes that, since the gospel is now even being preached in Afghanistan, the last remaining 'gospel free' nation, there is now nothing to hold up Christ's return and with it the end of satanic rule. (*The Challenge of Missions* pp. 9–16, especially p. 16).

59 Walker, *Fool and Fanatic?*, p. 43.

60 A. B. Simpson, *Missionary Messages*, p. 37.

61 Deryl Westwood Cartmel, Mission Policy and Programme of A. B. Simpson, MA, Hartford, 1962, pp. 70–97.

62 See also: Bacon, *From Faith to Faith*, pp. 12–26, 'Priority of the Unreached'.

63 *WWW*, 1882, p. 34.

64 But there was also a different reason behind this decision: the church had not done its duty to evangelize effectively. Therefore, to allow women to evangelize is to enhance the effectiveness of the church in fulfilling its commission. One of the first booklets Franson published was: *Weissagende Töchter*, Emden, 1890; also: *Gemeinschaftsblatt* (Emden) No. 16 and No. 17, 1890. The Swedish (revised) edition is: *Profeterande Döttrar*, St Paul, 1896; Stockholm, 1897.

65 Vinson Synan, *In the Latter Days. The Outpouring of the Holy Spirit in the Twentieth Century*, Ann Arbor, 1984, p. 33; *The Holiness-Pentecostal Movement in the United States*, Grand Rapids, 1972, p. 98.

66 Pyles, 'The Missionary Eschatology of A. B. Simpson' in Hartzfeld and Nienkirchen, *The Birth of a Vision*, pp. 29–47 (p. 37).

67 Editorial in *Alliance Life*, 14 September 1988, p. 30; Weber, *Living in the Shadow of the Second Coming* , p. 242.

68 See: Weber, *Living in the Shadow*, pp. 177ff.

69 There are several missions which did base their motivation to a lesser or greater part on the reality of communist expansion—those missions which worked by more or less secret means to reach people in communist countries. But their motivation was not eschatological.

70 See: Hal Lindsay, *The 1980s: Countdown to Armaggedon*, King of Prussia, PA, 1980.

71 John Jefferson Davis, *Christ's Victorious Kingdom. Postmillennialism Reconsidered*, Grand Rapids, 1986.

72 The best presentation of its history (but no sources given) is: Kenneth

Johnston, *The Story of the New Tribes Mission*, Sanford, 1985. The historical material for this book was collected by Terence Sherwood. He was US army historian in Taiwan, and after early retirement he joined NTM as its historian. Interviews with him and his wife Jane (Sanford, 20 March 1986; Ratingen, 20 May 1986) greatly helped me to understand NTM.

73 The Billy Graham Center Archives at Wheaton College contain a remarkable collection of primary sources relating to Rader. For his early development, see: W. Leon Tucker, *The Redemption of Paul Rader*, New York, 1918.

74 Most probably, the unfulfilled wish to marry Rader's daughter.

75 Alfred C. Snead, 'Robert A. Jaffray at Rest' in *The Alliance Weekly*, 6 October 1945. Jaffray became a CMA missionary in Kwangsi Province in 1896. In 1929 in Hong Kong, he helped to start one of the first Chinese Foreign Missions, the *The Chinese Foreign Missionary Union*, with Dr Leland Wang as president and himself as vice president (Nancy K. W. Ma, 'Chinese Missionaries in Indonesia', MA, Columbia Bible College, 1972, p. 33, based on Jason S. Linn, *The Light of the Gospel in Pagan Isles*, Djakarta, 1954, p. 59). Compared to other faith missions, CMA was very early in encouraging 'natives' in missionary work. Dr Leland Wang worked from 1945 to 1959 in Indonesia. In 1932, the Dutch East Indies Mission (CFMU) received $500 monthly from 'The Couriers', an organization which Rader had founded to foster the mission activities of independent churches (*The Courier*, 8 October 1932).

76 Most probably, this meant not full acceptance into the CMA, but acceptance into its Malaysia Mission (*Daily Prayer Calender for Malaysia Mission*, Ringlet, Cameron Highlands, F.M.S, PO Box 228, Singapore S.S.).

77 In the printed sources of NTM, Paul Lenn. Paul Lin (together with J. S. Linn) had worked at the East Coast of Borneo (Balik-Papan and Samarinda) as a missionary of the Chinese Foreign Missionary Union (Linn, *The Light of the Gospel*, p. 58). For his life, see: Terence Sherwood, 'Paul Lenn (Kwang Lin)' in *Family News*, 1885, p. 6f.

78 Johnston, *New Tribes Mission*, p. 19.

79 The churches still exist (1984) (Terence Sherwood, Chronology of NTM (database) for November 1947).

80 In his methods of presentation, Fleming was most innovative: he had 6,000 feet (800 metres) of 16 mm coloured motion picture film which, by using two turntables, record player and microphone, he made into a 45-minute multimedia show (Johnston, *New Tribes Mission*, p. 21). See also: Paul W. Fleming, *Spiritual Chain Reaction*, n.d. Translated into Dutch as: *Geestelijke Kettingreactie*, 1951, when an attempt was made to create a Dutch branch.

81 They were: Lance Latham (pastor of North Side Gospel Center, Chicago, a tabernacle similar to Rader's) (For his life, see: *A Tribute to the Memory of a Choice Servant. Lance B. Latham 1894–1985*, Sanford (NTM), 1985); Bob Dillon (Superintendent of the Sunshine Gospel Mission, Chicago); Bob Williams; Mervin Rossell; Roy Oestreicher; and Paul Fleming himself (Johnston, *New Tribes Mission*, p. 5).

82 Kenneth Johnston, *New Tribes Mission*, p. 27.

83 In 1947, there were renewed attempts for cooperation with Paul Lin, but they were foiled by the guerilla war (Terence Sherwood, Chronology of NTM [database] for 19 September 1947).

84 The first activity there, a trip to take pictures for mission promotion, was made with the active support of the Summer Institute of Linguistics (Terence Sherwood, Chronology of NTM (data base) for March 1942).

85 Jean Dye Johnson, *God Planted Five Seeds*, Sanford, [4]1981 (1966).

86 The ship soon turned out to be too large and too expensive (Johnston, *New Tribes Mission*, pp. 147–152).

87 United States Department of the Interior, National Park Service, Grand Teton National Park, narrative report of aircraft accident which occurred at Grand Teton National Park on 21 November 1950; Orrin and Lorraine Bonney, 'Plane Crash on Mt Moran in Teton' in *The Magazine of Jackson Hole, Wyoming*, 1978, pp. 10–15; pp. 52–57.

88 Eight of the first nine NTM missionaries came from the Saginaw Bible Tabernacle in Saginaw, Michigan (Terence Sherwood, 'In the Beginning' in *Family News*, 1985, p. 12).

89 Flood, *The Story of Moody Church*, pp. 15–20.

90 Niklaus, Sawin and Stoesz, *All for Jesus*, pp. 138–155.

91 The fact that he did not integrate his new tabernacle into CMA added to the existing frictions (Report of the Commission to the Board on official letter relative to the resignation of Mr Rader).

92 'We are out on a great revival—a revival that means a great return—a drastic readjustment of methods to those given by the Holy Spirit to the Apostle Paul [which organized religion has decidedly left]' (Rader in *The Courier*, 18 October 1932). 'The war is on! . . . It's over the Laymen's Mission Report. The split is here shown. Light and darkness cannot dwell together. The hour has come when each denomination must determine what place Christ is to have in their organization' (*The Courier*, 7 January 1933). On 29 April 1933 publication of *The Courier* stopped because of lack of money.

93 *New Tribes Mission* (Information leaflet, valid 1986).

94 'Self-propagation of the native churches shall be encouraged. Every means at our disposal shall be employed to bring the churches to a self-sustaining basis. Native workers shall be encouraged and trained to become effective Christian leaders, and the responsibility of the work shall be passed on to them as quickly as possible' ('Basic Principles' in Minutes New Tribes Mission, 17 July 1942). 'We pledge ourselves to pray daily for 5,000 New Tribes missionaries on pioneer fields doing New Testament missionary work; namely, building an indigenous church' (Covenant between Paul Fleming, Bob Williams, and Cecil Dye, 1 August 1942).

95 William S. Dillon, *Reaching the Last Tribe in This Generation. Via the Indigenous New Testament Methods*, n.d. (1945).

96 Dillon, *Reaching the Last Tribe*, p. 45. The book was written in 1945 by Dillon as a member of the NTM executive. It represents what he taught in the candidate courses and then became the text book. Fleming's foreword made it even more

official. Dillon first worked under Paul Rader, later he was a fellow worker of Dr Thomas Cochrane of World Dominion. For Cochrane, see: Floyd Hamilton and Thomas Cochrane, *Basic Principles in Educational and Medical Mission Work*, London (World Dominion), 1925.

97 *Field News from Inland South America. New Testament Missionary Union (Formerly Inland South America Missionary Union)* No. 5, November 1932. The British Council of the mission did not feel at ease with the new tendency: 'It was felt that any change of name would be detrimental to the interests of the Mission in the British Isles, and the new name proposed seemed to cast a slur upon other missionary bodies and to be an assumption that the New Testament Missionary Union was on New Testament lines whilst other Societies might or might not be so' (Protestant Inland South America Missionary Union, 30 April 1932). One group of the mission did not approve this new theology and founded in 1937 the Inland South America Missionary Union, using the older name (Prot. Inland South America Missionary Union Corporation, 7 March 1938; Prot. NTMU Council Minutes, 30 April 1943). Their leader was John Nairn Hay, doctor among lepers and brother of Alexander Hay, who had initiated the changes (Inland South America Missionary Union Continuing, November 1937; Prot. NTMU Council Minutes 7 March 1938). In addition to these theological reasons, another point of discontent was the cessation of medical work which Alexander Hay had brought about (W. Rownsfeld Brown, open letter, October 1937).

98 In his booklist in *Reaching the Last Tribe*, Dillon listed first Roland Allen, then Alexander R. Hay, *Practicing New Testament Methods in South America*, London, 1932. Hay claimed that after introducing the 'New Testament Methods' in NTMU, work in Brazil (the area of Iquitos) advanced twice as quickly as before.

99 Although as a mission NTMU is interdenominational, the churches are organized internationally, and there are also NTMU congregations in the United States (The New Testament Church of Wyoming, Michigan, *Bible Doctrines of the New Testament Church of Wyoming*, Michigan, 1978 (revised 1980); Interview Albert S. Robinson, 10 October 1985). Most NTMU churches are in South America, but there are also churches in Umuahia, Nigeria, which had started as an African Independent Church under Elder Amajo, who had been converted through a Canadian independent missionary and was then partly supported by the Brethren couple Lodge (Adrian Kooijmans, 'A Visit to Nigeria' in *NTMU Field News*, 61, 1 (1982)). The churches only slowly absorbed the NTMU 'New Testament Principles' ((Alexander Hay—Watson, 10 November 1964; 16 November 1964; 18 November 1964 ('a long way to go yet'); *NTMU Field News* July/September 1970; New Testament Church, Amazuta, Old Umuahia. Decisions adopted by the Church in a Prayer Meeting of 18 July 1884, after an address by Elder Amajo, declaring his intentions to implement the whole New Testament principle and order in the Local Church here; Interview Albert S. Robinson, 11 November 1985).

100An early formulation of this policy is: 'Local churches are... absolutely independent of each other so far as church government is concerned—no 'church federations' (Dillon, *Reaching the Last Tribe*, p. 12).

101To judge on the basis of my limited observations and discussions, I see this principle as counterproductive.

102James and Marti Hafley. *Uncle Cam*, London *et al.*, 1974.

103*Wycliff Bible Translator*, May/June 1982.

104Wycliffe today is the centre of much public controversy. One of the most inaccurate books (Arbeitskeis ILV, *Die frohe Botschaft unserer Zivilisation. Evangelikale Indianermission in Lateinamerika*, Reihe pogrom 62/63, Göttingen/Wien, 1979) does Townsend too much honour by crediting him with a translation of the whole Bible by that date (p. 15). Anti-Wycliffe sentiment is uncritically echoed by: Paul Gifford, *The Religious Right in Southern Africa*, Harare, 1988, p. 29.

105The WBT is sometimes called a mission which does not found churches. The opposite is true: 'We would be disappointed if the end result is not a church' (Interview Dr Gowan, Huntington Beach, 6 March 1986).

106For new developments in the philosophy of translation, see: Wayne Dye, *Bible Translation Strategy. An Analysis of its Spiritual Impact*, Dallas, [2]1985 (1980).

107For further information on COF, see Chapter 12.

108*COF Information Sheet*, valid 1987, p. 4 (author of the poem unknown, capitals added).

109Matthew 24:14 (CMF, *Taking Advantage of the Open Doors for Missions in 1987*, p. 3).

# 10

# Using (no longer) neglected forces: women

All men and women are equal before God. This theological truth was not necessarily applied in the church, nor in its mission. In the classical missions, women usually have no position of their own. Gustav Warneck, the leading missiologist of the German classical missions, made it clear: women are valuable in missionary work, but their position must clearly be inferior.[1] They are not to preach, because to do so would be 'unhealthy and contrary to the Scriptures'.[2] The role of a woman is either to be a missionary's wife or to be a 'third-class' missionary assistant.[3] First- and second-class missionary assistants are craftsmen and doctors.[4] Real missionaries are ordained men. If a women is married, Warneck does not count her in mission statistics; if she is unmarried, he does. Warneck is convinced that women (at least in Germany) need no missionary training. They can receive their training in teacher training colleges, deaconesses' houses and secondary schools.[5]

This attitude, quite widespread in the classical missions, did not, however, go unchallenged, at least in the English-speaking countries. Mrs Doremus, who started the Woman's Union Missionary Society (WUMS) in 1861, was one of those who protested against this attitude.[6] But it was the faith mission movement which developed a completely new theological and practical approach. Here again, Hudson and Maria Taylor set the standard. Right from the beginning, married women were counted as full missionaries and single women were missionaries in their own right,[7] not only being allowed to preach, but expected to.

When, in 1877, there was a severe famine in Shansi, Hudson Taylor sent his second wife Jennie and two single women from London into the area as yet unreached by missionaries. They started an orphanage and made it possible for CIM to establish a permanent mission station there.[8] Even more important for the development of the CIM was that Jennie Taylor and her two assistants had proved that, even in the unreached interior of

China, women can work as pioneer evangelists. So it became a regular thing for women to do pioneer missionary work and to open new mission stations.[9] This made CIM most attractive to young independent women.[10] Later, Taylor decided that in the Kwangsin Valley (300 km/190 miles long, 15 million inhabitants) only women were to be (Western) missionaries.[11] They did their work extremely well. Congregations and schools were established, 3,500 people were baptized and the church there produced its own leaders.[12] Fredrik Franson reported about women missionaries, who did similar work, although in a different area: 'They tend the work at the mission stations just as well as do the other missionaries, particularly when they have a married Chinese co-worker who preaches in the street chapel. They can then without difficulty reach both men and women... CIM, like us, has many stations staffed by women. One of the advantages of this arrangement is that the national pastor develops more rapidly than he would under the leadership of men.'[13]

All faith missions followed Hudson Taylor insofar as they always counted women, single or married, as missionaries in their own right.[14] This meant that, in principle, women were to receive the same training as men.[15] Married or engaged couples could not be accepted as a couple; each of them had to pass the process of being accepted into the mission individually. 'Candidates who are engaged will state this fact, and will not be accepted until both parties have been considered and found suitable... Married candidates may be accepted only after careful consideration of the suitability of both husband and wife... The Mission accepts men and women as full members in every sense, regardless of sex.'[16] If a single member of a faith mission wanted to marry someone who was not a member of the mission, the intended partner must undergo the full process of acceptance into the mission, or she or he had to leave the mission.[17]

That faith missions offered women the same possibilities as men resulted in many faith missions having two women to each man.[18] Although all faith missions followed Hudson Taylor in taking women to be missionaries in their own right, not all of them followed Taylor in giving women independent responsibilities, not immediately controlled by men.[19]

What about faith mission women in Africa? In the Livingstone Inland Mission they participated from the very beginning, but played no major role.[20] The situation was different with the North Africa Mission. It had a majority of women members, and

293

many stations were staffed by women only.[21] The same was true of the Gospel Missionary Union (1900)[22] and the Algiers Mission Band,[23] whose leader was even a woman.[24] The most extensive evangelistic effort of Moroccan evangelists, initiated in 1888, was directed by the NAM's Emma Herdman until her death in 1899.[25] She trained Moroccan evangelists and coordinated their work carefully from her station in Fez.[26] The first seven missionaries of the Egypt General Mission (1897)[27] were all single men, but their counsellor and mentor was the independent missionary Annie van Sommer, whose father, in 1853, had started his own missionary magazine, *The Missionary Reporter*[28] and, in 1905, was to found the Nile Mission Press.[29] Similarly in the Sudan-Pionier-Mission women also played a major role.[30]

During the early years of SIM, women were in the majority. In 1913, following the lead of CIM, the establishment of a 'ladies' station' for the Yagba-speaking area was decided upon.[31] Similarly, in AEF, women were in the majority. Many of them were single, and most of them worked as evangelists—even of the twelve 'deaconesses' in 1893 only eight did medical work.[32] In 1891, Miss Sheasby started missionary work among the (predominantly) Muslim Cape Coloureds.[33]

When the Scandinavian Alliance Mission (TEAM) was finally able to start its first mission station, there were only four women for the job. Franson, who happened to be nearby,[34] borrowed William Dawson, member of the Frie østafrikanske Mission, for half a year to 'build a house and to plant a field of maize' for the four women.[35] When Dawson and Miss Home, one of the four, decided to marry, Franson suggested that Dawson change mission and join SvAM as field leader for Swaziland,[36] which he did.

The most important SvAM missionary in South Africa became Malla Moe,[37] head of Bethel Station.[38] Her most important coworker was Johane (Mapelepele) Ngamede, her first convert. He became the leader of the emerging church and its first ordained pastor. Being a woman, Malla Moe was less of a threat to the chiefs than a male missionary, and Johane Ngamede, young, but polite, made up for Malla Moe's cultural clumsiness.[39] Malla Moe died in 1953 after fifty-eight years missionary service.[40]

The number of women was generally high in faith missions working in Southern Africa. In 1894, Petra Nielsen became the leader of the Frie østafrikanske mission's work in Ekutandane-ni[41] and, in 1895, Martha Sanne started the mission station at Umhlali.[42] Malla Moe regarded herself as an evangelist, and

preaching had become second nature to her,[43] but when someone asked for baptism, she got a man to administer that—first,
one of the male missionaries; soon, Johane Ngamede. This
separation between preaching and administering the sacraments
was usual.[44] No reason was given. With holy communion, that
rule was less strictly kept.[45] Occasionally women missionaries
are said to have conducted weddings[46] but, as a rule, women
kept away from the 'regular office of the church' (according to
Simpson, this comprised deacons, elders and ordained pastors)[47] on the mission field as they did at home. Though at
home there were exceptions, too, for example, in the case of the
'Église du Tabernacle' in Paris. When its pastor, Blocher, died in
1929, the congregation asked his wife to become his successor
and at the same time head of the Mission Biblique.[48] The
reluctance to allow women into the 'regular office of the church'
did not apply to the missions more directly connected to
holiness denominations or organizations. World Gospel Mission (Kenya) had always ordained women missionaries.[49]

## HOLINESS GAVE THEM A PROVINCE

Hudson Taylor had been the first to give women a province of
their own in missionary work in China. Later historians explained this away by arguing that simply there were no men
available. But nowhere had he employed women as second-rate
missionaries, so why should he have done so here?[50] That he
was able to give them a province was first of all due to the
theology which he had received from the holiness movement.
The holiness movement may have been started by a woman,
Phoebe Palmer, and women were always among its leading
exponents: Hannah Whitall Smith, Ruth Paxson, Charlotte Kerr,
Jessie Penn-Lewis and Gertrud Wasserzug, to name but a few.[51]

Their prominent role can be explained by the Wesleyan background of the holiness movement. In the early days of his evangelistic ministry, Wesley, being the ordained Anglican priest he after
all was, still rebuked women who did not keep quiet in the meetings
of the Methodist Societies. Quite a few women, burning with revival
fire as they were, did not obey, but instead evangelized. Wesley gave
them increasingly free reign. Later in his life, when asked why he
allowed women even to preach, he replied: 'If God owns them in the
conversion of sinners, who am I to hinder them?'[52]

Wesley had not simply become lenient, his decision was
theological:

◇ He gave priority to the unreached. If women were to convert them, that was infinitely better than men not converting them.

◇ He decided that theology must not just be deduced logically from certain scriptural verses, but also from observing what the Holy Spirit actually did. (He could well claim Peter in his favour who, after the conversion of Cornelius, argued: 'What was I, that I could withstand God' Acts 11:17(AV)).

## WOMEN'S RIGHT TO PREACH PROVEN FROM THE SCRIPTURES

In the years that faith missions were coming into existence, in almost all churches women, were not just not allowed to preach, but they had to keep completely quiet. When Fredrik Franson asked men and women to pray during evangelistic meetings in Wuppertal, he was sharply rebuked by Heinrich Neviandt, the Free Evangelical pastor there.[53] The first publication of Heinrich Coerper, leader of the German branch of the CIM (later Liebenzeller Mission), was a booklet arguing from scripture that women may pray aloud even with men being present, showing that this was New Testament pattern.[54]

Fredrik Franson took the argument further. In 1890, he published in Emden, Germany a booklet entitled: *Weissagende Töchter* ('Prophesying Daughters'). As for Wesley, though in a different fashion, the Holy Spirit was decisive for him in allowing women to preach: did not Peter claim Joel's prediction, that 'your daughters shall prophesy' (AV) for the 'last days' (Acts 2:17)? Fredrik Franson, as much as his readers, was convinced that he was living in the last days and, in good Reformed tradition, he identified prophesying with preaching. His subsidiary argument is based on faith missions' priority of the unreached: because the church does not effectively do its duty, it would be irresponsible to forbid women to execute the church's duty.[55]

Franson was not the only author who published a book arguing for women's right to preach. One of the very early books was written by Catherine Booth, co-founder of the Salvation Army,[56] to defend Phoebe Palmer's right to preach.[57] All arguments show a similar method of interpreting the New Testament they take the *life* of the early church as the pattern. If women prayed aloud in mixed company in the early church, that was the yardstick. If women taught men, as did Priscilla, who should forbid them from doing the same today? And if a Bible verse or two seemed to demand that women keep quiet and not teach at all, these must be interpreted in the context of how the

New Testament pictures the early church—in that early church, the women did not keep quiet.

## A HISTORIC COMPROMISE

Early faith missions, especially CIM, were rooted both in the holiness movement and the Brethren movement. One had an Arminian background, the other a Calvinist background; one gave women almost full scope for public ministry, the other full scope for keeping quiet.[58] How could the Brethren so whole-heartedly support CIM, which had such prominent women missionaries who did everything but keep quiet? Brethren theology provided the possibility. Being ardent Bible students, the Brethren were well aware that, especially in the Old Testament, there were women whom God had called into positions of leadership. That was explained by arguing that God always calls men, but if they fail, he has the freedom to call even a woman, just look at Deborah![59] On the mission field, men have failed, simply by not being available.[60] So God may send women, at least as pioneers. (If they are successful, men will be available to take over.) So Arminians and Calvinists, holiness people and Brethren, agreed on what should be done, in practical terms. But they agreed to and did the same thing with different theological concepts behind what they did. That was a historic compromise, indeed, but also a compromise which would, of necessity, become past history as soon as men had become available and were no longer 'failing'.

## AN EXCEPTION: KARL KUMM, THE BRITISH SUM AND THE USELESSNESS OF WOMEN MISSIONARIES

By the time that almost all the early faith missions were glad when women applied to join them, the British branch of the SUM felt them to be a nuisance. Karl Kumm was confronted with the problem that far more women applied to his nascent SUM than men. He was convinced that women were not qualified for pioneer work.[61] He considered wives to be a nuisance, albeit hard to avoid. But why should men, just as government officers did, not go to the Sudan without a wife, at least for one term?[62] Single women would be nothing but a burden for the whole mission.[63] When single women applied, they were rejected.[64] In 1909, they were at least entered into a waiting list,[65] but only when a home for rescued slave children was established in Rumasha were single women accepted, although exclusively for this job.[66] Dr Krusius, an old German friend of Kumm from Sudan-Pionier-Mission's days, made the British branch's position quite clear in a letter to the Danish branch: 'It should be quite clear to you that ladies cannot be counted as full members of the staff of a mission station in West Africa.'[67]

This restrictive attitude was not at all shared by the young Danish branch, but they complied insofar, at least, that, in addition to Dr Brønnum, only his wife and the nurse Dagmar Rose were sent out in 1911.[68] When Mrs Brønnum died in 1913, the British branch expressed the hope that the Danish branch might soon 'be able to welcome some more *men*, that pioneer work in Yola may not be delayed.'[69] Kumm also managed to reduce the possible number of single women in the South African branch.[70]

Even when, in 1914, Karl Kumm (because of his former German nationality) left Britain to work for the US branch, the British branch continued his restrictive attitude towards women. His attitude, though, was not at all shared by the US branch.[71] The most famous of the women pioneers sent out by SUM-US was Johanna Veenstra,[72] who left the United States in 1919.[73] Together with other single women,[74] she laid the foundation for one of the constituent churches (Benue)[75] of what is now the Church of Christ in Nigeria (COCIN). She was sent out by the interdenominational US branch, but she managed to convince her church to form its own denominational Christian Reformed Church Branch (1940) of SUM.[76] For ten years, she headed the Lupwe-Takum District of the SUM.[77] She never had men among her missionary co-workers.

In 1928, Johanna Veenstra attempted to change the restrictive attitude of the British branch ('Not to accept single ladies for service at present, unless they possess nursing, teaching or other special qualifications')[78] which was incomprehensible to her. She wrote to the London Committee, arguing that some of the best SUM (women) missionaries under these rules would never have reached the mission field.[79] Because the committee knew about her successful pioneer work, she was granted a hearing, and the harsh attitude was somewhat softened. It was decided 'that case papers should be sent to single women if they appear to have had some adequate training or to possess some special qualification'.[80] But opposition remained: Farrant, field leader of SUM-UK in Nigeria, insisted that only women with special qualifications were needed,[81] and when Dr Emlyn suggested the

appointment of women committee members or at least a statement that there was no objection to such an appointment in
principle, such a decision was seen as presently not advisable.[82]

Karl Kumm's restrictive attitude, so different from early faith
mission practice, is hard to explain, especially because his wife
was Lucy Guinness. She had never acquired any 'special qualifications' other than travelling,[83] public speaking,[84] writing [85] and
organizing a mission.[86] Had she applied to the British branch of
the SUM in 1908, she would not even have been put on the
waiting list. (The problem did not arise because she died in
1906.) Karl Kumm not only had quite an independent wife, but
also quite an independent sister, Pauline. She was a CIM
missionary and head of one of its stations.[87] I have not been
able to find out what made Karl Kumm and the British SUM
branch develop this attitude, so distinct from the general faith
mission attitude. But in view of later developments, one may
judge that Karl Kumm was just ahead of his time.

## Declining possibilities

Women like Malla Moe, Alma Doering or Johanna Veenstra are
counted among the 'heroes' of the early faith missions. They
were successful pioneers, and that was clearly recognized. By the
time books were written about them, however, they were no
longer held to be role models for young women missionaries,
whose role was increasingly reduced to 'female duties': nurses,
teachers, occasional doctors, secretaries, possibly wives. Typical
was the SIM decision of 1925 that all women should have some
nursing experience.[88] Sometimes, women were more cared for
than they actually wanted. In 1940, Lily Gsell of the Evangelische
Muhammedanermission (SPM) was refused permission to continue work in Aswan without male care.[89] When Malla Moe was
to be evacuated during the Boer War, she refused and asked no
one for permission. Her male colleagues waited a day for her but
did not try to make her change her mind.[90]

Over the years, it was made increasingly more difficult for
single women to be accepted by faith missions, compared to the
more rare men. In 1928, the SIM refused the application of a
Miss Jones, because it was felt that 'as more ladies were offering
than men it would be well to keep the standards high'.[91] If an
applicant was engaged to a man with qualifications, the standards
were liable to be lowered. 'Although the Committee could not

recommend her acceptance apart from Mr Evans, they are prepared to recommend her acceptance as the wife of Mr Evans'.[92] Sometimes, the home boards were more restrictive than the field leadership. When the SUM field leadership, after the retirement of the Rev. and Mrs Suffill, proposed to make two women their successors, the home board refused because of the 'large responsibilities involved' in the work at Forum.[93]

The cases shown here describe a development that took place in almost all faith missions, though at different speeds and to different extents. This development ran parallel to the decline of women's societies and possibilities in the classical missions.[94] In both movements, theological principles were (ab-)used: among classical missions, it was the principle of unity ('If men and women are all one, the women must not have their own organizations') among faith missions, it was the principle of scriptural authority ('Let your women keep silence in the churches, even if they prayed in New Testament times'). In 1968, Pierce Beaver judged that, nevertheless, faith missions still offered more opportunities to women than classical missions.[95] This is still true today for some faith missions, but not for all.

It is part of faith missions' lore that God sometimes calls a woman to do a man's job. Reports about such work are often given with a twinkle in the eyes[96] and in the firm conviction that what this or that woman is doing really is a man's job, and sooner or later the matter will be set right and a man will do it.

This attitude, usually shared by women and men alike, ensures that the successor of a successful women is always a man. Women can work as pioneers. That is acceptable. But Malla Moe's successor was a man. When Alma Doering grew older and could not successfully run the US side of the Unevangelized Tribes Mission, and there was no successor, the mission was closed.[97] When Johanna Veenstra died, the exceptional case took place and a woman, Nelle Breen, became her successor. Nonetheless, leadership passed into male hands not much later, when Edgar Smith married her and became field leader in her place. After the CIM women had successfully established the church in the Kwangsi River Bassin, even men could be spared to work in that area. The Bible schools reflect the same pattern: Prairie Bible Institute opened with L. E. Maxwell as director and three women teachers. One of them, quite old now, is still (1986) teaching theology on a part-time basis.[98] When she retires, there will be plenty of women teaching at PBI, but none of them in theology proper. The same is true of Beatenberg. Founded by a woman, her successor was a man. The last woman teacher, Frau Eiberle, retired in 1989, and was not replaced by a woman. Nor did a woman succeed Madame Blocher as pastor of the Tabernacle Church in Paris.[99]

When A. B. Simpson started his independent work, women were very prominent among his co-workers during the many conventions which shaped the early CMA.[100] The picture was the same on the early CMA board. About half the members were women, but whenever a woman's place became vacant a man took her seat. The final woman's seat was vacated by Mrs Simpson's death. One faith mission, the German Sudan-Pionier-Mission, had a women's committee as was frequent among the classical missions. This was later dissolved by 'integration'.

If a woman was successful in her pioneer work, the 'historic compromise' about women evangelists would break down, as men then became available. A decision then must be made: did she work as an evangelist in her own right or should a man now continue with what was rightly his? Usually, holiness theology lost and Brethren theology, in one guise or another, won.

One reason that the compromise was often dissolved in this way lay in the decline of the holiness movement. This decline started before the end of the century and was enforced by the recent pentecostal movement, which was born from the holiness movement and took with it a considerable section of that movement—the CMA, for example, losing one-third of its membership.[101] The pentecostal movement attracted many of the leading holiness women. As a backlash, this reduced women's chances in faith missions, as everything 'pentecostal' became suspect.

This development was part of the overall process of the re-Calvinization of Calvinism, which followed the period of the Arminianization of Calvinism. Holiness theology had much room for women; Calvinistic theology, usually little. The result was that those missions which kept much of the holiness teaching, such as WEC (see the case of Bessie Fricker later in this chapno) and Christian Literature Crusade, continued, and still continue, to grant women more possibilities than missions which have a strong Calvinistic base. This is the case with the American Unevangelized Fields Mission, which has the same origin as WEC, but an almost exclusively Calvinistic background.[102] Another mission which stresses very strongly the need for *men* is NTM.[103] Although in its early years NTM freely accepted even pentecostals, now its background is predominantly the usually Calvinistic independent churches.[104]

What has been described here as a process of re-Calvinization can also be described as part of the 'Great Reversal', in which the evangelicals after about 1910, in an overreaction against the 'social gospel' and 'liberal theology', lost much of their innovative power.

NO LONGER NEEDED?

A basic idea of faith missions was to 'utilize the neglected forces of Christianity'. They offered women a chance which society as a whole did not offer them in those years of the waning nineteenth century. When Fanny Guinness, appealing for the first students for Doric Lodge, wrote: 'We are increasingly convinced of the importance of well-trained female agents among the heathen, and of the fact that multitudes of women who have the natural and spiritual qualifications ... are wasting their time at home here in England'.[105] She had, besides spiritual fulfillment, also much self-fulfillment to offer to the young women. Now, three generations later, society as a whole has a lot more to offer to young independent women, and faith missions have far less to offer than they had three generations ago. This endangers the aim of faith missions to reach the unreached. In all missions women are welcome for the many 'female' jobs, but in many missions they are welcome only for those jobs. If faith missions give priority to evangelism,[106] this is now very often only a male priority.

This decline in the opportunities for women to work independently affected all missions, but some much less than others.[107] Of the larger missions, WEC was most probably least affected. Even in WEC there were tendencies, coming from Brethren theology, that women should keep quiet in the church. But the international conference of WEC ruled clearly that, although every woman is *allowed* to keep quiet, no one can be allowed to *demand* that a woman keep quiet. All positions of leadership are, in principle, open to women. Thus, WEC has a number of women as field leaders. In Gambia, there has never been a man as field leader; in Burkina Faso, Mady Vaillant was field leader for many years, resigning from that position only because she wanted to start a new pioneer work in West Mali;[108] for some time Annette Botting was field leader in Zaire and so on. The leadership ideal of WEC though, is not leadership by a man or by a woman, but by a 'mature couple'. This may look like a guise for simple male leadership, but that is not the intention. Leadership by a couple means that they both lead, and that the wife (for example, of the International Director) has a job description of her own.[109]

Women in leadership positions are otherwise less frequent. In TEAM, the Korean field elected a women as leader, though there were enough men around, and TEAM-US has appointed a woman as associate candidate secretary.[110] In OMF, women always had better chances than in other missions.[111] A mission which gives women equal rights is Wycliffe Bible Translators.[112] Two women can do (and very often do) pioneer translation work just as a couple would do (and does).[113] But because Wycliffe does not *directly* found churches and Wycliffe missionaries do little direct preaching, the position of women in the work of WBT does not contribute as much to faith mission *theology* as their numbers suggest. Nonetheless, the number of women working independently in WBT is high, and this suggests that, today as in the beginning, women respond eagerly and with a sacrificial spirit when a mission offers them independent pioneer work.

# Women's position in faith mission churches in Africa

In many of the early faith missions, women were effective evangelists and preachers of the gospel, and this greatly helped to speed up the spread of the good news[114] but, as a rule, the female missionaries' comparatively advanced position in the church was not passed on to African women. This is the more astonishing because, in Asia, classical missions and faith missions had both developed the institution of 'Bible women'.

In early faith mission magazines, there are occasional reports that women witnessed informally to their new-found faith, and WEC reports of a couple sharing their evangelistic efforts.[115] But when it came to full-time service, men were always chosen, even where women were the missionaries. The early 'Bible schools' (designed to train a *clerus minor* ('minor clergy') for the emergent churches, were for men. Often their wives attended, too, but they were not trained like the men. Most often, a reduced 'practical' programme for wives was administered.

In the time of the early faith missions in Europe, there were attempts to develop female office in the church, taking the deaconess (more correctly the woman deacon) Phoebe of Cenchreae (Romans 16:1) as an example; many fellowships had been founded by women, be they deaconesses, as in Germany,[116] or evangelists, as in Sweden.[117] Faith missions were not as involved with deaconesses, because that institution originated in the classical revival but, in some missions, there were a considerable number. In the beginning, they largely carried out evangelistic work but, later, they increasingly moved away from this.

Phoebe and her modern colleagues might have provided a pattern for the development of female offices in the nascent African churches, with no traditional church authority to hinder such innovations.[118] However, the missions, even their female missionaries who had claimed this right for themselves in Europe, did not transfer this to the African churches. Equally, when the young churches established councils and boards, sitting on them was men's business as far as African participation was concerned.

A parallel development can be observed in Germany. Fredrik Franson's activities in Eastern Prussia in 1899 interested a number of young women so much that they wanted to work as evangelists. The leaders of the *Gemeinschaftsbewegung* (fellowship movement) there channelled their enthusiasm into becoming deaconesses. They did not feel at ease in the classical deaconesses' houses, so one of the pastors founded, for six of them, a deaconesses' house with a strong emphasis on evangelism, which become known as Vandsburg. The Vandsburg Sisters (who later moved their centre to Marburg)[119] started many new fellowships in which they did the preaching there. But they never had 'ordinary' women preach, only ordinary men. They even organized a seminary for training the preachers, but no women preachers were trained.

This obvious difference between the women's position in faith missions and in the churches they started is usually explained as an accommodation to African customs; in Africa, the position of women is lower. And it is to this that the churches (or perhaps the missionaries already) conformed. This argument is not convincing, merely because it is so often repeated and widely accepted. There are a number of arguments and observations which contradict this notion. The missionaries, if they felt it to be necessary, did not budge even from all-out conflict—for example, in the case of polygamy. Why should they shrink from confronting African culture on such a matter as women's position in the church? The other observation is more important:there is no difference even in those areas of Africa where women have a much higher position in society, such as among the Baulé in the area of the Mission Biblique en Côte d'Ivoire. The reason is not African culture, but missionary subculture. The faith missionaries, who usually did not come from the established churches, did not try to create in Africa those structures[120] through which in Europe and the United States, they expressed their criticism of the established churches. As soon as the faith missionaries arrived in Africa they changed sides. There, it was they who erected a church establishment, and a church establishment is rarely in favour of independent women.

Two examples show that this change in the role of women is not due to African culture: in the 1930s, there was an advanced girls' school in each of the Lutheran Mission, on Kilimanjaro and the Anglican CMS in Central Tanzania. When Chagga girls (supported by their parents) asked to be trained as nurses or teachers,[121] the Leipzig missionaries declined their wish as being contrary to Chagga culture. A change in Chagga culture could only be expected after many years.[122] At the same time, in Mvumi, the CMS successfully trained women teachers.[123] And the 'Anglican' Gogo were usually considered to be 'less developed' than the 'Lutheran' Chagga. Even before the turn of the century, there were quite a number of women teachers in the CMS in Uganda and, in 1905, Gayaza High School was opened.[124] Faith missions never worked among the Gogo or the Chagga, but their cultures do not differ from cultures relevant to faith missions, such as Kikuyu or Kipsigi, to the extent that this difference could provide the explanation.[125]

The argument that the Bible does not object to women preaching, but that in African culture it is not advisable, is a frequent explanation for the fact that women do not preach in the Africa Inland Church. But the direct neighbour of AIC is the Africa Gospel Church, in which African women regularly preach. Whether a Kipsigi women is allowed to preach does not depend on her own culture, but on the missionaries' culture. If she belongs to a church which goes back, through the World Gospel Mission, to the Arminian holiness movement, she may preach. If she belongs to a church which goes back, through the AIM, to the more Calvinist historical fundamentalism, she may not.

The Africa Inland Church is the strongest church among the

Kamba, but more than 100,000 Kamba belong to the African Brotherhood Church which, in theology, hardly differs from the AIC, and whose head, Bishop Ngala, once belonged to the AIC. Bishop Ngala, himself a Kamba, did not conceive it as biblical to forbid women to preach, as was usual in the AIC. So he allowed women to preach in his church, even on Sunday morning.[126] If two churches in the same culture with basically the same theology, decide the question of women preachers so differently, one cannot assume that the reason can be found in 'African culture'. The reason is to be found in missionary culture, or the culture of the churches in their homeland on which they patterned 'their' African churches.

In the whole realm of faith missions in Africa, the African Brotherhood Church is the only church which has consciously developed women's offices. The Bible school, which the ABC opened very early in its history (1950), accepted women right from the beginning. After finishing the course, a woman is a preacher. After training, she becomes a 'sister'; after five more years, she may become a deaconess.[127] If she wants to marry, there is no objection to it.[128] If she observes certain intervals and marries a man who is no hindrance to her service to the church, she may keep her church office.[129] To take one example: for more than twenty years, a deaconess has been the treasurer of the church, for ten years she has been married.[130] Within ABC, the sisters and deaconesses have clearly defined positions, which include the right to preach and to teach, but they are not eligible for the 'regular office of the church'—that of the pastor. About 300 km (90 miles) south, among the Lutheran Chagga, there are also deaconesses, forming the Ushirika wa Neema. But they belong to a classical church and they follow the pattern of the German deaconesses, concentrating on teaching, congregational work and nursing, whereas the deaconesses in the African Brotherhood Church might be best classified as women deacons.

One of the African faith mission churches, the Igreja Evangelica de Guiné, was founded by a single woman, the WEC missionary Bessie Fricker. In 1898, Chapell, in his collection of essays on faith missions, writes that sometimes, where men fail, women succeed.[131] In WEC lore, this is expressed in the saying: 'If a job is too hard for men, God will send a woman'. All this is true for Bessie Fricker who, together with three young men, felt called to begin the first Protestant mission in what was then Portuguese Guinea. As a single women, she was not to travel with three single men, so it was decided that the three men should go ahead to establish a base for the mission in Bissau. Bessie Fricker was to go to Fogo, one of the Cape Verde Islands. The three men reached Bissau in 1939, but gave up after several months because they felt the problems to be insurmountable.[132] Norman P. Grubb, C. T Studd's son-in-law and successor, immediately called her back by telegram.[133] She replied: 'I hope you won't think me impertinent, but it was not you who sent me out; it was God. So I feel I should remain where I am and ask God His will.'[134] Once Bessie Fricker had 'disobeyed', Norman Grubb supported her wholeheartedly[135] and WEC coined the household word: 'A woman is the man to do the job.'[136] For health reasons, Bessie Fricker could only stay in Bissau from 1940 to 1941. During that time, she established a fellowship of about a dozen converts and a number of interested persons.[137] In 1945, she returned, married to Leslie Brierley, one of the first two WEC missionaries to Senegal. She entered the colony illegally from Senegal and convinced the governor to allow her to stay until Lisbon had approved her and her family's visa.[138] She left it largely to her husband to organize the church but, for the Christians, she remained the leader, the 'pastora'.[139]

Because of restrictive Portuguese immigration rules, women were always clearly in the majority in WEC Guinea Bissau, and in many areas they were the first preachers. Bessie Brierley was a fascinating preacher,[140] and other women missionaries also preached regularly. Some women from Cape Verde or Guinea were very close to Bessie Brierley, especially the Cape Verdian Juliana Evera,[141] but they did not preach because none of them could read.

What remained of these beginnings? Most obvious is the fact that the Igreja Evangélica da Guiné, for many years, has had one woman as a full-time worker: Benvinda Vaz Martins, daughter of one of the early converts of Bessie Fricker. Born in Cape Verde, she is not native to the country in the narrower meaning of the word. Everywhere in the church, women are allowed to preach. Women missionaries preach regularly on Sunday morning, local women do so less frequently, although they often contribute their testimonies or shorter exhortations to the services. About fifteen years ago, there seems to have been a movement in the church to make women keep quiet, but today, most probably supported by emancipatory political tendencies, the development has gone the other way. The missionaries had not created structures designed to give women a greater share, but their example has saved the church from being restrictive. An elder, when asked if women should preach, replied: 'If there had not been women preaching, I would not have been converted.'[142] With increasing education, Guinean women use the opportunities that were never, in principle, denied to them.

WOMEN PASTORS IN FAITH MISSION CHURCHES?

'The regular office of the church' is not for women. To this attitude there was at least one exception: Norman P. Grubb (WEC). When he had received a list of those proposed for ordination in Colombia, he replied to Pat Symes, the field leader: 'But why don't you ordain women? I think it is absurd to expect them to do the work of ministers such as they do all over the place, and yet refuse to ordain them. Plunge in brother, and recognize that the same Spirit works by women as by men. Make them all equal in the Gospel, neither male nor female'.[143] He was quite alone in his view, although there are tendencies in WEC today which point in the same direction: at the African Consultation of WEC-related churches, with fifty representatives from the various churches, it was decided that women, if they are leaders in the church, also have the right to baptize.[144]

Whereas the classical churches in Africa saw an increasing number of women being ordained, this is rare in the faith mission churches. I have only found information about two churches with ordained woman. In the Communauté Évangélique du Zaire, Kukangiza Nyambudi (ex-Julienne) was ordained in about 1978,[145] and, in 1985, the Église Évangélique du Congo ordained Mme Emilienne Boungou-Mouyabi.[146] Both churches have their roots in the Svenska Missionsförbundet, a Swedish mission with a strong holiness tradition and with many women pioneers (evangelists) in its early phase in Sweden. On the whole these days, the challenge to give women more leadership positions in faith mission churches comes less from their own holiness heritage than from classical churches and from the charismatic movement. The Africa Gospel Church, going back to the (holiness) World Gospel Mission, which all the time had ordained women missionaries, has never ordained women.[147]

WOMEN IN THE NEW AFRICAN FAITH MISSIONS

There are, despite Keyes' statistics, few interdenominational African missions yet. In them, women clearly play as important a role as they played in the early faith missions in Europe. CAPRO and Christian Missionary Foundation gave women full rights, whereas the older denominational Evangelical Missionary Society (Jos, ECWA) and the Africa Inland Church Missionary Board (Kenya) send out women only as wives.[148] With CAPRO, Naomi Famunore is training secretary, and both with CAPRO and CMF single women can even work abroad.[149]

**Notes**

1   Warneck, *Missionslehre*, pp. 217–231.

2   Warneck, *Missionslehre*, p. 248, basing his argument on 1 Corinthians 14:34 and 1 Timothy 2:12.

3   Warneck, *Missionslehre*, p. 247. Women's area of work is medical and social care and education (p. 249).

4   A woman doctor would be a member of the second class of missionary assistants.

5   Warneck, *Missionslehre*, p. 251.

6   R. Pierce Beaver, *American Protestant Women in World Mission. A History of the First Feminist Movement in North America*, Grand Rapids, [2]1980 (1968: *All Loves Excelling*), p. 91f. WUMS started as a specialized classical mission, but later accepted faith mission principles (Rupert,*The Emergence*, p. 123). This being so, WUMS is not, as Frizen sees it, the oldest American faith mission, although it is indeed the oldest of the seven IFMA founder members. For the history of WUMS, see: Edwin L. Frizen, *An Historical Study of the IFMA in Relation to Evangelical Unity and Cooperation*, DMiss, Trinity, Deerfield, 1981, pp. 67–71. In 1971, WUMS became United Fellowship for Christian Service in order to send out men, too. In 1975, it joined the Bible and Medical Missionary Fellowship (1978, BMMF Interview), which had been founded as a classical specialized mission in Glasgow in 1852 and later had accepted faith mission principles. The presence of extraordinary women was not limited to faith missions, as shown by the case of Mary Slessor (1848–1915) of the United Presbyterian Church of Scotland Mission in Calabar (W. P. Livingstone, *Mary Slessor of Calabar*, London, 1916).

7   Vgl. Broomhall, *Refiner's Fire*, p. 392f.

8   Phyllis Thompson, *Each to Her Post. The Inspiring Lives of Six Great Women in China*, London/Sevenoaks, 1982, pp. 57–61.

9   Warneck,*Abriß* divides the CIM missionaries as follows: 358 men, 290 single women, 231 married and 21 widowed. He can hardly comprehend that only 18 of the men were ordained, but for the CIM neither being male nor being ordained was considered to be a special qualification for missionaries (p. 114).

10  Even today in the United States, the percentage of unmarried women is highest in OMF.

11 Broomhall, *Assault on the Nine*, pp. 232–251 ('Women Inland'); p. 387; Appendix 1; Howard Taylor, *By Faith. Henry W. Frost and the China Inland Mission*, Singapore, [2]1988 (1938), pp. 163–165.

12 Bacon, *From Faith to Faith*, p. 66.

13 Fredrik Franson, 'Letter from Pingliang' in *Missionaeren*, 27 October 1904, quoted in: Torjesen, *Fredrik Franson*, p. 739.

14 In its early years, SUM-UK was an exception. They fell in line only in 1911: 'Resolved that the wife of a missionary be recognized a missionary' (Minutes SUM, 5 September 1911).

15 Until Fanny Guinness established Doric Lodge, ELTI had trained men only. From then onwards, nearly all Bible schools were co-educational, even though women and men were sometimes hardly allowed to speak to each other.

16 *SIM Manual*, 1984, p. 26. These rules are typical for faith missions in general.

17 Here, too, the current SIM regulation is typical: 'Since both husband and wife are members of the Mission, marriage to someone who is not a member of the Mission requires resignation from the Mission' (*SIM Manual*, 1984, p. 27).

18 This ancient statistic is still a regular part of today's faith mission lore, though the statistics contradict. But why check them?

19 The rationalization was that women could work well on their own in China, but not in Africa (Congo Missionary Conference, 1902).

20 Fanny Guinness, *The New World of Central Africa* (for the history of LIM, see pp. 173ff.). Miss Bosson, Henry Craven's fiancée, was in 1878 the first white women ever on the Lower Congo (p. 197). The role of women became much more important with the founding of the Congo Balolo Mission in 1889.

21 Warneck criticizes this severely: 'There are many missionaries indeed, though it is not clear if all 84 are in active service. Of them 64 (!) are ladies, who not only do house to house visiting, nurse the sick or teach school, but who also preach publicly (!) and on some stations are all alone' (Warneck, *Abriß*, p. 333, translation K. F., the exclamation marks are Warneck's).

22 George C. Reed, 'Memories of Morocco 1897–1914', unpublished, n.d. (55 pages).

23 Steele, *Not in Vain*, pp. 125.

24 Her biography is: Blanche A. F. Pigott, *I. Lilias Trotter. Founder of the Algiers Mission Band*, London/Edinburgh, n.d.

25 After her sudden death, the effort was continued until about 1909 (Steele, *Not in Vain*, p. 29). Contrary to E. F. Baldwin's (first NAM, then independent) her work was solid and convincing (p. 26).

26 By doing so, she took up Gützlaff's concept. But her sphere of work was much smaller and her control tighter.

27 Douglas D. Porter, *At Thy Disposal. The Beginnings of the Egypt General Mission*, London, 1934; George Swan, *Lacked Ye Anything? A Brief Story of the Egypt General Mission*, London, [3]1923 (1921).

28 Annie van Sommer had strong Brethren sympathies. Her father James van Sommer had founded the *Missionary Reporter*, to become the *The Missionary Echo* in 1872 (today, *Echoes of Service*) which, over the years, became the missionary magazine of the Brethren only.

29 Between 1905 and 1955, the Nile Mission Press produced nearly 1000 publications in twenty languages. In 1956, it fell victim to the Suez War. In 1957, it was restarted in Beirut under the name Arabic Literature Mission (*EMCM*, p. 40). In 1976, Arabic Literature Mission, Lebanon Evangelical Mission (1860) and Middle East General Mission (founded in 1898 as Egypt Mission Band; later, Egypt General Mission; after 1956, only EGM-UK) formed the Middle East Christian Outreach (MECO) (*UK Christian Handbook*, p. 359).

30 See: Margarete Unruh, *Hedwig von Hahn*, Wiesbaden, 1939. In 1926, Fräulein von Massenbach was head of station (Minutes SPM, 21 January 1926). 1983–84, Dr Elfriede Schmitt was field leader for Egypt; 1987–88, Irma Nübling was acting field leader.

31 Minutes SIM, 6 May 1913.

32 George Weeks, *W. Spencer Walton*, p. 73.

33 *South African Pioneer*, 1891, p. 228.

34 Franson has been called a 'world evangelist'. Nearly all the missionaries he sent out he also visited, in China as well as in India and South Africa. On the way, he evangelized everywhere and, if opportunity arose, baptized. For details of his travels, see: Torjesen, *Fredrik Franson*, pp. 589–629 (East Asia); pp. 704–764 (Australia and Asia); pp. 765–776 (South Africa); pp. 777–784 (South America).

35 Dawson, *History*, n.d. (1933), pp. 15, 18.

36 Dawson, *History*, p. 20.

37 Nilsen and Sheetz, *Malla Moe*.

38 Swanson, *Three Score Years*, p. 198.

39 Nilsen and Sheetz, *Malla Moe*, pp. 75ff. ('Trip to Chief Maja').

40 Nilsen and Sheetz, *Malla Moe*, p. 245.

41 Odd Ommundsen, 'Den frie østafrikanske mission' in *Det Norske Misjonsforbunds Ytremisjon. Utgitt til Det Norske Misjonsforbunds 100-årsjubileum*, n.p., n.d. (1984), p. 32f.

42 Kari Lorentzen, 'Det Norske Misjonsforbunds arbeid i Sør-Afrika' in *Det Norske Misjonsforbunds Ytremisjon*, p. 37.

43 Nilsen and Sheetz, *Malla Moe*, p. 145.

44 During the African Consultation 1985 in Vavoua, with fifty representatives of WEC related churches, the question if women, often having leadership positions in WEC, are allowed to baptize was answered in the affirmative (Christel Meyer—Fiedler, 30 March 1989).

45 When Benvinda Vaz in Guinea Bissau wanted to celebrate the Lord's table somewhere in a place where they were not yet used to doing so, she 'took one of the men and taught him while they were celebrating the Lord's supper' (Interview

311

Benvinda Vaz, 5 August 1986).

46  Reported, for example, about Marjorie Cheverton (WEC-UK, 1933–85) and Agnes Chansler (WEC-US, 1926) in Zaire.

47  Leslie A. Andrews, 'Restricted Freedom: A. B. Simpson's View of Women' in Hartzfeld and Nienkirchen, *The Birth of a Vision*, p. 223, based on: *CMA Weekly*, 27 March 1891, p. 195.

48  'Habitués par leur bien-aimé pasteur à n'écouter que les directions du Saint-Esprit, sans s'occuper des critiques ou de l'incomprehension, les membres du Conseil furent persuadés que celle qui avait été la collaboratrice de tous les instants de leur cher disparu, devait le remplacer, non seulement comme directrice de la Mission, mais encore comme Pasteur de l'église. L'église, à la quasi-unaminité, ratifia le choix du Conseil' ['Having been accustomed by their well-loved pastor to heed only the direction of the Holy Spirit, without concern over criticism or others' lack of understanding, the members of the council were convinced that she who had been the dear-departed's co-worker in all things should replace him, not only as director of the Mission but also as pastor of the church. The church ratified the choice of the council virtually unanimously.'] (Madame A. Blocher, *Par la Foi...*, Editions des Bons Semeurs, Paris, n.d. (*ca.* 1936), p. 90f.). Here, the argument was like Wesley's: 'If God uses a woman in the conversion of sinners, why should I hinder him'. The Holy Spirit had already made her a pastor; human choice was just to ratify this.

49  The number of ordained women missionaries has been declining over the years. In the Africa Gospel Church, women have never been ordained.

50  The Kwangsin Valley was not the only area entrusted to women only. The Friedenshort Mission (Eva von Thiele-Winkler) worked in Kweichow Province, and the Deutsche Frauenmissionsgebetsbund was entrusted with the Shungking area in Szechwan Province (Franz, *Hudson Taylor*, pp. 207–209, 214–218).

51  See Chapter 7.

52  For the growth (and later decline) of female ministry among Methodists (as well as for non-conformist precedents), see: Paul Wesley Chilcote, *John Wesley and the Women Preachers of Early Methodism*, PhD, Duke University, 1984 (UMI).

53  Heinrich Neviandt, *Die Heilsarmee und die Arbeit des schwedischen Evangelisten Franson*, Barmen, 1890.

54  Heinrich Coerper, *Über das Beten der Frauen und Jungfrauen in öffentlichen Versammlungen*, Neumünster, n.d. (*ca.* 1894).

55  Fredrik Franson, *Weissagende Töchter*, Emden, 1890; also published in: *Gemeinschaftsblatt* (Emden) No. 16 and No. 17, 1890. The Swedish (revised) edition is: *Profeterande Döttrar*, St Paul, Minnesota, 1896; Stockholm, 1897.

56  Catherine Booth, *Female Ministry; or, Woman's Right to Preach the Gospel*, London, 1859. See also: Minnie Lindsay Carpenter, *Women of the Flag*, London, 1945, and Flora Larsson, *My Best Men are Women*, London, 1974.

57  Together with her husband Walter, she was touring Britain. Of the two, she was the main attraction to the listeners. Mrs Booth, at that time, did not intend to preach herself, but she felt that women were entitled to do so. (She gave her first public address in 1860 and afterwards became as renowned a preacher as her

husband.)

58 There is some evidence that women in the earliest phase of the Brethren movement did not keep as quiet as later became the rule. See: Coad, *Brethren Movement*, p. 66. This needs more investigation.

59 Little thought was given to answer why Miriam (Exodus 15:20–21) was a prophetess, along with Moses and Huldah (2 Kings 22:14–20), along with Jeremiah.

60 In faith mission lore, Isaiah's answer to God's question: 'Whom shall I send?' had been transformed by men into: 'Here am I, send my sister!'

61 Kumm—Pedersen, 21 March 1911.

62 When in 1905, at a time when the SUM was in dire need of personnel, six holiness Quakers contacted SUM in Liverpool, SUM convinced them that they should work for an initial period with SUM in Benue. They accepted the condition that Mrs Ford, and Mrs Kurtzhals and her baby, remained in London (Minutes 17 January 1905, 'Grattan Guinness had written from US to commend them', *Lightbearer*, March 1905). Levi Lupton, William Smith, Jefferson Ford and Charles Kurtzhals left London for Nigeria on 21 January 1905.

63 Kumm—Juul, n.d. (*ca.* 1913).

64 Minutes SUM, 17 March 1904 (Miss Ross); *Lightbearer*, March 1905; Minutes SUM, 22 May 1905.

65 Minutes SUM, 2 April 1909.

66 'The British Executive Committee does not think it advisable to send out ladies unless there is a vacancy or a place has been prepared for them. If you send out three ladies now, they could not be accommodated at Ibi' (SUM—Juul, 19 December 1913). See also: Kumm—Pedersen, 21 March 1911.

67 Krusius—Pedersen, 5 September 1913. This letter and others can be found in the Riksarkivet, Copenhagen, No. 10.248.

68 Newspaper cutting in the Dansk Forenet Sudan-Mission's Minutes book for 1911.

69 SUM—Juul, 1 August 1913. Emphasis in the original.

70 See: Kumm—My dear friend, 26 September 1913: 'At the last meeting of the Executive of the Sudan United Mission, held at Swanwick on the 20th of this month, the attention of the Committee was drawn to the large number of lady missionaries, recently accepted by the various branches of the Mission. It was decided to consider at our next meeting on 8th October, the advisability of accepting no more ladies, for some time to come'. Including accepted candidates the ratios were (men: wives: single women): SUM-UK, 16:5:8; SUM-DK, 1:0:3; SUM-US, 2:2:2; and SUM-South Africa, 7:3:4. Altogether, there were six children in SUM.

71 They may have followed the example of the SIM, working side-by-side with the SUM in Northern Nigeria, which had a considerable number of women in pioneer work.

72 Johanna Veenstra, *Pioneering for Christ in the Sudan*, London, 1930.

73 Edgar H. Smith, *Nigerian Harvest*, Grand Rapids, 1972, p. 36.

74 In 1932, the missionaries of her district were: Johanna Veenstra, Nelle Breen, Jennie Stielstra and Bertha Zagers. When Johanna Veenstra died, Nelle Breen became her successor. When Nelle Breen married Edgar H. Smith, he became the field leader, being the first male missionary in that district.

75 The Church of Christ in Nigeria: Benue, counts (according to *WCE*) 232 congregations, with 9,259 adult communicants and a Christian community of 150,000.

76 Smith, *Nigerian Harvest*, pp. 74ff.

77 Smith, *Nigerian Harvest*, p. 49.

78 Minutes SUM, 18 December 1928.

79 Minutes SUM, 18 December 1928. Minutes SUM Executive Committee, 23 September 1954 report the retirement of Miss E. M. R. Webster after thirty-five years 'in charge of Sura District'. So she must have started to work there in 1929.

80 Minutes SUM, 22 January 1929; 28 February 1929.

81 Minutes SUM, 23 July 1929.

82 Minutes SUM, 24 May 1929.

83 With her father, she travelled to Egypt in 1900 to see if the Sudan Belt could be opened up to missionary work from its eastern end. There she met Karl, and they were married in Cairo.

84 Among other assignments, Karl had asked her to go to the United States to built up the SUM home base there. She died on that trip in 1906.

85 Among her books were: Lucy Guinness and E. C. Millard, *South America. The Neglected Continent*, London, 1894; Lucy Guinness, *To Help to Heal. A Missionary Study and an Appeal for Prayer*, London, n.d. (1896, dealing with Zaire); Guinness, *Enter Thou*, London, 1899.

86 It was she who brought the leaders of the British Free Churches and their missions to agree to and, to some limited extent, support the SUM. In 1897, she had crossed India, which led to the start of the Behar Mission (Lucy Guinness, *Across India at the Dawn of the 20th Century*, London, 1898).

87 'Nachklänge von unserer Jahresfeier' in *Chinas Millionen*, January 1901, pp. 4–7 (p. 5).

88 Minutes SIM, 20 March 1925. Such a demand was never put on men. That it caused problems even for women can be seen in Minutes, 9 June 1925, where it was pointed out that the new rule should not be applied too strictly.

89 Dessien, *Wasser auf dürres Land*, p. 41.

90 They waited a day at the prearranged meeting place, and having gained the (correct) impression that she did not want to be evacuated, continued their journey (Dawson, *History*, p. 74).

91 Minutes SIM-UK, 17 September 1928. The case of Lena L. Paris was similar: 'That she be notified that the Committee feels that she would stand a better chance of being accepted for missionary service by some other Board because of the

rulings of this mission relative to age and because the need at present is more for men than for women' (Minutes AIM Chicago Council, 27 October 1941).

92 Reply to Miss Kniveton (Minutes SUM, 7 February 1911).

93 'Committee decided to inform the Field Superintendent that they thought it inadvisable to make this appointment in view of the importance of the work at Forum, and the large responsibilities involved' (Minutes SUM, 24 May 1950).

94 Pierce Beaver, *American Protestant Women*, pp. 179ff. ('Integration and Sequel').

95 Pierce Beaver, *American Protestant Women*, p. 217. For developments among faith missions in general, see: Helena Wiebe, 'Toward a Complimentary Ministry: Women and Men as Full Partners in Christian Mission', MA, Fuller Pasadena, 1981, especially pp. 94ff. Wiebe bases much of her argument on Beaver, applying it to faith missions.

96 I remember quite well hearing a woman missionary speaking to the students of a Bible school. She spent quite some portion of her time of her talk explaining how she, a women, could do what she did. But it was obvious that she liked doing what she did.

97 The mission dissolved itself in 1952 (Juhnke, *A People of Missions*, p. 111).

98 *PBI Catalogue*, valid 1986.

99 Madame Blocher was Arminian, her 'clan' now is Calvinist (Interview Bernard Huck, Institut Biblique, Nogent-sur-Marne, 27 August 1986).

100 Prominent were Carrie F. Judd, Mary E. Moorhead and Harriet Waterbury, among others (Andrews, 'Restricted Freedom' in Hartzfeld and Nienkirchen, *The Birth of a Vision*, pp. 219–240 (pp. 230–235).

101 See: Charles Nienkirchen, 'A. B. Simpson: Forerunner and Critic of the pentecostal Movement' in Hartzfeld and Nienkirchen, *The Birth of a Vision*, pp. 125–164.

102 The UFM (United States) explicitly wants women only for nursing, teaching, office work, or as wives. In this, it differs strictly from WEC, which comes historically from the same roots. UFM (United States) has an almost exclusively Calvinistic home base.

103 At the back of its standard history, there is an advertisement: 'Men wanted!' which has a small appendix: 'Women—You Too!' (Kenneth Johnston, *The Story of New Tribes Mission*, Sanford, 1985).

104 This changing emphasis has found expression in additions to the original: 'We are not ecumenical, charismatic, or neo-evangelical.' Today, the NTM describes itself as being of 'fundamentalist and independent tradition' (p. 13, *NAPMO*).

105 *The Regions Beyond*, 1885, p. 110.

106 Bacon, *From Faith to Faith*, pp. 12ff.

107 According to statistics given in 13*NAPMO*, for the IFMA missions, the average is: married women, 40 per cent; single women, 17.5 per cent; married men, 40 per cent; single men, 2.5 per cent. The Overseas Missionary Fellowship (CIM) has the highest proportion of single women: 27.7 per cent. For the SIM, it is 25 per cent; for TEAM, 22.3 per cent; for Berean and AEF, 20 per cent.

108She is now deputy field leader. See: Mady Vaillant, 'Komonos of Burkina Faso' in Harley Schreck and David Barrett (eds.), *Unreached Peoples: Clarifying the Task*, Monrovia, CA, 1987, pp. 121–126.

109Present International Directors, Dr Dietrich and Dr Renate Kuhl (from Germany) at Bulstrode, Gerrards Cross, West London; the British homebase is also here.

110Interview Richard M. Winchell, General Director, TEAM, March 1986.

111Mrs Maureen Flowers has been 'Representative for [Ethnic] Special Ministries' for many years.

112In 1986, the Wycliffe membership consisted (including accepted candidates) of 1,977 couples, 855 single women and 158 single men (Andreas Holzhausen—Fiedler, 2 March 1993).

113There are eighteen teams of single women in Wycliffe, of whom at least one is a German, as against thirty-two married couples (Andreas Holzhausen—Fiedler, 2 March 1993).

114Many examples are given in Grubb, *Mit Studd im Kongo*, pp. 126ff, 175, 188.

115This was reported of the shared evangelistic activities of an African couple (WEC, northeastern Zaire, about 1918): 'At Poko, Maduga and his good wife, Namisa, began a fruitful ministry. They gave themselves tirelessly to the work—one going out each day to preach while the other stayed on the station to speak to any who came there' (Buxton, *The First Ten Years*).

116Important for faith missions were the deaconesses of the Deutsche Gemeinschaftsdiakonieverband, related to the Marburg Mission. But the DGDV deaconesses never passed on the right to preach to women who were not deaconesses, just as the WGM in Kenya did not pass on women's ordination to African women.

117In the Örebro Missionsförening, these women evangelists were sometimes called the 'Ongman girls'. The big painting in the foyer of Örebro Missionsskola shows one of these women evangelists preaching.

118I found the only case of a creative development of women's office in a so-called 'African Independent Church', the African Brotherhood Church (see below).

119Their foreign mission interest was directed to China: first through the Liebenzell Mission; then through the Yünnan Mission.

120In the same way, in Africa, faith missions did not create typical holiness movement structures.

121Elisabeth Vierhub, 'Berichterstattung über die Mädchenschule' in *Alt-Moshi*, 1938.

122Minutes Leipziger Mission, Prot. Missionarskonferenz, 1938.

123Irene Fiedler, *Wandel der Mädchenerziehung in Tanzania*, Saarbrücken/Ft Lauderdale, 1983, pp. 319–333.

124In 1905, Gayaza High School was founded (Gayaza High School 1905–55). For the context, see: Tom Watson, 'A History of Church Missionary Society High

Schools in Uganda, 1900–1924: the Education of a Protestant Elite', PhD, University of East Africa, 1968 (Gayaza, pp. 148–189; Iganga Girls' High School, pp. 300–310).

125 The rapid growth of women's orders in Tanzania points in the same direction. See, for example: Irene Fiedler, *Mädchenerziehung*, pp. 304–400.

126 Interview Bishop Ngala, 28 December 1986.

127 'Kanuni na sheria za African Brotherhood Church' in *Momanyisyo ma Atongoi ma Ikanisa*, Machakos, n.d. (valid 1986), p. 3.

128 'The Catholic nuns were the example, but required celibacy is not biblical' (Interview Bishop Ngala, 28 December 1986).

129 *Kanuni na sheria za ABC*, p. 8.

130 Interview Bishop Ngala, 27 December 1986.

131 F. L. Chapell, *The Eleventh-Hour Laborers'*.

132 'The Woman is the Man for the Job. The Story of a Lone Woman Who Dared to Believe and Obey God. Results? A Land Open Today to the Gospel' in *Worldwide*, jubilee year September/October 1964 in *Worldwide*, September/October 1964.

133 Macindoe, *Wo alle Wege enden*, p. 46.

134 Quoted like this in: 'The Woman is the Man for the Job' in *Worldwide*, September/October 1964.

135 'You are more upon our hearts and in our faith and prayer than any other WEC worker . . . They have been inspired to their roots by the heroism of your faith. You may feel weak, and the devil may tell you so, but the fact remains that in going in alone where others have failed, you have done something which, if you do not spoil it by turning back, will go down in the history of world evangelization. So stick to it, Bessie, for Christ's sake and your own, no matter how depressed and lonely you may sometimes feel. Stick to it even to death, if necessary. The Lord is evidently with you. Here another gift, I think of £150 has come in for you. If only the boys had stood steady, all the money they needed for building would be here. Now stand steady in their place, dear Bessie' (Norman P. Grubb—Bessie Fricker, 25 March 1941). 'Still I can only say: Go through, dear Bessie' (Norman P. Grubb—Bessie Fricker, 8 April 1941).

136 See the retrospective article: 'The Woman is the Man for the Job' in *Worldwide*, jubilee year September/October 1964, p. 1f.

137 Norman P. Grubb—Bessie Fricker, 8 April 1941 answering Fricker—Grubb, 1 February 1941.

138 The fact that she was a woman seems to have made it easier for the governor to support her application (oral tradition of the WEC missionaries in Guinea Bissau).

139 Interview N. N.; Macindoe, *Wo alle Wege enden*, p. 86.

140 Interview Amaro Lopez, 6 August 1986.

141 Interview Benvinda Vaz Martins, 5 August 1986. Donna Libania, also from Cape Verde, helped Bessie Fricker much at the start, but played no important role

later (Interview N. N.; see also: Bessie Fricker—Norman P. Grubb, 1 February 1941, quoted in Norman P. Grubb—Bessie Fricker, 8 April 1941).

142 Interview Amaro Lopez, 6 August 1986.

143 Norman P. Grubb—Pat Symes, 25 March 1941.

144 Christel Meyer—Fiedler, 30 March 1989.

145 Her husband is a pastor, too (*Le Chemin. Trimestriel de Liaison et d'Information*, Brazzaville III, 1985).

146 'Enfin une femme pasteur' in *Le Chemin* III, 1985). More women are in training for ordination.

147 Interview Bill Reincheld, 17 December 1987.

148 Poster: *Missionaries of AICMB*; Interview the Rev. Panya Baba, 4 February 1987.

149 Interview Naomi Famunore, 5 February 1987.

# 11
# Continuity and change: faith mission churches in Africa

Over the centuries, Christian theology grappled with the question of how to distinguish a true church from a false one. This grappling has not brought conclusive results but, in the course of the discussion, two sets of criteria have emerged which are acceptable to most churches: four attributes and two marks of the church. Faith mission leaders did not use the terminology, 'the attributes of the church', but they made a major contribution to each of the four attributes. To the attribute of unity, they contributed their concept and practice of individual unity. There is Christian unity, so we do not need first to unite the churches but can immediately start cooperating in effective evangelism where no church is doing the job. To the attribute of holiness, they contributed the concept and experience of holiness as *power for service*. The holiness of the church is not found in its holy sacraments, but in God empowering the individual Christian for holy living and service. To the attribute of catholicity, faith missions contributed their vision and their effort to make the church really worldwide. In doing this, they used the neglected forces of Christianity: laymen, women and the uneducated. To the attribute of apostolicity, they contributed the concept of missions as the main task of the church.[1] The apostolicity of the church is not to be found in its bishops or in its apostolic doctrine, but in doing what the apostles did, who were primarily missionaries.

The Reformation stressed the *marks* of the church more than its attributes. The basic mark of the church is the *word*: revealed, written and preached. Faith missions wholeheartedly agree with this: Christ the divine word, the scriptures witnessing to him; and the church preaching the word. The second mark of the church is the *sacraments*: baptism and the Lord's table. Because faith missions were interdenominational, they had to accept this mark of the church, too. How they did this is the topic of this chapno, and because faith missions' attitude to the churches was characterized by accepting and ignoring them at the same time, it can be expected that there was a similar attitude to the sacraments.

Besides the two 'official' marks of the church, there is a third one, the *ministry*, accepted *in theory* only by some theologians as a necessary mark of the church, but in practice by all the classical churches, centring in the idea of ordination. In this chapter, first, the attitude of the faith missions' to the marks of the church will be discussed, followed by how they applied it in Africa and, finally, what faith mission churches in Africa made of it.

# Faith missions' concepts of the church

As interdenominational missions, faith missions have to accept all churches, and their concept of individual unity makes it possible to accept even contradictory ecclesiologies. Indeed, in faith missions there were, and are, missionaries from practically all Protestant churches. Nevertheless, it has become clear from the study of the personal development of the early faith mission leaders that their private concept of the church was quite distinct and differed from the ecclesiology of the classical denominations. Faith missions never produced an ecclesiology of their own. They fully accepted the attributes of the church, but gave them each a special twist.

## THE CHURCH—THAT'S INDIVIDUAL

In classical ecclesiology, the corporate aspects are usually stressed. In faith mission ecclesiology, the individual aspects are stressed: it is not the churches which create unity, but individual Christians. Holiness is not a corporate aspect of the church for the individual to believe in, but a divine offer for everyone to claim individually. Catholicity of the worldwide church is not achieved by creating one church encompassing all the churches of the world, but by individuals from all countries sharing and working together. Apostolicity is everyone's duty: go, pray and give! This duty cannot be delegated; if there is a mission for a certain area, join it; if not, start one.

## THE CHURCH—THAT'S ACTIVITY

In faith mission theology, passive church membership does not exist. Every church member shares in the activities of the church, local and worldwide, and even the sick can actively pray. Theology is not speculative, but primarily applied. It does not matter as much whether one is saved as an Arminian or as a Calvinist, but if a theology does not actively encourage evangelism, it is not a good one. It does not matter as much exactly when Christ will come, but the contribution that eschatology makes to activate the missionary endeavour of the church.

Consider the attribute of holiness: for faith missions, holiness is clearly a gift of divine grace, but the individual who wants to receive that gift can take definite steps. He or she can give up all known sins, can consciously subordinate his or her will to God's will and, in a spiritual transaction, can put his or her whole self on the altar. It is not much different with the attribute of unity: do not wait for the churches to unite. All who personally believe in Christ are one, anyhow, and for those church members who do not personally believe in Christ, unity would be useless. Unity does not come about in a gradual process in which doctrinal differences are reduced by a growing consensus, but in evangelizing together.

In classical theology, the attribute of apostolicity serves more to safeguard continuity, whether in doctrine or in power. Faith missions take doctrinal purity for granted and define apostolicity as active missionary work.

## THE CHURCH—THAT'S CONVERSION

As in the revival of the second half of the nineteenth century, faith missions clearly distinguish between 'believers' and 'non-believers'. You may have been baptized and confirmed; you may even have undergone a full church wedding; and you may even attend church regularly but, if you are not saved, you are not a Christian.[2] It is not doctrine or the sacrament that makes you a Christian, but conversion. Billy Graham, the famous evangelist, who studied at a Christian and Missionary Alliance Bible college, formulated it in a more modern way than A. B. Simpson would have done, but with the same meaning: 'Conversion . . . is the impact of the kerygma upon the whole man, convincing his intellect, warming his emotions, and causing his will to act with decision. I have no doubt that if every Christian in the world would suddenly begin proclaiming the kerygma and winning others to an encounter with Jesus Christ, we would have a different world overnight'.[3] Conversion, then, is not only the necessary mark of faith, it is also the necessary and most basic mark of the church for faith missions, because he or she who is not converted is not in the church. For faith missions there was no difference in principle between a Christian non-believer and a non-Christian non-believer.[4] Small children presented a certain problem in this scheme, because Jesus had promised them the

321

kingdom of heaven unconditionally.[5] But, for all adults, conversion—as 'crossing the line' from unbelief to belief, from perdition to salvation, changing life permanently[6]—is of absolute necessity. Conversion may take place suddenly, as very vividly described by William F. P. Burton, Congo Inland Mission missionary candidate and then founder of the Congo Evangelistic Mission: 'On August 3rd 1905 I knelt by my bedside in Batley, Yorkshire, and claimed the promises in John 1:12, Romans 10:13 and John 6:37. Well do I remember the prayer which I prayed: I am only a lost undeserving sinner, O God, but I take the Lord Jesus to be my Saviour, and please take me to be Thy servant. I ask this in Jesus' Name' ... 'If I had died as I knelt down by my bed I should have dropped straight into hell, but I rose from my knees saved, rejoicing and on my way to glory'.[7] But conversion could also be a 'gradual turning of the heart toward God' as experienced by Harry Guinness.[8] In the process of conversion the 'personal testimony' of friends often played an important part. Quite often the decisive step of conversion was taken in connection with a public evangelistic meeting (such as those carried through by Fredrik Franson), but sometimes conversion was a calm and gradual affair.[9]

Conversion is not a human achievement, but God's gift, which people may or may not accept. In applied faith mission theology, there is no double predestination. The offer of salvation is for all, and it is assumed that everyone can accept it. That is Arminian practice, which very often runs hand- in-hand with a Calvinist conviction of election. That doctrine is, however, not part of preaching but of praise. Here again, the theological inconsistency of faith missions proves its worth. Norman P. Grubb of WEC formulated his attitude: 'I don't ask that the Bible should be a systematic theology to suit my theological mind. Revelation through the apostolic writings was a string of unsystematic letters, written existentially to meet some church need of the moment ... Why should I be more systematic than the Bible and Paul and the other apostles?'[10]

For faith missions, putting all emphasis on conversion did not lead them to abolish the sacraments or to spiritualize them, as the Salvation Army did.[11] But both are no longer marks of the church in the theological meaning of the term, and if to this one mark others should be added as secondary marks of the church, faith missions would not add baptism and communion, but fellowship and mission.

# Faith mission concepts for the African churches

Faith missions, not being nor intending to become churches themselves, had the aim of starting churches in the mission fields. They were not bound to any of the Western denominations, so there was, except for the few denominational branches of faith missions, no need to reproduce any denominational pattern. What were their ideas, consciously or less so?

## SAME DOGMATICS

One thing was clear to all the missionaries: the churches they planted had to have the same fundamental dogmatics (which for faith missions did not include any definite ecclesiology). In this, they fully succeeded, and if there are minor differences in the explicit statements of faith between a mission and one of its churches, the reason can usually be found in the missionaries' pecularities and not in independent decisions of the African church. The Africa Inland Church presents one such example: the AIC teaches the 'eternal security' of the believer, though this doctrine cannot be found in the AIM statement of faith. The reason is that, at the time that the church had to formulate its statement of faith, most AIM missionaries were Calvinists, the tide of Arminian influence having receded. Another example is RBMU. No special eschatology is required of its missionaries but, in all theological schools, RBMU missionaries either have to teach premillennial eschatology, or at least not oppose it, for the sake of unity. The African churches accepted premillennial eschatology because practically all missionaries held this view, though they were not required to do so. The same applies to the Communauté Évangélique Beréenne au Zaire (CEBZ19). Its statement of faith contains a section on baptism; that of the Berean Mission does not.[12]

The missions were not only able to transmit their dogmatics to faith mission churches, but also to the African Independent Churches which have sprung up from them. As a whole, faith missions and their churches did not produce many African Independent Churches. Most of them can be found in Kenya. The biggest, Africa Christian Churches and Schools, African Brotherhood Church and African Church, all have the same dogmatics as AIC, ACCS even uses the AIM catechism.[13]

## FAITH MISSIONS AS THE ECCLESIASTICAL ESTABLISHMENT

In Europe and the United States, faith missions accepted and ignored the churches at the same time. Their founders usually came from movements which were critical of the established churches, as all revival movements are. Faith missions and the revival movements they came from had been able to contribute innovative thoughts to various aspects of theology. Though they accepted the churches, faith missions were, to various degrees, critical of the churches. They had been critical of the centrality of the sacraments, they had not accepted for themselves ordination as the necessary precondition for leadership, and they had been able to give women a position which was unknown in the church establishment.

In Africa, faith missions had no established churches they could criticize or accept or reject. Immediately, they took over the role of those they had often criticized at home, and a faith mission became the church establishment as soon as it had founded a church. In this process, faith missions did not develop their critical possibilities (such as reliance on voluntary associations, para-church structures, not paying much heed to ordination) but, instead, developed official structures and a solid church establishment. This included the decision that within one mission field there could be only one mode of baptism, but that the form might differ between various fields of the same mission.

Though the early faith missions did not do much *thinking* on the structures of the nascent churches, they provided the nascent church everywhere quite effectively with an organizational structure, namely its own.

# Faith mission churches

With classical missions, comparisons are possible between the Western 'mother churches' and the African 'daughter churches'. Because faith mission churches have no mother churches, comparisons can only be drawn between how faith missions understood the church, how they portrayed the ideal church and how faith mission churches actually developed.

## CHURCH GOVERNMENT: THE MISSIONS' VERSION

In theory, faith missions accepted various forms of church government, and all forms can be found nowadays in faith mission churches. The AIM's work in West Nile (Uganda), from its beginning in 1918, has been part of the (Anglican) Church of Uganda,[14] and the Reformed and Lutheran branches of SUM have reproduced Reformed and Lutheran types of church government.[15]

Nevertheless, most faith mission leaders conceived church government to be primarily congregational. This is understandable, because most of them in their transdenominational movement had been strongly influenced by the Brethren, and often belonged to independent congregations or mission halls. In addition, a few early faith missionaries actually came from denominational congregationalism, were Quakers or, more often, Baptists. All the early faith mission leaders were reluctant to publish their concept of church government, but quite a bit of information can be gleaned from primary sources.

For faith missions, ecclesiology was a matter of personal choice, not of communal decision. When the church was in theological view, it was primarily the local church and the individual congregation. Both concepts were carried over to the mission field. Ecclesiastical matters were to be decided on the field. Sometimes this was done by the missionaries, deciding in committee how things should be handled, although often the decisions were made even more individually, or at least were attempted to be so. A typical case is the AIM. In the beginning, every missionary was free to decide on the structure of the church, as long as he was the founder of a mission station. His successor was not allowed to change the structures his predecessor had established. This congregational approach was confirmed in principle in 1909, but abrogated for all practical purposes and supplanted by a presbyterian[16] approach.[17] Thus, the African church was provided with a uniformity that reflected the presbyterian principles which the missionaries employed in their own organization.

The CMA experienced a similar development. Like the LMS 100 years before,[18] it had started its work with a purely congregational ideology. Every missionary and every local church was to introduce the form of church government that seemed best, according to the scriptures.[19] But, because the missionaries were of very varied origin and because they (and the local churches with them) differed in the interpretation of scripture, more uniformity was sought for. Therefore, it was decided in 1923 that the constitution of every congregation on the mission field was to be modelled along the lines of the CMA specimen constitution for US congregations contained in the CMA handbook.[20]

Efraim Anderson, Svenska Missionsförbundet missionary in Congo, summed up faith missions' experience with African church government:

◇ The congregational pattern of church government is not suited to Africa.

◇ All churches developed a presbyterian type of church government.

◇ This fits the African context much better, especially if combined with episcopal elements.[21]

Almost every faith mission church has undergone the development which Anderson describes for the Église Évangélique du Congo. All the churches have centralist constitutions, stress the uniformity of the church and provide for strong leadership. It is correct to define them with Anderson as 'presbyterian with an episcopal touch'.[22] In addition to this process, there is a process of administrative centralization going on in many churches. Especially, it can be seen that the centralized administration of finances creates centralized power structures.[23] In this, the churches would be following the precedent of the missions, whose missionaries also receive their pay ('living allowance') from a central office, usually associated with the field leader.

The momentous process of change from the congregationalist ideals of the early missionaries to the present-day presbyterian and episcopalian structures is seen by many contemporary faith missionaries as an adaptation to African culture which does appreciate strong chiefs and does not appreciate Western democracy.[24] Though firmly held, this explanation does not convince me. The argument does not detail how that process of adaptation worked and it does not explain why that process was not strongly resisted by the missionaries, who had shown themselves quite willing to join battle with African culture over some of its aspects. It also fails to explain why this process of centralization took place equally among the Yaka in Kwango, Zaire, with their strong king,[25] and among the Kenyan Kikuyu and Kamba, who never even had chiefs.[26]

Another explanation seems to me far more convincing. In centralizing their structures, the churches did not adapt to

African culture, but to missionary subculture. While the missionaries may have thought, and even taught, with a congregational approach, they organized their missions more or less with a presbyterian approach, while usually there was also a strong episcopal figure in the field leader. The churches did not pattern themselves after the New Testament, nor after the *ideals* of the missionaries, first of all but after their *organization*. The place of the annual missionary conference is taken by the Synod, the Great Assembly ('mkutano mkuu') taking place every one to three years. The missionaries' field council was the pattern for what is now the 'conseil exécutif' or 'halmashauri kuu'. The mission station is now the district,[27] what used to be preaching places in missionary terminology are now 'chapelles' or 'congrégations'. The field leader's position is now held by the president or the bishop of the church.

A typical case of such a church patterned on the model of the mission is CECA20 in Zaire, which goes back to the AIM. The smallest unit is the *Congrégation* (kundi la Wakristo) with its evangelist (mwalimu, teacher). A number of congrégations form an *église locale* (kanisa locale). A pastor (together with the elders) is in charge of this église locale, and he administers the sacraments there.[28] The église locale is the decisive administrative unit. All *locales* are equal in theory, but the bigger ones among them, especially those going back to a former mission station, have a somewhat leading position. Two to eight *locales* constitute one *sous-section*;[29] four to ten *sous-sections* constitute a *section*;[30] and two to ten sections constitute a *district*. The church's highest authority is the *Conseil de Administration* (baraza kuu).[31]

In the context of the present-day churches, the local churches are as dependant as they were under missionary leadership. In those days, they could not choose the missionary or their local evangelist;[32] now, equally, they cannot choose their evangelist or pastor. Higher authorities decide on appointments and transfers.[33]

Because of ever-increasing contacts between various churches, the question as to the appropriate title for the leader of the church often comes up. The Roman Catholic Church, existing almost everywhere in close proximity to faith mission churches, has bishops, as does the Anglican Church, with its often close relationship to faith missions. With other denominations, such as the Lutherans, there is an overwhelming tendency to appoint bishops,[34] and the pentecostal Assemblies of God in Tanzania even have an archbishop now.

Because faith missions had no doctrine of episcopacy, they had to find pragmatic solutions. The first faith mission church, the Kenyan Africa Inland Church created a bishop in 1973. The reason was the 1972 law restricting the term 'president' to the head of state. The AIC gave its regions the choice between chairman, moderator and bishop. They opted for bishop, because this title was found in the Bible. Therefore, President Mulwa became Bishop Mulwa, though this did not change his functions.[35] Later, AIC Tanzania also made its leader a bishop, although there the government did not require such a change. The present bishop of the Communauté Évangélique du Kwango (Zaire) also sees little difference between a president and a bishop, but prefers bishop, because that title is found in the Bible.[36]

In none of the three cases was there the intention of introducing the historic episcopate. A shift in this direction can easily develop when a neighbouring Anglican bishop is asked to participate in the consecration of a faith mission bishop. One step in the direction of the office of the bishop being understood in the classical way was the consecration of Assani Baraka Koy in 1978 as the first bishop of the Communauté Episcopale Évangelique au Zaire (founded by the Unevangelized Fields Mission), in which the German Lutheran Bishop of Lübeck, Heinrich Meyer, shared.[37] This episcopal consecration was as much resisted by the UFM as by many of the church's members. It resulted in the UFM terminating its relationship to the church.[38] In 1980, a considerable section of the church, led by the Rev. Masini, split from Bishop Assani's church[39] but, because in Zaire the government does not allow a church to split, the 'dissidents' were not able to organize legally, and their wish of joining the neighbouring CECCA16 was not granted.[40]

Although there is a strong tendency in East Africa and Zaire to opt for bishops, contrary tendencies can also be observed.[41] In CECA20 the issue of making the head of the church a bishop is still under discussion, but the number of supporters seems to decrease rather than to grow.[42] The developments in Zaire must always be seen in the context of the government enforced Église du Christ au Zaire, which leaves all its constituent churches to decide on their own constitution, but nevertheless strongly supports episcopal developments in order to strengthen its centralizing tendencies against the centripetal forces in the communautés.[43]

Although experience seems to have shown the futility of the attempt, younger missions or more recent branches of older missions nevertheless opt for congregational structures. This may happen simply through the missionary teaching that a church should have a plural (unpaid) eldership, without anyone actually trying to implement his teaching.[44] The WEC missionaries in Senegal, to the contrary, strictly implement congregational principles. Each of the few congregations has its own constitution; two neighbouring congregations even differ in minor points in their doctrinal statement.[45] But cooperation in a kind of union of all the churches is envisaged. The neighbouring mission, NTM, is equally congregational and insists that there be no formal organization beyond that of the local congregation.[46]

Older faith missions still tend to employ congregational principles when they start to work in new areas. A case in point is AEF (Africa Evangelical Fellowship, originally South Africa General Mission), which has already produced a number of presbyterian-type churches,[47] but employed strictly congregational principles in their new efforts on Mauritius[48] (1969) and Réunion[49] (1970). The Église Évangélique de la Réunion is organized as a union of independent congregations,[50] the two congregations on Mauritius are registered separately with the government, because the government there only recognizes a union of congregations if there are at least five of them.[51]

In all cases mentioned, the number of congregations is small and the missionaries' influence is large. It will be interesting to observe if these congregational structures will last because, up to now, faith missions have everywhere produced churches with presbyterian structures, without following directly presbyterian examples.[52] This means that a new type of churches has developed: presbyterian in church structure, baptistic in the practice of baptism. The presbyterian structures were not developed for theological reasons, but were patterned according to the 'presbyterian' structures of the missionary subculture.

These presbyterian structures are not only questioned by some of the more recent Western missions, but also by the new African faith missions. Due to bad experiences with the established churches,[53] CAPRO decided just to start 'simple New Testament congregations', without any central organization.[54] The missionary reports of the Nigerian Christian Missionary Foundation create a similar impression.[55] The Ghanaian Christian Outreach Fellowship mentions local churches only.[56] The

New Testament Church, a Nigerian organization at the border-line between a non-denominational mission and an African Independent Church, is also extremely congregationalistic.[57]

When faith missions started their work in Africa, they did not do much thinking on church structures beyond the congregational level. For one thing, they had not usually done any such thinking at home; secondly, they expected that the Lord's second coming was imminent; and thirdly, they never expected their work to be as numerically successful as it turned out to be after a few decades.

They also did not expect that whole populations would join their churches over the time span of a few generations, a development which had started in Africa before independence, but accelerated after *uhuru* ('freedom'). This means that, frequently, faith mission churches have become real folk churches, churches comprising perhaps not the whole population of a given area, but still a large section of it. To belong to a faith mission church no longer requires a clear-cut break with traditional religion and customs, when an area is already third-generation Christian. It has become socially acceptable to be a Christian. The thing to do is to join the church and, if conversion and baptism are required, to join the church in this way.

This has led to the spread of nominality as it has in the European folk churches. Contrary to what one might expect in terms of dogmatics, this development took place equally in the minority of faith mission churches with infant baptism and in the majority of faith mission churches with believers' baptism: this means that a new type of church has developed: folk churches with believers' baptism, but folk churches nonetheless.

# The ministry

A most important aspect of church government and church structure is ordination or its absence. In this field also, momentous changes have taken place between the ideas and practice of the early faith missionaries and the practice of the majority of today's faith mission churches. In general, faith missions had a 'low' view of the ministry in the church, though they were not hostile to it. The Brethren and the Quakers knew no ordained ministry, and for the Baptists and the independents it was mainly functional.[58] Ordination was accepted in faith missions, but little value was placed on it. The missionaries were convinced that they were indeed ordained, if not by human hands, then by the 'mighty ordination of the pierced hands'.[59]

When faith missions started their work in Africa, little *thought* was given to the ministry. Just as they had to establish churches without having *thought* too much about them beforehand, they also had to establish a ministry. This was simple in the beginning: no titles were used and no ordination was involved. Nevertheless, right from the very beginning the ministry was strictly hierarchical: field leader, head of station, ordinary missionary. The ministers usually were men, though not always. The ministry was purely functional.

The office bearers of the mission automatically became the office bearers of the nascent church. There, one level below the missionary, another office was added (for natives only): the office of evangelist/teacher. The evangelist had to be gifted, but no defined training was required, nor were any special spiritual rights accorded to him, except the right to preach, which was available anyway to anyone who was able to. In the early days, the evangelist usually lived at the mission station and regularly visited the surrounding villages. Later, he usually settled in one of the villages and so effectively became the pastor of that village congregation, but without any sacramental rights.[60] Though he was the pastor of the local Christian community, he usually spent most of his time teaching.

Often the teacher/evangelists were spoken of as 'native assistants', which clearly shows their relative position in the hierarchical structure of: field leader, head of station, ordinary (male) missionary, evangelist/teacher.

For missionaries, as much as for teacher/evangelists, ordination was of no importance, but there was one important difference: usually, some of the missionaries were ordained, whereas none of the teacher/evangelists was. In many of those missions which held ordination to be important, usually all male missionaries were functionally considered as being ordained.[61] For them, the 'ordination of the pierced hands' took the place of the 'ordination by the laying on of hands', but this was not applied to Africans.

ORDINATION INTRODUCED INTO THE AFRICAN CHURCH

A preliminary step, though not a conscious one, for the introduction of ordination in the African faith mission churches was the non-application of a functional understanding of the ministry to Africans. Unordained missionaries could administer the sacraments, unordained Africans could not. By this, race and sacramental rights were incidentally tied together.

The introduction of ordination and tying the sacraments to ordained office bearers was a break with early faith mission theology. Then, ordination had been a possibility; now, it became a necessity. Africans could not count on the 'ordination of the pierced hands'; they had to rely on the ordination by (white) human hands, an ordination much easier to regulate and control than the divine one.

The importance of ordination was enhanced by the fact that it had first to be granted to the African church. Just one example illustrates this point: in 1909, the Svenska Missionsförbundet (SMF), in erecting Madzia mission, started its work in (French) Congo. The first baptism was in 1913. In 1940, the Église Évangélique du Congo had 21,394 members, being pastored by 473 evangelists. Suddenly in 1942, eight of them were ordained as pastors.[62] Why had none been ordained earlier? And when the SMF decided to bestow ordination on the church, why only eight pastors?

In almost all faith mission churches, the process was the same. Usually ordination was bestowed quite late: SUM-UK granted the first ordinations in 1938 after thirty-four years of missionary work;[63] the World Gospel Mission in Kenya employed Johana Ng'etich in 1932 for pastoral work, but he was ordained only in 1960, when he was more than sixty years old.[64] The AIM in Kenya granted ordination in 1945, after fifty years of missionary work,[65] although in 1932 two men had been 'licensed' after finishing Bible school.[66] In Guinea Bissau, ordination was introduced in 1981, four decades after the first conversions and three decades after the first baptisms.[67]

There are three reasons for the late introduction of ordination:

◇ After 1900, missions in general were reluctant to ordain Africans simply because, after the scramble for Africa, Europeans (missionaries included) usually thought less of African capabilities than before the scramble.[68]

◇ Faith missions had started their work later than the classical missions. Their churches, therefore, were usually smaller, and the need for ordained African ministers seemed less obvious.

◇ Faith missionaries had not reflected much upon the issue of ordination. Before they could pass it on to the African church, they had to find out what it meant for themselves. To be able to do this, the missions had to *reflect* their concept of the church. By granting ordination, an interdenominational mission would recognize that *on the mission field*, it was a church. Some missions, for example, AIM in Kenya, were quite reluctant to admit this. Once this is admitted, immediately an additional question arises: would the mission now have to ordain those members who, incidentally, were not ordained?[69] Would they lose their sacramental rights, whereas up to now to be male and white had been a sufficient qualification? Another question was: is the African church to ordain or is the mission? Can a *mission* ordain at all?[70]

When ordination was introduced, it was only granted to the few.[71] In the churches, the first ordinations are usually seen as an important step towards independence. That is how the missionaries saw it, too. By ordaining only few Africans, the level of competition with them was kept low. The limited number of ordinations produced a marked change in the conception of the ordained ministry. In Europe and the United States, each congregation usually could get an ordained minister, in the United States, there were often several in one congregation. In Africa, only a few pastors were (and are) ordained, so ordination has become a stratifying factor in church government. The local pastoral work is mostly being done by those not even called pastors (evangelists, teachers, elders and so on), whereas the pastor (ordained or licensed) is the supervisor and the travelling dispenser of the sacraments. Ordination is not the church's blessing at the beginning of the full-time pastoral ministry, but a reward for good service and a promotion to the higher ranks of the ministry. This practice is even contrary to the *theology* of those churches which apply it. The *theology* of ordination is, just to take one example, expressed by CECA20 (AIM) as: 'Setting aside someone to do only the work of God all his life long'.[72]

With some exceptions, which will be treated below, faith mission churches have developed very similar structures. CEC-CA16 (WEC) has three levels of church leaders: catechists, evangelists and ordained pastors.[73] An ordained pastor may have to care for up to twenty congregations.[74] For each level, there are separate training institutes, and even ordained pastors often receive hardly any remuneration.

In the Angola Evangelical Mission, which had never had any structured training for its office bearers, there was nevertheless the rule that only a pastor of a central congregation was allowed to baptize, to administer communion and to conduct weddings. The deacons, leaders of the two to six village congregations under him, were to give baptismal instruction but were not allowed to baptize at the end of the course. For the quarterly celebration of communion, all had to go to the central congregation.[75]

In the AIM area, the stratification of the ministry has taken on even more drastic forms than usual: in Zaire (CECA20),at least half of the pastors are not ordained and in the Africa Inland Church in Kenya, three-quarters of all pastors never manage to be ordained. This may result in a whole district of the church not having even one ordained pastor.[76] The means of achieving this extraordinary stratification is the concept of 'licensing', which the AIM introduced in 1932, not being willing at that time to grant Africans full pastoral rights. The concept of 'licensing' is of Presbyterian origin. It grants certain rights above those a layperson has (such as preaching and administering the sacraments under special conditions), but a person licensed is clearly below a person ordained.[77] Licensing was usually used as an exceptional or as a preliminary measure. But in AIC and CECA20, licensing is neither a preliminary stage nor an exceptional case,[78] but the rule.[79] To be ordained, one has to accumulate distinctions and qualifications. If ordination is granted at all, it is granted only after many years of service.[80] Ordination enhances the pastor's status, and only after ordination may he be called 'Reverend'.[81] The licensed pastor may administer baptism and celebrate communion,[82] but only an ordained pastor is allowed to conduct a wedding and to collect the remuneration that goes with it.[83] The church has followed the early missionaries' example. African culture and missionary subculture obviously coincided. When the missions first granted ordinations, they did so sparingly, and today in AIC and CECA20, an élite group defines and defends its leadership role by the concept of licensing as being inferior to ordination.[84]

In the Africa Gospel Church, neighbour to AIC in the west, the situation is very similar, with the number of ordained pastors being efficiently kept low. According to the AGC statutes, ordination is possible after ten years of service, out of which four years may be spent in Bible school training. In reality, hardly anyone below fifty is ever ordained,[85] and some ordinations even have taken place after retirement.[86] At present, the average age of ordination is tending to become lower.[87] The consequence of requiring that many years must pass before ordination is that in the AGC's mission field in West Pokot, where Pastor Edward Tonnui has worked successfully since the 1970s,[88] baptisms and communion can only take place when one of the ordained pastors can be convinced to go on such a wearisome and expensive trip. For the whole church of more than 15,000 members, in 1985 there were only ten ordained pastors, some of them retired. Because there is no licensing and laypersons have no sacramental rights, AGC is practically a church without sacraments.[89]

In the smaller faith mission churches the stratification process has not (yet?) advanced this far. In the Église Chrétienne Évangelique du Mali (CMA), for example, there are only catechists and ordained pastors; similarly, in the Igreja Evangélica da Guiné (WEC) there are only evangelists and (since 1981) ordained pastors.[90] Nevertheless, even in the smaller churches, ordination has generally been introduced. This has made faith mission churches more respectable in their religious context. At the same time, they have lost much of faith missions' critical heritage.

Faith mission churches are now more respectable than before, but the price paid was to create a large *clerus minor* (minor clergy) doing most of the work in the church, and that the laity is barred from any leadership position in the church. People widely accept being governed by the ordained élite,[91] but the still small group of the better-educated laity can make their criticism felt.[92] In other areas, especially in Nigeria, the challenge to ordained superiority comes from participants in the charismatic movement.

In rare cases, attempts were made to develop churches without pastors. An example of this is the United Liberia Inland Church (WEC). In its northern section only the leader (president) of the church, Donald Wuanti, is a pastor. Nobody has received any training for the ministry, and there are also no evangelists or catechists. This came about because the missionaries patterned the church according to the indigenous church principle derived from Roland Allen. The result was not spontaneously expanding churches, but a small church with congregations led by authoritarian elders.[93] When WEC later started to work in the South of Liberia, they reacted to the developments in the north by arranging for the congregations to be led by trained (but largely unpaid) pastors.[94]

The New Tribes Mission in Senegal has only the offices of elder and deacon.[95] But, because only very few have been baptized there, it remains to be seen if this rule will produce spontaneous growth or stagnation.

# Changing concepts of baptism

## FAITH MISSIONS' TWOFOLD CONCEPT OF BAPTISM

The primary purpose of faith missions was evangelism, reaching the unreached areas of the globe with the gospel as speedily as possible. For this as many evangelist/missionaries as possible would be needed, so their denominational allegiance was not allowed to be a hindrance.[96] This cut deep into denominational concepts of the church, because the sacraments generally were seen as necessary marks of the church *notae ecclesia*. But, for faith missionaries, the second mark of the church (after God's word) was not the sacraments, but conversion.

The sacraments as such were taken for granted,[97] but neither their form nor the theology pertaining to them was fixed.[98] So infant baptism and believers' baptism were acceptable side-by-side and, if a missionary wanted to change his conviction, that was open to him, too. Conversion, in denominational theology often optional, became constituent; baptism, in denominational theology constituent, became optional, due to the priority of evangelism.[99]

Theory here, as it often does, differs from practice. Although both concepts of baptism were accepted, faith mission founders personally had clearly opted for believers' baptism, which for almost all of them had meant re-baptism, as they had been baptized as infants. However, they took their (re-) baptism not as an ecclesiastical decision but as a matter of personal spiritual development.[100]

Faith missionaries brought to Africa two versions of baptismal theology: the *conviction* that both modes of baptism were scripturally sound; and the *practise* of their founders (and many of their members) of preferring believers' baptism.[101]

## ONLY ONE MODE OF BAPTISM FOR THE AFRICAN CHURCHES.

Nowhere did missionaries pass on their twofold concept of baptism to the churches they founded,[102] and, because only one mode of baptism was acceptable, most missions opted for believers' baptism—even missions such as the QIM in Nigeria, whose early missionaries were all presbyterians. This can only be explained by the fact that the missionaries, where they felt uninhibited by the existence of churches with infant baptism, passed on that concept of baptism which they felt in reality to be the better one.[103]

This did not hinder many faith missionaries from personally holding on to their infant baptism and even having their children baptized. Such extraordinary baptisms however, were not to take place in the presence of Africans—in the same way as those missionaries who opted for personal rebaptism were expected to do it among themselves or back home.[104]

The fact that although in faith mission churches there was usually only believers' baptism, and that the missionaries were allowed not to teach differently but to believe and act differently, is obviously a lack in theological logic. How could they baptize believers, never having been baptized in this way? But that was, and is, a strength in faith mission theology: keeping together mutually exclusive things.

Though faith missions generally opted for believers' baptism, there were also cases where they opted for infant baptism. When AIM from North East Zaire started missionary work in the West Nile Province in Northern Uganda, this was done with the full consent of CMS and the agreement that the church there should be part of the Anglican Church of Uganda. Therefore, missionary work in West Nile Province was done by Anglican AIM missionaries, for whom the practice of infant baptism was unquestioned.[105]

When WEC, after its crisis in 1931, decided under the leadership of Norman P. Grubb to expand widely into unreached areas of West Africa,[106] missionary work was started in December 1933 in Spanish Guinea (today, together with Fernando Po part of Equatorial Guinea).[107] Dora and Alec Thorne were gladly received by the McNeills, representatives of the only Protestant mission (Southern Presbyterians, United States) in the colony.[108] Because they worked in the north, the Thornes and a few more WEC missionaries established a Protestant church in the south among the Okak in the area of Akurenan.[109] They did not join their church to the Presbyterian Church, but conformed to it in introducing infant baptism.[110] After independence the government integrated the Iglesia Evangélica Cruzada, in 1970, into the Iglesia Reformada de Guinea Ecuatorial. As a minority with quite a different piety and hardly a share in its leadership, however, they did not feel happy in that church.[111] After the reign of terror under Macias Nguema had come to an end in 1979, the church contacted WEC again, and today there are some missionaries working in that church.[112]

Because in SUM, unique among faith missions, there are interdenominational and denominational branches, the decisions on baptism were largely taken along these lines. With one exception, the denominational branches opted for infant baptism. The Danish (1912) and the Norwegian branch (1922) were right from the start *de facto* Lutheran. Proper denominational branches were: the Evangelical United Brethren branch (1926),[113] the only denominational branch which opted, contrary to practice in the United States, for believers' baptism;[114] Christian Reformed Church branch (1940); and Netherland Reformed Congregations branch (1974).[115] The South African branch was started in 1906 as an interdenominational branch. Baptism was not an issue because nobody at that time wanted to be baptized. In 1911, SUM-RSA started work among the Tiv.[116] Soon afterwards, the Dutch Reformed Church demanded a field of its own, where it could keep full ecclesiastical control.[117] In 1914, the RSA branch suggested that the whole Tiv area be reserved for the Reformed missionaries of the branch. The non-Reformed SUM-RSA missionaries were to work elsewhere with SUM.[118] This proposal was accepted,[119] but that did not keep the DRC in SUM for long. In 1916, the Reformed missionaries left the SUM;[120] in 1917, Salatu and Zaki Biam were officially handed over to the Dutch Reformed Church Mission.[121] In 1950, due to staffing problems, the DRC Mission handed missionary work in parts of the Tiv area over to the Christian Reformed Church branch. In 1961, for political and other reasons, the DRC Mission handed the whole area over, which thus returned to SUM, but with no change implied in the practice of baptism.[122]

While the missionaries, individually, had a choice between believers' baptism and infant baptism, this choice did not exist for Africans. For them, according to geography, the missionaries had decided. An AIM Christian in the West Nile had to bring his children to church to be baptized; if he lived a couple of miles further west across the border in Zaire, this was exactly what he was not to do.

Today, there is one faith mission church which accepts both modes of baptism: COCIN (SUM-UK) in Nigeria. The reason is historical. In 1907, the Cambridge Missionary Party (affiliated to CMS)[123] started to work among the Sura and Anga on the eastern

Jos Plateau.[124] In 1930, the CMS handed this, its easternmost area in northern Nigeria, over to the SUM, which was the predominant mission there.[125] Then it was decided to continue infant baptism for the stations of Panyam and Kabwir. Panyam stuck to that decision, whereas Kabwir later conformed to the rest of the church and adopted believers' baptism,[126] but even in Panyam parents can opt for not having their children baptized. The number who so decide is increasing. Mobility has grown enormously since 1930, so many Christians from Panyam and Kabwir now live elsewhere in the COCIN area. The COCIN General Church Council, therefore, decided that in urban congregations the pastor should, if requested by the parents, baptize infants.[127] In schools, baptisms and confirmations may be conducted in the same service.[128] Christians from a church with infant baptism, who join COCIN, can do so by undergoing confirmation. This applies even to Catholics, but they also may opt for believers' baptism. The possibility of believers' baptism is, on special request, also extended to COCIN Christians baptized in Panyam as infants who move into other COCIN areas.[129]

BAPTISM IN FAITH MISSION CHURCHES

For the very first converts, baptism was usually a daring step of faith into the unknown, and in the Muslim areas it remains so today. In most parts of Africa south of the Sahara, however, it gradually became less difficult to take this step. In a few areas, it soon became not only socially acceptable to become a Christian, but almost socially required. 'One has to have a religion' is a common saying, and the word 'religion' does not include African Traditional Religion.[130]

In faith mission theology, a clear profession of faith, usually expressed in conversion,[131] was considered as the only precondition for baptism. In Africa, secondary preconditions were soon added. Quite early on, a period of testing or probation was introduced to avoid 'baptizing the spurious convert'. Pre-baptism instruction about the faith was also considered to be necessary in Africa, and so faith missions followed the example of the classical missions in starting enquirer's classes. These usually lasted two years, but sometimes one year was considered to be sufficient. This meant that baptismal instruction became the required precondition for baptism. Conversion, so central to faith mission theology, was in turn considered as a precondition for baptismal instruction. But because conversion in a society where it is socially more or less required is easy to claim and difficult to check, baptism, in a large measure, depended just on the successful completion of the course.

To follow a two-year course faithfully was quite an achievement, especially for those who had to walk a distance to the place of instruction. The result was that baptism was no longer the sacrament of grace at the start of the Christian life but a sacrament of reward for good conduct (learning included), granted after quite some time in the Christian life.

Other secondary conditions were often added as well—learning to read often being prominent among them.[132] The theological reason for this was the Protestant principle of *sola scriptura*. If the scriptures are the definite revelation of God's will for mankind, every Christian should have direct access to them. So baptism classes were often reading classes, too. In many African languages, 'reader' and 'Christian' became synonyms,[133] supported by the fact that many of the converts were younger or older pupils of the mission's schools. Though it was held that everybody should learn to read, it was clear that some would not manage, so everywhere exceptions were made for those too old or otherwise unable to learn to read.[134] All this helped to enhance the notion that Christianity was something to be learned, an idea very different from the conversion theology of faith missions.

Another secondary precondition of baptism was soon added: monogamy. The problem was that the polygamous also experienced conversion. Of the many faith missions which allowed baptism of polygamous men in their early days, almost all retracted. For women, most missions tended not to see polygamy as a hindrance to baptism, choosing to ignore the fact that usually a woman entered into a polygamous union with her full consent. For men, the compromise with polygamy was differently arranged: polygamous men were simply excused from baptism. The genuineness of their conversion (and that is what makes a Christian) was not doubted,[135] but they would only be baptized when through their own efforts, through prayer or through circumstances beyond their control, the number of wives had been reduced to one. Here again, baptism has become a reward for success in Christian living, an aim to aspire to, not a divine gift being granted to start the Christian life with.[136]

These secondary preconditions to baptism and the possibility even to dispense with it, were somehow, though more or less subconsciously, congruent with faith missions' low estimation of baptism.[137] This may also have contributed to the fact that in a number of faith missions only a fraction of all believers are baptized, the percentage being sometimes as low as 10 per cent of the regular attenders at Sunday worship, and this in spite of the fact that perhaps 70 per cent see themselves, and are seen, as converted.[138] The explanation given is usually 'improper marital status' and/or 'insufficient break with heathenism'. This is only part of an answer. It must also be seen that in these churches the necessity of baptism is usually little proclaimed. It is quite common that converts, even after many years, still wait until the local evangelist tells them that he considers them to be mature enough for baptism.[139] This delay of baptism gives it, in theory, a very high value, in practice a very low one.[140]

In most areas of Africa south of the Sahara, neither African Traditional Religion nor Islam are seen as viable alternatives to Christianity, and baptism is the sacrament of initiation into Christianity. So many want to join baptismal instruction 'just to get themselves a religion' and, because in most faith mission churches infants are not baptized, the children or youths have to get themselves through the initiation process (baptism) to become adults. Thus, many profess conversion at the appropriate time in order to be admitted to baptismal instruction and not to reach baptism too late.[141] Thus, baptism is no longer the consequence of conversion and a personal commitment to Christ, but the successful conclusion of a social initiation rite. This often applies to adults, too.[142]

Almost everywhere in Africa, the age of initiation is declining, be it traditional, Muslim or Christian. This also applies to the Christian initiation of believers' baptism in faith mission churches.

According to general missionary conviction, adults and youths could be baptized; also, older children, if they were considered to be old enough to understand the faith *and* to understand the lifelong perspective of the decision. The earliest age for this was never defined, but twelve years can be regarded as the average.

In Africa, the missionaries tended even to regard twelve years as a bit early for baptism. Meanwhile, in many churches it is quite fashionable to become converted at the age of ten, so as to achieve baptism by the age of twelve. When asked about the minimum age for believers' baptism, church leaders almost always replied: twelve. This assumes conversion at the age of ten.[143] When I interviewed less official church members, it became clear that almost everywhere children are baptized much younger and that their number is increasing.[144] Often, parents take their children to be registered for baptismal instruction.[145] Occasionally, baptisms at the tender age of six or seven are reported.[146]

Among ethnic groups such as the Nandi and the Kipsigi, where the age of initiation is still higher than elsewhere, the minimum age of baptism also tends to be higher.[147] This also applies to the more recent areas of a church, such as the western sections of AIM. Because in various parts of East Africa even six-year-olds undergo initiation (into adult life!), it is to be expected that the minimum age for believers' baptism will lower itself further.

In addition, in most churches there is a tendency to reduce the period of pre-baptismal instruction—sometimes to one year, even to six months. This tendency was often enhanced by the fact that pentecostal churches usually baptize faster, sometimes much faster. And because some pentecostal churches work in the areas of faith mission churches, these are an attractive alternative for those who 'want to get themselves a religion' a bit more easily.

In East Africa, not only can the trend to lower the age of initiation be clearly discerned, but also the trend to shorten the period of initiation. Again, this applies to all three religions.[148] In former times, initiation, especially for boys, often lasted several months—nowadays, everywhere, it fits into the school holidays. This may also exert pressure on a reduction in length for baptismal instruction.

All these developments have brought about a phenomenon which, according to faith mission theology, should not exist: conversions after baptism.[149] Sometimes these 'late' conversions take place within the framework of the church, with the converts appropriating personally and existentially what they had learned previously.[150] But quite often such conversions occur under the influence of other churches or movements. So it happens that young AIC members are converted in meetings held by a charismatic evangelist[151] or organized by a DIGUNA team.[152] Often, such conversions find a positive echo in the church; sometimes they are rejected because, as baptism presupposes conversion, there cannot be a conversion after baptism. Therefore, such late converts are forced out of AIC into other churches, often of a charismatic character. This was the case with Silas Owiti, who had applied for baptism because everybody in his boarding school did so. When he was converted through contact with a pentecostal group, his local evangelist was very happy, but not the evangelist's superior, who demanded that he either keep quiet or leave the church. He then became founder, and presently bishop, of the Voice of Salvation and Healing Church.[153]

In almost all faith mission churches, only ordained or licensed ministers are allowed to baptize.[154] This, combined with the fact that the local minister (evangelist/teacher) is usually not ordained, makes for another exaltation of the sacrament of baptism which faith missions never intended, but which they definitely helped to bring about: for conversion as well as baptismal instruction, the local unordained minister is good enough, but not for the holy ritual of baptism. This supports the tendency to see baptism not just as the outward sign of the inward process of conversion, but as the real thing, far superior to conversion.

Faith missionaries had started their work in Africa with the firm conviction that it was conversion/faith (and that only) that made a Christian. For them, conversion was the *necessary* mark of the church, not baptism. In faith mission churches, this is changing or has already changed. Very often, baptism, irrespective of faith and conversion, has become *de facto* the mark of the church.[155] In theory, baptism is still believers' baptism with conversion as the necessary precondition; in practice, though, very often just regular attendence at baptismal instruction is sufficient. This, and the tendency to see baptism as a reward, have produced in faith mission churches a very different concept of baptism from that which their missionary founders brought to Africa. This obvious change of emphasis from 'subjective' conversion to 'objective' baptism did not come about in opposition to the missionaries, but as a continuation of the process that they themselves had initiated, though many missionaries may feel today that the churches have carried that process too far.

# Changing concepts of Holy Communion

If changes in the concept of baptism brought faith mission practice closer to that of the classical churches, this applied to the process of change in concepts of communion to a lesser degree. Here again, although many missionaries may claim that the changes have gone too far, they themselves initiated the process of change.

## FAITH MISSIONS' CONCEPT OF COMMUNION

As with baptism, faith missions took communion for granted and, being interdenominational, they did not interfere with the churches over their doctrines and practice of communion, accepting them all, as different as they were. This they could do only because they did not accord that much importance to the sacrament. Fellowship and Christian service were more important for the early faith missionaries.

In Europe and the United States, communion was often 'relegated' to the established churches,[156] but they could not do this in Africa because, there, they had to be the church establishment themselves.

In early missionary work, the administration of communion was not tied to ordination, but to being a missionary, usually a male one.[157] The policy of SUM was different in that only ordained men were to administer communion.[158] However, as even in SUM most male missionaries were not ordained, communion was also administered by them. This came to be criticized in some Anglican circles.[159] So it was then made the practice to license certain missionaries for administering the sacraments.[160]

For the missionaries, conversion/faith was the precondition for participation in communion, and baptism did not suffice. But then, could people participate who were converted but not baptized? In general, this possibility was excluded, although two exceptions are to be recorded. The Emmanuel Mission working in what was then Spanish Morocco admitted unbaptized believers to communion,[161] whereas the neighbouring NAM did not adhere to this practice. The Emmanuel Mission gave the reason that for many believers in that Muslim countries, baptism was a difficult proposition, which should not be pressed for by the missionaries.[162] For similar reasons, church leaders of, and missionaries in, WEC-related churches in Africa generally agreed that a believing woman whose husband hindered her from being baptized could indeed participate in communion and hold office in the congregation.[163]

## COMMUNION IN FAITH MISSION CHURCHES

Faith mission churches did not develop any *theology* of communion of their own different from that of their missionaries,[164] but dramatic changes did take place in the practice of communion, effectively depriving, at least in the larger churches, most members of the sacrament.[165] In the AIC parish Machakos Bomani in Kenya, communion can take place quite regularly. The parish has five pastors and sixteen places where services are held. If every pastor celebrated communion each Sunday at a different place, every congregation could, as the AIC rules prescribe, celebrate communion once a month.[166] In the western areas of AIC in Kenya, communion is celebrated much less frequently.[167] In many small congregations, communion is celebrated only once a year, and sometimes even this is missed out.[168] Even more extreme is the situation in the neighbouring Africa Gospel Church. According to their tradition, communion should be celebrated only quarterly; nevertheless, the ten or so ordained ministers, mostly very old, cannot provide this to such a widely dispersed church with such poor means of transport.[169] The AGC missionary work in West Pokot has never had a resident ordained minister.[170] In *practice*, communion is of little importance for AIC and AGC.[171]

In Zaire, the situation is similar, though less extreme. But even in the small Communauté Évangélique du Kwango, where communion is to be celebrated monthly,[172] there are many village congregations which celebrate communion as a festival at best.[173] Things are made more difficult by the fact that, for communion, people feel there must be bread,[174] but it is not available.[175] In many of the smaller congregations of CECCA16, communion is not celebrated for the whole year.[176]

In Nigeria in COCIN (SUM-UK), communion is to be celebrated monthly, but this rule is adhered to only in the central churches.[177] In ECWA, it is similar. Even where there are ordained pastors, communion is not often celebrated.[178] No theological reasons have been provided.

This practice of only rare celebrations of communion has brought about a two-class system: in the 'parish churches', communion is celebrated comparatively often, but the more out of the way a congregation is, the less important the sacrament becomes. The low appreciation of the sacrament is not only shown by the fact that it is celebrated rarely, but also by the fact that, when it is celebrated, only few participate. In the AIC, about 5–10 per cent of church attenders remain for communion to be celebrated.[179] In COCIN (Nigeria), the percentage is similar;[180] in CECA20 (Zaire), the percentage is higher, but declining.[181]

There are at least three reasons for this state of affairs:

◇ Church discipline. Obvious sins, such as drunkenness, adultery, theft and others, exclude from communion.[182]

◇ Then there is an almost magical fear of the sacrament, which makes many not participate, although there is no real hindrance in faith or conduct.[183] This fear is based on 1 Corinthians 11: 29: 'For he that eateth and drinketh unworthily, eateth and drinketh damnation to himself, not discerning the Lord's body'. (AV)[184]

◇ In many cases, ecclesiastical laws prevent many from participating in communion. In the AIC Tana District, anyone who is married must have been married in church in order to be permitted to share in communion. But, at the same time, there is no ordained pastor in the district, and licensed pastors are not allowed by their church to conduct marriages.[185] That so few members participate in communion is proof that the churches put little value on this sacrament.

While neglecting the sacrament in practice, a high theoretical value is assigned to communion by pegging it to ordination. Faith mission theology could have left other options, had the missionaries opted for them.[186] Not only by pegging communion to ordination was it made rare, but even more so by limiting the number of ordained men to a small fraction of those who actually are pastors. Thus, communion has become the means to define the powers of the leading élite over against the *clerus minor*, and over the laity, too.

Today's practice of communion is far from how the early missionaries had imagined it should be. There is one thing their practice and today's practice have in common: in both cases, communion is not important. The early missionaries 'relegated' communion to the established churches, faith mission churches delegate communion to an élite minority: the élite pastors are to distribute it, a small élite laity is to receive it. Communion has become an ecclesiastical status symbol and is no longer the joyous celebration of the forgiveness of sins and fellowship with Christ and all who belong to him. The developments over two or three generations have led to baptism becoming more and more easily accessible, and access to communion ever more difficult.

## A church wedding: the highest sacrament?

How many sacraments are there? Faith missionaries were quite clear that there were two: baptism and communion. This is by no means as clear in faith mission churches today. Upon enquiry, very often, three or four sacraments were named: always baptism and communion, very often marriage and sometimes dedication of children. This increase in the number of sacraments was facilitated by the fact that faith missions rarely taught what a sacrament was; often they did not even use the term, just speaking of baptism and communion or the Lord's table.[187] Not being taught to define a sacrament, the people had to trust their own judgment. To them sacraments were solemn rites of the church to which one has to be admitted first and which, after being admitted to them, grant a certain status. According to this yardstick, (church) marriage is distinctly the highest sacrament. It is far more solemn than baptism and more difficult to attain than communion, because its preconditions are not only baptism and the right to share in the Lord's table, but also the fulfilment of all civil requirements for a marriage, including the payment of the required bride price or at least a large part of it.[188]

It is not easy to fulfil the civil requirements for a church wedding. But to obtain one is being made even more difficult by a general increase in the size and the cost of the feast.[189] Not only is excellent food required, but also the bridal dress and the bridegroom's suit and, according to the solemnity required, special clothes for the bridesmaids, bestmen, parents and relatives, and perhaps transport for all the guests. In north-eastern Zaire, such a church wedding easily costs a quarter or more of the bride price of eight cows, so that one or two years' work are required just to finance the event.[190] In Kenya, the situation is similar: very few can afford a church wedding, but, for those who can afford it, it is a major status symbol.

This development has become possible by the early introduction of the church wedding into the African church and, at the same time, by assuming and ignoring customary laws on marriage. Customary law was assumed in that the civil preconditions for a marriage were accepted (especially the full payment of the bride price); it was ignored by making the church ceremony not the blessing of an existing marriage, but the wedding itself. The matter was further complicated by the naive transfer of Western customs: the bridal veil, bridesmaids, special dresses and suits and so on. Africans do not usually object to cultural mixtures, and it was not this mixture which caused today's problems, but two processes of social change: the one being the ever-rising bride price, the other the ever-growing stratification of African society. The rising bride price made it impossible for almost all

Africans to pay the full price before marriage,[191] the growing stratification makes it possible for a small group to celebrate ever more elaborate weddings.[192]

Another problem is due to that fact that the churches demand that the civil requirements for a wedding be fulfilled, but do not take into account that these civil requirements change. Because of the tremendeous bride price in many areas (for example north-east Zaire and Kenya), 'marriage by eloping' has become the rule. The churches do not accept this as a form of civil marriage, but regard it as concubinage, to be punished by excommunication. But 'marriage by eloping' these days is a thoroughly acceptable form of civil marriage. The young man finds his bride by using the traditional go-betweens, then he talks to her (bride price included); she takes her time to make enquiries about the suitor, and when she finally agrees, an evening is fixed for her 'eloping' from home. She is duly received with all honour by the bridegroom's family, and sometimes some good food is served, too. They start to live together. Immediately, the bride's family is informed so that a date for the bride price negotiations can be fixed.[193]

Many years ago, the church wedding was the norm; today, it is a rare event. In Kisangani Parish (formerly UMF), there has not been a church wedding for ten years.[194] In the northern CECA20 territory, there are practically none.[195] In the southern area around Oicha, there are church weddings (about 50 per cent), but the frequency is declining.[196] In the AIC Tana River District, hardly any church weddings occur.[197] The same has been true during half a generation of missionary work in the AGC mission field in West Pokot. One of the two Pokot evangelists there was dismissed because he had married in the traditional way.[198] Within AIC, only church marriages are considered as marriages; all other forms of marriage exclude from the sacraments[199] and from church leadership.[200] In CECCA16, the number of church weddings is low, too.[201]

It goes without saying that in the *teaching* of faith mission churches, there is no connection whatsoever between the church wedding and the (expensive) feast. But folk church practice seems to allow for no other option. Abolishing the church wedding altogether seems to me the only viable solution to the problems being described. Marriage not being a sacrament for Protestants, no church wedding is required and any type of civil marriage is regarded as a valid marriage.

One way to implement this might be along the lines of the 'marriage prayer' (*malombi ya marriage*) practised in CECA20 and some other churches.[202] It is usually applied to couples who 'eloped', but who want, after having settled their marriage with the families concerned, to return in the full fellowship of their church.[203] For this 'marriage prayer', the pastor visits the couple, reads the relevant scripture passages to them and prays for them.[204] Then usually some food is served. In theological terms, such a blessing of a marriage contains everything required, and the cost factor is negligible, but the fact that this 'marriage prayer' may only take place in the house, not in the church, shows that it is second class. It will remain second class as long as 'real' marriages are celebrated in church, as infrequently as that may be. As much as communion was 'relegated' to the few who can achieve that prize as a reward for their Christian efforts and good behaviour, so marriage, the highest sacrament,[205] has been 'relegated' to the few who can afford it, or who have to afford it for civil or religious reasons.[206]

## Notes

1  In this, they had precedents among classical missiologists, for example Alexander Duff, who saw missions as the chief end of the church.

2  Ludwig Doll, among the founders of faith missions the only active pastor of a classical denomination, was in conflict with his superiors, both political and ecclesiastical, on several counts (Bernd Brandl (working for a ThD at ETF/Heverlee on Neukirchen Mission history), 20 September 1993). He administered baptism and confirmation, but also preached that, without a sound conversion, anyone baptized and confirmed would go to hell (Affeld, *Er mache uns im Glauben kühn*, p. 7).

3  Billy Graham, 'Conversion. A Personal Revolution' in *Ecumenical Review*, 19 (1967), p. 284.

4  His critics said about Franson that he opened the doors of heaven for the awakened, but the doors of hell for the unconverted (*Östgöta Correspondenten*, 13 February 1882, quoted in Torjesen, *Fredrik Franson*, p. 214).

5  Matthew 19:14.

6  *WWW*, 1882, p. 31 (A. B. Simpson).

7  Womersley, *William F. P. Burton*, p. 25f.

8  'This "gradual turning of the heart toward God" exactly describes the growth of the Divine life in Harry Guinness ... Between his eleventh and twelfth birthday a deep and silent work took place in his heart, and though very gradual it proved to be the

real change from death unto life.' He was baptized on 29 August 1873 in Edinburgh Castle, Thomas Barnardo's mission hall (Mackintosh, *Harry Guinness*, p. 12).

9   A rare case, but one which exemplifies how different conversions may be, is that of Sheila Godfrey, later to become a WEC missionary to Zaire. From her youth, she had been a convinced Communist. A colleague at work showed her 1 Corintianths 13. Through this, she was gradually won over to a 'philosophy of love' (Interview Sheila Godfrey, 15 January 1987).

10   Grubb, *Once Caught, No Escape*, p. 79.

11   There is one small faith mission, working in eastern Zaire, the World Wide Grace Testimony, which does not practise water baptism, taking conversion as the baptism by the Spirit. For details, see: Fiedler, *Ganz auf Vertrauen*, pp. 472–474.

12   Interview Thomas Lindquist, 20 January 1987.

13   Barrett in *Kenya Churches Handbook*, p. 251, counts the pentecostal Voice of Salvation and Healing Church as 'schism from the AIC'. But Silas Owiti, its founder, stresses that he left the AIM as an individual only. His leading fellow workers come from very different churches and from African Traditional Religion (Interview Bischof Silas Owiti, 16 December 1987). In other parts of Africa, there are few African Independent Churches which split off from faith missions.

14   John Dobson, *Daybreak in West Nile*, London, n.d.

15   Church of Christ among the Tiv (1911); COCIN: Benue (1906); Lutheran Church of Christ in Nigeria (1913). See also COCIN: Muri (Methodist, 1923).

16   Here and elsewhere, the word is written with lower case 'p' to indicate that the word is not being used in its full historic meaning, but as describing a centralized corporate church structure based on the equality of all congregations and pastors.

17   'The missionary in charge of a station may elect the form of church government, but the final organization must be subject to the approval of Field Council and General Council' (AIM, *Constitution and Policy*, 1909, p. 16).

18   The 'fundamental principle' of LMS (then still The Missionary Society) runs: 'It is declared to be the fundamental principle of The Missionary Society that our design is not to send Presbyterianism, Independency, Episcopacy or any other form of Church government, but the glorious Gospel of the blessed God to the heathen and that it shall be left (as it ever ought to be left) to the minds of the persons whom God may call into the fellowship of His Son from among them to assume for themselves such form of church government as to them shall appear most agreeable to the Word of God' (Richard Lovett, *The History of the London Missionary Society 1795–1895*, London, 1899, I, p. 21f.).

19   'Each missionary and native community is free to adopt such form of church government as may be preferred, only requiring in every case that the doctrinal basis and practice shall be in strict accordance with the Word of God, and in harmony with evangelical truth' (The Evangelical Missionary Alliance, Constitution, 1887). See also: Thompson, *A. B. Simpson*, p. 131 and Daryl Westwood Cartmel, 'Mission Policy and Program of A. B. Simpson', MA, Hartford, 1962, p. 152f. Simpson held the same views for the United States (*WWW*, 1883, p. 165). His own congregation was an independent local church, but the fellowship movement he organized was presbyterian in its centralized

structures, with quite some episcopalian elements, as the crisis which developed after Simpson's death shows (see: Niklaus, Sawin and Stoesz, *All For Jesus*, pp. 143ff., 'Troubled Transition').

20  *CMA Annual Report 1923.*

21  Efraim Andersson (SMF), 'Den infödda kyrkans framtid' in *Svenska Missionstidskrift*, 1942, pp. 221–233. The article was written when the Église Évangélique du Congo (in WCE, still defined as PCon) adopted a modified presbyterian constitution (p. 232).

22  Danfulani Zamani Kore, 'An Analysis and Evaluation of Church Administration in the Evangelical Churches of West Africa, Nigeria', PhD, North Texas State University, 1980, reports that, of all the people he interviewed, one-third defined ECWA's structures as hierarchical. Among the highly educated church leaders and among the missionaries, this percentage was higher than among the pastors at the congregational level (pp. 80ff.).

23  In the Holiness Union Church in South Africa (Helgelseförbundet), many press for this course of action (Interview Håkan Wistrand, 13 June 1986). In doing this, they would continue the process of centralization started by the missionaries, but take it further than the missionaries would have wanted it to go.

24  These opinions were collected just before the current wind of democratic change began to blow over the continent.

25  For a detailed study of Yaka culture from the point of view of a Catholic missionary, see: Wilhelm Josef Otte, 'Religionsbedingte Sozialkonflikte im Congo aufgewiesen am Beispiel des Stammes der Bayaka', PhD, Cologne 1970. For the position of the king, see especially p. 159. The king of the Yaka made it possible to expel the BMM missionaries from Wamba-Luadi because they refused to establish government recognized schools.

26  Kenyatta, *Facing Mount Kenya*, pp. 186–230. Kenyatta starts with the statement: 'The Kikuyu system of government prior to the advent of the Europeans was based on true democratic principles.'

27  According to the original plan, AIM was to establish mission stations sufficiently far from each other 'to permit of the evangelization through native workers, under the supervision of missionaries, of large areas around each station' (AIM, *Constitution and Policy*, 1909).

28  Communion is celebrated each month at the *locale* for the members of all *congrégations* (Interview the Rev. Masangura Mbafele-Mussamba, 3 January 1987).

29  This applied in 1987. Under the new constitution, there are no more *sous-sections*, so that all *locales* may now be equal (Hank Schoemaker—Fiedler, 2 February 1993).

30  Originally, the districts were exactly the areas of the mission stations; later, districts were created which had never had a mission station, and in some districts the centre of gravity shifted from the mission station to the town.

31  La Constitution de la Communauté Évangélique au Centre de l'Afrique (CECA), (valid 1986).

32  Sandgren, *The Kikuyu*, pp. 139–193, shows how the AIM systematically

thwarted attempts of congregations to achieve some independence, starting, in about 1925, to use the concept of the 'new church', which stressed the authority of the missionaries as servants of God (pp. 178ff.).

33  In CECA20, transfers were decided upon by the annual Conseil Administratif or the semi-annual Conseil du District (Interview Rév. Masangura Mbafele-Mussamba, 3 January 1987). In practice, churches had considerable power in resisting an assignment, so that the respective councils frequently reassigned pastors (Hank Schoemaker—Fiedler, 2 February 1993). Under the new constitution, locals call their own pastor(s). 'The leaders and congregations don't like this one bit. The old system was more akin to their culture' (Hank Schoemaker—Fiedler, 2 February 1993).

34  For a critical assessment of these developments (including proposals for electing an archbishop), see: Cuthbert Omari, 'Bischöfliche Verfassung. Eine soziologische Tendenz in der Lutherischen Kirche in Tanzania' in Blick in die Welt, 1, 1988, pp. 1–3.

35  The decision of the regions coincided with President Mulwa's personal opinion (Jonathan Hildebrandt—Fiedler, 23 April 1988).

36  Interview Bischof Mukwalemba Ponzo, 26 January 1987.

37  Interview Donald E. Muchmore, 30 December 1986.

38  Herbert Jenkinson, 'A Brief History of the UFM in Congo/Zaire', unpublished, 1978, p. 11.

39  In 1987, Jenkinson was invited by both sides for a visit to find out if cooperation with UFM could be resumed. His report gives the impression that the dissident group comprises a considerable section of the church (Herbert Jenkinson, circular letter, 1987). Repeated attempts of dissident congregations to join CECCA16 were not acceded to. Thus government and churches practise 'comity' in a similar way to the former missions.

40  Dissident groups from other communautés were equally not accepted.

41  In his report at the triannual assembly of CECCA16, the Rev. Nonziodane, the réprésentant légal, stressed that CECCA16 was happy to be part of ECZ, but added: 'Or nous ne pouvons pas accepter que celle-ci nous impose des pratiques contraires à notre structure évangélique. C'est ainsi que j'invite cette Assemblée à présenter une position nette face au système épiscopale et la supression de mandat des serviteurs de Dieu. Ainsi nous demandons à la CECCA de prendre les dispositions nécessaires.'

42  Interview N. N. Dr Marini, president of the church (and at the same time second in command of ECZ after Dr Bokeleale), favours the introduction of the bishop's office in his church but the Rev. Etsea, the représentant légal (de facto leader of CECA20) opposes the idea. For him the New Testament office of bishop was a local congregational office (Ang'apoza Etsea Kila, L'episcopos, pasteur de l'église locale, Maître en Science Religieuses Faculté Libre de Théologie Évangélique Vaux-sur-Seine 1981, p. 50).

43  Interview N. N. This also can be seen by the fact that Dr Bokeleale has the title 'bishop', which his Communauté des Disciples du Christ au Zaire does not have.

44  Interview Glenn Crumley, 21 January 1987 reports this, but also that these

attempts achieve little in the Communauté Évangélique Beréénne.

45  Interview Alastair M. Kennedy, 10 January 1987. This is not usual WEC practice, but an African appropriation of the teaching of one missionary. An association of churches has now been formed (Kennedy —Fiedler, 3 March 1993)

46  In various NTM fields, loose fellowships of churches develop and are encouraged (Frank Lyttleton—Fiedler, 10 September 93). The WEC missionaries say of NTM: 'They out-WEC the WECers' (Interview Alastair M. Kennedy, 10 January 1987). This insistance on congregationalism does not tally with the centralized structures of NTM in Senegal. It remains to be seen if the churches will in the end copy the missionaries' doctrinal views or their organizational practice.

47  For example, Africa Evangelical Church, Malawi; Africa Evangelical Church, South Africa and Swaziland; Evangelical Church in South Africa (*AEF Guide for Daily Prayer*, 1985).

48  AEF took over the work in Rose Belle started by an independent English lady missionary (AEF, *Notes on Mauritius*, (n.d.) 1988).

49  AEF, *Notes on Reunion*, (n.d.) 1988.

50  The church 'is a fellowship of autonomous local churches. Each local church is directed by a committee of elders and deacons. All male missionaries are elders. Each local assembly develops within the structure as much liberty as possible' (*AEF Guide*, p. 74).

51  *AEF Guide*, p. 75.

52  This does not exclude occasional congregationalist elements. In the Zambezi Evangelical Church (ZIM), the big congregations may call their own pastor (Interview Leonhard Evans, 17 October 1985).

53  Interview Alastair M. Kennedy, 10 January 1987.

54  Among the Maguzawa, congregations are named like 'The Church in Bangu'. Among the Gwari, work had been begun before in Rumana Gbagi by Youth Corps people, who registered the church as 'Baptist Church' (not belonging to any Baptist Union). CAPRO saw no point in changing the name. The churches finance themselves and are in no way tied to CAPRO (Interview Naomi Fanumore, 5 February 1987). Fitting its rigid congregational principles is the individualized support system of the CAPRO missionaries (Interview Wilbur O'Donovan, 6 February 1987).

55  CMF, *Profile of CMF Missionaries*, 1986–87.

56  Christian Outreach Fellowship, *Information Sheet*, n.d. (1987).

57  In 1987, missionaries worked in Benin, Togo and Ghana (Samson Awumehab—Fiedler, 9 March 1987).

58  Among Baptists, ordination is usually practised, but just as a setting aside for full-time service, while neither preaching nor the administration of the sacraments are reserved for the ordained ministry. Early Methodism had the same view: Alan D. Gilbert, *Religion and Society in Industrial England. Church, Chapel and Social Change, 1740–1914*, London/New York 1976, p. 150.

59 For more details, see Chapter 6.

60 This development, typical for almost all missions, is well described in: David Langford, 'Equipping for Ministry in Zaire', unpublished, 1986, 30 pages. The paper was written with CECA20 (AIM) background.

61 Herein also CIM gave the lead (Moira J. McKay, *Faith and Facts*, p. 121).

62 Nkounkou *et al.*, *75e Anniversaire*, pp. 4–17.

63 Ordained were Toma Tok Bot (Forum), Bali (Langtang) and David Lot (Panyam) (SUM, *The SUM 75th Jubilee*, p. 8).

64 He was born about 1885. This means that at ordination he was about sixty-five (Fish, Mrs and Richard Adkins, *The Call to Battle*, pp. 5–7).

65 Benjamin N. Watuma (AIC, *First Anniversary of the AIC, 15th October 1972*, Kijabe, 1972, p. 25). In West Nile (Uganda), the first two ordinations took place in 1942 after twenty-four years of missionary work, but there the AIM work was part of the Anglican Church.

66 'Licensed to the ministry' (Clara Guilding—H. Campbell, 22 June 1932 in Gration, *The Relationship of the AIM*, p. 231).

67 *Trombeta. Boletim Informativo das Igrejas Evangélicas da Guiné-Bissau*, March 1985.

68 The Anglican CMS in Uganda, for example, around that time reduced the number of ordinations drastically.

69 Ernest Dalziel brought up the issue during the 1929 AIM annual conference: 'I asked the question, "Who gave us the right as members of the AIM to ordain native ministers, who was going to ordain them?" No one could give an answer although it has been taken for granted that we have the right. Then I contended that if the AIM has the right to ordain natives we also have the right to ordain missionaries on the Field [and] moved that all Senior Missionaries be ordained... who desired ordination' (Ernest Dalziel—H. Campbell, 22 March 1929 in Gration, *The Relationship of the AIM*, p. 231f.).

70 These issues were never solved in principle but only by history: AIM was finally integrated into the AIC, nowadays even missionaries can be ordained by the AIC. Ordination was twice offered to Jonathan Hildebrandt by the AIC (Interview Jonathan Hildebrandt, 14 December 86).

71 See also: David Langford, 'Equipping for Ministry in Zaire', unpublished, 1986 (30 pages).

72 'Ni kwa kuweka mutu awe kwa kazi ya Mungu tu katika maisha yake yote' (*Constitution ya Communauté Évangélique au Centre d'Afrique* (valid 1986)). One reason for not granting ordination after finishing pastoral training or after a brief period of being licensed is that 'the churches really want to see who is called by God and who are not. Many pastors fall by the wayside' (Hank Schoemaker—Fiedler, 2 February 1993)

73 Their ratio is about 1:3:10. The 1983 CECCA16 workers' list counts, on the male side, for fourteen parishes: sixty-eight pastors, 189 evangelists and 794 catechists (Communauté Évangélique du Christ au Coeur de l'Afrique, Majina ya Watumishi wa Mungu 1983).

74 In Lubutu Parish, for example, there were in 1986: 140 congregations ('chapelles'), 1,120 baptized and 4,139 unbaptized Christians, six ordained pastors, twenty-one evangelists and eighty-eight catechists (Rapport Statistique Paroisse de Lubutu 1986 CECCA16). Different from other faith mission churches, CECCA16 also list wives as church workers, and single women can be evangelists or catechists. This means, for Lubutu, an additional twenty-eight evangelists and 108 catechists. If wives are not counted separately, each congregation has one couple or individual to pastor it, but every ordained pastor in theory at least, must look after twenty-three or twenty-four congregations.

75 Mary Beard, In Times of Trouble, Toronto, 1964, p. 18.

76 Samson Kozi Maliwa, leader of Tana District with 18 congregations is only licensed (Interview Samson Kozi Maliwa, 20 December 1986). Pastor Maliwa was finally ordained in 1990.

77 With this differentiation, CMA managed to have its female missionaries counted in terms of insurance as ordained, without having to do so in matters ecclesiastical (Wendell Price, The Role of Women in the Ministry of the Christian and Missionary Alliance, DMiss, San Francisco Theological Seminary, 1977, pp. 57–66, describes this complicated process in detail).

78 The regulation still reads today: '[Licensing] is to test the candidate and to prepare him for ordination' (Constitution ya Communauté Évangélique au Centre d'Afrique (CECA20)).

79 The AIC Constitution 1954 (p. 31) makes provision for licensing; the 1972 Constitution does not. But this is completely ignored.

80 Of the about 200 male students who finished AIC Kapsabet Bible School, about five have reached ordination so far (Interview Mrs Naudé, Lecturer, Kapsabet Bible School, 16 October 1986).

81 Only ordination grants access to the higher offices of the church in AIC (Interview Alice and Henry Ndolo, 28 December 1986).

82 This applies to AIC; in CECA20, the licensed pastor may not baptize.

83 It is often claimed that a marriage officer must be ordained in Kenya, but in fact the government does not stipulate that but only that the minister be recognized by his church.

84 In several areas, there are moves under way to license earlier and to grant ordination sooner, for example in CECA20 and the Africa Gospel Church.

85 Interview Henry Ng'eno, AGC missionary in West Pokot, 18 December 1986.

86 Interview Richard Adkins, WGM (Kenya Highlands Bible College), Kericho, 18 December 1986.

87 Among those ordained in 1986, the four youngest were about fifty; for 1987, seven ordinations are envisaged, of them four for men between thirty and fifty (Interview the Rev. Jonah A. Chesengeny, Moderator, AGC Kericho, 18 December 1986).

88 In West Pokot, he has started ten congregations; some of these are pastored by AGC missionaries with several years of training (Kenya Highlands Bible College). (Interview Bill Reincheld, WGM, Kenya Highlands Bible College, Kericho, 16

October 1986; Interview Henry Ng'eno, Missionary of the AGC in West Pokot, 18 December 1986).

89  Interview Bill Reincheld, 16 October 1986.

90  *Trombeta. Boletim Informativo das Igrejas Evangélicas da Guiné-Bissau*, March 1985. Originally, Bessie and Leslie Brierley had appointed elders to do the pastoral work and evangelists for reaching the unreached, but the evangelists settled down to do the pastoral work that the elders had been assigned to do (Leslie Brierley—Fiedler, 26 February 1993).

91  For the ordinary Christian, there is a tremendous difference between laity and clergy (Langford, *Equipping for Ministry*, p. 10).

92  During the CECCA16 church conference of 1986, the question came up for discussion if ordination was required for the top offices of the church. The majority carried the motion, but the (better educated) representatives of the church's school and health systems voted against it.

93  Interview Alastair M. Kennedy, 10 January 1987.

94  Interview Alastair M. Kennedy, 10 January 1987. Over the last years some young Northerners attended the Bible school. On their return home, the elders refused to call them or, if they did so, demanded that they 'live by faith', but nobody gave them anything for their support.

95  Interview N. N., Sanford, 20–22 February 1986; Interview Frank Lyttleton, 28 July 1986.

96  '"Christ sent me not to baptize but to preach the Gospel". What did Paul mean? Did he not believe in Christian baptism? I think he meant that if baptism was going to become a matter of controversy and strife in the Church, it would be better to discard it rather than fight over it' (Bingham, *Seven Sevens of Years*, p. 114).

97  For example, CMA: 'The local church is a body of believers in Christ who are joined together for the worship of God ... and observance of the ordinances of baptism and the Lord's Supper.' TEAM states in its doctrinal statement: 'We believe that water baptism and the Lord's Supper are ordinances to be observed by the Church during this present age. They are, however, not to be regarded as means of salvation.' RBMU mentions in its 'Memorandum of Association' (1903) 'the divine institution of the Christian ministry, and the obligation and perpetuity of the ordinances of baptism and the Lord's Supper', but neither in 1930 nor in 1956 was this clause repeated. The 1982 version, written on request of RBMU-USA and for RBMU-UK even after the split of the mission, speaks of baptism, but not of water baptism: 'We believe that the Church, the Body of Christ, consists only of those who are born again, having been baptized into Christ by the Holy Spirit at the time of regeneration.'

98  A few missions opted for believers' baptism. The oldest example is possibly the Gospel Missionary Union: 'We believe in the great commission as the primary mission of the church, i.e., the preaching to all the world of the Gospel of the grace of God, teaching converts to obey the Lord in baptism by immersion, to remember Christ's death till He comes in the observance of the Lord's Supper, to be always careful to live godly lives in the world, and to pursue fellowship and seek ministry in visible, organized churches' (According to GMU—Fiedler, 2 November 1987,

the doctrinal statement of GMU is unchanged since its beginning). In the NTM doctrinal statement, formulated later but reflecting original practice, it is stated: 'We practice the baptism of believers by immersion.'

99 Rowland Bingham, after having had to abort his attempt to reach Northern Nigeria, had eventually become a Baptist pastor. For his next attempt, he contemplated to start a Baptist mission. But when a Presbyterian woman gave him a considerable sum for the new mission, he came to the conclusion that it would not be fair to accept Presbyterian money, but to refuse to accept Presbyterian missionaries. So he decided that the doctrine of baptism should be a matter of personal conviction in the new mission (Bingham, *Seven Sevens of Years*, p. 109).

100A. B. Simpson (1881) and A. T. Pierson (1896), for example, were baptized by Baptists, but never became Baptists.

101I have no detailed statistics, but the general impression is that in the early faith mission days, despite the example of the founders, most of the missionaries were happy with their infant baptism.

102Even Svenska Alliansmissionen, which in Sweden even today allows the baptism of infants, in South Africa does not recognize the validity of infant baptism for Africans (Interview N. N., Svenska Alliansmissionen, 16 June 1986).

103The comparative is deliberately chosen here. To hold believers' baptism to be *better* does not exclude holding infant baptism as *good*.

104One of the very first cases of such a private rebaptism: Peterson, one of the early SMF missionaries in Zaire, baptized his wife and a younger missionary secretly, 'lest the blacks might get the news and be caused to quarrel about baptism' (*AMZ*, 23 (1896), p. 435).

105Dobson, *Daybreak in West Nile*, p. 5.

106Grubb, *After C. T. Studd*, p. 64.

107Norman P. Grubb, *Penetrating Faith in Spanish Guinea*, Colchester, [3]1941 (1937); *After C. T. Studd*, pp. 63–76.

108Robert Munn, *These Forty Years. A Testimony of God's Faithfulness During Forty Years of Active Missionary Service*, published by the author, 1981, p. 98. The French edition is: Robert Munn, *Quarante ans d'aventure avec Dieu. Un témoignage de la fidélité de Dieu pendant quarante ans dans la mission*, Valence, 1985.

109November 1934, Lizzie Smith (Ma Lui), Aberdeen; June 1935, Emma Munn, Belfast. Both had finished Emmanuel Bible School, Birkenhead (Grubb, *Penetrating Faith*, p. 21; p. 31). For some time also, Emma Munn's brother Robert (Munn, *Quarante ans d'aventure avec Dieu*, pp. 101ff.).

110This explanation is based on WEC oral tradition only, not on primary sources. For the first baptism see: Grubb, *Penetrating Faith*, pp. 40–43.

111Because of their more limited training they have no chance to influence top level decisions, but even the Methodists who are better educated (about 5 per cent) are not content. Three couples finished training at the CMA Bible school in June 1988 (Dietrich Kuhl—Fiedler, 25 April and 19 May 1988).

112Interview Alastair M. Kennedy, 10 January 1987; Dietrich Kuhl—Fiedler 19 May 1988; *Praying Always*.

113Geoffrey Dearsley—Fiedler, 13 January 1988. Since 1968, the Evangelical United Brethren branch is the United Methodist branch, because in the United States, the Evangelical United Brethren Church joined the United Methodist Church.

114Geoffrey Dearsley—Fiedler, 13 January 1988.

115'Stichting voor de Zending der Gereformeerde Gemeenten' of the 'Gereformeerde Gemeenten in Neder land en Noord-America' (A. van der Vegt--Fiedler, 14 September 1988).

116For history, see: Rubingh, *Sons of Tiv*.

117Minutes SUM, 21 May 1913.

118Minutes SUM General Purpose Committee, September 1914.

119Minutes SUM, 10 June 1914.

120'We can only submit sorrowfully' (Minutes, 13 January 1916).

121Minutes SUM, 19 June 1917.

122Rubingh, *Sons of Tiv*, pp. 127–129.

123The information given in E. A. Ayandele, *The Missionary Impact on Modern Nigeria 1842–1914*, London, 1966, p. 142, that the Cambridge University Mission Party later became the SUM, is wrong. The SUM started 1904 in Wase, not the CUMP.

124Eugene Stock, *History of the Church Missionary Society*, Volume 4, London, 1916, p. 72. Panyam was started in 1907, Kabwir in 1910. The most important missionary in this work was Elsie Webster ('Nakam'), who changed to SUM in 1930 (Tett, *Road to Freedom*, pp. 102–103).

125Minutes SUM, 24 June 1930.

126Interview the Rev. Joel Gukas, Chairman of Panyam RCC of COCIN, 3 February 1987.

127Interview the Rev. Luther D. Cishak, President of COCIN, 3 February 1987.

128Interview the Rev. Joel Gukas, 3 February 1987.

129Interview th eRev. Luther D. Cishak, 3 February 1987.

130The East African version is: 'Lazima kuwa na dini'.

131The outward sign of conversion often was the burning or exposure of one's cult objects. For a typical example, see: Munn, *Quarante ans d'aventure avec Dieu*, pp. 144–149.

132In CECA20, this requirement is even laid down in the *Constitution ya CECA20*, but there is room for exceptions in specific cases.

133Among the Kikuyu (AIC), *athomi* means reader as well as Christian.

134The requirements for baptism in the World Gospel Mission in Burundi were, therefore: conversion; participation in the life of the congregation for at least a year; the faith becoming visible in daily life; financial contributions to the church; and *the attempt* to learn to read (Donald Hohensee, *Church Growth in Burundi*, Pasadena, 1977, p. 48).

135In Guinea Bissau, it happened repeatedly that polygamous men started congregations. As there was no one else, they were the leaders of the meetings. They could not understand when, after non-polygamous men became available, they were debarred from leading services (Interview N. N.).

136Altogether, *today's* faith missionaries are quite unhappy with this compromise, but attempts to make baptism available to polygamous converts are usually strongly resisted by the African church leaders because it would upset the established order.

137This is my judgment from observed *practice*; in theory, the missionaries would have a *high* view of baptism.

138This applies to large areas in CECCA16 as much as to the WEC- related churches in West Africa (*Report African Consultation in Vavoua 30.11.– 16.12.1985*).

139Interview Annette Botting (WEC/CECCA16), 14 January 1987. CECCA16 Lubutu Parish (1986) counts 1,120 baptized Christians and 3,493 unbaptized Christians, not including children (Rapport Statistique Paroisse de Lubutu 1986).

140Missionaries these days often deplore the long period when the church tests that the believer's life shows he or she believes (Margaret White—Fiedler, 22 February 1993).

141'I teach a baptismal class myself in my Nairobi congregation where I am an elder. One child was converted before, one is still unconverted, one was converted in my class etc. If baptized children are converted depends largely on the teacher. Some teach just as teaching' (Interview Joseph N. N., 10 December 1986).

142It is often assumed that 40 per cent do not lead a Christian life after baptism (Interview the Rev. Masangura Mbafele-Mussamba, 3 January 1987).

143In the Kikuyu area of AIC, children begin baptismal instruction even at six (Interview Joseph N. N., 10 December 1986).

144For example, Interview the Rev. Masangura Mbafele-Mussamba 3 January 1987; Interview Richard Adkins (WGM) 17 December 1986; Interview Alice and Henry Ndolo (AIC), 28 December 1986; Interview Hank Schoemaker (AIM/CECA20), 5 January 1987; Interview Samuel Schweizer (Communauté Cooperation Évangélique au Zaire), 28 January 1987; Interview Ursula Röthenmund (Communauté Évangélique du Kwango), 26 January 1987; Interview with six representatives of CECCA16, 11 January 1987. Alastair M. Kennedy reports that in December 1986, contrary to earlier practice, seven- and eight-year-olds were baptized. In the younger WEC-related churches in Africa, this process has not (yet?) taken place (Interview Alastair M. Kennedy, 10 January 1987).

145Interview the Rev. Kasali Yeiye, the Rev. Bakwanamaha Mutsungu, the Rev. Njialese Makambi, Pasteur Munyighulu Kambashu, 3 January 1987 (Oicha, CECA20).

146Interview Hank Schoemaker, 5 January 1987; Ursula Röthenmund—Fiedler, 14 October 1991.

147But in these ethnic groups also the age of initiation is going down (Interview Bill Reincheld, 16 October 1986).

THE STORY OF FAITH MISSIONS

148For the Muslim Zaramo around Dar-es-Salaam compare Anna von Waldow, 'Mwali Custom: Uzaramo Transformation', ca. 1935 (later published as: 'Mädchenerziehung bei den Zaramo' in *Afrika und Übersee*, 1961, pp. 292–306) with: Marja-Liisa Swantz, *Ritual and Symbol in Transitional Zaramo Society, Gleerup, 1970*, pp. 363–393.

149Alice Ndolo is typical (Interview, 29 December 1986): 'I wanted to be a good girl and please my mother, and more than anything else I wanted a real name. I wanted the name Alice. So I professed conversion and was admitted to baptismal instruction'.

150From the Evangelical Teacher Training College in Vryheid, Natal, started in 1948 by TEAM and five other missions, it is reported: 'Though entering students were always supposedly Christians, many dated their conversion from their time there' (Sheetz, *The Sovereign Hand*, p. 160).

151This was the case for both Alice and Henry Ndolo, who remained in the AIC and today serve their church as Bible School Teacher and Pastor respectively (Interview Alice and Henry Ndolo, 29 December 1987).

152DIGUNA is a predominantly German mission, which evangelizes within AIC/CECA20 and beyond in Kenya and Zaire, mainly through team efforts with lorries.

153Interview Silas Owiti, 16 December 1986.

154For a missionary to baptize, usually no ordination was required, but the same missionary required it from Africans.

155The tendency to see baptism instead of conversion as *nota ecclesiae*, can be seen in the following episode: due to a burial, the two pastors of Oicha congregation were not at home on 2 January 1987. An AIM female missionary asked if the deceased had been a Christian. The answer was: 'Not a Christian, only a believer.' The missionary: 'Why then was he not a Christian?' Answer: 'He was not baptized.'

156This was typical of the fellowship movements, especially on the European Continent. They had their own meetings, their own leadership, their organization as '*ecclesiola in ecclesia*' ('little churches within the church'). They did not usually administer the sacraments, leaving that to the established churches, even though they were often quite critical of these churches, counting many of their pastors as not even converted, and therefore not as Christians.

157Typical for this process is the missionary work started by the Africa Evangelistic Band in Booke, Zaire, in 1936. The AEB did not start churches in South Africa, and its 'pilgrims' are not ordained. But already in 1933, it was decided that they would administer the sacraments in Zaire (Peckham, *The Africa Evangelistic Band*, p. 62).

158SUM Constitution 1912.

159Minutes SUM, 17 April 1917.

160A typical minute runs: 'Permission was given to Mr. David Wilmshurst to administer the sacraments at Gindiri [School] for the usual period of one year' (Minutes SUM, 23 September 1954).

161Interview Mrs N. N., former Emmanuel missionary in Morocco 10 October 1985.

162The NAM missionaries shared this conviction, but did not draw the same conclusion.

163WEC *African Consultation Vavoua 30.11–16.12.1985.*

164The majority of the missionaries held broadly Calvinist views about communion, except in the clearly denominational branches of faith missions like AIM-Uganda (Anglican) or SUM-DK (Lutheran) or in strict holiness Missions (Arminian).

165In the smaller (and younger) this is not (yet?) the case. In the Église Protestante Évangélique in Burkina Faso (WEC), for example, a large majority of the baptized share in communion (Interview the Rev. Jean Kambou, 13 January 1987; Interview Alastair M. Kennedy, 10 January 1987).

166Interview Pastor Henry Ndolo, 28 December 1986.

167Interview N. N..

168Interview N. N., 20 December 1987: 'In Malindi comunion is celebrated about three times a year, in other congregations never'.

169'Functionally Africa Gospel Church is a non-sacramental organisation' (Interview Bill Reincheld, 16 December 1986).

170In spite of more than ten years' successful missionary work by Edward Tonui (Interview Bill Reincheld, 16 December 1986).

171'Communion seems to have no importance' (Interview Mrs Naudé, 16 December 1987); Interview N. N..

172Interview the Rev. Mwadi Mbubika and the Rev. Nyanga wa Mandamba, 27 January 1987.

173Interview Sr. Ursula Röthenmund, 26 January 1987. Even elsewhere, monthly communion is often the ideal but not the practice (Röthenmund—Fiedler, 16 October 1991).

174Faith missionaries in several cases tried to replace the 'European' elements in communion by 'African' elements, but usually the Christians prefer to celebrate communion in the 'right' way with bread and wine (or grape juice). In the recently founded NTM congregation at Chowo, the missionary used during the first communion service a local red juice, but for the next communion service the local Christians insisted on them buying proper grape juice (Interview John Mikitson, 27 July 1986).

175Interview Sr. Ursula Röthenmund, 26 January 1987.

176Interview Alastair M. Kennedy, 10 January 1987. The idea is that monthly communion is celebrated at some agreed-upon place in the congregation, where everyone should go, but, because CECCA16 is widespread, often great distances are involved. In the Ibambi area, the central church's congregation will often go to a 'communion meeting' at some agreed out-church, to encourage the Christians there (Margaret White—Fiedler, 22 February 1993).

177Interview the Rev. Luther Cishak, 6 February 1987.

178Crampton, *Christianity in Northern Nigeria*, p. 169.

179Interview Jonathan Hildebrandt, 14 December 1986; Interview N. N.

180Interview Eileen Owers, 6 February 1987.

181From the Communauté Episcopale Évangélique au Zaire (UFM), 25 per cent participation (tendency falling) is reported (Interview Donald Muchmore, 30 December 1986). For CECA20, the picture seems to be similar.

182'Ulevi, uasherati, wizi, magomvi, matukano, aishiye namna ili anajitenga mwenyewe' (Interview the Rev. Kasali Yeiye, the Rev. Bakwanamaha Mutsungu, the Rev. Njialese Makambi, Pasteur Munyighulu Kambashu, 3 January 1987, Oicha, CECA20). This is generally the case.

183Interview Sr. Ursula Röthenmund ,26 January 1987; Interview Pastor Samson Kozi Maliwa, 20 December 1986, Interview N. N.

184Interview Henry Ndolo, 28 December 1987.

185Interview Pastor Samson Kozi Maliwa, 20 December 1986. Pastor Maliwa has been ordained on 25 January 1990, so the number of church weddings has increased (Kozi Maliwa—Fiedler, 27 January 1993).

186From CEBK55 (UAM/CBFMS), it is reported that elders may celebrate communion (Interview the Rev. Paluku Kinyoma, 19 January 1987).

187In some languages, there is not even a word for 'sacrament', for example, in Kipsigi (Interview Bill Reincheld, 16 December 1986) and Yaka (Kwango) (Interview Sr. Ursula Röthenmund, 26 January 1986), or in the languages of the Berean Mission (Interview Kathy and Thomas Lindquist, 20 January 1987).

188In terms of social anthropology, 'bride wealth' would perhaps be more correct. But aren't the prices ever-rising and isn't bride wealth usually converted into cash payments?

189As for the solemnity of the rite, the missionaries set the example. Here is one from the early Congo Balolo Mission: 'Christmas Eve—dawned a glorious summer day—for the wedding of Mr Fred Gardner and Miss Elizabeth Henson. Preparations began in early morning. The native boys themselves decorated the church most beautifully. After the official State ceremony in French at Basankusu, the Bride and Bridegroom returned to the prettily decorated church at Ikan. Here in Lomongo, English and Lingala an impressive service was conducted by Mr. F. Antice before a large congregation. Much interest was aroused amongst the natives when the bridegroom endowed his bride with "all his worldly goods". The happy couple left the church amid scenes of rejoicing. A reception was given at Mr. and Mrs Anstice's house later in the day. After four days the bride and bridegroom returned to Bongandanga. We wish them every blessing in their service for the King' (Congo Mission News/Nouvelles Missionaires du Congo, No. 98).

190David Langford, 'Areas of Pastoral Concern—Marriage', (unpublished) 1985, p. 8. Others estimate that only a year is needed (Interview Donald Muchmore, 30 December 1986).

191The bride's parents and elders are not especially interested in full payment before marriage because that would drastically reduce the older generation's control over the younger.

192Just to see the wedding-report pages in Kenyan newspapers is sufficient to realize what social status a church wedding conveys or what social status makes a church wedding a necessity.

193Desribed in detail in: David Langford, 'Areas of Pastoral Concern—Marriage', p. 6. Langford describes the situation among the Hema in north-eastern Zaire (CECA20 (AIM)). But in very many areas of East Africa, the situation is basically the same.

194Meanwhile, even a legend helps to legitimize the neglect of church weddings: many years ago there was a church wedding, and the bride ran away from her husband that very night. Since then no church wedding has ever taken place—it was regarded as a bad omen for the success of a marriage (Interview Hilde Moro, 5 January 1987).

195David Langford, 'Areas of Pastoral Concern—Marriage', p. 8; Interview the Rev. Ang'apoza Etsea Kila, 30 December 1986.

196Interview the Rev. Musangura Mbafele-Mussamba, 3 January 1987.

197Interview the Rev. Kasali Yeiye, the Rev. Bakwanamaha Mutsungu, the Rev. Njialese Makambi, Pasteur Munyighulu Kambashu, 3 January 1987, Oicha, CECA20.

198Interview Henry Ng'eno, 18 December 1986.

199In Tana Distrikt, even government-registered civil marriage is not accepted as a valid marriage (Interview Pastor Samson Kozi Maliwa, 20 December 1986).

200It happened in west Kenya that an experienced Sunday School leader could not be made a church elder because he had not been married in church (Interview Jonathan Hildebrandt, 14 December 1986).

201The president of the Église Protestante Évangélique de Burkina Faso commented: 'Here the poor cannot marry' (Interview the Rev. Jean Kambou 13 January 1987).

202Constitution ya CECA.

203David Langford, 'Areas of Pastoral Concern—Marriage', p. 10.

204David Langford, 'Areas of Pastoral Concern—Marriage', p. 8; Constitution ya CECA (p. 20).

205In the Lutheran Church on the slopes of Mt Kilimanjaro, it is similar: the more experienced evangelists were accorded the right 'Wainjilisti wa Sinodi' to administer the sacraments, but only and ordained minister may conduct a wedding (Interview Kristosia Materu, 27 July 1972). The same applied to Moody, who in his North Market Mission conducted all rites, except weddings (William R. Moody, D. L. Moody, New York, 1930, p. 99).

206Even in CECCA16, where a church wedding is no precondition for participation in communion, applicants to the Institut Supérieur Théologique de Bunia must have it. In the Communauté Évangélique Beréenne au Zaire a government registered marriage is sufficient (Interview Kathy and Thomas Lindquist, 20 January 1987).

# 12
# A vision taken up:
# African missions

Within about a century, Africa south of the Sahara has changed
its religion and has become a Christian continent. The enormous
evangelistic effort that was required for this process of change
was initiated by European and US missionaries, but the biggest
amount of work was done by Africans, whether through informal
witness to their new-found faith or through part-time or full-time
service of the emerging church as teachers, evangelists or (later)
as pastors.[1] In this, the work of faith missions differed little from
that of classical missions,[2] except in that the early classical
missions, who had started their work already well before the
scramble for Africa with its ensuing feelings of European superiority, gave Africans a greater chance of working independently[3]
and/or of becoming ordained.[4]

Although faith mission churches often grow so quickly that
coping with the ever-increasing numbers is a major problem, they
usually lack missionary vision. One mission leader formulated it
drastically: 'Regions Beyond Missionary Union has founded a
church which does not look beyond'.[5] Faith missions, which had
so severely criticized the churches in their home countries for their
lack of missionary vision,[6] produced churches which lacked
exactly that. In Africa, the missionaries assumed the role of the
established church and did not create structures that were critical
of it, as mission societies usually are. (Even when they are not, they
still compete with the established church for its often meagre
resources.) It is true that their resources were often strained even
to reach the immediate neighbourhood, but faith missions believed
in the effectiveness of prayer, and mission prayer meetings would
have cost very little in money and personnel.

The missions introduced a clear dichotomy: mission is the
foreigners' affair, the church is for the 'natives'. Mission theology
supported this: the mission is the scaffolding of the church and,
after the church has been established, the scaffolding is to be
dismantled and used elsewhere. The scaffolding usually remained
much longer than originally envisaged, however, and the missionary vision was often not passed on to the 'young' churches.

This process was enforced by the indigenous church principle, applied within the framework of comity arrangements which assigned a limited territory to each church, to pass the borders of which was a transgression. Because the whole country was divided up by comity agreements, missionary work would have meant working abroad, but the churches could not afford that, and the indigenous church principle, as applied by faith missions, meant that 'white' money could not be used for black missionaries.

In spite of these theological and structural inhibitions, by the 1930s, there were already some missionary efforts. One example is the QIM. When they started a new field in Igala, four evangelists from the Qua Iboe River area shared in the effort,[7] and when George Curry started to work in Bassa, a teacher from the same area was his first assistant.[8] A (rare) example of African missionary work without European involvement, but still crossing colonial borders, was the effort of WEC Christians from Equatorial Guinea to establish a church at Coco Beach in Gabun. This church still exists today.[9]

More cases could be mentioned which could be classified either as the spontaneous expansion of the church or as missionary work. A more recent case, where the missionary motive was conscious but no organizational structure was involved, is the case of Evaristo and his wife, both Papel, from Guinea Bissau, who emigrated into the Casamance District of Senegal. There, they established a small congregation and built a small church. They spoke Balanta well, and when the Balanta expelled most Papel immigrants from that area nobody harmed Evaristo and his wife. As in Guinea Bissau, they felt part of the Église Évangélique (WEC).[10] Another couple from Guinea Bissau, Chico and Nang Dasilva, were converted in Senegal and, in a dream, they were called to go to Gambia. They settled at Sibanor and, after WEC had established a mission there, joined their efforts and are now playing a leading role in the small Gambia Evangelical Church.[11]

Although more examples could be added to these, they are not typical of the general attitude of faith mission churches. Conscious missionary efforts were very rare between the wars but, later, things began to change in a number of churches. Today, the impression is being created in Western publications that there is a tremendous number of 'Third World missionaries', or 'Two-thirds World missionaries'. These impressions go back to the research of Lawrence E. Keyes[12] and are sometimes published

# Critical analysis of the Kenyan missions mentioned by Keyes

| | 1972 missionaries | 1980 missionaries | 1980 members |
|---|---|---|---|
| **I: African Independent Churches Members[16]** | | | |
| African Gospel Unity Church[17] | 52 | 130 | 1,500 |
| Covenant Baptist[18] | 4 | 4 | ? |
| The Ethiopian Orthodox Holy Spirit and United Churches of East Africa[19] | | 100 | ? |
| Holy Spirit Church of East Africa[20] | | 200 | 3,000 |
| Holy Trinity Church in Africa[21] | | 3 | 50,000 |
| Independent Lutheran Church[22] | | 2 | 1,000 |
| Lost Israelites of Kenya[23] | | 28 | 20,000 |
| Musanda Holy Ghost Church[24] | 235 | 350 | 5,073 |
| **II: Organized missionary societies or church mission departments** | | | |
| Africa Inland Church Mission Board | | 28 | 300,000 |
| Fellowship of Spreading Good News (AIC) | 3 | 8 | |

less critically than even Keyes saw them.[13] The number of these missionaries is given worldwide as 15,000 or 20,000.[14] New research even counts 14,989 African 'transcultural missionaries' alone.[15] (See table: Critical analysis of the Kenyan missions mentioned by Reyes.)

In order to evaluate Keyes' statistics properly, the three missionaries and 50,000 members of the Holy Trinity Church should be moved to Group II. The three missionaries are most probably those who care for the few congregations in North Mara in Tanzania. Having done this, Group II has 350,000 members and 38 missionaries. This looks realistic. In Group I, then, there are 32,573 members and 779 missionaries. This extremely high missionary density (42 members to a missionary) is not due to the eager missionary spirit of the African Independent Churches, but to misconstructed and misunderstood questionnaires (responses printed in full in Keyes, pp. 137–140. Keyes assumes that he has not discovered all the Kenyan missions. In this he is correct, at least insofar as he did not discover the dozen or so Africa Gospel Church missionaries. To account for undiscovered missionaries, he extrapolates the (827)[25] he found to 1,002. Thus, he finds in Kenya one-thirteenth (less than 8 per cent) of the 13,000 transcultural Third World missionaries—but, of these, about 80–90 per cent exist only in the questionnaires.

Keyes' and Pate's approach has two serious shortcomings. One has been described above: the data are not solid, with too much data stemming from questionnaires which were not understood by those who filled them in. The other shortcoming is the definition of 'transcultural'. Culture is identified by language, which is fine, for instance, for Japan, Germany and Rwanda, but I think that no one can claim that Tanzania has about 126 different cultures just because there are this number of 'tribes' speaking this number of languages, not counting immigrants. If every African church worker working in a different language area from his own should be counted as a 'transcultural Third World missionary', then Keyes' and Pate's statistics are short by tens of thousands.[26]

Keyes is right when he claims that a missionary must not necessarily cross *national* boundaries; even crossing cultural boundaries is a missionary affair. But these cultural barriers must be high enough to warrant the term 'missionary': if, for example, a Kenyan missionary from a (southern) agricultural people such as the Luo moves to a cattle-keeping people in the north, the culture shock may be as intense as for a European who goes to work among the Luo.[27] Similarly, there are major cultural frontiers within Nigeria. Another aspect which may help to define who is a missionary is missionary consciousness, that is: if someone belongs to a mission organization, defines himself as a missionary or obviously does such a work. Therefore, in order to clarify matters and bring statistics closer to reality, I offer this definition: a missionary is someone doing primarily evangelistic or pastoral work in another country, or in an area of his or her own country, which in terms of culture and/or religion is *distinctly* different from his or her own background *and* who conceives himself or herself as a missionary, or, if not doing so, obviously does such a work.

Even if Keyes' statistics are mostly wrong, he is right in claiming that missions from the 'Third World' are a major phenomenon that will shape church history. In current classical missiology, the hoped-for result of missionary work is in equal partnership with the now-independent church and sharing in mission with the 'young' church, perhaps even sending a missionary as fellow worker into the area of the 'old' church.[28] The emergence of missions from former mission fields has brought, at least among faith missions, a new final aim: the end result is not just the church but, again, missions. If in the early years, mission was sometimes considered to be a one-way road, and if more recent classical missiology has stressed that mission is a two-way road, most recent faith mission missiology would see mission as never-ending dominoes: one domino always makes another fall, sometimes two, and so the domino line splits and the many lines finally cover the whole world.

In the area of Africa which I have studied, there are three types of missions, and I will describe some of each type: mission activities without any special organization with what is done being done by the ordinary organs of the church; denominational missions or mission departments; and interdenominational missions.

Now and again, faith mission churches send out missionaries as co-workers in other churches, often a sister church originating from the same mission. CECA20 has repeatedly seconded pastors to work with the AIM in southern Sudan, and the various branches of the SUM not only exchanged missionaries, but also African evangelists and teachers. The Holiness Union in South Africa, going back to the Swedish Helgelseförbundet, on the suggestion of Mokwena, a driver in a mine, started missionary work in Buchum/Transvaal.[29] Occasionally, missionaries are even sent to other continents, for example, Bounda Mabiala and his wife, who were sent by the Église Évangélique du Congo (SMF) to Ecuador in 1980.[30] All these activities, important as they individually may be, do not much influence the missionary vision of the churches concerned.

## AFRICA GOSPEL CHURCH—MISSIONARY DEPARTMENT

If the missionary activities are a regular department of a church, they usually receive more consideration. This is the case with the Africa Gospel Church. Its missionary department is small, comprising twelve missionaries in 1988, but it is clearly an entity of its own within the church structure.[31] It was organized in 1970, but its origins go back to about 1967, when Fredrik Makibior, a Kipsigi who grew up on the border of the Masai territory, was willing to start missionary work in Naikarra among the Masai. He learned Masai well, as did, later, his wife Raeli, and they overcame their traditional aversion against the Masai who, for the neighbouring Kipsigi, were those who 'stole their cattle and their women'. The Makibiors built up the mission, including a school and a polyclinic, and established a congregation. For the first six years, they worked together with a US missionary. Since then, they have worked alone, with assistants from the AGC. Their work is successful, and there is now a second branch 30 km (20 miles) away. A self-help *harambee* secondary school is being planned.[32]

From the very beginning in West Pokot, no white missionaries were involved. The work was initiated on the suggestion of George Kendagor, a Pokot member of the AIC, who was not happy that his church did not work in West Pokot.[33] In the early phase, there was some instability but, since 1969, work has continued steadily. Today, the AGC Mission in the Chepnyal area has ten churches and fifteen schools. During the 1984–85 famine, up to 4,000 families were cared for.[34] The AGC calls its workers in Masai and West Pokot 'missionaries'. The missionary work is supervised by a committee of the church, but the inspiration for the missionary work comes mainly from the Kenya Highlands Bible College and the missionaries teaching there.[35]

## AFRICA INLAND CHURCH MISSIONARY BOARD (AICMB)

Much more important, relative to its church, is the AICMB. It is not a mission that is independent of its church, but it has an organization of its own and thus competes in some way with other structures in the church. It was founded in 1959 as a joint effort between AIC (then with only limited independence) and AIM.[36] The first areas of activity were to be southern Sudan and Turkana in northern Kenya, both areas in which the AIM was also active.[37] Political developments prevented the AICMB from working in Sudan but, in 1960, Peter Kisulu and his wife started to work in Turkana—at first together with Dr Anderson, then independently in Kalokol on the shores of Lake Turkana ('Lake Rudolph'). Peter Kisulu started a number of churches and schools,[38] shared in relief work and in the running of a successful fishing cooperative in Kalokol,[39] and both he and his wife learned to eat fish.[40] In 1978, Peter Kisulu became Assistant Coordinator of the AICMB;[41] he served in this post until his original plan to work as a missionary in the Sudan became possible.[42]

AICMB work among the Giriama, not far from the Kenyan coast, was also very successful. Although the Giriama were not Muslim, the first missionary—the Rev. Mutandia, a Kamba—found very few open doors in the beginning.[43] When the response improved considerably, AICMB money was insufficient. Thus, in 1974, Bishop Mulwa (AIC) requested help from the Christian Nationals Evangelism Commission (CNEC); the help received sufficed for ten missionaries,[44] and the work among the Giriama today is a separate district of the AIC, the Kilifi District.[45] Turkana is also a separate district.

At present, about forty missionaries are fully supported by the AICMB, and about the same number by district church councils[46] or occasionally even by a local church council.[47] The missionary work of the AIC is financed mainly by two collections on the first Sunday of the month.[48] The AICMB missionaries work mainly in the border areas of Kenya,[49] which are quite distinct in culture from the core area of AIC (Kamba, Kikuyu) and where the AICMB, sometimes in cooperation with AIM, does pioneer work. The work which has recently started in the Kakamega District cannot be counted as pioneer work. The AIM had refused to work there because too many missions were already active in that district.[50]

A special case, but not at all unique in the process of growing religious pluralism in East Africa, is the AICMB missionary work in eastern Uganda where, without any input from AIC, AIM or the AICMB, an African Independent Church of about forty congregations had formed. Because of an understanding between what used to be AIM and CMS that the AIM would work in Uganda only in unreached territory (West Nile Province)[51] and only as part of the (Anglican) Church of Uganda, the AIC was reluctant to do anything in eastern Uganda but did accept a young man from that church into one of its Bible schools. Meanwhile the leader had been able to procure Uganda government recognition under the name 'Africa Inland Church'. After some time, the Church of Uganda freed AIC from the old understanding with AIM, because the Church of Uganda realized that it could exert no influence whatsoever on the Africa Inland Church Uganda.[52] This process of a newly founded African Independent Church asking a neighbouring mission or church for help is quite common, and contributes measurably to the process of religious diversification in Africa.

The AICMB experiences the same problems as other missions experienced, and still experience. In the early years, the missionary intentions were sometimes greater than the means available, so that occasionally their missionaries did not receive their allowances.[53] Today, the missionaries receive their stipends regularly, whereas pastors sometimes run into problems.[54] The early AICMB missionaries were as unprepared to come to terms with a strange culture as were their AIM collegues two generations before. They had trouble in accepting Turkana and Masai patterns of hygiene and, like their European predecessors, they had problems accepting that nudity and goat skins were decent ways to dress.[55] The lack of sensitivity for the cultural differences between the pastoral northerners and the agricultural low-country Kenyans has led to a church culturally dominated by missionaries—but this time not by white missionaries, but by Kenyan missionaries who assume that the AIC in the whole country must have the same faith, rules, customs and usages.[56]

When every missionary comes from the same country in which they work, the issue of the independence of the young church is more difficult to settle: missionaries from overseas know that at some point in time they have to hand the leadership of the church over to nationals, but are missionaries from the same country not nationals? This has led to severe tensions in Kilifi District between the 'national' (Giriama) pastors and the 'foreign' (Kamba) pastors,[57] because AIC had carefully thought through the issue of the euthanasia of the mission with regard to AIM, but not with regard to its own mission.

## THE EVANGELICAL MISSIONARY SOCIETY, JOS

The EMS in Nigeria, being the missionary arm of ECWA, is probably the largest African mission,[58] and its director, the Rev. Panya Baba, is known internationally.[59] Its origins date back to 1948, when two Nigerians (Basufwa and Dogo) and an SIM missionary (McElheran) tried to encourage Nigerian congregations to send out Nigerian missionaries. In 1949, SIM asked them to start the 'African Missionary Society'. In 1950, the first missionary was sent to Tsanyawa (Kano State) in northern Nigeria.[60]

The African Missionary Society was later renamed the Evangelical Missionary Society. As an organization, it is older than ECWA.[61] Despite its later integration into ECWA, EMS has retained its own administrative structures and its independence, because it administrates its own money and has its own income. The mission has a central office with a clearly defined leadership,[62] and there is an EMS district coordinator active in each of the thirteen district church councils.[63] Currently (end of 1987), the central office is being enlarged and, during the next few years, the number of EMS missionaries is expected to double to 900 or 1,000.[64] EMS missionaries work in all parts of Nigeria, but most of its approximately 500 missionaries work in the north, outside the original SIM/ECWA area.[65] It is EMS strategy to reach, first of all, those 'heathen' groups which have withstood the southward spread of Islam, partly by withdrawing into remote areas. The greatest 'discovery' in this respect were the Maguzawa, about 5 per cent (some 500,000) of all Hausa speakers,[66] who had 'run away' from Islam, as their name implies.

In 1975, Gerald Swank conducted a survey commissioned by the Nigeria Evangelical Fellowship to find all unreached people groups which were not more than 75 per cent Islamized.[67] This study made the EMS aware of the Maguzawa and of their readiness to change their religion. It soon became apparent that the envisaged ten EMS missionary couples were far too few. Today, seventy EMS couples work among the Maguzawa. As their readiness to become Christians was so unexpectedly great, many evangelists, especially Bible school students just after finishing their courses, worked for one year[68] or for even shorter periods among the Maguzawa,[69] although EMS tries, even among the Maguzawa, to work only with long-term missionaries.[70] Another emergency measure were three-month Bible courses for Maguzawa only, taught by ECWA pastors.[71] Today (1987), about 500 Maguzawa attend Bible schools full-time.[72]

In addition to working in the 'pagan' withdrawal areas of the north (which absorbs most of the missionaries), about twenty EMS missionaries also do 'diaspora work' in the south, in a few cases, in 'Catholic areas'.[73] An important—though in terms of numbers, still small—aspect of EMS's work is foreign missions. One couple works at Accra in Ghana and has established a Hausa diaspora congregation there.[74] In Niger, EMS cooperates with SIM in the context of the Églises évangéliques du Niger. EMS does the most independent foreign missionary work in Chad, where twelve EMS missionaries work. In 1987, the Chad government officially recognized EMS.[75] Most of the missionaries are Chad citizens who had lived in Nigeria for many years. Most of them had worked as EMS missionaries in Nigeria, but had to leave when Chadian residents were expelled. The EMS intends to increase its foreign activities.[76] The Nigerian currency regulations, restricting the transfer of money abroad, make this difficult[77] but, in the future, EMS also wants to include urban evangelism in its activities.

A comparison between the missionary work of ECWA and COCIN[78] suggests that independent structures serve missionary purposes better than full integration into the structures of the church. COCIN is half the size of ECWA,[79] both have their administrative offices in Jos, only three minutes walking distance from each other, and both work in similar areas of the country,[80] but ECWA has ten times as many missionaries as COCIN.[81] COCIN missionary work is centred in Bornu State in north-eastern Nigeria. One missionary also worked as a teacher of theology in Sudan.[82] The COCIN missionary work is similar to that of the EMS.[83] Over the past decades, the Qua Iboe Church has had little missionary consciousness, but it is now starting to develop a missionary vision.[84]

## TO AWAKEN THE MISSIONARY VISION: MISSION CECCA ZAIRE

Just as in the economically advanced countries of Western Europe (Britain, The Netherlands), the missionary spirit awoke first, and so Kenya and Nigeria are ahead of other countries in Africa. Compared to Kenya, north-east Zaire is equally evangelical, but extremely poor. It is astonishing that a church in such a situation tries to develop a missionary vision.

The origins go back to Kilcreggan in Scotland. Nonziodane Maronzi, Représentant Légal and leader of CECCA16, attended the worldwide WEC conference INTERCON I.[85] He came back with the question as to why his church was not sending out any missionaries.[86] Among the WEC missionaries in CECCA16, Margaret White, teacher at Ibambi Secondary School, took up the idea.[87] At the General Assembly in 1983, Nonziodane encouraged his church to decide in principle that it wanted to become a sending church.[88] After careful preparation, the first missionaries were to be sent out in 1987.[89] In 1983, a mission committee was formed and, since then, a regular two-page missionary leaflet has been published.[90] Attempts were made to interest the congregations in missions, and missionary representatives were selected for every area. Every pastor, evangelist and catechist received the magazine and, everywhere, mission prayer groups were formed. Money was collected for the first missionaries.[91] Mission information centred on the francophone countries, where WEC was working.

It was not easy to decide if the future missionaries of CECCA16 (or of Mission Mondiale, later renamed Mission CECCA Zaire (MCZ)) were to work for WEC or for CECCA16. The solution was that CECCA16 would send the missionaries through its missions department, called Mission CECCA Zaire, that they would work initially in West Africa within the respective churches and that WEC would assist and advise.[92] Another issue to be solved was that of financial support. It was decided to accept money from abroad, but not actively to solicit such support.[93] In 1985, three couples applied to become missionaries. The couple, Mbongo and Idoti, was sent to Kisangani to gain experience in diaspora work; the couples, Nefunga and Kanina, and Kokyakake and Ebayite, went through the candidate course conducted by Margaret White at Ibambi in 1986.[94]

Early in 1987, the CECCA16 general assembly decided to allocate some money towards sending missionaries.[95] CECCA16 appointed Sadeyna, who had perviously worked in his spare time for the missions department, to be its coordinator,[96] working in both the health service and for Mission CECCA Zaire. Margaret White became assistant coordinator.[97] The name of the mission had to be changed; because the name Mission Mondial sounded somewhat like 'Conseil Mondial des Églises' (World Council of

Churches) and misunderstandings had arisen, the name Mission CECCA Zaire (MCZ) was chosen.[98] Like other missions, there were problems in its early phase: Kokyakake, candidate for Chad, could not go there late in 1986[99] and, because of serious health problems, Nefunga could not leave for the Ivory Coast.[100] All this meant delay so, for a time, the main activity of the mission, for which Margeret White gave up teaching, remained mission-ary motivation.[101] Since the end of 1988, Nefunga and Kanina have successfully worked in the Ivory Coast.

AFRICAN INTERDENOMINATIONAL FAITH MISSIONS

The second stage in the development of African missionary initiatives is that of interdenominational faith missions.[102] Their number, contrary to Keyes' statistics, is still limited,[103] but it is growing. Three early West African faith missions may serve as examples.[104]

During an Easter house party, a number of young Ghanaians realized that many people in their country had never heard the gospel and would stand little chance of hearing it before the year 2000 if missionary progress were not speeded up. Immediately, the interdenominational Christian Outreach Fellowship (COF) was organized and, in 1976, legally incorporated, although it was only in 1982 that COF became really active. It is the aim of the COF to identify unreached areas and villages in Ghana, and to start missionary work there or to get other churches or missions to do so. Like the early classical missions, COF is organized as a voluntary association. The basic units are the COF core groups.[105] Like faith missions, COF is interdenominational, controlled by a council[106] and follows the 'faith principle'. COF has offices in Accra and Kumasi, its director is William Ofori Atta[107] and its ten missionaries work in various areas of Ghana.[108]

After finishing their university courses, Bayo Famunore and a few other young people from southern Nigeria were sent for their national service to Soba, not far from Zaria. With the permission of the Emir of Zaria, they evangelized in the town. They believed that northern Nigeria was to be the area of their future mission-ary service. After finishing national service, Bayo Famonure remained in northern Nigeria, working for NIFES (Nigeria Fellowship of Evangelical Students) and, together with Amos Aderonmu, who later became the first full-time worker of the new organization, he started to build up CAPRO (Calvary Productions/Calvary Ministries)[109] with the aim of evangelizing among the unreached people groups in Nigeria and abroad. About a dozen missionaries now (1987) work among the Maguzawa, Mumuye, Gwari and Dukkawa.[110] Abroad, CAPRO works in various countries. It has not yet established a mission field of its own, but it has been officially recognized in Senegal, being the first African mission there.[111] In addition, CAPRO has set itself the task of developing a missionary vision among Nigerian Christians, mainly by means of 'mission awareness seminars', and by visits to churches and groups.[112] 'The mind of Nigerian Christians is foreign to missions, we think of Whites' (Naomi Famunore). The missions centre was initially at Soba, then in Zaria. It then moved to Kafanchan, where the missionaries and candidates built their own buildings in simple style (now, the Discipleship Training School). The next step was to be in Jos, in rented premises. Induced by a prophetic utterance in a prayer meeting that they should have a 'mining compound', they enquired from the various mining companies and were welcomed into Gana Ropp Mining Compound (near Barkina Ladi, Jos). It was no longer needed and their occupancy of it saved the mining company from further vandalism. Gana Ropp is now the centre of the mission, and houses its Missionary Training Institute.

Much in CAPRO is reminiscent of the early faith missions: leaders, missionaries and students lead a kind of communal life in Gana Ropp; the churches and their structures are not being taken too seriously; a wide vision; lack of money and comfort; willingness to sacrifice; and contagious enthusiasm. There is another striking parallel: women are equals. They receive the same training as the men, both sexes share in the manual jobs, a woman (Naomi Famunore) is CAPRO's training secretary, and single women can do independent evangelistic work, whereas in the earlier Nigerian missions only married couples are accepted.[113]

The sociological background is unusual: for CAPRO's missionaries, university training is normal;[114] with EMS, it is the rare exception.[115] The language of communication among the missionaries, and of instruction at the training institute, is English.[116] Many of the students who work with CAPRO or maintain contact with it come from NIFES, and it is quite possible that the interdenominational character of CAPRO is patterned after NIFES, which has a charismatic spirituality similar to CAPRO and which does much to promote 'missionary awareness'.[117] CAPRO now (1993) has 145 missionaries,[118] the training schools and also a media department, which publishes two magazines and a few books, and contributes to films and radio programmes.[119]

Another Nigerian faith mission is the Christian Missionary Foundation (CMF), founded by Reuben E. Ezemadu in Ibadan. It comes from the background of the Christian Students Social Movement of Nigeria (CSSM).[120] After hearing a talk on the 'missionary challenge facing Nigerian Christians today' during the 1981 CSSM conference, fifty-seven volunteered and, in September 1981, the CMF was founded with the motto: 'Ministering the whole word to the whole man in the whole world.'[121]

Its aim is to establish churches in areas unreached or not well reached,[122] in Nigeria and abroad[123] but, at present, missionary motivation seems be prominent. This motivating effort is not confined to Nigeria. In other African countries, CMF also tries to establish missionary centres which finance themselves.[124] The first such centre, some of whose members were trained in Lagos, has been established in Malawi. From Kenya, evangelistic efforts were undertaken in the neighbouring countries. As far as possible, the missionaries are to earn their own support as 'volunteer missionaries' in the country where they work.[125] This is a variation on the industrial mission idea, also developed in a situation of financial stringency, because it is difficult to get permission to transfer money out of Nigeria.

## AFRICAN MISSIONARY TRAINING INSTITUTES

In the realm of faith mission churches, growing mission awareness has resulted not only in the birth of denominational and interdenominational missions, but also of the very first African missionary training institutes. One has already been mentioned: Gana Ropp, where CAPRO conducts a nine-month course for its own missionaries, but which members of other missions may attend. The most developed institute is currently the Missionary Training College in Eldoret, belonging to the Africa Inland Church.

When visiting AICMB missionaries in his capacity as a member of the board,[126] the Rev. Samson Bet (Eldoret) observed that the growing number of AICMB missionaries did not lack enthusiasm, but often encountered problems for which they had not been prepared.[127] In about 1979, he became convinced that Kenyan missionaries would also need specialized training, just as the Western missionaries had.[128] In his (western) section of AIC, he won support for his idea[129] to start the training institute for missionaries.[130] A committee was formed to bring the idea into reality.[131] In these developments, no non-Kenyans were involved—officially or unofficially. On 2 July 1982, the committee decided to ask Jonathan Hildebrandt, AIM missionary then on home leave, to be the director of the college.[132] About the same time, it was decided that the new institute was not to be part of an existing Bible school or college, but an independent institution in a separate locality. The question of locality was solved by Mr and Mrs Limo, farmers near Eldoret,[133] who donated thirty acres of their farm.[134] In all, Kenyan Christians donated more than 2 million Kshs for the college,[135] not counting the value of the land.[136] Later, overseas organizations also helped.[137]

In 1986, the Missionary College at Eldoret started its first course with twelve students.[138] Four couples ran the college and the course. The next course was to take in twenty-two students; full capacity will be one hundred.[139] The college is AIC property, but also accepts students from other churches. The prospective students must have finished four years' study of theology[140] and have sufficient command of English. If students are married, both husband and wife have to take part in the course, although usually the wives work only for the 'certificate in missiology', whereas the men work for the 'diploma in missiology'.[141] There is a kindergarten for small children. The theoretical subjects, mainly anthropology and missiology, are taught in the morning;[142] in the afternoon, the practical subjects are taught: agriculture, animal husbandry and mechanics. All students have to learn to care for cattle and goats, and to milk them, because most of them will work among people who keep cattle. The culture shock involved is sometimes considerable. They also learn to repair bicycles, to service motor cycles and to do basic repairs, because bicycles and motor cycles will be the normal means of transport. The full course lasts sixteen months, and consists of three terms' course work, with a longer and a shorter period of practical work. During the longer spell, the students are visited by a teacher at least twice.[143] The staff of the school is international: from the United States, Kenya and Korea.[144]

The Eldoret Missionary College's capacity is greater than the immediate needs of the Kenyan missions, so it may be expected that it will not only serve these missions, but also foster new developments. The first course has already helped AICMB missionaries to clarify their identity as missionaries in distinction from AIC pastors.[145]

The Nigerian missions have gone furthest in establishing their common identity. This process has found expression in the formation of the first evangelical national mission council, the Nigeria Evangelical Missions Association (NEMA). The idea goes back to Panya Baba (EMS) who, while attending a meeting of the World Evangelical Federation (WEF) Missions Commission, was challenged by Ernst Vatter of the German Liebenzeller Mission to start an organization of Nigerian missions. When Panya Baba tried, enthusiasm was, at first, very limited. When he tried again, he met with success because he was supported by CAPRO, which had meanwhile gained in stature.[146] NEMA now (1987) has seven members: three denominational missions with a background in faith mission churches (EMS (ECWA), COCIN (SUM), United Missionary Church);[147] three interdenominational missions (CAPRO, CMF and His Grace Evangelical Movement)[148]; one mission which at the same time is a church (Gospel Faith Mission)[149]; and the Nigerian Fellowship of Evangelical Students, which does not itself send out missionaries.[150] The general secretary of NEMA is Reuben Ezemedu, director of CMF.[151]

An important activity for which NEMA is responsible is the Nigeria Evangelical Missionary Training Institute (NEMTI) in Kagoro, south west of Kano.[152] It is the first interdenominational missionary training institute in Africa not tied to one mission. NEMTI has, as yet, no buildings of its own. Its three seven-week courses are held at Kagoro Bible Institute during its vacations. Its director, Wilbur O'Donovan, is an SIM missionary, seconded part-time to NEMTI. In 1987, the Missionary Church seconded Lois Fuller as a full-time teacher.[153]

NEMTI would not have come into existence without the growing interest of Nigerian students in missions. Wilbur O'Donovan was a frequent conference speaker and often appealed for mission volunteers. Many volunteered and asked where they could be trained, but he could only give them foreign addresses.[154] In 1984, during its general assembly in Ilorin, Panya Baba suggested to NEMA that it start its own missionary training institute.[155] When NEMA met again, in December 1984, O'Donovan was asked to establish the school for NEMA.[156] Because the school does not yet have any buildings of its own, every year only one term can be taught, which is not conducive to continuity.[157] An additional disadvantage is that the course has to take place during the rainy season.

In some faith mission churches, there is obviously a nascent missionary movement getting under way. Missions and missionary training institutes are fruits and bearers of this new missionary movement. Some of the larger Western and international faith missions, such as AIM, SIM and, especially, WEC, have taken note of this movement and try to contribute to it. Some developments seem to run parallel to those in Europe one or two centuries ago. It started with denominational missions, after which an interdenominational variety developed. The new African missions also seem to flourish best when they keep their distance from the churches. Obviously there is much energy for missions available on a level below that of the church leaders. It is also obvious that the resources for missions in countries such as Kenya or Nigeria, even in the financial realm, are not yet exhausted. Further growth of this new African missionary movement can be expected, but it will have to take place under severe financial restraints. It remains to be seen what influences will emanate from South Africa as a sending base for missions in black Africa, once South Africa has been fully integrated into black Africa.[158] The missionary training institutes have also made a start in creating an African missiology, not in the sense of creating a missiology that is independent of, and different from, European or US missiology, but nevertheless a missiology that is *relevant* to Africa.

**Notes**

1   The lives of far too few of them have been described in booklets such as: Gracie Bill, *David Ekong. Called. Chosen. Faithful. The Story of the First Convert and Pastor of the Qua Iboe Mission*, n.d.; Burnette and Gerald Fish and Richard and Mrs Adkins, *The Call to Battle*, Kericho, 1982 (Johana Ng'etich, AGC); Samuel Hussein Ali, *Aus meinem Leben*, Wiesbaden, 1920 (SPM).

2   The role of Africans, mainly Ganda, in the spread of Christianity in Uganda is thoroughly described in: Louise Pirouet, *Black Evangelists. The Spread of Christianity in Uganda 189–1914*, London, 1978. See also: A. D. Tom Tuma, *Building a Ugandan Church. African Participation in Church Growth and Expansion in Busoga 1891–1940*, Nairobi, 1980.

3   In 1896, Apolo Kivebulaya, from Toro in Uganda, at great personal risk and sacrifice, started missionary work in the then independent Mboga. This later

developed into the first francophone Anglican diocese (now Boga, north-eastern Zaire). See Pirouet, *Black Evangelists*, especially pp. 50–58. See: A. Luck, *African Saint: the Story of Apolo Kivebulaya*, London, 1963.

4   E. A. Ayandele, *The Missionary Impact on Modern Nigeria 1842–1914*, London, 1966, especially pp. 1–154. The story of Bishop Crowther dramatically shows the change of attitude in about 1885.

5   Interview Geoffrey Larcombe, 5 October 1985. The early comity agreements and the colonial mindset played a role in this, but so also did the geography of the Equatorial forest and the fact that the first CBM Bible school was only established in the 1930s (Larcombe—Fiedler, 7 April 1993).

6   A. B. Simpson, 'Christianity's Crime', Asbury Park Convention sermon, 31 July 1892, on Proverbs 24:11f. in Simpson, *Missionary Messages*, pp. 69–83.

7   *Qua Iboe Mission Annual Report 1933*.

8   *Qua Iboe Mission Annual Report 1936*.

9   Leslie Brierley—Fiedler, 29 October 1987.

10   Interview Frank Lyttleton, 28 July 1986.

11   Circular letter Maria Röbbelen, 2 May 1972.

12   Lawrence E. Keyes, *The Last Age of Missions. A Study of Third World Missionary Societies*, Pasadena, 1983.

13   For example, by Larry D. Pate and Lawrence E. Keyes, 'Emerging Missions and the Global Church' in *East Asia's Millions*, 1988, pp. 82, 87.

14   These figures are derived from Keyes' 13,000 missionaries in 1980, his projection of 15,249 for 1981 and from some extrapolation for future growth. Half of these missionaries would be Africans. For 1972, he computed 2,971 'cross-cultural third world missionaries' (Keyes, *The Last Age of Missions*, p. 64). Not to be overlooked is his critical assessment of the questionnaires received from Kenya and Nigeria, with their high figures.)

15   Larry D. Pate, *From Every People. A Handbook of Two-thirds World Missions*, Monrovia, CA, 1989, p. 47.

16   Membership according to *WCE* (mid-1970s).

17   Separated in 1964 from the African Gospel Church, with about 10 per cent of the membership (David Barrett *et al.*, *Kenya Churches Handbook*, Kisumu, 1973, p. 230). It has not experienced major growth since then (*WCE*: 1,500 members). My visit to the area confirmed this information.

18   Mentioned neither in *Kenya Churches Handbook* nor in *WCE*.

19   Mentioned neither in *Kenya Churches Handbook* nor in *WCE*.

20   Founded in 1927, 3,000 members (*WCE*).

21   Founded in 1960 as a split-off from Church of Christ in Africa, Masogo diocese has sixteen pastorates. There are also congregations in the area of Mombasa and in North Mara, Tanzania, 50,000 members (*WCE*).

22   Founded in 1961, 1,000 members (*WCE*).

23 Founded in 1960 in Kitale, 20,000 members (*WCE*), partly in west Uganda. In its questionnaire, the church only mentions missionary work in Uganda. There is little cultural difference between the people on both sides of the border.

24 Originated in a revival within CMS, forced into separation in 1934. In 1939, there were new splits, with more later. Slow growth, 5,073 members (*WCE*).

25 I can only arrive at a total of 817.

26 Klaus Fiedler, 'Wo sind die 20,000?—Eine kritische Analyse von Lawrence E. Keyes' Konzept der "transkulturellen Drittweltmissionare" und der ihm zugrundeliegenden Daten' in *Evangelikale Missiologie* 3, 1989, pp. 37–40.

27 That was definitely my experience when I travelled to Marsabit in northern Kenya in the company of students from the Eldoret Missionary Training College in December 1986.

28 Kambala Mangolopa, one such missionary, coming from a church that was originally founded by a faith mission, is now (1987) working in Dortmund in connection with the Vereinigte Evangelische Mission. He comes from the Communauté Baptistes du Kivu (CBK3), which has its roots in the Unevangelized Africa Mission.

29 Interview Håkan Wistrand, 13 June 1986.

30 Hilaire Nkounkou *et al.*, *75e Anniversaire de la Fondation de Madzia* 27; Interview Riitta Siikannen, 10 June 1986. They had to return after a severe accident in January 1983.

31 Pate, *From Every People*, p. 233.

32 Interview Richard Adkins, 17 December 1986.

33 In the area of Chepnyal, the Bible Churchmen's Missionary Society had evangelized some, but they were glad that the AGC was willing to work there intensively (Interview Richard Adkins, 17 December 1986).

34 Important missionaries are Edward and Evaline Tonui (Interview Richard Adkins, 17 December 1986). There is, as yet, only one Pokot evangelist, Paul Loboti (Interview Henry N'geno, 18 December 1986).

35 The moderator of AGC is at the same time responsible for the missionary department. This means that there are no competing structures and authorities.

36 Peter Mualuko Kisulu, *A Missionary Called Peter*, Kijabe, 1983, p. 15.

37 Tom Collins, AIM pioneer in East Pokot, had tried to win an entry into Turkana by evangelistic visits (K. N. Phillips, *Tom Collins of Kenya. Son of Valour*, London, 1965, pp. 101ff., see also p. 70). The first missionary allowed to settle in Turkana was Dick Anderson, a medical doctor, in 1959.

38 Raymond H. Davis, 'A Study of the AIC among Kenya's Turkana People', MA, Fuller, Pasadena, 1978, p. 65. See: Kisulu, *A Missionary Called Peter*, p. 20.

39 Kisulu, *A Missionary Called Peter*, p. 24; Davis, 'A Study', p. 104. The cooperative had 2,000 members in 1978. Kisulu began his missionary work in Turkana in a period of severe social change caused by population growth, draught periods and external influences.

40 Kisulu, *A Missionary Called Peter*, p. 22.

41 Kisulu, *A Missionary Called Peter*, p. 26. The coordinator was Michael Donovan.

42 See Kisulu, *A Missionary called Peter*, p. 27, for his intention to work in Sudan. *CNEC Partners Prayer Guide 1985–1986*, p. 51f. describes his work among the Toposa as a AICMB missionary, being supported by Christian Nationals Evangelism Commission (Partners International).

43 The first breakthrough occurred in Mashahini village. He had been invited there, because he had lent Kshs 60 to a woman who had come to Malindi for a difficult delivery (Interview Jonathan Hildebrandt, 14 December 1986).

44 Finley and Lutz, *The Family Tie*, p. 44f. CNEC assisted AICMB through 1991.

45 Interview Jonathan Hildebrandt, 14 December 1986. Interview Christian Friedrich, 20 December 1986.

46 Interview the Rev. Samson Bet, President of AICMB, 14 December 1986.

47 Interview the Rev. Samson Bet, 14 December 1986. Bet greatly approves of direct involvement of local congregations. AIC Machakos congregation, for example, paid for the first church building among the Giriama (Interview Jonathan Hildebrand, 14 December 1986). The AIC Eldoret women's group travelled several times to Pokot to help there (Interview Mrs Limo, 14 December 1986).

48 The fact that first Sundays (with larger offerings than other Sundays) were chosen shows the importance accorded to AICMB (Interview the Rev. Samson Bet, 14 December 1986).

49 Turkana, Wajir, Isiolo, Marsabit, Lungalunga (near the border with Tanzania); Masai, Malindi, Shimba Hills (south of Mombasa); West Pokot (Interview the Rev. Samson Bet, 14 December 1986). Two AICMB missionaries work in the AIC Tana District, and have founded two of its eighteen congregations (Interview Pastor Samson Kozi Maliwa, 20 December 1986).

50 The work in Kakamega is part of two developments: among the 'territorial churches' everywhere in East Africa there is a tendency to establish congregations outside its original territory; the area of Kakamega shows an extreme religious pluralism with a proliferation of so-called African Independent Churches. The Africa Inland Church effort in that area is part of that proliferation.

51 It started there in 1918 (John Dobson, *Daybreak in West Nile*, London, n.d.)

52 Interview Jonathan Hildebrand, 15 December 1986.

53 See, for example: Kisulu, *A Missionary Called Peter*, p. 25.

54 Interview Jonathan Hildebrand, 14 December 1986.

55 Kisulu, *A Missionary Called Peter*, p. 20f.; Interview Jonathan Hildebrandt, Eldoret, 14 December 1986.

56 In 1977, the Turkana District was led by two Turkana, four whites and four 'down-country' Kenyans. The white missionaries were generally more open to Turkana culture, for example, to their custom of drinking the blood of their cattle. They also had more tolerance for polygamy (Davis, 'A Study', pp. 77, 80ff.;

Interview Jonathan Hildebrandt, 14 December 1986). None of the 'down-country' Kenyans preaches in Turkana, not even the Chairman of Turkana District Church Council who is married to Ana Maraka, the only Turkana woman ever to have been to a Bible school (p. 81). Ana Maraka plays an important role in the church's women's work in Turkana. The basic attitude of the Kenyan missionaries is that AIC must be the same church in all of Kenya (Interview Malcolm Collins, 10 December 1987).

57  For a period of one year, the young Giriama pastors managed to take over the leadership from the old Kamba pastors (Interview Jonathan Hildebrandt, 14 December 1986; Interview Christian Friedrich, 20 December 1986).

58  Keyes, *The Last Age of Missions*, p. 142 counts 1,250 for the Church of the Lord 'Aladura', but Keyes himself questions (p. 66) if they all fit his definition of a 'cross-cultural missionary'. He applies the same to the Ghanaian Apostles Revelation Society (p. 69) with its 569 missionaries. According to WCE it has 60,000 members.

59  At present (1987), Panya Baba is also President of ECWA. See: Panya Baba, 'Arise and Let Us Rebuild ECWA. The Address of ECWA President at the Consultation Meeting of the DCC Chairmen and Secretaries, October 25th-26th, 1988, Jos' in *ECWA Today*, No. 6, April 1989.

60  N.N., *The Evangelical Missionary Society of the Evangelical Churches of West Africa*, Jos, n.d.

61  The organization of ECWA began in 1954. In 1956, it was registered officially (Ian M. Hay, *A Study of the Relationship Between SIM International and the Evangelical Missionary Society*, DMiss, Trinity, Deerfield, 1984, p. 151).

62  EMS headquarters are under the leadership of Panya Baba as director; his secretary is Ruth Cox, from the United States; and, as second in command, Pastor James Gabis, who studied for two years at All Nations Christian College in Britain; 'travel coordinator' is Samson Deba (1987).

63  *ECWA Prayer Guide and Directory*, Jos, 1985.

64  *EMS News 1987*; James Gabis, circular letter, end of 1986.

65  According to April 1986 statistics, EMS had 465 missionaries, of whom at least 285 were working in northern Nigeria beyond the original ECWA/SIM area.

66  Because the Maguzawa speak Hausa and live in different areas, they were recognized only at a late stage as a separate group of people. There were even a few mission stations among them, such as Malumfashi (SIM/ECWA), later to become the centre of EMS missionary work among the Maguzawa.

67  Published as Gerald O. Swank, *Frontier Peoples of Central Nigeria and a Strategy for Outreach*, Pasadena, 1977.

68  For 1979, a further 52 couples were to work in this way (the Rev. Panya Baba, *Progress Report of Work Among the Maguzawa*, December 1978).

69  Their employment had inflated statistics. The 1986 statistics contain only those missionaries who were to work at least three years for EMS. Three-quarters of the EMS missionaries stay longer in EMS.

70  Panya Baba, *Evangelism Report L. O. Seminar, Jos 16.–17.2.1982*; Interview the

Rev. Panya Baba, 3 February 1987.

71 Panya Baba, *Progress Report*, December 1978. Between January and March 1979, 800 participated in Bible courses. (Circular letter, Panya Baba, June 1979).

72 *EMS News*, 1987

73 For example, in Obudu, Cross River State (the Rev. David Thomas, 'Report on my Missionary Journey to Obudu C.R.S.', 1 October 1984). In 1987, the congregation was officially registered, but the officer refused the names EMS and ECWA as 'unknown' and suggested that it be registered under the name ELWA church, because their preaching was so similar to that of Radio ELWA, the SIM radio station in Monrovia, Liberia. The missionary Sabo Kurah accepted the name suggested to him (*EMS News*, 1987).

74 Circular letter, EMS, June 1979.

75 The original application dated 1985 (Interview the Rev. Panya Baba, 4 February 1987; *EMS News*, 1987).

76 Interview Panya Baba, 4 February 1987.

77 Interview Alastair M. Kennedy, 10 January 1987.

78 COCIN: Churches of Christ in Nigeria, going back to SUM.

79 According to *WCE*, COCIN has 220,000 members; and ECWA, 500,000.

80 ECWA was started by SIM in 1902; COCIN by SUM in 1904.

81 Interview Wilbur O'Donovan, 6 February 1987; Interview the Rev. Petrobas S. Oashi, 6 February 1987. The numbers are difficult to compare. Oashi counts thirty-two missionary couples, including those in Abuja, the country's new capital.

82 Interview the Rev. Petrobas S. Oashi, 6 February 1987.

83 See Jean Hamilton, *A Stranger Came. An Account of the Missionary Enterprise of the Church of Christ in Nigeria as Told Through the Lives of Some Nigerian Missionaries*, Sidcup, 1984.

84 Interview Wilbur O'Donovan, 6 February 1987. The missionary work in the Agenebode area on the western side of the Niger is now developing well (W. E. Leach—Fiedler, 12 May 1993)

85 WEC, *International Leaders' Conference. Report and Resolutions 3–26 June 78*, Gerrards Cross, 1978.

86 Interview the Rev. Nonziodane Maronzi, 12 January 1986.

87 Later, Douglas Craik also cooperated (Interview Annette Botting 12 January 1986).

88 Minutes Missionary Conference, 9–16 January 1983.

89 1983: information; 1984: information, prayer groups, collecting funds; 1985: preparing to train missionaries; 1986: first candidate course; 1987: first missionaries sent out (Interview the Rev. Nonziodane Maronzi, 26 April 1984).

90 In 1984 (Number 4), 1,600 copies were made: *Tazama* (Swahili) 800; *Botala* (Lingala) 600; *Regardez* (French) 200 (Minutes Comité de la Mission CECCA Zaire, 3 August 1984).

91 1984–1986: 42,165 Zaire. Double this amount was contributed from abroad (information shared at the meeting of the CECCA16 mission committee on 13 January 1987).

92 Interview Annette Botting, 14 January 1987; interview Alastair M. Kennedy 10 January 1987.

93 Minutes Mission Mondiale (MCZ), 23 May 1983.

94 *Tazama* No. 11, April 1986.

95 The Mission CECCA Zaire is responsible for its own finances; nevertheless, the church as such contributes the same amount as it pays for the leader of the church.

96 Sadeyna had organized regular mission motivation seminars in and around Ibambi. As it was in early faith mission days, he also reports conversions as a 'side effect' of these activities (Interview Sadeyna, 14 January 1987).

97 Lokanya Ntuafu (Lubutu), mission representative in the southern area of the church, suggested making Margaret White (who was at that time in Britain) the coordinator, because the constitution was designed in such a way as to require a European as coordinator and because money from Europe would come to a European coordinator. His argument was understood, but the general opinion prevailed that a Zairois, enthusiastic for world missions, would be a better coordinator, and that money from Europe would still come to Margaret White even if she were only assistant coordinator (meeting of Comité Mission Mondial, 14 January 1987).

98 Meeting of Comitée Mission Mondial, 14 January 1987.

99 The small WEC team in Chad deemed the situation too difficult. Early in 1987, he was elected to lead the church as Réprésentant légal (*The Frontiersman*, 2, 1988, p. 14). Renewed plans to go to Chad were blocked by the November 1991 disturbances. Having been released from leadership responsibilities in 1993, he is planning a new attempt for November 1993. (Margaret White—Fiedler, 13 April 1993).

100Margaret White—Ans van Wageningen, 3 December 1987.

101Margaret White—Fiedler, 17 October 1987. One result is that CECCA16 tries harder to reach the few small unreached people groups in its area (Tazama 16 and 17, July and October 1987). Through Botala, a pastor received the call to work in Lowa (Meeting of Comitée Mission Mondial, 14 January 1987).

102In Asia, too, interdenominational missions are the second stage. For one of the more important interdenominational Asian missions, see: Esther Williams, *Sacrifice or Investment. Indian Evangelical Mission 1965–1985*, Bangalore, 1985.

103Keyes counts twenty-nine of his seventy-seven African missions as interdenominational. With twenty-two of them he is obviously wrong—as their names show (for example: Church of Melchizedek; Musanda Holy Ghost Church; Evangelical Lutheran Church of Tanzania, Department of Missions and Evangelism). AEF (South Africa) and Dorothea Mission (Zimbabwe) are branches of international faith missions, I could not find out the nature of two missions. This means that there remain three (possibly five) interdenominational African missions: Souls Salvation Society (Egypt), African Enterprise (South

Africa, not mentioned in Kenya) and Christian Outreach Fellowship (Ghana), with all in all fifty-four missionaries. Instead of 44 per cent, only 4 per cent or 6 per cent of Keyes' African missions are interdenominational.

104An untypical interdenominational African mission is African Enterprise, founded in 1964 by white South Africans and black Kenyans. Its piety is close to that of the East African Revival, Bishop Festo Kivengere being one of its early leaders. It wants to testify that black and white Africans are one in Christ and do evangelistic team work, especially in urban situations. It also organized the Pan African Christian Leadership Assembly (PACLA) in Nairobi during 9–19 December 1976 (Michael Cassidy and Gottfried Osei-Mensah, *Together in One Place. The Story of PACLA*, Kisumu, 1978; Michael Cassidy and Luc Verlinden, *Facing the New Challenges. The Message of PACLA*, Kisumu, 1978).

105'As part of its strategy, COF seeks to establish a cadre of core members throughout Ghana, who will place the affairs of COF among their highest priorities. These core members should gather in their own localities to form COF core groups. These core groups are to be responsible, self-motivating, practically self-governing constituencies of COF.'

106The council is composed of representatives of leading denominations and organizations such as SIM, WEC, Scripture Union, Maranatha Bible College, Christian Service College, Campus Crusade and Navigators.

107COF—Fiedler, 17 June 1987.

108Mentioned are: Chiana (Upper East Region), Klonu and Anfoe Mafi (Volta Region), Hebron and Mensah Krom (Rural Accra).

109Unless otherwise stated, all information based on: interview Naomi Anne Famunore, Training Secretary of CAPRO, 5 February 1987.

110Work among the Kanuri and Hausa (in Kaduna State) is planned. For more details on the people groups mentioned, see: *LOOK* (Nigeria), special celebration 1986 issue.

111Workers abroad to date as follows: Gambia (with WEC) Victoria Hasan (she now (1987) works among the Gwari in Nigeria (*Occupy*, special celebrations edition, 1986)) and Amos Aderonmu, two years each; presently no one. Senegal: one couple, two young men. (see: Amos Aderonmu, 'Country Profile Senegal' in *LOOK* (Nigeria), 1, 1986, p. 5). Guinea (in cooperation with WEC): two couples, since 1987, also Amos Aderonmu. North Cameron: independent work in the Mandara Mountains. Liberia: one women working for Scripture Union. Niger: from the outset, evangelistic efforts in connection with the Église Évangélique du Niger, but no resident missionaries.

112This activity has now (1993) been extended to the Ivory Coast. There, CAPRO has created a mission agency (Action Missionaire Intrafricaine (AMI)) and opened a School of Missions (Institut Intrafricaine de Formation Missionaire) with six students.

113In recent years, EMS also has accepted unmarried men, but they must marry within three years if they want to remain EMS missionaries (Interview the Rev. Panya Baba, 6 February 1987).

114Interview the Rev. Panya Baba, 6 February 1987; Interview Alastair M.

Kennedy, 10 January 1987; Interview Nike Akinkunmi, 5 February 1987; Interview Taiwo Rotibi, 5 February 1987.

115Therefore, Panya Baba sees CAPRO not as competing with EMS, but as a necessary alternative (Interview the Rev. Panya Baba, 6 February 1987).

116Naomi Famunore, 'Focus on School of Missions' in *Occupy*, special celebrations edition 1986, p. 4f.

117NIFES—Fiedler, 4 March 1987.

118They work in five zones of northern Nigeria and in five other countries (Kennedy—Fiedler, 3 March 1993).

119Headed by Timothy O. Olonade. Olonade is very much interested in missiology and is important in NEMA, the Nigerian Evangelical Missions Association (Interview, 5 February 1987).

120Reuben E. Ezemadu, 'Focus on the Christian Missionary Foundation', draft for *Mission Focus Magazine*, 1987, p. 3. CSSM (also called Christian Evangelical Social Movement) was organized in May 1977 by students from the universities of Ibadan and of Ife as a movement to mobilize students in higher institutions towards evangelism (Matthew Ojo, 'Charismatic Movements in Africa', unpublished, p. 37).

121'[CMF] sponsors career missionaries, volunteer missionaries and short-term missionaries to fulfil the call of God upon them, and supports them with prayers and gifts. CMF also engages in health, agricultural and other services aimed at improving the physical lives of the people' (*Introducing the Christian Missionary Foundation*, n.d.).

122CMF, *Taking Advantage*, p. 1; 'It has an express purpose of reaching areas in Nigeria, Africa and other parts of the world where the Gospel of our Lord Jesus Christ is yet to gain roots' (*Introducing the CMF*).

123To date, work has been started in eleven countries, but not in unreached areas. The work done is usually evangelism and training, for example: in St Rita near Cotonou, Benin (Mrs and Mr Zinsou); in the slums of Pt Bouet, Ivory Coast (Gloria and James Kwarteng); in the suburbs of Entebbe, Uganda (Mrs and Mr Gichuru); or among the poor in Zimbabwe (Rose Kubeyinje). John Adeniji works as a school teacher in Gambia, in fellowship with WEC (Interview, 30 July 1986), Chinwe Onochie works with Child Evangelism Fellowship in the Ivory Coast (*Profile of CMF Missionaries 1986/1987* and so on).

124'The role that CMF aims to play in emerging Missionary work in Africa is to stimulate Christians in various parts of Africa and to organize local Christians to finance, pray for and support the sending out of indigenous missionaries within their own countries and to their neighbouring states' (Ezemadu, *Focus on the CMF*).

125A traditional example is that of Stella Okoronkwo, who works in Nairobi for a Christian organization producing literature for francophone Africa. An innovative example is that of N. N., who established a travel agency on Equatorial Guinea, serving also as a base for evangelistic efforts there (*Profile of CMF Missionaries 1986/1987*).

126The Rev. Samson Bet is now AICMB chairman.

127 Interview the Rev. Samson Bet, 15 December 1986.

128 His visit to All Nations Christian College in England also somewhat contributed to his ideas (Interview the Rev. Samson Bet, 15 December 1986).

129 Among others, the Rev. Birech, Chairman of Nandi District Church Councils and of Rift Valley Regional Church Council, who then succeeded Bishop Mulwa. The information given in *Africa Inland Church Missionary College Catalogue 1986*, p. 4, that Bishop Birech and Tim Kendagor had the original vision, is not correct.

130 Parallel to these ideas, Tim Kendagor developed ideas to expand Kapsabet Bible College, whose director he was (Interview the Rev. Tim Kendagor, 15 December 1986). A secondary motive in both ideas may have been the wish to enhance the role of the western (younger) AIC districts (Nandi, Rift Valley and Eldoret). But to expand Kapsabet would have been seen as competition to Scott Theological College, as the only Theological College at the top of AIC's hierarchy of training institutes.

131 No minutes of this time seem to exist. The earliest available ones are: minutes Curriculum Committee, 22 January 1982. But the general committee had started to meet in 1979 or 1980.

132 Minutes Curriculum Committee (Eldoret), 2 July 1982.

133 Due to the tremendous growth of Eldoret, the farm is now on its outskirts. Close by, Moi University is being erected as the second Kenyan state university. A polytechnic is already in existence. Though Eldoret is centrally situated, several insufficiently evangelized people groups live not more than 100 km (60 miles) away, especially the Pokot.

134 Mr and Mrs Limo are members of the AIC and very active in the East African revival movement. Mrs Limo suggested to her husband that they donate to the missionary training school a piece of their land out of gratitude for God's blessings. At the time of independence, Mr Limo was an agricultural officer. The South African who owned the farm wanted it to 'remain in Christian hands' and allowed payment in smaller installments over a longer period of time (Interview Mrs Limo, 14 December 1987; Interview Mr Limo, 14 December 1986). The piece of land was donated in 1981 and handed over officially to Eldoret MTC in 1984.

135 *Catalogue*, p. 7. On 9 May 1985, President Moi, as an AIC member gave Kshs 150,000 without publicity from his private account (copy of the cheque); interview Jonathan Hildebrandt, 13 December 1986).

136 About 1 million Kshs.

137 *Catalogue*, p. 8. Hilfe für Brüder (Germany) helped with grants for building and by seconding a handyman for some time (interview Jonathan Hildebrandt, 14 December 1986).

138 For further developments, see: Jonathan Hildebrandt, 'Africa Inland Church Missionary College, Eldoret, Kenya' in William D. Taylor (ed.), *Internationalizing Missionary Training: A Global Perspective*, Exeter/Grand Rapids, 1991, pp. 97–109.

139 The first course finished in April 1987. Of the six couples, five work as missionaries (among the Sabaot, Somali, Pokot, Masai and Boya (South Sudan)). One couple works in urban missions (*The A.I.C. Missionary College Messenger*, April 1988).

140Occasional exceptions are possible (p. 23).

141*Catalogue*, pp. 45–48. If wives do not know enough English, special arrangements can be made (p. 23).

142'Cultural Anthropology'; 'The Missionary Movement and Africa'; 'Principles of Evangelism and Church Planting'; 'Structure and Policies of a Mission Society' (*Catalogue*, 1986).

143*Catalogue*, pp. 32–44; Interview Jonathan Hildebrandt, 12 December 1986 and 14 December 1986; Interview Malcolm (10 December 1986) and Barbara Collins, 14 December 1986; Interview Jin Ju, 14 December 1986.

144The Hildebrandts and the Collins are from the United States, the Jus are Koreans, the Ng'ang'as (with ten years' missionary experience in Turkana) and the Mutungas are Kenyans (Kikuyu and Kamba).

145This became clearly visible in comparing the interview with the Rev. Wilson Bartwol (AICMB missionary in Marsabit), 11 December 1987, with that with Ruth and Ally Towett (Eldoret MTC students there on practical), 10 December 1987. For Bartwol, it was difficult to decide how far he was a diaspora pastor and how far a missionary. Bartwol is to attend the next MTC course. The Towetts were better equipped for the culture shock awaiting them.

146Interview Wilbur O'Donovan, 6 February 1987.

147The United Missionary Church goes back to CMA. Influences from Simpson and CMA led to the establishment of a similar fellowship movement amongst the Mennonites in 1891, which later became (like the CMA) a denomination, the Missionary Church (Eileen Lager, *Merging Streams*, Elkhart, 1979, pp. 12–75). The plan of a union between Missionary Church and CMA (Harry L. Turner, President CMA, Tillman Habegger, President, The Missionary Church Association, 17 June 1959; Tillman Habegger, Harry L. Turner, 2 June 1959); file: MCA Fraternal Committees, Missionary Church Association, Ft Wayne) just missed the required two-thirds majority, receiving only 3,405 of the 3,447 votes needed. The Missionary Church is the Mennonite denomination with the highest percentage of members from a non-Mennonite background.

148According to Pate, *From Every People*, p. 253, it was started in 1975. In 1988, it had twenty-two missionaries: four of them in Brazil, Florida and Benin; eighteen in Oyo, Ondo, Kwara and Bauchi States of Nigeria. Its headquarters are at Ibadan, its character is pentecostal, the leader is the Rev. Nicholas D. Osameyan.

149The Gospel Faith Mission is not mentioned by Pate. A similar group, but not an NEMA member, is New Life for all Nations. Both groups began as evangelistic teams. They made so many converts that they had to establish churches for them. Preaching, conversion and missionary involvement are the main emphases (Interview Wilbur O'Donovan, 6 February 1987).

150NIFES—Fiedler, 4 March 1987.

151Interview Wilbur O'Donovan, 6 February 1987.

152All information from interview Wilbur O'Donovan, 6 February 1987.

153She joined NEMI in July 1987 as Dean of Studies. The courses are now being held in Jos, and land for a permanent campus has been acquired near Abuja. See:

Lois Fuller, 'Nigeria Evangelical Missionary Institute: A Case Study' in William D. Taylor (ed.), *Internationalizing Missionary Training: A Global Perspective*, Exeter/ Grand Rapids, 1991, pp. 81–95.

154 The Assemblies of God have instituted a branch for missiological training, which could possibly accept a few outside students after 1990.

155 He made this proposal on the basis of a report O'Donovan had written for Ian Hay, Director of SIM, on the situation among Nigerian students.

156 'NEMA and Panya Baba gave credibility, but I was on my own'.

157 The first term was in 1986 with eighteen students.

158 WEC-RSA sent out its first non-white missionary in 1978, its first black missionary in 1981. Presently many applications from neighbouring countries have to be turned down because these countries do not allow finances to be sent out of the country (Fernando Mouro—Fiedler, March 1993).

# 13
# Sufficient challenges for faith missions

Faith missions share many challenges, such as secularism and the Islamic resurgence, with any other missionary movement. This final chapter will concentrate on those challenges which are specific to faith missions or which, due to their history, principles or pecularities, have a special 'colouring' for faith missions.

## THE CHALLENGE OF THE UNREACHED

The first and foremost aim of faith missions was to reach the unreached, those who had never heard of Jesus. In terms of geography, this challenge has been greatly reduced, and faith missions played a leading role in that process over the past century and a quarter, but the challenge is still sufficiently great. Most of the unreached areas and their 'hidden peoples' are within what evangelical missiologists now call the *10/40 window*, which means that part of the northern hemisphere from 10 degrees to 40 degrees latitude, from North Africa to Asia.[1] This area contains much of the Muslim belt, and this means that it contains the areas most unresponsive to Christian evangelism.[2] A special feature of this 'window' is that it contains a number of peoples in the former Soviet Empire, which have now become accessible to foreign missionaries.[3]

Though the responsive (non-Muslim) areas of Africa have mostly been evangelized, there are pockets of responsive areas left, especially in West Africa. Whereas in early faith mission thinking, the category was unreached *areas*, this has now often been replaced by unreached or hidden *peoples* or *people groups*. This new concept takes sociology more seriously: in an area which is reached, has churches and so on, it may still be that certain social or ethnic groups are quite untouched by any missionary activity.[4]

In terms of numbers, the challenge of the unreached is ever-growing. Now there are at least 2 billion who have never heard the gospel in any meaningful way and, with worldwide population growth, their numbers are still increasing. Although missionary work is reaching new groups, and faith missions had, and still have, a fair share in this, even the percentage of

Christians in the world is either not growing or only slightly so.[5]

Faith missions were never content simply to 'christianize' people—they always sought to bring them to a living and saving faith. They had come into existence out of a revival movement which was a challenge to nominal Christianity. But nominal Christianity is not, and never was, only a 'Northern' phenomenon. The challenge of nominal Christianity is an ever-present challenge for the faith missions, not excluding the churches which they themselves founded.

Another aspect of the challenge of the unreached is the worldwide population shift to the cities, especially to the megacities.[6] With their geographical concept of reaching the unreached, faith missions have achieved much, often even literally reaching 'the last tribe',[7] but often, too, this idea has led to their concentrating on areas with small numbers, thereby neglecting the unreached millions in the mushrooming cities of the two-thirds world.[8] Pentecostal missions and churches have shown themselves more adaptable to the cities than have faith missions.

## THE CHALLENGE OF INTERDENOMINATIONALISM

Recalling Hudson Taylor's statement that the most important feature of faith missions is not their 'faith principle' of financing them, but their interdenominational character, how then did this aspect fare in the course of history? As a whole, it has not only survived, but seems to be gaining new strength. The overall picture includes both a process of denominalization and a process of interdenominationalization, and both processes run concurrently.

Denominationalization: many interdenominational missions received their main support from one particular interdenominational revival movement. If and when such a revival movement changes its ecclesiology and becomes a free church denomination, as many fellowship movements do after one or two generations, the mission it supports usually becomes a denominational mission. Examples of this process of denominationalization include the Christian and Missionary Alliance, the Örebro Missionsfrening, and the Swiss and French sections of the Chrischona-Mission.[9] Clearly perceptible as this process has been, it never reached the proportions of the process of denominationalization which took place in the interdenominational classical missions. The large majority of faith missions kept their interdenominational character and, since the 1960s, with growing denominational pluralism, especially in the Free Church sector, their interdenominational character has usually been strengthened. Overall, the Free Church element in faith missions seems to have been gaining some ground over the years, which can be explained by the fact that, over the same period, most mainline churches have experienced decline and most Free cChurches have experienced relative growth.[10] Nevertheless, the faith missions have by no means become a Free Church movement.[11]

The concept of interdenominationalism has been taken up strongly by parachurch movements.[12] Many of these parachurch movements are also foreign missions.[13] They often share a common spirituality with faith missions, and often cooperation is strong. Since they are basically related to the same home base as faith missions, they also compete to some extent for that home base's missionaries and money.

THE CHALLENGE OF NEW REVIVAL

The most basic pecularity of faith missions was their origin in the 1858/1873 revival, and the theology and spirituality derived from it. Though changes in both theology and spirituality took place,[14] as they do in any Christian movement, faith missions kept quite close to their unique heritage.

Revivalists pray for ever-new revival, but they also seem to share a subconcious feeling that their revival should be the last. They are thrilled to see a new revival breaking, but it usually comes to them as a shock that this new revival is so different from their own, having a new piety and a new theology. In this, the new revival is not different from their own, but because the revivalists perceived their message, theology and piety not as something new, but as 'originally Christian', it is not easy for them to come to terms with the fact that a new revival claims to be as 'originally Christian' as theirs, albeit differing considerably.

The first new revival to break after the holiness revival was the pentecostal revival. Because of the new pentecostal piety and theology there was an early parting of the ways, but the common heritage was strong enough for pentecostal missions to pattern their work, in many respects, on faith missions. This becames clear in their adoption of the Bible school pattern for theological training[15] and in the pattern of mission structures, but also in their common veneration for the indigenous church principle and its high church Anglican apostle, Roland Allen.[16]

In 1960, a new revival broke, which some called 'neo-pentecostal' but which is more commonly known as the charismatic movement or the charismatic revival. Unlike the pentecostal revival, it was not expelled from most of the denominations. Some sections of the faith mission home base were not affected, because the charismatic movement did not touch them, and other sections of the home base consciously rejected it,[17] but many sections of the faith mission home base were strongly touched by the charismatic renewal, so that charismatics soon applied to become faith missionaries. Often, charismatic existence in faith missions is somewhat uneasy, especially in those with a strong US and/or Calvinistic background, but many faith missions have been able to accommodate charismatic missionaries in one way or another.[18] With this charismatic revival having reached its second—the denominational—stage, its challenge is by no means over. It is still an open question whether the faith missions in general will be able to come to terms with the growing number of charismatic churches and with their new missiological emphasis.[19] The possibility also seems to exist of the rise of an interdenominational charismatic missionary movement.

The charismatic revival confronts faith missions with two challenges which were not strange to them in their original piety: the concept of a 'second blessing' (then sanctification, now baptism/fullness of the Holy Spirit); and the idea of up-to-date forms of worship (then the harmonium and Sankey songs, now praise choruses and prayers with raised arms). Judging from the overall picture of the worldwide evangelical movement, there is considerable chance of a growing covergence, but also the chance of increasing divergence.[20]

## THE CHALLENGE FROM THE FEMINIST MOVEMENT

In their first decades, faith missions challenged society in general, and the churches in particular, by their tremendous willingness to give women positions of responsibility and leadership.

For more recent decades, and therefore for the larger part of this century, the challenge was usually the other way round. If the missions (and faith missions prominent among them) were—though perhaps unconsciously—in the vanguard of the first feminist movement,[21] today they tend more to make up the struggling rear. To some extent, evangelicals have managed to keep clear of the second feminist movement, whose start can be dated in the revolutionary 1960s, but its influence among the home base and among evangelical missionaries is making itself increasingly felt. One reason is overall societal influences, but the other reason is the revival of what now, looking back, one can term the first wave of evangelical feminism. Did not evangelical stalwarts such as Wesley allow women to preach freely? And does not the New Testament show that women's ministry was not restricted to children, charity and serving the menfolk?

In faith missions today, as in their home bases, there are strong tendencies, among both women and men, to assign to women 'their rightful Biblical place',[22] but among both women and men there are also tendencies to regard women not only as of equal value, but as equals, thus opening for them all avenues of ministry. This comes closer to the original faith mission attitude than the 'biblical' position.[23] In some missions, this attitude is gaining ground, but it is far from clear to me which way most missions will go. I think they may eventually go this way, but there is a good chance that, by then, faith missions will have lost an unnecessarily high number of gifted women, either to other missions, to marriage or to social and secular concerns.[24] Would it not be better for many people worldwide to hear the gospel from a woman than not at all?

## THE CHALLENGE OF GROWING QUALIFICATIONS

Faith missions started on the principle that missionary candidates from all educational backgrounds would be welcome. Their educational level was not to be decisive but, rather, their spiritual level. Much emphasis was put on spiritual growth and also on practical experience in evangelism at home as qualifications for missionary service.

Faith missions quickly realized that good training is an additional qualification. This realization ran parallel to the social upward mobility of those evangelical Christian groups that constituted the major part of the home base of faith missions, so that faith missions became more of a middle class affair than in their early years.

In a world which is growing ever-more educated (though not necessarily ever more enlightened), both in the 'sending' and in the 'receiving' countries, it might be fatal to try to reverse this trend. This should not hinder faith missions from devising ways for those with less formal education to serve in missionary work. One attempt to do just this are the short-term missions, such as Youth With a Mission and Operation Mobilization. There are also short-term missionaries in many of the older faith missions. In some cases, these are just stop-gaps. In other cases, a period as a short-term missionary is a test for, or the initial step to, a missionary career. On the other hand, short-term service may tend to make the missionary calling 'cheap' and a bit of an episode or an adventure. Still, the challenge to use 'the neglected forces of Christianity' for missionary work remains—and remains unanswered in many cases.

## THE CHALLENGE OF GROWING INTERNATIONALIZATION

There is much to support the argument that in our day many of the 'neglected forces of Christianity' that should be employed in the missionary endeavour are no longer to be found in the sending countries of the West, but in the former 'receiving' countries. Very early in their history, faith missions grew to be international, and by this they opened to many who were touched by the revival in the remoter areas of the West (such as Germany, Norway, New Zealand and South Africa) the needed avenues for missionary involvement. Although there are always tendencies to make faith missions more national, the tendency towards internationalization seems to be keeping pace well with the growing internationalization of the world on all levels, facilitated by the growth of fast and comparatively cheap international communication.

Since the 1960s, the racial barriers which had come into faith missions around the turn of the century have collapsed, and in many of the larger faith missions the percentage of 'non-whites' is steadily growing.

The distinctions of race have been overcome, but the distinctions of wealth are more difficult to overcome, because most of the 'white' countries are still far more wealthy. If one compares, for example, Germany and Brazil as sending bases, there is a considerable difference in resources. Nonetheless, missionaries from both countries are working side by side, for example in Guinea Bissau. Faith missions have sucessfully attempted to create an awareness of worldwide missions in some of their mission fields, but if they continue to be successful in this, it will necessitate massive adjustments in their international structures, both in terms of personnel and in terms of finance.

## THE CHALLENGE OF INTERNATIONAL SHARING

It is interesting to note that nearly all non-Western missionaries in the international faith missions do not come from the poor countries. Most come from the so-called 'threshold nations', such as Korea, Singapore, Taiwan and Brazil. Their home bases are perhaps less affluent than those in the West, but they can contribute financially. Must God's call to missionary work be dependent on the economic level of a nation?[25]

Faith missions obviously need to rethink the 'faith principle' of support on a *worldwide* scale. The issues are: how much of the 'faith principle' operates by faith and how much by culture? And is God in any way interested in national borders? If a well-qualified African from Zaire, with its ruined economy and rampant inflation, is to go forth as a missionary to Chad, will he find financial support?

Over many decades, the idea of faith support was closely tied to the indigenous church principle. This, in effect, not only separated money according to race, but also created the impression that it was the divine will that every country should support its own missionaries. Because African churches cannot support missionaries financially (unless they work very close from home), they may not send any. But can the sending of missionaries be simply a function of economic surplus?

If the remaining missionary task of reaching the unreached is to be taken seriously, missionaries from the West and from those countries which can afford to pay them, simply will not suffice. In addition, it must be taken into account that Western missionaries, even Western faith missionaries with their comparatively low income, are quite expensive. If the 'faith principle' is applied positively to the cost-intensive Western missionaries, why should it not be applied equally positively to missionaries from poorer countries who also have God's call and whose work will be often far less expensive?[26]

One of the very first faith missions to take up this challenge is what is now Partners International, but was then the Chinese Nationals Evangelism Commission and later the Christian Nationals Evangelism Commission (1943).[27] Some other attempts at worldwide faith sharing have also been made.[28] In several contexts, a process of worldwide evangelical sharing has begun, but many tread very hesitantly and many, if not most, missions do not seem to have become aware of the immensity of the challenge.

THE CHALLENGE FROM THE FALL OF COMMUNISM

The sudden demise of Communism was as much of a surprise to faith missions as to everyone else. Some faith missions had always contended that Eastern Europe, though technically 'closed' to Western missionaries, was nevertheless a worthy field of missionary endeavour, although innovative means might have to be employed, such as Bible smuggling, 'visitation' ministries, distant theological education, public relations or literature production.[29]

For most faith missionaries and missiologists, the Eastern bloc was 'closed' to missionary work, and was often seen simply as the nucleus of an ever-growing number of countries with closed doors. For early faith missions, the imminent end of the world had been characterized by new doors opening, together with the missions' attempt to reach the unreached, who thus became accessible, whereas of late the eschatological scenario had changed gradually but perceptively: the end time was now qualified by ever-more doors closing. The identification of the antichrist had also changed in this process. Though early faith missionaries had never come to an agreement as to who the antichrist was or would be, there were many who, like Grattan Guinness, saw the antichrist either to be the Pope, the Papacy as an institution (more frequently) or as coming from that institution in the near future. Over the past decades of the Cold War, many expected the antichrist and the preceding evils to come from the communist system, which was usually perceived as growing in strength. This position was never officially accepted or shared by a large majority, but it was a potent force in eschatological thinking, especially so because the methods of interpretation of some biblical texts claimed to be in the heritage of the prophetic movement, which was extremely influential at the time faith missions were born.

The rising power of Communism fitted well with the negative aspects of premillennial eschatology: the expectation of growing decline, of a world developing rapidly from bad to worse.[30] This could be seen as a call to greater missionary activity before the closing of the age, but it could also lead to depression or to political militancy.

With the demise of Communism, all these eschatological scenarios must be revamped. 'Prophetic interpretation' seems to be quite flexible, and it is possible to substitute new 'realms of evil' for the previous one just lost—'militant Islam' or 'worldwide environmental deterioration'. The tendency to avoid repentance for false prophecies by creating new scenarios is certainly there but, for faith missions, this could be an opportunity to scrupulously avoid speculative eschatology and to re-embrace applied eschatology: the great eschatological task is worldwide missions, reaching everyone, everywhere, with the gospel.

The fall of Communism has brought two further challenges: the open doors to the East mean that faith missions can now reach many unreached areas that had seemed to be closed forever, such as the Asian republics of the old Soviet Union.[31] Both Western and Asian faith missions have started to take up this challenge.

The former communist bloc countries must be seen not only as new mission fields, but also as a challenge as possible new sending bases. When there was a chance, missionaries from Eastern Europe had participated in various Western missionary movements, including faith missions.[32] The political changes in Eastern Europe make it possible for faith missions to extend their sending base, but this extension, too, may not reach far without financial innovations.

## THE CHALLENGE OF MISSIOLOGY

Evangelical missions (and faith missions as a major constituent part) have always had their own identity and thus, from the beginning, have had their own practical missiology. Because their identity was undemarcated compared to other missionary movements, they could use some of the scholarly work and thinking of the classical mission movement.[33]

But over the decades, with growing personal and educational resources, faith missions started to make their own contribution to missiology as a science. Because the two movements, which had never been one, drifted further apart in this century, the evangelicals had to formulate their own missiology. They were somewhat slow in talking up this challenge, but they are increasingly doing so. The lead in this was taken in the United States, where there are a number of thriving evangelical graduate schools and programmes in missiology, but the challenge to develop fully an evangelical missiology still exists. In many countries, very little is being done; the history of many missions and churches has never been written in any scholarly way, so that much identity is in danger of being lost. Also, some subjects do not receive the necessary attention, such as the study of non-Christian religions, the evaluation of Catholic missionary work or the indigenization/contextualization of theology. Much more creative thinking needs to be done on special faith mission issues: the faith principle of financial support, the challenge of the unreached, Third World missionary involvement, the role of women as missionaries, and the relationship between institutional missionary work and direct evangelism. A creative missiology will help faith missions avoid becoming just another group of institutions surviving from a bygone revival.

## THE CHALLENGE OF THE 'YOUNG' CHURCHES

When faith missions started their work in Africa, they did not think much in terms of ecclesiology for their converts, because they simply did not expect the developments that took place. But now they are here, the 'churches on the mission field'—young, vigorous and growing. This poses for faith missions the challenge to take conscious ecclesiology seriously. It is not enough to open the Bible and to quote a few verses, because that reflects more the missionaries' ecclesiastical tradition or their personal inclinations, based on the New Testament and applied to a particular place on the globe at a particular time in history.

What is needed is a conscious ecclesiology which takes seriously the young churches' identities, the missions' doctrinal traditions, and the social and political context in which the churches exist. The missions cannot provide this alone, but by making a conscious contribution they can contribute to the development of an indigenous ecclesiology.[34]

One aspect of this necessary ecclesiological thinking will be to provide an answer to the issue of wider unity for faith mission churches. Is wider unity for them to be found in the National Christian Council (or perhaps in the National Evangelical Fellowship)? Are there sister churches in other countries, even if there can be no mother church overseas?

The other ecclesiological issue faith missions have to face is rather a thorny one. How do they relate to the churches they have helped to bring into being? The issue is thorny insofar as the larger churches among them developed into folk churches with many non-converted and non-committed members. The priority of the faith missions was always evangelism. How will they evangelize among those who are full members of those churches that they themselves founded? Is their job simply to provide specialized support for the 'young' churches and to leave evangelism to them?

## SUFFICIENT CHALLENGES

The faith mission movement originated from the realization that the risen Lord's commission to evangelize the world had not yet been completely carried out—that more had to be done. Innovative steps needed to be, and were indeed, taken. Since then, more than 125 years have passed. The worldwide missionary task is still unfulfilled. Over the generations, faith missions have been able to meet many challenges. They have kept their vitality, perhaps not in every individual mission, but in the movement as a whole. This inspires confidence that faith missions will be able to meet the present challenges and to continue their distinct contribution to the worldwide missionary task. If they succeed in this, their contribution will not be the only one, as it never was.

**Notes**

1  Compare Garry Corwin (SIM) in *Evangelical Missions Quarterly*, 1992, pp. 118ff.

2  It must not be overlooked, though, that faith missions especially do a considerable amount of missionary work among Muslims. Although the response is very limited, there has been an increase in the number of conversions over the past decade or so, and a number of ex-Muslim Christian congregations have come in, or are being or have been stabilized.

3  One mission which is taking advantage of these new opportunities is WEC International.

4  The concept of unreached or hidden people is still far from clear, because definitions of what constitutes such a group vary greatly. A recent attempt to clarify some issues is: Harley Schreck and David Barrett (eds), *Unreached Peoples: Clarifying the Task*, Monrovia, CA, 1987.

5  According to David B. Barrett, 'Annual Statistical Table on Global Mission: 1993' in *IBMR*, 1993, p. 22f., Christians comprised 33.7 per cent of the world's population; in 1993, the percentage was 33.53 per cent. This means that losses in some areas, especially in Europe, make up for the considerable missionary advances elsewhere. For the year 2000, Barrett expects the Christian percentage to rise slightly to 34.07 per cent.

6  In 1970, Barrett counted 161 mega-cities with populations in excess of one million; in 1993, he counted 360; and, for the year 2000, he expects 433.

7  This is the motto of the New Tribes Mission, and Wycliffe Bible Translators are convinced that even a distinct linguistic group of 100 speakers deserves translation of the New Testament.

8  There were always exceptions, for example, the Dorothea Mission in South Africa. In city missionary work, that among the 'urban poor', the 'slum-dwellers'

constitute a special challenge. In literature and practice, this challenge is now being taken up. See: Viv Grigg, *Companion to the Poor, Pasadena 1984; The Cry of the Urban Poor*, Pasadena, 1992.

9   Those faith missions which turned denominational usually retained some interdenominational traits (such as accepting missionaries from outside their denomination), and these traits are mostly growing at the present time.

10   This process of change was especially vivid in the United States, where the mainline denominations related to the National Council of Christian Churches are now a minority among Protestants.

11   In some faith missions, missionaries from the mainline denominations are increasingly represented, for example in WEC-Germany. Faith missions offer an alternative venue of missionary service to those members of mainline denominations who do not agree wholeheartedly with the dominant mainline theologies or spiritualities.

12   I define a parachurch organization as a service-oriented Christian organization, which does not intend to plant churches but has its own distinct tradition and spirituality, which often claims and/or receives the primary spiritual allegiance of its members, though they all retain membership in their respective churches. I distinguish parachurch organizations from specialized Christian service organizations (such as the Bible Societies), which do not develop their own spirituality.

13   For example, Youth With A Mission (YWAM) and Operation Mobilization (OM).

14   Such changes, for example, were the de-historization of eschatology and the de-emphasizing of holiness spirituality.

15   In the United States, the New York Missionary Training College of A. B. Simpson (CMA) became the model (L. F. Wilson, 'Bible Institutes, Colleges, Universities' in *Dictionary of Pentecostal and Charismatic Movements*, pp. 57–65), although Simpson always remained critical of the pentecostal movement (Charles Nienkirchen, 'A. B. Simpson: Forerunner and Critic of the Pentecostal Movement' in Hartzfeld and Nienkirchen, *Birth of a Vision*, pp. 125–164.

16   On the pentecostal side, Allan's ideas were strongly taken up by Melvin Hodges. His book *The Indigenous Church. A Complete Handbook On How to Grow Young Churches* is still in the programme of the Assemblies of God Gospel Publishing House, Springfield. For 'national' church planters, he wrote: *Build My Church*, Springfield, 1957.

17   This applies, for example, to many of the independent Bible churches, which became the major home base of the New Tribes Mission in the United States. This led to the NTM defining itself as specifically non-charismatic.

18   An international faith mission which consciously attempted (and managed) 'to straddle the charismatic divide' is WEC International.

19   It seems to me to be too early to make an overall assessment of the charismatic movement as a missionary movement. There seems to be a widespread trend to establish large independent city churches in the United States and Europe, which tend to send out their own foreign missionaries into various parts of the world

without using the services of a missionary organization. In its very early phase, the faith mission movement attempted to accommodate independent missionaries, but it could not do so without losing one of its basic achievements, the centralized structures. Therefore, there seems to be little chance of reaching such an accommodation now.

20 This seems to me obvious from the two world congresses: Lausanne I (1974) and Lausanne II in Manila (1989). In Lausanne, the pentecostal and charismatic elements were by no means excluded, but in Manila the charismatic presence was much more visible, even dominating some of the meetings, which also provoked some evangelical resistance.

21 See: R. Pierce Beaver, *American Protestant Women in World Mission. A History of the First Feminist Movement in North America*, Grand Rapids, 1980 (1968: *All Loves Excelling*). Beaver concentrates on classical missions and shows how they lost the 'feminist cutting edge' in the process of integration. In faith missions, a similar process took place, though somewhat later and under the influence of different ideological premises. See Chapter 10.

22 To see that rightful place as clear subordination under men is a view strongly supported in various segments of the charismatic renewal.

23 Although in most early faith missions women were given much scope in ministry, the regular distribution of the sacraments was mostly reserved for men.

24 On the lower level of faith mission 'career' there is still quite a surplus of women, for example, in the Bible schools, for which reason admission rules are often relaxed for male students.

25 WEC-RSA, for example, regularly receives applications from suitable candidates from the southern African nations. They cannot be accepted, because they either have no home base which can support them or because currency regulations make it impossible to send money for missionaries out of the country.

26 A strong claim that Western missionary money should be employed is made by the US-based Gospel for Asia, led by K. P. Yohannan. His views, radical if taken seriously, are laid down in: K. P. Yohannan, *The Coming Revolution in World Missions. God's Third Wave*, Altamonte Springs, FL, [5]1989 (1986). Yohannan argues that it is largely a waste of precious resources to send Western missionaries (some specialists, such as trainers for Bible translation, excluded) to countries where indigenous missionaries are available. He strongly contradicts equally the 'indigenous church principle' and the current concept that the Western churches should fund 'projects', but never pay for spiritual work. For him 'projects' are not to be the objective of the mission but of the local churches (if and when they can afford them). Gospel for Asia now supports more than 3,000 missionaries in ten Asian countries, some of which are inaccessible to foreign missionaries, such as India.

27 See Chapter 5. Their concept of missions and worldwide sharing is less negative towards previous missionary work than Yohannan's. See: Luis Bush and Lorry Lutz, *Partnering in Ministry. The Direction of World Evangelism*, Downers Grove, 1990.

28 The first and, to date, only missionary couple of Mission CECCA Zaire is, to a considerable extent, supported by foreign money coming in on the basis of the

faith principle. The effects of their service in the Ivory Coast obviously justify this international application of the faith principle.

29 Only a few can be mentioned: Licht im Osten (1920), Slavic Gospel Association (1934), Open Doors with Brother Andrew (1955) and Biblical Education by Extension.

30 A major 'prophet' of this kind of political eschatology was the best-selling author Hal Lindsay, whose book *Great Late Planet Earth* sold by the millions in English and by the tens of thousands in many other languages. He did not belong to a faith mission, but to a parachurch organization, Campus Crusade for Christ. In a later book, he predicted confidently that the final battle was close at hand (*The 1980s: Countdown to Armaggedon*), that the antichrist was already alive and a member of the European Parliament, and that Russian expansion would be stopped only in the final battle by divine intervention. In this book, he grafted eschatology successfuly onto extreme US militarism. He has not yet published any explanation why things did not happen as the Bible had 'clearly' predicted them. My claim is not that Lindsay represented the thinking of faith missions, but that a considerable number of faith missionaries were influenced by it or by similar eschatological (mis-)conceptions.

31 But, to some, these areas were not closed for information and intercession; for example, people around Leslie Brierley, the veteran WEC researcher (and early missionary to Guinea Bissau as Bessie Fricker's husband) started the NAMECA concert of prayer for the Non-Arab Muslim Ethnic Groups in Central Asia.

32 From Hungary, for example, between the two wars six Hungarians joined the interdenominational German Liebenzeller Mission, and recently a Hungarian branch of the Liebenzeller Mission has been reestablished. See Ang la Beliczay, *Tod im Pazifik*, Bad Liebenzell, 1988 (*Engem v rnak a szigetek*, Budapest, 1987).

33 This can be seen, for example, in the fact that the German Sudan-Pionier-Mission, whose foundation in 1900 was highly resented by the leading classical missiologist, Gustav Warneck, nevertheless warmly recommended his mission history to its readers.

34 One such conscious contribution is: Alastair M. Kennedy, *The Church. An Ecclesiology Study Manual*, Abidjan, 1992. Another contribution are regional meetings of WEC related churches, where ecclesiology was thoroughly discussed.

# Bibliography

In order not to increase the number of pages unduly, not all the materials used in this book are listed here. The book is largely based on primary sources collected in Europe, Africa and the United States. For archival material, such as letters and minutes, for journals published by the faith missions, and for interviews and letters to the author, please refer to the endnotes. The list of books and articles includes only those titles directly related to faith missions or to the movements which influenced them. I have attempted to look at, as far as possible, all dissertations related to faith missions. The following list of books and articles also includes unpublished items.

A Tribute to the Memory of a Choice Servant. Lance B. Latham 1894–1985, Sanford (NTM), 1985

Åberg, Göran, Enhet och Frihet. Studier i Jönköpings missionsförenings historia, (Acta Universitatis Ludensis), Jönköping, 1972

Account of the Union Meeting for the Promotion of Scriptural Holiness, Held at Oxford, Aug. 29 to Sept. 7, 1874, London, Boston/New York, 1874

ACTEA, ACTEA Directory of Theological Schools in Africa, Nairobi, [2]1985

Adams, Kenneth R., The Foolishness of God is Wiser than Men, Ft Washington, 1981

Adeyemo, Tokunbah, The Indigenous Church in Africa, Achimota, 1988

Affeld, Ulrich, Er mache uns im Glauben kühn. Einhundert Jahre Neukirchener Mission, Wuppertal, 1978

Africa Evangelical Fellowship, Fellowship, Organisation and Administration, Reading, 1985

Africa Evangelical Fellowship, Guide for Daily Prayer for Personnel of the Fellowship and Associated Churches, Reading, 1985

Africa Evangelistic Band, The Africa Evangelistic Band. Its Aims, Principles and Methods, London, n.d.

Africa Inland Church, Constitution, 1954

Africa Inland Church, First Anniversary of the Africa Inland Church, 15th October 1972, Kijabe, 1972

Africa Inland Mission, Constitution and Policy, 1909

Africa Inland Mission, Constitution and Policy, 1912

African Brotherhood Church, Momanyisyo ma Atongoi ma Ikanisa, Machakos, n.d.

Allen, Roland, Missionary Methods, St Paul's or Ours. A Study of the Church in the Four Provinces, London, 1912, (London (rev. 1927), [3]1953, [5]1960, [6]1968)

Allen, Roland, Missionary Principles, London, 1913 (Grand Rapids [2]1964, London, 1968), also published as Essential Missionary Principles, New York, 1913

Allen, Roland, The Spontaneous Expansion of the Church, and the Causes which Hinder it, London, 1927 ([2]1949)

Anderson, Gerald H., 'American Protestants in Pursuit of Mission: 1886–1986' in IBMR, 1988, pp. 98–118

Anderson, John, The Struggle for the

School. The Interaction of Missionary, Colonial Government and Nationalist Enterprise in the Development of Formal Education in Kenya, Nairobi/London, 1970

Anderson, Theodor (ed.), Svenska Missionsförbundet. Den uppkomstoch femtioårigs verksamhet, Stockholm, 1928

Andersson, Efraim, 'Den infödda kyrkans framtid' in Svenska Missionstidskrift 1942, pp. 221–233

Andrews, John S., 'Frances Bevan: Translator of German Hymns' in Evangelical Quarterly, 1962, pp. 206–213, 1963, pp. 30–38

Andrews, Leslie A., 'Restricted Freedom: A. B. Simpson's View of Women' in Hartzfeld and Nienkirchen, The Birth of a Vision, pp. 219–240.

Arbeitskreis ILV, Die frohe Botschaft unserer Zivilisation. Evangelikale Indianermission in Lateinamerika, Reihe pogrom 62/63, Göttingen/Wien, 1979

'Are The Heathen Lost?' or 'Will Those Who Have Never Heard The Gospel Go To Hell?', Toronto, [5]n.d.

Arms, Goodsil Filley, History of the William Taylor Self-Supporting Missions in South America, New York, 1921

Armstrong, W. D., Sunrise on the Congo. A Record of the Earlier Years of the Congo Balolo Mission, unpublished (283 pages), n.d.

Pierson, Arthur Tappan, A Spiritual Warrior, Mighty in the Scriptures; a Leader in the Modern Missionary Crusade, New York et al., 1912

Austin, Alvyn J., 'Blessed Adversity: Henry W. Frost and the China Inland Mission' in Carpenter and Shenk, Earthen Vessels, pp. 47–70

Bacon, Daniel W., From Faith To Faith. The Influence of Hudson Taylor on the Faith Missions Movement (DMiss, Deerfield, 1983), Singapore, 1984

Baker, Ashley, Publishing Salvation. The Story of Scripture Gift Mission, London, 1961

Baker, Eric, A Herald of the Evangelical Revival. A Critical Inquiry into the Relation of William Law to John Wesley and the

Beginnings of Methodism, London, 1948

Barrett, David B. (ed.), World Christian Encyclopedia. A Comparative Survey of Churches and Religions in the Modern World AD 1900–2000, Nairobi/Oxford/New York, 1982

Barrett, David et al., Kenya Churches Handbook, Kisumu, 1973

Barrett, David, 'The 20th Century Pentecostal/Charismatic Renewal in the Holy Spirit, with Its Goal of World Evangelization' in IBMR, 12, 3 (July 1988), pp. 119–129

Battersby, Thomas D. H., Memoir of T. D. Harford-Battersby. Together with Some Account of the Keswick Convention by Two of His Sons, London, 1890

Beard, Mary, In Times of Trouble. A Look at the Christian Church in Africa with Reference to Canadian Baptist Witness Among the Angolan People from 1961 to 1964, Toronto, n.d. (1964)

Beaver, R. Pierce, American Protestant Women in World Mission. A History of the First Feminist Movement in North America, Grand Rapids, 1980, (1968: All Loves Excelling)

Beliczay, Angla, Tod im Pazifik, Bad Liebenzell, 1988, (Engem vrnak a szigetek, Budapest, 1987)

Bevan, Frances, Hymns of Ter Steegen, Suso and Others, London, 1894

Bezzenberger, Günter, Mission in China. Die Geschichte der Chinesischen Stiftung, Kassel, 1979

Bill, Gracie, David Ekong. Called. Chosen. Faithful. The Story of the First Convert and Pastor of the Qua Iboe Mission, n.p., n.d.

Bingham, Rowland V., 'A New Name for an Established Mission' in The Missionary Witness, 17 October 1905

Bingham, Rowland V., 'Modern Industrial Missions. A Plea for Self-supporting and Self-propagating Industrial Missions in Africa' in The Faithful Witness, 19 July 1898

Bingham, Rowland V., 'Rev. H. Grattan Guinness' in Faithful Witness, 3 August 1889

Bingham, Rowland V., Seven Sevens of Years and a Jubilee. The Story of the Sudan Interior

Mission, Toronto, (1958), 1943, (New York/Toronto)

Bingham, Rowland V., *The Bible and the Body. Healing in the Scriptures*, London/Edinburgh, [4]1952, ([1]1921, [3]1939)

Bingham, Rowland V., *The Pentecost Plan or The Manna Method of Missionary Maintenance*, Toronto, n.d.

Bingham, Rowland V., 'Unity the Key Word—But at Too Great a Cost' in *The Missionary Witness*, 1910, p. 27

Bingham, Rowland V., 'Why Work Interdenominationally?' in *The Evangelical Christian*, January 1913, p. 4

Blakeslee, H. Virginia, *Beyond the Kikuyu Curtain*, Chicago, 1956

Blanc, Ren; Blocher, Jacques; Kruger, Étienne, *Histoire des Missions Protestantes Françaises*, Flavion, 1970

Bliss, Edwin M. (ed.), *The Encyclopedia of Missions*, New York, 1891

Blocher, Jaques, 'Les Missions Périphriques' in Ren Blanc, Jacques Blocher, tienne Kruger, *Histoire des Missions Protestantes Françaises*, Flavion, 1970, p. 353

Blocher, Madame A., *Par la Foi*, editions des Bons Semeurs, Paris, n.d., (ca. 1936)

Boardman, Mary M., *Life and Labours of Rev. W. E. Boardman*, New York, 1886

Boardman, William Edwin, *Faith-Work or the Labours of Dr Cullis*, London, 1874

Boardman, William Edwin, *In the Power of the Spirit, or Christian Experience in the Light of the Bible*, Boston/London, 1875

Boardman, William Edwin, *The Higher Christian Life*, Edinburgh/London, 1859, (London 1870, revised)

Boardman, William Edwin, *The Lord that Healeth Thee (Jehovah-Rophi)*, London, n.d., (ca. 1881)

Boer, Harry R., 'My Pilgrimage in Mission' in *IBMR* 1987, pp. 172–175

Boer, Jan Harm, *Missionary Messengers of Liberation in a Colonial Context: A Case Study of the Sudan United Mission*, Amsterdam, 1979

Boer, Jan Harm, *Missions: Heralds of Capitalism or Christ?*, Ibadan, 1984

Boer, John H., *The Gospel of Liberation in a Colonial Context. A Partial and Introductory Case Study of the SUM 1904–1918*, Amsterdam, 1974

Boer, John H., *The Last of the Livingstones: A Study of H. Karl W. Kumm's Missiological Conceptions of Civilization*, Free Reformed University of Amsterdam, 1973

Booth, Joseph, *Africa for the Africans*, Baltimore, 1897

Braekman, E. M., *Histoire du protestantisme au Congo*, Bruxelles, 1961

Brandl, Bernd, 'Ludwig Doll: Der Gründer der ersten deutschsprachigen Glaubensmission' in *EM*, 1988, pp. 41–46

Brchet, Rudolphe, *J'ai ouvert une porte devant toi. Essai sur l'histoire de la Mission Philafricaine*, Lausanne, n.d., (1972)

Bredberg, William, *P. P. Waldenströms verksamheit til 1878. Till frågan om Svenska Missionsförbundets uppkomst*, Stockholm, 1948

Bredberg, William; Lövgren, Oscar, *Genom Guds Nåd. Svenska Missionsförbundet under 75 år*, Stockholm, 1953

Brierley, Peter; Longley, David (eds), *UK Christian Handbook*, 1987–88 edition, Bromley/London/Swindon, 1986

Brierley, Peter; Martin, Sharon (eds), *UK Christian Handbook*, 1985–86 edition, London/Swindon, 1984

Brierley, Peter; Merckx-Stringer, E. (eds), *Handboek van Christelijk Nederland/Netherlands Christian Handbook*, Bromley/Driebergen/Kampen, 1986

Brookes, James H., 'How I Became a Premillennialist' in *HD*, July 1899

Broomhall, A. J., *Barbarians at the Gates*, Sevenoaks/London, 1981, (I)

Broomhall, A. J., *Over the Treaty Wall*, Sevenoaks/London, 1982, (II)

Broomhall, A. J., *If I Had A Thousand Lives*, Sevenoaks/London, 1982, (III)

Broomhall, A. J., *Survivors' Pact*, Sevenoaks/London, 1984, (IV)

Broomhall, A. J., *Refiner's Fire*, Sevenoaks/London, 1985, (V)

Broomhall, A. J., *Assault on the Nine*, Sevenoaks/London, 1988, (VI)

Broomhall, A. J., *It is Not Death to Die!*, Sevenoaks/London, 1989 (VII)

Broomhall, Marshall, *The Jubilee Story of the China Inland Mission*, London, 1915

Brown, David, *Christ's Second Coming: Will it be Pre-Millennial?*, Edinburgh/London, [2]1849, reprinted, available from Great Christian Books

Brümmer, N. J., 'Dr. Kumm' in *De Kerkbode*, (RSA), 1907, p. 306

Budd, Jack, *Read Sea Mission Team Story*, n.d., typewritten, 405 pages, printed version expected, Bonn, 1994

Buddeberg, Ernst, *Heinrich Coerper. Aus dem Leben und Wirken des Gründers der Liebenzeller Mission*, Bad Liebenzell, n.d., (1936), [3]1988, (widely rewritten)

Burgess, Alan, *Daylight Must Come. The Story of a Courageous Woman Doctor in the Congo*, Minneapolis, n.d., (London, [1]1975, New York, 1977); *Daylight Must Come: The Story of Dr Helen Roseveare*, London, 1977

Burgess, Stanley M., McGee, Gary B. and Alexander, Patrick H., *Dictionary of Pentecostal and Charismatic Movements*, Grand Rapids, 1988

Burton, William F., *When God Makes a Missionary. The Life Story of Edgar Mahon*, London, 1936, (revised by Alfred J. and Margaret Mahon, Zion, [2]1961)

Buscarlet, A.F., 'Aperçu sur la Mission Philafricaine' in *Les Rapports de la Mission Philafricaine 1898–1905*, Lausanne, 1905

Bush, Luis; Lutz, Lorry, *Partnering in Ministry*, Downers Grove, 1990

Bushnell, Katherine C., *God's Word to Women*, Piedmont, 1923; reprint: North Collins, New York, n.d. (1987 still available)

Bushnell, Katherine C., *God's Word to Women. 101 Questions Answered. A Woman's Catechism*, Southport/Lancashire, n.d.

Buxton, Alfred B., *A Triplet of Years 1920–1922*, London, 1923

Buxton, Alfred B., *Evangelise to a Finish (Inter-Varsity Missionary Paper No. 1)*, n.d.

Buxton, Alfred B., *Nala Missionary Methods*, London, 1916

Buxton, Alfred B., *Nala Missionary Methods. A Description and Scriptural Explanation of Them*, based on an article by C. T. Studd, London, 1916

Buxton, Alfred B., *The First Seven Years of the Heart of Africa Mission and A Triplet of Years 1920–1922. With Nine Years Ago and Now by Mrs C. T. Studd*, London, 1922

Buxton, Alfred B., *The First Ten Years of the Heart of Africa Mission 1913–1922*, London, (Heart of Africa Mission), [5]1927

Buxton, Edith, *Reluctant Missionary*, London, 1969

Buxton, Edith, *Reluctant No Longer. Address Given by Mrs Buxton at a Luncheon to Mark the Publication of the Paperback Edition of Reluctant Missionary, at the Westminster Theater*, London, [2]1974, (1973)

Cairns (Mrs), *Pastor Charlie Bonongwe. Chosen, Called and Faithful*, Wroughton, n.d.

Carpenter, Joel A., 'Propagating the Faith Once Delivered: The Fundamentalist Mission Enterprise, 1920–1945' in Joel A. Carpenter and Wilbert R. Schenk (eds), *Earthen Vessels. American Evangelicals and Foreign Missions, 1880–1980*, pp. 92–132

Chamberlin, Margaret, *Reaching Asians Internationally. A History of International Missions*, Wayne NJ, 1984

Chapell, F. L., *The Eleventh-Hour Laborers. A Series of Articles from 'The Watchword'*, Nyack/New York, n.d., (1898)

Chatelin, Alida, *Héli Chatelin. L'Ami de l'Angola. Fondateur de la Mission Philafricaine. D'après sa correspondence*, Lausanne, 1918

Chatelin, Héli, *Grammatica elementar do Kimbundu*, Geneva, 1888–89

Chatelin, Héli, *Grundzüge des Kimbundu oder der Angola Sprache*, Berlin, 1889–90

Chatelin, Héli, 'The First Expedition Successful!' in N. N., *Les Rapports de la Mission Philafricaine 1898–1905*, Lausanne, 1905

China Inland Mission, *Principles and Practice*, 1885

Choy, Leona, *Andrew Murray. Apostle of Abiding Love*, Ft Washington, (Christian Literature Crusade), 1978

Christian and Missionary Alliance, *Annual Report* 1897, 1899–1900, 1900–01, 1901–02, 1907–08, 1923

Christian and Missionary Alliance, *Missionary Atlas*, 1960

Christian and Missionary Alliance Congo, *Eleventh Annual Report*

Christian Missionary Foundation, *Profile of Missionaries*, 1986–87

Christian Missionary Foundation, *Taking Advantage of the Open Doors for Missions in 1987*

Church of Scotland, Confidential Memorandum Prepared by the Kikuyu Mission Council on Female Circumcision, Kikuyu, 1 December 1931, (National Archives of Scotland ACC 7548 D64)

Clark, Rufus W., *The Work of God in Great Britain: Under Messrs Moody and Sankey, 1873 to 1875*, New York, 1875

Cleverdon, Irene V., *Pools on the Glowing Sand*, Melbourne, 1936

Coad, Frederick Roy, *A History of the Brethren Movement. Its Origins, its Worldwide Development and its Significance for the Present Day*, Exeter, 1968

Coad, Frederick Roy, *Prophetic Developments. With Particular Reference to the Early Brethren Movement*, Pinner/Middlesex, 1966, (Christian Brethren Research Fellowship Occasional Paper No. 2)

Cocoris, Michael, *70 Years on Hope Street. A History of the Church of the Open Door 1915–1985*, Los Angeles, Glendora, 1985

Cole, Stuart G., *The History of Fundamentalism*, New York, 1931

Conwell, Roy E., *Samwiil of Sudan*, Ashgrove (AUS), 1985

Cooley, John K., *Baal, Christ and Mohammed. Religion and Revolution in North Africa*, New York/Chicago/San Francisco, 1965

Corbett, Jean S., *According to Plan. The Story of Samuel Alexander Bill, Founder of the Qua Iboe Mission*, Nigeria, Worthing, [2]1979, (1977)

Corbett, Jean S. and Dickson, Herbert W., *All the Days of My Life. Recollections of Herbert W. Dickson as Told to Jean S.*

Corbett, Belfast, 1981

Coslet, Dorothy Gawne, *Madame Jeanne Guyon. Child of Another World*, Ft Washington (Christian Literature Crusade), [2]1985, (1984)

Cotterell, Peter, 'An Indigenous Church in Southern Ethiopia' in *Bulletin of the Society for African Church History*, 1969–70, pp. 68–104

Cotterell, Peter, *Born at Midnight*, Chicago, 1973

Cotterell, Peter, 'Dr T. A. Lambie. Some Biographical Notes' in *Journal of Ethiopian Studies*, 10 (1), January 1972, pp. 43–53

Cousins, Peter and Pam, *The Power of the Air. The Achievement and Future of Missionary Radio*, London, 1978

Cowan, George M., *The Word that Kindles. People and Principles that Fueled a Worldwide Bible Translation Movement*, Chappaqua, NY, 1979

Crampton, Edmund P. T., *Christianity in Northern Nigeria*, London, [3]1979, (1975)

Cullis, Charles, *Faith Cures or Answers to Prayer in the Healing of the Sick*, Boston, 1879

Cullis, Charles, *Tuesday Afternoon Talks*, Boston, 1892

Cuninghame, William, *Pre-Millennial Advent of Christ Demonstrated from the Scriptures*, (1813)

Dahms, John V., 'The Social Interest and Concern of A. B. Simpson' in Hartzfeld and Nienkirchen, *The Birth of a Vision*, pp. 49–74

Daniels, W. H., *D. L. Moody and His Work*, Hartford, 1876

Daniels, W. H., *Dr Cullis and his Work*, Boston, 1885

Davidsson, Birger, *Det började med ett bönemöte . . . Missionssällskapet Helgelseförbundet. En presentation av Missionssällskapet Helgelseförbundets uppkomst, utveckling och verksamhet*, Kumla, 1955

Davis, Raymond J., *Fire on the Mountains. The Story of a Miracle —the Church in Ethiopia*, Scarborough, [12]1981, (1980)

Dawson, William E., *History of the Scandinavian Alliance Mission work in*

*Africa 1892–1920*, n.d., (1933)

Dayton, Donald W. (ed.), *The Higher Christian Life. A Bibliographical Overview*, New York, 1984

Dayton, Edward R.; Wilson, Samuel (eds), *The Future of World Evangelization. The Lausanne Movement*, Pasadena, 1984

Dessien, Eberhard von; Ehrbeck, Ulrich; Troeger, Eberhard, *Wasser auf dürres Land. 85 Jahre Sudan-Pionier-Mission/ Evangelische Mission in Oberägypten*, Wiesbaden, 1985

Diakubikwa, Komy-Nsilu, *L'Église du Christ au Zaire à la Recherche d'une Unit 1902—1977*, DTheol., Brussels, 1984

*Die Saat geht auf. Fünfzig Jahre Missions- und Kirchengeschichte im Kwango-Zaire*, Basel, 1990

Dieter, Melvin E., *The Holiness Revival of the Nineteenth Century*, Metuchen, 1980

Dillon, William S., *God's Work in God's Way*, River Grove, Illinois, n.d.

Dillon, William S., *Reaching the Last Tribe in This Generation. Via the Indigenous New Testament Methods*, n.d., (1945)

Dinnen, Stewart R., *Here We Stand. Foundations for Effective Christian Service*, Gerrards Cross, n.d.

Dinnen, Stewart R., *When I Say Move*, Ft Washington, 1972

Dinnen, Stewart R.; Woodford, Brian, *Serving Together. Manual on Intercultural Relationships within WEC International*, Gerrards Cross, 1987

Dobson, John, *Daybreak in West Nile*, London, n.d.

Doering, Alma, *Leopard Spots or God's Masterpiece. Which? An Attempt to Answer After 18 Years of Missionary Service Among Races of Three Colors, White, Black and Copper*, Cleveland Ohio, n.d., (1914)

Doering, Alma, *Röster från Kongo*, Stockholm, n.d.

Doering, Alma, 'The Winning Side' in *The Christian Evangel*, December 1914, pp. 443–445; p. 480

Dollar, George W., 'The Early Days of American Fundamentalism' in *Bibliotheca Sacra*, pp. 115–123

Dorothea Mission, *Some Vital Facts About*

*The Dorothea Mission*, Rosslyn, n.d., (valid 1987)

Douglas, William M., *Andrew Murray and His Message—One of God's Choice Saints*, London/Edinburgh, 1926, (Ft Washington, 1957)

Du Plessis, Johannes, *The Life of Andrew Murray of South Africa*, London, 1920

Duff, Clarence W., *Cords of Love. A Testimony to God's Grace in Pre-Italian Ethiopia as Recorded in Memorabilia of One of the Sudan Interior Mission's 'C.O.D. Boys'*, Phillipsburg, NJ, 1980

Dunkelberger, Stella C., *Crossing Africa. Being the Experiences of a Home Secretary in Primitive Parts of the Black Continent*, Germantown, 1935

Dye, T. Wayne, *Bible Translation Strategy. An Analysis of its Spiritual Impact*, Dallas, [2]1985, (1980)

Edwards, Jonathan, *A Humble Attempt to Promote Explicit Agreement and Visible Union Among God's People in Extraordinary Prayer, for the Revival of Religion and the Advancement of Christ's Kingdom on Earth, Persuant to Scripture-Promises and Prophecies Concerning the Last Time*, Boston, 1747 (republished Northampton, 1789 by John Sutcliffe)

*Efter Tjugufem år. Minneskrift med anledning af Helgelseförbundets tjugufemårige verksamhet bland Kineser och Zuluer*, Torp, (Kumla), 1915

Eidberg, Peder A., 'Debora-expedisjonen. Et norsk fors k på kolonisering og misjon' in: 'For kirke og misjon, Festskrift til professor dr. theol. Nils Egede Bloch-Hoell på 70-årsdagen 26. september 1985', *Norsk tidsskrift for misjon*, Nos 3–4, 1985, pp. 152–161

'Enfin une femme pasteur' in *Le Chemin. Trimestriel de Liaison et d'Information*, Brazzaville, III, 1985

Engen, Charles E. van, 'A Broadening Vision' in Carpenter and Shenk, *Earthen Vessels*, pp. 203–232

Evangelical Missionary Alliance (CMA), *Constitution*, 1887

Famunore, Naomi, 'Focus on School of Missions' in *Occupy*, Special Celebrations Edition, 1986

Fiedler, Klaus, 'Aspects of the Early History of the Bible School Movement' in Festschrift Donald Moreland and Marthinus W. Pretorius (eds), *The Secret of Faith. In Your Heart—In Your Mouth*, Heverlee, 1992, pp. 62–77

Fiedler, Klaus, 'Bishop Lucas' Christianization of Traditional Rites, the Kikuyu Female Circumcision Controversy and the "Cultural Approach" of Conservative German Missionaries in Tanzania' in Noel Q. King; Klaus Fiedler (eds), *Robin Lamburn—From a Missionary's Notebook: The Yao of Tunduru and Other Essays*, Saarbrücken/Ft Lauderdale, 1991, pp. 207–217

Fiedler, Klaus, *Christentum und afrikanische Kultur. Konservative deutsche Missionare in Tanzania 1900–1940*, Gütersloh, 1983, the German version of the original thesis (to be published in 1994): *Missionary Cultural Conservatism: Attempts to Reach an Integration Between African Culture and Christianity in German Protestant Missionary Work in Tanzania 1900–1940*, PhD, Dar-es-Salam, 1977)

Fiedler, Klaus, 'Der deutsche Beitrag zu den interdenominationellen Missionen' in Hans Kasdorf; Klaus Müller (eds), *Bilanz und Plan: Mission an der Schwelle zum Dritten Jahrtausend*, Festschrift George W. Peters, Liebenzell 1988, pp. 184–199

Fiedler, Klaus, 'Fundamentalismus' in Karl Müller; Theo Sundermeier, *Lexikon Missionstheologischer Grundbegriffe*, Berlin, 1987, p. 115

Fiedler, Klaus, *Ganz auf Vertrauen. Geschichte und Kirchenverständnis der Glaubensmissionen*, Giessen/Basel, 1992

Figgis, J. B., *Keswick from Within*, London/Edinburgh/New York, n.d.

Finley, Allen; Lutz, Lorry, *Is Supporting Nationals Biblical?*, San Jose, n.d.

Finley, Allen; Lutz, Lorry, *The Family Tie. An Exciting Approach That Could Revolutionize World Missions*, Nashville/Camden/New York, [2]1983, (1981), also published as: *Mission: a World-Family Affair. Sharing Resources in the Church around the World*, San Jose, n.d.

Finney, Charles Grandison, *The Baptism of the Holy Ghost and the Enduement of Power*, London, n.d., (1870)

Finney, Charles Grandison, *Views of Sanctification*, Oberlin Ohio, 1840, (Christian Literature Crusade: *Sanctification* (ed. William Ernest Allen), London, 1950)

Fish, Burnette and Gerald, and Adkins, Richard and Mrs, *The Call to Battle*, Kericho, 1982

Fish, Burnette and Gerald, *The Place of Songs*, Nairobi, 1989

Flood, Robert G., *The Story of Moody Church. A Light in the City*, Chicago, 1985

Frank, Douglas W., *Less Than Conquerors. How Evangelicals Entered the Twentieth Century*, Grand Rapids, 1986

Franson, Fredrik, *Himlauret*, Stockholm, [2]1898

Franson, Fredrik, *Profeterande Döttrar*, St Paul, 1896, Stockholm, 1897

Franson, Fredrik, *Weissagende Töchter*, Emden 1890, also *Gemeinschaftsblatt*, (Emden), Nos 16 and 17, 1890

Franz, Andreas, *Mission ohne Grenzen. Hudson Taylor und die deutschsprachigen Glaubensmissionen*, Giessen/Basel, 1993

Frizen, Edwin L., 'An Historical Study of the Interdenominational Foreign Mission Association in Relation to Evangelical Unity and Cooperation', DMiss, Trinity/Deerfield, 1981

Fuller, Harold, *Mission-Church Dynamics. How to Change Bicultural Tensions into Dynamic Missionary Outreach*, Pasadena, 1980

Fuller, Harold, *Run While the Sun is Hot*, Toronto et al., 1967

Fuller, Lois, 'Nigeria Evangelical Missionary Institute: a Case Study' in William D. Taylor (ed.), *Internationalizing Missionary Training: A Global Perspective*, Exeter/Grand Rapids, 1991, pp. 81–95

Garrard, David John, 'The Congo Evangelistic Mission/Communaut Pentecôtiste au Zaire', PhD, Aberdeen, 1983

Garrard, Mary N., *Mrs Penn-Lewis. A Memoir*, London, 1930

Gasper, Louis, *The Fundamentalist Movement 1930–1956*, Grand Rapids,

[2]1981 (1963)

Getz, Gene A., *Moody Bible Institute. The Story of Moody Bible Institute*, Chicago, 1969

Glenny, Edward H. and Rutherford, J., *The Gospel in North Africa*, London, 1900

Goddard, Burton L. (ed.), *The Encyclopedia of Modern Christian Missions. The Agencies*, Camden, NJ et al., 1967

Goen, C. C., 'Jonathan Edwards: A New Departure in Eschatology' in *Church History*, XXVII, (March 1959), pp. 25–40

Gordon, Adoniram Judson, *How Christ Came to Church. The Pastor's Dream. A Spiritual Autobiography, with Life-Story by A. T. Pierson*, Philadelphia/London, 1895

Gordon, Adoniram Judson, *The Holy Spirit in Missions*, New York/London, 1893, also London, [3]1900, today available as a reprint with slight alterations, A. J. Gordon, *The Holy Spirit in Missions*, Harrisburg, 1968

Gordon, Adoniram Judson, *The Ministry of Healing; or, Miracles of Cure in All Ages*, London/Boston, 1882

Gordon, Adoniram Judson, *The Ministry of the Spirit*, London/Philadelphia, 1894

Gordon, Adoniram Judson, 'The Overflow of Missions' in *WWW*, March 1893

Gordon, Adoniram Judson, *The Twofold Life, or, Christ's Work for Us and Christ's Work in Us*, London, 1884

Gordon, Ernest B., *Adoniram Judson Gordon. A Biography*, New York, 1896

Gospel Missionary Union, *Handbook*, n.d., (valid 1987)

Govan, I. R., *Spirit of Revival. The Story of J. G. Govan and the Faith Mission*, Edinburgh, [4]1978, (1938)

Govan, John George, *In the Train of His Triumph. Reminiscences of the Early Days of the Faith Mission* (ed. I. R. Govan), Edinburgh, n.d.

Gration, John A., *The Relationship of the Africa Inland Mission and its National Church in Kenya Between 1895 and 1971*, PhD, New York University, 1973, Ann Arbor (UMI), 1974

Grauer, O. C. (ed.), *Fifty Wonderful Years. Missionary Service in Foreign Lands*, Chicago, 1940

Gray, James M., 'Are the Heathen Lost?' in *Hearing and Doing*, No. 1, 1900

Groves, Anthony Norris, *Journal of a Residence at Bagdad, During the Years 1830 and 1831*, London, 1832

Groves, Anthony Norris, *Journal of Mr Anthony N. Groves, Missionary, During a Journey from London to Bagdad Through Russia, Georgia, and Persia. Also, a Journal of Some Months Residence at Bagdad*, London, 1831

Groves, H., *Memoir of the Late Anthony Norris Groves, Containing Extracts from His Letters and Journals, Compiled by his Widow, London 1856; (Memoir of Anthony Norris Groves, Compiled Chiefly from His Journals and Letters, to Which is Added a Supplement, Containing Recollections of Miss Paget, and Accounts of Missionary Works in India, etc.)*, by his widow, London, [3]1869

Grubb, Norman P., *After C. T. Studd*, London/Redhill, [4]1945 (1939)

Grubb, Norman P., *Alfred Buxton of Abyssinia and Congo*, London/Redhill, 1942

Grubb, Norman P., *C. T. Studd. Cricketer and Pioneer*, London, 1933, (Ft Washington, 1965, and further editions, for example, Guildford, 1982)

Grubb, Norman P., *Continuous Revival*, London, 1952

Grubb, Norman P., *J. D. Drysdale, Prophet of Holiness*, London, 1955, (with Drysdale's autobiography pp. 1–184)

Grubb, Norman P., *Jack Harrison*, Basel, n.d.

Grubb, Norman P., *Leap of Faith. The Story of Christian Literature Crusade*, Ft Washington, [3]1984, (1962)

Grubb, Norman P., *Mighty through God. The life of Edith Moules*, London, 1951

Grubb, Norman P., *Mit Studd im Kongo*, Wuppertal, 1961

Grubb, Norman P., *Once Caught, No Escape. My Life Story*, Ft Washington, 1963

Grubb, Norman P., *Penetrating Faith in Spanish Guinea*, Colchester, [3]1941(1937)

Grubb, Norman P., *Rees Howells.*

*Intercessor*, Guildford/London, [8]1983, (1952)

Grubb, Norman P., *Successor to C. T. Studd. The Story of Jack Harrison*, London, 1949

Grubb, Norman P., *The Law of Faith*, London/Redhill, 1947

Grubb, Norman P., *The Liberating Secret*, London, 1955

Grubb, Norman P., *Touching the Invisible*, London, 1940

Grubb, Norman P., *Who Am I?*, London, 1974

Guinness, Fanny E., *An Answer to the Question 'Who are the Plymouth Brethren?'*, Philadelphia, 1861

Guinness, Fanny E., *Hulme Cliff College, Curbar, or, the Story of the Third Year of the East End Training Institute*, London, n.d.

Guinness, Fanny E., *Other Seventy Also; or, the Story of our Fifth Year at the East London Institute for Home and Foreign Missions*, London, 1878

Guinness, Fanny E., *Sitwana's Story*, London, 1882

Guinness, Fanny E., *Some are Fallen Asleep, or, the Story of our Sixth Year at the East London Institute for Home and Foreign Missions*, London, 1880

Guinness, Fanny E., *The First Christian Mission in the Congo*, London, 1880, (enlarged edition, [4]1882)

Guinness, Fanny E., *The New World of Central Africa. With a History of the First Christian Mission on the Congo*, London, 1890

Guinness, Fanny E., *The Wide World and Our Work in It; or, the Story of the East London Institute for Home and Foreign Missions*, London, 1886

Guinness, Fanny E., 'Transfer of the Congo Mission' in WWW, 1884, pp. 148–150

Guinness, Geraldine, *Story of the China Inland Mission*, London, 1894

Guinness, Grattan, *A Letter to the 'Plymouth Brethren' on the Recognition of Pastors*, London, 1863

Guinness, Grattan, *A Plea for Believers' Baptism. An Address Delivered in Somerset-Street Chapel, Bath, Sept. 29, 1860, Previous to his Baptism*, by the Rev. H. Grattan Guinness of New College, St John's Wood, London, 1860, Sydney, 1861, Dublin, [2]1863, (revised and enlarged)

Guinness, Grattan, *Creation Centered in Christ*, 2 vols, London, 1896

Guinness, Grattan, 'Evangelizing Nubia', (typewritten, 5 pages)

Guinness, Grattan, *Fallacies of Futurism: a Reply to Futurist Objections to the Historic Interpretation of Prophecy*, London, n.d., (ca. 1882)

Guinness, Grattan, *History Unveiling Prophecy; or, Time as an Interpreter*, New York, 1905

Guinness, Grattan, *Key to the Apocalypse; or, The Seven Interpretations of Symbolic Prophecy*, London, 1899

Guinness, Grattan, *Light for the Last Days. A Study Historical and Prophetical*, London, 1886, [2]1917

Guinness, Grattan, *Lucy Guinness Kumm. Her Life Story. With Extracts from Her Writings*, London, 1907

Guinness, Grattan, *Mosaic History and Gospel Story, Epitomized in the Congo Language with Translations of Several Passages of Scripture*, London, 1882

Guinness, Grattan, *Romanism and the Reformation from the Standpoint of Prophecy*, London, 1887

Guinness, Grattan, *The Approaching End of the Age*, Frome/London, 1878, New York, 1881

Guinness, Grattan, *The City of the Seven Hills. A Poem*, London, 1891

Guinness, Grattan, *The Congo Crisis*, London, 1908

Guinness, Grattan, *The Divine Programme of the World's History*, London, 1888

Guinness, Grattan, 'The East-End Training Institute for Home and Foreign Missions, by an "Hon. Sec." in *The Illustrated Missionary News*, 1874, pp. 96, 108, 120, 131

Guinness, Grattan, *The Heresy, Taught by the Rev. G. O. Barnes ('The Kentucky Evangelist') Exposed and Answered*, London, n.d.

Guinness, Harry, *Congo Slavery. A brief survey of the Congo Question from the humanitarian point of view*, London, n.d., (*ca.* 1905)

Guinness, Harry, *Not Unto Us. Record of Twenty One Years' Missionary Service*, London, n.d.

Guinness, Henry Seymour; Guinness, Brian, *The Guinness Family*, n.d., ²1969

Guinness, Lucy, *Across India at the Dawn of the 20th Century*, London, 1898

Guinness, Lucy, *Enter Thou. Pages from the Life Story of Fanny E. Guinness*, London, 1899

Guinness, Lucy, *Only a Factory Girl*, London, 1886

Guinness, Lucy, *To Help to Heal. A Missionary Study and an Appeal for Prayer*, London, n.d., (1896)

Guinness, Lucy and Millard, E. C., *South America. The Neglected Continent*, London, 1894

Guinness, Michele, *The Guinness Legend*, London *et al.*, 1990

Gundry, Stanley N., 'Hermeneutics or Zeitgeist as the Determining Factor in the History of Eschatologies?' in *Journal of the Evangelical Theological Society*, 1970, p. 50

Gundry, Stanley N., *Love Them In. The Life and Theology of D. L. Moody*, Grand Rapids, 1982 (1976)

Hafley, James and Marti, *Uncle Cam*, London *et al.*, 1974

Hägg, Fritz, *Svenska Alliansmissionen genom hundra år*, Jönköping, 1953

Hall, Douglas, *Not Made for Defeat. The Authorized Biography of Oswald J. Smith*, London, ²1970 (1969)

Hall, John and Stuart, George H., *The American Evangelists D. L. Moody and Ira Sankey In Great Britain and Ireland*, New York, 1875

Hamilton, Jean, *A Stranger Came. An Account of the Missionary Enterprise of the Church of Christ in Nigeria as Told Through the Lives of Some Nigerian Missionaries*, Sidcup, 1984

Handy, Robert T., 'The American Religious Depression, 1925–1935', (Presidential address, American Society of Church History, 1959)

Harris, Leonard F., *Our Days Are in His Hands. A Short History of the Unevangelized Fields Mission*, London, n.d.

Harrison, Mary, *Mama Harri—and No Nonsense. Missionary Memoirs of a Congo Casualty*, London, 1969

Hartzfeld, David F. and Nienkirchen, Charles, *The Birth of a Vision. Essays by Members of the Faculty of Canadian Bible College and the Faculty of Canadian Theological Seminary Regina, Saskatchewan, the Official College and Seminary of The Christian and Missionary Alliance in Canada on the Occasion of the Centennial of the Christian and Missionary Alliance 1887–1987*, Regina, 1986

Hay, Alexander R., *Practising New Testament Methods in South America*, London, 1932

Hay, Ian M., *A Study of the Relationship Between SIM International and the Evangelical Missionary Society*, DMiss, Trinity/Deerfield, 1984

Hay, Ian M., *Unity and Purity: Keeping the Balance*, Scarborough *et al.*, (SIM), 1983

Haye, Sophie de la, *Byang Kato. Ambassador for Christ*, Achimota, 1986

Haye, Sophie de la, *Tread upon the Lion. The Story of Tommie Titcombe*, Toronto *et al.*, ³1980 (1974)

Heggoy, Willy N., *Fifty Years of Evangelical Missionary Movement in North Africa, 1881–1931*, PhD, Hartford, 1960

Held, Johannes, *Anfänge einer deutschen Muhammedanermission. Rückblick auf die ersten 25 Jahre der Sudan-Pionier-Mission 1900–25*, Wiesbaden, 1925

*Helgeseförbundet 1887–1937*, Torp, 1937

*Helgeseförbundets missionsverksamhet. En återblick vid 25-årsjubileet, den 23–25 Juni 1912*, Torp, 1912

Henkel, Reinhard, *Christian Missions in Africa. A Social Geographical Study of the Impact of Their Activities in Zambia*, Berlin, 1989

Henry, Carl F., *The Uneasy Conscience of Modern Fundamentalism*, Grand Rapids, 1949

Henry, Marie, *The Secret Life of Hannah*

Whitall Smith, Grand Rapids, 1984

Jenkinson, Herbert, A Brief History of the UFM in Congo/Zaire, (unpublished), (1978)

Heyer, Friedrich, 'St Chrischona in Äthiopien' in Fides pro mundi vita, (Festschrift Hans-Werner Gensichen), Gütersloh 1980, pp. 133–147

Hildebrandt, Jonathan, 'Africa Inland Church Missionary College, Eldoret, Kenya' in William D. Taylor (ed.), Internationalizing Missionary Training: a Global Perspective, Exeter/Grand Rapids, 1991, pp. 97–109

Hillyer, H. S., Being Sent Forth. The Story of Canadian Baptist Missionary Advance into Angola, Toronto, n.d.

Hjelm, K. A., Swedish Alliance Mission e South Africa 1901–1951, Piet Retif, 1951

Hocken, Peter D., Charismatic Movement, in DPCM, pp. 130–160

Hocken, Peter D., 'Polhill, Cecil H.', in DPCM, p. 718

Hodges, Melvin L., Build My Church, Springfield, 1957

Hodges, Melvin L., The Indigenous Church, Springfield, 1953

Holmes, Kenneth, The Cloud Moves, London, [5]1974 (1963)

Holthaus, Stephan, Protestantischer Fundamentalismus in Deutschland— Geschichte und Erscheinungsbild, Bonn, 1993

Hotchkiss, Willis Ray, Sketches from the Dark Continent, London, 1903, [2]1906

Hotchkiss, Willis Ray, Then and Now in Kenya Colony. Forty Adventurous Years in East Africa, London/Edinburgh, 1937

Houghton, George Gerald, The Contribution of Adoniram Judson Gordon to American Christianity, ThD, Dallas Theological Seminary, 1970

Hughes, George, Fragrant Memories of the Tuesday Meetings and The Guide to Holiness, and their Fifty Years' Work for Jesus, New York, n.d.

Hughes, George, The Beloved Physician Walter C. Palmer, M.D. His Sun-Lit Journey to the Celestial City, New York, 1884

Hunter, J. H., A Flame of Fire. The Life and Work of R. V. Bingham, Toronto, 1961

Hussein, Samuel Ali, Aus meinem Leben, Wiesbaden, 1920

'In A Strange Land. Two Topeka Missionaries Lose Their Lives' in The Topeka Daily Capital, 13 August 1890

Irvine, Cecilia, The Church of Christ in Zaire. A Handbook of Protestant Churches, Missions and Communities, 1878–1978, Indianapolis, 1978

Johanson, Bernhard A., We Watched it Grow. A Story of the Union Bible Institute, Durban, 1971

Johnson, John Dye, God Planted Five Seeds, Sanford, [4]1981 (1966)

Johnston, Kenneth, The Story of the New Tribes Mission, Sanford, 1985

Johnstone, Patrick, Operation World, Bromley/Waynesboro, GA/Gerrards Cross, 1993 (1974)

Jones, Charles Edwin, A Guide to the Study of the Holiness Movement, Metuchen, NJ, 1974

Jones, Charles Edwin, Perfectionist Persuasion: the Holiness Movement and American Methodism, 1867–1936, Metuchen, NJ, 1974

Jooste, Die Africa Evangelistic Band in Wese en Praktyk, Bloemfontein, 1957

Juhnke, James C., A People of Mission. A History of General Conference Mennonite Overseas Missions, Newton Kansas, 1979

Kallam, James Gray, A History of the Africa Evangelical Fellowship From Its Inception to 1917, PhD, New York University, 1978

Kane, J. Herbert, Faith Mighty Faith, Wheaton, 1956

'Kanuni na sheria za African Brotherhood Church' in Momanyisyo ma Atongoi ma Ikanisa, Machakos, n.d., (valid 1986)

Karlson, Elsa, Med Gud i Kongo. Personliga minnen och upplevelser, Örebro, 1956

Kato, Byang H., African Cultural Revolution and Christian Faith, Jos, 1976

Kato, Byang H., Biblical Christianity in Africa, Achimota, 1985.

Kato, Byang H., 'Black Theology and African Theology', (Public lecture delivered at the University of Nairobi, 27

September 1975) in *Perception* (AEAM, Nairobi)

Kato, Byang H., *The Spirits: What the Bible Teaches*, Achimota, 1975

Kato, Byang H., *Theological Pitfalls in Africa*, Kisumu, 1975

Keyes, Lawrence E., *The Last Age of Missions. A Study of Third World Mission Societies*, Pasadena, 1983

Kila, Ang'apoza Etsea, *L'episcopos, Pasteur de l'Église Locale*, Maître en Science Religieuses Facult Libre de Thologie Evanglique Vaux-sur-Seine, 1981

Kisulu, Peter Mualuko, *A Missionary Called Peter*, Kijabe, 1983

Klassen, Jacob P., 'A. B. Simpson and the Tensions in the Preparation of Missionaries' in Hartzfeld and Nienkirchen, *The Birth of a Vision*, pp. 241–259

Kore, Danfulani Zamani, *An Analysis and Evaluation of Church Administration in the Evangelical Churches of West Africa, Nigeria*, PhD, North Texas State University, 1980

Kouakou, Andr Konadio, *Les méthodes d'évangelisation utilisés par les missionaires évangliques en Côte d'Ivoire*, Vaux, 1975

Kouakou, Andr Konadio, 'Les Ministéres dans les églises Protestantes d'Afrique Francophone', DTh, Strasbourg, 1980

Kruger, Etienne, 'Histoire de la Société des Missions évangliques de Paris' in Blanc, Blocher and Kruger, *Histoire des Missions Protestantes Françaises*, Flavion, 1970

Kumm, Karl, 'A Crisis in the Mission Field', (Prot. SUM, February 1906)

Kumm, Karl, *African Missionary Heroes and Heroines*, New York, 1917

Kumm, Karl, 'Crisis in Hausaland—Cross or Crescent' in *Lightbearer*, 1908, p. 173

Kumm, Karl, *From Hausaland to Egypt Through the Sudan*, London, 1910

Kumm, Karl, *Khont-Hon-Nofer. The Lands of Ethiopia*, London/Edinburgh, 1910

Kumm, Karl, *The Sudan. A Short Compendium of Facts and Figures about the Land of Darkness*, London, 1907

Kumm, Karl, 'To all Christians in England, Scotland, Ireland and Wales' in Prot SUM September 1904

Kumm, Karl, *Versuch einer wissenschaftlichen Darstellung der wirtschaftsgeographischen Verhältnisse Nubiens von Assuan bis Dongola*, Diss Freiburg, 1903

LaBerge, Agnes O., *What God Hath Wrought*, n.p., n.d.

Lager, Eileen, *Merging Streams*, Elkhart, 1979

Lagergren, David (ed.), *I Kongo. Svensk baptistmission under 50 år i ord och bild*, n.p., 1969

Lagergren, David, *Mission and State in the Congo. A Study of the Relations Between Protestant Missions and the Congo Independent State Authorities With Special Reference to the Equator District, 1885–1903*, (Studia Missionalia Uppsaliensia XIII, 1970)

Laird, Margaret N., *They Called Me Mama*, Chicago, 1975

Lang, G. H., *Anthony Norris Groves*, London, 1949

Lange, Dieter, *Eine Bewegung bricht sich Bahn. Die deutschen Gemeinschaften im ausgehenden 19. und beginnenden 20. Jahrhundert und ihre Stellung zu Kirche, Theologie und Pfingstbewegung*, Giessen/Gnadau/Berlin(East), 1979

Langworthy, Emily Booth, *This Africa Was Mine*, Stirling, 1952

Latourette, Kenneth Scott, *A History of The Expansion of Christianity*, 7 volumes, New York, 1937–45. References in the text refer to the Zondervan edition Chicago [5]1976, (1970)

Law, William, *A Practical Treatease Upon Christian Perfection*, London, 1726

Law, William, *A Serious Call to a Devout and Holy Life, Adapted to the State and Condition af all Orders of Christians*, London, 1729, [2]1732, [6]1753, [10]1772, also Philadelphia, 1948, (Westminster Press) *et al.*

Law, William, *The Power of the Spirit. With Additional Extracts From the Writings of W. Law*, selected and with an introduction by A. Murray, London, 1896

Linden, Jane and Linden, Ian, 'John Chilembwe and the New Jerusalem' in

*Journal of African History,* 12 (4), 1971, pp. 629–651

Lindsay, Gordon, *John Alexander Dowie. A Life Story of Trials, Tragedies and Triumphs,* Dallas, 1980

Lindsell, Harold, 'Faith Missions Since 1938' in W. C. Harr (ed.), *Frontiers of Christian World Mission Since 1938,* New York/London, 1962 (Latourette Festschrift)

Linn, Jason S., *The Light of the Gospel in Pagan Isles,* Djakarta, 1954

'List of Nyasa Mission Schools With Names of Supporters and Native Teachers, (n.d., copy in Yale University Day Missions Library)

Loewen, Melvin J., *Three Score. The Story of an Emerging Mennonite Church in Central Africa,* Elkhart, 1972

Lohrentz, Kenneth P., 'Joseph Booth, Charles Domingo and the Seventh Day Baptists in Northern Nyassaland, 1910–1912' in *Journal of African History,* 12 (3), 1971, pp. 461–480

Lorentzen, Kari, 'Det Norske Misjonsforbunds arbeid i Sur-Afrika' in *Det Norske Misjonsforbunds Ytremisjon. Utgitt til Det Norske Misjonsforbunds 100-års-jubileum,* n.p., n.d.

Lundahl, J. E., *Vår yttre mission. Svenska Missionsförbundets mission i Kongo, Kina, Ost-Turkestan m.n.,* Stockholm, 1916

Lutz, Lorry, *Born to Lose. Bound to Win. The Amazing Journey of Mother Eliza George,* Irvine, CA, 1980

Lyall, Leslie T., *A Passion for the Impossible. The Continuing Story of the Mission Hudson Taylor Began,* London, [2]1976 (1965)

M'Keown, Robert L., *Twenty-Five Years in Qua Iboe. The Story of a Missionary Effort in Nigeria,* London/Belfast, 1912

Ma, Nancy K. W., *Chinese Missionaries in Indonesia,* MA, Columbia Bible College, 1972

Macindoe, Betty, *Going for God,* London, 1972

Mackintosh, C. W., *Dr Harry Guinness. The Life Story of Henry Grattan Guinness,* London, 1916

Maclean, J. Kennedy, *Dr Pierson and his*

*Message. A Sketch of the Life and Work of a Great Preacher, Together With a Varied Selection From His Unpublished Manuscripts,* New York, 1911

Maddox, Randy L., 'Responsible Grace' in *Wesleyan Theological Journal. Bulletin of the Wesleyan Theological Society,* Asbury Theological Seminary, 1984, pp. 7ff.

Magama, Luyeye; Ndolila, Malenso; Mlemvo, Mbenga-Bohuma, *Église du Christ au Zaire. Cent ans de présence protestante au Zaire,* Kinshasa, 1978

Magnusson, J. (ed.), *50 år i ord och bild 1892-1942. Jubileumskrift for Örebro Missionsförening,* Örebro, 1942

Magnusson, John, Lagerquist, Sven and Sollerman, Samuel (eds), *Örebro Missionsskola 1908–58,* Örebro, 1958

Mahan, Asa, *Autobiography. Intellectual, Moral, and Spiritual,* London, 1882

Mahan, Asa, *Christian Perfection,* London, [2]1875, (1874)

Mahan, Asa, *Out of Darkness into Light; or The Hidden Life Made Manifest,* London/Edinburgh, 1875, Louisville, n.d. (1876)

Mahan, Asa, *The Baptism of the Holy Ghost,* New York, 1870, London, 1872

Mahan, Asa, *The Promise of the Spirit; or, The Scripture Doctrine of the Baptism of the Holy Ghost,* London, 1874

Mangolopa, Kambale, *Histoire de la Communaut Baptiste au Kivu 'C.B.K.'. Son origine et son volution au cours de ses deux premières décénies 1959 à 1979,* Goma, [2]1984, (1979)

Marsh, Charles R., *Streams in the Sahara,* Bath, 1972

Marsh, Charles R., *Too Hard for God?,* Bath, [5]1973, (1970)

Martin, Roger, *R. A. Torrey. Apostle of Certainty,* Murfreesboro, 1976

Massenbach, Gertrud von, *Als Mohrenland noch christlich war,* Wiesbaden, 1930

Massenbach, Gertrud von, *Mohrenland wird seine Hände ausstrecken zu Gott,* Wiesbaden, 1952

Mavumilusa, Makanzu, *L'histoire de l'E.C.Z.,* Kinshasa, 1973

Maxwell, J. Lowry, *Half a Century of Grace. A Jubilee History of the Sudan United*

*Mission*, London, n.d.

Maxwell, L. E., *Prairie Pillars*, Three Hills, 1971

Mayor, Henri-Samuel, *L'Évangile en Kabylie*, Lausanne, 1883

Mbodo, Nsafu, *La Communaut Évanglique de l'Alliance au Zaire*, grad. theol., Kinshasa, 1984

McClung, L. Grant, '[Pentecostal] Missiology' in *DPCM*, pp. 607–609

McGee, Gary B., 'Missions, Overseas (North American)' in *DPCM*, pp. 610–625

McGee, Gary B., *This Gospel Shall Be Preached*, Springfield, 1986

McIlwain, Trevor, 'Key Old Testament Passages for Translation' in *Outreach*, December 1983, p. 1

McIlwain, Trevor, 'Old Testament Teaching for New Testament Saints' in *Outreach*, September 1984, pp. 1–3

McIlwain, Trevor, *The Chronological Approach to Evangelism and Church Planting* (provisional edition), Sanford, 1985

McIlwain, Trevor and Nancy Everson, *Firm Foundations. Creation to Christ*, Sanford, 1991

McKay, Moira J., *Faith and Facts in the History of the China Inland Mission 1832–1905*, MLitt, Aberdeen, 1981

Meyer, Frederick Brotherton, *The Call and Challenge of the Unseen*, London, 1928

Meyer, Frederick Brotherton, *The Soul's Pure Intention*, London, 1906

Miller, Basil, *A Beautiful Life. The Story of Esther K. Miller*, Pasadena, 1970

Miller, Basil, *Arms Around the World*, Pasadena, 1971

Miller, Basil, *Dreams Fulfilled*, Pasadena, 1971

Miller, Basil, *Those were the Days*, Pasadena, 1970

Miller, Basil, *Years to Remember*, Pasadena, 1971

Miller, David L., 'Building New Relations of Production During the Transition to Colonial Rule: the Case of Christian Missions and Lower Pokomoni' in Niels-

Peter Moritzen and J. C. Winter, *Ostafrikanische Völker zwischen Mission und Regierung. Referate einer Arbeitskonferenz 16–18 June 1982*, pp. 131–142

Miller, David L., 'Problems and Possibilities in the Period of Colonial Consolidation: Christian Missions and Lower Pokomoni, *circa* 1900–1920' in *Ibid.*, pp. 43–163

*Minneskrift vid Helgelseförbundets fyrtioårsjubileum 1. Juni 1927*, Götabro, 1927

Minter, Georgie B., 'To Die Is Gain. An Appreciation of Carrie E. Merriweather' in *Alliance Weekly*, 25 April 1931

Moody Bible Institute, *Here We Stand*, Chicago, 1986

Moody, Dwight Lyman, *Power from on High*, London, n.d.

Moody, Dwight Lyman, *Secret Power; or, The Secret of Success in Christian Life and Christian Work*, Chicago, 1881

Moody, William R., *The Life of D. L. Moody*, New York, 1900

Mortenson, Vernon, *This is TEAM*, Wheaton, [3]1985, (1967)

Moules, Leonard (ed.), *WEC Leadership Manual*, (especially: 'Leadership Under C. T. Studd', pp. 2–11)

Muhr, Marlène, *Along Unfamiliar Paths . . . Proclaiming God's Light in Man's Night. The Story of Gospel Recordings Europe*, Glendale, 1982

Muinde, Philip K., *Missionary Attitudes and Assumptions Regarding Tribal Societies. A Study of the Africa Inland Mission Pioneers in Ukambani (1895–1900)*, MLitt, Aberdeen, 1976

Müller, George, *A Narrative of Some of the Lord's Dealings with George Müller Written by Himself*, London, [9]1895, ([1]1837)

Müller, George, *Autobiography*, Bristol/London, 1905

Munn, Robert, *These Forty Years. A Testimony of God's Faithfulness During Forty Years of Active Missionary Service*, n.p., 1981, (*Quarante ans d'aventure avec Dieu. Un témoignage de la fidélité de Dieu pendant quarante ans dans la mission*, Valence, 1985)

Murray, Andrew, *Abide in Christ. Thoughts on the Blessed Life of Fellowship With the Son of God*, London, 1882, (1895, 68th thousand, London/Edinburgh, 1963 *et al.*)

Murray, Andrew, *Absolute Surrender. Addresses Delivered in England and Scotland*, London 1895 (*et al.*, London/Edinburgh, 1957)

Murray, Andrew, 'De Soedan' in *De Kerkbode*, 1907, pp. 443, 481

Murray, Andrew, *Divine Healing. A Series of Addresses and a Personal Testimony*, London, 1934, (1900)

Murray, Andrew, 'George Müller and His Second Conversion', appendix to: *The Two Covenants and the Second Blessing*, London, 1899

Murray, Andrew, *Holy in Christ. Thoughts on the Calling of God's Children to be Holy as He Is*, London, 1888

Murray, Andrew, *The Full Blessing of Pentecost. The One Thing Needful*, London, 1908

Murray, Andrew, *The Key to the Missionary Problem. Thoughts Suggested by the Report of the Ecumenical Missionary Conference Held in New York*, April 1900, London, 1901

Murray, Andrew, *The State of the Church. A Plea for More Prayer*, London, [3]1912, (written for Edinburgh, 1910)

Murray, Andrew, *The Two Covenants and the Second Blessing*, London, 1898

Murray, Jocelyn, *The Kikuyu Female Circumcision Controversy, With Special Reference to the Church Missionary Society's Sphere of Influence*, PhD, UCLA, 1974

Mutiso, Ruth M., *African Brotherhood Church. Miaka Arobaini ya Kazi 8.4.1945–8.4.1985*, Machakos, 1985

N. N., 'Are the Heathen Safe?' in *South African Pioneer*, 1891, p. 193

N. N., *Dr Guinness Self-Refuted. Inconsistency of the Congo Balolo Missionaries*, Edinburgh, 1905, ('A Congolese Pamphlet')

N. N., *Founded on the Word, Focused on the World. The Story of the Conservative Baptist Foreign Mission Society*, Wheaton, 1978

N. N., *Promoted! or, A Brief Life Sketch of P. Cameron Scott*, New York, 1897

N. N., *Root from Dry Ground. The Story of the Sudan Interior Mission*, London, 1966

N. N., *Swedish Alliance Mission e South Africa 1901–1951*, Piet Retief, 1951

N. N., *The Evangelical Missionary Society of the Evangelical Churches of West Africa*, Jos, n.d.

N. N., *The Jubilee of the Nyasa Mission 1893–1943*, Cowley, 1943

N. N., *The Mutilation of Natives. The Cutting off of Hands*, Brussels, 1905, ('A Congolese Pamphlet')

Nangle, E., *The Baptism of Infants, as Taught and Practised in the Church of England, A Divine Institution. With Strictures on a Pamphlet by Henry Grattan Guinness, on 'Believers' Baptism'*, London/Dublin, n.d.

Nienkirchen, Charles, 'A. B. Simpson: Forerunner and Critic of the Pentecostal Movement' in Hartzfeld and Nienkirchen, *The Birth of a Vision*, pp. 125–164

Niklaus, Robert L., Sawin, John S. and Stoesz, Samuel J., *All For Jesus. God at Work in The Christian and Missionary Alliance Over One Hundred Years*, Camp Hill, 1986

Nilsen, Maria and Sheetz, Paul H., *Malla Moe*, Chicago, [8]1980, (1956)

Nkounkou, Hilaire *et al.*, *75e Anniversaire de la fondation de Madzia et de l'évangelisation du Congo par les missionaires protestants*, Brazzaville, 1984

Nyasa Mission, *The Jubilee of the Nyasa Mission 1893–1943*

Ommundsen, Odd, 'Den frie östafrikanske mission' in *Det Norske Misjonsforbunds Ytremisjon*

Ongman, John, *Finnes det frälsning efter döden?*, Örebro, 1925, 1926

Ongman, John, *Samleda skrifter*, 3 volumes, Örebro, 1931, 1931, 1934

*Örebro Missionsskola 1909–1933. Minneskrift med porträttsamling*, Örebro, 1933

*Örebro Missionsskola 75 år, 1908–83*

Orr, James Edwin, *The Eager Feet. Evangelical Awakenings 1790–1830*,

Chicago, 1975

Orr, James Edwin, *The Fervent Prayer. The Worldwide Impact of the Great Awakening of 1858*, Chicago, 1974

Orr, James Edwin, *The Flaming Tongue. Evangelical Awakenings, 1900–*, Chicago, ²1975, (1973)

Orr, James Edwin, *The Second Evangelical Awakening in Britain*, London/Edinburgh, 1949

Orr, James Edwin, *The Second Evangelical Awakening. An Account of the Second Worldwide Evangelical Revival Beginning in the Mid-nineteenth Century* (an abridgement of two theses—'The Second Evangelical Awakening in America' and 'The Second Evangelical Awakening in Britain'), London, 1955

Ottersen, Roger W., *The Christian Catholic Church Around The World*, Zion, 1985

Overseas Missionary Fellowship, *Principles and Practice*, 1966

Pache, Ren, *Dr Pierre de Benoit 1884–1963. Notice biographique*, Vennes, 1965

Palmer, Phoebe (ed.), *Pioneer Experiences*, New York, 1868

Palmer, Phoebe, *Faith and its Effects*, New York, 1854

Palmer, Phoebe, *The Way of Holiness*, Boston, ⁵⁰1867

Palmquist, Frank, 'Några korta anteckningar om Skandinaviska Alliansmissionens verksamhet i Kulesa och Lemu, Öst-Afrika, från år 1893 till år 1908' in Josephine Princell (ed.), *Alliansmissionens Tjugufemårsminnen 1891–1916*, Chicago, 1916

Paxson, Ruth, *Life On the Highest Plane*, 3 volumes in one, Chicago, 1928

Pearson, B. H., *The Vision Lives. A Profile Of Mrs Charles E. Cowman*, Los Angeles, 1961, London, 1962

Peckham, Colin N., *The Africa Evangelistic Band. An Historical and Doctrinal Appraisal*, Diploma of Theology, Theological College, Johannesburg, 1973

Penn-Lewis, Jessie, *The 'Magna Charta' of Woman 'According to the Scriptures'*, Bournemouth, 1919, (*The Magna Charta of Women*, Minneapolis, 1975)

Percy, Douglas C., *Doctor To Africa. The Story of Stirrett of the Sudan*, Toronto/New York, 1948

Philafrican Liberators' League, 'The First Expedition Successful, New York 1897' in Alida Chatelin (ed.), *Les Rapports de la Mission philafricaine 1898–1905*, Lausanne, n.d.

Phillips, K. N., *Tom Collins of Kenya. Son of Valour*, London, n.d., (1965)

Phiri, D. D., *John Chilembwe*, Blantyre, 1976

Pierson, Arthur Tappan, *A Spiritual Clinique. Four Bible Readings Given at Keswick in 1907*, London, 1907

Pierson, Arthur Tappan, *Catherine of Siena: An Ancient Lay Preacher. A Story of Sanctified Womanhood and Power in Prayer*, New York/London, 1898

Pierson, Arthur Tappan, *Forward Movements of the Last Half Century. Being a Glance at the More Marked Philanthropic, Missionary and Spiritual Movements Characteristic of Our Time*, New York/London, 1900 (Garland Reprint New York/London, 1984)

Pierson, Arthur Tappan, *George Müller of Bristol*, London, ⁶1901, (1899)

Pierson, Arthur Tappan, 'Promoting Missions by Indirection. A Tribute to the Work of D. L. Moody' in WWW, 1910, pp. 276–280

Pierson, Arthur Tappan, *The Acts of the Holy Spirit*, Harrisburg, 1980, (¹1895), London, 1913 *et al.*

Pierson, Arthur Tappan, *The Crisis of Missions or, The Voice out of the Cloud*, London, ⁴1904, (1886)

Pierson, Arthur Tappan, *The Divine Enterprise of Missions. A Series of Lectures*, London, 1892

Pierson, Arthur Tappan, *The Greatest Work in the World; or, the Evangelization of All People in the Present Century*, New York/Chicago, 1891, London (revised), 1891

Pierson, Arthur Tappan, *The Heart of the Gospel. Twelve Sermons Delivered at the Metropolitan Tabernacle, in the Autumn of 1891*, London, 1892

Pierson, Arthur Tappan, *The Keswick Movement in Precept and Practice*, New

York/London, 1903

Pierson, Arthur Tappan, *The Miracle of Missions, or the Modern Marvel in the History of Missionary Enterprise*, London, 1891

Pierson, Arthur Tappan, *The Modern Mission Century, Viewed as a Cycle of Divine Working. A Review of the Missions in the Nineteenth Century*, London, 1901

Pierson, Arthur Tappan, *The New Acts of the Apostles; or, Marvels of Modern Missions*, London, 1894

Pierson, Arthur Tappan, *The Story of Keswick and its Beginnings*, London, 1897

Pierson, Arthur Tappan, 'The World's Want and the Church's Neglect' in *WWW*, 1883, p. 29

Pierson, Delavan Leonard, *Arthur T. Pierson. A Biography by His Son*, London, 1912

Pigott, Blanche A. F., *I. Lilias Trotter. Founder of the Algiers Mission Band*, London/Edinburgh, n.d.

Pollock, John, *Hudson Taylor and Maria. Pioneers in China*, London, 1962

Pollock, John, *Moody Without Sankey*, London et al., [2]1983, (1963)

Pollock, John, *The Cambridge Seven*, Basingstoke, [2]1985, (1955)

Pollock, John, *The Keswick Story. The Authorized History of the Keswick Convention*, London, 1964

Polnick, Bertha, *Carl Polnick. Ein Lebensbild*, Barmen, 1920

Porter, Douglas D., *At Thy Disposal. The Beginnings of the Egypt General Mission*, London, 1934

Price, Oliver, 'The Historical Background of the Five Fundamentals' in *Bibliotheca Sacra*, p. 118, (1961), pp. 35–40

Price, Wendell W., *The Role of Women in the Ministry of the Christian and Missionary Alliance*, DMiss, San Francisco Theological Seminary, 1977

Prince, John and Moyra, *No Fading Vision. The First 50 Years of the Asia Pacific Christian Mission*, n.p., 1981

Pritchard, Elizabeth, *For Such a Time as This. God's Faithfulness Through the Regions Beyond Missionary Union for a Hundred Years*, Lottbridge Drove, 1971

Procter, John Craig, *The Cross in Southern Africa. A History of the South Africa General Mission Prepared for the American Council South Africa General Mission*, New York, 1945, (typescript)

Pyles, Franklin Arthur, 'The Missionary Eschatologie of A. B. Simpson' in Hartzfeld and Nienkirchen, *The Birth of a Vision*, pp. 29–48

Qua Iboe Mission, *Annual Report*, 1916, 1918, 1933, 1936

Qua Iboe Mission Association, *First Annual Report for the Year Ending 31st December 1889*, Belfast, 1890

Qua Iboe Mission Mountpottinger Auxiliary. *Its origin and management*, Belfast, n.d.

Qua Iboe Mission Occasional Paper, January, 1891

Qua Iboe Mission Occasional Paper, March 1896

Qua Iboe Mission Occasional Paper, November 1890

Qua Iboe Mission Occasional Paper, October 1893, 'Memoirs of Keswick 1893. By a first attender'

Ratzlaff, Dwayne, 'An Old Mediaeval Message. A Turning Point in the Life of A. B. Simpson' in Hartzfeld and Nienkirchen, *The Birth of a Vision*, pp. 165–194

*Record of the Convention for the Promotion of Holiness Held at Brighton, May 29, to June 7th, 1875*, Brighton, n.d., (Garland Reprint, NY, 1984)

Rediger, C. E. (ed.), *25 Years of Mission Work in Belgian Congo*, Chicago, 1938

Reed, George C., *Memories of Morocco 1897–1914*, n.d., (unpublished, 55 pages)

Reed, Jane and Jim Grant, *Voice Under Every Palm. The Story of Radio Station ELWA*, Grand Rapids, [2]1970, (1968)

Regions Beyond Missionary Union, *Principles and Practice*, Revised Edition, 1956

Reinmiller, R. J., *Gospel Missionary Union. Early History*, (unpublished), (1964)

Rennstich, Karl, *Nicht jammern, sondern Hand anlegen! Christian Friedrich Spittler. Sein Werk und Leben*, Metzingen, 1987

Report of the Proceedings of the Conference, held at Freemasons' Hall, London, from August 19th to September 2nd inclusive, 1846, London, 1847

Reynolds, Lindsay, Footprints. The Beginning of The Christian and Missionary Alliance in Canada, Toronto, 1981

Richardson, Kenneth, Garden of Miracles. The Story of the Africa Inland Mission, London, [2]1976 (1968)

Robeck, Cecil M., 'National Association of Evangelicals' in DPCM, pp. 634–636 (p. 635)

Robert, Dana L., ' "The Crisis of Missions": Premillennial Missions Theory and the Origins of Independent Evangelical Missions' in Carpenter and Shenk, Earthen Vessels, pp. 29–46

Robert, Dana L., 'The Legacy of Adoniram Judson Gordon' in IBMR, 1987, pp. 176–181

Roberts, W. Dayton and Siewert, John A. (eds), Mission Handbook. USA/Canada Protestant Ministries Overseas, Monrovia/ Grand Rapids, [14]1989

Roche, John Alexander, The Life of Mrs Sarah A. Lankford Palmer, Who for Sixty Years was the Able Teacher of Entire Holiness, New York, 1898

Root, Jean Christie, Edward Irving. Man, Preacher, Prophet, Boston, 1912

Roseveare, Helen, Doctor among Congo Rebels, London, [2]1965

Roseveare, Helen, Doctor Returns to Congo, London, 1967

Roseveare, Helen, Give Me This Mountain. An Autobiography, London, 1966, Leicester, 1985

Roseveare, Helen, Living Holiness, London, 1986

Roseveare, Helen, Living Sacrifice, London, 1979

Roseveare, Helen, Living Stones. Sacrifice, Faith, Holiness, Fellowship: 75 Years of WEC, London et al., 1988

Roth, Alfred, Otto Stockmayer. Ein Zeuge und Nachfolger Jesu Christi, Gotha, 1925, ([2]1938)

Rowbotham, Elsie, It Happened in Scotland. Would You Believe It!, Gerrards Cross,

[5]1982 (1963)

Rowdon, Harold H., The Origins of the Brethren Movement: 1825–1850, London, 1967

Rubingh, Eugene, Sons of Tiv. A Study of the Rise of the Church Among the Tiv of Central Nigeria, Grand Rapids, 1969

Ruscoe, Alfred W., The Lame Take the Prey. An Autobiography, Ft Washington/ Toronto, 1968

Salliens, Reuben, 'The Religious State of France and the McAll Mission' in WWW, 1888, pp. 896–902

Sandeen, Ernest R., The Roots of Fundamentalism. British and American Millenarianism, 1800–1930, Chicago, 1970

Sandgren, David P., The Kikuyu, Christianity and the Africa Inland Mission, PhD, University of Wisconsin-Madison, 1976, Ann Arbor (UMI), 1976

Sauer, Eileen, The Dynamics Affecting Faith Mission Finance, MA, Columbia Bible College, 1969

Sawin, John, 'The Fourfold Gospel' in Hartzfeld and Nienkirchen, The Birth of a Vision, pp. 1–28

Schenk, Raymond, A Study of the New Testament Bases for the Teaching of Dr Albert B. Simpson on Divine Healing, MA, Wheaton, 1964

Schick, Erich; Haag, Klaus; Christian Friedrich Spittler. Handlanger Gottes, Giessen/Basel, [2]1982

Schirrmacher, Bernd, Baumeister ist der Herr. Erfahrungen göttlicher Kleinarbeit in einem Missionswerk, Neuhausen, 1978

Schlansky, Elisabeth; Doering, Alma, Die Kongo-Inland Mission, Brieg, n.d. (1915)

Schlyter, Herman, Der China-Missionar Karl Gützlaff und seine Heimatbasis. Studien über das Interesse des Abendlandes an der Mission des China-Pioniers Karl Gützlaff und über seinen Einsatz als Missionserwecker, Lund, 1976

Schlyter, Herman, Karl Gützlaff als Missionar in China, Lund, 1946

Schrupp, Ernst, 'Die gemeindliche Sendung' in EM, January 1987, pp. 10–14

Scofield, Cyrus Ingersoll, Rightly Dividing

*the Word of Truth*, many editions, some of them altered, today easily accessible in the unaltered 14th edn, Grand Rapids, 1976

Sell, Alan P. F., *The Great Debate. Calvinism, Arminianism and Salvation*, Worthing, 1982, Grand Rapids, 1983

Sheetz, Paul H., *The Sovereign Hand*, Wheaton, 1971

Shelley, Bruce L., *A History of Conservative Baptists*, Wheaton, [3]1981 (1971)

Shepperson, George A. and Price, Thomas, *Independent African: John Chilembwe and the Origins, Setting and Significance of the Nyasaland Native Rising of 1915*, Edinburgh, 1958

Sherwood, J. M., 'Mr Moody's Training School' in *WWW*, 1889, p. 945f.

Sherwood, Terence, 'In the Beginning' in *Family News*, 1985, p. 12

Sherwood, 'Terence, Paul Lenn (Kwang Lin)' in *Family News*, 1885, p. 6f.

Siikanen, Riitta, 'Die finnischen Missionen' in *EM*, 1987, p. 41f.

SIM International, *Manual*, 1984, 1986

Simpson, Albert B., 'A New Missionary Movement' in *WWW*, 1882, pp. 33ff.

Simpson, Albert B., *Baptism and the Baptism of the Holy Spirit*, New York, 1902

Simpson, Albert B., *Christ Life: or, the Life of Christ Made Real in the Life of the Believer*, London, 1895, [2]1911

Simpson, Albert B., 'Christianity's Crime', Sermon During the Asbury Park Convention (31 July 1892) on Proverbs 24:11f. in: Simpson, Albert B., *Missionary Messages*, pp. 69–84

Simpson, Albert B., *Divine Healing and Natural Law*, New York, 1896

Simpson, Albert B., *Friday Meeting Talks, or Divine Prescriptions for the Sick and Suffering*, New York, 1895

Simpson, Albert B., 'How I Was Led to Believe in Pre-Millennarianism' in *Christian Alliance and Missionary Weekly*, 13 November 1891

Simpson, Albert B., *How to Receive Divine Healing. An Address at the London Conference*, New York, 1896

Simpson, Albert B., *Larger Outlooks on*

*Missionary Lands. Descriptive Sketches of a Missionary Journey Through Egypt, Palestine, India . . . China*, New York, n.d. (1894)

Simpson, Albert B., 'Looking For and Hastening Forward' in *The Christian and Missionary Alliance*, 8 June 1898, p. 533

Simpson, Albert B., *Missionary Messages*, New York, n.d. (1925)

Simpson, Albert B., 'New Testament Missionary Types', Sermon on Philemon 17 during the Nyack Covention on 29 July 1906 in Simpson, Albert B., *Missionary Messages*, pp. 48ff.

Simpson, Albert B., *The Fourfold Gospel*, New York, n.d., (1895), today available as: Simpson, Albert B., *The Fourfold Gospel. A. B. Simpson's Conception of the Complete Provision of Christ for Every Need of the Believer . . . Spirit, Soul, Body*, updated and revised, Camp Hill, 1984

Simpson, Albert B., *The Gospel of Healing*, New York, 1887, London, 1885 (and further editions to date)

Simpson, Albert B., *The Gospel of the Kingdom. A Series of Discourses on the Lord's Coming*, New York, n.d., (ca. 1890)

Simpson, Albert B., 'The Logic of Missions', Sermon on Romans 10:14f. in *New York Tabernacle* (9 October 1904, in Simpson, Albert B., *Missionary Messages*, p. 65)

Simpson, Albert B., 'The New Testament Pattern of Missions', Sermon on Ezra 43:10f (New York Tabernacle, 11 December 1892), in Simpson, Albert B., *Missionary Messages*, p. 23

Simpson, Albert B., *The New Testament Standpoint of Missions*, New York, 1896

Simpson, Albert B., *Wholly Sanctified*, New York, 1890

*Svenska Missionsförbundets Kongomission*, Stockholm, 1911

Smith, Edgar H., *Nigerian Harvest*, Grand Rapids, 1972

Smith, Hannah Whitall, *The Christian's Secret of a Happy Life* (reprinted from the pages of *The Christian's Pathway to Power*, a monthly periodical edited by Robert Pearsall Smith, 1875, [2]1876, (revised and enlarged)

Smith, Hannah Whitall, *The Unselfishness of God and How I Discovered it. A Spiritual Autobiography*, New York/London, 1903

Smith, Oswald, *The Challenge of Missions*, Bromley, 1986, ([19]1978), (1959: *The Cry of the World* (14 editions))

Smith, Robert Pearsall, *Holiness Through Faith*, London, 1870, [2]1875

Smith, Robert Pearsall, *On Sinless Perfection*, London, 1875

South Africa General Mission, *Statement of Position*, February 1903

Spartalis, Peter J. et al., *The History of COCIN*, unpublished, expected to be published, Bonn, 1994

Spartalis, Peter J., *To the Nile and Beyond. The Birth and Growth of the Sudanese Church of Christ*, Homebush West, NSW, 1981

Spartalis, Peter J. with Roy Conwell and Christof Sauer: *Karl Kumm: The Last of the Livingstones. Pioneer Missionary and Statesman*, Bonn, 1993 ([2]1994)

'Statement No. 3. Success of the Philafrican Liberators League' in *Les Rapports de la Mission Philafricaine 1898–1905*, Lausanne, 1905

Staub, Hans, *Wir sind sein Werk. 125 Jahre Pilgermission St. Chrischona bei Basel*, Giessen/Basel, 1965

Stauffacher, Gladys, *Faster Beats the Drum*, New York, [2]1978 (1977)

Steele, Francis R., *Not in Vain. The Story of North Africa Mission*, Pasadena, 1981

Steer, Roger, *George Müller. Delighted in God*, London, 1975

Steffen, Tom, 'Pre-Evangelism' in *Outreach*, September and December 1981

Steinhilber, Wilhelm, *Der feuerspeiende Berg. Aus der Frühzeit der Liebenzeller Mission* (revised and enlarged by Lienhard Pflaum), Bad Liebenzell, [4]1985, (1979)

Steinhilber, Wilhelm, *In aller Welt am Netz. Festschrift zum 75-jährigen Jubiläum der Liebenzeller Mission*, Bad Liebenzell, 1974

Stoesz, Samuel J., 'The Doctrine of Sanctification in the Thought of A. B. Simpson' in Hartzfeld and Nienkirchen, *Birth of a Vision*, pp. 107–123

Stoll, David, *Fishers of Men or Founders of Empire? The Wycliffe Bible Translators in Latin America*, London/Cambridge, Mass., 1982

Strayer, Robert W., *The Making of Mission Communities in East Africa. Anglicans and Africans in Colonial Kenya 1875–1935*, Nairobi et al., 1986 (chapter 4 written in conjunction with Jocelyn Murray)

Strong, Polly, *Burning Wicks. The Story of Baptist Mid-Missions*, Cleveland, [2]1986, (1984)

Studd, Charles T., *Christ's Etceteras. Heart of Africa Mission Constitution*, London, 1915 (facsimile edition, Gerrards Cross, 1988)

Stunt, W. I., *Turning the World Upside Down*, Eastbourne, 1972

Sudan United Mission, *Constitution*, 1907

Sudan United Mission, *Constitution, revised*, 11 September 1912

Sudan United Mission, *The Sudan United Mission 75th Jubilee 1904–1979*, Sidcup, 1979

Summer Institute of Linguistics, *Bibliography*, Volume I, (1935–75), Volume II (1976–82)

Swan, George, *Lacked Ye Anything? A Brief Story of the Egypt General Mission*, London, [3]1923, (1921)

Swank, Gerald O., *Frontier Peoples of Central Nigeria and a Strategy for Outreach*, Pasadena, 1977

Swanson, J. F., *Three Score Years... and Then. Sixty Years of Worldwide Missionary Advance*, Chicago, n.d. (1950)

Synan, H. Vinson, 'Fundamentalism', in *DPCM*, pp. 324–327

Synan, H. Vinson, *The Holiness-Pentecostal Movement in the United States*, Grand Rapids, 1972

Taylor, Geraldine and Howard, *Biography of James Hudson Taylor (Abridged Version)*, London, 1965, new version, 1973, [5]1985

Taylor, Geraldine and Howard, *Hudson Taylor and the China Inland Mission: the Growth of a Work of God*, London, 1918

Taylor, Geraldine and Howard, *Hudson Taylor in Early Years. The Growth of a Soul*, London, 1911

Taylor, Geraldine and Howard, *Hudson Taylor's Spiritual Secret*, Chicago, 1982, [1]1932

Taylor, Geraldine, *The Story of the China Inland Mission*, 2 volumes, London, [2]1893–94

Taylor, Geraldine and Howard, *By Faith. Henry W. Frost and the China Inland Mission*, Singapore, [2]1988 (1938)

Taylor, J. Hudson, *A Retrospect*, London, 1894, [2]1899, [3]1903, [18]1974

Taylor, J. Hudson, *Brief Account of the Progress of the China Inland Mission, From May 1866 to May 1868. With a Preface by W. T. Berger*, London, 1869

Taylor, J. Hudson, *China; its Spiritual Need and Claims; with Brief Notices of Missionary Effort, Past and Present*, London, 1865, [2]1866, [3]1868, [5]1884, (revised and enlarged) [8]1890

Taylor, J. Hudson, 'The Relation of Itinerant to Settled Work' in James Johnston (ed.), *Report of the Centenary Conference on the Protestant Missions of the World. Held in Exeter Hall (June 9th–19th)*, London, 1888, Volume II, pp. 29–34

Taylor, William D. (ed.), *Internationalizing Missionary Training: a Global Perspective*, Exeter/Grand Rapids, 1991

Taylor, William D., *Four Years' Campaign in India*, London/New York, 1876

Taylor, William D., *Pauline Methods of Missionary Work*, Philadelphia, 1879

Taylor, William D., *Story of My Life*, New York, 1896

Taylor, William D., *Taylor of California, Bishop of Africa. An Autobiography*, London, 1897 (New York, 1896)

Taylor, William D., *Ten Years of Self-Supporting Missions in India*, New York, 1882

Teinonen, Seppo A., *Gustav Warneck und Robert Pearsall Smith. Eine Begegnung der deutschen neupietistischen Missionstheologie mit einer amerikanischen Heiligungsbewegung*, Helsinki, (Studia Missiologica Fennica I), 1957

Tett, Mollie E., *The Road to Freedom. The Sudan United Mission 1904–1968*, Sidcup, 1968

'The Beauty of Holiness. A Letter to the Newark Presbytery, by a Pastor of the Free Presbyterian Church, Newark, N.J., America' in *Wesleyan Methodist Magazine*, (November) 1849, pp. 1144–1150, 1270–1274

'The Woman is the Man for the Job. The Story of a Lone Woman who Dared to Believe and Obey God. Results? A Land Open Today to the Gospel' in *Worldwide*, Jubilee Year September/October 1964, p. 1f.

Thompson, Albert E., *The Life of A. B. Simpson*, Brooklyn, 1920, (revised: Thompson, Albert E., *A. B. Simpson. His Life and Work*, Camp Hill, PA, 1960)

Thompson, Phyllis, *A London Sparrow. The Story of Gladys Aylward —The Small Woman*, London, [2]1972, (1971)

Thompson, Phyllis, *Capturing Voices. The Story of Joy Ridderhof*, London, 1978

Thompson, Phyllis, *China. The Reluctant Exodus. The Untold Story of the withdrawal of the China Inland Mission from China*, London, 1979

Thompson, Phyllis, *Each to Her Post. The Inspiring Lives of Six Great Women in China*, London/Sevenoaks, 1982

Thompson, Phyllis, *Faith by Hearing. The Story of Gospel Recordings*, Glendale, [8]1973 (1960)

Tinou, Tite, 'Recapturing the initiative in theology in Africa' in *Evangelical Review of Theology*, 1987, pp. 152–156

Tinou, Tite, *The Theological Task of the Church in Africa*, Achimota, 1985

Tinou, Tite, 'Theological task in Africa. Where are We Now and Where Should we Be Going?' in *East Africa Journal of Evangelical Theology*, (6:1) 1987, pp. 3–11

Torjesen, Edvard, *A Study of Fredrik Franson. The Development and Impact of his Ecclesiology, Missiology, and Worldwide Evangelism*, (PhD, International College, 1984), Ann Arbor (UMI), 1985 (855 pages)

Torjesen, Edvard, *Fredrik Franson. A Model for Worldwide Evangelism*, Pasadena, 1983

Torjesen, Edvard, *In the Expectation of Christ's Return. A Study of Premillennialism*

*In the Perspective of Church History and the Writings of Fredrik Franson*, prepared for the Second Consultation of Organizations with a Franson Heritage, Ewersbach, Germany, August 29–September 2 1983, (cyclostyled booklet)

Torrey, Reuben Archer, Dixon, Amie C. *et al.*, *The Fundamentals. A Testimony to the Truth*, Los Angeles (BIOLA), 1917, reprint edition, Grand Rapids (Baker), 1972

Tozer, Aiden Wilson, *Wingspread. Albert B. Simpson. A Study in Spiritual Altitude*, Harrisburg, PA, 1943

Trachsel, Laura Cammack, *Kindled Fires in Africa*, Marion, 1960

Trachsel, Laura Cammack, *Kindled Fires in Asia*, Marion, 1960

Trachsel, Laura Cammack, *Kindled Fires in Latin America*, Marion, 1961

Truby, David, *Not So Much a Story . . . More a Work of God*, Worthing/London, 1968

Trumbull, Charles G., *The Life Story of C. I. Scofield*, New York *et al.*, 1920

Tucker, W. Leon, *The Redemption of Paul Rader*, New York, 1918

Tulga, Chester E., *The Foreign Missions Controversy in the Northern Baptist Convention 1919–1949*, Chicago, 1950

Turner, W. G., *John Nelson Darby*, London, [3]1944 (1901)

Udo, E. A., 'The Missionary Scramble for Spheres of Influence in South-eastern Nigeria 1900–52' in Ogbu Kalu (ed.), *The History of Christianity in West Africa*

Unruh, Margarete, *Fünfzig Jahre evangelische Missionsarbeit unter Muhammedanern*, Wiesbaden, 1950

Unruh, Margarete, *Hedwig von Hahn*, Wiesbaden, 1939

Upham, Thomas Cogswell, *Principles of the Interior or Hidden Life*, Boston, 1846

Vaillant, Mady, *Historique des missions protestantes en Haute-Volta avec un tat de la formation actuelle des autochthones*, December 1975

Veary, Victor E., 'Pentecost on the Plains', special twenty-first anniversary number of *The Lightbearer* containing the Rev. Victor E. Veary's report of the joys and sorrows, trials and triumphs of twenty-one years of effort to the glory of God in French Equatorial Africa, New York/Toronto/Calgary, n.d.

Veenstra, Johanna, *Pioneering for Christ in the Sudan*, London, 1930

Vincent, Eileen, *C. T. Studd and Priscilla. United to Fight for Jesus*, Bromley/Gerrards Cross/Eastbourne, 1988

Vinton, Samuel R., *Elimu Kubwa za Biblia. Les Grandes Doctrines de la Bible*, Bukavu, [5]1984, (rev.) (1959)

Vinton, Samuel R., *Kawaida Ya Mafundisho*, Kama, n.d.

*Vittna och vinna 1887–1962. Missionssälskapet Helgelseförbundet*, Kumla, 1962

Vollenhoven, E. van, 'Enkele grepen uit de vroege geschiedenis (1937–1953) van het CAMA-Werk in Ned. Oost-Indi' in *De Pionier*, May 1986, pp. 7f., 14

Walan, Bror, *Församlingstanken i Svenska Missionsförbundet. En studie i den nyevangeliska rörelsens sprängning och Svenska Missionsförbundets utveckling till o. 1890*, Stockholm, 1964

Walker, Andrew, *Restoring the Kingdom. The Radical Christianity of the House Church Movement*, London, ?1989 (1985)

Walker, Jean, *Fool and Fanatic? C. T. Studd. Quotations From His Letters*, Gerrards Cross, 1980.

Wall, Ernest, 'I Commend unto you Phoebe' in *Religion in Life*, 1957, pp. 396–408

Walls, Andrew F., 'Missionary Societies and the Fortunate Subversion of the Church' in *Evangelical Quarterly*, 88:2 (1988), pp. 141–155

Wargenau-Saillens, M., *Ruben et Jeanne Saillens. Évanglistes*, Paris, 1947

Wasserzug, Gertrud, 'By the grace of God I am what I am', n.d. (unpublished)

Wasserzug, Gertrud, *Wunder der Gnade Gottes. 50 Jahre 'Bibelheim Beatenberg'*, 30 Jahre 'Bibelheim Böblingen', Festschrift, Böblingen, 1984

Watt, Eva Stuart, *Floods on Dry Ground*, London, 1940

Weaver, William B., *Thirty-Five Years In The Congo. A History of Demonstrations of

*Divine Power In the Congo*, Chicago, 1945

Weaver, William B. and Bertsche, Harry E., *Twenty-five Years of Mission Work in Belgian Congo*, Chicago, 1938

Weber, Timothy P., *Living in the Shadow of the Second Coming. American Premillennialism 1875–1982*, Grand Rapids, [2]1983, (1969)

WEC International, *International Leaders' Conference. Report and Resolutions 3–26 June 78*, Gerrards Cross, 1978

WEC International, *Praying Always*, 1984–85, 1986–87, 1988–89

WEC International, *Principles and Practice*, 1982

WEC International, *Report African Consultation in Vavoua 30.11.–16.12.1985*

WEC International, *Report and Resolutions of the International Leaders' Conference 26 May–18 June 1984, Gerrards Cross*, 1984

WEC International, *The World of WEC*, Gerrards Cross, n.d.

Weeks, George, *W. Spencer Walton*, London/Edinburgh/New York, n.d., (between 1914 and 1918)

Wesley, John, 'A Plain Account of Christian Perfection as Believed and Taught by the Reverend Mr John Wesley' in John Wesley (ed. Wesleyan Conference Office), *The Works of Rev. John Wesley. With the Last Corrections of the Author*, London, [3]1872, volume 11, pp. 366–446

Westgarth, J. W., *The Holy Spirit and the Primitive Mind*, typewritten, Belfast, n.d.

Westgarth, J. W., *The Qua Iboe Mission Makes History*, 1946, (unpublished)

Westmeier, Karl-Wilhelm, *Reconciling Heaven and Earth. The Transcendental Enthusiasm and Growth of an Urban Protestant Community, Bogot*, Colombia, Bern/Frankfurt/New York, 1986

Wheatley, Richard, *Life and Letters of Mrs Phoebe Palmer*, New York, 1876

Wheatley, W. L., *Sunrise in Nigeria. A Record of Missionary Service from 1920 to 1952*, Belfast, 1977

Widman, Ragnar, *Trosförestӓllningar i Nedre Zaire från 1880—talet*, Stockholm, 1979 (with English summary)

Williams, Cecil Peter, *The Recruitment and Training of Overseas Missionaries in England Between 1850 and 1900. With Special Reference to the Records of the CMS, the Wesleyan Methodist Missionary Society, the London Missionary Society and the China Inland Mission*, MLitt, Bristol, 1977

Williams, David and Bridget, *The Wind Blowing*, Sidcup, 1973

Wilson, J. Christy, *Today's Tentmakers. Self-support: An Alternative Model for Worldwide Witness*, Wheaton, [4]1984, (1979)

Wilson, Lewis F., 'Bible Institutes, Colleges, Universities' in *DPCM*, pp. 57–65

Wilson, Samuel (ed.), *Mission Handbook: North American Protestant Ministries Overseas*, Monrovia, [12]1980.

Wilson, Samuel; Siewert, John (eds), *Mission Handbook. North American Protestant Ministries Overseas*, Monrovia, [13]1986

Wiseman, Nathaniel, *Elizabeth Baxter (Wife of Michael Paget Baxter). Saint, Evangelist, Preacher, Teacher, and Expositor*, London, 1928

Womersley, Harold, *William F. P. Burton, Congo Pioneer*, Eastbourne, 1973

Woodward, David B., *A Flame for God. Biography of Fredrik Franson, Founder of The Evangelical Alliance Mission*, Wheaton, [3]1981 (1966)

Zambezi Industrial Mission, *Facts of Interest*, London, 1911

Zambezi Mission, *Principles and Practice*, revised edition, 1946